D0469127

Taiwan

Robert Kelly

Joshua Samuel Brown

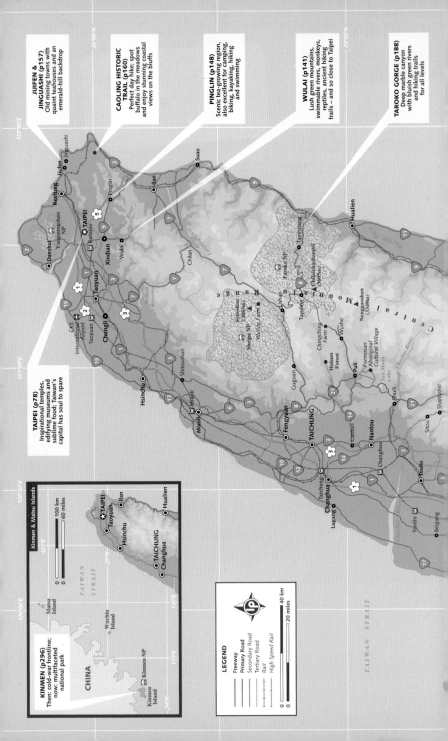

JIUFEN & JINGUASHI (p157)
Old mining towns with quaint teahouses and an emerald-hill backdrop

CAOLING HISTORIC TRAIL (p160)
Perfect day hike: spot buffalo in the meadows and enjoy stunning coastal views on the bluffs

PINGLIN (p148)
Scenic tea-growing region, also excellent for camping, biking, kayaking, hiking and swimming

WULAI (p141)
Lush green mountains, swimmable rivers, monkeys, reptiles, ancient hiking trails – and so close to Taipei

TAROKO GORGE (p188)
Deep marble canyon with bluish green rivers and hiking trails for all levels

TAIPEI (p78)
Inspirational temples, edifying museums and sublime food; Taiwan's capital has soul to spare

KINMEN (p296)
Then: cold-war frontline; now: multifaceted national park

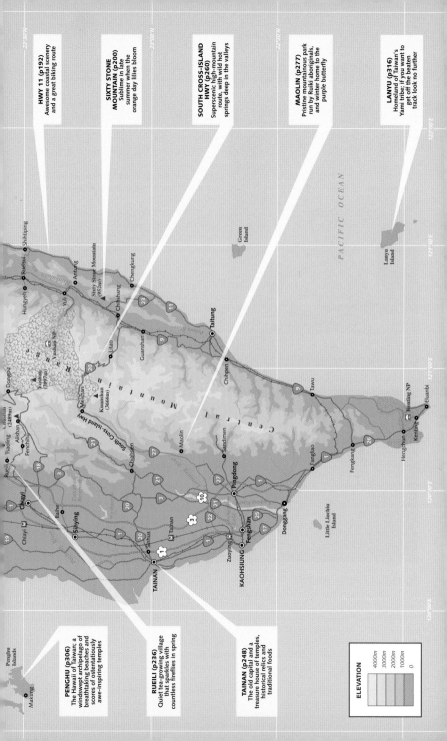

HWY 11 (p192)
Awesome coastal scenery and a great biking route

SIXTY STONE MOUNTAIN (p200)
Sublime in late summer when the orange day lilies bloom

SOUTH CROSS-ISLAND HWY (p260)
Superscenic high-mountain route, with wild hot springs deep in the valleys

MAOLIN (p277)
Pristine mountainous park run by Ruiki aboriginals, and winter home to the purple butterfly

LANYU (p316)
Homeland of Taiwan's Yami tribe; if you want to get off the beaten track look no further

PENGHU (p306)
The Hawaii of Taiwan; a windswept archipelago of breathtaking beaches and scores of ostentatiously awe-inspiring temples

RUEILI (p236)
Quiet tea-growing village that sparkles with countless fireflies in spring

TAINAN (p248)
The old capital and a treasure house of temples, historical relics and traditional foods

ELEVATION

4000m
3000m
2000m
1000m
0

PACIFIC OCEAN

On the Road

ROBERT KELLY Coordinating Author

I am tired, so tired in this picture, and not even a cup of freshly pounded *lei cha* (a fortified field-worker's drink) from the Well teahouse in Beipu can revive me. Nor can the owner's tales of frontier life in Beipu. When I get too weary I rest my head on the wooden boards. No-one cares. It's that kind of place.

There are three things I love to do most in Taiwan: try new teas, visit hot springs and hike. Going to Beipu I can indulge in them all. For tea, there's Hakka *lei cha* and also a local oolong called Oriental Beauty. Just don't ask how it gets its sweet flavour!

A new hot-spring resort opened outside Beipu two years ago, and my friends and I often drive there from Taipei – it's that good. Before a dip, we cruise around the mountains. Areas like this always yield some new little treasure whenever you visit.

JOSHUA SAMUEL BROWN

The Lonely Planet writer is a veritable travel-literature magnet: maps, magazines, brochures, business cards from restaurants, guesthouses and hotels. By the end of this project I'd accumulated around 30kg of assorted Taiwan tourist propaganda, some of it pretty good. I celebrated finishing the project by having this photo of me taken covered head to toe in the stuff.

What I dig most about life in Taiwan is constantly discovering new spots. Even after living in Taipei for years, I still regularly stumble into little neighbourhoods I've never heard of before; places with temples, markets, and the inevitable food stand offering some item or flavour only available at that one place.

During the course of doing this guide I switched residences from Taipei to the Penghu Archipelago. Here, my regular 'wow' moment involves stumbling across some hitherto undiscovered temple in the middle of nowhere, such as a beautiful statue-filled complex on Paisha Island.

See full author bios page 373

Highlights

Taiwan's hot springs (p75) are favourite
spots for families, couples and just about
everyone else

Hike in the bamboo forests near Fenchihu
(p235) for a full body work-out

More than five million visitors a year flock to the stunning 18,000 hectare Kenting National Park (p282)
in southern Taiwan to hike, swim, dive, snorkel, visit hot springs and take in the views

Highlights

SIMON FOALE

Take a break from shopping and reward yourself with some roasted cuttlefish from Snake Alley (p100)

SIMON FOALE

Immerse yourself in the colour and sound of Taipei and do as the locals do – ride a scooter

Breakdancers gyrate on Taipei's footpaths (boom-box not included)

BRENT WINEBRENN

Highlights

SIMON FOALE

Worshippers have been visiting the revered
Longshan Temple (p97) in Taipei since 1738

TOM COCKREM

Colourful Taoist deities watch over visitors
at some of Taiwan's temples (p22)

Traditional temple performances are a part of the cultural fabric of Taiwan's oldest city, Tainan (p248)

MARTIN MOOS

Highlights

TOM COCKREM

Taiwan's temples are often covered with decorative detail, such as these painted doors

SIMON FOALE

Expect the quintessential temple experience, complete with imposing dragon columns, at Longshan Temple (p97)

There is no better place to view Taiwan's world-class pottery and ceramics than at the Yingge Ceramics Museum (p151)

TOM COCKR

Taipei

Worshippers from all walks of life make frequent trips to the multidenominational Longshan Temple (p97)

Dusk brings out the glow from the world's (current) tallest building, Taipei 101 (p101)

A typical night market in Taipei is not complete without masses of people, snacks galore and enough shopping to drain even the deepest pockets

BRENT WINEBRENNER

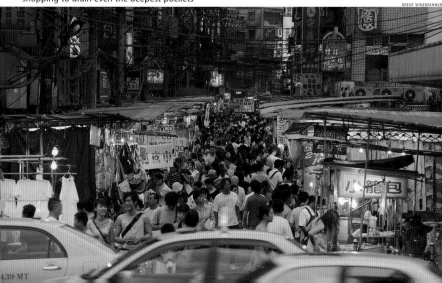

139-MT

Northern Taiwan

HELENE ROGERS / PHOTOLIBRARY

Fishing boats ply the waters at the little port town of Suao (p164), renowned for its odourless 22°C cold springs

PER-ANDRE HOFFMANN / LOOK DIE BILDAGENTUR DER FOTOGRAFEN GMBH / PHOTOLIBRARY

Keelung Island (p155), with its strange geological formations and emerald peak, makes a perfect day trip from Taipei

East Coast

JUPITERIMAGES / CREATAS / ALAMY

Marble-walled Taroko Gorge (p188) has trails once used by the indigenious Atayal people, which offer majestic scenery for hikes

HELENE ROGERS / PHOTOLIBRARY

Bathers relax in the soothing 32°C sodium bicarbonate water at the Chihpen Hot Springs (p205)

Western Taiwan

JUPITERIMAGES / CREATAS / ALAMY

The Alishan Forest Train (p241) takes passengers to a height of 2200m above sea level, over 77 bridges, 71km of track, 49 tunnels and three climatic zones in 3½ hours

Don't miss the Wenwu Temple that overlooks Taiwan's largest body of water, Sun Moon Lake (p222)

JTB PHOTO COMMUNICATIONS INC / PHOTOLIBRARY

Southern Taiwan

JUPITERIMAGES / CREATAS / ALAMY

Long stretches of beach in the Kenting National Park (p282) dispel the notion that national parks are strictly for hiking

Carved turtles carrying Qing dynasty tablets greet visitors at Tainan's Chihkan Towers (p250)

JUPITERIMAGES / CREATAS / ALAMY

Taiwan Islands

HENRY WESTHEIM PHOTOGRAPHY / PHOTOLIBRARY

Only 2km from China, Kinmen (p296) is home to many military-related relics such as this abandoned bunker

HENRY WESTHEIM PHOTOGRAPHY / PHOTOLIBRARY

The wind- and water-eroded coastlines of Penghu (p306) feature stunning basalt cliffs and reefs

Indigenous Yami tribes have occupied Lanyu Island (p316) for centuries

PER-ANDRE HOFFMANN / LOOK DIE BILDAGENTUR DER FOTOGRAFEN GMBH / PHOTOLIBRARY

Green Taiwan

Dense forests cover more than half of Taiwan and are home to more than 4000 species of plants (p71), 1000 of them native to the country

RON YUE / PHOTOLIBRARY

HENRY WESTHEIM PHOTOGRAPHY / PHOTOLIBRARY

Taiwan's many lakes offer more than just good views – visitors can expect walking trails, boating and more

Majestic scenery awaits visitors to Taiwan's top tourist destination, Taroko Gorge (p188)

CHRISTIAN KLEIN / PHOTOLIBRARY

台北捷運路網圖
Taipei Metro System Map

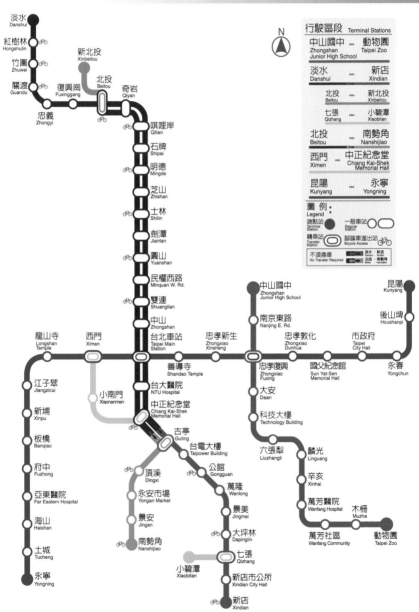

Contents

Regional Map Contents

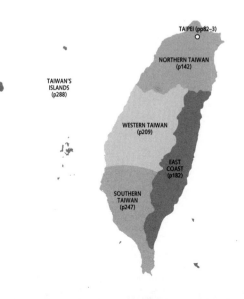

TAIPEI (pp82–3)

NORTHERN TAIWAN (p142)

TAIWAN'S ISLANDS (p288)

WESTERN TAIWAN (p209)

EAST COAST (p182)

SOUTHERN TAIWAN (p247)

Destination Taiwan

Ilha Formosa – Beautiful Island.

This is what a group of Portuguese sailors, said to have been the first Westerners to lay eyes on the island, uttered upon seeing Taiwan for the first time. We imagine they must have been pretty enamoured. While not every Westerner has the same love at first sight reaction to Taiwan, our Portuguese seafaring friends were just the first of many. With lush jungles, pulsating cities, great beaches, excellent hiking and biking, not to mention some of the world's best hot springs, Taiwan cuts a figure as one of the most diverse destinations in Asia.

True, Taiwan hasn't yet made it to the top of everybody's 'to visit' list, but we think this is partially a result of people not quite knowing what Taiwan has to offer. But within the borders of this small, sweet-potato-shaped island barely the size of many American states lies a world of contrasts and a melange of cultural influences you're not likely to find anywhere else on the planet.

In the first decade of the 21st century, Taiwan is increasingly drawing travellers of all stripes: from spiritual seekers looking to experience the island's religious heritage to gourmands in search of the perfect night-market meal to computer geeks scanning the horizon for the latest high-tech gadgets. Taiwan offers visitors a hypermodern skin, an ancient Chinese skeleton and an aboriginal soul. And more than that, Taiwan has some of the world's warmest people, affable to a fault and so filled with *rénqíng wèi* (which, roughly translated, means 'personal affection') that few who come to Taiwan a stranger leave that way.

Much has changed in the centuries since the Portuguese first saw Taiwan. Still, we think if the same group of sailors came back in the present day, they'd call it *Ilha Formosa* all over again.

Getting Started

Travelling to Taiwan takes relatively little advanced preparation, as there are no serious challenges compared with other Asian destinations. The big cities are easy to get around, roads are signed in English, and transport is comfortable and affordable by western standards. In addition, there are now visitor centres inside most major train stations, airports (and now high-speed rail stations), with English- and Japanese-speaking staff to help with bus transfers, hotels and the like. There's even a helpful 24-hour tourist hotline (☎ 0800 011 765) you can call anytime you need help.

For the budget traveller, more and more hostels and campsites are opening, the former often by well-travelled, English-speaking Taiwanese. The proliferation of B&Bs and swanky hot spring resorts finally gives those on a higher budget options beyond sterile midrange hotels or generic 5-stars.

See Climate Charts (p333) for more information.

Adventure travellers will be happy to discover that the old permit system for climbing high mountains has been relaxed, maps are easy to find, and there are now many sources of good clear information about outdoor activities.

WHEN TO GO

People often remark that Taiwan has no seasons, but in reality you must take the time of year into account when travelling. In general, autumn (September to November) is best, as conditions tend to be warm and dry, air pollution is at a minimum, and prices lower. Visiting in spring (March to May) is a crapshoot: it can be clear and dry, or wet and grey, or even blighted by a sandstorm from China. Sometimes you get all three conditions in one day.

Summer (June to August) is a great time to visit the east coast, especially for outdoor activities, but be aware of typhoons, which can hit the island from June to October. Summer is not a good time for travel to the outer islands as they are crowded with tourists and flights and hotels are difficult to secure. Try October to November when rates have dropped but the weather is still great. The cities are always hot and sticky in summer.

Beach lovers can swim comfortably anywhere from May to October. But if you want to swim in winter, head south, not southeast.

Avoid travelling during the Chinese New Year holiday as the entire country pretty much shuts down. Some good holidays not to avoid, however, include Lantern Festival, Dragon Boat Festival, and the Matsu Pilgrimage (p336).

In general, July and August, Saturday night, and Chinese New Year are considered high season and accommodation prices are often double the off-season rates. Outside touristy areas, however, there is little change in price from month to month (only perhaps weekday and weekend).

COSTS & MONEY

A bed in a dorm room will cost from NT300 to NT400 on average, while a room in a hotel your mother might find acceptable starts at NT1200. Campsites average NT200 per person if you have your own tent. Consider B&Bs if your budget is NT2000 to NT4000 a night as they are much better value than most midrange hotels. Top-end hotels are overpriced in general (even the tourism board thinks so), especially when full rates are charged. The corollary is they are often good value in the off-season.

The typical lunch or dinner might cost NT80 to NT250. A bowl of noodles or dumplings costs NT40 to NT50 but is not usually enough to be considered a meal. Realistically, backpackers should budget NT200 to

HOW MUCH?

Basic fare on Taipei's MRT (underground railway): NT20

Taxi ride: NT70 for the first 1.5km

Adult admission to National Palace Museum: NT100

Train fare, Taipei to Hualien (for Taroko Gorge): NT343

Motor scooter rental: NT200–600 per day, average NT400

TOP 10

TAIWAN

Kinmen (Taiwan)
Taiwan Strait
Taipei
Penghu

TOP 10 SUPERLATIVES

The best of Taiwan in a variety of categories:

1 Keelung Miaokou (Street Food; p154) Let our Taipei-city friends scoff; here is the best street fare in Taiwan!

2 Lantern Festival (Traditional Festivals; p149) With modern high-tech displays and traditional lantern releases, this festival has mass appeal.

3 Erkan Old Residences, Penghu (Traditional Villages; p314) A living museum of culture in a beautiful setting.

4 South Cross-Island Hwy (Drives; p260) This route has it all: mountain views, wild hot springs, aboriginal villages, ancient cypress forests, and some great hikes.

5 Caoling Historical Trail (Day Hikes; p160) A six-hour walk along stunning coastal bluffs.

6 Chipei Beach, Penghu: (Beaches; p306) In an archipelago known for beaches, this ranks among the finest.

7 Spring Scream, Kenting (Music Festivals; p285) Still Taiwan's best venue for independent music.

8 Cochin Ceramic Museum, Chiayi (Small Museums; p233) The figurines from a master 19th-century ceramicist express fluid natural movements with amazing life-likeness.

9 Core Pacific City, Taipei (Buildings; p101) An alien golf-ball? Even if you don't shop here, we promise you won't soon forget Taipei's strangest mall.

10 Old British Consulate at Takou, Kaohsiung (Cafes; p268) Watch ships sail into the harbour from this great old vantage point.

TOP 10 TEMPLES

Taiwan's temples are often both beautiful historical relics and lively centres of folk worship.

1 Longshan Temple, Lukang (p217) The largest and best-preserved Qing dynasty temple in Taiwan, ready at last after years of repairs.

2 Longshan Temple, Taipei (p97) An important place of worship and a great spot for photographers looking for that quintessential temple atmosphere.

3 Matsu Temple, Matsu (p251) One of the most sacred temples in Taiwan, once thought to hold the bones of Matsu.

4 Tzushr Temple, Sansia (p152) A masterpiece. Restoration of this temple has been progressing steadily for over 50 years.

5 Shitoushan (p175) Not one temple but a whole mountainside of them.

6 Chung Tai Chan Temple, Puli (p226) A modern temple filled with gorgeous works of art. English-speaking nuns can show you around.

7 Zhinan Gong, Maokong, Taipei (p138) Float up to this 19th-century temple on the new gondola and take in the views.

8 Confucius Temple, Tainan (p251) The first and best of the sage's temples in Taiwan. Expect calm and dignified beauty.

9 Nankunshen Temple, Tainan County (p258) Exorcisms and other expressions of extreme religious faith are often on display.

10 Dongyue Temple, Tainan (p252) The masterful wall paintings depict the agonies of Hell in disturbing detail.

DON'T LEAVE HOME WITHOUT

- Tissues – many public toilets don't have paper towels or hand driers. Antiseptic baby wipes are good too.
- Business cards – people here like to exchange them.
- At least one nice outfit – even if you're only here to teach kids English.
- Quick-drying clothing – for outdoor activities; cotton never dries.
- Photocopies of diplomas, certificates, etc – if you plan on seeking employment.
- Good rain gear – the weather changes very frequently!
- Tampons – if you're travelling outside Taipei.
- Underwear – especially for women; you won't like what's here.
- Makeup – especially if you're dark skinned as local makeup is designed to make Chinese look whiter.
- Shoes and clothing – if you're above or below average size.
- A towel – if you're staying at cheaper hotels and don't like to dry with tea towels.
- Warm clothing – if you'll be here for winter.
- Vitamins – expensive here.
- Earplugs – don't ask us why; literally, our hearing's shot.
- A smile – showing anger will do more harm than good.

NT300 a day for food and water; those on a higher budget, NT500 to NT1000. Breakfast tends to be cheap, NT40 for an egg sandwich and a soy milk drink, and many hotels, including budget ones, include it free.

For the budget traveller, then, basic expenses could run from NT400 to NT600 a day. For the greatest savings, hit resort areas midweek and areas that have dorms or campgrounds on the weekends. Adventure travellers, such as cyclists and hikers will spend little except on food and water (and some transport), as you can usually camp in the mountains or on the beaches for free. Midrange travellers should budget for at least NT2000 per day (based on double occupancy as hotels charge by room, not person). For those opting for resorts and western style meals, NT3000 to NT5000 a day (again, based on double occupancy) is a good start.

TRAVEL LITERATURE

Formosan Odyssey by John Ross (2002) is a quirky personal account of one writer's journey across Taiwan just after the 21 September 1999 (921) earthquake. Dead-on descriptions of small-town life in Taiwan.

Keeping Up With the War God by Steven Crook (2000) is a series of short articles on life in Taiwan – from politics to folk religion – by a shrewd observer.

Vignettes of Taiwan by Joshua Brown (2006) An anthology of short stories, travel essays, photographs, random meditations and political meanderings about life in present-day Taiwan.

From Far Formosa by George Mackay (1896) is a chronicle of the famous Presbyterian minister's life in Taiwan around the turn of the 19th century. You can still find copies in some Taipei bookstores.

INTERNET RESOURCES

Please refer to regional chapters for websites of local interest.

Forumosa (www.forumosa.com) Expat community website that collectively has the answers to all your questions: from visa and citizenship issues, to where to find whole wheat pasta. This is where we hang out online.

SOUVENIRS

Paper umbrella: NT600 and up

Chinese-style coat: NT1000 and up

Good traditional teapot: NT500 and up

Hand made Kinmen knife: NT800 and up

Reproduction Chinese scroll: NT1000 and up

Information For Foreigners (http://iff.immigration.gov.tw/enfront) Lists everything from getting a visa to what days the garbage trucks accept recycling materials.

Lonely Planet (www.lonelyplanet.com) Don't forget to visit the Thorn Tree site for updates from fellow Lonely Planet readers and fans.

The View From Taiwan (http://michaelturton.blogspot.com) Good local political coverage.

Welcome to Taiwan (www.tbroc.gov.tw) Official website of the Tourism Board.

Zhongwen.com (www.zhongwen.com) A nifty intro to the Chinese language and a good links section to books on Taiwan.

Itineraries

CLASSIC ROUTES

THE EAST COAST LOOP   Two Weeks / Hualien to Taitung and Back

From Hualien, it's a quick hop to **Taroko National Park** (p188), site of Taroko Gorge, a rugged marble canyon that's been Taiwan's premier natural attraction since the '30s. After a few days exploring this treasure, head down the coast on **Hwy 11** (p192) to Taitung. This stretch of road takes you past some of the most scenic stretches of coastline in the country. Spend three or four days en route, stopping at sandy beaches, ocean-side campsites, fishing harbours, and aboriginal villages.

South of Taitung, take a stroll through **Chihpen Forest Recreation Area** (p205) with its monkey-filled banyan forests. Then head back north but this time go up the rift valley on **Hwy 9** (p196). You're between two mountain ranges here, in the rice belt of Taiwan, and the contrast with the coastline is dramatic. Check out the organic farming scene at **Loshan** (p201), walk at least part of the historic **Walami Trail** (p200), raft the Hsiukuluan River at **Rueisui** (p198), relax in the many hot springs, and feast on some very exotic aboriginal food in **Mataian** (p197) before returning to Hualien.

TAIWAN STRAIT

Taroko National Park

Hualien

9

Mataian

11

Rueisui

Walami Trail

Loshan

11

9

Taitung

Chihpen Forest Recreation Area

PACIFIC OCEAN

The contrast between the coastline and the countryside will amaze, and the endless outdoor activities will exhaust you on this 400km, two-week loop on the east coast.

DOWN THE WEST COAST   One Month / Taipei to Kenting

Almost every trip to Taiwan will start in the capital, Taipei. Don't miss the **National Palace Museum** (p90) with the world's foremost collection of Chinese art, and **Longshan Temple** (p97) a centre of Taiwanese folk worship. If you have time, ride the new gondola to Maokong for an afternoon of fine oolong tea, followed by an evening visit to **Shilin Night Market** (p99).

History soaked **Danshui** (p126) makes for a pleasant day trip as does the **Juming Museum** (p156), which features Taiwan's best modern sculptures. Heading south, fans of traditional arts and crafts will enjoy a smorgasbord in **Yingge** (p151), a town devoted to ceramics; at Hsinchu's relic-rich **Guqifeng** (p173); in the woodcarving shops in **Sanyi** (p178), and around **Lukang** (p216), home to master lantern, fan and tin craftsmen.

Further south in **Chiayi** (p233), visit the small collection of Cochin pottery while you wait for the train to **Alishan** (p232). The narrow-gauge alpine railway, called the **Alishan Forest Train** (one of three left in the world; p241), takes you from 0m to 2200m in just a few hours. For a great side trip, stop halfway at **Fenchihu** (p235) and hike through bamboo forests to the pretty tea-growing village of **Rueili** (p236). In spring, countless fireflies light up the night.

After returning to Chiayi, continue south to the old capital of **Tainan** (p248) for a few days of temple- and relic-hopping, and sampling of traditional foods. During the winter, take a detour east to see the purple butterflies at **Maolin** (p277).

Returning to the coast, head south to **Kaohsiung** (p265). Lunch in this bustling harbour city at the old **British Consulate at Takou** (p268) before continuing to **Kenting National Park** (p282) to wind down your journey on the beach.

A month-long, 600km route that lets you visit the best museums, the most relic-rich small towns, and a splendid mountain retreat (without working up too much of a sweat). Along the way sample tasty local foods, relax in teahouses, and shop for traditional crafts.

ROADS LESS TRAVELLED

ISLAND HOPPING   Three Weeks / Matsu to Lanyu

Start with **Matsu** (p289) to get a taste of maritime Fujian culture you can't find in Taiwan proper. Give yourself at least four days, unless you're only exploring Nangan and Beigan Islands. In any event, definitely spend a night in the traditional houses of Beigan.

From Matsu, fly to **Kinmen** (p296) via Taipei and spend two days exploring the ancient towns and military presence on the main island. Birdwatchers will want to include an extra day for walking around Little Kinmen; the saltwater marshes here are home to a unique mixture of waterbirds.

If the weather's fine, you'll want to spend at least five days getting in some beach-time (or windsurfing) on **Penghu** (p306) via Taipei; and don't miss the opportunity to explore the archipelago's myriad temples.

When moving on from Penghu, we recommend flying to Kaohsiung. If the seas aren't too rough, try the Penghu–Kaohsiung boat. From Kaohsiung, take a two-hour train ride across southern Taiwan's flat banana and betel nut growing country to Taiwan's easternmost city, Taitung. From here, you can either boat it (if you have the stomach) or fly to both eastern outposts, **Green Island** (p320) and **Lanyu** (p316). Don't miss the seawater hot springs on Green Island. Both islands are worth three days each.

The autumn months offer the most pleasant weather to visit the islands, not to mention a respite from the crowds that can make getting to Penghu and Green Island difficult. But autumn can also bring typhoons, a definite consideration for anyone travelling the islands.

Three weeks of short air-hops and ferries will take you around Taiwan's island outposts for glimpses into her military, maritime and aboriginal heritage. Ancient villages, beautiful beaches, amazing temples, and one of the world's only seawater hot springs await.

A CROSS-ISLAND TOUR   Two Weeks / Taichung to Jiaoshi

Leave **Taichung** (p209) with a full stomach as there's little to satisfy you until you reach the Chung Tai Chan Temple in **Puli** (p226) – and this amazing centre of Buddhist art and research will only help with the spiritual pangs.

After Puli the highway starts to rise into the Central Mountains and it's just one gorgeous landscape after the other begging for a photo from here on in. For a side trip, head down to **Aowanda Forest Recreation Area** (p230) and spend the night in little Beatrix Potter–approved cabins among cherry and plum trees. Keep an eye out for the birds; this is a top-twitching venue.

Returning to Hwy 14, continue to the end to the start of the **Nenggao Cross-Island Historic Trail** (p230). You don't need to do the whole thing (which takes you all the way down to the east coast) but think about hiking in and spending the night in a cabin.

Retrace your route, and head north up Hwy 14甲. Prepare for endless windy roads and numerous wash outs. Also prepare for a stunning landscape of receding blue mountain ranges.

After Wuling Pass (3275m), the highest point on the road, stop in **Hehuanshan Forest Recreation Area** (p231) to photograph (and maybe stroll) the treeless emerald hills. Then head up Hwy 8 to Hwy 7. Follow this north to **Wuling Forest Recreation Area** (p169) for thick forests, high waterfalls, and cool mountain streams, some of which are home to the endangered Formosan landlocked salmon.

Past Wuling Forest Recreation Area, the road winds down past quaint aboriginal villages with their trademark church and steeple, past countless streams just asking to be traced, until it reaches the Lanyang River plains. Continue to **Jiaoshi** (p163) and treat yourself to a hot-spring bath.

You'll need your own vehicle for this 300km route but it's quintessential Taiwan: from the temples to the landscapes – high-altitude farms, maple forests, rolling alpine meadows, grassy plains – to the washed out roads. And of course it ends with a hot spring.

TAILORED TRIPS

HOT SPRINGS

For star resorts head to **Yangmingshan** (p133), **Jinshan** (p156) or **Beitou** (p131). **Paolai's** (p261) spas are perched on mountainsides. We love the traditional brick design at the resort in **Nanzhuang** (p176). In scenic **Sun Moon Lake** (p222) and **Carp Lake** (p229) hotels have drilled for water. In **Jinluan** (p206), facilities overlook the ocean. In **Dongpu** (p245) people hot spring after climbing Yushan. For wild springs hike to **Sileng** (p169) and **Fan Fan** (p169) on the North Cross-Island Hwy. Pretty **Bayen Hot Spring** (p156) is on the back of Yangmingshan. **Wulai's** springs (p141) bubble by the river. Don't miss sublime **Lisong** (p264) and eerie **Mokenan** (p265).

   Jinfeng (p206) offers simple tiled pools beside a campground. A similar setting exists at the **Taitung Hongye Hot Springs** (p201). At **Nanao** (p165), villagers have built primitive pools by a rushing river. The park's board did the same at **Maolin** (p278). **Jiaoshi** (p163), on the northeast coast, has slightly salty spring water. **Suao** (p164) possesses a rare cold spring. **Green Island** (p321) boasts one of only three saltwater springs worldwide. Iron-rich springs are found at **Rueisui** (p198) and nearby **Hungyeh** (p199). **Sichongsi** (p287) gives bathers an alternative to the beaches. The silky waters at **Taian** (p176) leave the skin glowing. At **Antung** (p200), spring water is used to make coffee.

A HIKING GUIDE TO TAIWAN

For day hikes around Taipei, head to **Yangmingshan** (p132), **Maokong** (p137), and **Pingxi** (p144). **Huangdi Dian** (p150), **Wuliao Jian** (p152) and **Bijia Shan** (p150) are exciting ridge walks not far from the capital. **Wulai's** trails (p143) were once aboriginal hunting routes: hike all the way to the east coast, or south and connect with more trails in **Manyueyuan** (p152). The aboriginal trails in **Taroko National Park** (p188) run through valleys, and alongside blue-green rivers to waterfalls.

   Scenic coastal routes include the **Caoling Historic Trail** (p160), the **Bitou Cape Trail** (p159), the path from Jialeshui to Lake Nanren in **Kenting National Park** (p282), and the 10km circuit around **Little Kinmen Island** (p305). For a hike through bamboo forests, head to **Fenchihu** (p235). To see some of the best-preserved subtropical forests in Asia hike the **Walami Trail** (p200). Experience the tropical forests along the Qing dynasty **Jin-Shui Yin Old Trail** (p280). For 3000m+ mountains, try **Snow Mountain** (p170), **Hehuanshan** (p231), and **Yushan** (p243).

   For cross-island thrills, hike the **South Cross-Island Hwy** (p260). The two- to three-day **Nenggao Cross-Island Historic Trail** (p230) crosses the island midway, while several week-long trails cross **Yushan National Park** (p243). **Lanyu** (p318) and **Green Island** (p321) don't have long hikes, but views are spectacular. For strolling through pretty forests try **Alishan** (p242), **Chihpen** (p205), **Fuyuan** (p198), **Shuangliou** (p287), **Mingchih** (p168), **Aowanda** (p230) and **Neidong** (p144) forest recreation areas. For more on hiking, see also p329 and p330.

Snapshot

There's no question about it. From Keelung to Kenting, the winds of change are blowing, and Taiwan in 2007 stands at a crossroads. Ideas once unthinkable are now openly debated; changing the titular China of various state-owned entities to Taiwan; rewriting the constitution of the Republic of China itself to reflect a growing sense of Taiwanese identity; perhaps most revolutionary of all, removing many (some voices cry for all) traces of the once-sacrosanct former dictator Chiang Kai-shek – smiling statues, commemorative plaques, even the name Chiang itself – from military bases, city squares and just about all public spaces.

But Taiwan is no stranger to transformation (if anything, the island has long thrived on it): from pirates' nest to fortress for the Ming dynasty's last futile stand; from Qing dynasty backwater to coveted Japanese possession; from former colony of a defeated empire to enforced 'loyal subjects' of an authoritarian regime; from one-party state to full-fledged democracy.

Economically, Taiwan has proven itself nothing if not eminently flexible. In a few short decades this one-time maker of textiles and cheap consumer goods transformed itself into the world's leading high-tech producer, fuelling the digital boom of the late 20th century, becoming in the process one of Asia's most durable and dynamic economy. But even this is subject to change. Across the straits, the economic power of once-impoverished and technologically backwards China is growing exponentially (in no small part thanks to Taiwanese investment), and many in Taiwan feel that the days of regarding China as the unsophisticated, muscular cousin wearing a cheap suit are over. Cross-Strait relations are a major issue in Taiwan, but it's far more complex than the question of independence versus unification.

However, the more important question is one of identity, of what it means to be Taiwanese. While many in Taiwan feel a strong connection to Chinese culture and history, not all feel the same pull. Many Taiwanese feel no more kinship with China than, say, a third generation Italian-American might feel towards Italy. Sure, they like Peking Duck and might have vague plans to visit the Great Wall one summer, but they aren't really interested in tying their entire identity to the nation that their ancestors left generations ago. Many Taiwanese, young and old, are instead increasingly defining their identities by the shared memories of Taiwan. It's a rich history indeed, one of colonisation and oppression, rags to riches, and the island's long journey from dictatorship to democracy.

While Taiwan's relationship with China is a major issue, perhaps even the defining one, it isn't the only issue being discussed. Not by a long shot. So what are Taiwanese office workers chatting about around the water cooler (or water boilers) in most offices? Politics, not surprisingly, is a big topic, with a variety of high-level scandals involving figures from all parties being very much in the news. Of course the economy looms large in the collective unconscious. As more and more manufacturing moves from labour-expensive Taiwan to labour-cheap China, Taiwan is increasingly manoeuvring itself to redefine its niche in the global economy.

Ecology and the environment are big issues as well. Whereas the Taiwanese were once flagrantly callous about pollution, the last 10 years have seen a veritable renaissance of environmental awareness. As decades of environmental neglect are reversed, many hope that Taiwan's international image (already changed from 'Asia's bargain-basement factory' to 'global high-tech powerhouse') might, through promotion of its

FAST FACTS

Population of Taiwan
(July 2006): 23,036,100

Mobile phones in use:
22.1 million

Percentage of population
under 14: 19.4%

Estimated percentage
of population (including
infants) without mobile
phones: < 5%

Highest Point: Yu Shan
(Jade Mountain) 3952 m

Percentage of homes connected to the internet:
75%

Percentage of Taiwanese
who shop online: 45%

Percentage of male
population who chew
betel nut: 25%

Number of street vendors
in Taiwan (2003):
291, 064

Number of betel-nut
vendors in Taiwan (2003):
17,604

unparalleled natural beauty, make yet another transformation: 'Switzerland of Asia' anybody?

Still, the question of Taiwan's future vis-à-vis China looms large. While political leaders from one side creep slowly towards codifying the island's de facto independence, those from the other camp have been making highly publicised pilgrimages to China in order to create a framework for eventual unification. In the middle stand those who'd prefer to keep the status quo, neither admitting nor denying either Taiwan's independence from or inclusion within the greater Chinese nation. Many say that 2008 will be a decisive year, and that once China's Olympic hosting duties are over, the nation will turn towards settling the question once and for all.

So is Taiwan at a crossroads, or a precipice? Only time will tell.

History

Writing a historical overview of any place in under 5000 words necessitates being both sweepingly general and highly selective. For a travel guide, this is generally a fine way to go; after all, the only questions travel guides need answer are those of the 'why should I go?' and 'what should I eat/see/do if I do?' variety. But writing about Taiwan's history is especially tricky, because it's a history of two entities: Taiwan, the island, and Taiwan, a political entity known as the Republic of China (ROC). Though unified currently, the history of the former is far older, and the origin of the latter is found many miles elsewhere. Since history is a big part of Taiwan's appeal to travellers, and because Taiwan's history is so mired in politics, we endeavour to tread delicately, but boldly.

Information about Taiwanese history (from the point of view of the Taiwanese) can be found on www.taiwandc .org/history.htm. The site has a lot of interesting photographs and an excellent recommended reading list.

EARLY HISTORY

There is evidence of human settlement in Taiwan dating as far back as 30,000–40,000 years ago; current prevalent thinking dates the arrival of the Austronesian peoples, ancestors of many of the tribal people who still inhabit Taiwan (p47), between 4000–5000 years ago.

For most of her long history, China seemed fairly indifferent to Taiwan. Early Chinese texts from as far back as AD 206 contain references to the island, but for the most part it was seen as a savage island, best left alone. Contact between China and Taiwan was erratic until the early 1400s, when boatloads of immigrants from China's Fujian province, disillusioned with the political instability in their homeland, began arriving on Taiwan's shores. When the new immigrants arrived, they encountered two groups of aboriginals: one who made their homes on the fertile plains of central and southwestern Taiwan and the other, seminomadic, lived along the Central Mountain Range.

Over the next century, immigration from Fujian increased, these settlers being joined by the Hakka, another ethnic group leaving the mainland in great numbers. By the early 1500s there were three categories of people on the island: Hakka, Fujianese and the aboriginal tribes. Today, Taiwan's population is mainly descended from these early Chinese immigrants, though centuries of intermarriage makes it likely a fair number of Taiwanese have some aboriginal blood as well.

The bilingual 10-book series *A History of Taiwan in Comics* (認識台灣 歷史) is a fun way to learn about Taiwan's history. It can be ordered at http://edu .ocac.gov.tw/local/ history%5Fof%5Ftaiwan

EUROPE AND THE MING IN TAIWAN

In 1544 a Portuguese fleet 'discovered' the island. Enamoured by the lush plains, rugged mountains and rocky coasts, they declared Taiwan *Ilha Formosa*, meaning 'beautiful island'. Less romantically minded Europeans soon took notice, and before long the Dutch (national proprietors of the recently formed Dutch East India Company) set up a trading base on the Penghu Islands (p306) in the Taiwan Strait.

This did not sit well in China's Ming court, who sat up suddenly and took notice of Taiwan. The Ming government sent its navy to Penghu, and before long had thrown the Dutch off the island. But being particularly tenacious, the Dutch soon returned and established a colony in Penghu in

TIMELINE	c 10,000 BC	AD 1544
	Prehistoric people living in Taiwan	Portuguese sailors 'discover' Taiwan and like it enough to call her *Ilha Formosa*

1622, remnants of which can still be seen in the Dutch Fort ruins (p313), a few kilometres out of present-day Makung City.

The first thing the Dutch did on their return was to establish a trading route between Batavia (now Jakarta), Makung, China and Japan. For a short period of time, Dutch trade dominated the Taiwan Strait, much to the chagrin of the Ming court, who issued a decree in 1623 banning all entry of ships into the Taiwan Strait from southeast Asia. Realising the ineffectiveness of the decree, Ming troops were sent to attack the Dutch, who gave in and agreed to remove themselves from Penghu. Oddly, the Ming allowed the Dutch to establish trading ports in Taiwan proper.

Spain, ever envious of the Dutch hold on Taiwan and their growing wealth, decided they wanted in on the action themselves. In 1626 the Spanish invaded what is now Keelung and established their territory all the way down the west coast to Danshui and eventually all over northern Taiwan. Unfortunately, Taiwan's climate took revenge and a series of catastrophes took its toll on the Spanish traders. Typhoons and malaria devastated the Spanish and attacks by local aboriginals caused them to relinquish their territory. In 1638 the Spanish withdrew from Danshui and the Dutch (ever tenacious) moved in to snatch up the remains, taking control of Keelung in 1642.

> Taiwan was once a haven for pirates in the 15th and 16th centuries.

TAIWAN UNDER CHENG AND QING

Though continued western encroachment into Taiwan undoubtedly displeased the Ming court, over in Beijing the emperor had bigger problems; the dynasty itself was in collapse. One staunch Ming loyalist in exile would have a lasting impact on Taiwanese history; Admiral Cheng Cheng-kung, also known as Koxinga, sought refuge with his troops on the small island of Kinmen (p296) off China's Fujian province. On Kinmen, Cheng met a disgruntled former interpreter for the Dutch East India Company who convinced Cheng to invade Taiwan and overthrow the Dutch.

Intrigued, Cheng somehow managed to amass an army on Kinmen and build a fleet of ships (in the process deforesting the island, from which it's now only just recovering). Cheng set sail for the Penghu Islands, where he swiftly deposed the Dutch before moving on to Taiwan proper. Arriving in Taiwan, Cheng he was greeted by local supporters anxious to be free of the Dutch once and for all. Realising their days in Taiwan were numbered, the Dutch surrendered to Cheng in 1662 and left for good.

With Cheng came 30,000 mainland Chinese, who established Taiwan island as their home. Others soon followed, and would do so for the next 200 years. Taiwan's growing population accelerated development on the island, especially in the north and along the fertile plains of the west coast. To manage Taiwan's fast growth, Cheng set up an efficient system of counties, some of which remain today. However, his dreams of overthrowing the Manchu remained unfulfilled; he died a year after landing on Taiwan. Many Taiwanese today regard Cheng as a hero for driving the Dutch out of Taiwan.

After Cheng's death, his son and grandson ruled the island but their ineptness caused widescale poverty and despair. In 1683, the Qing government overthrew Cheng's descendents and took over the island, placing it under the jurisdiction of Fujian province. Having 'retaken' Taiwan, the Qing court's attitude towards Taiwan was about as lax as the Ming's before

1624–1662	1662
Dutch set up Taiwanese colonies	Dutch surrender to Ming Admiral Koxinga

them, and Taiwan was again mostly ignored by China, save the boatloads of Chinese immigrants yearning for space to spread out.

In the West, however, Europeans were not blind to Taiwan's advantageous position, and the 'beautiful island' was quite well known among traders both for its strategic location and hazardous coastline. (The latter factor would eventually play a part in the Qing court's surrender of Taiwan to Japan.) After the second Opium War ended, Taiwan was opened to trade with the West in Keelung and Suao. The southern ports of Kaohsiung and Tainan were also opened. Foreign trade increased rapidly, with Taiwan's main exports being camphor, rice, tea and opium.

JAPANESE OCCUPATION (1894–1945)

Despite Taiwan's importance as a trading centre, the island remained a wild and unruly place, and the Qing government did little to control the frequent unrest between settlers, foreign sailors and the aboriginal population. In 1872 the crew of a shipwrecked Japanese junk was executed by an aboriginal tribe; after being told by the Qing emperor that the aboriginals on the island were beyond the his court's control, Japanese troops invaded Taiwan. Before the annexation was complete, the Qing government offered compensation to the families of the dead sailors, as well as pledging to exert more control over Taiwan. Placated for the time being, the Japanese withdrew from Taiwan.

In 1894 war broke out between Japan and China over the Japanese invasion of Korea. China's poorly equipped navy was no match for Japan's modern fleet, and in 1895 China was forced to sign the humiliating Treaty of Shimonoseki which ceded the Ryukyu Islands (Okinawa), Taiwan and the Penghu Archipelago to Japan.

Taiwan responded to the treaty with alarm and a group of intellectuals formed the Taiwan Democratic Republic, writing a Declaration of Independence and claiming the island as a sovereign nation. Japan was not deterred, and after subduing the areas of Keelung and Danshui, the Japanese took over the ex-Qing governor's office in Taipei. Control over the rest of the island was not as easy as in the north and the Japanese met strong resistance as they moved further south. Employing over a third of its army in Taiwan, the Japanese eventually overcame the Taiwanese who'd confronted the modern weapons of the invaders with bamboo spears and outdated weapons.

The hopes of the nascent Taiwan Democratic Republic were crushed, and Japan was to stay on the island for 50 years. It's believed that in the first several months after the Japanese arrived, over 10,000 soldiers and civilians lost their lives.

Once the Japanese felt they had things under control, they set out to modernise the island, building highways and railways to improve trade and to open up formerly isolated areas, especially along the east coast. They also constructed hospitals, schools and government buildings in an effort to improve the infrastructure of the island. Despite these improvements, the Japanese rule on the island was harsh, with brutal crackdowns on political dissent.

THE REPUBLIC OF CHINA

The loss of Taiwan to Japan was merely one in a string of humiliations heaped by foreign hands upon the tottering Qing dynasty, and by 1900 it was obvious that a strong breeze would bring about its collapse. That wind

Taiwan was declared a Chinese province only in 1887, just a few years before being ceded to Japan.

Over 80,000 Taiwanese served in the Japanese military during WWII.

1895	**1912**
China cedes Taiwan to Japan after defeat in first Sino-Japanese war	Sun Yat-sen declares Republic of China after Qing dynasty collapse

came in the form of a revolutionary doctor named Sun Yat-sen, founder of China's Nationalist party, Kuomintang (KMT). In 1911, China's last dynasty finally collapsed; Sun's KMT stepped in to fill the void, and Imperial China became the ROC. By this time Taiwan had been under Japanese control for nearly two decades, and the nascent ROC had far bigger things to worry about than reclaiming Imperial China's former and farthest-flung possession. From the creation of the ROC in 1911 until the defeat of Japan in 1945, Taiwan remained firmly in Japanese hands, while the ROC battled for its very existence on the Chinese mainland.

Richard C. Bush's *Untying the Knot: Making Peace in the Taiwan Strait* provides a number of interesting insights into the difficulties inherent in the Taiwan-China conflict.

All this would change on 25 October 1945 (known as Retrocession Day in Taiwan). Japan, defeated in WWII, was forced to cede all overseas possessions. Taiwan, now a spoil of war, was handed over to the ROC.

Though some say the Taiwanese were relieved to be rid of the Japanese, others maintain that most already grown accustomed to the stability offered by the Japanese. In any event, any goodwill towards their Chinese 'liberators' would be short-lived. Almost immediately following the defeat of Japan, civil war broke out on the mainland between the KMT (led by Chiang Kai-shek) and Chairman Mao's communist forces. Embroiled in civil war, Chiang sent an inept general named Chen Yi to govern Taiwan; Chen Yi and his thugs plundered Taiwanese homes and shops, sending anything of value back to the mainland to help support the Nationalist fight against the communists. Riots against the KMT broke out, leading to the deaths of tens of thousands of civilians.

TAIWAN UNDER CHIANG

Though adept at slaughtering civilians, Chiang's KMT proved less so at fighting soldiers, and before long Mao's communist forces had driven the

2-28 INCIDENT

On 27 February 1947, a trivial incident led to a massacre that still reverberates to this day. Having declared a government monopoly on the sale of all tobacco, the KMT went after merchants selling black market cigarettes. In Keelung, police from the Alcohol and Tobacco Bureau seized cigarettes and money from a middle-aged widow and pistol whipped her into unconsciousness. Angry crowds formed and attacked the officers, who responded by shooting into the crowd, killing an innocent bystander.

The next morning, crowds protested outside the Taipei branch of the Monopoly Bureau, attacking employees and setting the offices on fire. This was followed by a protest outside the governor's office. But the KMT was in no mood for negotiations. On the order of Governor Chen Yi – orders handed down, many maintain, by Chiang Kai-shek himself – troops fired on the crowds, killing dozens. A state of emergency was declared, and all public buildings were shut down as civilians took to the streets. Soon, news of the event spread and riots erupted island wide. Government offices and police stations were attacked and mainland immigrants were targeted for beatings.

The government's crackdown was brutal, and in the weeks following the incident intellectuals, political activists, and innocents were arrested, tortured and executed. Some estimate that up to 30,000 Taiwanese were murdered.

The 28 February incident evokes powerful memories even today for those who lived through the event. To commemorate those who died during the tragedy, 28 February was declared a national holiday 50 years later and Taipei New Park was renamed the 2-28 Peace Park (p87).

1945	**1947**
Japan defeated; Taiwan ceded to ROC control	2-28 massacre

THE AUGUST 23RD ARTILLERY WAR

On the morning of 23 August 1958, Beijing, determined to take Kinmen from the Chiang Kai-shek's Nationalist army, launched a ferocious bombardment against the island. In just two hours the island was hit with over 42,000 shells. Alarmed, the US acted to defend Kinmen, realising that if it fell, the security of America's 'unsinkable battleship' (as Harry Truman called Taiwan) would be in severe jeopardy. The US sent a shipment of jet fighters and anti-aircraft missiles to Taiwan, along with six aircraft carriers.

Communist forces created a tight blockade around Kinmen's beaches and airstrip, preventing any military supplies from getting in. On 7 September, the US sent several warships into the Taiwan Strait to escort a convoy of ROC military-supply ships; the convoy got within 5km of the blockade and was surprised that the communists refused to fire.

Realising that its navy was outclassed (and no doubt wary of factions in America threatening China with nuclear bombs), Beijing offered the nationalists a very odd ceasefire – it would only fire on Kinmen on odd-numbered days. The deal was agreed to, and the Chinese side continued to shell Kinmen throughout September and October only on odd-numbered days. By November, tensions had decreased and the bombing stopped, but not before nearly half a million shells had struck Kinmen, killing and wounding thousands of civilians and soldiers.

KMT from the mainland. Fully defeated, Chiang Kai-shek fled to Taiwan, followed by a steady stream of soldiers, monks, artists, peasants and intellectuals. One of the first things Chiang did when he arrived in Taiwan was to send Chen Yi back to the mainland (he was later executed). By 1949, the ROC consisted of Taiwan, Penghu, and a number of islands off the Chinese coast including Matsu and Kinmen. These straits islands were quickly set up as military zones, both to rebuff any mainland attack and to set up a base of operations from which Chiang vowed he would use to retake the Chinese mainland.

On Taiwan, Chiang proved the able state governor that he never had been in China, instituting a series of land reform policies that successfully laid the foundation for Taiwan's future economic success. While advertising his government in exile as 'Free China,' based on the democratic ideals of Sun Yat-sen, Chiang's Taiwan was anything but free. While economic development was swift, Chiang's rule was quick to crush any political dissent. The White Terror (opposite) era of the 1950s was a frightening time in Taiwanese history, when people literally disappeared if they spoke against the government. Political dissidents were either shipped to Green Island (p320) to serve long sentences or executed outright.

During the Korean War, the Americans were protective of Taiwan, assuring the Taiwanese that they would repel any communist attacks. Military outbreaks between China and Taiwan were common in the 1950s and 1960s, with Kinmen subjected to regular shelling. Events such as the August 23rd Artillery War kept Chiang's 'Free China' firmly entrenched in the hearts and minds of anti-communist America. At the time of the KMT arrival, the Taiwanese had been heavily indoctrinated by the Japanese and spoke little Mandarin. They were also accustomed to a higher standard of living than the mainland Chinese and felt an ingrained superiority towards the poorer and less well-educated immigrants, especially soldiers who often came from humble backgrounds. The KMT issued laws requiring all Taiwanese to speak

1949	1971
KMT driven from China; seat of ROC government moved to Taiwan	ROC loses UN seat to PRC

Mandarin, in an attempt to 'resinicise' the population. The Taiwanese resented the heavy handedness of the KMT, and there were various outbreaks of rebellion and clashes with military police.

Though Taiwan prospered during the 1950s and 1960s, her economy becoming one of the richest in Asia, and her population growing to 16 million, big changes were on the horizon as the 1970s began. In 1971, Chiang Kai-shek withdrew the ROC from the UN Security Council after the council's admission of the People's Republic of China (PRC). In 1979, America, the ROC's staunchest international ally, switched official recognition from the ROC to the PRC. US policy towards Taiwan would now be dictated by the Taiwan's Relations Act, which, while promising to protect Taiwan militarily in the case of attack by mainland China, recognised Beijing as the sole capital of a China which included Taiwan.

Chiang Kai-shek died in 1975, his presidential duties taken over by his son, Chiang Ching-kuo. The younger Chiang's rule over Taiwan was softer than that of his father; in an effort to improve relations with native Taiwanese, Chiang allowed more Taiwanese to take up political positions. The late 1970s saw increasing political dissent in Taiwan. One of the most noteworthy uprisings of the late martial law–period place occurred in December 1979.

Considered a turning point in Taiwan's shift from authoritarian rule to democracy, the Kaohsiung Incident occurred when editors of *Meilidao,* a publication often critical of the government, organised a rally to celebrate International Human Rights Day. The day before the rally, two organisers were arrested and beaten by police when they were caught handing out promotional flyers. On the day of the rally, scuffles broke out between police and protestors and the situation turned violent, changing from a peaceful event into a full-scale riot. Eight of the organisers were arrested, including Taiwan's current vice president Annette Lu. Among the lawyers who represented the organisers was future Taiwanese president Chen Shui-bian. Though it was a short-term defeat for the democracy advocates, the violence brought increasing support for democratic reforms. Public sentiment eventually forced the KMT to make political concessions. In 1986, with martial law still in effect, Taiwan's first opposition party, the Democratic Progressive Party (DPP), was formed. Chiang Ching-kuo, surprisingly, did not shut the party down, resulting in a large number of DPP candidates being elected to office, and culminating in the official formation of Taiwan's first opposition party.

Denny Roy's *Taiwan: A Political History* is a very readable and balanced account of Taiwan's progress towards democracy.

TAIWAN'S WHITE TERROR

One of the bleakest times in Taiwan's history was the White Terror, when the government started a large-scale campaign to purge the island of political activists during the 1950s. Many who had spoken out against government policies were arrested, charged with attempting to overthrow the government and sentenced to death or life imprisonment. Some who were arrested were indeed political spies but most, it's believed, were unjustly accused. Over 90,000 people were arrested and at least half that number were executed. Taiwanese were not the only targets; a large number of mainland Chinese were arrested or killed. Today Taiwan's White Terror period, though an unpleasant memory, is not forgotten. Green Island's once-notorious political prison, now empty of prisoners, has been transformed into a human rights museum, serving both as a focal point for mourning and a reminder of the human cost of tyranny.

1975	**1979**
Chiang Kai-shek dies; Chiang Ching-kou becomes ROC president	Kaohsiung Incident; US recognition switched to PRC

TAIWAN'S DIPLOMATIC ALLIES

There are currently 22 nations maintaining official diplomatic relations with Taiwan (as the ROC) over the PRC. These are: Belize, Burkina Faso, Dominican Republic, El Salvador, Gambia, Guatemala, Haiti, Honduras, Kiribati, Malawi, Marshall Islands, Nauru, Nicaragua, Palau, Panama, Paraguay, Saint Kitts and Nevis, Saint Vincent and the Grenadines, São Tomé and Príncipe, Swaziland, Solomon Islands, Tuvalu and the Vatican.

In 1987, Chiang Ching-kuo announced the end of martial law. The following year, Chiang passed away and his vice president, Lee Teng-hui, became the first Taiwanese-born ROC president. For Taiwan, a new era had begun.

POST–MARTIAL LAW UNTIL NOW

With Taiwan all but excluded from the international community and China growing economically and militarily, Lee Teng-hui had his work cut out for him. Early in his presidency, Lee paid lip service to the 'One China policy,' but as the years progressed he developed a more pro-independence stance. Mistrustful of Lee, China launched a series of missiles only 25km away from the Taiwanese coast in 1995. But the scare tactics backfired, and Taiwan reelected Lee Teng-hui in open elections the following year.

Sensing that the 'stick' approach had failed, China switched to carrots, and in 1998 offered to lift the ban on shipping and direct flights. The offer was rebuffed by Lee, who incensed China even further the next year by declaring openly his belief that China and Taiwan, as two separate countries, should enjoy 'state to state' relations.

In 2000, with Taiwan's presidential elections looming on the horizon, there was much cross-Strait sabre rattling. Despite this, DPP candidate Chen Shui-bian won in a three-party race, ending 54 years of KMT rule in Taiwan. Though the election signalled pro-independence, Chen was widely seen as a disaster by Beijing. The newly elected Chen soon softened his stance somewhat, declaring in his inauguration speech that the status quo would be maintained as long as China did not attempt to take Taiwan by force. But Beijing was hardly won over by Chen's words, demanding a firm commitment to the 'One China principle.'

Chen found himself between a rock and a hard place, unable to please either his supporters or his detractors. As a result, cross-strait relations stalled during Chen's first term, with the only glimmer of improvement being the opening of limited trade and travel between China and Taiwan's offshore islands. Though often overshadowed by the more high-profile presidential election, Taiwan's legislative election of 2001 was equally revolutionary, reducing the KMT (albeit temporarily) to minority party status in a legislature they'd once controlled with an iron grip.

Chen's reelection in 2004, by the slimmest of margins, was surrounded by strange circumstances to say the least; an assassination attempt on the day before the election resulted in both president and vice president being mildly wounded, both by the same bullet. Needless to say, some felt the event was staged for sympathy. China, fearing that Chen's reelection would embolden pro-independence factions, caused cross-strait tensions to be ratcheted to

1988	**1996**
Chiang Ching-kou dies; Lee Teng-hui becomes first Taiwanese-born ROC president	Lee Teng-hui reelected in first democratic ROC presidential election

their highest level in years with the issuing of an 'anti-secession law'. The law, in brief, codified China's long-standing threat to attack Taiwan should the island's leaders declare independence. Though Beijing's move was protested by massive rallies throughout Taiwan, cross-strait tension seems to have abated somewhat since, and there's been little outside of the usual sabre rattling for the past two years.

NOTABLE POLITICAL FIGURES OF POST–MARITAL LAW TAIWAN

Lee Teng-hui

Even Lee Teng-hui's worst enemies grudgingly concede that the first democratically elected president of the Republic of China (1988–2000) was one smart cookie. After all, only the most clever of men could possibly rise to the highest office in the land (a position once held by Chiang Kai-shek), all the while holding political views diametrically opposed to the very party he led. Taiwanese-born Lee, a Hakka, had been a KMT apparatchik since the early 1970s. After taking over the presidency on the death of Chiang Ching-kuo in 1988, Lee skilfully consolidated his power base by stalwartly defending the KMT party line while simultaneously continuing the democratisation of Taiwan which was started by his predecessor. During his term, Lee was a supporter of the Taiwanese localisation movement, which sought to restore the identity of Taiwan as more than just an appendage of Mainland China. While president, many suspected that Lee was a secret supporter of Taiwan independence. After the KMT loss in 2000 (a loss which many still feel was due in part to Lee's having sown the seeds of discord within his own party), Lee was expelled from the KMT, immediately becoming the spiritual leader of the staunchly pro-Taiwan-independence Taiwan Solidarity Union party.

Chen Shui-bian

Loved by some and despised by others, the ROC's current president Chen Shui-bian (or A-bian, as he's colloquially referred) was elected in 2000. His election ended more than 50 years of KMT rule in Taiwan, and though previously a strong supporter of Taiwanese independence, Chen's current official stance seems to be one of conciliation towards both sides of the issue. A lawyer by trade (Chen was one the defence lawyers following the crackdown on democracy activists in what would later be called 'the Kaohsiung Incident'), Chen's tenure as mayor of Taipei in the mid-90s made him the DPP's most prominent figure in the decade following the lifting of martial law. (Chen would lose his mayorship in 1998, only to redeem his political career in a big way in the presidential election of 2000.) Reelected by the narrowest of margins in 2004, Chen's second term as ROC president has been marked by scandals involving family members and island-wide protests that have widely gridlocked the government. Constitutionally barred from seeking a third term in 2008, it is likely that Chen, like his predecessor Lee Teng-hui, will become an elder statesmen of sorts.

Ma Ying-jeou

Current KMT chairman and former Taipei mayor Ma Ying-jeou is widely considered the front-runner for the 2008 presidential election. Though Ma's squeaky-clean image has been tarnished in recent years due to a number of scandals, Ma has defended his innocence and maintained his intention to run for the presidency in 2008. Whether Ma will be able to withstand the veritable typhoon of mudslinging that's part and parcel of Taiwan's current political environment with his image intact still remains to be seen; nonetheless, the charismatic former justice minister's image looms large over Taiwan's future political landscape.

2000	**2000**
Chen Shui-bian elected ROC president, ending KMT rule	'Three small links' opens trade between Taiwanese-held islands and Mainland China

2006 brought a number of interesting political developments, as two major figures from Taiwan's 'old guard' made much-touted visits to mainland China. Other major political stories of 2006 and 2007 have been the changing the names of various state-run departments and buildings to incorporate the word 'Taiwan' instead of 'China,' and the large scale removal of thousands of statues of former dictator Chiang Kai-shek from many public spaces in Taiwan. As of this writing, there's even talk of removing Chiang's statue from one of Taipei's most famous landmarks, Chiang Kai-shek Memorial Hall (p90); the hall's name itself might have been changed to the National Taiwan Democracy Memorial Hall by the time this edition goes to print. Probably the biggest political story of 2007 has been Taiwan's extended state of political gridlock thanks to a number of high-profile corruption charges involving major figures from both the KMT and the DPP. What affect this will have on Taiwan's internal and external situation in the coming years is anybody's guess.

The Culture

THE NATIONAL PSYCHE

Taiwan offers travellers food and festivals, mountains and beaches, temples and museums; still, the first thing that people usually mention after visiting the island is the kindness of the people. Taiwan's overall social friendliness can be seen in the island's overall low crime rate, general receptiveness to new ideas, and overall *joie de vivre* of its citizenry. A western visitor standing around in a train station trying to decipher the train schedule can pretty much take it for granted that some earnest young person (we say young person simply because the older generation is less likely to speak English, and not because Taiwanese kindness knows any particular generation gap) will approach them asking, 'Can I help you?' within a few minutes. 'Friendly' is often used to describe the Taiwanese, often followed by 'relaxed'. The latter is especially true when compared with Taiwan's close neighbours (physically, and to some extent, culturally), Japan and South Korea, where people there are often described as 'industrious', 'polite', and 'reserved' – but rarely 'relaxed'.

Why is this? It's interesting to compare the national psyche of the three countries. Economically the three have followed roughly similar trajectories (low-tech agrarian to high-tech industrial) to roughly similar demographics featuring largely middle-class populations. Though dissimilar in many ways, the 20th century was filled with periods of trauma for all three nations. South Korea, like Taiwan, bears the scars of foreign colonialism, oppressive dictatorship, military occupation and the always-looming spectre of catastrophic war. The Japanese psyche is scarred by military defeat and occupation. But Taiwan, which endured the shackles of colonialism, decades of brutal martial law and dictatorship, continual low level threat of invasion, and the added ignominy of existing in the strange political limbo of being an officially politically unrecognised entity (by all but a handful of nations; see p38), has managed to produce a population of 21-odd million citizens whose disposition could be summed up with the word 'sunny'.

Strange indeed. Or is it? Consider the possibility that the same factors that have brought about Taiwan's unique geopolitical position have also had a great hand in shaping the disposition of its people. Taiwanese people are painfully aware of their island's diplomatic isolation. Though hobbled by (among other factors) imposed nonparticipation in the UN, the Taiwanese government has gone to great lengths to make itself heard on the international stage. Rarely does a week goes by in which the Taiwan government doesn't attempt to join various international agencies. Though generally blocked, these attempts are always big news in Taiwan. Taiwan's lack of 'official' international recognition is a big part of the Taiwanese psyche, so much so that every victory – the occasional recognition by any nation, no matter how small – is cause for national celebration.

This may be part of why Taiwanese people are so genial. By the very act of applying for a visa, or of passing through customs at Taoyuan Airport, a foreign visitor is recognising (in some sense at least) Taiwan's legitimacy to control its own borders.

There's another possible way in which Taiwan's curious diplomatic situation may have helped to shape the disposition of its people. Although the United States does not technically recognise Taiwan as a sovereign nation, it has pledged to come to Taiwan's aid in the event of military conflict. Thus, like Japan and Korea, Taiwan enjoys the 'protection' of the world's most powerful

Articulate advice and acerbic arguments can be found on www.forumosa .com; if there's something about Taiwan you've got to say, don't be shy, join the fray.

Wan An Taipei (Goodnight Taipei; http://wan antaipei.blogspot.com) is a regularly updated blog and podcast. It's a good resource for students of language and culture.

Andres' Photoblog (http://drepix.blogspot .com) is the photoblog of a Taiwanese expat who has a definite eye for colour.

Anyone in Taipei can tell you how to order a pizza from Dominoes. The number – 2882 5252 in mandarin sounds like, 'Hungry Daddy hungry, I'm hungry, I'm hungry!'

military force. However, unlike either of the other nations, Taiwan has long been free from the obligation of having to quarter American soldiers. Though older people might recall the days when American servicemen were stationed in Taiwan, or patronised brothels in Taipei's Combat Zone (p117) while on R&R from Vietnam, for people under 40 those days are forgotten history.

By comparison, nearly every Seoulite has witnessed at least a few incidents involving American soldiers, ranging from minor cultural misunderstandings to fully fledged street brawls between young foreign soldiers and locals. In Okinawa, as well in other parts of Japan, the presence of American military bases are to the Japanese a source for feelings ranging from mild irritation to fear and anger. Perhaps this is another way in which the curse of Taiwan's political isolation has spit up a gift, and why western visitors to Taiwan don't have to learn to say 'I'm a tourist, not a soldier' in Mandarin.

Perhaps both of these theories are mostly hogwash. Maybe Taiwanese people are friendly because of the weather (hot and wet, and down south usually sunny). Maybe its because Taiwan has been blessed with a mixture of Buddhist philosophy and hefty (though somewhat underestimated) contribution of relaxed Polynesian DNA to the overall gene pool.

Or maybe there is something in the theory of collective national hunger for recognition from the world community, a sentiment that filters down only partly through the lips of people on the street. Perhaps when a Taiwanese person is especially nice to a Western visitor (as often happens), following some random act of kindness with the commonly spoken words, 'Welcome to Taiwan', they're only telling part of the story.

Maybe what they're really saying is, 'Thank you for realising that we are here.'

Tealit.com, an acronym (sort of) for 'Teach English and Live in Taiwan', has helped launch many an expat life in Formosa.

LIFESTYLE
Education

To foreign eyes, the Taiwanese generally seem a fairly relaxed bunch, at least on a superficial level. But beneath the surface, Taiwanese society is plagued by much the same pressures that bedevil Japanese, Korean, Hong Kong, and increasingly of late, middle class Chinese society; namely an education system that's an absolute pressure cooker for pathos.

One of the elements cited as a factor both in Taiwan's economic success and its successful transition from authoritarian dictatorship to representa-

---

CULTURAL COMPASSION MOMENT #1

If you're a Westerner in Taiwan, chances are that you'll have had the following experience:

A parent will push their child – sometimes an adolescent, often younger – in your direction, saying in vaguely scolding-sounding Mandarin, punctuated with poorly pronounced English, 'Hello' or 'How do you do?'

What the parent is probably saying is some variation of, 'Mummy and daddy have spent thousands on English lessons you didn't want in the first place. Now show us that we haven't wasted all that money!'

If the child is the confident sort, they'll then say a few words in English in your direction. This is fine. Greet them back, always smiling.

More often than not, the child will fall into personality type 'B', and will look distinctly uncomfortable. They might even look as if they hate you, but don't take it personally. Instead, imagine your own parents, first forcing you to study a completely alien language when you'd rather be playing video games, then trying to get you to perform like a trained monkey for some random funny-looking stranger on the footpath. Just keep smiling. But remember this moment for Cultural Compassion Moment #2.

tive democracy is the emphasis Taiwan society has placed on education. But this has come at a price, one especially paid for by the young. For most Taiwanese, the pressure begins in early adolescence. Competition to get into 'good' universities is fierce, and university admission in Taiwan is done on the basis of the results of standardised testing. Mastering these tests requires rote memorisation, offering students little incentive for creative 'out of the box' thinking. Beginning in high school, and often earlier, most Taiwanese students will spend long hours at one of tens of thousands of *bǔxíbān* (cram schools), where, well…they'll do just that; cramming as much studying and memorisation in as possible. One of the subjects they'll be tested on is English, but generally speaking, learning useful conversational English takes a backseat to memorising the grammatical patterns they'll see in their all-consuming tests. Many an idealistic Westerner has come to teach at one of these cram schools with the idea that they'll be beloved by gearing the preexisting curriculum towards fun and useful language skills, only to learn that their efforts are not appreciated. 'Teach us the English we need to pass the test', will commonly be the response of young Taiwanese towards their earnest foreign educators. 'When we've gotten into university then we can learn English we can actually use.'

You might be able to detect the long-term detrimental effects of this type of education when interacting with educated Taiwanese, who often feel shy and awkward when confronted by a Westerner. Often times, what's going on in their head at the time is, 'Dammit, I studied English for years but I still can't tell this Western guy how to get to the train station.' Because of the overall friendliness of the Taiwanese, combined with their desperate desire not to lose face, they'll try their best. This is another reason Taiwanese people tend to flatter to the point of obsequiousness a Westerner who can barely string together three words of Chinese. Part of it is cultural (the Taiwanese are, in general, pretty prone to flattery), but another part is that they're generally impressed with someone who has the courage to risk losing face by speaking a language not their own.

Access Koshering (http://accesskaohsiung.blogspot.com) is a public-service site for English speakers living in Kaohsiung.

Tolerance

A primarily Buddhist nation, Taiwan is, by and large, a highly tolerant society. Though no Sydney or San Francisco, Taipei has a flourishing gay culture scene, with plenty of bars, cafés, bookstores and other places where gay, lesbian and transgender people hang out. In 2006, then-mayor Ma Ying-jeou officiated the opening of the city's annual Gay, Lesbian, Bisexual and Transgender Festival, ceremonially hoisting a rainbow flag contributed

---

CULTURAL COMPASSION MOMENT #2

Also common among Westerners visiting Taiwan is an experience of the following sort: You are at a bank, a restaurant, or someplace else, desperately wishing that the local with whom you're briefly interacting could understand just a few words of simple English. But they can't; in fact, you seem to be making them visibly uncomfortable by your presence. Perhaps they're fidgeting, or stammering something unintelligible, or just giggling nervously. They certainly aren't helping you get your money changed, your coffee sweetened, or whatever it is that you came for. You find yourself wondering, 'Does this individual dislike foreigners?'

Consider instead the reluctant performing child of Cultural Compassion Moment #1. It's entirely possible that this nervous person before you is that child, all grown up, and that your current interaction is bringing up memories about which they'd rather not be reminded.

Though this only *might be* the case, smile sweetly, practising the compassionate patience of the Buddha.

by San Francisco mayor Gavin Newson, and stating that he felt the festival demonstrated that Taiwan society placed a premium on 'peace, compassion, and respect for all voices and cultures'. Certainly 'traditional' values hold sway in certain families, so a young, gay Taiwanese is probably slightly less likely to be comfortable coming out to their parents than, say, their North American counterpart might be. But the difference is probably not all that pronounced.

Drugs

Though Taiwan has liberalised in many ways, drugs are still as illegal as they've always been, and even possession of 'soft' drugs like cannabis is dealt with harshly. The Western traveller or expatriate caught with illegal drugs (in any quantity) soon discovers that the Taiwanese tendency to be overly kind towards westerners does not extend itself into the criminal justice system. Really – we can't stress this enough – if you need to catch a buzz during your visit to Taiwan, consider the mixing of *Whisbih* (p58) and betel nut to be your safest option.

Charlie in Wonderland (http://taiwan.atashi -anta.net) is a Taiwan blog in Spanish!

Home Life

Taiwanese home life is about as diverse as that of Australia, Canada, or other countries where a large percentage of families are urban and a small percentage lead more rural lifestyles. More typical Confucian family structure is still strong in some parts of society – especially in more rural areas, where an extended family living under one roof is common (opposite) – but nowadays most urban Taiwanese families wouldn't seem much different from their Western counterparts. Sexual equality has been the norm for decades in Taiwan, so two working parents are a feature of a good many families. Since most kids go to after-school programs of one sort or another (*bǔxíbān*, usually), there isn't the same level of outcry over children being left unattended in the afternoons as in the West. Furthermore, its still fairly common in Taiwan to have one or more surviving grandparents living within the nuclear family, taking more of a role in child-raising than in the west.

When entering a family household, greet the oldest person first unless said person is a middle-aged woman, who may not be pleased by your presumption.

ECONOMY

Taiwan has long been known as a serious economic success story, its economy being one of the strongest and most stable in Asia. Once known as a producer of cheap textiles and low-grade electronics, nowadays the 'Made in Taiwan' label can be found on a wide variety of high-end products, from laptop computers and LCD monitors to aluminium and carbon-fibre bicycle frames. Over the past several years, Taiwan's economy has begun to shift away from that of a purely manufacturing-based one. The reasons behind this shift won't come as a surprise to those familiar with current trends in the global economy; though political relations between the People's Republic of China (PRC) and the Republic of China (ROC) are frosty, both governments have long since recognised the benefits of encouraging strong business relations between the two sides. This has allowed Taiwanese companies like Acer, Giant, and many others to take advantage of the mainland's cheaper labour and highly motivated workforces to maximise profits for the company.

Though his face appears on Taiwan's currency, Sun Yat-sen never made it to the island in his lifetime.

Though this policy has certainly increased corporate profits, it has also raised unemployment levels in Taiwan. At about 4%, Taiwan's unemployment rate is relatively low for the region, but still high for a nation used to near-full employment levels. Still, Taiwan's economy remains pretty strong; you don't tend to see former salary men sleeping on cardboard boxes in parks in Taipei, something quite common in Tokyo, Seoul, and other cities that have experienced marked economic downturns. Compared to the level of

A 'TYPICAL HAKKA FAMILY HOME' *Joshua Samuel Brown*

In the mid 1990s I lived with the Yeh family, Hakkas living in a medium-sized village just a stone's throw away from Hsinchu Science Park, one of Taiwan's major computer and high-tech manufacturing centres. The Yehs lived in a four-storey house, part of a chain of row houses that stretched fairly far in either direction along the town's main street. Half of the first floor was taken up by an indoor garage. The garage had a prominently displayed aquarium filled with goldfish, which, according to feng shui principles, is meant to bring good luck. If the fish weren't enough, the garage was also home to the family dog, Lai-fu, whose name meant 'Come Fortune'. The garage also had two nice cars, three or four motorcycles, and some bicycles for the kids. Lai-fu and the fish, it seemed, were earning their keep.

Behind the garage was the living room where at any given time friends, family and extended family might be found drinking tea, eating sunflower seeds or otherwise just hanging out. The centrepiece of the living room was an expensive, beautifully ornate wooden table carved from a single piece of wood. Next to the living room was a kitchen in which meals were cooked but almost never eaten. Instead, Yeh Tai-tai ('Mister Yeh's Wife', which was how I always addressed the family matriarch) and Mr Yeh's mother (who I called Ah-yi, or Auntie) brought the meals they cooked into the kitchen of the house next door through a side door that was never closed. This was the home of Mr Yeh's brother and his wife. Their kitchen was equipped with a large round table with a lazy Susan. There was always a pot of soup on sister-in-law's stove, as well as a rice cooker filled with rice.

Grandfather and Grandmother lived in an apartment somewhere behind the two kitchens. They were only home around half the year; the rest of the time they were off travelling around the world, a popular pursuit for Taiwanese retirees of decent physical and economic health.

The second floor contained the bedrooms of Mr and Mrs Yeh, across the hall from which was that of Chien-chiu (or 'Jem') a cute, chubby preadolescent who was almost always never seen without a big grin on his face. The Yehs had the idea that renting a room to a foreigner would be a good way for Jem to practice his English, but Jem wound up teaching me more Chinese than I ever taught him English.

The third floor contained the bedroom of the Yehs' oldest sons, who only came home for the holidays, and a parlour with a fold-up Ping-Pong table and disused snooker table that Mr Yeh had bought some years ago when snooker had been a passing craze in Taiwan.

The fourth floor was divided into two sections. In the back was the little apartment I lived in; two medium-sized rooms with wooden Japanese-style floors and a bathroom with a shower. The front of the fourth floor was the most beautiful room in the house; the front half was an outdoor garden, complete with a tiled fish pond and dozens of plants. The back half was a large, open room with an ornately tiled ceiling, an incense brazier, and a large mahogany table pressed against the northern wall.

This was the shrine of Yeh Ken-fu, the grandfather of Mr Yeh. It was here that the family came on holidays to pay their respects. Most of the time it was only me, the foreign boarder, who spent any time on the fourth floor, except on weekends when Mrs Yeh would come upstairs to clean and dust, and very early in the predawn hours when Mr Yeh's father would come up to tend to his own father's shrine.

poverty visitors to the PRC will see, poverty levels in the ROC are negligible. Street beggars, ubiquitous in China, are a rarity in Taiwan.

Currently, one of the major factors slowing the pace of capital and investment growth between Taiwan and mainland China is the restrictions placed on travel between the two. While the lack of direct travel links between Taiwan and the Mainland is little more than a nuisance to the casual traveller (who needs to fly from one to the other via a 'neutral' political territory like Hong Kong), some in Taiwan – particularly the current administration – feel that such links would unduly accelerate the rate of job loss in Taiwan. The issue of direct links are discussed in greater detail in our History chapter (p32).

The Daily Bubble Tea (http://toddalperovitz .blogspot.com) has good pictures and cultural insights from an expat living in Taiwan.

POPULATION

As far as population density is concerned, Taiwan is second only to Bangladesh. The majority of Taiwanese live in crowded urban areas, and the most crowded of these is unquestionably Taipei; the capital and the surrounding areas, including the port city of Keelung, accounts for over 40% of Taiwan's entire population. Visitors will notice the crowds (if they try to travel between cities during the holidays, they'll notice them rather intimately); but in everyday circumstances, Taipei doesn't feel quite as elbow-to-elbow congested as Shanghai, Guangzhou or Hong Kong. If Taiwan were a man, people might comment 'He's fat, but he carries his weight gracefully.'

On the surface, Taiwan's ethnic breakdown seems fairly straightforward – an overwhelming majority of people are of Han Chinese stock, with a tiny minority being of aboriginal descent. But appearances are deceiving, for in recent years, as Taiwan has sought to create a national identity for itself distinct from that of mainland China (which is itself not nearly as culturally homogenous as many would believe), its people have tended to look for diversity in their own cultural backgrounds wherever these might be found. For example, it isn't unusual to chat to a shopkeeper or taxi driver in Taipei affecting a few items of aboriginal-style clothing, only to have them tell you about their having some blood lineage (however slight), to one of Taiwan's nine major aboriginal tribes.

The population of Taiwan's indigenous tribes is under half a million, though the numbers become blurry when intermarriage is taken into consideration. These groups live throughout Taiwan, though the majority are concentrated in the Hualien and Taitung Counties, the Central Mountain Range and Nantou County. However, a fair number of Taiwanese people who wouldn't consider themselves as being aboriginal still have some aboriginal blood.

Then there are distinctions among the Han Chinese themselves. Some of the earliest Han Chinese immigrants were from China's Fujian province. They spoke the Hoklo dialect, which some now refer to as Taiwanese. These Fujian immigrants make up roughly 70% of Taiwan's current population. The Hakka people followed the Fujian people into Taiwan in the 17th century, settling themselves into the foothills of the Central Mountain Range. Nowadays, most Hakka live in the northwestern counties of Taoyuan, Miaoli and Hsinchu, and make up between 10% and 15% of Taiwan's population. Some Hakka also live on the east coast.

But the main distinction – some even call it a divide – has to do with the remaining 12% to 15% of Taiwan's population, the descendents of those who came over from mainland China with the Kuomintang (KMT) between 1945 and 1949; it was this group that by and large controlled the reigns of politics and business during the Chiang Kai-shek era. This situation only began to be reversed after the lifting of martial law, and though Taiwan can easily lay claim to being one of the most peaceful societies in Asia, old wounds and divides still linger under the surface.

ABORIGINAL SOCIETY

Though Taiwan's aboriginal people represent less than 2% of the overall population, celebration of their culture is experiencing a serious heyday in Taiwan. Part of this has to do with the ongoing quest for a true 'Taiwanese' identity; not one necessarily independent from that of Han China, but one not totally viewed through the prism of China either. Taiwan's aboriginal culture has been touted especially heavily in various tourist campaigns, both internationally and regionally throughout Taiwan, so much so that first-time travellers to Taiwan might be led to believe that Taiwanese of non-Han descent represent a larger percentage of the population than the actually do.

Business cards should be handed and received with both hands and never put in a back pocket.

If you're working for a Taiwanese company and your boss says she's serving you some fried squid, don't look forward to sharing a tasty snack. To serve someone fried squid is slang, meaning 'You're fired!'

Ben Goes to Taiwan (Not Thailand), http://taiwanben.wordpress.com, is full of random ravings from a roving rambler.

TAIWAN'S INDIGENOUS TRIBES

With a few exceptions, most of Taiwan's indigenous communities are found in the mountains or along the eastern coast. Nearly all aboriginal people speak Mandarin in addition to their own tribal languages. Some villages offer Disneyesque recreations of 'traditional' tribal life and others are hardly distinguishable from any other small Taiwanese town.

- With a population of around 140,000, the **Amis** are the largest aboriginal tribe in Taiwan. You'll find people of Ami descent all over Taiwan, and predominantly Ami towns and villages on the east coast, from Taitung to Hualien.

- The second largest tribe in Taiwan, is composed of roughly 90,000 **Atayal** people living in the hills and mountains of northern Taiwan. Some of the businesses in Wulai County are owned by Atayal people.

- Originally from the central and southern mountains of the Island, the **Bunun** are the third largest tribe in Taiwan, with about 40,000 people.

- Around 40,000 people identify themselves as members of the **Truku** tribe, whose villages can be visited around Hualien, on Taiwan's central east coast.

- The **Rukai** and the **Puyama** dwell on Taiwan's south east coast, though the Rukai historically ranged out a bit further west than did the Puyama. About 9000 people belong to each tribe.

- The **Tsou** tribe settled in Kaohsiung north of Chiayi, and the **Paiwan** people settled in Kaosiung south of Pingtung. Each tribe claims membership of around 7000.

- Settled in the hills around Hsinchu and Miaoli, the **Saisiat** are a small tribe of around 4000, about the same size as the indigenous population of enchantingly beautiful Lanyu island, home of the **Yami** tribe.

- Taiwan's two smallest tribes are the **Kavalan** of Ilan, with around 1000 members, followed by the 400 or so **Thao** people, who live around Taiwan's most famous tourist spot, Sun Moon Lake.

- *Hold the presses!* Numbering between five and ten thousand, until recently the **Sakizaya** people had been classified as Ami; though the Sakizaya have lived among the Ami for the past century following conflict with Han settlers in late 19th century, in 2005 tribal elders petitioned the government for official recognition as a separate tribe. In January, 2007 the Sakizaya became Taiwan's 13th officially recognised indigenous tribe.

Some are cynical of Taiwan's usage of aboriginal imagery in light of the fact that for decades, prosperity largely bypassed aboriginal communities.

While we don't wish to be overly Pollyana-ish about it, what we hear while travelling among aboriginal communities is that a fair majority of Taiwan's aboriginals are taking a 'better late than never' attitude towards the sudden government and societal recognition of their contributions. To be sure, many issues remain unresolved (particularly on Lanyu, where hundreds of barrels of nuclear waste still remain buried on the island's southern end, continuing to affect the health of the native Yami tribe). But on the whole, travel and tourism seems to be playing a positive role in the empowerment of Taiwan's aboriginal people.

One of the most comprehensive sites on Taiwan's aboriginal peoples is www.atayal.org. The site provides detailed information on the history and customs of the nine major tribes in Taiwan.

SPORT

Since the establishment of the five-day work week, increasing numbers of Taiwanese are finding the time to pursue outdoor activities and organised sports. Land developers and government have really, er, stepped up to the plate. Newest is the Taipei Arena (p102), a state-of-the-art sports complex that seats 15,000 within its cavernous dome. The Tianmu Baseball Stadium seats 10,000, and is where many of Taiwan's professional baseball games are played.

If you really want to get to know a tribe, your best bet is to spend a few days in a homestay. Lanyu is a particularly good place to do this.

Those interested in sporting events for the disabled will want to head to Taipei in 2009 when the city will play host to the summer games for the Deaf Olympics.

Lánqiú (basketball) and *bàngqiú* (baseball) are two of the most popular organised sports in Taiwan. The teams in Taiwan's Chinese Professional Baseball League include the Brother Elephants, China Trust Whales, President Lions, Makoto Gida, Sinon Bulls and First Securities Agan. Because the teams don't have a home stadium, games rotate at various local stadiums around the island.

Basketball is popular largely because it can be played indoors and is not dependent on Taiwan's volatile weather. Amusingly, the most strident fans of basketball in Taiwan are junior high school girls, who have fan clubs devoted to their favourite stars.

Gāoěrfū (golf) is the oldest organised sport in Taiwan and a favourite pastime for the well-to-do. Most golf clubs are open to the public and only require a guest membership to play. Fees can be hefty, though, reaching NT3000 for 18 holes. The Professional Golf Association of the ROC holds annual tournaments in Taiwan and participates in international competitions.

Martial arts have always been practised in Taiwan as a way to keep fit and keep healthy by regulating ones *chi* (*qì*; vital energy). There are more than 20 different kinds of martial arts including the one most foreigners are familiar with, *tàijíquán* (taichi). Taichi is graceful but powerful slow-motion shadow-boxing and is commonly practised in the early morning as the sun rises. The 2-28 Peace Park or the Sun Yat-sen Memorial in Taipei are good places to watch taichi practitioners.

Dragon boat racing, another traditional sport, takes place in June. The Taipei International Dragon Boat Race Championships attracts local and international competitors.

Qing emperor Kangxi was not enamoured of Taiwan; he refused to allow it on official maps, calling it 'a ball of mud beyond the pale of civilisation'.

MEDIA

Unbiased…Reserved…Nontitillating…aren't words you often hear used to describe the Taiwanese media. Newspapers feature, as often as not, no-holds-barred political slugfests, with a number of papers clearly supportive of one political camp and mercilessly skewering the other. Rupert Murdoch might not understand the language, but he'd feel right at home collecting the cheques. Magazines with scantily clad sexpots in suggestive poses can be found everywhere from the backs of taxicabs to dentists' waiting rooms. Sex sells, and magazines, newspapers, and TV news programs grow more vapid and titillating by the year. Reporters on the Taiwan news beat are known – and feared – for being aggressive (Sir Elton John had a few words for the Taiwanese media on a recent trip, but we shouldn't reprint them in a family oriented guidebook). And they're crafty as well, so much so that its likely that any Taiwanese politician or celebrity thinks twice before removing their clothes anywhere but in the privacy of their own homes. Taiwan's media is free, not merely in the sense of being neither government censored nor controlled, but free in the purest 'free for all' sense. This is what a couple of decades of change brings after the near half-century of state-controlled propaganda the Taiwanese endured under martial law.

Though revered in Taiwan for deposing the Dutch, Ming general Koxinga is mostly remembered in Kinmen for cutting down all the trees.

Over on the Mainland, the Communist Party justifies censorship and government control of the press by warning that a Taiwan-style free press will lead to spiritual pollution and moral decay; bollocks. Though Taiwan currently has one of the most sensationalistic medias in the world, most Taiwanese are about as personally lascivious as a Norman Rockwell painting.

RELIGION

Religion on the island is syncretic, dominated by ancestor worship, Taoism and Buddhism. The Taiwanese approach to spirituality is eclectic and not particularly dogmatic; many Taiwanese will combine elements from various religions to suit their needs rather than rigidly adhering to one particular spiritual path. This is something that many Christian missionaries have found frustrating; many Taiwanese don't feel that a conversion to Christianity should imply giving up the myriad folk beliefs that have long-standing meaning to their culture.

Religion plays a number of roles in Taiwanese society. It fosters a sense of shared culture and identity, creating a kind of spiritual glue that brings together people from different economic backgrounds. Temples, especially in less urbanised areas, are usually not just places of worship, but community centres as well. And of course, religion gives Taiwanese people an excuse to get together many times a year and throw massive parties, complete with fireworks, huge multicourse meals, gifts and much making of toasts all around.

But there's a supernatural component too. Most Taiwanese homes have shrines, meant as a sacred place to burn incense and place offerings for ancestors. In a well-to-do household, this shrine will often be on the fourth floor (the word for 'four' and the word for 'death' are almost the same in Mandarin). Many Taiwanese wear amulets for good luck and the jade bracelets that adorn many women's wrists were once thought to have supernatural powers to protect the wearer from harm.

Looking to learn more about religious life in Taiwan? Pick up a copy of Mark Caltionhill's *Private Prayers and Public Parades – Exploring the Religious Life of Taipei.*

Folk Religion

Most residents of towns and villages practise special folk customs that pertain to a historical event or person particular to that area. Folk temples are dedicated to the myriad gods and goddesses that populate Taiwanese folk religion. Some of these deities were actually real people who later became deified due to their earthly reputation as a hero or a healer. The warrior Guan Yu, the famous general from China's legendary Three Kingdoms, has temples dedicated to him all over Taiwan. The most popular deities in Taiwan are the god of heaven, who personifies justice, the earth god, who watches over the harvest, and the house god, who protects families when they move into new homes.

Probably the most popular deity in Taiwan is Matsu, goddess of the sea (p216), who watches over fishermen when they go out to sea. Matsu's birthday, which falls on the 23rd day of the third lunar month, is one of the most important religious festivals in Taiwan and Matsu temples around the island host celebrations to honour the goddess.

Taoism

There are some 4.55 million Taoists and over 7000 Taoist temples in Taiwan. Taoist deities in temples sometimes share space with folk deities and the two religions are often intertwined. At the heart of the faith is the philosophy of *Dàojiào* (Taoism), based on the *Tao Te Ching,* attributed to the 6th century BC sage/philosopher Lao-tzu. The Tao, or way, according to Lao-tzu, is the essence of all things in the universe but ultimately cannot be defined. A central facet of Taoism is the concept of *wúwéi* (nonaction), meaning to live in harmony with the universe without forcing things to your will.

In time, Taoism split into two branches – religious Taoism and philosophical Taoism, each taking very different approaches to Lao-tzu's teachings. Religious Taoism, borrowing concepts from Buddhism and folk religion, became ultimately concerned with the afterlife and achieving immortality. Taoist magicians banished demons through exorcisms and won over the public with demonstrations of their supernatural powers. China lost several emperors who died after drinking elixirs given to them by Taoists promising eternal life. Philosophical Taoism remained a way of life for hermits and for sages, who withdrew from the public life.

Taiwan has world's largest person/temple ratio.

Chuang-tzu is one of the most interesting Taoist writers and the Chinese often quote him today. Numerous translations of his work exist and are easy to locate in bookshops around Taipei.

During the Japanese occupation of Taiwan, many Taoist temples were forced to become Buddhist. It wasn't until the KMT arrived that the Taoist temples were restored to their original status. Many of the Chinese immigrants who came after 1945 considered themselves Taoist and established Taoist organisations and fellowships in addition to schools, hospitals and publishing houses.

Confucianism

Rújiā Sīxiǎng (Confucian values and beliefs) form the foundation of Chinese culture. The central theme of Confucian doctrine is the conduct of human relationships for the attainment of harmony and overall good for society. Confucius (551–479 BC), or Master Kong, lived during the upheavals of China's Warring States era, a time of disunity and fear. Master Kong took it upon himself to re-educate his fellow citizens in the words and deeds of earlier Chinese rulers, whom he believed had wisdom that could be applied to his chaotic times. His goal was to reform society through government. Society, he taught, was comprised of five relationships: ruler and subject, husband and wife, father and son, elder and younger, and friends. Other things he taught were deference to authority and devotion to family.

> If you take but one of the great sage Confucius' sayings with you on your journey, we suggest the following: 'Wheresoever you go, go with all your heart.'

Over the course of his lifetime Confucius attracted a steady following of students. After his death at age 72, disciples carried on his work and thousands of books were published with sayings and advice attributed to the philosopher. The five classics of Confucianism are the *Wujing,* consisting of the *I Ching (Book of Changes), Shijing (Book of Poetry), Shujing (Book of History), Liji (Book of Rites)* and *Chuzu (Spring and Autumn Annals).* Confucian disciples also published other collections of his work, including the *Great Learning, Doctrine of the Mean* and *Classic of Filial Piety.* Perhaps the single most influential book attributed to Confucius is the *Lunyu (Analects),* a collection of essays and dialogues between Confucius and his students. This slim little book contains the central teachings of Confucianism and is standard memorisation for Chinese children.

KNOW YOUR TEMPLES

Taiwanese temples are where most travellers will get their first exposure to Taiwan's rich religious heritage. The amazing craftsmanship found in temples is a science in itself. The shape of the roof, the placement of the beams and columns and the location of deities are all dictated by the use of feng shui, a complex cosmological system designed to create harmonious surroundings in accordance with the natural laws of the universe.

To the untrained eye, Taoist, Buddhist and Confucian temples look similar, but the three are actually quite distinct. Buddhist temples have fewer images, except for statues of the Buddha seated in the middle of the temple on an altar. Guanyin is the next most common deity you'll see, sometimes accompanied by other Bodhisattvas.

Taoist and folk temples are the gaudiest of the three, featuring brightly painted statues of deities, colourful murals of scenes from Chinese mythology, and a main altar with the temple's principal deity (often flanked by lesser-ranked gods). Fierce-looking temple guardians are often painted on the doors to the entrance of the temple, something you won't see at a Buddhist temple.

Confucian temples are the most sedate and lack the colour and noise of Taoist or Buddhist temples. Confucius was a studious sort, so his temples are generally located in park-like settings, or other locales that are well suited for study, contemplation, or other academic pursuits. About the only time you'll find a serious ruckus at a Confucian temple is on the sage's birthday.

Over time Confucianism developed as a philosophy, with Confucius' words and teachings adopted by Chinese emperors. One of his most important followers was Meng-tze (Mencius; 372–289 BC) who continued to spread the Confucian teachings and expand on Confucian thought.

Confucianism's influence on modern Taiwan society remains strong, as it does in most Chinese communities around the globe. Family is the most important unit of society, friends come second and country comes last. The close bonds between family and friends are one of the most admirable attributes of Chinese culture, a lasting legacy of Confucian teachings.

Buddhism

When Buddhism reached China in the 1st century AD it was already about four centuries old in India and had split into two schools: the Hinayana and Mahayana. In the Hinayana tradition, it was believed that Siddhartha Guatama was the sole Buddha who had given humans a simple path to attain freedom from suffering. The Hinayana stressed that Buddha was not a god but a man who had attained perfection and left the cycle of suffering. In the Mahayana school, Siddhartha was believed to be the reincarnation of a series of Buddas, stretching from the past into an indefinite future. In later Mahayana beliefs, Buddas became gods of transcendence and listened to the prayers of followers. It was Mahayana Buddhism that entered China and eventually made its way to Taiwan and other parts of northeast Asia.

Buddhism came to Taiwan in the 17th century, after the Ming loyalist Cheng Cheng-kung drove out the Dutch and relocated his troops to Taiwan. With him came a steady stream of Buddhist monks who had faced persecution in China and wanted to set up temples and monasteries on the island.

Many Japanese were devout Buddhists and supported the growth of Buddhism during their occupation. They were active supporters in the building of temples on the island and financed the construction of Buddhist schools and hospitals.

Buddhists in Taiwan largely follow the Mahayana school, believing in redemption for all mankind. In many Buddhist temples on the island, visitors will see the female Bodhisattva Guanyin, the goddess of mercy, who watches and protects people from harm. Translated, the name Guanyin means 'the one who listens to complaints'.

WOMEN IN TAIWAN

As far as sexual equality is concerned, Taiwanese society is about as equitable as you're going to find anywhere in Asia. The Taiwanese constitution forbids discrimination on the base of gender, and women are found in the upper echelons of many companies and businesses. And of course, vice president Lu, a heartbeat away from the presidency, is a woman.

In education there are a few interesting gender gaps; while graduating classes of both high schools and universities tend to be evenly split, graduate programs skew heavily on the male side, with roughly three of five Masters students being men, and only one in three doctorate students being women. A similar skew can be seen in the teaching profession; women dominate the profession at kindergarten and grade school levels while high school positions skew slightly towards men and the majority of Taiwan's university professors are men.

Foreign women travelling in Taiwan should be as cautious here as anywhere else, but on the whole Taiwanese men are pretty respectful (though they're known to sometimes gawk a bit too much). Incidences of actual harassment, though not unheard of, are on the low side for Asia in general.

ARTS

Art in Taiwan is alive and well in great abundance. Generally, a discussion of art can be divided into three fairly broad categories; traditional, contemporary and indigenous.

As far as the traditional is concerned, the fact that Taiwan is home to some of the world's finest repositories of classical Chinese art ranks among the world's worst kept secrets. Chiang Kai-shek was a voracious collector of valuable items, including art. In keeping with his passion for 'collecting,' he ordered his retreating forces to collect as much art as they could get their hands on while retreating from the Mainland in 1949. These treasures were added to the already voluminous collection that had been liberated earlier from the former imperial collection housed for centuries in the Forbidden City in Beijing. Much of this collection is housed at the National Palace Museum in Taipei (p90), but amazing examples of classical Chinese art – from paintings and scrolls to ceramics and bronze – can also be found in various museums throughout the island.

The storing of so many borrowed precious *objets d'art* on Taiwan is one of many long-standing sore spots between the ROC and PRC. However, the fact that much of the art currently on display in Taiwan would very likely have been destroyed during the Cultural Revolution (1966–76) had it remained in the Mainland leads most on both sides to believe that Chiang's having taken them to Taiwan turned out to be, in the long run, a good thing.

While many aspects of traditional Chinese arts can be seen in much contemporary art coming out of Taiwan today, over the past few decades, Taiwanese artists have sought to create an artistic vision that is more Taiwanese, and less connected with the themes found in classical Chinese art. This quest for a Taiwanese identity is one of the most important themes in the contemporary Taiwanese art world. Taiwanese artists have pursued this not only through traditional media such as oil painting and ceramic sculpture, but also through more modern approaches such as multimedia installations and videos, and performance art and film. Taipei's Fine Arts Museum (p93) and the Museum of Contemporary Art (p93) are both must visits. Fans of sculpture should make the trek into northern Taipei County to visit the Juming Museum (p156), which houses a vast collection of works created by Taiwan's most revered modern sculptor.

The art of Taiwan's aboriginal people is also becoming quite popular throughout the island; quite distinctive from Chinese and Chinese-influenced artwork, Taiwanese aboriginal art tends to be more earthy, and almost Polynesian. Traditional arts among Taiwan's aboriginal cultures include woodcarving, weaving and basket making. The Shung Ye Museum of Formosan Aborigines (p91) is an excellent place to learn about the arts and crafts of Taiwan's aboriginals. The Ketagalan Cultural Centre (p131) in Beitou, Taipei, features aboriginal culture exhibitions, a multimedia showroom, an aboriginal theme library, research facilities, and conference and performance space. Taitung's National Museum of Prehistory (p93) also has worthy exhibits devoted to traditional arts and crafts. Should you make it to Lanyu (p316), you'll be able to interact with local artists from the Yami tribe who create artwork unique to their tribe.

Cinema

Taiwanese cinema has a long history, going all the way back to 1901, with Japanese-made documentaries and feature films. Silent-era films often used a Japanese convention called *rensageki,* a mix of film and theatre with moving images supplementing performances on stage. When the KMT took over

Chinese pronunciation of the number 'four' is similar to the word for 'death'; hence, the number is considered unlucky.

Eight is a lucky number. This accounts for the high number of businesses paying big bucks to have phone numbers like xxxx-8888.

MANY SCULPTURES, MANY STORIES

British art critic Ian Findlay has proclaimed Juming's work 'the most instantly recognisable of Taiwan's contemporary sculptors.' An afternoon spent at the Juming Museum in Taipei County's Chinshan is kind of like an intensive course in short story appreciation, with every tale created by a master of the genre, its text made of stone, metal and other mediums instead of words. Within the 12+ hectare sculpture garden and museum, myriad tales are told indeed.

One painted bronze sculpture shows a man and woman sitting beneath an umbrella while behind them a third woman sits with arms folded, a dour, petulant expression creasing her face. The couple are lovers, that much seems certain, but is the third woman a jealous paramour or disapproving auntie? If the artist himself knows, he isn't saying. One of Juming's most oft-quoted views is his belief that the interpretation of art is the domain of the viewer and not the artist. Visitors to the Juming Museum may well be struck by how few of his works bear titles aside from the names of the series to which they belong. The artist has been quoted as saying that he feels that naming his sculptures would just 'get in the way' of the viewer's interpretation.

While many of his sculptures (most notably those in his most famous series, *Tai Chi*, which feature gigantic blocky stone monoliths in various martial-arts poses) have clearly Taiwanese – or at least Asian – themes, the majority of Juming's works are slice-of-life features, moments frozen in amber, scenes that could be taking place anywhere in the world.

It is fitting, we believe, to consider Juming's artwork as highly representative of modern Taiwanese art as a whole. The artist – and his personal artistic philosophy – seems to fit well with the spirit of 'strategic ambiguity' that Taiwan itself has used so well to navigate the potentially hazardous waters of a political entity that, while clearly independent, dares not declare itself as such.

Is Taiwan a nation or a province? Is the scowling woman a jealous suitor or an over-protective auntie? Different people have different interpretations, but the 'official' answer to both of these questions is roughly the same:

'Have a look. Draw your own conclusions.'

Taiwan, they set up their own movie industry as a way to 'educate' the Taiwanese population in all things Chinese. The movie business was short-lived, however, because there was little interest in KMT morality plays and, on top of that, only a few of the older residents of the island could speak Mandarin.

In the 1960s the government created the Central Motion Picture Corporation (CMP) and the movie industry finally took off. During the 1960s and 1970s, audiences were treated to a deluge of romantic melodramas and martial-arts epics and in the late 1970s a disturbing subgenre emerged called 'social realism', full of brutal violence and sex.

In the 1980s the Taiwanese grew tired of the repetitive films of the past two decades and film makers had to find a way to compete with foreign-made films. During this time, two film makers emerged who would have a strong impact on how Taiwanese cinema was seen abroad, though most locally made movies from this point forward would only be seen in art houses. Hou Hsiao-hsien, considered the most important director of this New Wave movement, broke away from escapist movies and chose instead to make movies that depicted the gritty reality of Taiwan life. *The Sandwich Man* (1983) is one of the best examples of Taiwan's New Wave ideals, establishing it as a realistic artistic movement. The movie is an adaptation of three short stories by the Taiwanese author Huang Chun-ming, which explore life in Taiwan during the 1950s and 1960s. One segment of the movie is taken from the story 'The Taste of Apples', and is about a young boy from the countryside who encounters tragedy when he moves from the countryside to Taipei.

Another of Hou Hsiao-hsien's movies, *A Time to Live and a Time to Die* (1985), also explores childhood in rural Taiwan during the Cold War era.

Probably Hou Hsiao-hsien's most successful film is *City of Sadness* (1989), which follows the lives of a Taiwanese family living through the KMT takeover of Taiwan and the 2-28 Incident. This movie was the first to break the silence surrounding the tragedy. *City of Sadness* won the Golden Lion award at the 1989 Venice Film Festival. Hou Hsiao-hsien has continued to produce some masterful work, including the brilliant *The Puppet Master* (1993), an examination of the life of 84-year-old puppeteer Li Tien-lu, who is considered a 'living treasure' by the Taiwanese. Most recently, Hou Hsiao-hsien shot *Millennium Mambo* (2001), a more conventional story about a woman torn between two men.

'By far the most famous director to come out of Taiwan is Tainan-native Ang Lee. Though his megahit *Crouching Tiger, Hidden Dragon* (2000) made him a household name in the West, Lee had long made the A-list of Hollywood directors with the English language films *Sense and Sensibility* (1995) and *The Ice Storm* (1997). Lee's first film was *Pushing Hands* (1992), filmed in New York with funding from the CMP, followed by *The Wedding Banquet* (1993), which took a bold step in exploring homosexuality in Chinese culture. *Eat Drink Man Woman* (1995) was an art-house favourite in America, featuring both a beautiful storyline and some of the best food scenes ever filmed. Lee's Academy Award for Best Director for the 2006 film *Brokeback Mountain* was cause for major celebration throughout Taiwan, especially in his hometown of Tainan.

> 'By far the most famous director to come out of Taiwan is Tainan-native Ang Lee'

Taipei hosts some notable film festivals every year, including the Taipei Golden Horse Film Festival. Attending the Golden Horse is a wonderful way to support a struggling industry and see some great films that won't make it into the general theatres. The best place to see indie movies, both local and foreign, is at the SPOT Taipei Film House (p121).

Music

To discover the roots of traditional Taiwanese music, you need to go back a ways, centuries in fact. Early Chinese music was brought to Taiwan by immigrants from Fujian province, who brought with them both the informal folk music and the more stylised operas of their native province. Soft and melodic Nanguan and its more cacophonous sibling Beiguan can be found played around the island. Taiwanese folk music today is called Hoklo, or Holo, and generally features melodic songs played on the *yuèqín* (moon guitar; a kind of two-stringed lute), and accompanied by lyrics in the Taiwanese dialect. Taiwanese and Hakka language opera are also popular, and can be watched both in theatres and at ad-hoc performances on warm nights in small towns around the island. The older generation are naturally more fond of opera than the younger.

As different from traditional Taiwanese music as it is diverse, Taiwanese aboriginal music is also reaching a wide audience, both in and out of Taiwan. Though you've probably never heard of Yingnan and Xiuzhu Guo, you've almost definitely heard their voices; the polyphonic vocals of this elderly Ami couple were sampled by Enigma, becoming the backing vocals for their smash hit, 'Return to Innocence.' (When the couple discovered that their voices were being heard around the world, they filed suit against Enigma, settling out of court for an undisclosed sum.) The more touristy aboriginal theme parks and villages around the island stage regular performances, and you can buy music recorded by various tribal groups all over Taiwan.

However, the most widely listened to music in Taiwan tends to be fairly generic pop. Ask most Taiwanese people what kind of music they listen to, and nine times out of ten you'll hear some variation of 'I like music that

WHAT IS TAIWAN HIP-HOP?

You don't need to understand Chinese to realize that Kou Chou Ching doesn't fit the mold of the stereotypical Western hip-hop aping Asian rap-act. The Taipei Based hip-hop band has been playing clubs, festivals and events around Taiwan since 2003, mixing politically charged lyrics in Mandarin, Hoklo (Taiwanese) and Hakka with sampled flavours drawn from the far corners of Taiwanese musical history. Kou Chou Ching's MC Fan Jiang spoke a bit about Taiwanese hip-hop, music and identity:

'What can I say about Taiwan hip-hop? Like everywhere else in the world, hip-hop is getting more popular in Taiwan, and like everywhere else, Taiwan has its share of 'pop' hip hop artists making money from rhyming over beats, guys like Jay or Wang (two rappers currently popular in Taiwan). A lot of Taiwanese hip-hop artists start by mixing music on computers, then mixing in various Western influences, including of course old and new school rap from African-American hip-hop artists.

But some groups try to take it in a different direction aiming for a more clearly Taiwanese-flavoured hip-hop music. Kou Chou Ching draws its influences not primarily from the West, but from the music of our home, from traditional Taiwanese music; Kou Chou Ching songs sample Beiguan and Nanguan, Taiwan Opera, Hakka Ba-yin and Mountain Songs, South Chinese Huamei Diao, with some Peking Opera and Classical Chinese music thrown into the mix.

Kou Chou Ching's language and lyrics reflect the new generation of Taiwan, people who have transcended so-called 'ethnic differences'. Our song 'Confluent People', attempts to realise this desire for harmony among Taiwan's diverse ethnic groups. The name of the song itself mixes Hoklo and Hakka language elements, using the Hakka phrase for youth and a Hoklo expression that means 'becoming close friends with just one word'. Together, this name represents young people shaking hands and coming to agreement, singing together and forming friendships.

Another songs is called 'Your name is Taiwanese'. Modelled on an old Taiwanese folk-song called 'Moonlit Sighs', our song has a background beat that sounds kind of pensive, as if reminding the listeners to think things over. The word 'Taiwan' is sung many times throughout this song. This repetition, the beat and lyrics combined remind listeners to use their hearts when considering their roots.

These days many people forget their roots. Caught up with J-Pop and the K-wave, young people don't remember their own culture. Parents send their children to study English, but where do the children learn to speak their mother tongue? Kou Chou Ching songs are about reminding people that it doesn't matter what language you speak at home; if you grew up eating Taiwanese rice, drinking Taiwanese water, then you are a Taiwanese person.'

Check out Kou Chou Ching's music online at www.myspace.com/koucc or www.kou.com.tw.

makes me feel happy.' Mainstream Taiwanese musical tastes would hardly be categorised as 'edgy'. (Kenny G albums sell well here, and the prince of saccharine-spiced sax plays to a full house when he tours around.) Most Taiwanese pop music falls well within this mold, and is best avoided by those with family histories of diabetes. (The curse of a reasonably well-adjusted society? Perhaps.)

There are exceptions, of course. Wu Bai, Taiwan's 'King of Live Music' is probably the edgiest of Taiwan's mainstream rockers. An excellent guitarist and lyricist, Wu Bai is among the best-known Taiwanese rockers, playing to sold-out arenas in and out of Taiwan with his band China Blue. Those who understand Mandarin or Taiwanese (the artist records equally in both) can detect a certain amount of pathos in Wu Bai's lyrics, unusual for Asian pop in general.

The Daily Lomo (http://lomodiary.blogspot.com) showcases Taiwan through a fisheye lens. Very cool!

Another extremely popular Taiwanese artist is A-mei, a singer/songwriter from Taiwan's Puyuma tribe. A-mei is one most well-known faces on Asia's pop scene, and since 2000 her career has been flavoured with cross-strait controversy. Early in that year A-mei did a Sprite beverage commercial; shortly thereafter, she performed the ROC national anthem at the first inauguration of newly elected president Chen Shui-bian. This did not sit well with the Beijing Government, who subsequently banned the singer from visiting mainland China and banned her songs from Mainland airwaves. Though the ban has since been revoked, A-mei performances in China are often marred by protests by Chinese nationalists; to make matters worse, the singer's Taiwanese patriotism has been questioned back home (by, among others, vice-president Annette Lu). Nonetheless, her career is still going strong, and her face has graced the cover of magazines such as *Time* and *Newsweek*, making her one of the most well-known Taiwanese entertainers in the world.

Of course, Taiwan's underground music scene, small though it is, is definitely flourishing; though you might not understand the lyrics, if you're a fan of underground music you'll definitely understand the sentiment if you can manage to catch a few of Taiwan's indie rock bands in full bloom. Some of our favourite Taiwanese punk bands are The White Eyes, Ladybug, Chicken Rice and Chthonic (the last would technically fall under the 'Death Metal' category). Taiwan also has a number of bands started by expatriates; Consider the Meek, Milk and the Deported being three well worth catching. There are a good number of venues for independent music around Taiwan. These include small clubs like Underworld (p119) and larger places like The Wall (p119).

A French blog from Taipei (http://michaelataipei .canalblog.com) covers music, sports, culture, and much more.

Serious indie music fans should definitely try to time their visit to catch one of Taiwan's weekend-long (sometimes longer) music festivals. Our favourite is the long-running Spring Scream Festival, currently in its 13th year. Held in Kenting during spring break, the multistage festival brings together names big and small in Taiwan's indie music scene, along with a few imported bands. Festival grounds rotate from year to year, with guests and bands alike camping out together in the fields inside the site. Check www.springscream.com/for more details.

A MOVING SOUND

Tom Pryor, of WorldMusic.NationalGeographic.com describes Taiwan's A Moving Sound (AMS) as, 'one of the most original outfits working in the world music arena today'. Performing both locally and internationally since 2002, AMS is comprised of five extraordinary performers who bring their diverse backgrounds together to create music that transcends the East–West barrier as only the highest art can.

Mixing elements of modern dance, taichi and deep-breath work, vocalist and dancer Mia Hsieh provides sublime vocals and movement in a unique performance style she calls 'Singing Body.' Percussionist Wu Cheng-chun combines Eastern and Western drumming styles, while Lo Tang-hsuan, an *èrhú* (mandolin) player since the age of eight, takes his traditional Chinese instrument and uses it to call forth a hybrid of Chinese, Indian and Western sounds. Equally skilled in both Western six-string guitar and the *zhōng ruǎn* (Chinese guitar), Hua Chou-hsieh uses both instruments to create a fusion of sounds drawing from influences as diverse as American jazz and Taiwanese aboriginal sounds. American-born Scott Prairie plays both bass and *zhōng ruǎn*, his compositions mixing his New York and Taiwan influences. Together, this diverse group of performers creates a sound that is both ancient and modern, at once universal and distinctly Taiwanese. In short, a sound that is truly moving.

Though AMS tour internationally, catching them on their home turf is an especially unique experience; check their website www.amovingsound.com for performance schedules and updates.

Theatre & Dance

Taiwan has a number of home-grown drama and dance troupes. The best known internationally is the Cloud Gate Dance Company, founded in the early 1970s by Lin Hwai-min. Lin was a student under Martha Graham and upon his return to Taiwan in 1973 desired to combine modern dance techniques with Chinese opera. While Lin's first works were based on stories and legends from Chinese classical literature, his more recent works have tended to explore Taiwanese identity. *Legacy,* one of Lin's most important works, tells the story of the first Taiwanese settlers. More recently still, Cloud Gate's performances have included Tibetan, Indian and Indonesian influences. The company tours most of the year, both domestically and internationally. Check their website, www.cloudgate.org .tw, for performance schedules.

Food & Drink

No doubt about it, there's a lot to love about Taiwanese food, and a lot of it to love. And crickey, do the Taiwanese love food. Taiwanese people tend to eat out often, and are hardly known as sombre diners. Looking for a good restaurant? Just follow the noise. But some of the best food is not found in restaurants but on the street, and gourmands know that some of Asia's best street eats are found in night markets in and around Taiwan's cities.

But first things first…

STAPLES
Rice

Rice is an inseparable part of virtually every Taiwanese meal; as in China, the phrase used to ask someone if they've eaten is to say 'you eat rice yet?' Rice comes in many forms – as a porridge (congee) served with plates of pickled vegetables at breakfast, fried with tiny shrimps, pork or vegetables and eaten at lunch or as a snack. Plain steamed white rice accompanies most restaurant meals, except formal banquets, where you'll often need to ask for it. While plain white rice is still the norm, many restaurants – especially vegetarian buffets, as well as more health-oriented eateries, offer a choice between white and *quán mài* (whole-grain rice).

Noodles

Noodles are thought to have originated in northern China during the Han dynasty (206–220 BC) when the Chinese developed techniques for large-scale flour grinding.

Taiwan has several types of noodles which are worth mentioning. *Lā miàn* (hand-pulled noodles) is created when the noodle puller repeatedly stretches a piece of wheat-flour dough, folding it over and stretching again, until a network of noodle strands materialise. Thin, translucent noodles made from rice flour are common in the city's Southeast Asian restaurants. And of course, for the carnivore no visit to Taiwan would be complete without trying the wares of at least a few beef noodle restaurants; the best of these

The long, thin shape of noodles symbolises longevity. For this reason, its considered inauspicious to break noodles before cooking them.

A RECIPE FOR OVERVIEW OF TAIWANESE CUISINE

Assemble following ingredients:

- One medium-sized subtropical island well suited for growing rice, vegetables, tubers and fruit;

- One surrounding ocean teeming with fish (seafood-rich outer islands optional);

- Several thousand years of indigenous Pacific Islander culinary tradition;

- Several hundred years of southeastern Chinese culinary tradition;

- Equal parts of Buddhist, Taoist and indigenous culinary roots;

Mix well, adding long dash of Japanese culinary influence. Continue to cook under subtropical heat until 1949.

In 1949, RAPIDLY infuse long and slow-cooking mixture with traditions of chefs from all corners of China fleeing political turmoil; continue cooking under high pressure for around 35 years.

Begin liberalizing in 1987: Continue to infuse and then mix regularly with random dashes of international influence and increasing aboriginal seasonings to taste.

Serve hot, cold, or in-between, and until all diners are fit to burst.

Serves around 22 million locals as well as guests.

places shave each noodle individually from a cinder block–sized lump of dough before tossing them into the pot of beef stock.

REGIONAL CUISINES IN TAIWAN

Taiwanese cuisine can be divided into several styles of cooking, though the boundaries are often blurred. You'd be hard pressed to find some of Taiwan's more emblematic dishes (stinky tofu, for example) anywhere in China outside of restaurants specialising in Taiwanese cuisine, though you'll find much food of close comparison in Fujian province. Straddling both sides of the straits, Hakka food is distinct enough to warrant its own category, though Hakka cuisine you'll find on Taiwan will be more seafood heavy than what you'd find in China's inland regions. And of course, anything you'd find on the Mainland – Cantonese, Sichuanese, Beijing, Shanghainese and so forth – you'll find in Taiwan. See the Menu Decoder (p66) for pinyin and Chinese spellings of dishes described in the following sections.

For a quick and cheap snack, *cháyè dàn* (tea eggs) can't be beat. A cauldron filled with these hard-boiled (in black tea, naturally) eggs can be found in any convenience store. The darker they are, the longer they've been cooking.

Taiwanese

As our recipe at the head of the chapter shows, Taiwanese cooking has a long, storied and complex history, with influences ranging from all over China mixed with a rather unique aboriginal/Polynesian base. In general, food that you'll see people enjoying at roadside markets and restaurants tends to emphasise local recipes and ingredients (though often curious about things foreign, most Taiwanese tend to buy local when it comes to their food). Seafood, sweet potatoes, taro root and green vegetables cooked very simply are at the heart of most Taiwanese meals. Chicken rates second in popularity to seafood, followed by pork, beef and lamb. *Xiǎoyú huāshēng* (fish stir-fried with peanuts and pickled vegetables) is an example of a Taiwanese favourite. *Kézǎi* (oysters) is popular, and *kézǎi tāng* (clear oyster soup with ginger) is an excellent hangover cure and overall stomach soother. Something completely unique to Taiwan is its use of a local variant of *jiǔcéngtǎ* (basil), which frequently flavours soups and fish dishes. The Taiwanese like to cook with chilli, though dishes are never as mouth searing as those in Sichuanese cuisine.

Ah, Stinky Tofu!
Really, quite odious.
Truly Taiwanese.

Hakka

Hakka cuisine is having a renaissance in Taiwan, with Hakka-style dishes being featured in restaurants across the country. The dishes of the Hakka are very rich and hearty, suitable for people who historically made their living as farmers and needed plenty of energy to work the fields. Dishes are often salty and vinegary, with strong flavours. Pork is a favourite of the Hakka, often used in dishes cut up into large pieces, fried and then stewed in a marinade.

Hakka cuisine is also known for its tasty snacks. Some of these include *zhà shūcài bǐng* (fried salty flour balls made from mushrooms), *kèjiāguǒ* (shrimp and pork turnip cakes) and *kèjiā máshǔ* (sticky rice dipped in sugar or peanut powder).

'RICE OR NOODLES…'   *Joshua Samuel Brown*

…was the question I heard pretty much daily from my first Taiwanese girlfriend when the subject of what we should eat for dinner came up. New to Taiwan and somewhat unschooled in the culinary culture as I was at the time, I took this as a sign that everyday Taiwanese cuisine was none too diverse. It took me a while to understand that this question would actually lead to a wide variety of meal choices, that the two staples were mere starting points, as limiting to the Taiwanese gourmand as choosing between oil paints or watercolours would be to an artist.

Fujianese

Much of Taiwanese cuisine has Fujianese roots, as the earliest wave of Han Chinese immigration to the island comprised primarily Fujian mainlanders who immigrated in the 18th and 20th centuries. Fujianese cuisine particularly abounds on the Taiwan Strait islands of Matsu and Kinmen (both of which are a stone's throw away from Fujian province), but you'll find Fujianese cuisine all over Taiwan. Really, most people won't call it Fujianese cuisine, as so much of its basic elements have been incorporated in Taiwanese cooking. Cuisine in Fujian is best known for its seafood, often cooked in red wine and simmered slowly in dark soy sauce, sugar and spices. One of the most popular dishes in the Fujianese food canon is *fó tiào qiáng*, 'Buddha Jumps Over the Wall', a stew of seafood, chicken, duck and pork simmered in a jar of rice wine. The dish got its name because it is believed that the smell is so delicious Buddha would climb a wall for a taste, ironic considering the fact that the Buddha is generally thought to have been a vegetarian.

On that subject, Fujian is where Chinese vegetarian cuisine reached its apex, partly thanks to the availability of fresh ingredients and partly because of the specialisation of generations of chefs. The Taiwanese, however, have taken vegetarian cuisine to heights that easily rival that of India, a fact worthy of a heading all its own (opposite).

Chopsticks stuck vertically into a bowl of rice is reminiscent of incense sticks stuck in a brazier; it reminds the Taiwanese of death, and is therefore considered a terrible faux pas.

Cantonese

This is what non-Chinese consider 'Chinese' food, largely because most émigré restaurateurs originate from Guangdong (Canton) or Hong Kong. Cantonese flavours are generally more subtle than other Chinese styles – almost sweet, with very few spicy dishes. Sweet-and-sour and oyster sauces are common. The Cantonese are almost religious about the importance of fresh ingredients, which is why so many restaurants are lined with tanks full of finned and shell-clad creatures.

Cantonese *diǎnxīn* (dim sum) snacks are famous and can be found in restaurants around Taiwan's bigger cities. Apart from barbecued pork dumplings, you'll find *chūn juǎn* (spring rolls), *héfěn* (flat rice noodles), *zhōu* (rice porridge) and, of course, *jī jiǎo* (chickens' feet) – an acquired taste.

Sichuanese

Sichuan food is known as the hottest of all Chinese cuisines, so take care when ordering. Lethal red chillies (introduced by Spanish traders in the early Qing dynasty), aniseed, peppercorns and pungent 'flower pepper' are used, and dishes are simmered to give the chilli peppers time to work into the food. Meats are often marinated, pickled or otherwise processed before cooking, which is generally by stir-frying.

CULINARY COURSES & MORE

Those looking to take more than memories of great Taiwanese cuisine back home will be glad to know that the **Community Services Centre** in Taipei conducts cooking courses where visitors to Taiwan can learn all the secrets to preparing amazing traditional Chinese and Taiwanese dishes. Call ☎ 02-2836 8134 or visit their website www.community.com.tw for information on current courses, prices and scheduling.

Located in Taipei, the **Lu-Yu Tea Culture Institute** offers basic, intermediate and advanced courses in tea arts, culture and lore. All courses are in English. Course length and schedules vary; call ☎ 02-2331 6636 for more information or email **Steven R Jones** (icetea8@gmail.com) for details on current courses.

TRAVEL YOUR TASTEBUDS

Eating in Taiwan can be an overwhelming experience, especially with so many delicious foods to try. It's important to venture beyond the more conventional dishes of *chǎofàn* (fried rice) or *chǎomiàn* (fried noodles) that seem to be available at every hole-in-the-wall roadside stand. What about trying a savoury dish of *húntún* (wontons), filled with leeks and minced pork?

For a meal on the run, consider picking up some *jiānbǐng* (omelette stuffed with pickled radishes, spring onions and filled with hot sauce). If time is not an issue, sit down to *huǒ guō* (simmering pot of vegetables and meats, cooked in a spicy broth).

For adventurous eaters, may we suggest delectable *chòu dòufu* (stinky tofu) – some say it's the equivalent to European stinky cheese. Or how about *chǎo shāchóng* (fried sandworms), a speciality of Kinmen and best served hot, and last but not least, Hakka-style *jiāngsī chǎo dàcháng* (stir-fried intestines with ginger).

Famous dishes include *zhāngchá yāzi* (camphor tea duck), *mápó dòufu* (Granny Ma's tofu; spiced mincemeat sauce and tofu) and *gōngbǎo jīdǐng* (spicy chicken with peanuts). Sichuan is an inland province, so pork, chicken and beef – not seafood – are the staples.

Other Chinese Cuisine

In the north of mainland China, wheat or millet, rather than rice, is traditional. Its most common incarnations are steamed dumplings and noodles, while arguably the most famous Chinese dish of all, Peking duck, is also served in Taiwan with typical northern ingredients: wheat pancakes, spring onions and fermented bean paste. Shanghainese cuisine is popular, especially in Taipei. Expect dishes to be generally sweeter and oilier than China's other cuisines, and to feature a lot of fish and seafood, especially cod, river eel and shrimp. The word for fish, *yú*, is a homonym for 'plenty' or 'surplus'; fish is a mandatory dish for most banquets and celebrations.

Common Shanghainese fish dishes include *sōngrén yùmǐ* (fish with corn and pine nuts), *lúyú* (Songjiang perch), *chāngyú* (pomfret) and *huángyú* (yellow croaker). Fish is usually steamed but can be stir-fried, pan-fried or grilled. Shanghai-style steamed fish, cooked lightly and covered with ginger or spring onions is a mainstay at any banquet.

Vegetarian cooking was already an independent school of Chinese cuisine by the 14th century.

VEGETARIAN CUISINE

Vegetarian visitors to Taiwan may well consider applying for citizenship once they've experienced the joys of Taiwanese vegetarian cuisine. Taiwan's Buddhist roots run deep, and while only a small (but still sizable) percentage of Taiwanese are vegetarian, a fair chunk of the population abstains from meat for spiritual or health reasons every now and again, even if only for a day or a week.

Buddhist vegetarian restaurants are easy to find. Just look for the gigantic *savastika* (an ancient Buddhist symbol that looks like a reverse swastika) hung in front of the restaurant. If the restaurant has a cassette or CD playing a soothing loop of *ami tofo* (Buddhist chant) and a few robed monks and nuns mixed among the lay patrons, you're in business. Food at these places tends to not merely be 100% vegan friendly (no animal products of any kind), but also garlic and hot-pepper free (fiery belching being disruptive to meditation). Every neighbourhood and town will generally have at least one vegetarian buffet; some are a bit on the plain side, others are places of unparalled food artistry. Taipei has a number of vegetarian buffets (p115) that keep us coming back. Buffets are especially cool because there's no language barrier to deal with. Take what looks and smells the best, pay by weight, and enjoy.

Soybeans have been cultivated in China since 2700 BC.

The Taiwanese are masters at adding variety to vegetarian cooking and creating 'mock meat' dishes made of tofu or gluten on which veritable miracles have been performed. Some of our vegetarian friends shy away from some of the dishes at Taiwanese vegetarian restaurants because, in look and texture, they're just 'too meat-like for comfort'.

DRINKS
Tea & Coffee

Tea is a fundamental part of Chinese life. In fact, an old Chinese saying identifies tea as one of the seven basic necessities of life, along with fuel, oil, rice, salt, soy sauce and vinegar. Fujian settlers introduced tea to Taiwan over 200 years ago; a fondness for the beverage quickly took hold and tea became one of Taiwan's main exports. Taiwan's long growing season and hilly terrain are perfectly suited for growing excellent quality tea, especially high mountain oolong, which is prized among tea connoisseurs the world over.

Tea Island (http://chadao .blogspot.com) is dedicated to the appreciation of tea from Taiwan and the Mainland.

There are two types of tea shops in Taiwan. The first are traditional teashops (more commonly called teahouses) where customers brew their own tea in a traditional clay pot, sit for hours playing cards or Chinese chess, and choose from several types of high-quality leaves. These can be found tucked away in alleys in most every urban area, but are best visited up in the mountains. Taipei's Maokong (p136) is an excellent place to experience a traditional Taiwanese teahouse. The second type are the stands found (almost literally) on every street corner. These specialize in bubble tea, a mixture of tea, milk, flavouring, sugar and giant black tapioca balls. Also called pearl tea, the sweet drink is popular with students who gather at tea stands after school to socialise and relax, much in the way that the older generation gathers at traditional teahouses.

Tea Arts (http://teaarts .blogspot.com) is a beautiful website with pictures and lore about Taiwan's tea culture.

Bubble tea comes in an infinite variety of flavours; passionfruit, papaya and taro are a few of the most common. The pastel-coloured drinks are served in clear cups with straws fat enough to suck up the chewy tapioca balls that rest at the bottom. A cup usually costs from NT15 to NT25. Some find the gummy texture of the tapioca balls gross, but if bubble tea sales in Taiwan are anything to go by, these people are a quiet minority. As the saying goes, there's no accounting for taste.

Coffee, once hard to come by, is now widely consumed all over Taiwan, at prices ranging from cheap (NT35 per cup) to expensive (NT100 and up). Not only is Taiwan big on coffee consumption, the island is experimenting with

---

COFFEE IN TAIWAN

Twelve years ago, one of the writers working on this guide was teaching an adult English class in a major Taiwanese city, and as a conversational exercise divided the classes into groups, giving each one a business idea with the plan that they should discuss how best to make their business successful. One group was handed a card reading 'Open a coffee shop in Taipei.' After considerable conversation, the group came back and told the teacher that they felt as if they'd drawn the short straw. 'A coffee shop in Taipei would be a failure, teacher,' complained the group. They concluded, 'Taiwanese people are tea drinkers. We don't like coffee.'

Fast forward a dozen years. Coffee, once an alien beverage available only in McDonalds, expensive hotels, or the rare-as-hen's-teeth specialty shop, has become completely ubiquitous throughout Taiwan (not just in big cities but smaller towns as well). Popular chains include Barista, Mr Brown, Chicco D'Oro, Dante, Doutor, Is Coffee, E-Coffee, and, of course, Starbucks.

As for the students, we don't know what became of them, but we can say with certainty that, if they live anywhere in Taipei, their homes are no more than a ten-minute walk – probably less – from a coffee shop.

coffee growing as well; in the past few years a number of coffee plantations in southern Taiwan have begun producing coffee for domestic consumption and export. Though Taiwan isn't likely to replace Brazil anytime soon, Taiwanese coffee – smooth, nonacidic and definitely flavourful – may well find niche market in the next few years. Stay tuned.

Juices

Fresh-fruit stands selling juices and smoothies are all over Taiwan, and these drinks make wonderful thirst quenchers on a hot summer day. All you have to do is point at the fruits you want (some shops have the cut fruit already mixed in the cup) and the person standing behind the counter will whizz them up in a blender for you after adding water or milk. Especially good are iced-papaya milkshakes.

Generally, you'll find that fresh-fruit juices sold on the streets are cheaper than in the West. Expect to pay around NT50 a cup.

Harder Stuff

On the drunk scale, the Taiwanese tend to be fairly moderate drinkers (with some exceptions, banquets being a time where much drinking abounds). But Taiwan does have a number of locally produced inebriants well worth trying. The most famous of these is *gāoliáng jiǔ* (Kaoliang liquor). Made from fermented sorghum, Kaoliang is produced on Kinmen and Matsu, the islands closest to Mainland China. A running joke among locals is that, were mainland Chinese troops to invade the islands, they wouldn't get much further than the Kaoliang factories. Another local favourite is *wéishìbǐ* (Whisbih), an energy drink with a fine mixture of dong quai, ginseng, taurine, various B vitamins, caffeine, and some ethyl alcohol to give it a kick.

WHERE TO EAT & DRINK

You can find restaurants on the main streets of most every city. For eats on the cheap, you can find generic-looking eateries on the main streets, back streets and alleys of any city or town. Small restaurants often open in the morning and stay open until late at night, sometimes closing for a few hours in the afternoon if business is light.

In the mornings, every town, village and small city neighbourhood has one or more places serving breakfast. These places open at dawn, and are usually scrubbing the grills clean by 10am. Breakfast shouldn't cost more than NT50, usually less.

All Taiwanese cities have Western-style restaurants, and the bigger the city the more and varied the restaurants. Taipei has a large international restaurant scene with places serving cuisine from around the globe. Restaurants generally open between 11am and noon for lunch, close around 2pm and reopen in the evening for dinner. Some stay open all day, while others don't. Bars often keep long hours in Taiwan, opening in the afternoon and closing late at night. Most bars offer a limited menu and some offer full-course meals. Expect to pay around NT150 or more for a beer.

Quick Eats

One experience you can't miss out on is eating at a night market. Though Taipei's night markets are arguably the most famous, all cities in Taiwan have at least a few of their own, and even a medium-sized town will have a street set up with food stalls selling traditional Taiwanese eats late into the night. We've listed our favourite night markets in our city headings, but you're sure to find ones you like all over the island.

The Chinese were the first to cultivate tea, and the art of brewing and drinking tea has been popular since the Tang dynasty (AD 618–907).

Like wine tasters, who spit rather than imbibe the wine to prevent drunkenness, some connoisseurs of fine teas do the same to avoid getting too wired.

This Hungry Girl is a Taipei blogger who writes restaurant reviews and takes fine food shots. Her website (http://hungryin taipei.blogspot.com) is definitely worth a visit!

A Tainan specialty, *guāncái bǎn* (coffin sandwiches) are fat toast planks hollowed out and filled with a thick chowder of seafood and vegetables.

So what kind of eats can you expect to find on the fly in Taiwan? Some items won't surprise people used to eating Asian food back home. Taiwanese *shuǐjiǎo* (dumplings) are always a good bet, especially for those looking to fill up on the cheap. Stuffed with meat, spring onion and greens, *shuǐjiǎo* can be served by the bowl in a soup, and sometimes dry by weight. Locals mix *làjiāo* (chilli), *cù* (vinegar) and *jiàngyóu* (soy sauce) in a bowl according to taste. Vinegar and soy sauce look almost identical, so Taiwanese people won't mind if you give the plastic bottles a squeeze and a sniff. Dumplings are often created by family minifactories – one person stretches the pastry, another makes the filling and a third spoons the filling into the pastry, finishing with a little twist to seal it.

Other street snacks include *zhà dòufǔ* (fried tofu), *lǔ dòufǔ* (tofu soaked in soy sauce) and *kǎo fānshǔ* (baked sweet potatoes), which can be bought by weight. Probably the most recognizable Taiwanese street snack is *chòu dòufu* (stinky tofu). This deep-fried dish is something of an acquired taste, like certain European cheeses. Generally speaking people either love the stuff or they can't stand it. Another strange food to keep an eye open for are *pídàn* (thousand year eggs – ducks' eggs that are covered in straw and stored underground for six months). The yolk becomes green and the white becomes jelly. More interesting snacks available at markets include *jī jiǎo* (chickens' feet), *zhū ěrduo* (pigs' ears), *zhū jiǎo* (pigs' trotters) and even *zhū tóupí* (pigs' faces).

Senorita Pequeña, a Taiwanese girl with a Spanish soul has lovingly put up a website (http://senoritapequena .blogspot.com). It has restaurant reviews in Chinese and English and is complete with pictures too!

Meals

A traditional breakfast in Taiwan usually consists of watery rice with seaweed, clay-oven rolls and steamed buns, served plain or with fillings. This is generally washed down with sweetened or plain hot soybean milk. Other popular breakfast foods include rolled omelettes, egg sandwiches, and turnip cakes. Most breakfast places open at about 7am and close midmorning.

The Taiwanese generally eat lunch between 11.30am and 2pm, many taking their midday meal from any number of small eateries on the streets. *Zìzhù cāntīng* (self-serve cafeterias) are a good option, and they offer plenty of meat and vegetable dishes to choose from.

Dinner in Taiwan is usually eaten from 5pm to 11pm, though some restaurants and food stalls in bigger cities stay open 24 hours. Taiwan's

---

EATING DOS & DON'TS

- Every customer gets an individual bowl of rice or a small soup bowl. It is quite acceptable to hold the bowl close to your lips and shovel the contents into your mouth with your chopsticks. If the food contains bones, just put them out on the tablecloth or into a separate bowl, if one is provided. Restaurants are prepared for this – the staff change the tablecloth after each customer leaves.

- Remember to fill your neighbours' tea cups when they are empty, as yours will be filled by them. You can thank the pourer by tapping your middle finger on the table gently. On no account serve yourself tea without serving others first. When your teapot needs a refill, signal this to the waiter by taking the lid off the pot.

- Taiwanese toothpick etiquette is similar to that of neighbouring Asian countries. One hand wields the toothpick while the other shields the mouth from prying eyes.

- Probably the most important piece of etiquette comes with the bill: although you are expected to try to pay, you shouldn't argue too hard, as the one who extended the invitation will inevitably foot the bill. While going Dutch is fashionable among the younger generation, as a guest you'll probably be treated most of the time.

cities – especially the larger ones – all have a fair to excellent selection of international restaurants; don't be surprised to run into a small Indonesian, Indian, or even Mexican eatery on a back alley.

EATING WITH KIDS

Taiwan is a kid-friendly place and children often have free run of the restaurants when eating out (often to the consternation of those hoping for a quiet meal). Budget eateries won't have special menus for children (you'll be lucky if they have English menus), but some might have booster seats. Higher-end restaurants usually have both kids' menus and booster seats. A good bet for dining with kids on the cheap is to take them to a buffet restaurant, where they can pick and chose from colourful dishes to their heart's content. Another fun bet is to bring them to a pet-friendly restaurant, a new trend in Taiwan. Why just eat when you can eat surrounded by puppies and the occasional pot-bellied pig, eh?

Travellers with infants will find everything they need from baby formula to puréed baby foods as well as infant cereals. Every Taiwanese supermarket has at least an aisle for newborn baby fare.

BANQUETS

If you ever get the chance to go to a Taiwanese banquet, jump at it. As in China, Taiwanese banquets are amazing experiences. Like anywhere else, banquets are held to celebrate holidays and special events. Business banquets are also common, and many a significant business deal in Taiwan is clinched at the banquet table.

Dishes at a Taiwanese banquet are served in sequence, beginning with cold appetisers and continuing through 10 or more courses, usually comprised of the most expensive ingredients available. Vegetarians invited to a banquet should inform their hosts as early as possible so that a few suitable

> Popular in Taiwan, *pídàn* (thousand year eggs) are ducks' eggs that are covered in straw and stored underground for six months. If this sounds less than appealing, consider that the traditional recipe has them soaked in horses' urine before burial!

A VERY TAIWANESE BANQUET

The *weiya* is a company dinner party held at the end of the lunar year, usually on the last Saturday night before everyone takes off for the holiday. Much wine or Kaoliang liquor will be drunk by all, usually in response to toasts made by the boss complimenting various employees for having done a good job, or to the company in general. Gifts will almost always be given by the boss, sometimes in the form of *hóng pāos* (red envelopes stuffed with money), or actual gift items, or both.

Always paid for by the boss, *weiyas* are massive spreads featuring the best dishes money can buy. You can generally expect a couple of expensive seafood dishes, like prawns, crabs (even lobster if it's been a good year for the company), and of course some sort of beautifully cooked whole fish. There'll be vegetable dishes and a few meat dishes as well, usually something interesting like *huíguō ròu* (twice-cooked pork), all served in an atmosphere of good cheer and revelry.

However, one dish always served at a *weiya* will be anticipated with some trepidation. This is the chicken course, whose manner of serving is fraught with meaning. Traditionally, a *weiya* is the event in which an unwanted employee is informed that their services will no longer be needed in the coming year, a message conveyed by the direction in which the chicken's head (left on, and not removed as with Western chicken dishes) is facing at the time of serving. An employee who finds themselves facing a just-served chicken at a *weiya* is being told not return to work after the lunar new year's break.

If the boss is happy with everyone's performance that year, the kitchen staff is instructed to serve the chicken facing him or her, or as part of a claypot dish like *réncān jītāng* (ginseng chicken soup), with the head tucked into the pot. For this reason, the serving of a headless chicken dish at a *weiya* is a cause for celebration for all.

Except, of course, for the chicken.

replacement dishes can be rustled up. Soup, often a broth made with medicinal herbs to aid digestion, is generally served after the main course.

Generally speaking a Taiwanese banquet usually ends when the food and toasts end. You may find yourself being applauded when you enter a large banquet. Applauding back is fine; bowing is considered gauche.

Ang Lee's *Eat Drink Man Woman* is a wonderful movie about a Taiwanese chef and his three estranged daughters. The best part about this movie are the close-ups of food!

EAT YOUR WORDS

See also the Language chapter (p361) for additional useful terms and phrases to help you enjoy eating out in Taiwan.

Useful Phrases

I don't want MSG.	*Wǒ bù yào wèijīng.*	我不要味精
I'm vegetarian.	*Wǒ chī sù.*	我吃素
Not too spicy	*Bù yào tài là.*	不要太辣
menu	*càidān*	菜單
bill (check)	*mǎidān/jiézhàng*	買單/結帳
set meal (no menu)	*tàocān*	套餐
Let's eat.	*Chī fàn.*	吃飯
Cheers!	*Gānbēi!*	乾杯!
chopsticks	*kuàizi*	筷子
knife	*dāozi*	刀子
fork	*chāzi*	叉子
spoon	*tiáogēng/tāngchí*	調羹/湯匙
hot	*rède*	熱的
cold	*bīngde*	冰的

Menu Decoder
TAIWANESE DISHES

chòu dòufu	臭豆腐	stinky tofu
kézǎi jiān	蚵仔煎	oyster omelette
kézǎi tāng	蚵仔湯	clear oyster soup
cháyè dàn	茶葉蛋	tea egg
guāncái bǎn	棺材板	coffin sandwiches
chǎo pángxiè	炒螃蟹	sautéed crabs
zhū xiě gāo	豬血糕	congealed pig's blood
luóbuó gāo	蘿蔔糕	turnip cake

When dining on whole fish, don't lift the fish and turn it over; its considered inauspicious.

RICE DISHES

jīròu chǎofàn	雞肉炒飯	fried rice with chicken
dàn chǎofàn	蛋炒飯	fried rice with egg
báifàn	白飯	steamed white rice
lǔroù fàn	魯肉飯	pork mince in soy sauce with rice
sān bǎo fàn	三寶飯	BBQ pork, chicken & roast duck with rice
shūcài chǎofàn	蔬菜炒飯	fried rice with vegetables
tǒngzǎi mǐgāo	筒仔米糕	sticky rice
xīfàn/zhōu	稀飯/粥	watery rice porridge (congee)
zhà páigǔ fàn	炸排骨飯	deep-fried pork chop with rice

NOODLE DISHES

gān miàn	乾麵	noodles (not soupy)
húntún miàn	餛飩麵	wonton with noodles
jīsī chǎomiàn	雞絲炒麵	fried noodles with chicken
jīsī tāngmiàn	雞絲湯麵	soupy noodles with chicken
májiàng miàn	麻醬麵	sesame-paste noodles
niúròu chǎomiàn	牛肉炒麵	fried noodles with beef

niúròu miàn	牛肉麵	soupy beef noodles
ròusī chǎomiàn	肉絲炒麵	fried noodles with pork
shūcài chǎomiàn	蔬菜炒麵	fried noodles with vegetables
tāngmiàn	湯麵	noodles in soup
xiārén chǎomiàn	蝦仁炒麵	fried noodles with shrimp
zhájiàng miàn	炸醬麵	bean & mincemeat noodles

BREAD, BUNS & DUMPLINGS

cōngyóu bǐng	蔥油餅	spring-onion pancakes
guōtiē	鍋貼	pot stickers/pan-grilled dumplings
mántóu	饅頭	steamed buns
ròu bāozǐ	肉包子	steamed meat buns
shāobǐng	燒餅	clay-oven rolls
shuǐjiǎo	水餃	boiled dumplings
shǔijiān bāo	水煎包	pan-grilled buns
sùcài bāozǐ	素菜包子	steamed vegetable buns
xiǎo lóng tāng bāo	小籠湯包	steamed meat buns & meat sauce

SOUP

gě lì tāng	蛤蠣湯	clam & turnip soup
gòng wán tāng	貢丸湯	Taiwanese meatball soup
húntún tāng	餛飩湯	wonton soup
ròu gēng tāng	肉羹湯	meat *potage*
sān xiān tāng	三鮮湯	three kinds of seafood soup
suānlà tāng	酸辣湯	hot and sour soup
yóu yú gēng	魷魚羹	cuttlefish *potage*

VEGETABLE & TOFU DISHES

báicài xiān shuānggū	白菜鮮雙菇	bok choy and mushrooms
càifǔ dàn	菜脯蛋	omelette with pickled radishes
cuìpí dòufu	脆皮豆腐	crispy skin tofu
hēimù'ěr mèn dòufu	黑木耳燜豆腐	tofu with wood ear mushrooms
jiangzhí qīngdòu	薑汁青豆	string beans with ginger
lúshǔi dòufu	滷水豆腐	smoked tofu
shāguō dòufu	砂鍋豆腐	clay pot tofu
táng liánǒu	糖蓮藕	sweet and sour lotus root cakes

BEEF DISHES

háoyóu niúròu	蠔油牛肉	beef with oyster sauce
hóngshāo niúròu	紅燒牛肉	beef braised in soy sauce
niúròu fàn	牛肉飯	beef with rice
tiěbǎn niúròu	鐵板牛肉	beef steak platter

CHICKEN DISHES

háoyóu jīkuài	蠔油雞塊	diced chicken in oyster sauce
hóngshāo jīkuài	紅燒雞塊	diced chicken braised in soy sauce
jītǔi fàn	雞腿飯	chicken leg with rice
tángcù jīdīng	糖醋雞丁	sweet and sour chicken

PORK DISHES

dōng pō ròu	東坡肉	stewed pork with brown sauce
gūlǔ ròu	咕嚕肉	sweet and sour pork
háoyóu ròusī	蠔油肉絲	pork with oyster sauce
jiàngbào ròudīng	醬爆肉丁	diced pork with soy sauce
páigǔ fàn	排骨飯	pork chop with rice
ròu yuán	肉圓	deep-fried pork-mince buns

DUCK DISHES

yāròu fàn	鴨肉飯	duck with rice
yāxiě gāo	鴨血糕	congealed duck blood

SEAFOOD DISHES

gélì	蛤蠣	clams
gōngbào xiārén	宮爆蝦仁	diced shrimp with peanuts
hóngshāo yú	紅燒魚	fish braised in soy sauce
kē zǎi jiān	蚵仔煎	oyster omelette
lóngxiā	龍蝦	lobster
pángxiè	螃蟹	crab
xiǎoyú huāshēng	小魚花生	fish stir-fried with peanuts and pickled vegetables
yóuyú	魷魚	squid
zhāngyú	章魚	octopus

MAINLAND CHINESE SPECIALITIES

Hakka Dishes

bǎntiáo	板條	flat rice noodles
chéngzhī jīliǔ	橙汁雞柳	chicken and orange sauce
kèjiāguǒ	客家粿	shrimp and pork turnip cakes
kèjiā máshǔ	客家麻糬	sticky rice dipped in sugar or peanut powder
kèjiā xiǎo chǎo	客家小炒	stir-fried cuttlefish, leeks, tofu and pork
kǔguā xiándàn	苦瓜鹹蛋	salty eggs and bitter melon
zhà shūcài bǐng	炸蔬菜餅	fried salty flour balls made from mushrooms

Cantonese Dishes

chāshāo sū	叉燒酥	barbecued pork pastry
dōngjiāng yánjú jī	東江鹽焗雞	salt-baked chicken
héfěn	河粉	flat rice noodles
hóngshāo dàpái chì	紅燒大排翅	stewed shark's fin with pork and chicken feet
mì zhī chāshāo	蜜汁叉燒	roast pork with honey
tàiyé jī	太爺雞	smoked chicken with tea and sugar
zhōu	粥	rice porridge

Fujianese Dishes

fó tiào qiáng	佛跳墙	Buddha Jumps Over the Wall
méicài gān kòuròu	梅菜干扣肉	steamed pork with dried mustard
qīxīng yúwán tāng	七星魚丸湯	fish-ball soup with eel, shrimp and pork

Sichuanese Dishes

guàiwèi jī	怪味雞	shredded chicken in a hot pepper and sesame sauce
gōngbǎo jīdīng	宮保雞丁	spicy chicken with peanuts
huíguō ròu	回鍋肉	twice-cooked pork with salty and hot sauce
málà dòufu	麻辣豆腐	spicy tofu
mápó dòufu	麻婆豆腐	Granny Ma's tofu (spicy mincemeat sauce and tofu)
zhāngchá yāzi	樟茶鴨	camphor tea duck

Shanghainese Dishes

dàzhá xiè	大閘蟹	hairy crabs
jīngdū páigǔ	京都排骨	Mandarin-style pork ribs
lúyú	鱸魚	Songjiang perch
shīzi tóu	獅子頭	lion's head (steamed pork meatballs)

sōngrén yùmǐ	松仁玉米	fish with corn and pine nuts
xiánshuǐ jī	鹹水雞	cold salty chicken
xiāngsū jī	香酥雞	crispy chicken
xièfěn shīzi tóu	蟹粉狮子頭	lion's head meatballs with crab
zuìjī	醉雞	drunken chicken

DRINKS
Alcohol

bái pútáo jiǔ	白葡萄酒	white wine
hóng pútáo jiǔ	红葡萄酒	red wine
mǐjiǔ	米酒	rice wine
píjiǔ	啤酒	beer
gāoliáng jiǔ	高粱酒	Kaoliang liquor

Nonalcoholic

liǔdīng zhī	柳丁汁	orange juice
dòujiāng	豆漿	soybean milk
kuàngquán shuǐ	礦泉水	mineral water
niúnǎi	牛奶	milk
qìshuǐ	汽水	soft drink (soda)
shuǐ	水	water
yézi zhī	椰子汁	coconut juice

Tea & Coffee

hóng chá	紅茶	black tea
júhuā chá	菊花茶	chrysanthemum tea
kāfēi	咖啡	coffee
lǜ chá	綠茶	green tea
luòshén chá	洛神茶	hibiscus tea
mài chá	麥茶	wheat tea
mòlìhuā chá	茉莉花茶	jasmine tea
wūlóng chá	烏龍茶	oolong tea
zhēnzhū nǎi chá	珍珠奶茶	milk tea with tapioca balls

Environment

An overcrowded and polluted hive of human industry or scenic seashore surrounding an interior comprised of equal parts jungle and mountains? A factory island pumping out high-tech or Asia's semi-tropical Switzerland, only with lovely beaches and cheaper food?

Would you believe Taiwan is all this and more?

THE LAND

Lying 165km off the coast of mainland China, separated by the Taiwan Strait, Taiwan straddles the Tropic of Cancer and is shaped kind of like a sweet potato, 394km in length and 144km wide. The territory includes a number of other islands, including the Penghu Archipelago and the islands of Matsu and Kinmen in the Taiwan Strait, and Green Island and Lanyu, off the east coast.

At 36,000 sq km, Taiwan is roughly the size of the Netherlands, and about a third more populous. But whereas most of Holland is flat, Taiwan is a different story entirely. Being mostly mountainous, the majority of Taiwan's 23 million people live on the small expanses of flat land to the west of the Central Mountain Range, a series of jagged mountain peaks that stretches for over 170km from north to south. It's this topography that makes Taiwan's capital Taipei feel considerably more crowded than Amsterdam.

Crisscrossed with many small rivers that empty into the sea, the plains and basins of western Taiwan essentially provide the only land suitable for either agriculture or industry. The east coast, with its towering seaside cliffs and rocky volcanic coastline, is utterly spectacular; outside of the three cities of Ilan, Hualien and Taitung, it's sparsely populated as well.

CLIMATE

Taiwan's climate is subtropical. Though often damp, winters can be pleasant enough, especially in the south. Up north, it tends to get chilly and damp, and many Taipei residents find themselves pining for some sunshine come mid-February. Typhoon season hits in late summer to mid-autumn, and tends to strike the east coast particularly hard. Summers are hot and humid: walking out of an air-conditioned mall in August feels like being wrapped in a steaming towel. Perfect Taiwan weather? In our opinion, autumn and spring are best. Summer's fun, but prepare to sweat, and as for winter, down south it's nice most of the time, but up north, well, Taipei has plenty of indoor malls!

There's no more environmentally friendly way to travel than by bicycle. Definitely check out the Yangmingshan Cycling Club's website (http://taipeiycc.blogspot.com/) if you're interested in riding in northern Taiwan.

Taiwan is also prone to earthquakes, sitting as it does on the colliding Eurasian and Philippine plates. Before you curse the forces of geology, consider that these grinding plates are also responsible for the beautiful mountains and amazing hot springs that make a trip to Taiwan truly worthwhile. Most of these quakes are small earth tremors. Some are far more devastating, particularly the one that occurred on 21 September 1999, which measured 7.3 on the Richter scale and killed thousands. A more recent quake off the southern coast in late 2006 caused only a few casualties, but severed several underground cables, disrupting telephone and internet service across Asia.

WILDLIFE

Lush and mountainous, Taiwan is home to a wide range of flora and fauna, particularly bird life.

Fauna

Though many of Taiwan's larger mammals were driven to near extinction through hunting (much of it to make Chinese medicine), increased environmental education and awareness since the mid-'90s has helped to save a number of species native to the island. The Central Mountain Range has the largest amount of remaining forest in Taiwan and is home to a wide range of animals including the wild boar, Formosan macaque, Formosan black bear, sambar deer and pheasants.

The Formosan black bear is the largest mammal on the island and lives at altitudes above 2000m. It's highly unlikely you'll see one as they're very elusive; judging by the fact that some humans still seem to view them as walking medicine chests, this is probably a wise characteristic for them to have developed. Another elusive animal is the Formosan clouded leopard, which lives in the lowlands of the Central Mountain Range. Sadly, the last sighting of the leopard was in 1985 and authorities are not certain if any more of these animals remain in the wild.

AnimalsTaiwan provides aid to animals in need throughout Taipei, and welcomes visiting volunteers. Learn more about volunteering through http://animalstaiwan.org.

Monkeys live in the mountains of Taiwan as well, some of them rather close to major cities; you stand a good chance of running into a Formosan macaque on the trail from Tianmu to Yangmingshan (p102). Snakes also call Taiwan home, and though the majority of these are nonvenomous, the ones that are poisonous fall into that rare 'last animal you meet in this life' category. Hikers should tread with caution (and with good boots).

Flora

More than half of Taiwan is covered with dense forest. Experts claim that the island is home to over 4002 types of plants, 1000 of them found only in Taiwan. Some of these include the Chinese juniper and cowtail pine, though the most common species are bamboo, spruce, fir and cypress found at higher altitudes. Taiwan was once covered with camphor forests but, sadly, most of these have been logged to near extinction. The largest one remaining is at Fuyuan Forest Recreational Area (p198) in the Eastern Rift Valley.

TAIWAN FOR TWITCHERS

Taiwan is for the birds. We mean this in the best possible way.

According to the Taiwan Birding Association, Taiwan has 15 generally accepted endemic bird species (some authorities say 17 to 19, or more) and more than 60 endemic subspecies. Among the species endemic to Taiwan are the Taiwan partridge, Mikado pheasant, Taiwan whistling-thrush, white-whiskered laughing thrush and Taiwan bush-warbler.

Furthermore, Taiwan's geographic position makes it something of a massive food court for countless more species of migratory birds who stop by as they fly south in the winter and back again in the spring. And birds aren't the only ones making Taiwan a migratory stopover: twitchers (bird-watchers) are flocking to Taiwan as well, drawn by opportunities to spot a huge variety of creatures feathered and fowl. Serious twitchers will definitely want to visit the outer islands; Kinmen, in particular, is home to a number of species not found on the Taiwanese mainland. However, even Taipei's parks hold surprises for birding enthusiasts. Taipei's Botanical Gardens are considered one of the best places in the world to see the rare Malaysian night heron, which is fairly amazing considering that the gardens are in the centre of a major metropolis.

For serious birding enthusiasts, there are a number of resources to help you plan your trip. The Wild Bird Society of Taipei has a fairly good website (www.wbst.org.tw) charting recent bird sightings around Taiwan. It also sells two excellent books, *Bird Watching in Taiwan* (NT600) and *100 Common Birds of Taiwan* (NT200), and can arrange birding tours all over the country.

The Taipei City government also puts out a useful reference book, *Birdwatcher's Guide to the Taipei Region* (NT320), available at most bookstores.

RESPONSIBLE TRAVEL

In an age of dwindling forests, melting icebergs and politicians in deep denial, Taiwan is a nation that seems to have managed to pull itself back from the precipice of environmental disaster. So what can tourists do to encourage the island to keep moving boldly forward towards its goal of becoming the 'Switzerland of Asia'? Sure, there are the obvious ways to minimise a person's personal environmental footprint. When buying snacks, avoid taking a plastic bag if you don't really need one. Nowadays most of the larger shops charge for bags as a way to minimise rubbish. Smaller stores still hand them out freely; try saying *bú yào xièxie* (no thanks) whenever possible. Recycling is the rule in most places, so place your rubbish in the appropriate bins. Most 7-Elevens also take used batteries, though at this point you really should be using rechargeable ones as your digital cameras will run longer on them anyway. And on that subject, Taiwan offers myriad temptations for those turned on by technology; just keep in mind that improperly disposed mobile phones, laptop and MP3 players wind up contributing to the growing and ever toxic high-tech trash heaps of southern China, India or Africa. Chose your purchases wisely and dispose of them even more so.

Another area for concern for visitors is visiting aboriginal villages. Tourism is becoming especially important economically for Taiwan's native tribes and for tourists, staying at an aboriginal family homestay is a great way to learn about the culture and contribute to the local economy. We've met more than a few Taiwanese aboriginals who've commented that tourists (city-bred Taiwanese are most often cited) treat the locals with less respect than the locals would prefer; extensive gawking, taking photographs without asking, entering private spaces uninvited and littering are oft-mentioned complaints. Try to be especially mindful when taking photos or when wandering around aboriginal areas. It never hurts to ask for permission to do so.

NATIONAL PARKS & RESERVES

The Republic of China (on Taiwan) National Park Act was passed in 1972, and since then six national parks have been established. This puts the percentage of Taiwan's acreage designated as national parkland at around 9%, which is pretty substantial for a country of Taiwan's relatively diminutive size.

National Park	Features	Activities	Best Time to Visit	Page
Kenting	popular beach resort with 'Cancún of Taiwan' vibe	swimming with tropical fish, diving in pristine coral reefs, migratory bird-watching, surfing, camping, 3-day rock concerts	year-round	p282
Kinmen	once off-limits military outpost transformed into a beautiful island park	hiking, history, bike riding, ancient villages, temples, bird-watching	summer, autumn	p296
Sheipa	second-highest mountain in Taiwan, diverse terrain, Formosan landlocked salmon	hiking, bird-watching	summer, autumn, spring	p178
Taroko	spectacular gorge, Formosan macaque, pheasants	hiking	summer, autumn, spring	p188
Yangmingshan	beautiful mountain park with varied climate, butterflies	hiking, hot springs, bird-watching	summer, autumn, spring	p132
Yushan	tallest mountain in Taiwan, rare Formosan salamander, Formosan black bear	hiking alpine, tundra and cedar forests	summer, autumn, spring	p243

There are also 18 nature and forest reserves around Taiwan, and it seems as though Taiwan is making up for lost time when it comes to preserving what untouched areas it has left. In addition to national parks, designated scenic areas have been established across the island, including the East Coast National Scenic Area between Hualien and Taitung.

Some of the most scenic spots in Taiwan can be found on the outer islands. Beautiful and replete with culture, history and wildlife, the island of Kinmen (p296) is itself a national park; just off the coast of mainland China, both Kinmen and Little Kinmen are excellent places to spot rare waterbirds. Halfway between China and Taiwan, the windswept Penghu Archipelago (p306) offers a surprising variety of topography, from flat white-and-black sand beaches to dramatic, jagged cliffs. And both Lanyu (p316) and Green Island (p320) offer otherworldly landscapes more reminiscent of Polynesia than East Asia.

In 1998 American actor and animal-rights activist Steven Seagal met with then-president Lee Teng-hui and convinced him to sign legislation limiting animal cruelty.

ENVIRONMENTAL ISSUES

When Chiang Kai-shek's nationalist troops were driven off the mainland, they brought more than just millions of Chinese people fleeing communism with them: they also brought capital, much of which was used to transform

TAIWAN'S ENVIRONMENT: TWO STEPS FORWARD, ONE STEP BACK

Taiwan well deserves the name given to it by the Portuguese centuries ago – *Ilha Formosa*, beautiful island. Lush green mountains jut up from the alluvial plain of the west coast, and on most of the east coast the mountains drop straight into the blue ocean. The central spine of the mountain ranges reaches nearly 4000m. The forest is semitropical; huge fern trees with fronds like green ostrich feathers, plus birds-nest ferns, hang overhead. The rice paddies are grass-green when the rice is young.

But the economy of the island has been industrialising pell-mell since the 1970s; 'Made in Taiwan' has evolved from sweaters and shoes through to colour TVs, computer components and biotech. With population density among the highest in the world, Taiwan became the workshop of the world, with both mega-factories and local homes getting into the production business. The outfall has been noxious industrial dumping, poorly planned residential and industrial sprawl through farm areas, and the urban concrete jungle of high-rise offices and apartments. Now several major freeways, waterways with flood walls, the railway and the bullet train compete for space on the western coast.

In 1988 Taiwan's environmental movement emerged in the wake of Chernobyl and the conclusion of half a century of martial law left over from the Cold War. It failed to stop the country's fourth nuclear power plant, but it delayed it by 14 years and put further nuclear-power projects on hold. Communities refusing to serve as sites for new garbage dumps or incinerators finally spurred city schemes for rubbish reduction and recycling; as a result garbage per capita has since been halved. Now a functioning democracy, Taiwan's elected leaders compete through populist projects such as modernised vegetable markets, riverside parks, community centres and children's museums. There is a continuing effort to clean up the rivers and create a modern sewerage system.

However, the island's wealth brings new challenges to environmental sustainability – Taiwan ranks poorly in this in world comparisons. Pork-barrel politics has spawned huge appropriations for 'flood control', which has resulted in streams and rivers and even some of the coastline being lined with cement walls and wave-breaker structures. The country's emissions per capita of greenhouse gases, about 60% of US emissions per capita, surpass Japan and most of Europe. Total carbon dioxide emissions have doubled since 1990, and are expected to soar further with planned industrial development as well as consumer preferences that ape the US, including 4WDs. Environmental concerns are paid lip service by the government, but hard choices lie ahead.

Environmental activist Linda Gail Arrigo is the International Affairs Officer of the Green Party Taiwan and former wife of former DPP Chairman Shih Ming-deh

Want to learn more about environmental regulations in Taiwan? Check out the Taiwan Environmental Protection Administration's website at www .epa.gov.tw/english.

a primarily agrarian society into a major industrial powerhouse. Taiwan became wealthy, quickly, but it also became toxic, with urban air ranking among the world's worst, and serious pollution in most of its waterways. Indeed, Taiwan's 'economic miracle' came at a serious price, and pollution, urban sprawl and industrial waste have all taken a heavy toll on the island. In the name of economic wealth, vast tracts of Taiwan's forests have been destroyed, decimating animal habitats and causing extensive soil degradation.

But over the recent years, much has been done to reverse decades of environmental derogation throughout Taiwan. Some of this can be attributed to a 'happy' accident of global economics: much of Taiwan's most polluting industrial production has shifted to mainland China. But some of the improvement can be attributed to increased government oversight. Environmental laws, long 'on the books with a wink towards industry', are now enforced far more stringently across the board, and the results have been tangible, eg the Danshui and Keelung Rivers in Taipei, once horribly befouled, are significantly cleaner in sections. We've even seen people swimming at the foot of the Danshui River in Bitan, and the Keelung, while hardly pristine, is home to a variety of waterfowl. Urban air quality has improved markedly, thanks to a combination of improved public transport, more stringent clean-air laws, and a switch to unleaded petrol. Taipei's air quality, once almost as bad as Mexico City's, now hovers somewhere around London's.

The Taiwanese collective unconscious has changed as well: so much of the emerging 'Taiwanese identity' is tied in with having a clean and green homeland that people are tending to take environmental protection far more seriously. This isn't to say that you won't see people chucking garbage into the street (or along wooded trails), but you tend to see far less of it than you would have a decade ago. (A notable exception to this is betel-nut-chewing taxi drivers. They still hack their blood-red spit and throw their chewed-betel-nut-filled Dixie cups out on the road, and they're about as *tái kè*, or 'truly Taiwanese' as you can get.)

Taiwan's Green Party is active in issues of ecological sustainability and social justice in Taiwan, coordinating with other environmental organisations throughout the island.

There's still much more to be done, of course. As travellers, we can't promise that you won't find empty beverage cans while hiking along a pristine mountain trail, or the remains of somebody else's picnic in a city park. The issue of decaying barrels of nuclear waste buried on the aboriginal island of Lanyu has also yet to be resolved to anybody's satisfaction. The environmental implications of the just-completed Taiwan High-Speed Rail are also something worth considering. Though proponents claim it will have a positive environmental impact by reducing car and air travel, some environmentalists feel that the positioning of the stations (outside of city centres in what was once farmland) will create urban sprawl and other environmental problems.

So while it's fair to say that Taiwan has made great strides on the environmental front, it's clear that yet more remains to be done.

Hot Springs

Taiwan had been in the imperial sights of the Japanese empire long before her colonisation in 1895. Though conventional wisdom holds that Taiwan's neighbour to the north was seduced by the island's abundant wood, coal and metal deposits, we think the real reason (in part, at least) might have lain elsewhere. For a people as *wēnquán* (hot spring) crazy as the Japanese, the thought of having some of the world's finest hot springs so close to home yet not under imperial control must have been discomforting to them to say the least. And of course, there's the issue of prestige; for the rest of the world to discover that the finest hot springs in Asia were anywhere else but in Japan might have implied an unbearable loss of face. Clearly Taiwan, and her amazing geothermal waters, would have to be incorporated into the empire. The Japanese knew the truth, one the rest of the world is slowly finding out; when it comes to hot springs, Taiwan is second to none.

Taiwan is ranked among the world's top 15 hot-spring sites and harbours a great variety of springs including hot springs, cold springs, mud springs, and even sea-bed hot springs. Its worth noting that the most vociferous pilgrims to Taiwanese hot springs come from – you guessed it – the land of the rising sun. And as in Japan, the same geological forces that frequently shake Taiwan have caused the island to be riddled with hot springs (talk about the curse spitting up a gift).

When it comes to hot springs, earthquakes giveth and earthquakes taketh away. The popular Cingcyuan springs were closed by an earthquake after WWII only to be reopened by a devastating quake on 21 September, 1999.

WHAT'S IN THE WATER?

Water bubbling up from underground picks up a variety of minerals that offer a veritable bouquet of health benefits. Aficionados claim that Taiwan's waters are practically magical when it comes to healing various infirmities, and that knowing which waters are good for what ailments is a key to health. While we can't attest to the miraculous qualities of all Taiwanese hot springs, we do know that after a long hike, we always head for the nearest one (aching muscles being one condition on which all hot springs seem to work like a charm).

Bathers in Yangmingshan will notice waters there have a milky colour and mildly sulphurous odour. Waters in Beitou have an even stronger sulphur reek, which some find overpowering. Waters from Yangmingshan are said to be excellent in the treatment of ailments such as arthritis, measles and gout, while those from more acidic and sulphuric Beitou are said to be especially good for dermatitis and other skin ailments. Places such as Renze and Hungye (both on Taiwan's east coast) produce waters

The first mention of Taiwan's hot springs came from a 1697 manuscript, *Beihai Jiyou* (裨海紀遊), but hot springs were not developed until 1893, when a German businessman discovered Beitou and later established a small local spa.

HOT-SPRING ETIQUETTE

- Some resorts separate bathers by gender, while others do not. If you're at the former, get naked. If you're at the latter, doing so is probably a bad idea.

- Shower thoroughly using soap and shampoo before getting into the tub. If you're going to dunk your head, wash your hair.

- Once you're in the tub (to quote the sign at Lengshuikeng in Yangmingshan National Park), 'Do not do anything that will make other users uncomfortable.' We assume you know what that means.

- Some remote hot springs have a tendency to attract a more rough-and-tumble type of clientele. Comparing tattoos is fine; mentioning scars or missing fingers should be avoided.

OUR 10 FAVOURITES

- **Jiaoshi** (p163) From the minute you get off the train, you'll know you're in a hot-spring town. Don't believe us? Just ask one of the locals (you're sure to find one soaking a foot or two in the spring-fed fountain in front of the train station).

- **Taian Hot Springs** (p176) The springs produce silky, smooth bicarbonate water, said to be excellent for treating arthritis. It sure makes your complexion glow. The facilities are lovely outdoors and in, and the mountain surroundings are marvellous.

- **East River Spa Garden, Nanzhuang** (p176) The spa drills down for their water here (no, it's not cheating). We love the traditional Taiwanese red brick and wood design and the natural setting.

- **Tienlai, Jinshan** (p156) This high-class resort has more than a dozen pools, high-pressure water jets, saunas, and other spa fixings; all with a picture-perfect view of surrounding Yangmingshan.

- **Lisong Hot Spring, South Cross-Island Hwy** (p264) Simply one of the most beautiful natural springs in Taiwan. Don't miss this one.

- **Sileng Hot Spring, North Cross-Island Hwy** (p169) A wild spring on the wild North Cross-Island Hwy. You won't find a four-star hotel here, and that suits us just fine.

- **Paolai** (p261) Hosting one of the nicer southern hot-spring resorts, the area offers a number of lovely new hotels set in isolated pockets of the mountains, and the waters themselves are mineral rich.

- **Beitou** (p131) Though often crowded (it is in the city, after all), Beitou is still a great place for a quick dip. The waters are highly sulphuric, and come out of the ground extremely hot. Our favourite spot in Beitou? The humble public springs right in Beitou Park – the best NT40 we've ever spent.

- **Jauri, Green Island** (p321) One of only three saltwater hot springs in the world, the waters of Jauri are sulphuric, but only mildly so. The spa itself is on the beach, and an absolutely perfect place to stargaze on autumn nights.

- **Suao Cold Springs** (p164) OK, they're not hot, but after hiking around in the summer nothing feels better than a dip in the naturally carbonated 22°C water of Suao's cold springs. Good for body and spirit alike.

of an alkaloid nature, and are favoured by people who don't like the 'rotten egg' smell of the northern sulphuric springs. These waters are said to have a calming effect on the nervous system, as well as being good for stiff muscles and skin ailments. Closer to Taipei, the Jiaoshi springs also produce water that is clear and odourless, slightly salty and calcium- and potassium-rich to boot. This water offers similar benefits to the alkaloid springs down south.

Antung is the only place you can get hot-spring coffee. Try some and tell us how it is.

THE TAIWAN HOT-SPRING EXPERIENCE

Setting is a major part of the appeal of any Taiwan hot-spring experience. The best developed springs are found in valleys or meadows surrounded by green mountains, on hillsides overlooking the ocean, or (as is the case with Jauri springs on Green Island) actually *on* the beach itself. Sometimes the facilities, which include restaurants and cafés and rooms for an overnight stay, are almost as nice as the views. But the popularity of such places sometimes comes at the expense of water quality (more on that later).

Some of our absolute favourites are the wilder ones that lie beside cool rivers in deep remote valleys. We like them not only because they are free in the 'born free' way, but also because they literally cost nothing. Wild springs can be found around the island, most often up in the mountains. One of Taiwan's most famous wild springs lies in a river bed deep inside Taroko Gorge; unfortunately, this spring has been closed by recent landslides, and whether it will be opened again by the time you read this is anybody's guess.

If you are looking to explore wild springs beyond the ones we mention (and there are scores more), pick up a copy of *Taiwan Wild Hot Springs* (台灣溫泉地圖), by Sunriver Press (上河文化), at any outdoor shop. The book is in Chinese but the maps are good, and with minimal help translating walking times and locations, you should be able to use it.

Hot-spring resorts come in a variety of shapes and sizes. In addition to having rooms (available by the night or hour) with tubs waiting to be filled with pumped-in spring water, most spa areas also have large public bathing complexes, with multiple pools, jets and showers. Charges typically range between NT300 and NT500 for an unlimited time, though prices are higher around Taipei. We have started to really enjoy using the outdoor facilities as the range of bathing options is entertaining and the views are usually better than from out the window of a hotel room. Room tubs are also often a little too small for a single Western frame (to say nothing of two).

Legend has it that after Japan lost Taiwan, one Japanese police officer jumped into Hell Valley springs (p131), boiling himself alive rather than return to Japan.

THINGS TO AVOID

It's unfortunate but many of Taiwan's springs are victims of their own popularity. Random health checks are showing a disturbing trend of overuse. Hotels and resorts must often dilute natural hot spring water, and even recycle water between bathers. This is common around the world, even in Japan, but we still don't like it. So our recommendation is twofold: first, generally speaking, the less developed the area, the purer the water quality; second, since many of the worst offenders come from among the oldest and most expensive hot-spring resorts, avoid these unless we indicate otherwise. If you're going to be soaking in diluted mineral water, or water mixed with a little sulphur powder, you might as well not pay top dollar.

Taipei 台北

Once upon a time, Taipei's streets were chock-full of taxis, buses and racing scooters, and its sidewalks congested with people and trash. The air was foul, and the architecture – shrines, temples and old colonial buildings aside – was ugly. Central planning seemed sporadic or even nonexistent. In the late 1980s, as the scars of former martial law began healing, citizens realised that while they were materially rich, their quality of life was poor. They demanded change and over the next decade, city planners did what you'd expect those schooled in Asia's most computer-savvy society to do: they played a protracted game of SimCity, only for keeps.

'Traffic is hideous!' cried Taipeiers, and a light-rail network was built. 'The rivers are putrid, and our kids have nowhere to play!' was the next complaint. 'Strengthen environmental laws and build parks on every river bank', was the answer. 'Ugly buildings, we can't stand looking at 'em,' moaned the people of Taipei. 'Then let's build interesting-looking places!' was the Solomonic decision of city planners.

Naturally, this explanation is a vast oversimplification; a myriad of other complex political, economic, and social changes were also taking place. Still, in a veritable blink of the eye, Taipei has gone from an ugly duckling of Asia to one of the region's most dynamic, comfortable and liveable cities. Most important to the intrepid traveller, Taipei is also fun. If you take some time to explore, we think you'll agree that Taipei is a city that's managed to strike a fine balance between business and beauty, and between chaos and convenience.

HIGHLIGHTS

- Chill with the young and trendy set in ultraconsumeristic **Ximending** (p99)

- Experience some of Asia's finest street cuisine at the **Shilin Night Market** (p99) or if more nautically themed culture and cuisine is your thing, at **Danshui** (p126)

- Bike, skate or stroll along Taipei's lovely new **riverside leisure paths** (p102)

- Hike, soak or do both in **Beitou** and **Yangmingshan National Park** (p133)

- Relax over a fine cuppa and enjoy the spectacular view from the tea-growing hills of **Maokong** (p136)

- Explore Taiwan's prehistoric past at the **Shihsanheng Museum of Archaeology** (p129) or experience global spiritual beliefs at the **Museum of World Religions** (p138)

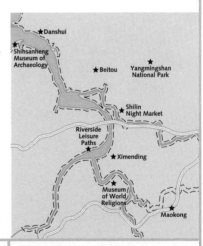

- TELEPHONE CODE: 02   - POPULATION: 2.63 MILLION

HISTORY

Prehistoric Taipei (Táiběi) was wet. The mountains surrounding present-day Taipei were majestic then as now, but the basin in which a great metropolis would one day rise was under water. It was a pretty lake, we've no doubt, but it was completely lacking in restaurants, museums, hotel rooms and even people. We'd have advised all but the most adventurous travellers to postpone their trip for a few million years.

At some point, over 6000 years ago, the now (mostly) dry basin between the mountains began to be settled by people who'd sailed over from other islands in the Pacific. Anthropologists would later collectively describe the first settlers as 'Pingpu' or 'plains aboriginals'. Their descendants still live in Taiwan.

Fast forward to the last millennium. Having been 'discovered' by Han Chinese, Taipei (along with the rest of Taiwan) was subject to a slow but inexorable influx of settlers from China's east coast. These settlers forced the original inhabitants of Taipei to retreat into the surrounding mountains. They then renamed the displaced aboriginals 'mountain people', perhaps to make themselves feel better for having evicted them from the plains.

During Western Europe's great age of conquest, Taiwan was 'discovered' again, and in fairly rapid succession by the Portuguese, Dutch and Spanish, all of whom decided that they liked the place well enough to plant their respective flags around the island. The Spanish took a particular interest in Danshui (now part of Taipei County) and before leaving they built a fortress that still stands today (p127). Sensing that European interlopers were getting too attached to the island, in 1709 the Qing court reversed a Ming decree forbidding settlement on Taiwan and granted citizens in China's Fujian province permission to emigrate.

Many of these Fukkienese settlers came to present-day Taipei, founding communities along the Danshui River in areas that today are considered central Taipei. These early communities became trading ports for tea and camphor and set the stage for more settlement from China as well as economic development.

By 1882 Taipei had become a fully fledged city, large enough to warrant the construction of a wall. Though the wall is long gone, four of the five gates leading into the city can still be visited. Alas, the city wall – the last to be built under the Qing – proved merely cosmetic to the Japanese, who took the city (along with the rest of Taiwan) through strong-arm diplomacy rather than arms, in 1895.

Under Japanese rule (1895–1945), Taipei became the administrative headquarters for the island. Although the Japanese ruled with an iron hand, their engineers left behind good basic infrastructure. Buildings remaining from that era are among the city's most prized. After the decampment of Chiang Kai-shek's Nationalist forces to Taipei in 1949, the city expanded, growing to its present size (272 sq km) and governmental structure of 12 districts. It's in this present-day city that your tour begins.

ORIENTATION

First, the good news: finding your way around Taipei is much easier today than it was 10 years ago. Now the bad: it can still be pretty complicated.

The Taipei Metro (MRT) makes getting around the city pretty easy and every MRT station has a map (labelled in Chinese and English) that points the way to almost every sight worth visiting as well as street names both major and minor. If that wasn't enough, most people in Taipei are extremely friendly. If you look lost, chances are good someone will give you directions. Ready to head out? Not so fast. Here comes the complicated part.

Central Taipei is constructed on a grid, with major streets running east–west and north–south. These streets are named according

---

SISTER CITIES

Taipei may well have more sister cities than just about any metropolis in the world. These number somewhere around 50 and America boasts the largest number of ceremonial urban siblings with the Taiwanese capital paired with the urban heavyweights of Boston, Dallas and Los Angeles. Other notable sister cities include Perth, Jeddah and Guatemala City. The likely reason behind the large number of ceremonial relationships is the Republic of China's (ROC) peculiar diplomatic status, necessitating the building of international relations at a more low-key municipal level.

to direction and broken up further into sections, numbered according to the distance from the central axis (roughly speaking, the Taipei Main Station). The lower the section number, the closer to the centre of the city the address tends to be; Zhongshan N Road sec.1 is close to Taipei Main Station; sec.7 is in the wilds of Tianmu, 25 minutes by taxi in good traffic.

But wait, it gets more complicated. Taipei also has numbered 'lanes', which generally run perpendicular to the main streets. Major sights, hotels and restaurants are located along the main streets, but many addresses include lanes. So if you're looking for, say, Grandma Nitti's Restaurant (p111), at 8 Lane 93, Shida Rd, you need to first find Shida Rd, then look for where number eight would be. But instead of finding a building, you'll find the lane where you'll find Nitti's.

Then there are alleys, which are to lanes as lanes are to streets. Though the system's a bit complicated, it's actually quite logical. But before you head out, there's one more thing you should know: though Taipei is an increasingly English-friendly city, with all street signs featuring both Chinese and English lettering, over the past few years there have been a number of, er, interesting developments concerning the spellings of nearly every street name in the city. Our spelling decoder, opposite, should help a bit, but visitors to the city should be aware that the Taiwanese approach to English translation is about as rigidly dogmatic as their approach to religion (ie not very dogmatic as all). As a result, don't be surprised to find a restaurant whose business card address reads Chunghsiao East Road under a street sign reading Zhongxiao E Road.

Districts

Though Taipei proper is divided into 12 *qū* (districts), most of what we've listed in our inner Taipei section can be found in one of six general areas.

OLD TOWN CENTRE 萬華區
The first part of the city to be developed, this proto-Taipei (also known as Wanhua) was once encircled by a wall. Though the wall is gone, four of its five gates still stand, adding to the historic character of this district. It's in and around this area where you'll find sights traditional (Longshan Temple), contemporary (Ximending) and

historically edifying (2-28 Museum). It's in the Old Town Centre where you'll find the government district, often a hub of activity in Asia's most vibrant democracy.

MRT Stations: Taipei Main Station, Ximen, Longshan Temple, Xiaonanmen, NTU Hospital, Chiang Kai-shek Memorial Hall.

DA'AN & SHIDA 大安區, 師大區
These districts in the southern part of the city centre are built around Shida (home to Taiwan Normal University) and Da'an Park. Thus, Shida, sometimes spelt, amusingly enough, Shita, is filled with students and funky, while Da'an is breezy and more grown up, yet without the slick modernity of Xinyi in Eastern Taipei. Both feature famous food streets (Shida Night Market, Yongkang St and Tonghua Night Market) and Da'an is also known for the weekend jade and flower markets.

MRT Stations: Guting, Taipower Building, Gongguan, Da'an, Technology Building, Dingxi, Yongan market.

ZHONGSHAN 中山區
This area north of the Zhongshan (Zhōngshān) train station and south of the Keelung River features museums (large and small, and even a miniature one), beautiful parks and some of Taipei's most important temples. The western part of this district, near the Danshui River, is sometimes known as Dadaocheng or Datong. In general, most of the major sights listed are within walking distance of the Xindian/Danshui MRT line.

MRT Stations: Zhongshan, Shuanglian, Minquan W Rd, Yuanshan.

EASTERN TAIPEI 東台北市
With rivers and established subcities to the north and west, and mountains to the south, when it came time for Taipei to expand there was but one direction left. Encompassing Songshan, Xinyi and pretty much everything east of Fuxing Rd, Eastern Taipei is fast becoming a second city centre of Taipei. While central Taipei is characterised by its older neighbourhoods and winding lanes, neighbourhoods in the eastern districts are laid out in a grid, and feature spiffy new high-rise office blocks, five-star hotels, city hall and some of Taipei's trendiest night spots and restaurants. And of course, there's one edifice that sticks out, both literally and

SPELLING DECODER

One complication for visitors to Taipei is that streets go by so many English spellings. Until roughly the beginning of the 21st century, the city used the Wade-Giles system of Romanisation of Chinese place names, then it switched to Hanyu Pinyin, the current standard in the Chinese-speaking world. But in practical terms there's no common approach to street names; spellings can be one way or the other, or worse, a hybrid of the two.

To make matters more confusing, the city recently instituted a system of numbering its major streets. Numbered 'boulevards' run east–west, and numbered 'avenues' run north–south. The numbers of the boulevards (1st, 2nd etc) start at the southern end of the city, while the numbers of the avenues start at the western end. Theoretically, this numbering system was designed to help foreigners make sense of it all, but in practice locals have no idea which street corresponds to which number.

Chinese	Wade-Giles	Pinyin	Number
East–West Streets			
和平路	Hoping Rd	Heping Rd	1st Blvd
信義路	Hsinyi Rd	Xinyi Rd	2nd Blvd
仁愛路	Jen-ai Rd	Renai Rd	3rd Blvd
忠孝路	Chunghsiao Rd	Zhongxiao Rd	4th Blvd
市民大道	Civil Blvd	Shimin Blvd	5th Blvd
長安路/八德路	Chang'an/Pateh Rds	Chang'an/Bade Rds	6th Blvd
南京路	Nanking Rd	Nanjing Rd	7th Blvd
民生路	Minsheng Rd	Minsheng Rd	8th Blvd
民權路	Minchiuan Rd	Minquan Rd	9th Blvd
民族路	Minchu Rd	Minzu Rd	10th Blvd
North–South Streets			
環河路	Huanho Rd	Huanhe Rd	1st Ave
中華路	Junghua Rd	Zhonghua Rd	2nd Ave
延平路	Yenping Rd	Yanping Rd	3rd Ave
重慶路	Chungching Rd	Chongqing Rd	4th Ave
承德路	Chengteh Rd	Chengde Rd	5th Ave
中山路	Chungshan Rd	Zhongshan Rd	6th Ave
林森路	Linsen Rd	Linsen Rd	7th Ave
新生北路/金山南路	Hsinsheng N/Chingshan S Rds	Xinsheng N/Jinshan S Rds	8th Ave
松江路/新生南路	Sungchiang/Hsinsheng S Rds	Songjiang/Xinsheng S Rds	9th Ave
建國路	Chienkuo Rd	Jianguo Rd	10th Ave
復興路	Fuhsing Rd	Fuxing Rd	11th Ave
敦化路	Tunhwa Rd	Dunhua Rd	12th Ave
光復路	Kongfu Rd	Guangfu Rd	13th Ave
基隆路	Keelung Rd	Jilong Rd	14th Ave

figuratively; the world's (at time of writing) tallest building, Taipei 101 (p101).

MRT Stations: Zhongxiao Fuxing, Zhongxiao Dunhua, Sun Yat-sen Memorial Hall, Taipei City Hall, Yongchuan, Houshanpi, Kunyang.

SHILIN 士林區

North of the city centre and south of Tianmu, Shilin (Shìlín) is home to some of Taipei's best known cultural attractions such as the National Palace Museum, the CKS Shilin Residence Park, and of course, the Shilin Night Market. Shilin is also where you'll find some of Taipei's most kid-friendly venues, including the Astronomical Museum and the National Taiwan Science Education Centre. Bustling, crowded and usually noisy, Shilin is a must to visit.

MRT Stations: Jiantan, Shilin.

TIANMU 天母區

Just north of Shilin, in many ways Tianmu (Tiānmǔ) is its diametrical opposite. Whereas

Danshui River

A B C D

Danshui
淡水
Danshui

See Danshui Map (p126)

See Yangmingshan National Park
& Beitou Map (p134)

Beitou

Shamaoshan
(643m)

Bali

Hongshulin

Zhuwei

Fuxinggang

Xinbeitou

Zhongyi

Beitou

Guandu

Qiyan

Qilian

See Shilin & Tianmu
Map (p100)

Shipai

Zhongshan

See Zhongshan Map (p92)

Chongqing N Rd

Xincheng Rd

Datung

Taipei Main Station

Zhongcheng

To Taoyuan
(24km)

Danshui River

Jiangzicui

Wanhua

Xinpu

Roosevelt Rd

Old Town Centre, Da'an
& Shida Map (p88)

Gongguan

Banqiao

Banqiao
Train Station

Dingxi

Yongning

Yongan
Market

Far Eastern Hospital

Jingan

Haishan

Nanshijiao

Tucheng

Yongning

Jingmei

Waolong

Dapinglin

Xindian
City Hall

Xindian

Bitan

Heimen River

To Hsinchu (70km)

1 2 3 4 5 6

0 |=====| 10 km
0 |=====| 6 miles

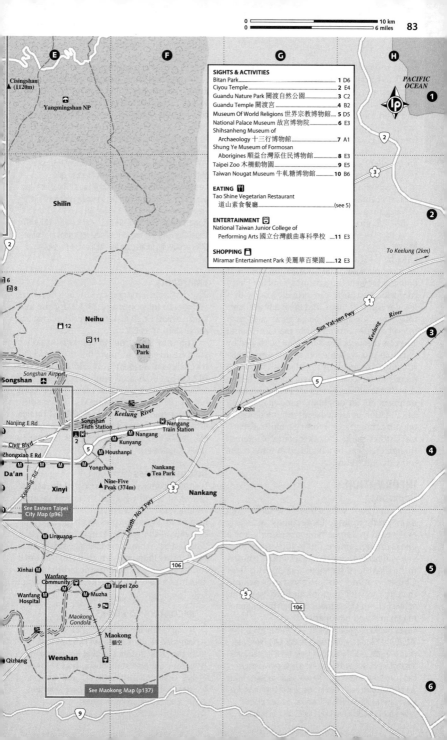

PACIFIC OCEAN

Cisingshan ▲ (1120m)

Yangmingshan NP

Shilin

To Keelung (2km) →

Sun Yat-sen Fwy

Keelung River

Neihu

12

11

Tahu Park

Songshan Airport

Songshan

Keelung River

Nanjing E Rd

Songshan Train Station

Nangang Train Station

Xizhi

5

Civit Blvd

Nangang

Kunyang

Zhongxiao E Rd

Houshanpi

Da'an

Yongchun

Xinyi

Nine-Five Peak (374m)

Nankang Tea Park

Nankang

See Eastern Taipei City Map (p96)

North No 2 Fwy

Linguang

106

Xinhai

Wanfang Community

Wanfang Hospital

Taipei Zoo

Muzha

9

Maokong Gondola

Maokong 貓空

Qizhang

Wenshan

See Maokong Map (p137)

106

5

Shilin is usually crowded and noisy, Tianmu tends to be quieter, less crowded, with wider avenues and more spread-out neighbourhoods. Shilin is where you go for street food and Tianmu is the place for sit-down restaurants. Though once thought of as kind of a foreigner ghetto, a nice place to live without much to draw the casual visitor, Tianmu has an excellent mountain park complete with temples and pavilions as well as some of Taipei's posher malls. Tianmu is also a great place to start or finish a hike into the volcanic wilds of Yangmingshan (p132).

MRT Stations: Zhishan, Mingde, Shipai

Maps
Once hard to find, good English-language maps are now plentiful. The information booths at both the Taoyuan (international) and Songshan (domestic) airports can provide you with a few government maps, and the freely available magazine *Taiwan Fun* has a great inlay map in every issue. Our favourite map for central Taipei is the *Taipei Visitor's Map* published by Asiamap and available free at hotels and tourist points. It's regularly updated and has street names in the current Pinyin spelling. It also depicts the all-important lanes and building numbers. As for neighbourhood maps, every MRT station boasts a decent mounted map of the surrounding area featuring temples, department stores, parks and other points of interest, though these can be a bit faded in some of the more distant stations.

INFORMATION
Bookshops
You'll find book sellers, from hole-in-the-wall newsstands to large local chains, at nearly every turn in Taipei. Not surprisingly, most books are in Chinese, but in the larger stores you will find foreign-language books (mostly in English) filed by subject along with their Chinese counterparts. Newsstands around the city (at MRT stations and the like) typically carry an assortment of English-language magazines and newspapers.

Caves Books (Dūnhuáng Shūjú) Tianmu (Map p100; ☎ 2874 2199; 5 Lane 38, Tianyu St; Bus 220) Zhongshan (Map p92; ☎ 2537 1666; 103 Zhongshan N Rd, sec.2; MRT Shuanglian) Frayed and fading like a long-owned paperback, Caves was once one of the only places in Taipei where Westerners could find a decent selection of English books. Nowadays though Caves is still among the best places to find books on both teaching English and on learning

Chinese, selection-wise Caves has been well outdone by Taipei's newer and flashier generation of book sellers.

Eslite (Chéngpǐn; Map p96; ☎ 2775 5977; 245 Dunhua S Rd; MRT Zhongxiao Dunhua) Taipei's most renowned bookshop, with locations all over town. The flagship Dunhua S Rd location is the first place most locals look for foreign-language books, particularly on travel.

GinGin's Taiwan (Jīngjīng Shūkù Jīngpǐndiàn; Map p96; ☎ 2364 2006; 8 Alley 8, Lane 210, Roosevelt Rd, sec.3; MRT Guting) Gay and lesbian bookshop and café.

Le Pigeonnier Bookshop (Xìngē Fàguó Shūdiàn; Map p96; ☎ 2517 2616; 9 Lane 97, Songjiang Rd) Specialist in French books.

Page 1 (Map p96; ☎ 8101 8282; 4th fl, Taipei 101; MRT Taipei City Hall) Has one of the finest selections of English titles in the city, located on the 4th floor of the world's tallest building.

Emergency
The national emergency contact numbers are ☎ 110 for police and ☎ 119 for fire and ambulance. English-language directory assistance is ☎ 106.

You may find English speakers at police stations throughout town, but the **Central District police station** (Map p88; ☎ 2556 6007; 33 Chengde Rd, sec.2) has dedicated English-speaking staff who can help if you're in a jam. If you need help with immigration or visa extensions, you'll be told to go to the **Ministry of Foreign Affairs** or the **National Immigration Agency** (Map p88; ☎ 2388 9393; www.immigration.gov.tw; 15 Guangzhou St; MRT Xiaonanmen).

Internet Access
It should come as no surprise that the capital city of an island whose main export is semiconductors is pretty much totally wired when it comes to internet access. With the exception of a few of the smaller hotels (generally the 'love hotels', whose customers generally have needs other than ready email access), all hotel rooms in the city have in-room broadband, and many have wi-fi in the lobby. Internet

---

SECONDHAND BOOKS

If you're looking to stock up on cheap on-the-road reading, there are two restaurants in the Shida district boasting not just sandwiches but also secondhand books. These are Grandma Nitti's (p111) and Bongos (p111). Bongos has Taipei's best selection of science fiction paperbacks.

cafés abound, especially (but hardly limited to) neighbourhoods surrounding universities. And if you happen to be travelling with a laptop or another wireless device, you're pretty well set; when it comes to wi-fi access, cities don't get much friendlier than Taipei. You can buy stored-value wireless cards at 7-Eleven. The **National Central Library** (below) is a good place to check your email. There are also a couple of free kiosks on the 3rd floor of the **Nova Computer Arcade** (p122).

Laundry

All of the hostels in our lodgings listings have washing machines on site, as does the YMCA. Getting your washing done at high-end lodgings can get expensive. If neither of these options works for you, there are some small clothes-cleaning shops and coin-operated laundromats. You'll find these shops in the alleys and lanes of many districts, especially those surrounding universities. One such place is **Shida Zizhu Xiyi** (Shīdà Zhìzù Xǐyī; Map p88; ☎ 2362 1047; 72 Longquan St; MRT Taipower Building), which will get your laundry back to you in about six hours (NT60 per load).

E-clean (Mèishì Zhìzù Xǐyī) Shida (Map p88; ☎ 0952-763 132; 159-1 Shida Rd; ☺ 24hr; MRT Taipower Building) Taipei City Hall (Map p96; 47 Zhongxiao E Rd, sec.5; ☺ 24hr; MRT Taipei City Hall) is the most prominent laundromat chain in the city (NT60 per load). If you're up around the Minquan E Road area, **Shabon Coin Laundry** (Map p92; 122 Minquan E Rd, sec.2; ☺ 24hr) has washers for NT60 per load, and the dryers are NT10 for six minutes.

Left Luggage

The basement floor of the Taipei Main Station has several rows of coin-operated lockers, as does the food court in the Shingong Tower across the street and the SOGO department store (p120). English instructions and regulations are clearly marked. The Songshan Domestic Airport has small/large lockers for NT80/120 per 24 hours, with a six-day limit. Most hostels also offer left-luggage service.

Library

Right across the street from the Chiang Kai-shek memorial sits the **National Central Library** (NCL, Zhōngyāng Guójiā Túshūguǎn; Map p88; ☎ 2361 9132; 20 Zhongshan S Rd; ☺ 9am-9pm Tue-Fri, 9am-5pm Sat & Sun), inside whose hallowed halls you'll find an extensive collection of Chinese-language tomes, current and back issues of more than

650 foreign magazines, a dozen newspapers in English, rare books and an art gallery on the 4th floor. The NCL also offers dozens of computers for free internet use, and a like number of desks with handy DSL ports for those travelling with their own laptops. If you're planning a trip to Taiwan's hinterlands, the NCL is a fine place to get photocopies of various road atlases and topographic maps (2nd floor). To enter, you'll need a library card; temporary (one day) cards can be picked up at the entrance with some ID, and for a permanent card you'll need your passport and a photo.

Media

If you're after a steady stream of nonthreatening English-language pop tunes punctuated by light banter, traffic reports and news on the hour, then Taiwan's International Community Radio Taipei (ICRT; 100.7FM, 576AM) is the station for you. ICRT is Taiwan's only English-language radio station and possibly single-handedly responsible for making Taiwan's youth think that people in the West are actually still listening to ABBA and Hootie and the Blowfish. See p327 for general information on newspapers, magazines and TV stations in Taiwan.

Several free magazines published in English have loads of useful Taipei-specific information. These include *Wow Taipei* (published by the city government) and *Taiwan Fun* (www.taiwanfun.com), which has a great city map.

Medical Services

Almost every hospital in Taipei has English speakers on staff; most also have an English-speaking, information-booth attendant close to the entrance. Most of the phone numbers below lead to recordings with English options. Three hospitals we've heard good things about are **Heping Hospital** (Map p88; ☎ 2192 6068; 33 Zhonghua Rd, sec.2, MRT Xiaonanmen), **Mackay Hospital** (Mǎjiē Yīyuàn; Map p92; ☎ 2543 3535; 92 Zhongshan N Rd, sec.2, MRT Shuanglian) and **Veterans General Hospital** (Róngmín Zōng Yīyuàn; Map p100; ☎ 2875 7346; 201 Shipai Rd, sec.2; MRT Shipai).

Other hospitals include:
Adventist Hospital (Táiān Yīyuàn; Map p96; ☎ 2771 8151; 424 Bade Rd, sec.2; MRT Zhongxiao Fuxing)
Air Force Hospital (Kōngjūn Yīyuàn; Map p96; ☎ 2764 2151; 131 Chiankang Rd)
Cathay General Hospital (Guótài Zōnghé Yīyuàn; Map p96; ☎ 2708 2121; 280 Renai Rd, sec.4; MRT Zhongxiao Dunhua)

Chang Gung Hospital (Cháng Gēng Yīyuàn; Map p96; ☎ 2713 5211; 199 Dunhua N Rd)
National Taiwan University Hospital (Táidà Yīyuàn; Map p88; ☎ 2312 3456; 1 Changde St; MRT NTU Hospital)
Yangming Hospital (Yángmíng Yīyuàn; Map p100; ☎ 2835 3456; 105 Yusheng St, Tianmu; MRT Zhishan)

The Taiwanese enjoy subsidised medical coverage, but even as a visitor you won't find yourself paying too much for treatment for run-of-the-mill illnesses or injuries. If you're interested in checking out traditional medicine, the **Hospital of Traditional Chinese Medicine** (Táiběi Shìlì Zhōngyī Yīyuàn; Map p88; ☎ 2388 7088; 100 Kunming St; ☯ 8-11.30am & 1-4.30pm Mon-Fri, 5-8.30pm Tue-Fri, 8-11.30am Sat; MRT Ximen) has English-speaking doctors. The same building also houses the **STD clinic** (Táiběi Shìlì Xingbìng Fángzhì Sǔo; ☎ 2370 3739).

Money
You shouldn't have much problem accessing your cash in Taipei as most Taiwanese banks are connected to either the Cirrus or Plus network. These networks generally accept foreign cards from banks aligned with those systems. You'll also find cash machines in the strangest places, such as McDonalds and 7-Elevens. We've found the latter to be especially trouble free in dispensing cash for out-of-town cardholders. The ATM on the ground floor of the Nova Computer Arcade (p122) across from Taipei Main Station also takes foreign cards. Most Taiwanese ATMs ask you to chose a language before entering your PIN. See p339 for further information.

Post
Taipei's main post office, the **North Gate Post Office** (Map p88; Zhongxiao W Rd), is southwest of Taipei Main Station. Come here to claim poste restante packages. There are post offices throughout the city; easy to find because of their bright green facades and large signs in English. Post-office workers can generally understand a bit of English and are overall pretty helpful, but avoid going between noon and 2pm if at all possible; that's when busy time coincides with nap time.

Tourist Information
There are eight Taipei Visitor's Information Centre booths scattered around the city, all with the usual assortment of maps and pamphlets, stacks of free magazines and generally helpful English-speaking staff.

Taipei Visitor's Information Centre Taipei Main Station (Map p88; ☯ 8am-8pm) Songshan Airport (Map pp82-3; ☯ 8am-8pm) These branches keep the longest hours. Taipei Travel Net (http://taipeitravel.net) has locations for the other six, plus loads of other useful information.
Tourism Bureau (Guānguāng Jú; Map p96; ☎ 2349 1500; 9th fl, 290 Zhongxiao E Rd, sec.4; ☯ 8am-5pm) Has similar information, though its location deep inside the building makes it a bit trickier to locate.

Travel Agencies
There are a number of travel agencies located just south of the Songshan Airport by the junction of Minquan E and Dunhua N Rd and English-speaking agents advertise in all of the English-language newspapers. Low advertised prices without taxes and fees are often quoted, so clarify the total price before you buy any tickets. If you need to make a visa trip to avoid overstaying a landing or 60-day visa, the three cheapest spots to fly to are generally Manila, Okinawa, and of course, Hong Kong.

SIGHTS
Taipei's sights can be extreme, from Qing dynasty temples with burning incense and chanting monks to wide plazas where teen-aged vixens with mobile phones seem to be engaging in tight-skirt beauty pageants. Wide and noisy neon-lit roads offer shopping malls (one of which is shaped like a golf ball and surrounded by wooden horses) with all the modern conveniences. Warrens of lanes and alleys, punctuated by the occasional playground, jungle gyms and health and pain inducing foot-massage paths (take off your shoes, walk steadily, and breathe deeply. Nothing better than some self-induced reflexology to keep you in shape) offer a quiet reprieve from the urban sprawl. With places to go, culture to experience, and things to eat, Taipei offers a plethora of exploration opportunities. We've listed some of our favourite spots, divided roughly by category. But we feel that the real joy of travel lies not in the destination, but in exploration itself. Taipei is particularly well suited for exploration, so make sure you leave yourself some time to investigate this truly dense – and often unexpectedly strange – city.

Parks, Monuments & Memorials
Taipei has spectacular gardens, history from varying angles and more statues than you can shake a stick at: fancy a walk in the park?

CKS SHILIN RESIDENCE PARK 士林官邸

Once upon a time this multifaceted botanical garden, the **CKS Shilin Residence Park** (Shìlín Guāndǐ; Map p100; 60 Fulin Rd; admission free; 🕑 8.30am-5pm Mon-Fri, 8am-7pm Sat & Sun; MRT Shilin) was part of the sprawling estate of Generalissimo and Mrs Chiang Kai-shek. They ruled the gardens with an iron hand, overseeing the pruning, weeding and other daily gardening tasks from their palatial home overlooking the estates, all the while dreaming of their inevitable triumphant retaking of mainland China. When the Generalissimo died, Madame Chiang (who never cared much for Taiwan), wasted no time in moving her official residence to America. For decades the estate and the surrounding gardens were closed to the public.

In the late 1990s, then-mayor (now president) Chen Shuibian decided to turn the whole area into a park. This did not please Chiang's widow, who, though in her late nineties, still claimed title to the property. Eventually a compromise was reached and the gardens were opened to the public while the house remained closed.

The main features of this sprawling estate, one of 15 of Chiang's estates still left over around the country, are its fabulous Chinese- and Western-style gardens. There is also a horticultural exhibition hall often filled with artistic displays of flowers and plants. Rafts of gardeners take care of them all.

The estate is just off Zhongshan N Rd, sec.5. The main entrance is about 10 minutes' walk from the Shilin MRT station. Keen observers might note that though the initials 'CKS' still appear on all signs, the former dictator's full name, as well his name in Chinese, have been removed from much of the signage within the property. Can it be too long before 'the little people' are wandering around Chiang's personal sanctuary? Who knows?

DA'AN PARK 大安公園

If Taipei has a central park, then this is it. Bordered on all sides by the major urban thoroughfares of Xinyi, Jianguo, Heping and Xinsheng Rds; this large park (Dà'ān Gōngyuán; Map p88) is where the city comes to play. And play it does, from kiddies rollerblading and playing tag to teens playing basketball and ultimate Frisbee to old men whomping each other in *xiàngqí* (Chinese chess). The park is a great place to hang out on sunny afternoons; take off your shoes and walk barefoot on the foot-massage path or just stop and smell the flowers. In the early mornings, you'll see folks practising taichi. Perhaps more incongruous for visitors expecting Asian-themed pursuits are the ad hoc ballroom-dancing classes that often occur on cool summer evenings. Find a partner and join in. On big holidays, especially Christmas, New Year and Chinese New Year, the amphitheatre hosts free stage shows featuring some of the biggest names in Taiwanese entertainment. There's also a row of restaurants with outdoor seating across the street from the park's northwest corner.

2-28 PEACE PARK 二二八和平公園

At first glance the lovely **2-28 Peace Park** (Èrèrbā Hépíng Gōngyuán; Map p88; MRT NTU Hospital) doesn't seem more significant than any of the other dozen or so parks in Taipei. There's a band performance stage, some lovely shrines and pavilions, paths and playgrounds. But there is a certain air of solemnity to this place, for it is dedicated to the memory of a massacre that began on 28 February 1947 (hence the 2-28), an event that heralded the start of Taiwan's martial-law era. In the centre of the park stands the memorial itself, a steepled sculpture surrounded by three enormous cubes turned on their corners. The memorial is surrounded by a moat that is crossed by a bridge. In the early mornings, the park is a good place to watch people practising taichi and you can join in if you're so inclined. At night, it's said that 2-28 park is a popular cruising ground for gay men. This park is home to both the 2-28 Memorial Museum (p92) and the National Taiwan Museum.

BOTANICAL GARDENS 植物園

A beautiful oasis in Taipei's funky west side, this **park** (Zhíwùyuán; Map p88; ☎ 2381 7107; 53 Nanhai Rd; admission free; 🕑 4am-10pm; MRT Xiaonanmen) has greenhouses featuring a vast variety of lush plants, literature- and Chinese-zodiac-themed gardens and a marvellous lotus pond. Taipei's Botanical Gardens are also considered one of the best places in the world to see the rare Malaysian Night Heron, making the park a major stop on foreign birding tours. That such a rare bird can be seen so close to, let alone inside, a major urban centre is quite amazing, or so our twitcher friends tell us. The Botanical Gardens are where you'll find the National Museum of History (p93).

ZHISHAN CULTURAL & ECOLOGICAL GARDEN 芝山花園

Just south of Tianmu's Yangming hospital and a few blocks east of the Zhishan MRT sits one of our favourite Taipei **parks** (Zhīshān Huāyuán; Map p100; MRT Zhishan), a jungle-filled mountain just north of the Shuangxi River (also a lovely park in its own right). It's filled with gardens and shrines and the top of the mountain has a temple dedicated to a much revered sage and general called Chen Yuan Kwang who lived 1500 years ago. Though the temple itself is lovely enough, more interesting still are the statues surrounding it – carved stone representations of characters well known to anyone familiar with the Chinese classic *Romance of the Three Kingdoms*.

And what really makes the climb worth it is the view, a sweeping panorama of the whole of Taipei city. The park itself offers a wide variety of hikes, both on dirt trails as well as wooden boardwalks that skirt sections of the mountain.

CHILDREN'S RECREATION CENTRE 兒童育樂中心

Just south of the Keelung River, this large **park** (Értóng Yùlè Zhōngxīn; Map p92; ☎ 2593 2211; 66 Zhongshan N Rd, sec.3; NT30, additional for planetarium shows; ◷ 9am-5pm, closed Mon; MRT Yuanshan) features a 'world of yesterday' with historical Chinese toys and folk arts, and a 'world of tomorrow' with, among other things, a planetarium.

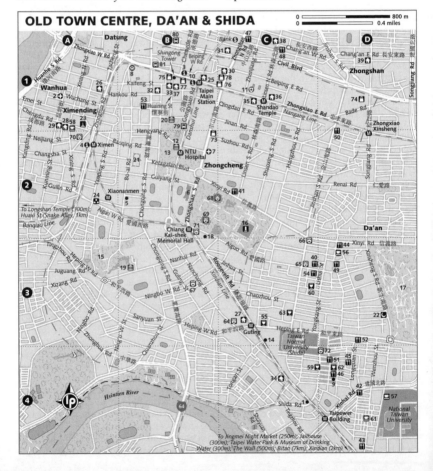

OLD TOWN CENTRE, DA'AN & SHIDA

SUN YAT-SEN MEMORIAL HALL 國父紀念館

Occupying an entire city block, this **hall** (Guófù Jìniànguǎn; Map p96; ☎ 2758 8008; 505 Renai Rd, sec.4; admission free; ☉ 9am-5pm; MRT Sun Yat-sen Memorial Hall) serves as a cultural centre (concerts, performances and special events), a large public park and a museum of the life of the man considered the founder of modern China. A huge statue of Dr Sun sits in a cavernous lobby facing the park to the south. It's guarded by two implacable sentries – you can watch the changing of the guards, an intricate choreography involving much spinning of bayoneted rifles and precision stepping. This happens twice a day. Morning visitors practising taichi on the grounds provide another kind of choreography. You'll also find the excellent Discovery Centre of Taipei (p93) on the grounds.

MARTYRS' SHRINE 忠烈祠

Against a backdrop of mountains across the Keelung River from the city centre, the monumental **National Revolutionary Martyrs' Shrine** (Zhōngliècí; Map p92; ☎ 2349 1635; 139 Beian Rd; admission free; ☉ 9am-5pm) enshrines the dead of the wars fought on behalf of the ROC. The complex covers around 5000 sq metres and the main sanctuary was modelled after the Taiho Palace in Beijing. Plaques, paintings and friezes in the arcade surrounding the main sanctuary describe the details of various 20th-century rebellions and battles. A bell tower and drum tower are used during memorial ceremonies.

The main reason most people come here, however, is to see the hourly changing of the guards. Blue uniformed, silver-helmeted, implacable and silent, they wield and spin their bayoneted rifles with the precision of a drill team. The public is able to march along with the guards as they tread the path from the sanctuary to the main gate hundreds of metres away. The shrine is about 10 minutes' walk east of the Grand Hotel (p107).

CHIANG KAI-SHEK MEMORIAL HALL
中正紀念堂

Whether this imposing **hall** (Zhōngzhèng Jìniàn Táng; Map p88; ☎ 2343 1100; 21 Zhongshan S Rd; admission free; ☺ 9am-5pm; MRT Chiang Kai-shek Memorial Hall) will still go by the same name by the time this book goes to print is anybody's guess. Many and strident are the voices in the high halls of Taiwan's government calling for this 70m-tall memorial to Taiwan's one-time dictator to be renamed, and the massive statue removed. For now, this iconic monument with its white walls and blue octagonal roof still stands as a grandiose, ostentatious and perhaps fitting memorial to the man who, in life, was known in some circles as 'General Cash-my-check'. On the ground floor you'll find a museum dedicated to Chiang's life, with an assortment of military uniforms, medals, paintings and manuscripts, along with two humungous black, bulletproof Cadillacs he used. You'll also find in this museum an interesting version of history in which Chiang's Kuomintang (KMT, Nationalist Party) forces nearly single-handedly defeated the Japanese empire, and the Chinese communist revolution is reduced to a mere speed bump in history.

The sculpture of the man himself is equally ostentatious. To get to it visitors ascend a flight of 89 steps (representing Chiang's age when he died), where the gigantic bronze sculpture occupies a cavernous hall, and looks out over the gate and towards China. The statue is flanked by two motionless guards with bayoneted rifles and, behind him, carved into the white marble walls, are Chinese characters reading 'ethics', 'democracy' and 'science', the 'Three Principles of the People'. A sign in front of the hall, opened in 1980, five years after Chiang's death, states that those with slippers or slovenly dress shall not be admitted.

The grounds (250,000 sq metres) also include the **National Theatre** and **National Concert Hall**; it's here that the Taipei City Classical Chinese Orchestra often performs (check schedule for times). The plazas and gardens around the three buildings are among Taipei's grandest and best used, and on weekends you'll often find anything from outdoor art exhibitions to hip-hop concerts. The grounds are also used by marching bands and drill teams to rehearse their routines.

At press time, one of the most dramatic examples of Taiwan's break from the Chiang Kai-shek era is still in progress. As of mid-July the cavernous entrance to the upper portion of the monument has been covered by scaffolding, and the plaque above the doorway bearing Chiang's name taken down. Green and blue banners reading 'National Taiwan Democracy Monument' have been hung just under the eaves on three of the monuments. The name of the park and corresponding MRT station remains unchanged. Will this sight still be called 'Chiang Kai-shek Memorial' by the time you read this, or should you look for a building called 'National Taiwan Democracy Monument'? And will the colossal generalissimo still be seated upstairs? Time (and future editions of this book) will tell for sure.

Museums

If it's museums you like, you'll find no shortage of them in Taipei.

NATIONAL PALACE MUSEUM 故宮博物院

This **museum** (Gùgōng Bówùyuàn; Map pp82-3; ☎ 2881 2021; 221 Zhishan Rd, sec.2; adult/concession/infant NT100/ 50/free; ☺ 9am-5pm) is home to what could quite easily be termed the world's largest and finest collection of Chinese art; it is unfortunate that the overall interior setup of the museum does not match with the grandeur of the collection. Its renovation, ongoing for several years, was pronounced 'completed' with great fanfare in 2007; however, we have to liken the National Palace Museum to a sumptuous gourmet banquet made with the finest ingredients, but prepared by a disinterested chef and arranged by colour-blind kitchen staff.

The museum's interior is poorly lit and for the most part its grand collection is laid out with little sense of theme or design, giving the museum a stagnant feel overall. This is especially strange in light of the fact that the exhibits are rotated frequently; the vast collection (much of it liberated from mainland China during the last retreat of the KMT) is far too large to exhibit at any given time. Nonetheless, the sheer volume and beauty of the museum's treasures still makes it a must visit.

ONE-DAY TAIPEI TOURS FOR THE...

Spiritual Traveller

Rise at dawn and head to **2-28 Peace Park** (p87) for some taichi and morning contemplation, followed by walking 200 steps along the stone foot-massage path to build inner resilience. Go to **Longshan Temple** (p97) to mingle with morning devotees and fellow travellers. After that, head over to the **Museum of World Religions** (p138) and check out exhibits until noon, then have lunch at the **Tao Shine Vegetarian Restaurant** (p139). Afterwards, visit the compact yet beautiful **Tien-Ho Temple** (p98), located in the heart of ultrachic Ximending. The walk from the MRT will test your resolve against a variety of forms of sin. Travel north to the Yuanshan neighbourhood to check out **Confucius Temple** (p95) and the surrounding temples in the area until dusk. Head to Shilin for a meal at **Haw Kuang** (p115). Afterwards, get to **Beitou** (p131) for a soak in the hot spring. You've earned it.

Culture Vulture

Spend the morning in the government district getting your historical bearings. To glean two very different versions of Taiwanese history, visit the **Chiang Kai-shek Memorial Hall** (opposite) and the **2-28 Memorial Museum** (p92). Then visit the **Presidential Building** (p102), letting the very fact that you can visit give you an idea of how far Taiwan's democracy has evolved. After an early lunch in the neighbourhood, head up to Shilin and divide the rest of the afternoon between the **Shung Ye Museum of Formosan Aborigines** (below) and the **National Palace Museum** (opposite) as they're close to each other. When the museums close, head up to **Danshui** (p126) for the evening, checking out the old shops and eating on Danshui 's Gongming St (also known as Danshui Old St).

Glutton

Get up whenever. If it's before 10am, find any restaurant that has a sign reading 早餐店 (Zǎocān Diàn, Breakfast Shop) and get yourself two *qǐ sī dàn bǐng* (rolled cheese and egg omelettes), a side of *luóbuógāo* (turnip cake – trust us, they taste better than they sound), and maybe a *wēn dòujiāng* (warm soymilk) to settle your stomach. If it's after 10am, go to the **Taipei Main Station food court** (p110) and try some Hakka food. After lunch, head back to your hotel, crank up the air-con, and rest up for a long night. For dinner, head out to the **Shida neighbourhood** (p111). Eat liberally from any of the stalls that appeal to you and don't forget to buy some fruit (to aid digestion). Hit the nearest 7-Eleven for a bottle of Whisbih (an energy drink) and take a taxi up to the **Shilin Night Market** (p99). Share your Whisbih with the driver and if he offers you betel nut, take it. Spend a few hours eating light snacks such as *zhū xiě gāo* (congealed pigs blood) and *chòu dòufu* (stinky tofu) before heading to the food court across from the station for a nice *táiběi niúpái* (Taiwanese beefsteak) nightcap. Bon appetit!

Among the treasures on rotation at the National Palace Museum are painting, calligraphy, statues and ceramic and jade. Some pieces date back thousands of years into Chinese history and even prehistory. The museum also has an amazing collection of Buddhist artifacts inherited from the Forbidden City. Some of the most popular items are always on display – check with the front desk to find out where they are during your visit.

The museum offers free guided tours in English at 10am and 3pm. Tour contents vary with each guide, but all offer a good overview. If you prefer to move about at your own pace, there's an English headphone guide (NT200).

To reach the museum, take the MRT to Shilin station (Red Line), exit to Zhongzheng Rd (north exit), and catch bus 304, 255, red 30, minibus 18 or 19 or culture bus 101.

SHUNG YE MUSEUM OF FORMOSAN ABORIGINES 順益台灣原住民博物館

This **museum** (Shùnyì Táiwān Yuánzhùmín Bówùguǎn; Map pp82-3; ☎ 2841 2611; www.museum.org.tw; 282 Jishan Rd, sec.2; adult/concession NT150/100; ✆ 9am-5pm, closed Mon & 20 Jan-20 Feb) features highlights of nine Taiwanese indigenous tribes. These Austronesian peoples are related through blood or linguistic ties to people across precolonial Oceania, as far away as Madagascar. The tribes developed pottery, basketry, wood carvings, musical instruments and colourful costumes. The museum is tastefully put together and features soft lighting and an interesting array of exhibits. Fine examples of Taiwanese aboriginal handicrafts are displayed and video footage offers an educational summary of the histories of the tribes themselves.

While the culture of Taiwan's aboriginal people was nearly subsumed as Han Chinese overtook the island both culturally and demographically, in the past decade, there's been a remarkable upswing of interest among Taiwanese people towards their aboriginal brethren, due perhaps in part to the wish of many in Taiwan to establish a cultural identity distinct from that of mainland China.

The museum is about 200m past the bus stop for the National Palace Museum, across the street.

2-28 MEMORIAL MUSEUM 二二八紀念館

Located inside 2-28 park (p87), the **2-28 Memorial Museum** (Èrèrbā Jìniànguǎn; Map p88; ☎ 2389 7228; 3 Ketagalan Blvd; adult/concession NT20/10; ☉ 10am-5pm, closed Mon; MRT NTU Hospital) offers an explanation of the events and repercussions of the 28 February 1947 massacre. Acknowledgment of the 2-28 incident was a pivotal part of Taiwan's transformation from dictatorship to democracy. Though there is little in the way of English signage in the museum, a multilingual walking tour device is available for NT50, plus NT1000 rental deposit. However, there

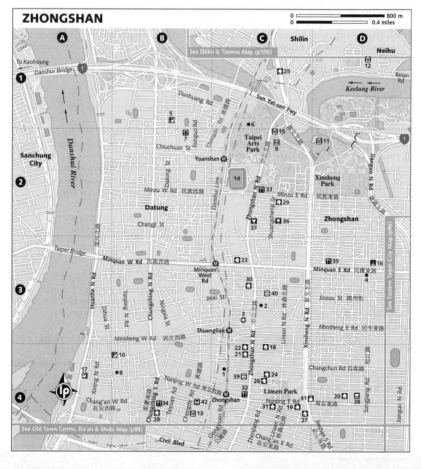

ZHONGSHAN

are generally bilingual volunteers on hand willing to walk you through the displays. The building itself is significant, for it was from this, the former KMT radio station, that officials tried to calm the masses as panic swept the island.

Just north of the museum (by the park's northern gate) is the National Taiwan Museum (Guólì Táiwān Bówùguǎn; Map p88), with exhibits on the flora and fauna of the island, as well as special exhibits. Its lack of English signage, however, may make it less accessible to non-Chinese-speaking visitors.

FINE ARTS MUSEUM 市立美術館

Constructed in the 1980s, this airy, four storey box of marble, glass and concrete showcases contemporary art, with a particular focus on Taiwanese artists. Although the **museum** (Shìlì Měishùguǎn; Map p92; ☎ 2595 7656; 181 Zhongshan N Rd, sec.3; student/adult/senior NT15/30/free; ☺ 9.30am-5.30pm, closed Mon; MRT Yuanshan) features exhibits that change annually, and works from the permanent collection. These include pieces by Taiwanese painters and sculptors from the Japanese period to the present.

South of the museum is the Zhongshan Fine Arts Park, a gently sloping green-grass space with ancient trees, sculptures, and various rotating exhibits and happenings. The park is a popular weekend hangout for members of Taipei's *kabayan* (Philippine guest worker) community, who come here to picnic, play music and otherwise chill out on days off.

MUSEUM OF CONTEMPORARY ART TAIPEI 台北當代藝術館

Taiwan's first **museum** (MOCA, Táiběi Dāngdài Yìshùguǎn; Map p92; ☎ 2552 3721; www.mocataipei .org.tw; 39 Chang'an W Rd; admission NT50; ☺ 10am-6pm, closed Mon; MRT Zhongshan) dedicated explicitly to contemporary art occupies an important Japanese-era building that was once Taipei's city hall. Shows are all special exhibits and fill anything from one gallery to the entire museum; they might include architecture, design, fashion, digital and video art and even comic books. Check the website for current exhibition information.

DISCOVERY CENTRE OF TAIPEI 台北探索館

Inside Taipei City Hall, this **complex** (Táiběi Tànsuǒguǎn; Map p96; ☎ 2725 8630; 1 Shifu Rd; admission free; ☺ 9am-5pm, closed Mon; MRT Taipei City Hall) is a good place to get your bearings on the city and its history. You can see maps and models depicting Taipei's evolution from a walled, gated city in 1882 to the bustling metropolis it is today. You can find out more about its geography, topography, commerce, famous residents and natural resources here too. There's a free audio guide in English, and guided tours are available with advance notice.

NATIONAL MUSEUM OF HISTORY 國立歷史博物館

Just outside the Botanical Gardens, Taiwan's first **museum** (Guólì Lìshǐ Bówùguǎn; Map p88; ☎ 2361 0270; 49 Nanhai Rd; adult/concession NT20/10; child & senior free; ☑ 10am-6pm, closed Mon; MRT Chiang Kai-shek Memorial Hall, Xiaonanmen) is still an anchor of local arts and culture housed in an elegant Japanese-era building. 'History' is actually a misnomer – Chinese *art* history would be more accurate, with thousands of Chinese artifacts from the Tang, Shang and other dynasties. The tea room on the 3rd floor has views of the Botanical Gardens' lotus pond. A tour in English takes place at 3pm each afternoon.

SU HO PAPER MUSEUM 樹火紀念紙博物館
Don't blink or you might walk right past the store front housing this four-storey **museum** (Shùhuǒ Jìniàn Zhǐ Bówùguǎn; Map p96; ☎ 2507 5539; 68 Chang'an E Rd, sec.2; admission NT100, NT180 with paper-making session; ☑ by appointment 9.30am-4.30pm Mon-Sat; MRT Zhongxiao Fuxing). Fulfilling the lifelong dream of Taiwanese paper-maker Mr Chen Su Ho, this museum features special exhibits of ultracreative uses of paper (such as paper sculpture or installation art). No matter when you visit, you can make your own sheet of paper in the museum's workshop and learn about materials and processes. An English audio guide is available. Exhibits change two or three times a year.

The museum shop sells cards, elegant kites and other trinkets constructed from handmade paper.

MINIATURES MUSEUM OF TAIWAN 袖珍博物館
Bigger is better, so some say; but not at the **Miniatures Museum of Taiwan** (Xiù Zhēn Bówùguǎn; Map p96; ☎ 2515 0583; B1, 96 Jianguo N Rd, sec.1; adult/student/child NT180/150/100; ☑ 10am-6pm, closed Mon; MRT Zhongshan Junior High School) where quite the opposite is true. This small, private museum is dedicated to the exhibition of the minuscule, the tiny, the 'Sweet Jesus, I can't believe someone had the patience and steadiness of hand to create something so small and intricate!' Among the most (of many) astounding articles on display is a 40-bulb chandelier no bigger than a single grain of rice. A most impressive little museum indeed.

TAIPEI STORY HOUSE 台北故事館
Just north of the Fine Arts Museum, this **house** (Táiběi Gùshìguǎn; Map p92; ☎ 2587 5565; 181-1 Zhongshan N Rd, sec.3; adult/student NT30/20, child & senior free; ☑ 10.30am-6pm, closed Mon; MRT Yuanshan) was built in 1914 by an aristocratic tea trader. Its style

---

TAIPEI FOR CHILDREN

Children should have a good time visiting Taipei, as the number of kid-friendly venues is growing each year. This isn't so much to attract Western visitors who travel with children, though that may be a happy by-product; academic pressure starts early for Taiwanese kids, and over the last decade more enlightened souls in the country have sought to balance this pressure with play, giving rise to a cottage industry of child-friendly places.

There are obvious choices, of course, such as the **Taipei Zoo** (p136) and the **Children's Recreation Centre** (p88). There are also a number of museums geared towards children's edutainment. Our favourite of these is the newly opened **National Taiwan Science Education Centre** (opposite). Likewise, kids will like the **Taipei Astronomical Museum** (opposite) and **Taipei Sea World** (opposite). The little ones should find enough to occupy them inside the weirdly mystical **Wonderland of Love** (p139) to allow the parents a solid hour to explore the decidedly more mature **Museum of World Religions** (p138) to which it's attached.

Danshui (p126) is also a good place to bring kids. The waterfront plaza and Old St are car-free, and there are a number of odd venues (such as the Believe it or Not Museum and Starbugs) with plenty of gross-out factors that kids should enjoy. Just across the river, **Bali** (p129) is also a fine place for travellers with children, as the bike-rental shops seem to do a good business with various tandem bikes equipped with child seats – a great way to bring the little ones to the surprisingly kid-pleasing **Shihsanheng Museum of Archaeology** (p129). Of course, if the risk of severe insulin shock isn't daunting, a visit to the **Taiwan Nougat Museum** (p139) is fun for the whole family.

Naturally, Taipei also offers great opportunities to expose children to Chinese culture. Try a **Chinese opera performance** (p120) or a puppet show. Kids also seem to love marching with the guards at the **Martyrs' Shrine** (p89), while the **Chiang Kai-shek Memorial Hall** (p90) offers plenty of space for them to run around. And the night markets are always alluring, and offer lots of messy-dining meals for kids of all ages.

was said to have been inspired by a building he saw while visiting the 1900 Paris Expo. Today the house is an exhibition space for Taipei nostalgia and history. Exhibits change frequently and might include goodies such as toys, matchboxes and comic books.

The gift shop features the work of a dozen local artists and the tearoom serves afternoon tea and French-style cuisine.

TAIPEI ASTRONOMICAL MUSEUM
天文科學教育館

Opened in 1997, this **museum** (Tiānwén Kēxué Jiàoyùguǎn; Map p100; ☎ 2831 4551; www.tam.gov.tw; 363 Jihe Rd; adult/concession NT40/20; ☼ 8.50am-5pm, closed Mon; MRT Jiantan) houses four floors of constellations, ancient astronomy, space science and technology, telescopes and observatories. Though a good place to while away an hour with the kids, what keeps this otherwise excellent museum from being a must-visit is a dearth of English content, though every exhibit features English and Chinese, but most of the actual information is in the latter language only. Plans are underway to put full bilingual information online, so theoretically non-Chinese speaking visitors could download exhibit information and study up before arriving. More English-friendly attractions (at an extra charge) are an IMAX theatre, a 3-D theatre (presentations change frequently) and the 'Cosmic Adventure', an amusement-park ride through outer space.

NATIONAL TAIWAN SCIENCE EDUCATION CENTRE 國立台灣科學教育中心

If this place doesn't bring out the kid in you, than there's no kid in you to be brought out. The **National Taiwan Science Education Centre** (NTSEC, Guólì Táiwān Kēxué Jiàoyù Zhōngxīn; Map p100; ☎ 2837 8777; 189 Shihshang Rd; NT100; ☼ 9am-6pm Tue-Fri, 9am-7pm weekends & holidays, closed Mon; MRT Shilin) is one of the coolest children's museums we've yet to find in Asia. Interactive exhibits cover the gamut of scientific knowledge, from anatomy (a walk-through digestive tract!) to zoology (a cat-head-shaped helmet that gives the wearer feline hearing powers). Though NTSEC is not fully bilingual, museum staff have gone to great length to include enough English content to make all sections of the museum accessible to non-Chinese speakers.

Like the Astronomical museum, NTSEC has a 3-D theatre (admission is an extra NT120). You also have the option of paying

an extra NT100 to take a short ride on a bicycle. Why would you want to do this, you ask? We'll let that be a surprise, suffice to say that it has to do with where the bicycle is located and what the short ride entails. Keep pedalling and for Buddha's sake, don't look down!

TAIPEI CHILDREN'S ART MUSEUM
蘇荷兒童美術館

Opened in 2003, this highly interactive children's **museum** (Sūhé Értóng Měishùguǎn; Map p100; ☎ 2872 1366; www.artart.com.tw; B1, 20 Alley 50, Tianmu W Rd, ☼ 10am-5.30pm, closed Mon except holidays & closed Tue following holidays; Bus 220) features artwork by children and regular programmes to encourage children to participate in the creation of art. Dedicated to the nurturing of children's hearts and minds through art, the museum offers an excellent counterpoint to the rote 'learning through repetition and imitation' educational methods prevalent in Taiwan. Though generally frequented by teachers with school groups, activities and guided tours for travellers with children can be arranged by calling in advance.

TAIPEI SEA WORLD 台北海洋館

Though this **aquarium** (Táiběi Hǎiyángguǎn; Map p100; ☎ 2880 2310; 128 Jihe Rd; adult/concession/senior NT480/430/350; ☼ 9am-10pm; MRT Jiantan) probably won't win any awards from the Jacques Cousteau foundation, it's OK as a quick diversion. The fish are pretty, and kids should have a good time checking out the reasonable variety of sea creatures on display. Probably the only aquarium we've ever seen in a high-rise building.

Must-Visit Temples

Many are Taipei's houses of worship; some are even surrounded by snack vendors.

CONFUCIUS TEMPLE 孔廟

Modelled after the temple in Confucius' native town of Shandong, this **temple** (Kǒng Miào; Map p92; ☎ 2592 3934; 275 Dalong St; admission free; ☼ 8.30am-9pm Tue-Sat, 8.30am-5pm Sun; MRT Yuanshan) is based on classical Chinese temple architecture. Confucius (551–479 BC) is generally acknowledged as China's greatest educator and scholar. In his day, education was exclusive to nobility but Confucius successfully promoted popular education.

Confucius valued simplicity, a trait seen in the temple's architecture and relatively muted

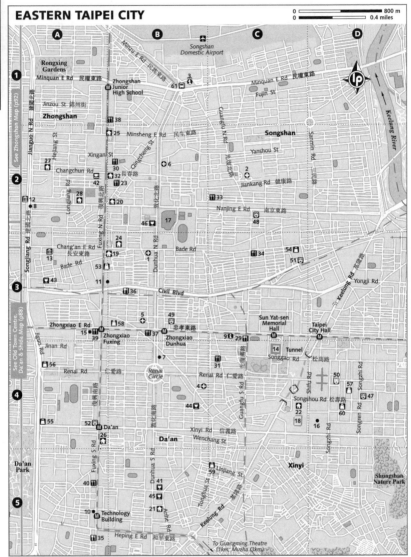

EASTERN TAIPEI CITY

adornments. Inscriptions that might be found on columns, doors and windows in other temples are banned here; who would have the temerity to think his or her writing could compare with that of the great master? Do take note of the detailed carvings of dragons on the temple's Ling Xing Gate and the fired pottery on the Yi Gate. The central Ta Cheng hall is one of the few traditional wooden buildings in Taiwan and contains a Confucius tablet. A seven-storey pagoda in the centre of the roof is said to drive away evil spirits. A total of 186 tablets representing the Confucian disciples are located on the premises.

The temple at this site (13,935 sq metres) dates back to 1928, replacing the original 1879 temple that was damaged beyond repair during a rebellion under Japanese occupation.

The temple's biggest day of the year is Confucius' birthday, celebrated on 28 September. Events begin at 6am with a ceremony presided over by the mayor of Taipei and officiated by rafts of attendants, supervisors and officers, all dressed in elaborate costumes. Confucius' spirit is welcomed with drumming, music, bowing, incense, chanting, a sacrificial feast and the burning of spirit money. Tickets go on sale at the temple about five days in advance and always sell out. At other times of year the Confucian tradition of education continues with weekly Chinese calligraphy classes (2pm to 4pm every Wednesday) and poetry readings (2pm to 4pm every Saturday). Classes are informal and free so just turn up.

LONGSHAN TEMPLE 龍山寺
Religious life in Taiwan is alive and kicking seven days a week at the Longshan **temple** (Lóngshān Sì; Map p88; 2302 5162; 211 Guangzhou St; admission free; 6am-10.20pm; MRT Longshan Temple). Though not the biggest temple in the city,

there is something unique and beautiful about the vibe at Longshan that keeps people coming back.

The temple dates back to 1738. As the story goes, a passer-by left an amulet of the Guanyin (goddess of mercy) hanging on a tree on the site of the present temple, and the amulet shone so brightly, even after dark, that all who passed by knew the site was blessed. Nearly three centuries later, the spot still exudes a certain warmth. The stones that line the courtyard of the temple were originally ballast on the ships that ferried immigrants from Fujian province across the often treacherous Taiwan Straits, and the waterfall inside the courtyard is a favourite spot for shutterbugs. Once you enter the main building, expect a riot of scarlet and gold in the form of enormous bronze incense burners and carved-stone columns. The best times to visit are around 6am, 8am and 5pm when crowds of worshippers gather and engage in hypnotic chanting.

Like many temples in Taiwan, the Longshan temple is multidenominational. Although the Guanyin is still the central deity worshipped here, the temple enshrines 165 other deities. Along the back wall are several bays containing different gods – on the right is the patron of scholarly pursuits, while on the left is the god of military pursuits and business people. The goddess Matsu (p216) is in the centre, and provides for the safe return of travellers by sea or land (air travellers pay their respects to the Guanyin). Matu is flanked by two male guards, one is said to see 1000 miles, while the other can hear 1000 miles.

The lights on columns at the back of the temple represents one person whose family has made a donation in his or her honour.

Outside of the front gate of the temple, old monks sit selling cedar-wood beads, and old women sell magnolias. The number of vendors increases markedly on weekends. Across the street from the temple is an underground market and the entire neighbourhood is good for shopping for religious items and trinkets of all sorts.

XINGTIAN TEMPLE 行天宮

This **temple** (Xíngtiān Gōng; Map p92; ☎ 2502 7924; 109 Minquan E Rd, sec.2; admission free; ⏱ 5am-11pm) is one of the city's busiest. It's dedicated to Guangong (AD 162–219), a famous red-faced general who became deified and is worshipped as the god of war and, by extension, martial arts. Business people also flock here as Guangong was said to be adept at finance.

Although it does not have the long history of other temples (the present building dates from 1967), it has heft. One distinctive feature is the large shed that covers the central courtyard. This is where supplicants leave their daily offerings on tables. Temple officials wear handsome royal-blue robes.

Xingtian Temple is also popular for fortune-telling. Within the temple grounds you'll hear, and then see, visitors dropping oracle blocks. Fortune-tellers can often be found even in the pedestrian underpass outside the temple.

The temple god is celebrated on the 24th day of the sixth lunar month, and at smaller festivals during the third and ninth lunar months.

BAO-AN TEMPLE 保安宮

It began with humble Qing-dynasty origins, but today this Taoist **temple** (Bǎoān Gōng; Map p92; ☎ 2595 1676; 61 Hami St; admission free; ⏱ 7am-10pm; MRT Yuanshan) is one of the city's leading religious sites. The original, wooden structure

was completed in 1760 by immigrants from Fujian province who brought their own materials with them. The current temple, dating from 1805, took 25 years to build.

The temple deity is the emperor Baoshen, famous as a doctor and great healer. As such, the temple gets many visitors who come to pray for good health. Enshrined in the bell tower is the goddess of birth. She is flanked by 12 female aides, each of whom assists with childbirth during a particular month, so naturally it's long been popular with pregnant women. Other gods commemorated here are patrons of business and good fortune.

The two open-mouthed lions (one male, the other female) are said to be an appeal for the rule of law and good government.

HSIAHAI CITY GOD TEMPLE 霞海城隍廟

Others may be larger and grander, but this **temple** (Xiáhǎi Chénghuáng Miào; Map p92; 61 Dihua St, sec.1) teems with character and characters. It's also one of the best-preserved temples in the city and has had the same appearance for over a century. Visit on the city god's birthday (the 13th day of the fifth lunar month) for one of Taipei's biggest, loudest and most lively celebrations.

In addition to being protector of the people of the city, the city god also keeps track of good and evil deeds performed by mortals, and monitors the movements of souls and demons in the afterlife. The powers of the city god are almost carrot-and-stick in nature, the power to motivate good thoughts on the one hand, and the ability to strike fear through punishment on the other.

TIEN-HO TEMPLE 天后宮

More proof that good things come in small packages, this **temple** (Tiānhòu Gōng; Map p88; 51 Chengdu Rd, Ximending) seems, from the outside, but a narrow (though exceptionally ornate) storefront in the busy Ximending district. But walk through the narrow gate and you'll find one of Central Taipei's most beautiful Buddhist temples, complete with statues of Matsu, ancient Chinese generals, a bell tower and a small dragon-shaped pond filled with huge carp. The original temple was built during the mid-Qing period and demolished during the last years of Japanese rule to make way for a roadway. The current temple was built in 1948 and holds several ancient statues brought over from mainland China hundreds of years ago.

Then there's the matter of the smell. For reasons which we can't quite explain, the temple often smells of burning hemp. But worshippers seem to be walking straight, so we assume it's an industrial blend.

CIYOU TEMPLE 慈佑宮

Right across from Songshan train station, this **temple** (Cíyòu Gōng; 761 Bade Rd, sec.4) is dedicated to the goddess Matsu and is one of the oldest in the city. But Ciyou temple has another thing going for it besides age; noise. Specifically this takes place, on the day of Matsu's birthday (p216), when the temple is said to hold the loudest, most colourful birthday celebrations in Taiwan. Proceedings are resplendent with gongs, music and firecrackers. If you see us at Ciyou temple during the festival, don't bother yelling. We might see you at Ciyou, but we won't be able to hear you…or anything else for the rest of the day, for that matter.

TAIPEI MOSQUE 台北清真大寺

Built in 1960, the Taipei **mosque** (Táiběi Qīngzhēn Dà Si; Map p88; 62 Xinsheng South Rd, sec.2; www.taipeimosque.org.tw) seems at first strangely out of place in this city of Buddhist, Taoist and Confucian temples. But with its green crescent-peaked domes and tall minarets, the mosque adds additional depth and texture to the spiritual cloth of Taiwan's capital city.

Night markets & Notable Neighbourhoods

Replete with fascinating neighbourhoods and world renowned for its night markets, Taipei is an urban explorer's dream.

SHILIN NIGHT MARKET 士林夜市

Considered by many to be the king of Taipei's night markets, the sprawling **Shilin Night Market** (Shìlín Yèshì; Map p100; MRT Shilin) is a nightly carnival of snacking and shopping. Teeming with stalls selling delectable edibles far beyond our ability to describe (though we try – see p113), the latest in trendy clothing from shoes to hats (and everything in-between), games of skill and chance and much, much more. If you have only one night to spend in Taipei, spend it here. Appetite not whet yet? Fear not, Shilin Night Market is covered in greater detail in our food section.

XIMENDING 西門町

Like Tokyo's Ginza, **Ximending** (Xīméndīng; Map p88; MRT Ximen) is the ultraconsumerist heart of Taipei's mainstream youth culture. This eight-branched intersection dates from the Japanese era and is now chock-full of shops selling fashion, fast food, sneakers, sunglasses, scarves, Sanrio, Sony and spaghetti. If it's young and trendy, it's here. The pedestrian streets northwest of the main intersection (between Chengdu Rd and Wuchang St) is more or less the epicentre, but for the full Ximending experience you'll really want to explore the smaller alleys. It's here you'll find the edgier side of Taiwan's youth culture, the places they hang out and the stores in which they work and shop.

There are restaurants for all tastes in Ximending, from coffee shops and steak houses to sushi bars both cheap and expensive, and plenty more. Though there are gift shops aplenty in Ximending, you may want to bring home something a bit more permanent to remember your Taiwan trip. Hanzhong Lane 50 is where you'll find your tattoo parlours and piercing joints. If it can be inked, pierced or otherwise modified, chances are good you can get it done in Ximending.

While it's busy most of the time, nights and weekends are prime time, especially Friday and Saturday nights. You might catch a musical act on a temporary stage set up on the streets and if you want to see a film, Wuchang St is home to many cinemas as well as some fine examples of Japanese-period architecture, notably the **Red Pavilion Theatre** (p102).

Ximending is also where you'll find one of our favourite urban holy spots, the **Tien-Ho temple** (opposite).

DIHUA MARKET 迪化街

The several blocks that make up this **market** (Díhuà Shìchǎng; Map p92; MRT Zhongshan) are Taipei's best-preserved examples of historic architecture. Building styles range from Fujianese to Baroque to modernist. The area is sometimes called 'Grocery Street', and for most of the year it's thought of as a good place for buying traditional Chinese medicines and herbs, bolts of cloth and sundries. If you're lucky enough to be in Taipei for the weeks leading up to the Lunar New Year celebrations, Dihua market's true colours shine, as the area is considered Taipei's best for traditional New Year foods, party supplies and gifts of all kinds. During these weeks, a festive spirit of bonhomie

SHILIN & TIANMU

descends on the market, manifesting itself in a veritable orgy of giving as merchants offer samples of their edible wares to all passersby. Should you come during this period, be prepared to be fed.

No matter when you come, be sure not to miss the nearby **Hsiahai City God Temple** (p98).

SNAKE ALLEY 華西街夜市

Once considered a Taipei must see, nowadays, Snake Alley, aka Huaxi St Night Market (Huáxijiē Yèshì; Map p88; Huaxi St; ☉ 7pm-midnight; MRT Longshan Temple) is more of a window into Taiwan's less enlightened past, when the live skinning of reptiles for the benefit of passing tourists was considered an appropriate form of cultural expression. In decades past, Taipei dwellers might bring their visitors from abroad to Snake Alley and express mild amusement as their foreign guests squirmed at the sight of a local merchant baiting a cobra with a hooked metal rod before slitting its belly and offering the foreigners a shot glass of snake bile mixed with Kaoliang liquor. These days, Snake Alley is considered somewhat passé and cruel by many.

If you'd like to watch a snake handler barking like a carnie while ('Careful, ladies and gents, don't get too close! One bite from this beast and you'll be dead before you hit the ground!') taunting a poisonous viper before disembowelling it, than by all means a trip to Huaxi St should be high on your agenda. The snake meat ends up in soup or stir-fried with vegetables, while the blood is mixed with liquor, a cocktail said to be good for virility and a host of ailments. Snake meat tastes like a blend of chicken and monkfish, and many of the restaurants in this brightly lit covered alley are worth visiting. Another interesting facet of this neighbourhood is that, until a few years ago, it was a legal brothel district. For this reason, Snake Alley is also a good place to find shops selling herbal aphrodisiacs, sex toys and Viagra. The foot-massage parlours on the bright end of the street are fine, but avoid the karaoke bars on the dark end as they're vile. The surrounding alleys are good places to by religious items.

Buildings

Taipei's reputation for boring architecture is so over. Here are a few reasons why.

TAIPEI 101 台北國際金融中心

Towering above the city like the gigantic bamboo stalk it was designed to resemble, **Taipei 101** (Táiběi Guójì Jīnróng Zhōngxīn; Map p96; 45 Shifu Rd; www.taipei101tower.com; MRT Taipei City Hall) is impossible to miss. At 508m, Taipei International Financial Centre 101, as it's officially named, is the world's tallest building (Dubai eat your heart out, until next edition at least!). Construction began in 1997 and the exterior was completed in 2003. In addition to holding the world record for height, Taipei 101 also holds the record for having the world's fastest elevator. The pressure-controlled lift travels at 1010m per minute and takes 40 seconds to get from ground level to the 89th floor observation deck.

In the basement of the structure is an excellent food court, and the lower five floors are taken up by swank malls and several banks. Floors 89 to 91 are the observation decks offering incomparable views of the surrounding city, mountains and horizon. The hefty admission price for the observation floors (NT350, NT4500 for the outdoor deck) does not deter the hordes of locals and visitors who line up to catch the view from almost atop the world's tallest building.

At the time of this writing, the planned plush restaurants set to open on the floors just below the observation tower weren't open, but may well be by the time you read this. As for the floors between the mall and future restaurants, these are home to some of Taipei's choicest and most expensive office spaces. But don't get any bright ideas about pretending to work on the 80th floor just to sneak up and catch the view from a bathroom window without paying the observation deck fee, business floor elevators are strictly monitored and controlled. As for the stairway, well, there are frequent 'stair master' races held in Taipei 101, but as far as we know individual travellers are, shall we say, discouraged from using this method to around the ticket counter. But if you make it, let us know.

CORE PACIFIC CITY 京華城

Some people call it **Core Pacific City** (CPC, Jīnghuáchéng; Map p96; ☎ 3762 1888; 138 Bade Rd, sec.4). We like to think of it as The Great Golf Ball of Taipei. Designed by Jon Jerde, the Pablo Picasso of the architecture world, Core Pacific City is quite probably the weirdest shopping mall in Asia. A building inspired (by MC Escher or perhaps LSD) to say the least, from the outside CPC looks like a gigantic golf ball being embraced by a stone sarcophagus. Though you can get in through the basement, for maximum weirdness take the escalator from the street into the main lobby. Just keep reminding yourself that you are going shopping and not being taken via conveyor belt deep into the heart of an alien hive. Do not panic, the colour lights along the ceiling are there to soothe. Soon, you will be inside the structure, calm and refreshed, ready to experience all the shopping, eating, karaoke and cinema-going magic that the 'Living Mall' has to offer.

Since the initial rush of publicity over its grand opening in 2001, Core Pacific City seems to have had a bit of a mixed ride. Though unquestionably unique from the outside, most of the stores found inside can be found elsewhere in the city. Furthermore, despite

TAIPEI

the free shuttle bus service from the nearest (but rather distant) Sun Yat-sen Memorial Hall MRT, Core Pacific City is considered less convenient to visit as some of Taipei's other malls. As a result, this wonderfully strange, egg-shaped behemoth can sometimes feel a bit empty, though it tends to be more crowded on the weekends.

TAIPEI ARENA 台北體育館

'Build it and they will come', seems to be the motto behind this brand-new **Taipei Arena** (Táiběi Tǐyùguǎn; Map p96; www.tpa.com.tw) on the corner of Tunhua and Nanjing Rds. Vast, cavernous and shaped like a flying saucer, the Taipei Arena hosts concerts, sporting events and noteworthy performances such as the 2007 Taipei running of *Cats* (the musical, not actual felines themselves). Check out the website for the latest schedule. Even if there's nothing in particular going on, it's a good place to visit because of the swish shops on the first level, and it's a good place for the kiddies thanks to the amusement centre in the basement.

PRESIDENTIAL BUILDING 總統府

Built in 1919 as the headquarters of the then-occupying Japanese forces, this **building** (Zǒngtǒng Fǔ; Map p88; ☎ 2311 3731; www.president .gov.tw; 122 Chongqing S Rd, sec.1; admission free, passport required; ☺ 9am-noon Mon-Fri; MRT Ximen) has housed the offices of the president since 1949. Its ornate brickwork is typical of the Japanese era, and at 85m it was the tallest building in town for decades.

Exhibits include documents from Taiwanese history (both originals and copies) and artifacts from the Japanese occupation (lacquerware, statues etc). Although most signage is in Chinese, there is usually an English speaker on hand to guide you through. At the gift shop you can pick up a presidential windbreaker (NT500).

Taiwan's democracy can at times be extremely active. For a few weeks in 2006, large-scale protests were centred around the Presidential Building, making casual tourism in the area somewhat more interesting. Needless to say, should your visit coincide with any future mass acts of democratic expression, plan your trip to the Presidential Building accordingly (and don't be surprised if visiting hours are curtailed). In any case, most of the time, visitors are permitted to see only the gardens and ground floor exhibition

halls. However, the rest of the building does open but only for six days each year; check the website or inquire for details.

LIN ANTAI OLD HOMESTEAD 林安泰古厝

This is Taipei's oldest **residential building** (Línántài Gǔcùo; Map p92; ☎ 2598 1572; Binjiang St; admission free; ☺ 9am-9pm Tue-Sat, 9am-5pm Sun; MRT Yuanshan). The southern Fujian–style 30-room house was built during 1783–87, near what is now Dunhua S Rd. It was gradually expanded as this wealthy merchant family grew. The home reached its present size in 1823.

However, the city also expanded and in the 1970s this historic home was slated to be destroyed as the road was being widened. Thankfully, public outcry saved it; the building was painstakingly dismantled and, in 1983, rebuilt on this field across from Xinsheng Park. Today the house is notable for its central courtyard, swallowtail roof and period furniture. We're not sure the Lin family would have wanted their house in the shadow of an expressway (as it currently is) but we bet they'd be glad it's been preserved.

RED PAVILION THEATRE 紅樓劇場

The **Red Pavilion Theatre** (Hónglóu Jùchǎng; Map p88; ☎ 2311 9380; 10 Chengdu Rd; admission free except during events; ☺ 1-10pm Mon-Fri, 10am-10pm Sat & Sun; MRT Ximen) is one of Taipei's older buildings. The wooden, octagonal structure was originally a public market, then a theatre for Chinese opera as well as a second-run cinema. Since beginning life anew as a multipurpose centre for vocal and visual arts it has hosted a variety of performers and performances, such as Taiwan-based world music group A Moving Sound (p56) and the Taipei run of the *Vagina Monologues*. Exhibits and performances change frequently, but even if you come just to check it out (or have a coffee), it's worth the time.

ACTIVITIES
HIKING & BICYCLING

First-time visitors will be astounded by just how thin the line between Taipei's urban jungle and jungle-jungle can be. Head south at either end of the MRT blue line and before long you're hiking through mountain foothills with only the occasional glimpse of Taipei 101 to remind you of how close to the city you still are. Head east out of the Xinbeitou MRT station and before long you'll be walking through jungle that's dotted with sulphur-spewing steam vents.

One our favourite hikes is the Tianmu Trail, beginning at the very top end of Zhongshan N Rd, sec.7. It's here that Taipei's longest street becomes a dirt trail and later a stone staircase that pretty much leads to the front gate of Yangmingshan National Park (p132). Expect to pass by mountain streams and dense jungle on the way in. Though we can neither confirm nor deny tales of monkeys prowling the upper sections of the trail, looking to waylay travellers, signs warn of the dangers of monkey-feeding and help lend such rumours official credence.

The **Taipei Rapid Transit Corporation** (☎ 2181 2345; www.trtc.com.tw) puts out an excellent free booklet you can pick up at some MRT stations and at all tourism offices. The booklet, *Guide to Hiking & Cycling*, lists 20 excellent hiking and biking trails throughout and around the city. One of the best things is that the trails are well marked, with trailheads generally well signposted on the front map of its nearest MRT station.

Cycling opportunities abound as well, and cyclists would do well to pick up a free *Taipei City Cycling Map* from any of the Taipei Visitor's Information Centres (p86). This publication shows some of great trails running along the banks of Taipei's rivers. The booklet also lists seven city-run, bike-rental stores, and you can pick bikes up at one and leave it off at another. Charges vary depending on bike quality and you'll be asked to leave a deposit and show your passport. You can find bike-rental places close to the Muzha and Guandu MRT stations or you can call the **Taipei Cycling Lifestyle Foundation** (☎ 2719 2025) to get English directions to the nearest bike-rental place. The trails ranges from nine to 18km in length and you can easily get from one end of the city to the other along the rivers.

BIRD-WATCHING

For a city, Taipei sure has a lot of bird-watching opportunities. **Shuangxi park** (Map p100) is a great place to spot cormorants and herons, and the **Botanical Gardens** (Map p88) is said to be a good place to spot the rare Malaysian Night Heron. The **Wild Bird Society of Taipei** (Táiběi Shì Yědiǎo Xuéhuì; Map p96; ☎ 2325 9190; http://www.taipeibird.org.tw; 3 Lane 160, Fuxing S Rd, sec.2) arranges bird-watching tours around Taipei and Taiwan and stocks a number of English

books for the devoted twitter. See p71 for more details about bird-watching in Taipei and around Taiwan.

IN-LINE SKATING

Taipei boasts a small but dedicated group of in-line skaters. Most of the cycling trails work just as well for blading, though some are a bit rough in spots. The trail running under the MRT north of Shilin station is perfect, as are most sections of the Shuangxi river path. A Kiwi, Geoff, and his wife, Xiaoling have been teaching skating and hockey to children since the mid-90s. Their business, **Mono Club** (Map p88; ☎ 2321-2065; www.monoclub.com.tw; 20-1 Aiguo E Rd; skate rental per day NT150; MRT Chiang Kai-shek Memorial Hall), is the city's best skate shop. People at Mono Club will let you know what skating events are going on during the time of your visit. Some of Taipei's more hardcore skaters meet up for a Friday night skate through the city, weather permitting. Call the shop for details. There's also a small park for skateboarders in Zhongshan that aggressive in-liners might enjoy. The park has jumps, ramps and a serviceable quarter pipe and is south of the Yuanshan MRT station (Map p92).

FITNESS CLUBS & SWIMMING POOLS

There are a few public outdoor swimming pools around town and some hotels have arrangements where you can use their pools for a fee. We've noted hotels with pools under Sleeping (p104). However, outdoor swimming is a seasonal thing in Taipei and is usually reserved for warmer months. People do swim in the river up in Wulai (p141) and there are a number of good beaches on the northeast coast. One excellent place to swim is **Yuquan Park Pool** (Yùquán Gōngyuán Wēnshuǐ Yóuyǒng Chí; Map p92; ☎ 2556 2539; 28 Xining N Rd; admission NT110; ☒ 5.30 7.30am, 8am-5pm & 6-10.30pm). The pool was constructed in 2004 and is near the centre of town. Its glass atrium features a water slide that empties into hot-water baths and there are nearby 'massage waterfalls'.

The **California Fitness** (Jiāzhōu Jiànshēn Zhōngxīn; Map p88; ☎ 2311 7000; 100 Zhongxiao W Rd, sec.1; guest pass NT500 per day; ☒ 6am-midnight Mon-Sat, 8am-midnight Sun; MRT Taipei Main Station) gym is as cutting edge as the health clubs in its namesake home state. You'll find the latest equipment and shiny metallic locker rooms fitted with steam and sauna baths. It's affiliated with California and 24-Hour Fitness clubs in other countries, so if you have a regular membership card for either of these you can use the facilities for free. There's also a branch in Tianmu (with a pool) and another in Ximending. Get more details from the main branch.

Another gym is **Being Sports** (☎ 2369 9299; B1, 19 Roosevelt Rd, sec.2; ☺ 7am-11pm; MRT Guting). Though Being doesn't offer day passes, it does offer contract-free, one-month memberships for NT3000. Somewhat more low key than California Fitness, Being has weights, exercise machines, a sauna and a Jacuzzi.

YOGA

The Swami Salami School of Yoga (Map p96; ☎ 0918 494 082; www.theswamisalamischoolofyoga.com; Lane 251, Alley 3, 8 Zhongxiao E Rd, sec.3; MRT Zhongxiao Fuxing) Regular classes are taught by a Yogi named Rob Ogle, a man with a definite sense of humour (hence the business's name). Check his website for more details.

Space Yoga (Yújiā Kōngjiān; Map p100; ☎ 2877 2108; www.withinspace.com; Lane 43, 5 Tianmu E Rd; Bus 220) This upscale boutique yoga studio often hosts visiting international teachers. Visit their website for information.

Chiu Su Jen Yoga Centre (Map p96; ☎ 2740 2688; www.csjyoga.com.tw; 36 Fuxing S Rd, sec.1; MRT Zhongxiao Fuxing) This school has branches around Taiwan and Taipei and conducts both English and Chinese classes. The website has classes and branch information.

TOURS

You won't have any trouble finding an organisation to take you on a bus tour of Taipei. The companies listed under Tours (p351) all offer them. Three-hour city tours (adult/child NT700/600) take in the Martyrs' Shrine, National Palace Museum, Chiang Kai-shek Memorial Hall, a temple visit and some shopping, although at three hours you won't get more than a taste of any one site. Other options

---

include a visit to a Wulai aboriginal village (adult/child NT900/700, four hours), a Taipei-by-night tour (NT1200, 3½ hours) and a culture tour that takes in Chinese opera (NT1200, three hours).

The **523 Mountaineering Association** (523 Dēngshān Huì; ☎ 2555 7523; Map p92; 28-2 Chifeng St; www.523.org .tw/English; MRT Shuanglian) has been a government-approved nonprofit organisation since 1999. The 523 can help travellers obtain mountain permits for a small fee as well as arrange transport to and from trailheads. It organises day and overnight trips to the high mountains and low jungle trails, some along paths you simply won't be able to find on your own. Its website has tour schedules and staff speak English.

FESTIVALS & EVENTS

In addition to national festivals, interesting events include the celebrating of the birthdays of the city god at the Hsiahai City God Temple (p98) and Confucius at the Confucius Temple (p95). Christmas eve has become a de facto holiday too with bars and restaurants throwing big parties. The weeks leading up to the Lunar New Year's festivities are a great time to visit the Dihua Market (p99) and if you're around during the Lantern Festival be sure and hit both Chiang Kai-shek Memorial for the official festivities and Xindian's Bitan Park for ad-hoc pyrotechnics.

Trade shows are big business in Taiwan, with dozens taking place each year. While usually the domain of the business and not the casual traveller, trade shows are actually pretty cool if you're interested in the wares being traded. And what wares indeed, ranging from orchids to motorcycles to every high-tech gadget you can imagine. Trade shows are a great place to get cool samples, make connections and often buy things at rock-bottom prices (especially on the last day when vendors are looking to lighten their take-home loads). Most trade shows take place in or around the **Taipei World Trade Center** (Map p96), though smaller ones tend to be held elsewhere. To check out what trade fairs are happening and when, check out the website: www.taipeitradeshows.com.tw.

SLEEPING

Budget lodgings have basic rates of up to about NT1600 per room and dorm beds in hostels start at about NT250. Midrange rates are up

---

COMMUNITY SERVICES CENTRE

The **Community Services Centre** (Map p100; ☎ 2836 8134; www.community.com.tw; 25 Lane 290, Zhongshan N Rd, sec.6; MRT Mingde) is a clearing house for foreigners looking for practical information on living in Taipei. It offers newcomer orientation, continuing education, cooking classes, travel outings, 12-step meetings and Western-style counselling.

to about NT4000 and anything above that is considered top end. Top-end accommodation in Taipei is easy to locate, so we've just culled our favourites from that end of the pool. (On the subject of pools, you'll generally only find swimming pools in a few of the top-end hotels and indoor pools are scarce).

Note that when Taipei hotels list rates for a 'single' room, it often refers to a room with one queen-size bed that most travellers will find big enough for two. Many hotels also throw in breakfast, though you may have to ask when you make reservations. Upmarket hotels tend to charge a 10% service fee and 5% value-added tax (VAT) on top of their rates.

The rates listed here are rack rates, the base rate charged at peak times. However, most midrange and top-end hotels offer reductions of up to 30% on weekdays as well as during nonpeak periods. Further, we've made note where hotels offer deep discounts on their websites. With various discounts factored in, some top-end hotels can be booked for midrange rates, and midrange for close to budget so plan your trip wisely.

Budget options are scattered around town, but the highest concentration is within striking distance of Taipei Main Station (see Old Town Centre and Zhongshan listings). The nexus for hostels in the Old Town Centre is the Taipei Key Mall (K-Mall), right across from the train station, and barring holidays, your chances of getting a bed are pretty good if you just turn up without reservations. Also, look out for boutique hotels in places just outside of the main city, as well as a new category of short-term residences that, while not really a good choice for a day or two, are good for those looking to spend a week or more in Taipei. These are listed in 'Around Taipei' (p126). And finally, another option for cheaper lodgings are 'love hotels'; just specify that you're renting for the night and not to 'take a rest'.

Old Town Centre, Da'an & Shida
BUDGET

World Scholar House (Map p88; ☎ 2541 8113; www.worldscholarhouse.com; 8th fl, 2 Lane 38, Songjiang Rd; 松江路38巷2號8樓; dm/d NT350/650; ⚇ 🖳) The Taipei hostel with the erudite name has been spruced up in recent years, and now offers both dorms and double rooms, cable TV, laundry and ironing facilities, and wi-fi. Weekly and monthly rates make this a popular spot for

expat English teachers, though we've heard that the atmosphere here can sometimes be a bit too wild for tamer travellers' tastes. Air conditioning costs an extra NT20 to NT30 per hour (depending on room size).

Happy Family Hostels I, II & III (Kuàilè Jiātíng; Map p88; ☎ 2375 3443; www.taiwan-hostel.com; 2 Lane 56, Zhongshan N Rd, sec.1; 中山北路1段56巷2號; dm/s/d from NT300/400/600; 🖳) The three facilities are close to one another, but the office is at the address listed here (look for 'Happy Family' in red letters on the 2nd-floor window). Although all of the facilities are very simple, Happy Family III is the newest and nicest. Happy Family II gets a younger, more party-oriented crowd. There are shared toilets and hot-water showers on each floor, cable TV in the living rooms and free use of washing machines. Owner John Lee has been in the business for many years and enjoys a good reputation among travellers for hospitality. The reception for all three locations are at Happy Family I.

Taipei Hostel (Map p88; ☎ 2395 2950; www.taipeihostel.com; 6th fl, 11 Lane 5, Linsen N Rd; 林森北路5巷11號6樓; dm/s/d NT300/500/550; 🖳) An institution in itself, the Taipei Hostel has been a launching pad for many a Taiwan expat's career. This aged dame may be a bit frayed around the edges, but she still attracts guests from all points on the map. On a quiet backstreet, the hostel has a large room for socialising, kitchen facilities, washer/dryer, free ADSL use for laptop users and a rooftop garden. Long-term rates are available, and as the hostel is a nexus of sorts for early stage Taiwan expats, there's always a buzz about jobs, visas and what-have-you on Taipei life. The website has tips and links to information on Taipei and teaching English.

Hostelling International Taipei Youth Hostel (Táiběi YH Qúnxiánlóu Wénhuà Jiāoliúzhàn; Map p88; ☎ 2388 0885; www.yhtaiwan.com; 13th fl, 50 Zhongxiao W Rd, sec.1; 忠孝西路1段50號13樓; dm 650) This is a clean and cheerful place smack in the heart of Taipei. The proprietors have gone all out to make travellers feel welcome in Taipei. Services include tours, free films, a snooker table and use of the in-house musical instruments. There's also a nice kitchen, lockers and a laundry facility. The hostel also has a left-luggage service for travellers. International Youth Hostel (IYH) members get a discount here.

Holo Family House (Ā Luó Zhùsù Jiēdài Jiātíng; Map p88; ☎ 2331 7272; 22nd fl, Taipei K-Mall; 50 Zhongxiao W

Rd, sec.1; 台北自助旅行家 忠孝西路1段50號22樓; dm/s/d 550/680/1280) Yet another fine, clean and fun hostel run by a Taiwanese fellow who goes by the name of 'Hello'. This place is a bit quirkier than your usual hostel and offers free breakfast for guests. It also offers left-luggage service.

MIDRANGE

Li-Yuan Hotel (Líyuán Fàndiàn; Map p88; ☎ 2365 7367; 98 Roosevelt Rd, sec.3; 台北市羅斯福路3段98號; r incl breakfast from NT1480; 💻) Small, comfortable and clean, the Li-Yuan is on the south side of the Shida night market, and popular with friends and family who are visiting students at the local university. There's also free wi-fi.

Taipei YMCA International Guest House (Táiběishì Zhōngguó Jidūjiào Qīngniánhui; Map p88; ☎ 2311 3201; rv@ymca-taipei.org.tw; 19 Xuchang St; 許昌街19號; s/tw from NT1800/2800, f NT4200; 💻) Not quite cheap enough to make the budget category, the Taipei Y is nonetheless still popular with students and business people. Rooms are plain but well-kept and there's a laundry on site for guests.

Han She Business Hotel (Hánshè Shāngwù Lǚdiàn; Map p88; ☎ 2371 8812; www.handsomehotel.com.tw; 4th fl, 68 Chengdu Rd; 成都路68號4樓; r incl breakfast from NT1880; 💻) Museum-lit *objets d'art* in the corridors, clean, handsomely furnished rooms and kind staff are just a few reasons that make finding this 55-room business hotel worthwhile. While the address is on Chengdu Rd, the entrance is on a small side street. Look for the sign reading 'hotel' and you've found the place.

Cosmos Hotel (Tiānchéng Dàfàndiàn; Map p88; ☎ 2361 7856; www.cosmos-hotel.com.tw; 43 Zhongxiao W Rd, sec.1; 忠孝西路1段43號; d/tw from NT3200/4000; 💻) Ah, the Cosmos, if it were any closer to Taipei Main Station it would be inside it. This is where visiting midlevel businessmen on expense accounts, working for companies with tight-fisted accountants stay. The décor is a bit mismatched, but overall the hotel is immaculately kept and there's a gym and sauna.

Keyman's Hotel (Huáiníng Lǚdiàn; Map p88; ☎ 2311 4811; www.keymans.com.tw; 1 Huaining St; 懷寧街1號; r from NT2080) The rooms are a bit small, but the hotel is well kept, and as far as location goes the place is a good deal.

Hotel Flowers (Huáhuá Dàfàndiàn; Map p88; ☎ 2312 3811; 19 Hankou Rd, sec.1; 漢口街1段19號; r from NT2000) This is two hotels run by the same management really. One building is on the north and the other on the south side of the street (the latter is slightly newer, but both are fine). The location is not quite a quiet corner, but you won't have to change out of your flip-flops to get great snacks outside. It's just a few minutes walk from Taipei Main Station.

East Dragon Hotel (Dōnglóng Dàfàndiàn; Map p88; ☎ 2311 6969; www.east-dragon.com.tw; 23 Hankou St, sec.2; 漢口街2段23號; s/tw from NT2100) The East Dragon is a comfortable 70-room hotel on the far and quiet end of Ximending's pedestrian plaza, making it an ideal place to rest and heal up from any gruelling 12-hour, liquor-fuelled piercing-and-tattoo session. Popular with Korean and Japanese tourists.

Good Ground Hotel (Guó Guāng Dàfàndiàn; Map p88; ☎ 2371 8616; www.goodground.com.tw/en; 6 Lane 27, Chengdu Rd; 成都路27巷6號; r from NT2200, f NT4800; 💻) The faux-jade stone-pattern lobby floor makes the hotel feel like something out of the Flintstones. As laptop-toting geeks, we like the fact that the hotel is wireless down to the 1st-floor coffee shop (which also serves a good java). The six-person family room has three large beds but it's a bit cramped and we wouldn't recommend it for argument-prone families.

Tango Hotel (Kělù Tiāngé; Map p88; ☎ 2531 9999; www.thetango.com.tw; 15 Lane 83, Zhongshan N Rd, sec.1; 中山北路1段83巷15號; r incl breakfast from NT3600; ✗ 💻) Formerly known as Kodak III, this small hotel gives more expensive hotels a run for their money. Rooms feature a flat-screen TV with DVD player, silk bedspreads and a Jacuzzi bathtub. Nonsmoking rooms are available. Although the address is a lane off Zhongshan N Rd, the hotel is actually closer to Linsen N Rd.

Friends Star Hotel (Yǒuxīng Fàndiàn; Map p88; ☎ 2394 3121; fax 2386 7791; 11 Heping Rd, sec.1; 和平路1段11號; r incl breakfast from NT2300) Fairly popular with travellers with budgets falling between hostel and four star, this newish hotel next to the Guting MRT is a quick hop to both the Shida nightlife and the cultural attractions of downtown Taipei. Friends Star staff speaks English well enough to help you arrange your day. Small, windowless rooms cost the least and are good if you like things quiet.

TOP END

Sheraton Taipei (Táiběi Xǐláidēng Dàfàndiàn; Map p88; ☎ 2321 5511; www.sheraton-taipei.com; 12 Zhongxiao E Rd, sec.1; 忠孝東路1段12號; r from NT9000; 💻 🖳) This recently renovated 686-room hotel smack in the centre of Taipei's government district is the height of luxury. It's here that visiting high-ranking diplomats often stay, so if you're looking to see and be seen by the ambassador of Nauru or any other of about two dozen countries, this is the place to be. But be prepared to pay for it as luxury ain't cheap, and with a price tag of close to US$80 million, the bill for all these renovations might not be paid yet.

Zhongshan
BUDGET

Formosa Hostels I (Map p92; ☎ 2511 9625, 0910 015 449; 3rd fl, 16 Lane 20, Zhongshan N Rd, sec.2; 中山北路2段20巷16號3樓; dm/s/tw NT250/350/260) This hostel is decently kept, but extremely basic. Simple cooking and laundry facilities are available.

Formosa II (Map p92; ☎ 2511 9625, 0910 015 449; 2nd fl, 5 Lane 62, Zhongshan N Rd, sec.2; 中山北路2段62巷5號2樓; dm/s/tw NT250/350/260) A basic hostel and a branch of Formosa I. When we dropped by there was major construction going on next to Formosa II, though hopefully that'll be done by 2008.

Queen Hotel (Huánghòu Bīnguǎn; Map p92; ☎ 2559 0489; 2nd fl, 226 Chang'an W Rd; 長安西路226號2樓; s/d from NT700/800) Obviously budget but comfy. Rooms have a phone and some of their original 1950s tile work. There's no English sign out the front and you'll be lucky to find an English speaker inside, but it's right off a colourful market alley, and with the money you're saving on hotel rooms you'll be able to do more shopping.

MIDRANGE

The Moon Hotel (Map p92; ☎ 2521 3301; fax 2521 3309; 122 Xinsheng N Rd, sec.1; 新生北路1段122號; s incl breakfast from NT1800) 'A lovely place for lovers' reads their business card, and if it's a real Taipei 'love hotel' experience you're looking for, well, you've found it. Conversation with the concierge is kept at a minimum; a softly glowing board next to the counter shows pictures and prices of available rooms – all you need do is ask for your room of choice by number and pay the lady behind the desk. Go ahead, we know you want to check it out. We won't tell a soul.

Friends Spring Hotel (Yǒuchūn Fàndiàn; Map p92; ☎ 2597 2588; fax 2598 6664; 55 Minquan W Rd; 民權西路55號; s/tw incl breakfast from NT2500/3200; 🖳) This nice little budget hotel was redecorated a few years back and seems to get a lot of trade from Western business people. On weekdays, rates can dip as low as NT1875. Rates include a

copy of an English-language newspaper in the morning and there's free ADSL if you've got your own laptop. Close to the MRT Minquan West Rd stop.

First Hotel (Dìyī Dàfàndiàn; Map p92; ☎ 2551 2277; www.firsthoteltaipei.com; 63 Nanjing E Rd, sec.2; 南京東路2段63號; s/tw incl breakfast from NT2700; 🖳) The First makes the most of its four-decade-old shell and smallish rooms with renovated facilities, free wi-fi and several restaurant options. For friendliness, the staff can't be beat.

Emperor Hotel (Guówáng Dàfàndiàn; Map p92; ☎ 2581 1111; emperhtl@ms9.hinet.net; 118 Nanjing E Rd, sec.1; 南京東路1段118號; r incl breakfast from NT3400; 🖳) Its décor is a little dated and the rooms are a bit musty. However, its location is excellent, near shopping and surrounded by dining (with lots of Japanese restaurants nearby).

Taipei Fortuna Hotel (Fùdū Dàfàndiàn; Map p92; ☎ 2563 1111; www.taipei-fortuna.com.tw; 122 Zhongshan N Rd, sec.2; 中山北路2段122號; r from 3400; 🖳) Around the corner from the Minquan West Rd MRT station, this high-rise is often busy with tour groups. It's ageing only moderately well, but rooms are a decent size for the price. There's a health club with sauna on the premises. Book online for deep (up to 40%) discounts.

TOP END

Grand Hotel (Yuánshān Dàfàndiàn; Map p92; ☎ 2886 8888; 1 Lane 1, Zhongshan N Rd, sec.4, Shilin; 士林區中山北路4段1巷1號; r from NT4800; 🖳 🖭) This is it, the big Kahuna of Taiwan's hotels and a tourist attraction in itself. This 1970s reconstruction of the original 1952 building is a Chinese-style high-rise just across the Keelung River. Resplendent with red columns and painted beams, the lobby itself pretty much screams 'Old Chinese Money'. Rooms, too, are suitably spacious and decorated in old-style Chinese, offering both city and mountain views. Recreation includes a golf driving range, tennis courts, year-round swimming, a fitness centre and sauna and there are eight in-house restaurants. Even if you're too broke to stay, paying the Grand Hotel a visit on the way to the Shilin Night Market is a great way to see how the other half lives.

Hôtel Royal Taipei (Lǎoyé Dàjiǔdiàn; Map p92; ☎ 2542 3266; www.royal-taipei.com.tw; 37-1 Zhongshan N Rd, sec.2; 中山北路2段37之1號; r from NT8000; 🖳 🖭) A member of the Nikko hotel group, this contemporary hotel features a subtly understated French design (dark wood and white linen) that goes well with its overall quality of service. It offers fine attention to service, a gym and sauna. Each of the 202 rooms has bathrobes, a safe, a minibar and free ADSL connections. We are less impressed with the pair of elephant tusks in the lobby, however.

Ambassador Hotel (Guóbīn Dàfàndiàn; Map p92; ☎ 2551 1111; www.ambassadorhotel.com.tw; 63 Zhongshan N Rd, sec.2; 中山北路2段63號; r incl breakfast from NT4500; 🖳 🖘) Crisp, contemporary and international in style, the 430-room Ambassador is a beautiful hotel that's popular with business travellers and flight crews. There is blonde wood and marble throughout, and there's a spa with massage services.

Riviera Hotel (Óuhuá Jiǔdiàn; Map p92; ☎ 2585 3258; www.rivieritaipei.com; 646 Linsen N Rd; 林森北路646號; d/tw from NT6000/7000; 🖳) With its European exterior and comfortable rooms, the Riviera is a favourite with business travellers and those looking for a quiet oasis within walking distance of some of Taipei's busiest nightlife districts, not to mention the Fine Arts Museum. The health centre is excellent and the rooftop jogging track is a unique topping for this high-class hotel.

Grand Formosa Regent (Jīnghuá Jiudiàn; Map p92; ☎ 2523 8000; www.grandformosa.com.tw; 41 Zhongshan N Rd, sec.2; 中山北路2段41號; r from NT8400; 🖳 🖳 🖘) Set back from busy Zhongshan road, the Regent is tops in every way, from the gold-leaf accents and exclusive shopping to the mountain views from the rooftop pool. Standard rooms are large and well furnished, complete with lovely deep-soaking tubs. If you want to pamper yourself further, the 20th floor Wellspring Spa is one of the loveliest we've seen anywhere.

Taipei International Hotel (Táiběi Guójì Fàndiàn; Map p92; ☎ 2562 7569; fax 2531 8376; 66 Nanjing E Rd, sec.1; 南京東路1段66號; r incl breakfast from NT4320; 🖳) Eurasian in feel and well located at the corner of Linsen N Rd, the International opened in 2003. It has reasonably sized rooms with dark wood trim and cool bathroom faucets. Other amenities include a gym, free wi-fi and daily newspaper delivery.

Eastern Taipei
BUDGET
One-Star Hotel (Wànshìdá Lūdiàn; Map p96; ☎ 2752 8168; www.onestartaipei.com.tw; 12th fl, 219 Chang'an E Rd, sec.2; 長安東路2段219號12樓; r from NT1580 incl breakfast; ✗) We say that the management

is being far too humble, for One-Star gets at least a three-star rating in our book. This cool little boutique hotel is clean, well furnished and offers no-smoking rooms (a rarity in the price range). There's free breakfast in the morning and a fruit basket on the bed when you arrive just to thank you for staying. The only catch is that the place is a bit tricky to find. Follow the blue One-Star sign just off Chang'an Rd.

MIDRANGE
Baguio Hotel (Bìyáo Dàfàndiàn; Map p96; ☎ 2781 3121; www.baguio-hotel.com.tw; 367 Bade Rd, sec.2; 八德路2段367號; d/tw from NT2300/2600; 🖳) Some might say the Baguio Hotel is a bit long in the tooth, but we prefer to use the phrase 'old-school' Taipei. Expect Chinese art on the walls, and a well-kept interior. Rooms are clean and comfortable and the staff are quite friendly. Seasonal discounts are available.

Hotel Delight (Dàlái Fàndiàn; Map p96; ☎ 2716 0011; 432 Changchun Rd; 長春路432號; s/d incl breakfast from NT2727; 🖳) This delightful little hotel has a classy, subdued feel, free wi-fi and an excellent free breakfast. The overall package gives more expensive hotels a run for their money. There's a little lounge area on the 1st floor with a small business centre.

Brother Hotel (Xiōngdì Dàfàndiàn; Map p96; ☎ 2712 3456; www.brotherhotel.com.tw; 255 Nanjing E Rd, sec.3; 南京東路3段255號; r from NT4300 incl breakfast; 🖳) Well situated on the corner of Nanjing and Fuxing roads, the Brother becomes a midrange hotel when the 20% discount (often available) is factored in. The hotel is popular with business travellers.

Waikoloa Hotel (Wéikèlè Fàndiàn; Map p96; ☎ 2507 0168; www.waikoloa.com.tw; 187 Changchun Rd; 長春路187號; r incl breakfast from NT2640; 🖳) Located in an interesting neighbourhood, the Waikoloa is decorated in a mix of Japanese and Chinese via Versailles styles. There's also free internet access. Not a bad place at all.

Taipei Fullerton 315 Hotel (Táiběi Fùdūn Fàndiàn; Map p96; ☎ 2703 1234; www.taipeifullerton.com.tw; 315 Fuxing N Rd, sec.2; 復興北路2段315號; r incl breakfast from NT2800; 🖳 🖘) This is one of a pair of boutique hotels on Fuxing Rd. The Fullerton 315 has a lobby furnished like a classical British sitting room, comfortable rooms and pretty much anything the business traveller might want. It's also slightly cheaper than its sister hotel, the Fullerton 41.

TOP END

Taipei Fullerton 41 Hotel (Táiběi Fùdūn Fàndiàn; Map p96; ☎ 2703 1234; www.taipeifullerton.com.tw; 41 Fuxing S Rd, sec.2; 復興南路2段41號; r incl breakfast from NT5200; 🖳 🖳) The Fullerton 41 has 95 rooms offering slick, contemporary décor that would not be unexpected in places such as San Francisco or Tokyo. Rates include use of the business centre, sauna and fitness centre. Internet discounts can often make the 41 almost as inexpensive as its sister hotel, 315.

Far Eastern Plaza Hotel (Yuǎndōng Guójì Dàfàndiàn; Map p96; ☎ 2378 8888; www.shangri-la.com; 201 Dunhua S Rd, sec.2; 敦化南北路2段201號; s/d from NT7200/8200; 🖳 🖳) Fancy indeed, with Chinese art features throughout and rooms with walk-in closets. Even the bathrooms have TVs and Jacuzzi tubs, but don't pass up the glorious Jacuzzi and pool on the rooftop. There's a hefty charge for in-room ADSL, but we get the feeling that people who stay here consider NT600 chump change.

Grand Hyatt Hotel (Táiběi Jūnyuè Dàfàndiàn; Map p96; ☎ 2720 1234; www.taipei.grand.hyatt.com; 2 Songshou Rd; 松壽路2號; r from NT6200; 🖳 🖳) The Grand Hyatt is massive (over 850 rooms) and looms like a massive stone hawk, wings outspread in the shadow of nearby Taipei 101. Rooms have three phone lines, there's a business centre, health club and the very upscale Ziga Zaga nightclub. This is where the company sends you when the shareholders are very happy.

Westin Taipei (Liùfú Huánggōng; Map p96; ☎ 8770 6565; www.westin.com; 133 Nanjing E Rd, sec.3; 南京東路3段133號; r from NT9400; 🖳 🖳) If American-style hotels are what you like, then the high-rise Westin with its 288 rooms, piano bar and dozen food and beverage outlets, won't disappoint. Front-desk reception seems a bit on the snooty side, but an indoor pool means that you can swim all year. There's also a health club.

SHORT TERM RESIDENCE

Mandarin Hostel (www.mandarinhostel.com; stay@mandarinhostel.com; d NT3000/4000 weekly; 🖳) Catering primarily to those coming to Taipei to look for work or study Chinese, the Mandarin Hostel has a few locations throughout the city, generally near MRT stations. The one that we stayed at was close to the NTU student district, and was a typical hostel with TV, computers and a decent kitchen. Add NT1000 per week for double occupancy rooms. Check the website or email for more details.

EATING

Beijing has its duck and Shanghai its dumplings. Singapore has its fish-head curries and Hong Kong its dim sum. But at the risk of sounding hyperbolic, Taipei has it all and more, and goes toe-to-toe with any of Asia's culinary capitals.

Some say that the reason behind Taiwan's culinary diversity is its history. It's true that among the millions who fled the Mainland in the great exodus of 1949 were skilled chefs bringing with them little more than the clothes on their backs and long-kept secret recipes. Others maintain that Taipei's position as a rising star on the Asian culinary scene has more to do with the tastes of the city's denizens themselves. Taipei people are well travelled, by and large, with a substantial percentage of the population a bit too worldly in culinary tastes to accept substandard food. Geographical influence plays a role, with Taiwanese cuisine in general borrowing bits and bobs from that of eastern China and Japan with a healthy dose of aboriginal influence thrown in for good measure. Taiwan is a paradise for anyone with a taste for fresh fruit, vegetables and seafood. In addition, Taiwan's large Buddhist population makes the city a veritable heaven for those looking for vegetarian cuisine.

So numerous are the restaurants worth visiting in Taipei that listing each candidate would require a separate book entirely devoted to restaurants. For now, we've decided to list fewer individual restaurants than we have in the past, focusing instead on the various neighbourhoods, alleys and streets known to local food lovers as places to get good Taiwanese food of all varieties. Your job is to get out there and enjoy.

Old Town Centre

The Old Town Centre offers myriad eating opportunities for diners of all tastes and budgets. The warren of roads stretching southwest from the Taipei Main Station to Ximending is popular with students and has scores of coffee shops, cheap noodle joints, and midpriced restaurants. The crowd in this neighbourhood tends to skew towards the young side, though there are also a number of wallet-lightening fancy restaurants in the hotels by the Taipei Main Station. Very politically incorrect on a number of levels, Huaxi St Night Market, otherwise known as Snake

Alley, has a few restaurants worth visiting. And lest we forget, the Shingong Tower and the main station itself are home to two of our favourite food courts.

BUDGET

Xiangyi Vegetarian Heaven (Xiángyì Sùshí Tiēndì; Map p88; ☎ 2361 1755; 15 Wuchang St sec.1; meals from NT100; ☷ lunch & dinner; MRT Taipei Main Station) Easily one of the best vegetarian buffets in Taipei, this narrow two-storey restaurant is usually crowded, with the ground-floor seating generally taken by the monks who eat here daily. A beautiful assortment of Taiwanese vegetarian cuisine is cooked fresh and served to the lilting sounds of Buddhist songs coming from an overhead boom box. The restaurant has no English signboard, just look for a yellow sign above the door or follow the sounds of soft Buddhist chanting.

Amigo Mexican Food (Āmígē Mòxīgē; Map p88; ☎ 2393 2488; 85 Linsen S Rd; dishes NT100; ☷ lunch & dinner; MRT Chiang Kai-shek Memorial Hall) Got a hankering for Mexican? Amigo has tacos, burritos, home-made soups and other 'south of the border' favourites just one block north of the Chiang Kai-shek memorial. Dishes are served with flair matching a genuine taco-stand ambiance.

MIDRANGE

Yuan Thai (Yuán Tài; Map p88; ☎ 2389 5763; 25, Lane 10, Chengdu Rd; dishes from NT150; ☷ lunch & dinner; MRT Ximending) A nice little Thai restaurant behind Ximending's Red Pavilion Theatre, Yuan Thai is a stone's throw away from the serious youth bustle of Ximending without actually being in the middle of it. Though a bit plain in ambiance, the restaurant gets points for price and quality, and is a good place to get your *Pad Thai* fix.

TOP END

Momoyama (Táoshān; Map p88; ☎ 2321 5511, ext 8085; 12 Zhongxiao E Rd, sec.1; set lunch NT500-1300, set dinner NT1300-3300, dishes NT100-1500; ☷ lunch & dinner; MRT Shandao Temple) One of Taipei's top Japanese restaurants, Momoyama is located on the ground floor of the upmarket Sheraton Taipei. The stunning décor might remind you of Kyoto, especially if you book a private tatami room (at extra charge). Popular with politicos.

Tainan Tan-tsu-mien (Huáxījiē Táinán Dànzǎimiàn; Map p88; ☎ 2308 1123; 31 Huaxi St; dishes NT1200-1500; ☷ lunch & dinner; MRT Longshan temple) Odd though it may seem to have rooms decorated like Versailles and Vienna in Snake Alley, that's what you'll find here. Select your own fish and

---

A (FOOD) COURTING WE WILL GO!

So you're a vegetarian, but your date absolutely must have Korean BBQ? Or perhaps you've got a strange hankering to eat a three-course meal of beef-noodle soup, sashimi and French fries? Fancy some freshly baked mini donuts for desert? Or maybe it's just raining and you don't feel like searching for just the right restaurant. If so, hungry traveller, a trip through one of Taipei's fabulous food courts might be just your thing. Some of our favourites include:

- **Taipei Main Station, 2nd floor**: An oldie but a goodie, the cavernous upstairs of the main station offers a plethora of noodle stands, BBQ joints and other assorted Taiwanese favourites.

- **Shingong Tower, basement**: Two floors of food stalls to chose from, including hard-to-find items such as duck-meat sandwiches and fish-ball soup. Many of the shops on the lower level offer samples, making the Shingong food court a moocher's paradise.

- **Tianmu Takashimaya, basement**: Korean BBQ, sashimi, Indian food and donuts. What more could you ask for in the basement of an upscale department store?

- **Taipei 101, basement**: Though most people are drawn to Asia's tallest building by its height, it's what's in the basement that keeps us coming back. Expect sandwich, sushi, pasta and prime rib and more. And lest we forget, there's also a very upmarket supermarket doling out free samples daily.

- **Jiantan Food Court**: After the old Shilin Night Market central food court was declared a fire hazard, an uproar ensued, forcing the municipal government to build a new food court across from the Jiantan MRT station to house some of Taipei's most venerable grease pits. Expect oyster omelettes, Taiwanese beef steak and of course, plenty of stinky tofu on tap day and night.

seafood out the front and the chef will suggest a preparation method (grilled, steamed, fried etc). Don't forget to try the shop's namesake noodles (made with ground pork). A bargain at NT50 for a small bowl.

Da'an & Shida

For the student crowd, the grid of roads south of Shida University, in between Heping and Roosevelt Rds, is the place for a feed. It's an excellent choice for the traveller with an appetite as well. At night the main drag is packed, as are most of the alleys, side streets and restaurants. You can buy everything from meat skewers to oyster omelettes to stinky tofu, and the stalls in the area tend to be pretty cheap. Our favourite vendor is a woman known for years to Shida students as *shuǐguǒ āyí* (fruit auntie). Her stall is on the corner of Shida Rd and Longquan St (Map p88) and her freshly cut fruit must be tasted to be believed. There are also a number of self-serve buffets in the Shida neighbourhood that charge by weight (the foods' weight, not yours). The best time to hit these places is between 11.30am and 12.30pm for lunch, and 4.30pm and 6.00pm for dinner as that's when the dishes are freshest.

Looking for a slightly more upscale dining experience? The stretch of Yongkang St south of Xinyi Rd is lined on both sides with excellent restaurants reflecting a range of culinary styles. Just a bit further to the east lies Heping E Rd, sec.2, a long street chock-full of excellent restaurants. Alley 54 runs roughly parallel to Fuxing Rd and has at least two dozen restaurants of all sorts.

BUDGET

Vegetarian Paradise (Sùshí Tiāntáng; Map p88; 182 Heping E Rd; meals from NT100; ☻ lunch & dinner; MRT Taipower Building) Because of its location (right across from Shida University), this is usually the first vegetarian buffet many newly arrived students visit. The owners haven't let success go to their heads, though, and they still serve the same sublime vegetarian cuisine as they did when some of us came here as students, way back when. Price is by weight, and unless your eyes are far bigger than your stomach, shouldn't ever exceed NT130.

Ice Monster (Bīngguǎn; Map p88; ☎ 2394 8279; 15 Yongkang St; dishes NT80-150; ☻ 10.30am-midnight summer, 11.30am-11pm winter) It's hard to imagine anything more refreshing on a hot summer day or after a big winter-time dinner than shaved

ice topped with chunks of strawberry, kiwi fruit or (most famously) mango and a scoop of mango sorbet.

Yang's Bakery (Yángjiā Shuǐjiǎoguǎn; Map p88; ☎ 2772 1190; 278 Zhongxiao E Rd, sec.3; dumplings NT50-70; ☻ lunch & dinner) This 40-plus-year-old, northern-Chinese style place is unpretentious to the max and has no English menu, but that doesn't matter. Order yourself some *dàguōtiē* (long-rolled dumplings, steamed then fried) or *yángjiāshuǐjiǎo* (pork dumplings) and you'll see what we mean. Yang's is also a good place to get yourself a bowl of *niúroù miàn* (beef-noodle soup), one of Taiwan's most famous dishes.

MIDRANGE

Dintaifung (Dīngtàifēng; Map p88; ☎ 2321 8927; 194 Xinyi Rd, sec.2; dumplings NT140-290; ☻ lunch & dinner) With Taipei's most celebrated dumplings, Dintaifung is deservedly popular for Shanghai-style treats made fresh to order. Try the classic *xiǎolóng bāo* (steamed pork dumplings). Very popular with locals and visitors alike, so either phone in reservations (they speak enough English) or prepare to queue up.

Grandma Nitti's (Zhōngxī Měishí; Map p88; ☎ 2369 9751; 8 Lane 93, Shida Rd; dishes NT150-400; ☻ 9am-11pm Mon-Sat, 10am-11pm Sun; MRT Taipower Building) A mainstay of Taipei's Western community, Nitti's serves comfort food such as waffles, burgers, Philly-cheese steaks, Mexican dishes and family-size pastas. Breakfast is served until dinner time. There's a comfy street-side terrace and the windowed space upstairs is a great place to mull over newspapers. There's a long bookcase on the 1st floor with an excellent selection of secondhand books for sale, and the restaurant's owner is a mainstay in Taiwan's animal-protection community.

Bongos (Map p88; ☎ 2365 6059; 3 Alley 5, Lane 74, Wenzhou St; dishes NT150-300; ☻ 11am-11pm; MRT Taipower Building) Have a hankering for *poutine* (French fries topped with cheese curds and gravy) and pasta, or perhaps some salad served with a secondhand science-fiction paperback? Bongos, then, is undeniably the place. In addition to serving good Western-style lunches and dinners, including the aforementioned Canadian favourite, Bongos also has a comfortable reading area, outdoor seating, and a huge collection of second-hand paperbacks for sale.

Yuan Shu Vegetarian (Yuánsù; Map p88; ☎ 2393 3489; 2 Lane 14, Lishui St; set lunch from NT300; ☻ lunch

& dinner; MRT Guting) Since its opening in 2005, this restaurant has received a fair amount of press coverage for its new-school renditions of traditional Taiwanese favourites. Vegetarian meals are prepare in the classic Buddhist way, not merely meat but also garlic and pepper free. Hotpots are a specialty as are the pumpkin rice noodles and delicious tofu dishes. The sign outside reads simply 'Vegetarian'.

Lan Ji (Lánjī Málà Huǒguō; Map p88; ☎ 2322 4523; 19 Jinshan S Rd, sec.1; ingredients NT50-400; ⏰ 5.30pm-5am, closed Sun; MRT Zhongxiao Xinsheng) It's a hole in the wall, but a can't-miss spot for Taiwanese hotpot. Order yours with any number of meats and/or vegetables and choose your desired level of spiciness. Special pots with dividers in the centre allow companions with different tastes to still share the same pot.

Alleycats (Xiàngmāo; Map p88; ☎ 2321 8949; B1, 6 Lishui St; pizzas from NT150; ⏰ lunch & dinner) This dark and swank basement pizzeria not only serves the best stone-oven pizza in Taipei, but is also the only place we've found so far to get hard cider on tap.

Zhongshan

This is the neighbourhood that stretches north from the city centre, roughly encompassing the neighbourhoods along the Danshui Line from the train station until the point that the subway becomes an elevated train line. Located in this area is Taipei's once-infamous bar and brothel zone, aka the Combat Zone (p117), now more noteworthy for the Shuangcheng Street Night Market to the south (great place for late-night eats and livelier than the Zone, in our opinion). Linsen Rd and the surrounding alleyways is popular among Japanese businessmen and tourists, so if you're looking for sake, teppanyaki, Kobe beef or tekka maki, you'll find it there.

BUDGET

Joy Yuan Taiwan Buffet (Qiáoyuán Zìzhùcān; Map p92; ☎ 2550 0777; 171 Chang'an W Rd; dishes NT10-50; ⏰ lunch & dinner; MRT Zhongshan) Always busy, this perennial favourite offers a cafeteria-style buffet with dozens of selections, encompassing a fairly wide chunk of the omnivore dietary spectrum. As a general rule, high turnover at a buffet ensures fresh food, making this among the best bang-for-buck buffets. Most dishes are under NT30 and a *biàndāng* (premade takeaway lunch box) costs NT70.

MIDRANGE

Celestial Restaurant (Tiānchú Cāntīng; Map p92; ☎ 2521 1097; 3rd fl, 1 Nanjing W Rd; dishes NT165-380, Peking duck from NT750; ⏰ lunch & dinner) Lovers of Beijing-style cooking have been coming to this restaurant for generations. In addition to Peking duck (expensive but meant for sharing), try the elegant, comforting 'green beans (actually peas) with shredded chicken'. Enter off Nanjing W Rd.

Green Leaf (Qīngyè Cāntīng; Map p92; ☎ 2571 3859; 1 Lane 105, Zhongshan N Rd, sec.1; dishes NT128-298; ⏰ lunch & dinner; MRT Zhongshan) This local favourite literally serves everything Taiwanese from dumplings to full plates in vintage 1964 décor. Pluses are its friendly service and the well-translated menu. Some more expensive seafood options cost up to NT1288, so unless your wallet is deep as the ocean you might want to steer clear of the lobster.

Haibawang (Hǎibàwáng Qíjiàndiàn; Map p92; ☎ 2596 3141; 59 Zhongshan N Rd, sec.3; dishes NT100-600; ⏰ lunch & dinner; MRT Yuanshan) The speciality at this multistorey restaurant is Taiwanese hotpot. Expect an elegant setting, eight storeys above ground and overlooking the Taipei Arts Park and the Fine Arts Museum. If you're not up for hotpot (or some lovely Taiwanese seafood plates), some floors feature Italian or buffet-style dining.

Hatsuho (Chūsuì Jūjiǔwū; Map p92; ☎ 2522 1251; 112 Nanjing E Rd, sec.1; dishes NT80-320; ⏰ lunch & dinner; MRT Zhongshan) Just steps from the Emperor Hotel is where you'll find this country-Japanese-style place for sashimi, grilled fishes, *yakitori* (grilled chicken skewers) and *okonomiyaki* (savoury pancakes). You can choose *horikotatsu* seating, with your feet in a well under the table.

Taipei Story House Tearoom (Táiběi Gùshìguǎn; Map p92; ☎ 2587 5565; 181-1 Zhongshan N Rd, sec.3; dishes NT250-650, Chinese-/English-style tea NT320/280; ⏰ lunch Tue-Sun, dinner nightly) Part of the Taipei Story House (p94), this place serves excellent snacks and tea.

TOP END

Cosmopolitan Grill (Map p92; ☎ 2508 0304; 218 Changchun Rd; www.cosmo.com.tw; dishes NT400; ⏰ lunch & dinner) An upscale Western-style eatery on the southwest corner of Changchun Rd and Jianguo Rd offers dinner, business lunches and delicious weekend brunches of the type that have helped make people around the world corpulent. Check their website for specials, map, and even an online menu.

NIGHT MARKETS WE LOVE

■ **Shilin** (Map p100; MRT Jiantan) If you can eat it, wear it or give it a name and bring it home with you (stalls selling puppies are big here, though we question the ethics of a spur-of-the-moment puppy purchase), you'll find it here.

■ **Shida** (Map p88; MRT Taipower Building) If Shilin is king, than Shida is queen. You'll be met with a mind-boggling array of stuff to eat as well as some very cool shops.

■ **Jingmei** (MRT Jingmei) Though a bit on the dark and grotty side, there's something about the realism of this night market on the southern end of the city that we respect.

■ **Yingchuan Rd** (Map p126; MRT Danshui) While Danshui's Old Street is a great place to explore, don't leave before checking out the Yingchuan Rd Night Market.

■ **Shipai** (MRT Shipai) Where people in Tianmu go for night-market food when they can't stand the crowds at the Shilin market. A good place to hit after soaking at Beitou Hot Springs.

Paris 1930 (Bālìtíng; Map p92; ☎ 2597 1234; 41 Minquan E Rd, sec.2; meals NT1800-3000; ☺ dinner) This restaurant in the Landis Hotel is consistently rated as having the best French food in town. Dinners will often run over six courses. There's piano music and a refined atmosphere, and the hotel's Art Deco setting provides a suitably sophisticated backdrop.

Golden Dragon (Huángjīn Lóng; Map p92; ☎ 2886 8888, ext 1262; Lobby, Grand Hotel, 1 Lane 1, Zhongshan N Rd, sec.4; dishes NT150-500; ☺ lunch & dinner; MRT Jiantan) Popular with politicos and visitors alike, the Golden Dragon is the gorgeous Hong Kong–style restaurant inside the Grand Hotel (which is possibly one of Taipei's best known landmarks). Excellent dim sum and other Cantonese favourites are served in style. Diners have a panoramic view of the Keelung River.

Eastern Taipei City

Taipei city east of Fuxing Rd is vast and offers a plethora of flavours. While some of the city's most expensive restaurants are located here, there's no shortage of budget and midprice places. If street eats are your thing, have a walk up Da'an Rd just north of the Zhongxiao Fuxing MRT station, where you'll find a bunch of noodle shops and stalls selling everything from roast corn to stinky tofu. Just to the south, the stretch of Zhongxiao E Rd between the Zhongxiao Fuxing and Zhongxiao Dunhua stations are chock-full of eateries for all budgets.

There's a stretch of Fuxing Rd just beneath the Muzha elevated train line on the west side, right between the Technology Building and Da'an stations worth visiting. Certain friends of ours call this 'breakfast alley', though this

moniker is somewhat misleading. It's not traditional Sunday brunch that these friends come here for (they're rarely out of bed that early), but rather the postbarhop-get-something-in-stomach-before-passing-out meal so important to the health and well being of booze hounds in the know. Though the specialty of restaurants along this stretch are stomach-soothing items such as *wēn dòujiāng* (warm soymilk) and *qīngzhòu* (thin rice porridge served with chunks of sweet potato), a full variety of typical Taiwanese snacks are also available.

BUDGET

Yonghe Congee King (Yǒnghé Qīngzhōu Dàwáng; Map p96; ☎ 2702 1226; 132 Fuxing N Rd, sec.2; dishes NT20-80, ☺ 24hr) One of our favourite postdrinking-binge breakfast joints, Yonghe Congee King is clean, well lit (but not too bright) and serves perfect post and prehangover foods such as home-made *dòujiāng* (soymilk), *luóbuógāo* (turnip cake) and *qīngzhòu*. If this doesn't settle your stomach, consider laying off the Taiwan beer and Whisbih for a while.

Liaochen Niuroumian (Liàochén Niúròumiàn; Map p96; 1 Alley 9, Lane 133, Nanjing E Rd, sec.4; noodle soup NT70-80; ☺ lunch & dinner, closed Sun) On a lane loaded with street-food stalls, come here for its famous beef-noodle soup and ignore the basic atmosphere.

Sababa (Map p96; ☎ 2738 7796; 8 Alley 54, Lane 118, Heping E Rd, sec.2; dishes NT150 ☺ lunch & dinner) This excellent new eatery serving falafel, hummus and other Middle Eastern food is already so popular that the kitchen exhausts their supply of delicious home-made pita before we get there for our typically late dinners. But it would be selfish to not list Sababa just to keep the pita for ourselves. Instead, we're just going to exaggerate how hard the place is to find. Really. It's so very hard to find! You'll probably have to settle for one of the three dozen other restaurants on Alley 54, leaving the pita for us regulars. Good luck.

MIDRANGE

G'day Café (Qíngxī Cānfáng; Map p96; ☎ 2717 5927; 180 Xingan St; dishes NT120-320; ☾ 10am-10pm Mon-Sat, 10am-5pm Sun, closed last Mon of month) A popular hangout for local expats. The G'day is a good place to go for burgers, tacos, steak, Western-style brunches, apple pie with ice cream and a bottomless cup of coffee.

Ostrich (Tuó Niǎo; Map p96; ☎ 2748 4047; 67 Guangfu S Rd; dishes from NT300; ☾ lunch & dinner) Welcome to Ostrich, Taipei's first and only (at least to our knowledge) restaurant specialising in the tall and gamey bird. Ostrich steaks, ostrich burgers and ostrich noodle soup are all on the menu at this upscale restaurant just around the corner from Core Pacific City. (That's the mall shaped like a large ostrich egg. Coincidence? We think not.) Ostrich also serves drinks and has a good selection of wines from California, Australia and France.

Very Thai (Fēicháng Tài Gàiniàn Cāntīng; Map p96; ☎ 2546 6745; 319 Fuxing N Rd; dishes NT150-450; ☾ lunch & dinner) Very dark and very cool, this mod-Thai spot has black-on-black décor and lovely dishes. It's open, you guessed it, very late.

Sweet Dynasty (Tángcháo Tiánpǐn Zhuānméndiàn; Map p96; ☎ 2772 2889; 160 Zhongxiao E Rd, sec.4; dishes from NT350; ☾ lunch & dinner; MRT Zhongxiao Dunhua) Though specialising in Chinese desserts, Sweet Dynasty also serves a wide variety of mouth-watering dishes such as Shanghainese prawns, braised beef ribs with bitter melon and other Chinese classics. Desserts, of course, are amazing, so top off your meal with a slice of taro cake or a dish of mango pudding. Lines can be long, especially on the weekends, so make reservations or be prepared to spend some time people watching on the footpath outside.

Capone's Lounge Bar (Kǎbāng Xīnyìshí Měishí; Map p96; ☎ 2773 3782; 312 Zhongxiao E Rd, sec.4; dishes NT350; ☾ Lunch & Dinner; MRT Sun Yat-sen Memorial Hall) Named after noted Italian-American gourmand, merrymaker and racketeer, Capone's serves Italian food at prices you can't refuse. A popular watering hole with upscale expats, especially after 9pm when the house band plays.

TOP END

Hooters (Map p96; ☎ 2716 5168; www.hooters.com.tw; 18 Qingcheng St; dishes from NT400; ☾ 11am-midnight Sun & Mon, 11am-1am Fri & Sat) The opening of Hooters in Taipei caused quite a stir. If you've ever been to a Hooters in the USA, you know that the women who work here are chosen for their looks, outgoing personalities, and willingness to join in spontaneous hula-hoop performances. The ladies of Hooters Taipei live up to the franchise's expectations. Food and décor is pure Americana – how you feel about that depends on your personal bias.

Lawry's The Prime Rib (Láoruìsī Niúlèipái Cāntīng; Map p96; ☎ 3762 1312; 12th fl, Core Pacific City, Living Mall, 134 Bade Rd, sec.4; mains NT790-1690; ☾ lunch & dinner) This institution from Beverly Hills has now landed in Taiwan with its huge roast-beef dinners and a signature 'spinning bowl' salad prepared beside your table.

Shabu-jan (Chán; Map p96; ☎ 8761 6677; 11th fl, Core Pacific City, Living Mall, 134 Bade Rd, sec.4; dishes NT620-1680; ☾ lunch & dinner) Lots of places around Taipei claim to serve *shabu-shabu*, a Japanese hotpot of thinly sliced beef which you dip into sauces, but Shabu-jan (Japanese name, Shabu-zen) has the home-country pedigree to go with it.

Geneva (Rìnèiwǎ; Map p96; ☎ 2731 7641; www .geneva.com.tw; 9 Alley 5, Lane 345, Renai Rd, sec.4; dishes from NT600; ☾ dinner, closed Mon) We were saddened to learn that Ticino's (our old favourite Taipei Swiss restaurant) had closed its doors, but happy that Geneva has picked up the flaming fondue torch. Though pricey, Geneva uses only the finest cheese to make its fondues and the best home-baked breads and imported meats for dipping. Leave room for desert, an amazingly decadent chocolate fondue served with fresh strawberries. And of course, don't forget to order the sparkling wine.

Shilin & Tianmu

Avoiding food in Shilin is a bit like avoiding casinos in Las Vegas; you really need to be committed to manage it, for the very name 'Shilin' is synonymous with Taipei's most celebrated night market. Quiet during the day, once the sun goes down the Shilin Night Market becomes a frenetic buzz of food carts offering tasty Taiwanese treats such as grass jelly soup, stinky tofu, beef-noodle soup, fresh cut fruit, and more meat-on-a-stick than you can shake a stick at. Until recently the centre of the night market had a food court with teppanyaki booths, noodle stalls and milk-tea joints, but after many artery-clogging decades, city elders deemed the place a fire risk, and moved most of the food court's purveyors of tasty grease to their new home in the **Chiantan Food Court** (Map p100; MRT Jiantan), located just across from the Jiantan station. Specialities of the Shilin Night Market are numerous and wonderful, ranging from the recognisable, *chǎo pángxiè* (sautéed crabs), to the mysterious, *zhū xiě gāo* (congealed pig blood, usually served on a stick). There are also a number of more traditional style sit-down restaurants in the neighbourhood.

Though the two neighbourhoods border one another, culinary wise, Tianmu is Shilin's diametric opposite. While Shilin is the place for crowded night markets and street food, Tianmu is generally more upscale, offering a wide variety of sit-down restaurants. Tianmu does have a night market (p113), though it's a bit of a walk. Check out a little place called **Escargot** (24 Chung Yi St) for some of the best cakes in the neighbourhood.

BUDGET

Beitou Squid (Běitóu Yóuyú; Map p100; 98 Dexing E Rd; dishes NT30-50; ☺ lunch & dinner) It isn't in Beitou (though we're told there's another one there), and there's no squid. But we like this funky little eatery in Tianmu because, aside from the eats – great pork and seafood dumpling soup and tasty Taiwanese side dishes such as cold cucumber salad and tofu with thousand year eggs – the place is just way cool. Old 1960s Taiwanese movie posters adorn the wall (they're for sale) and the shop sells kitsch nostalgia items including wind-up cars and candy cigarettes. John Waters would just love this place.

He Xiang Delicious Food (Hé Xiāng Měishí; Map p100; 60 Fuguo Rd; dishes NT50; ☺ lunch & dinner; MRT Zhishan) A long-standing favourite street-side eatery in Tianmu, He Xiang has kept the same tiny menu for decades (the picture menu on the wall behind the counter has almost totally faded). The specialty of the house, and a local must-try, is the bamboo-steamed sticky rice with red pork and vegetables, wrapped in a lotus leaf and served with hot sauce. Look for the faded picture of this dish above the entrance. The restaurant is on the north side of the street, just east of the Zhishan MRT. Another excellent dish is the shrimp ball soup. Nothing fancy, just cheap, good and very Taiwanese.

Haw Kuang Vegetarian Restaurant (Háoguāng Sùshí; Map p100; ☎ 2883 2168; 357 Zhongzheng Rd; meals from NT100; ☺ lunch & dinner; MRT Shilin) Words can't describe how much we love this vegetarian buffet just a few blocks northwest of the Shilin Night Market. The chef is a genius, with an eye for both colour and flavour. Imagine yourself a painter and the white cardboard tray your canvas. Arrange your meal from dozens of beautifully prepared vegetarian dishes and enjoy. If you visit one vegetarian buffet during your time in Taipei, make it this one.

MIDRANGE

Lavender Garden (Tiānmǔ Gǔdào Sēnlín Huāyuán; Map p100; ☎ 2873 7581; 4 Alley 1, Lane 232, Zhongshan N Rd, sec.7; dishes NT250-350; ☺ lunch & dinner, closed Mon) At the bottom of a long, steep stairway that (eventually) leads up into Yangming Mountain lies this excellent restaurant set inside a two-storey home that's surrounded by an aquatic garden. Amazing health-oriented Chinese dishes such as 'health tonic hotpot with 10 Chinese herbs' will give you strength for the climb ahead. Then again, as Lavender Garden's deserts are delicious as well, you might want to save the meal as a reward for the climb down.

Doggy & Yummy (Dòjí Yǎmǐ; Map p100; ☎ 2874 5341; 2nd fl, 59 Chungshan N Rd, sec.7, Tianmu; dishes NT250; ☺ lunch & dinner) One of the latest trends in Taipei is pet-friendly restaurants, that is, places where pet-loving city dwellers can take the pooch (or pot-bellied pig for that matter) out for a good meal. Though most tourists tend not to bring their own pets, doggy restaurants are fun places, especially for travellers with children (besides, we couldn't resist listing at least one of these odd eateries). Doggy & Yummy has decent Western food such as pasta and fried chicken and an English menu that's definitely dog (and kid) friendly.

Lanka Curry Restaurant (Lánkǎ Kālǐ; Map p100; ☎ 2832 0153; 48 Zhongyi Rd; dishes NT100-200; ☺ lunch & dinner, Mon dinner only) One of the less flashy (and less expensive) South-Asian restaurants in Taipei, Lanka has been serving excellent curries, sambals and dhal dishes for nearly two decades. If you're feeling especially adventurous, try the fish-head curry (the priciest item on the menu, but well worth it). Whatever you get, order their special appetizer, 'Lunu Dehi', it's diced onion mixed with lemon pickle.

Fang's Restaurant (Fāngjiā Xiǎoguǎn; Map p100; ☎ 2872 8402; 7 Tianmu E Rd; dishes NT160-560; ☻ lunch & dinner) You can find excellent plates of Jiangzi-style (Shanghai regional) cooking at this local favourite that is well regarded by both long-term expats and locals alike. Just about every table also seems to order a tray of 'mini-mall steamed buns', tiny soup dumplings (NT260 for a serving of 20).

Organic Markets

Need something to balance out the night markets' stick-meat, fried tofu and assorted artery-clogging goodness? Taipei has a number of places to get organic fruits, vegetables and other healthy products. Our favourite place is **Cottonfields** (Map p88; ☎ 2364 8899; 273 Roosevelt Rd, sec.3), which sells the sort of stuff you'd find at a farmer's market in places such as San Francisco. It also sells salads and have a great juice bar with upstairs seating.

With branches all over the city, **Santa Cruz** is another organic chain. We've marked one of their branches on our Eastern Taipei map (p96). Santa Cruz is a good place to stock up on vitamins, though they tend to be pricier than those you'd find in North America or Australia.

DRINKING
Cafés

Once hard to find, coffee shops abound throughout Taipei. Typical opening times are 7.30am to 10pm and you might find folks, particularly students, camped out at them for hours studying or chatting over a coffee, pastry or light meal. As finding a coffee shop in Taipei has become as easy as, well, finding a coffee shop in Taipei, we've skipped the chain shops and listed some of our favourite unique spots. Many of these are as much chill-out and event spots as they are places to get coffee.

Fong Da (Fēngdà Kāfēi; Map p88; ☎ 2371 9577; 42 Chengdu Rd; coffee NT100; ☻ 8am-10.30pm) One of Taipei's original coffee shops, Fong Da dates from the 1950s and still uses some of the origi-nal equipment. Drip ice coffee with biscuits costs NT100. Whenever we've been away for a while we always stop in as absence makes the heart grow Fong Da.

Chocoholic (Qiǎokèhākè Qiǎokèlì Zhuānyìndiàn; Map p88; ☎ 2321 5820; 2 Lane 7, Yongkang St; drinks NT90-130; ☻ noon-11pm) Leave room for desert. This tiny, brightly painted café is an old favourite, dating back to the days when good choco-late was impossible (as opposed to merely inconvenient) to find. Expect cakes, choco-late drinks and a clientele of smiley young things galore.

Norwegian Wood (Nuówēi Sēnlín; Map p88; ☎ 2363 3714; 182 Wenzhou Rd; ☻ noon-midnight; MRT Gongguan) A very cool coffee house serving espresso drinks as well as alcohol. Known as a hangout for Taipei's literary crowd, as well as being a gay and lesbian friendly venue.

Orange Music Cafe (Kàn Diànchē; Map p100; ☎ 2888-1220; 302 Wen Lin Rd; ☻ 11:30am-1am, Sun-Friday, 11:30am-3am Fri & Sat; MRT Shilin) Orange is the predominant colour of this bar and café located across from Shilin MRT station's exit 2. An up and com-ing chill-out spot, Orange serves food, but is better known for another fire-related activity, the 'fire dance' performances, which begin every Friday night at 10.50pm. Admission for the performance is NT150, but if you come in costume it drops to NT80.

Corridor Cafe (Huíláng Kāfēiguǎn; Map p88; ☎ 8369 5656; Sports Bldg, National Taiwan University, 312 Roosevelt Rd, sec.4; ☻ 10am-10pm Mon-Sat, 10am-6pm Sun; MRT Gong-guan) Smack in the middle of Taiwan's most respected institute of higher learning, the Cor-ridor Cafe offers a small-stage performance space for both planned and ad-hoc perform-ances. Good coffee, artistic vibes and a good place to meet up with Taipei artists.

Tea Shops

Tea is an institution in Taiwan as well as a major export, and Taipei has a great variety of shops that serve it. You'll find tea shops in places as varied as atop serene mountains down to stands in crowded markets.

HYPNOTIZED IN TAIPEI

'Hey Rocky, watch me pull a rabbit out of this hat!' No, seriously. Local legend-in-waiting Brian David Philips doesn't do the old rabbit-in-the-hat trick, but the expatriate magician/hypnotist's performances packs 'em in all the same. Power of suggestion, mind over matter and experiential trance are all part and parcel of Philips' bag-o-tricks. Shows are held in Chinese and English at various clubs around Taipei. Check out www.BrianDavidPhillips.com for upcoming gigs.

THE ZONE

The Combat Zone got its name back when Taiwan was still known in some circles as 'Free China'. Then, American soldiers came here in droves. They were either stationed in Taiwan or on R&R leave from Vietnam. The neighbourhood was a major red-light district, a little slice of Bangkok, or perhaps of Amsterdam.

Times have changed and nowadays it's difficult to say exactly who the habitués of these few grungy alleys really are. Japanese businessmen perhaps, though the section of alleys across Linsen Rd to the southwest seems more geared towards such clientele. Shuangcheng St, the main road from which the alleys branch off, is a night market to the south, not much different from many of Taipei's other small night market streets. North of the night market on the main drag are a few pubs. There, places like B52 seem to be more popular with Filipino and Indonesian migrant workers than either locals or Westerners. As for the girlie bars, nowadays only one alley in the Combat Zone is still dedicated to them. While we're reluctant to advertise it by name, it isn't too hard to either find or avoid.

Though eschewed by tea purists, *zhēnzhū nǎichá* (pearl milk tea) is way popular with everyone from kids to secretaries. This sweetened tea with chewy black balls of tapioca is served in a plastic cup with a seal as tight as a bongo head and drunk through a straw thick enough to suck up marbles. Order yours *rè* (hot) or *bīng* (cold). Another favourite is *paòmò hóngchá* (bubble black tea), which is tea frothed until it has a head not unlike that of beer. Both are available at tea stands and stalls citywide for about NT25.

Rose House (Gǔdiǎn Méiguī Yuán; Map p92; 95 Nanjing E Rd, sec.2) Readers have written in praise of this teahouse, which, despite its normal store front, looks like it could have been decorated by Laura Ashley inside. Among its dozens of varieties are Earl Grey and Mango. Teas are sold by the cup, the set or the tin.

Maussac (Mósàikǎ Fàshì Cháguǎn Cāntīng; Map p88; ☎ 2391 7331; www.m-tea.com; 24 Lishui St, sec.1; dishes from NT350) Maussac is an upscale teahouse, complete with a bookshelf's worth of jars featuring teas from around the world. In addition to tea, set-meal specials, including pasta, meat and seafood dishes, are all served with a haute European flair. Maussac's charming jazz atmosphere makes it a popular spot for Taipei's chic looking to unwind with a meal, tea or both.

ENTERTAINMENT
Bars & Clubs

Ah, where to begin? Taipei is a city where the young heading home from a night of hard clubbing pass through parks where the old have been practicing taichi since dawn. There is no lack of clubs, pubs, bars, musical venues or other places to drink, hear music, or if you're drunk enough, to make music of your own. Typically, beers sell for between NT100 and NT150. Hard liquor might set you back NT250. Ask around for happy hours or drink specials.

Clubs come and go, but we've done our best to list ones that should still be around when this book goes to print. A loose affiliation of pubs have come together to promote their latest menus and events. Check out their website, www.taipeipubs.com. Another excellent site to find out what bands are playing and where is www.taiwannights.com.

2F (Map p88; ☎ 2392 2222; 15 Heping W Rd, sec.1) This large club (capacity more than 1000) is home to both commercial and underground scenes, with everything from techno to house to trance. It often hosts a selection of international DJs.

45 (Map p88; ☎ 2321 2140; 45 Heping E Rd, sec.1) Go up the narrow stairs and join the huge crowd (which includes many foreigners), especially on Friday and Saturday nights. It's festooned with Americana, from licence plates to movie-star photos and the food is American style too.

B1 (Map p88; ☎ 2397 0506; 71 Aiguo Rd) If you're young, hip and dress like the latest pop or hip-hop star, you'll find loads of company here. Pay the cover charge and it's all you can drink, all night.

Brown Sugar (Hēitáng; Map p96; ☎ 8780 1110; www .brownsugar.com.tw; 101 Songren Rd; admission NT380 Sun-Thu, NT550 Fri & Sat) A swank place with lots of right angles and silk curtains, Brown Sugar has live jazz Monday to Saturday nights and salsa on Sunday. It serves good food as well.

TAIPEI

GAY & LESBIAN NIGHTLIFE

Foreign-born gay and lesbian travellers will find Taipei to be no less friendly than anywhere else. An open-minded city, Taipei hosted one of Asia's first Gay Pride parades (in 2-28 Peace Park), which has now become an annual autumn event. Gay life here is well documented in film and literature. While there isn't really a 'gay district' in Taipei, there's no lack of bookshops, bars, saunas and social options scattered throughout town to choose from.

Like the rest of the city's nightlife scene, the hot club when we go to press may not even exist by the time you read this, but the establishments we've listed have been around for a while. *G-spot* magazine puts out an informative little Taipei map listing some of the city's hot spots and you can usually pick up a copy at some of the venues listed below. Visitors should check out www.fridae.com. And of course, the folks at **Utopia** (www.utopia-asia.com) keep the data fresh for those looking to hook up in Taipei and elsewhere.

Men's Saunas
Rainbow Sauna (☎ 2370 2899; 2nd fl, 142 Kunming St; MRT Ximending); **Garden of Eden** (☎ 2311 8681; 2nd fl, 120 Xining St; MRT Ximending); **24 Men's Sauna** (☎ 2361 1069; 5th fl, 72, sec.1 Zhongxiao W Rd; MRT Taipei Main Station)

GLBT Venues
■ **Fresh** (Map p88; ☎ 2358 7701; 2nd fl, 7 Jinshan S Rd) Taipei's gay club *du jour* has three floors of fun; a bar floor, a dance floor and a chill room. In addition, there's a roof garden. It's friendly and the crowd is international.

■ **Jailhouse** (☎ 2364 1623; 3 Alley 8, Lane 316, Roosevelt Rd, sec.3) A long-standing favourite among the Taipei lesbian scene, this tiny bar in the Gongguan neighbourhood has a small dance floor and occasional drink specials. If you're just popping in to check things out, be advised that you'll be hit for a 'minimum charge' of NT500.

■ **Source** (Map p88; ☎ 3393 1678; 1-2 Roosevelt Rd, sec.1) There's a small bar downstairs and a dance floor upstairs and the handsome top floor is reminiscent of a old-world Chinese salon. Foreigners aren't just welcome here, they're encouraged.

Carnegie's (Map p96; ☎ 2325 4433; 100 Anhe Rd, sec.2; dishes NT260-780) Carnegie's caused quite a stir when it first opened in 2001, what with patrons dancing on the bar and all, but even if it has calmed down a notch, it's still one of the liveliest nightspots in Xinyi. It's a popular meeting place for after-work drinks. The menu includes steaks, halibut and lamb.

Green Bar (Map p100; ☎ 2873 3263; 85 Tianmu E Rd) Green Bar is another icon of the foreign community. Here you'll find darts, table games and the latest sports on TV.

Indian Beer House (Map p96; ☎ 2741 0550; 196 Bade Rd, sec.2; meals from NT400; ☻ dinner) A Taipei institution. Dine among the dinosaurs (huge fossils dress the interior) and huge crowds of young professionals nightly.

Jr Caffé (Map p88; ☎ 2366 1799; 80 Shida Rd) It's in the heart of the student pub zone but everyone is welcome here. Glass doors means that it doesn't get too smoky on street level and there are foosball and pool tables downstairs.

Living Room (Map p96; ☎ 8787 4154; www.living roomtaipei.com; 3rd fl, 8 Nanjing E Rd, sec.5; ☻ 6pm-1am) Part supper club, part music lounge, this low-key venue is a great respite from everything huge, noisy and self-consciously trendy. It's filled with sofas, curtains and has classy wooden flooring. Living Room is popular among musicians, and every night features a different theme. Expect jazz, jam sessions, electronica dance parties and more. Check the website to see what's going on and for images of the place.

Luxy (Map p96; ☎ 2772 1000; www.luxy-taipei.com; 5th fl, 201 Zhongxiao E Rd, sec.4) A massive club that often features international bands, DJs and some of the hippest live entertainment in Taipei. Check the website for the latest offerings.

Malibu West (Map p92; ☎ 2592 8228; 9 Lane 25, Shuang-cheng St) There's a pool table and a menu with dishes including burgers, pastas, pizzas and snacks. Happy hour is between 4pm and 9pm.

TAIPEI

In the heart of the Combat Zone (p117), it has a tropical feel and is popular with business people and airline pilots.

My Place (Map p92; ☎ 2591 4269; 3-1 Lane 32, Shuang-cheng St) Also in the Zone, My Place bills itself as Taiwan's first pub (established 1975) and is still going strong. This Brit-owned establishment boasts friendly hostesses, a pool table and a huge 100-inch-screen TV for sports broadcasts.

Naomi (Map p96; ☎ 2709 8295; 65 Anhe Rd, sec.1) Metal-bead curtains, mirrored columns, red padded walls and dim lighting provide a great backdrop for this lounge bar where well-dressed 20- and 30-somethings sip scotches and single malts.

Peacock (Map p88; ☎ 3365 2997; 5 Lane 93, Shida Rd; ⏱ 6pm-2am, closed Tue) A recent entry into Taipei's world of nightspots, Peacock's sets itself apart by offering not just the usual snacks (pizza, fries and an assortment of tasty Mediterranean-themed items, all well presented) and alcoholic beverages, but also for renting Arab-style *shisha* (flavoured tobacco) pipes complete with a full variety of imported *shisha*. Food is reasonably priced and *shisha* pipes go for NT400 (NT10 for each extra mouthpiece).

Pig (Map p100; ☎ 2874 0630; 78 Tianmu E Rd; dishes NT250-425) This friendly Tianmu pub certainly feels very British and the menu includes steaks, chops, chicken and, er, enchiladas. There's no cover charge but when there's a band on (usually from 9.30pm) there's a minimum spend of NT400 for food and drink (NT500 on Friday and Saturday).

Room 18 (Map p96; ☎ 2345 2778; Warner Village, 124 Songshou Rd) This dark and atmospheric basement club offers dancing, spinning, hip-hop and house, and would be very much at home in New York or London. It gets a lot of fashionable locals and ABC (American-born Chinese) visitors. Taiwanese stars might find themselves in the VIP room. A warning: cover charges can be steep.

Roxy 99 (Map p88; ☎ 2358 2813; 69 Jinshan S Rd, sec.2) Popular with students, workers and assorted 20- and 30-somethings, Roxy 99 has a great CD collection and a food menu that includes pastas, fried rice and more adventurous fare. It's in the basement, yet manages not to feel claustrophobic.

Saints & Sinners (Map p96; ☎ 2739 9001; 114 Anhe Rd, sec.2; dishes NT150-550) This bar attracts Taiwanese and foreigners alike. Expect a pool table, foosball and darts and a couple of big screens to watch sports broadcasts. Menu choices include Thai, Chinese and British pub food. The house drink, the 'upside down', includes, among other things, vodka, honey, plum powder and cherry brandy.

Shannon (Map p96; ☎ 2772 0948; 6 Dunhua N Rd) This cosy Irish-style pub opened in 2002 and is hugely popular with guests from overseas. There's live music (think R&B) Thursday to Sunday.

Wall (B1F, 200 Roosevelt Rd, sec.4; www.the-wall .com.tw; ⏱ 8pm till late; MRT Gongguan) Fast becoming Taipei's premier venue for alternative music, the cavernous Wall is tucked into the end of a grunge and punk-focused minimall. Live bands play Wednesday to Saturday.

Underworld (Map p88; ☎ 2369 0103; Basement, 45 Shida Rd; admission NT250) A little bit psychedelic, a little bit smoky and very friendly, this cosy, graffiti-painted basement pub pours lots of beer and Long Island iced tea. Come here after having dinner at nearby Shida Night Market and stay for DJs spinning house music or watch a live band on weekends.

Velvet Underground (Dìxià Sīróng; Map p88; ☎ 2314 1868; www.velvet-underground.com.tw; Basement, Key Mall, 50 Zhongxiao W Rd, sec.1) Rock and roll lives, baby, at this underground (literally) club across from Taipei Main Station. Live bands, full bar, Mexican food and walls covered with kick-ass rock

---

NOT THE MTV YOU EXPECTED

Another interesting choice for watching films are the once-ubiquitous MTV houses. These have nothing to do with the music channel of the same name. Rather, a Taiwanese MTV is a place where, for about the same cost as a normal movie ticket, you can rent a DVD and watch it a private room complete with a wide-screen TV, comfy couch and your choice of beverage. Favoured by teens looking for a quiet spot to make out on the cheap, most MTVs have a pretty decent collection of movies and are open 24 hours. Once found all over Taipei, there seem to be fewer and fewer every year. There are a few still open around Taipei and we know of at least two in Ximending. To find one, look for big signs with the words 'MTV'.

TAIPEI

art not unlike something out of the a museum of album covers. ROCK ON!

Vacuum Space (Map p96; ☎ 2700 6535; B1, 208 Fuxing S Rd, sec.2) Vacuum Space was an overnight media sensation a few years back, and not just thanks to the nightspot's hip décor, talented fire-juggling bar staff or excellent music, but rather because of its amateur fight nights. Think the movie *Fight Club*, only with gloves, a few safety rules and prizes for the winners and you've kind of got the idea. Fight night is held on the first Saturday night of the month, the entry fee is NT500 and participants are required to sign a waiver releasing the management from responsibility should they be mashed to pulp.

Chinese Opera & Theatre Venues

While some venues around town host touring Chinese-opera companies, there are regu-larly scheduled performances at the following places. Both of these venues project English-language subtitles during the performance so you can understand the action.

Taipei Eye (Táiběi Xìpéng; Map p92; ☎ 2568 2677; www.taipeieye.com; 113 Zhongshan N Rd, sec.2; tickets NT880; ⏳ 8pm Thu-Sat) Situated in Zhongshan, this new venue showcases Chinese opera together with other rotating performances including pup-pet theatre and aboriginal dance. Audience members have the unique opportunity to watch the actors as they rehearse and put on make-up, wigs and costumes. Enter from Jinzhou St.

National Taiwan Junior College of Performing Arts (Guóli Táiwān Xìjù Zhuānkē Xuéxiào; Map pp82-3; ☎ 2796 2666; 177 Neihu Rd, sec.2; adult/child NT400/200; ⏳ 10am Mon & Thu) Students begin their study on this campus (also known as Fuxing Arts Acad-emy) at the age of 10. Junior and advanced

---

SHOPPING MALLS & DISTRICTS OF NOTE

You'll have no difficulty finding cool places to spend money as well as interesting stuff to spend it on. Here are just some of the places we recommend, along with a brief description of what you'll find there.

■ **Breeze Centre** (Wéifēng Guǎngchǎng; Map p96; ☎ 6600 8888; 39 Fuxing N Rd, sec.1; MRT Zhongxiao Fuxing) Nine floors above ground and three below, Breeze Centre houses worldwide brands including Ralph Lauren, Coach, Marc Jacobs, Omega and Prada…and that's just on the ground floor. The top floors features the Ambassador cinemas.

■ **Core Pacific City 'Living Mall'** (Jīnghuáchéng; Map p96; ☎ 3762 1888; 138 Bade Rd, sec.4; ⏳ 11am-11pm Sun-Thu, 11am-11pm Fri & Sat) This is one of Taipei's most unique buildings owing to it's funky architecture. The 'Living Mall' has clothing, home wares, a great bookshop and a 13-screen movie theatre that runs 24 hours.

■ **Warner Village** (Huá'nà Wēixiù Yǐngchéng; Map p96; 124 Songshou Rd) The centrepiece of this mall is the 18-screen Warner Village cinema. The centre is busy all day (and especially so on week-ends). You'll find international boutiques such as the oddly named (but maybe we're just im-mature) FCUK, Monique Japan, Maybelline, Boots and Aveda. The food court is also popular.

■ **Shin Kong Mitsukoshi Department Store** (Xīnguāng Sānyuè Bǎihuò; Map p96; ☎ 8780 1000; 11 Songshou Rd) This is a ritzy shopping centre not far from Warner Village.

■ **Ximending** (p99) Pierced punks and glam girl a-go-go.

■ **Dinghao District** (Dǐnghǎo Shāngjuàn; Map p96; Zhongxiao E Rd, sec.4) Anchored by not one but two **SOGO Department Stores** (Tàipíngyáng SOGO Bǎihuò; Map p96; ☎ 7713 5555; 45 Zhongxiao E Rd, sec.4), it's Taiwan's most famous shopping street complete with shops both big and small, restau-rants, cafés and nightspots.

■ **Dayeh Takashimaya** (Dàyè Gāodǎowū; Map p100; ☎ 2831 2345; 55 Zhongcheng Rd, sec.2) Where Tianmu folk go when they want a change from outdoor ritz to indoor ritz. We like the food court.

■ **Miramar Entertainment Park** (Měilìhuá Bǎilèyuán; ☎ 2175 3456; 20 Jingye 3rd Rd, Neihu) Part mall, part amusement park, all fun. This entertainment facility in the Neihu suburb northeast of the city boasts the world's second-largest Ferris wheel, located on its top floor. Panoramic views, and of course, plenty of stuff to eat in Miramar's fine food court.

SPECIALITY SHOPPING STREETS

Taipei has a number of streets offering an abundance of items relating to particular pursuits. While some items on our list (camping gear and silk jackets) are the sort of things you may well want to buy in Taiwan, it's doubtful that the average traveller will make spurious purchases of wedding dresses or funeral urns. Still, browsing around the streets dedicated to the selling of said items is a good way to catch a peek into local tradition.

- **Wedding dresses** Aiguo E Rd, across from the Chiang Kai-shek Memorial Hall, and also at Zhongshan N Rd, near Minquan Rd.
- **Religious articles** Xiyuan Rd, west of Longshan Temple.
- **Menswear** Tacheng St, just south of the Dihua Market.
- **Footwear** Yuanling St between Chongqing S Rd and Boai Rd.
- **Cameras** Beimen Camera Shopping Area on Hankou St, southwest of Taipei Main Station.
- **Outdoor/backpacking gear** Zhongshan N Rd, sec.1, just north of the intersection of Zhong-xiao E Rd, on west side of the street.
- **Chinese silk jackets and embroidered shoes** Yuanling St, west of Chongqing S Rd, just north of Baoqing Rd.

---

students, some teachers and alumni participate in twice-weekly performances of acrobatics and Chinese opera. Admission includes a guided visit of the Beijing opera museum (which is upstairs) as well as an educational video (in English) about Chinese opera. If you arrive early, you may be lucky enough to catch students participating in outdoor classes.

Puppetry Art Centre of Taipei (Táiběi Ǒuxìguǎn; Map p96; ☎ 2528 7955; www.pact.org.tw; 2-4 fl, 99 Civic Blvd, sec.5; tickets NT100; ☒ 10am-5pm, closed Mon) This theatre sits in the shadow of the extraterrestrial-looking Core Pacific Mall. Born of a love of puppets and puppetry, the puppets on display and those used for performances all come from the vast collection donated by Lin Jung-fu, chairman of the board of the Tai-Yuan art and culture foundation. Call or check the website for performance times.

Gu Ling Experimental Theatre (Gǔlíngjiē Xiǎojùchǎng; Map p88; ☎ 2391 9393; 2 Lane 5, Guling St) This grass roots, community-based, avant-garde company presents music, drama, dance and children's theatre. Performance are contemporary if not exactly experimental. The majority of the shows are not culturally specific, meaning that even those without Chinese-language skills will be able to follow. The building, which dates from 1906, was originally a police station and during some performances the audience can see all the way through to the former jail cells.

Both the **National Theatre** at Sun Yat-sen Memorial Hall (p89) and the **Novel Hall for Perform-**

ing Arts (Map p96; ☎ 2722 4302, ext 7999; www.novelhall.org .tw; 3 Songshou Rd) host large-scale concerts and cultural events including dances, musicals, Chinese or Western opera and concerts of Chinese or Western classical or popular music.

Cinemas

The place to head for an old-school movie experience is Ximending. There's a cluster of movie theatres with character along Wucheng St. Leading multiplexes are at Warner Village (opposite), the Core Pacific 'Living Mall' (opposite) and Breeze Centre (opposite). The theatres at the 'Living Mall' operate 24 hours. Ticket prices there are adult/concession/matinee NT280/250/220.

SPOT – Taipei Film House (Táiběizhījiā Diànyǐng Zhǔtíguǎn; Map p92; ☎ 2511 7786; www.spot.org.tw; 18 Zhongshan N Rd, sec.2; nonmember/member tickets NT220/170) An excellent cinema with a bookshop and outdoor café. The building, a landmark that dates back to 1925, was once the home of the US ambassador.

Though sadly a dying breed in today's upscale Taipei, a few second-run theatres offering double features in a more 'downtown' setting have managed to survive. One of the last of the great film movie houses is called the **Guangming** (260 Muzha Rd, sec.1; tickets NT80). It's just off Yusheng St and runs four films on two screens, mostly in English with Chinese subtitles. Prices are for a double feature.

SHOPPING

Taipei is a paradise for shoppers of all stripes. For those who like their shopping old school, the city has a plethora of streets and alleys chock-full of stores selling everything from antiques to religious items, herbal medicines to high-tech gadgetry. If you like your shopping new school, have we got malls for you. There are big malls, small malls, tall malls (p101) and even a mall shaped like a golf ball (p101). Prices are very reasonable and you can often bargain.

Jade, Chinese Handicrafts & Clothing

There's no shortage of browsing for clothing in the city's night markets, but the highest concentration in one place is at the **Chinese Handicraft Mart** (Táiwān Shǒuyè Tuīguǎng Zhōngxīn; Map p88; ☎ 2393 3655; 1 Suzhou Rd; ⏰ 9am-5.30pm; MRT Taipei Main Station, NTU Hospital). You'll find four storeys of clothing, jade, porcelain, ceramics, tea sets, jewellery, scrolls, paintings and prints and that's just a small selection of the variety on offer here.

Probably the most fun place to shop for knick-knacks in Taipei are the **weekend markets** that are set up under the Jianguo Fwy. On weekdays all one sees is empty asphalt; but all day Saturday and Sunday the area springs to life with stalls, tables, merchants and people coming out of the woodwork.

North of Renai Rd lies the **Holiday Jade Market** (Jiàrì Yùshì; Map p96), perhaps the largest market for jade and other semi-precious stones in Asia. The Jade Market is also a great place to buy jewellery, *objets d'art* both small and large, religious items and everything you might need to set up your own feng-shui practice back home (outside of actual knowledge of Chinese geomancy of course).

South of Renai Rd the Jade Market becomes the **Holiday Flower Market** (Jiàrì Huāshì; Map p96), a veritable cornucopia of plants, flowers and incredibly impressive bonsai trees. This market is also a good place to buy tea and tea supplies as well as dried fruits, nuts and some locally grown organic produce.

The markets are a must-visit, even for people who don't particularly like shopping in general. Noise and crowds are the norm, so if you're bringing your kids keep them close.

The **Shilin Night Market** (p99) is always a fun place to shop for clothing. Any of Taipei's shopping malls and districts are good for hours, if not days, of retail therapy too.

Taibei Shanshui (Táibei Shānshui; Map p88; ☎ 2361 9507; 12 Zhongshan N Rd, sec.1) and **Tingshaniou** (Dēngshānyǒu; Map p88; ☎ 2311 6027; 18 & 22 Zhongshan N Rd, sec.1) are two popular options for outdoor clothing and gear.

Computers & Electronics

Where do we even start? We have friends who come to Taipei just to buy laptops, mobile phones and other electronic whatnots.

Guanghua Market (Guānghuá Diànnǎo Shìchǎng; Map p88; cnr Civic Blvd & Jinshan Rd; MRT Zhongxiao Xinsheng) This is a cyberpunk's paradise. Here are several square blocks of stores, alleys and underground malls that are to electronics what a night market is to clothing and foods. Software, hardware, laptops, peripherals, mobile phones, gadgets of all kinds.

Nova Computer Arcade (NOVA Zīxùn Guǎngchǎng; Map p88; ☎ 2381 4833; 100 Guangjian Rd) Across from Taipei Main Station, this arcade has about 130 shops and booths dealing in computers, components, digital cameras, mobile phones and just about any electronic peripheral you can imagine.

Tea & Tea Supplies

Traditional Chinese teapots can be found in teashops all over Taiwan. They come in a mind-boggling array of sizes, shapes and quality. Some are truly works of art, decorated with poems and exquisitely carved. Oolong tea is one of Taiwan's most celebrated exports and a number of shops stock it. You'll find small shops in every corner of the city and there are a number of stalls inside of the Jianguo Weekend Holiday Flower Market selling tea supplies; for most you'll need to speak Chinese.

Ten Shang's Tea Company (Tiānsháng Míngchá; Map p92; ☎ 2542 7113; 45 Nanjing E Rd, sec.2) Hailing from a tea-growing mountain community in Central Taiwan's Nantou, Mr and Mrs Chang have been selling organically grown oolong teas from all over Taiwan for a quarter of a century. Visitors are welcome to come in and chat over a pot or two of their exquisite high-mountain tea while shopping for tea and tea supplies.

GETTING THERE & AWAY

Western visitors tend to come into Taipei straight from Taiwan Taoyuan International Airport. If you're taking a bus (a wise and money-saving choice indeed), you'll be let off either around the Taipei Main Station, at Songshan Domestic Airport in the north end of the city or in front of one of the hotels along the way.

Getting out of Taipei is about as easy as getting into it, and intercity travel in Taiwan is now even easier thanks to the completion of Taiwan's High-Speed Rail (HSR; p352), which can traverse (nearly) the length of the island in a mind-bending 90 minutes. The HSR leaves from Taipei Main Station and makes a stop in Banqiao (MRT Banqiao) before heading south. Of course, the regular-speed rail (TRA) is always an option. Trains leave from both the Taipei Main and Songshan stations, with the latter being a good choice for trains heading north and down the east coast. TRA schedules are online at http://new.twtraffic.com.tw/TWRail_en.

Buses are also a good intercity option. Several companies run buses ranging in luxury and price, up and down both coasts of the island. Generally speaking you'll never have to wait more than an hour (usually less) for a bus to any city in Taiwan, though you may have to wait longer over the holidays, when every student in Taiwan seems to be going somewhere. Kuo Kuang Hao buses leave from the city bus station a block west of the Taipei Main Station, while the luxury bus companies operate from the terminal about a half a block past that. The luxury bus companies (Aloha and Ubus are two popular ones) have wider seats, movies, and occasional light refreshments. They're also priced about 15% higher than the government-run buses and have a somewhat dicey reputation for being lax when it comes to road safety.

GETTING AROUND

Fast and easy to use, the Taipei MRT makes Taipei city one of the easier Asian capitals to navigate. Another cool bonus of MRT travel is that every station has bilingual wall maps pointing out the neighbourhood's attractions. Compass-toting travellers beware, for whatever reason, some stations have maps in which south is facing upwards. Make sure to line their north arrow with that of your compass. In addition to operating the MRT, the Taipei Rapid Transit Association (TRTA) also runs many of Taipei's public bus routes and private bus lines that crisscross the city. Nowadays most buses have English as well as Chinese route signs. You can find fares, route maps and lots of other information at www.dot.taipei.gov.tw.

To/From the Airport

Two airports serve Taipei (see p345 for information on both). The international airport is the Taiwan Taoyuan International Airport. Its airport code is TPE and it's situated about 50km west of the city centre. Songshan Airport, just north of the city centre, handles domestic traffic. If you're heading to any other city in Taiwan or to one of the outer islands (p288), this is the airport you will be going to. If you are transiting through Taipei between an international flight and a domestic flight you must first get from one airport to the other. The bus is your best bet.

To get to Songshan Airport from downtown's Taipei Main Station, take bus 275 or 262. A taxi will cost around NT200.

Unless you're travelling very late at night or are carrying way more than you can handle, there's no real reason to take a taxi to and from the international airport. Buses to Taipei city (NT125, one hour) run every 15 minutes until midnight and tickets can be bought at either terminal (just follow the signs for 'Long Distance Buses'). Buses run either to Taipei Main Station or Songshan Airport, usually stopping at major hotels along the way. Because different buses stop at different hotels, make sure you let the ticket staff and driver know where you want to be let off.

Taxis from TPE Airport to the city centre cost NT1200, but NT1000 going the other direction. It's more expensive from the airport to the city because of an airport surcharge. Many hotels also offer private car services (at a mark-up, of course), but some offer free and discounted tickets on the buses.

Car & Motorcycle

There isn't much reason to drive in Taipei, though both cars and motorcycles can be a good thing to have to explore the mountains around the city. For information on car and motorcycle hire, see p349. If you do ride around Taipei on a motorcycle or scooter, make sure your paperwork is in order. Random traffic checks for unlicensed, drunk (or both) motorcyclists are now the rule, not the exception, and the days when a foreign face and lack of Mandarin-speaking ability would get you off the hook are long over.

TAIPEI

Public Transport
SUBWAY (MRT)

Having already mentioned just how much Taipei transport has improved thanks to the MRT, we can skip the additional praise (deserved though it is) and get down to brass tacks.

The ever-expanding Taipei MRT (Map p16), though it might have expanded further by the time you read this) pretty much goes everywhere you want to get to. Trains are comfortable and you can usually get a seat except during peak hours. Signage is bilingual and announcements are actually quadlingual (all stations are announced not merely in Mandarin and English, but in Taiwanese and Hakka as well). Most places within the city centre are (or soon will be) within about a 20-minute walk of an MRT station. Our one complaint about the MRT is that we wish it would run even later than 1am, but we've been saying the same thing about San Francisco's BART for decades.

OFF THE RAILS

Taipei's transformation from an ugly duckling of Asia to garden city has been nothing short of revolutionary. Though myriad are the factors involved in her rebirth, the greatest kudos probably goes to the Taipei MRT. Completed in 1999 (though 'completed' isn't quite appropriate as the system is still expanding to connect ever-distant suburbs to the city centre), the Taipei MRT was instrumental in greatly reducing the capital city's once-noxious pollution. Equally important, the MRT turned travel in and around Taipei from hellish to pleasant, making for convenient exploration of neighbourhoods that might otherwise have been overlooked by the casual tourist. Some of our favourite, and often overlooked, stations include:

- **Yuanshan** The first above-ground station on the red line marks Taipei's change from claustrophobic to suburban, and from business to spiritual. This is a good neighbourhood for temple hopping, quiet meditation and tea drinking. In addition to the being home to Taipei's well-known Confucius temple, Yuanshan also boasts a Buddhist temple and monastery (directly across from the station) built in the 1890s. Climbing the gnarled stone stairs that wrap around the complex's back brings you past several shrines and statues, and eventually to a small grass park with old stone tablets and a few stone stools and tables. It's a good place to sit in silence, though your meditation may be punctuated by the regular sound of an airplane coming in for a landing at Songshan airport, which lies directly east.

- **Xiaonanmen** Though in the city centre, this is another often overlooked station as it sits smack in the middle of a line with only three stops. Though there's only one cultural relic of serious note here, the old 'little south gate' (Map p88) for which the station is named after, it's well worth the 90-second ride from Chiang Kai-shek Memorial Hall station.

- **Kunyang** The eastern end of the blue line sees little tourist action. It's a shame, really, as Nankang park is just a short walk south of Kunyang station. A wide expanse of green grass, ponds, greenhouses, trees, pavilions and a lovely running track with a spectacular view of Taipei 101 to the west and mountains to the east, Nankang park is an oasis on the city's edge.

- **Xindian** The red line's southernmost stop, Xindian station, is the last neighbourhood in Taipei proper. Beyond here lie mountains and rural splendour. Xindian is where the Danshui River comes down from the mountains and sitting on both sides of the river is Pitan park, home to various semiregular fairs and festivities that offer the requisite games of chance and grilled meats. Xindian is also where you'll find the very cool, ever-swaying Bitan suspension bridge.

- **Tucheng** Very nearly the end of the western end of the blue line, Tucheng is a suburb of Taipei city that has a number of interesting temples, including the Buddhist Guang Cheng Yian and the Taoist Wugusiandi temples. If you follow the main road westward towards the Yongning station, you'll pass a park on your left that's used for traditional Taiwanese funeral parties, with a massive statue of a black dog straddling the park's entrance. We don't know the canine's proper name, but we're told he's there to keep watch for wayward spirits. It's a bit spooky, to be honest.

MRT fares are based on distance. The base fare is NT20 and you'll pay NT65 for the longest trip. Single tickets can be purchased from machines located in every MRT station. The fare for each destination is noted in both English and Chinese on a map beside the machine. Coins and bills are accepted, and change is provided.

If you're going to spend any length of time in Taipei, buy yourself an Easy Card, the TRTA's stored-value card. Adult/child Easy Cards sell for NT500/300, of which NT100 is a deposit. The rest is valid for MRT and bus fares and even for payments at certain car parks. It saves the hassle of queuing for tickets and fumbling for change and the best part, the Easy Card gives users a 20% discount on MRT fares. Additionally, if you use your Easy Card and transfer between the MRT and a bus within two hours, the bus ride is half-price. If you're taking a bus on your way to the MRT, the same discount applies.

To use your Easy Card, wave it across a reader device (Savvy Easy Card users wave the card through their wallet or handbag). The reader will then tell you how much value you have left. When the value drops below NT100, the reader will beep.

Easy Cards can be purchased from machines at many MRT stations (instructions available in English). Cash is accepted at most stations and you can add value to your Easy Card using either cash or bank/credit cards, although foreign cards tend not to work. Some stations have both cash and card versions of the Easy Card machines.

When you're done using your Easy Card, simply take it to an MRT ticket booth and your deposit plus any remaining value will be refunded.

BUS

Taipei's bus system is decidedly harder to figure out as compared with the MRT, mostly because there are so many more bus lines than there are subway lines. But most buses in the city have English signs, generally names of the neighbourhoods or their terminal points, making Taipei's most time-honoured mode of transport a good bet for visitors as well.

There are several types of buses, run by several companies, although that won't matter to most travellers as all of them accept Easy Card (see opposite). Each bus is numbered on the front and sometimes on the

---

TAIPEI BUS MAP ONLINE

Need to know what bus goes where? Then check out http://www.taipeibus.taipei.gov .tw (click on the English button) for an excellent online bus map put out by the Taipei City Government.

---

side, and larger buses display the start and end points of the routes in Chinese and English. Note, however, that it's not always clear which direction the bus is headed. There are also minibuses, sometimes called *hóng* (red) buses, with the character 紅 appearing before the route number.

All MRT stations have a map marking bus stops in its vicinity. If you can't find the map, just ask the attendant. Once you've located the bus stop, stand by the sign for your bus and if you see it coming be sure to flag it down. As there may be several different bus routes converging at the same stop, drivers often assume that passengers will identify themselves for pick-up. Note that Taipei's buses may not necessarily pull all the way up to the kerb. Occasionally the bus will stop a lane away, though you usually do not have to step through traffic to board the bus.

Fares are NT15 on most routes within the city centre, though that can double or triple on longer routes. If the sign over the fare box reads 上車 (*shàngchē*), that means you pay getting on and 下車 (*xiàchē*) means you pay getting off.

Taxi

Taipei's distinctively yellow taxis are metered and charge by distance and waiting time. Base fare is NT70 for the first 1.5km plus NT5 for each 300m thereafter. After midnight, the base fare is NT70 for the first 1.2km plus NT5 for each 250m thereafter. Taxis also charge NT5 for every two minutes that the car is idle (eg sitting in traffic or at a red light). These two minutes are cumulative and appears on the meter.

You won't have any trouble finding a taxi in the city centre as they're everywhere. There are taxi stands around the city but most people just hail one from the side of the road. If an approaching taxi is available, it will have a red light in the windscreen. A taxi may well honk and just stop for you if you look like you need a ride.

AROUND TAIPEI

Not to put too fine a point on it, but one of the many reasons for our boundless love for Taipei's MRT is that it has made once-difficult places a mere subway ride away. Even mountain spots such as Yangmingshan (p132), Maokong (p136) and Wulai (p141) are much easier to get to from the city centre thanks to the mass transit system.

DANSHUI 淡水
pop 110,000

Start with a charming Taipei-river suburb as your soup base, add equal parts college-town youth vibe and oceanside-boardwalk festivity. Toss in a healthy sea breeze and a hefty dash of old-world colonial architecture and you've got **Danshui** (Dànshuǐ), possibly among the coolest, and most unique, hangout spots in Taipei.

History

Also known as Tamshui, the long and storied history of this once-important fishing village has been shaped primarily by its geographical position at a place where the Danshui River meets the Taiwan Straits. Danshui was initially settled by the Ketagalan tribe, then at various times by the Spanish, Dutch, Japanese and of course, the Han Chinese. By the mid-19th century Danshui was a bustling port city thanks to its natural harbour, and it boasted a sizable foreign population and even a British embassy.

By the end of the 19th century, Danshui's importance as a port had waned, and once Taiwan reverted to Chinese control after WWII, the town slowly settled into a comfortable position as farthest suburb of a major metropolis. With the opening of the Danshui line of the Taipei MRT in 1998, Danshui suddenly found itself a popular weekend travel destination.

Orientation

Travelling from the Danshui MRT station towards the centre of town, the river front is on your left, while the town itself gradually slopes up the hills towards Tamkang University to the right. Directly north of the station is a great park for kite flying and past

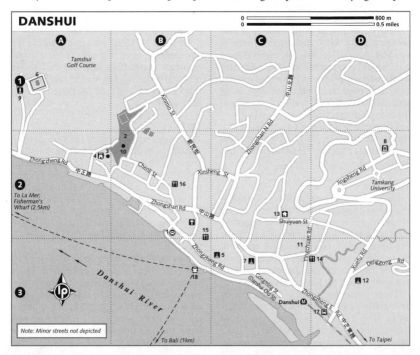

this is Danshui's famous Gongming St and waterfront pedestrian plaza. Across the river is Guanyinshan mountain and the town of Bali, both a quick ferry ride away. Ferries also leave for Danshui's Fisherman's Wharf tourist area, near the mouth of the river. Though buses from the station take you to the various sights around town, most of Danshui is reachable on foot, and the town, though crowded, is particularly pedestrian friendly.

Sights

A street filled with renovated colonial architecture, Danshui's Gongming St (also known as Danshui Old St) is a favourite with visitors. Lined with shops and food stalls, the pedestrian street gets pretty crowded on the weekends, so if you're averse to crowds, weekdays are the best time to visit. In addition to the shops and stalls, Gongming St also has a branch of Taiwan's (no affiliation with Ripley's) **Believe it or Not** where, for a mere NT90 entry, you can see a live two-headed lizard and a dead (and pickled) two-headed calf. Just look for the stuffed gorilla by the door. Fun for the whole family!

Gongming St runs adjacent to a river-side promenade, which, though lacking an actual boardwalk, still manages to have a boardwalk vibe thanks to its seafood restaurants, outdoor seating, carnival amusements, but

with just a few shrines to let you know you're still in Taiwan. From here you can catch a ferry across the river to Bali and the Guanyinshan area (see p130), or upriver to Danshui's newly renovated Fisherman's Wharf, which is a great place to drink beer while watching the sun go down over the Taiwan Straits after you've exhausted yourself walking around Danshui all day. Details on how to get there are on p129.

Gongming St ends at Zhongzheng Rd, but keep walking north as there's still plenty to see. Right next to the **Longshan Temple** (Lóngshān Sì; Map p126) sits the Danshui **morning market** (Map p126; ☼ sunrise-noon), the traditional centre of town. Nestled in its alleys are a cacophony of shops and stalls selling fish, vegetables, meats, clothing and the like. About 100m further along Zhongzheng Rd is **Fuyou Temple** (Fúyòu Gōng; Map p126). Built in 1796, this beautiful low-lying structure is the oldest temple in Danshui. Naturally the temple is dedicated to Matsu, goddess of the sea. In bygone days, wives and families would come here to pray for the safe return, and sometimes the souls, of their menfolk.

Hiking further up Zhongzheng Rd takes you past a plethora of shops, shrines and alleyways. Do you like bugs? Don't miss **Starbugs Insect Mall** (Map p126; Lane 11 Zhongzheng Rd; ☼ 3-9pm), a shop specialising in the care, breeding and raising of gigantic beetles. Browsers are welcome but a strict no-petting policy is enforced. But if you need tactile stimulation you can stick your hands inside puppets at the **Classical Chinese Glove Puppets Art Centre** (4 Lane 11, Zhongzheng Rd; ☼ 10am-9pm).

Further up the road sits Danshui's most famous sight, **Fort San Domingo** (Hóngmáo Chéng; ☎ 2623 1001; adult/student NT30/20; ☼ 9am-5pm, closed Mon). The hill on which it sits has been home to a fort since the Spanish occupation of northern Taiwan from 1626 to 1641. The original fort no longer exists and there are two theories on its demise: either the Spanish destroyed it during their 1641 retreat from the Dutch, or that the Dutch razed it in order to build a stronger structure. In any case, the basic structure of the current fort dates from 1642.

The fort was under Chinese control from 1683 to 1867 until the British took it over in 1868, painted it red and made it their consulate. Adjacent to the fort is the 1891 **former British consular residence**, a real throwback to the British Raj complete with original tiles from

Java, ceiling fans, and furnishings recreated from photographic records. The consulate was closed under Japanese occupation but reopened after WWII, and the British retained it until 1972 when diplomatic relations with Taiwan were severed.

The fort's present-day offices and ticket booth near the entrance were once guards' and servants' quarters. Inside you can view the jail cells they built for insubordinate sailors and businessmen. There are sweeping views from the fort itself.

Up the hill from the fort is **Alethia University** (Zhēnlǐ Dàxué), the first Western-style university in Taiwan. It was founded by a Canadian Presbyterian missionary, Dr George Leslie Mackay, who first came to Taiwan in 1872 and is revered in certain Taiwanese circles for introducing Western techniques of education and medicine. Thanks in no small part to Mackay's influence, Presbyterian is the most popular Christian denomination in Taiwan. The university's original building, **Oxford College** was built in 1882 and fronts a Chinese-style pond and a large, more recent, chapel.

About 1km beyond Fort San Domingo, **Huwei Fort** (Hùwěi Pàotái; adult/student NT25/15; ♥ 9am-5pm, closed Mon) is less flashy but no less interesting. This well-camouflaged fort dates from 1886. If Fort San Domingo is meant to convey authority, Huwei Fort was built for military action. It has thick walls, massive gates, four batteries and steep steps to its ramparts to deter intruders (try it and you'll see what we mean, but watch your step!). An inscription above the main entrance reads 'key to northern gate', denoting the fort's importance in the defence of the island. It was also used by the Japanese but never saw military action. In April and May, the fort's chinaberry trees are awash in purple flowers.

Back in the MRT station part of town is **Yinshan Temple** (Yínshān Sì; Map p126; ☎ 2625 2930; cnr Denggong & Xuefu Rds; admission free; ♥ 6am-6pm May-Oct, 6am-4.30pm Nov-Apr), considered Taiwan's best-preserved example of temple architecture from the Qing dynasty (AD 644–1911). Although small, it's a riot of sculpture, especially obvious in the tiny glass and ceramic figurines and flowers among the roofing tiles. This is also the city god temple for Danshui. Another unique feature is that the temple, founded 300 years ago, remains in the control of the 21 families who founded it. The current building dates

to 1822 and it was most recently renovated in 1992.

From here, Xuefu Rd leads up to the campus of Tamkang University. Aside from being one of the prettiest university campuses in Taiwan, boasting gardens and Qing-dynasty-style pavilions, Tamkang is also home of the **Maritime Museum** (Hǎishì Bówùguǎn; Map p126; admission free; ♥ 9am-5pm, closed Mon), a four-storey museum shaped like an ocean liner. How appropriate, as it used to be a training centre for sailors and maritime engineers. The museum's collection is anchored by dozens of large model ships from around the world. Expect steamers, frigates, explorers' ships and aircraft carriers as well as an aboriginal canoe from Taiwan's Lanyu Island. You can learn about the treasure ship of Taiwanese admiral Cheng Ho, who was said to have navigated the Red Sea, Persian Gulf and East Africa 87 years before Columbus sailed. On the 4th floor, the 'ship's bridge' offers excellent views of distant buildings and Guanyinshan.

Finally, though not a big tourist magnet, one of our favourite Danshui neighbourhoods also happens to be among our favourite Taipei night markets. **Yingchuan Rd** (Map p126) and the surrounding alleyways are a great place to get cheap eats, shop for socks and observe genuine Taiwanese youth culture. Mind the speeding scooters though.

Sleeping & Eating

Life is quieter in the outskirts and hotels outside of the city centre tend to be a mixture of midrange boutiques, with some 'love hotels' thrown in. We're convinced that Danshui and the surrounding areas are cool enough to warrant more than a quick trip; apparently we're not alone. Though there are a number of hotels in the area, **RegaLess Hotel** (Fúgé Dàfàndiàn; Map p126; ☎ 2626 8165; www.regalees-hotel.com.tw; 89 Shie-fu Rd, Danshui; 台北縣淡水鎮學府路89號; r from NT2800), built in 2004, is particularly good value for the price. It's a few blocks east of the Ying Chuan Rd Night Market and within good walking distance of all Danshui's sights and smells, and not too far from the ferry to Bali.

Dining on a budget is no problem in Danshui. Yingchuan Rd is chock-a-block with restaurants and food stalls. Chenli St, on the way to Alethia University, is filled with **restaurants** catering to local students.

If you want seafood, there are dozens of restaurants on Danshui's harbour-front promenade serving a 'catch of the day' likely caught just that day. And for Taiwanese favourites, Gongming St can't be beat as it's loaded with food stalls serving Taiwanese from-the-grill Specialities such as squid, chicken and corn. One local dish you'll find in abundance is called 'iron eggs' – these are regular eggs that have been boiled, shelled and roasted until they turn black and leathery. If you don't like the flavour, you can always use them to play marbles. Another Danshui delicacy is *A-gi*, fist-sized pouches of fried tofu filled with bean-thread noodles and served in hot broth.

The **Dongdong Vegetarian** (Dōngdōng Sùshí; Map p126; ☎ 2623 7692; 15 Ren Ai Jie; dishes NT40-100; ☺ lunch & dinner) is a nice little vegetarian place with daily specials. There's no English signage, so remember that the sign is yellow with green characters and it's across the street from a guitar shop.

The **Red Castle 1899** (Dáguānlóu; Map p126; ☎ 8631 1168; 6 Lane 2, Sanmin St; dishes NT180-360; ☺ lunch & dinner) is a Victorian-style building and a well-known architectural landmark in Danshui, dating back to the late 19th century. Beautifully restored and reborn as a swank eatery, the Red Castle serves both Western and Chinese dishes. We've heard mixed reviews on the food, but the ambiance can't be beat. Anyway, you'll be ready to eat after climbing the 106 steps from the front gate to the restaurant.

Another good place to spend an evening is Fisherman's Wharf, just a few kilometres downriver. The upper deck of the promenade is a great place to watch the sun set after a day spent bopping around Danshui, and the shops, restaurants and amusements below are a fine way to while away the evening. Located roughly in the middle of the strip **La Mer** (45-12 Bei Shi Zi, San Chih) is a cool jazz and blues bar and grill. Their regular band is made up of both foreign and local musicians. Their Saturday night gig (7pm to 10pm) has been a regular feature for the past two years and looks set to continue for more to come.

Getting There & Around

Danshui is at the end of the MRT Danshui (red) line. The journey from Taipei Main Station takes about 35 minutes and costs NT50. The **Danshui Motor Transport Company** (Map p126; ☎ 2621 3340) runs buses along the north coast to Baishawan (p156), Keelung (p153), and points beyond.

If you're going to Fisherman's Wharf, take red bus 26 from Danshui MRT station (NT15, 15 minutes). A more interesting option is the 15-minute ferry trip operated by **Suen Fung Ferry Company** (☎ 8630 1845; Danshui Ferry Pier; adult/child NT40/20; ☺ 9am-8pm Mon-Fri, 9am-10pm Sat & Sun).

BALI 八里

West of Danshui is the charming riverfront /seacoast town of Bali (no relation to the Indonesian paradise of the same name). Just across the wide mouth of the Danshui River where it meets the sea, Bali is quickly becoming a magnet for Taipeiers, especially families with children looking to get out of the big city for an afternoon. The entire bank of the river is taken up by the aptly named 'Left Bank Park', a waterfront park with 14km of biking and hiking trails and wooden boardwalks skirting wetlands teeming with plant and marine life. The area has also become a magnet for bird-watchers, as a number of species of birds either make their homes here or stop by for a quick feast on their migratory routes.

Sights & Activities

Bicycles can be rented for NT50 per hour at a number of shops right off the boat dock from Danshui. Most of the bikes available are serviceable, but hardly in 'Tour de France' condition, so check to make sure yours has working brakes before you take off. A variety four-wheeled 'family bikes' are also available. These are pedal-powered minicars. In addition to the park and bike trails, Bali is also home to the Guanyinshan scenic area and an excellent new museum.

The newly built and very cool **Shihsanheng Museum of Archaeology** (Shísānxíng Bówùguǎn; Map pp82-3; ☎ 2619 1313; 200 Bowuguan Rd, Bali Hsiang, Taipei County, admission NT100; ☺ 9.30am-5.00pm, closed Mon) offers exhibits on the archaeological history of Taiwan's earliest residents. A variety of installations show the earliest evidence of aboriginal culture on the island, tracking the movements of the various tribes from prehistory to the present day. Highly interactive, the museum is surprisingly kid friendly for a museum devoted to as scholarly a pursuit as archaeology; kids will especially like the aboriginal weaponry displays. English signage abounds and the museum staff will be happy to arrange a tour.

TAIPEI

Getting There & Around

The same ferry company that goes to Fisherman's Wharf also operates regular boats from Danshui to Bali (adult/child NT18/10; ☉ 6.15am-8pm). However, if you're not planning to rent a bike but are planning to hit the museum, you can save some NT by taking the MRT to the Guandu station and buying a roundtrip bus ticket at the station that will bring you to the Bali waterfront, the museum, and back to Guandu station. The entire ticket is NT99 and includes museum entry.

GUANDU 關渡區

Two stops south of Danshui, Guandu is home to both an excellent nature park and Taiwan's oldest temple.

Sights & Activities

GUANDU NATURE PARK 關渡自然公園

Ten years in the planning, this **nature reserve** (Guāndù Zìrán Gōngyuán; Map pp82-3; ☎ 2858 7417; 55 Guandu Rd; adult/concession/children below 90cm NT50/30/free; ☉ 9am-5pm, closed 3rd Mon each month) opened in 2001 under the control of the Wild Bird Society of Taipei. Over 100 species of birds, 150 species of plants and 800 species of animals live here on about 58 hectares of grass, mangroves, saltwater marsh and freshwater ponds at the confluence of the Danshui and Keelung Rivers (and their smaller tributaries).

On weekdays, it's rather busy with school groups, and with other tourists on weekends. Monday mornings are the least crowded.

GUANDU TEMPLE 關渡宮

Dating back to 1661, this is one of Taiwan's oldest **temples** (Guāndù Gōng; Map pp82-3; 360 Zhixing Rd). Though it doesn't look like much from the street, this temple to Matsu is actually quiet lovely. To the right of the main hall is a 100m-plus tunnel through the mountain (lined with brightly painted deities enshrined in cases). At the end of the tunnel is a balcony with sweeping views of the Danshui riverscape. Naturally, the balcony has a rich assortment of stone carvings; take special note of the intricately carved and painted ceiling. Around the marble façade of the back of the temple, there's a hill-side park where you can contemplate an impressive frieze.

Legend has it that three banyan trees on the site died on the same day in 1895, and locals took it as an omen of impending disaster. Was it coincidence that the Japanese occupation began the same year?

Getting There & Around

Take the MRT Danshui (red) line to Guandu station. Leave by exit 1 and cross under the overpass to reach the nature park and temple. Both are about 15 minutes' walk from the station along Zhixing Rd (where there are a number of casual restaurants for a quick lunch). To reach the nature park, turn left when you see a playground. To reach the temple, continue on to the end of Zhixing Rd. Alternatively, Bus 302 from Guandu station terminates at the temple. It's an easy walk (less than 10 minutes) between the nature park and temple.

BEITOU北投

Beneath the soil of Taiwan bubbles a veritable cauldron of sulphurous water, and though most hot-spring resorts are well away from major urban areas, Taipei's Beitou (Běitóu, sometimes spelled Peitou) is a notable and welcome exception. It's here that locals and travellers alike come for a quick soak in sulphurous waters.

The wēnquán (hot springs) in this district have been a lure for tourism as far back as the Japanese era.

Not too long ago, the waters themselves were the priority and comforts such as attractive baths, meals and massages came a distant second. Nowadays Beitou offers dozens of bathing options, from simply soaking your feet in the roadside creeks (cost: nothing) to glamorous private baths in ritzy high-rise resorts (cost: prepare your credit card for a workout). The latter might include the use of several public pools, with optional massages and multicourse dinners and even karaoke. Popular day-trip packages combine a hot-spring visit with lunch or dinner. There are also public hot springs with cheap admission to somewhat downmarket private baths that won't set you back more than a few hundred NT. But be warned, thought Beitou is lush and lovely, its position as a quick skip from the city centre means that the area can get crowded, especially on chilly winter weekends.

Orientation & Information

The resort area is a few minutes' walk from Xinbeitou MRT station. Inside the eye-shaped Beitou Park are the Beitou Hot Spring Museum and public hot springs. A number of hot-spring hotels line Guangming Rd on the park's southern side. The park is bordered to the north by Zhongshan Rd, where you'll find the Ketagalan Culture Centre and the route towards the Di-re Valley, the source of the many resorts' hot springs. Where Guangming and Zhongshan Rds converge at the far end of the park, you can continue along the mountain roads to some deluxe resorts. Most of these have shuttle buses to and from Xinbeitou MRT station.

During the Hot Spring Carnival in October, Beitou's resorts offer special packages.

Sights & Activities

BEITOU HOT SPRING MUSEUM
北投溫泉博物館

On the site of one of the original Japanese-era hot-spring baths, this handsome **museum** (Běitóu Wēnquán Bówùguǎn; Map p134; ☎ 2893 9981; 2 Zhongshan Rd; admission free; ☷ 9am-5pm, closed Mon) mixes a Victorian-style exterior with a variety of other architectural designs inside. Upstairs, wooden verandas surround a large Japanese-style tatami room where bathers once took tea and relaxed after their baths. The former baths downstairs feel almost Roman in their construction. Old scrubbing brushes, buckets and other implements of Taiwanese hot-spring bathing are displayed. You have to remove your shoes at the entrance and wear loaner slippers to enter the museum, but don't let this fool you into getting your hopes up; there is no actual bathing allowed at this museum.

DI-RE VALLEY 地熱谷

Throughout the Japanese occupation this **geothermal valley** (Dìrè Gǔ, Hell Valley; Map p134) was considered one of the country's great scenic wonders and a visit by the Japanese crown prince sealed Beitou's reputation as the hot-spring destination in Taiwan. These days it's interesting to walk through, and the valley's 3500 sq metres of bubbling waters and sulphurous gases leave no question as to the origins of its name. Although the waters are not suitable for bathing – in some spots they reach 90°C – it is the source of many of the hot springs used by the resorts in town.

The name Di-re refers to what first came to mind when folks first walked through this area of mountains filled with smoking craters and cracks from which steam and sulphurous fumes arose, 'This must be what hell is like!'.

Since than, the scenic Di-re Valley has been tamed somewhat.

KETAGALAN CULTURE CENTRE
凱達格蘭文化館

Opened in 2002, this multistorey **centre** (Kǎidágélán Wénhuàguǎn; Map p134; ☎ 2898 6500; 3-1 Zhongshan Rd; admission free; ☷ 9am-5pm, closed Mon) exploring Taiwan's aboriginal culture is worth a stop. Exhibits are mostly on the 2nd and 3rd floors, while there are performance stages and various seasonal exhibits on other floors. The upper floors house study centres and a library. Although signage is in Chinese, English-language leaflets explain Taiwan's tribes in detail.

HOT SPRINGS

Practically next to the Beitou Hot Spring Museum, Beitou's **outdoor public bath** (Gōnggòng Lùtiān Wēnquán; Map p134; ☎ 2893 7014; Zhongshan Rd; weekday/weekend NT20/40; ☷ 8.30-11.15am, noon-2.45pm, 3.30-6.15pm & 7-9.45pm) is one of the least expensive options in town. The outdoor public bath is set into a hillside and offers bathing for men and women. Bring your own swimsuit and towel as bathing au naturel is not permitted. This public hot spring boasts a number of pools ranging in temperature from comfortably warm to damn near scalding. There's also a frigid pool off to the side for those of especially strong constitution. The pools are emptied every few hours for cleaning, so be sure to allow yourself enough time to enjoy it.

On the other end of the spectrum is the **Asia Pacific Resort** (Yàtài Wēnquán Shēnghuóguǎn; Map p134; ☎ 2898 2088; http://www.apresort.com.tw; 21 Yinguang Lane; ☷ 8.30am-1am Mon-Fri, 8.30am-2am Sat & Sun), a magnificent bathing/dining/meeting complex with Japanese raked-sand gardens and indoor and outdoor baths, including white-water mineral baths. Guests can rent private rooms with both indoor and outdoor hot-spring baths; some of these feature tea-service and others have setups for hot-pot dining. Pricing depends on a variety of options. The bilingual website lays these out nicely.

See p75 for bathing options inside large resorts.

Sleeping

Whispering Pine Inn (Yíngsōnggé Lǚshè; Map p134; ☎ 2895 1531; fax 2891 2037; 21 Youya Rd, Beitou; 北投區幽雅路21號; d NT3600) More than 80 years old, this Japanese-style inn is a registered historic landmark. Expect indoor stone baths and rooms in which you can sleep on either beds or tatami. It's worth a stay here just to be around the beautiful original woodwork. The Whispering Pine Inn is unusually retro; not only don't rooms have internet, they don't have phones or TVs. Soaking and relaxing are what this place is all about.

Broadway Hotel (Bǎilèhuì Wēnquán Fàndiàn; Map p134; ☎ 2895 6658; 99 Wenquan Rd, Beitou; 北投區溫泉路 99號; www.broadway-hotspring-hotel.com.tw; d NT3000) One of the newest of Beitou's hot-spring resorts, the gorgeous Broadway has a wide variety of room types, ranging from Japanese-tatami rooms to Taiwanese to more Western-style rooms. There are a number of common areas furnished with mahogany Chinese tea tables, sculptures, and other works of art. It's an especially good deal on the weekdays, when prices drop nearly low enough for it to be considered in the budget range.

SweetMe Hot Spring Resort (Shuǐměi Wēnquán Hùiguǎn; Map p134; ☎ 2898 3838; www.sweetme.com.tw; 224 Guangming Rd, Beitou; 北投區光明路224號; d/tw incl breakfast from NT5600/6200) Across from Beitou Park and an easy walk from Xinbeitou MRT station, the SweetMe has an odd name but beautiful facilities. It opened in 2003 as the latest incarnation of an older, high-rise resort. There are indoor and outdoor baths, extensive spa and dining facilities and Japanese touches throughout. Even standard guest rooms have handsome bathtubs.

Getting There & Around

Beitou is easily reached by MRT. Take the Danshui (red) line to Beitou station and transfer to a spur train to Xinbeitou station. Before 7am and after 9pm, services between Beitou and Xinbeitou may be by a free shuttle bus.

YANGMINGSHAN NATIONAL PARK
陽明山國家公園

How fortunate Taipei is to have this **national park** (Yángmíngshān Guójiā Gōngyuán) at its doorstep, complete with majestic mountains, hot springs, tall grasses, forests of bamboo and broad-leaf trees and some handsome lodgings and restaurants. Among its 1200-plus species of plants, the area is particularly known for rhododendrons, azaleas and Japanese cherry trees. An excellent escape from the city for hikers, bikers (of the gear and motor-head variety), hot-spring lovers, twitters, or just about anyone getting away from it all.

Like Beitou, a major attraction of Yangmingshan is the hot-spring baths. The park is filled with kēng (sulphur steam vents), the largest being Xiaoyoukeng in the northwestern part of the park. To the east, Lengshuikeng has hot-spring baths open to the public for free.

Yangmingshan is protected and no new construction can take place. This can also mean that some of the lodgings are not as spiffy as those in Beitou but the trade-off is that they feel more historic.

The area just outside the park's boundaries tends to be more developed. Many well-to-do Taiwanese and expats live on the mountains' lower reaches and there are schools and churches serving the community.

Orientation & Information

The centrepiece of the park is **Cisingshan** (Qīxīngshān), northern Taiwan's tallest peak at 1120m.

Yangmingshan bus station (Map p134) is near the south entrance of the park, and from here you can catch a shuttle bus around the park. There are some cafés and convenience stores near the bus station and nearby Jianguo St turns into an ad-hoc food festival on nice days.

There are visitors centres at major tourist sights within the park and most usually have an English speaker on hand. All these centres have simple maps of the park that includes basic information and hiking-trail details in English. You can pick up a detailed map of the park for NT50 at the **National Park Visitors Centre** (Map p134; ☎ 2861 3601; www.ymsnp.gov.tw).

Yangmingshan tends to be a bit cooler than central Taipei, so like mom used to say, bring a sweater. July to September has the most stable weather, though afternoon thunderstorms then are common. Autumn brings monsoons and humidity, chilly rain and fog. Though it doesn't often happen, when it snows on the peaks the roads are clogged with Taiwanese who never see snow driving up to see it.

Sights

Chiang Kai-shek had 15 villas, of which **Yangming Shuwu** (Yángmíng Shūwū, Yangming Villa; Map p134; ☎ 2861 1444; adult/concession NT50/30; ☷ tours 9am & 1.30pm, closed Mon) was the last (built in 1970) and the grandest. Its valley setting makes for quite a sight, especially in March when its gardens are in full bloom. It also provides quite an insight into the life of the president and madame. Even before you reach the house, you'll see bushes pruned into five clumps (symbolising Chiang's rank as a five-star general) and the hidden guard posts where an entire military police battalion could be stationed.

Inside the house are several dining rooms, both Chinese and Western, a life-size portrait of Chiang with eyes that seem to follow you around the room, and other memorabilia from the lives of Taiwan's last dictator. While the furniture is mostly reproduction, most of the building itself is original and quite grand.

Tours are held in Chinese and Japanese, although English-language tours can be scheduled by phoning the **national park visitor centre** (☎ 2861 3601; www.ymsnp.gov.tw) at least one week in advance. The centre also offers general information about recreation in Yangmingshan.

Activities

HIKING

Hiking is the main thing people do in Yangmingshan and no matter what else brings you here (bird-watching, flower gazing, hot springing), it's more than likely it will take some hiking to get you there. Serious hikers can spend days here exploring dozens of amazing trails, some of which can be done in a couple of hours and others which can take up the day. It would take a whole book to describe 'em. Luckily Richard Saunders went and wrote *Yangmingshan The Guide*, available at **Caves Books** (Dūnhuáng Shūjú) Tianmu (Map p100; ☎ 2874 2199; 5 Lane 38, Tianyu St) Zhongshan (Map p92; ☎ 2537 1666; 103 Zhongshan N Rd, sec.2; MRT Shuanglian), **Eslite** (Chéngpǐn; Map p96; ☎ 2775 5977; 245 Dunhua S Rd; MRT Zhongxiao Dunhua), and the **Community Service Centre** (Map p100; ☎ 2836 8134; www.community.com.tw; 25 Lane 290, Zhongshan N Rd, sec.6; MRT Mingde). The book outlines hikes both short and long in loving detail.

Casual visitors will not have any problems finding trails. There are English signposts and maps with 'you are here' symbols are all over the park, and you can pick up a simple map with trail instructions at the **National Park Visitor's Centre** (Map p134). One popular hike on Cisingshan starts at Xiaoyoukeng, northwest of Cisingshan, and goes to the top of the mountain. The hike takes you past the brimstone-reeking sulphur pits for which the region is famous; it's really quite a sight (and aroma). There are high-plains buffalo (mind the cow pies!) and the panoramic view is stunning when the fog lifts.

To get to the trailhead, take minibus 15 from the Shilin MRT station to the end of the line. From here, signs are clearly marked.

HOT SPRINGS

The public **Lengshuikeng** (Lěngshuǐkēng; Map p134; ☎ 2861 0036; admission free; ☯ 9am-5pm, closed Mon) bath on the park's eastern side has separate men's and women's indoor baths, although free admission means there can be long queues to enter. Its name means 'cold water valley', and by comparison to other local hot springs it's chilly, at 40ºC. High iron content makes its waters reddish brown. Technically, Lengshuikeng is open to 5pm, but it's often open later, so phone ahead if you're considering an after-hours visit.

BIRDWATCHING

Yangmingshan is definitely on the international birders circuit, being one of the best places to see endemic species such as the Taiwan Blue Magpie (an adorable bird with a tail almost twice its body length). The optimum time for bird-watching is early in the morning, with early autumn being the best season. The **Wild Bird Society of Taipei** (Map p96; ☎ 2325 9190; http://www.taipeibird.org.tw; 3 Lane 160, Fuxing S Rd, sec.2) organises tours from their Taipei office.

Sleeping

Yangming Sunrise Spring Hotel (Rìchū Yángmíng Wēnquán Huìguǎn; Map p134; ☎ 2862 0668; www.sunrise-spring.com.tw; 5 Lane 23, Yangming Rd, Beitou; 北投陽明路一段23之5號; r from NT2500) Close to the entrance of the park, this cute hotel sits along a hot-spring river rolling down the mountain towards Beitou. Rooms are comfortable, but the main feature in each are the deep, stone Japanese tubs for extended hot-spring soaking. The lower level of the hotel is taken up by tub-only rooms, rented by the hour. Costs are steep on the weekends (NT800 for a 90-minute soak) but with the weekday 50% discount, the tubs alone make it worth the trip.

International Hotel (Guójì Dàlǚguǎn; Map p134; ☎ 2861 7100; 7 Hushan Rd, sec.1; r incl breakfast from NT2310) Built in 1952 and maintaining its original character, the International has a rustic stone façade and charming rooms that are a great deal. The hotel is close to the hot-spring source and has both public and in-room hot-spring baths. Both Japanese and Western-style rooms are available. Three-hour use of rooms (including hot springs) is NT990.

Landis Resort Yangmingshan (Yángmíngshān Zhōngguó Lìzhì Dàfàndiàn; Map p134; ☎ 2861 6661; www .landisresort.com.tw; 237 Gezhi Rd; r from NT7000) With its low-slung profile, slate surfaces and lots of grainy wood and plate glass, this grand yet intimate resort feels inspired by Frank Lloyd Wright. Rooms in the deluxe category and up have hot-spring baths but any guest may use the spa and indoor pools. The Landis has an easy to use internet booking system that can get rooms down as low as NT5000.

Eating

About a kilometre away from the entrance to Yangmingshan National Park sits Yang-mingshan University, surrounding which is a plethora of student-type restaurants for quick and cheap eats. There's also a Subway sandwich shop if you'd like to carry a hoagie into the park with you. On weekends and most nice days during the high season, Jian Guo St (on the south side of the bus station) turns into an open-air food court serving Tai-wanese favourites such as Hakka-style salt pork, seafood dumpling soup and a variety of noodle dishes.

Among a number of small eateries near the bus station, country-style café **Ping Shan** (Map p134; ☎ 2861 4162; 2 Lane 11, Hushan Rd; meals NT260-280; ✼ breakfast, lunch & dinner) does lovely versions of Western classics (salmon, steaks, squid-ink pasta) plus a few Japanese choices and Thai curries. Many dishes are part of set menus that include starters, drinks and/or desserts.

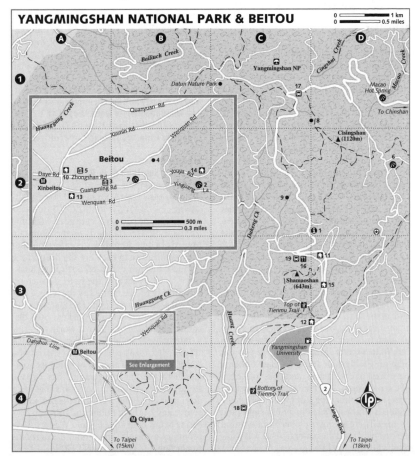

YANGMINGSHAN NATIONAL PARK & BEITOU

Getting There & Around

Bus 260 comes all the way from Taipei Main Station (NT30) via Zhongshan N Rd. From Shilin MRT station you can catch red bus 5 (NT15). Buses run frequently between 5.40am and 10.30pm. Bus 230 and minibus 9 also run into the park from Beitou while Daohan minibus 15 heads into the park from Jiantan.

Note that if approaching from the park's main entrance on Yangte Blvd, passenger cars require permits from 8am to 3pm, weekends and holidays. Only residents can obtain permits. Other forms of transport are permitted within the park without a permit and some locals circumvent the permit requirement by approaching the park via Tianmu or Beitou.

On weekends and holidays, a shuttle bus does the circuit around Yangmingshan's main road every 15 minutes (hourly on weekdays), beginning at Yangmingshan bus station. The cost is NT15 per ride, or NT60 per day during flower-viewing season (late February to early March).

SOUTH OF CITY CENTRE
Xindian & Bitan 新店 碧潭

The Xindian station is the last stop on the red (Danshui to Xindian) line or the first, depending on your perspective, which is fitting as Xindian is the far end of Taipei city, beyond which lies kilometres of mountainous splendour, bucolic scenery, and, if you take the right bus, a little town called Wulai (p141). The main attraction of Xindian is **Bitan park** (Map pp82–3), which straddles both sides of the Danshui River as it rolls down the mountain. It's in this park where you'll find various semiregular fairs and festivities. Should you be in town during the Lantern Festival (which caps the Lunar New Year's festivities), Bitan park is a great place to come to see Taipei's 'unofficial' lantern festival. While Chiang Kai-shek Shilin Residence Park is where folks go to see the floats, Bitan park is where locals come to write out their wishes on paper lanterns before setting them alight and aloft. The burning lanterns usually sink slowly into the river, but occasionally they'll be carried by the wind into the surrounding neighbourhoods. The Lantern Festival is usually a busy time for the local fire brigade.

Old Xindian St runs behind the station and stretches south along the river. The street boasts a small unspectacular night market that's good for a snack. Some stands sell grilled chicken, doughy octopus balls, and various other night market fare. From the market you can follow the river towards the mountains, checking out some of the old pumping stations along the way. You can also hang a right onto the pedestrian bridge and cross the river into Bitan. A marvel of low-tech engineering, the Bitan cable suspension bridge is extremely light. As a result, it has a peculiar tendency of bobbing and swaying in the near-constant breeze, offering the closest sensation you can get to seasickness without boarding a boat. Speaking of boats, small two-person pedal boats are available for rent on weekends at the river pier for NT100 per hour. Either side of the river is a great place to be during the Dragon Boat Festival (p337).

Bitan itself is increasingly becoming the main tourist attraction of the area. This small neighbourhood on the left bank of the river is home to the **Bi Ting** (Bì Tíng; ☎ 2212 9467; right side of suspension bridge; tea NT200), a rustic, 50-year-old teahouse built on a rocky cliff overlooking the river where you can while away the afternoon or evening while brewing endless pots of tea. If you're looking for a fancy meal, **Rosemary's Kitchen** (Mǎliyàde Méiguī Xiāngliào Chúfáng; ☎ 2218 9689; left side of suspension bridge; dishes from NT300) is a beautiful Western restaurant with an odd Bavarian theme and a balcony overlooking the river. Otherwise, there's plenty of street food on this side of the river as well.

Taiping Temple (Tàipíng Sì), a multistorey Taoist temple is just a few blocks north of the suspension bridge and worth a visit. Perhaps oddest of the area's offerings is a small roadside shrine on the right side of the road leading off the bridge. One feature of this otherwise ordinary-looking shrine to Guanyin stands out; a line of water bottles on a table, beneath which a sign in Chinese reads 'Blessed Water – 100 NT'. Apparently the water has been blessed, either by the goddess herself or one of her earthly representatives. The bottles have red labels upon which a various blessings have been written. The shrine is generally unmanned, with payment based on an honour system. It seems unlikely that any believer in the benefits of blessed water would even consider pilfering the stuff.

Bitan has a number of decent hotels should you decide to base yourself a bit (but not too far) out of the city. The **Bitan Hotel** (Bìtán Fàndiàn; ☎ 2211 6055; www.bitan.com.tw; 121 Bitan Rd; 臺北縣新店市碧潭路121號; d incl breakfast from NT1690; MRT Xindian) is pretty little boutique hotel with a view of the river and mountains. All rooms have flat-screen televisions and some have swinging porch chairs. We have no idea why, but it's a nice, though somewhat odd, touch. Free airport pick-up is available too.

A more upscale choice is the boutique **Beautiful Hotel** (Měilì Chūntiān Dàfàndiàn; ☎ 8666 9999; www .beautifulhotel.com.tw; 8 Taiping Rd, Bitan; 北縣新店市太平路8號; r incl breakfast from NT4200) in the Xindian/Bitan neighbourhood. This hotel seems about the same as the Bitan Hotel, only at twice the price and without the swinging porch chairs. Excellent lobby décor, though.

Taipei Zoo 木柵動物園

The **Taipei Zoo** (Mùzhà Dòngwùyuán; Map pp82–3; ☎ 2938 2300; 30 Xingguang Rd, sec.2; adult/concession NT60/30; ☺ 9am–5pm; MRT Muzha) attracts five million visitors each year, making it one of Taiwan's top attractions. Its sprawling (165 hectares of land that's 1.5km across) grounds include a wide variety of simulated geographical regions, including a tropical rainforest zone, extensive gardens and a beautiful aviary that rivals the one in Hong Kong Park in size and splendour. There's even an enclosed 'nocturnal world' section, kept dark during the day for the benefit of visitors. The zoo features more than 300 species. Eating opportunities abound inside the zoo and lunch boxes are available for around NT70 and snacks cost less. If you feel like something more substantial there's a food court with a Ponderosa Steakhouse next to the zoo.

On the subject of eating, if you feel like feeding the animals, don't. If you must, the crocodiles get peckish around midday; your hands might make a nice snack.

If you don't feel like walking the entire zoo, there's a minitrain (adult/senior NT5/3) that will take you around a circuit. If you really don't feel like walking at all but still want to see the zoo, the newly opened gondola system (see p138 for more details) actually goes over it, with a stop fore and aft, before climbing up to Maokong.

Maokong 貓空

The hills of southern Taipei, known as **Maokong** (Māokōng, cat holes), have a history of tea growing that goes back to the 19th century. These days, however, the money is not in growing tea but selling a pleasing atmosphere for drinking it. Dozens of teahouses now dot the green hills, many with lovely interiors and splendid views. At the time of writing a new gondola was about to open, making these teahouses completely accessible from the city.

SITES & ACTIVITIES
Teahouses

Most teahouses are open from around noon to at least 10pm (later on weekends). Typically you pay for a small packet of tea (enough for a group of four to enjoy for hours) and a 'water fee' of NT50 to NT100 a person. On weekdays you can bring your own tea and just pay the 'water fee', though do note that many teahouses close on Mondays. Teahouse designs vary, allowing you to choose one according to your mood and the weather; indoor or outdoors, traditional or modern, city view or nature view. Most serve food as well as coffee and flower-based drinks and it's usually no problem to visit just for a meal.

PLC Tea Tavern (Hóngmùwū Xiūxián Cháguǎn; Map p137; ☎ 2939 9706; 33 Lane 38, Zhinan Rd, sec.3; 指南路3段38巷33號; dishes NT100-200; ☺ 9.30am-midnight) One

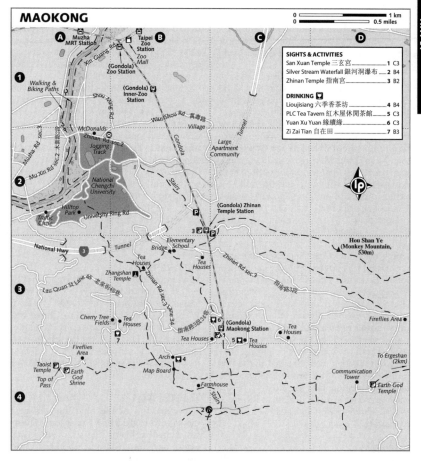

MAOKONG

0   1 km
0   0.5 miles

SIGHTS & ACTIVITIES
San Xuan Temple 三玄宮.................................**1** C3
Silver Stream Waterfall 銀河洞瀑布 **2** B4
Zhinan Temple 指南宮..................................**3** B2

DRINKING
Lioujisiang 六季香茶坊................................**4** B4
PLC Tea Tavern 紅木屋休閒茶館......**5** C3
Yuan Xu Yuan 緣續緣..................................**6** C3
Zi Zai Tian 自在田......................................**7** B3

of our favourites for its old-style brick design and verandas with excellent views across the valley. The food here is quite good too. The chicken soup is tasty and great on a chilly, foggy evening.

Yuan Xu Yuan (Yuán Xù Yuán; Map p137; ☎ 2936 7089; 2nd fl, 16-2 Lane 38, Zhinan Rd, sec.3; 指南路3段38巷 16-2號2樓; dishes NT100–400; ۞ 11am-2am Sun, Tue-Fri, 10am-4am Sat, closed Mon) Just a minute's walk from Maokong station, this fancy-looking place has one of the best city views in Maokong. It's also the only place with private booths where you can spread out on the glass floor with cushions and pillows. Why is the floor glass? So you can watch fish and turtle swim under you.

Zi Zai Tian (Zìzài Tián; Map p137; ☎ 2938 1113; 27 Lane 45 Lao Quan St; 老泉街45巷27號; set meals NT180;

۞ 10am-10pm Mon-Thu, 10am-midnight Fri & Sat, closed Mon) Another gem with a traditional atmosphere inside (the building is a remodelled traditional brick house) and a lovely garden setting outside. Set meals are simple but tasty and there is a veggie option.

Lioujisiang (Liùjìxiāng; Map p137; ☎ 2939 4371; 53 Lane 34, Zhinan Rd, sec.3; 指南路3段34巷53號; ۞ 1pm-midnight) The teahouse is pretty rustic, but the tea (grown on site) is excellent. Try the namesake *liùjìxiāng* (six-seasons fragrant) tea. The arch beside the teahouse leads to the network of trails around Maokong.

Hiking
Maokong's a fantastic area for getting away from it all. The trails are in good shape, natural

(not staired like Yangmingshan) and many thickly wooded sections feel delightfully remote despite the fact that Taipei is just over the ridge. Few trails have any signs on them, however, so bring a compass.

One fun two- to three-hour return hike goes to the **Silver Stream Waterfall** (Yínhé Dòng Pùbù; Map p137). You can get behind the waterfall via a temple built into the cliff beside the falls. Enter the temple and follow the passage to the end. From Maokong station follow the trail beside **San Xuan Temple** (Sān Xuán Gōng; Map p137) up to the ridge, then head straight down. At the bottom head downstream until you reach the falls. An easier route, also on the map, starts beside Lioujisiang teahouse.

Ergeshan (二格山; Èrgéshān; elevation 678m) is the highest point in Maokong. To get to the top, again follow the trail from the temple up to the ridge. Go left this time (not down) and keep to the right side of the ridge for the first while. Look for signs at junctions to keep you on the right path (it's not hard at all if you have any hiking experience). When you reach the paved track by a communication tower (after about 1½ hours), follow it to a small earth-god temple and take the natural trail on the temple's right up. The path runs along a wooded ridge all the way to the platforms at the top of Ergeshan (1½ hours). Returning, take the dirt road by the earth-god temple down to Zhinan Rd, sec.3. Walk a kilometre west for a bus 10 or 15 back to the zoo.

Fireflies

Fireflies appear in Maokong in late April, early May. They are most visible just after sunset for an hour or so. See the map for locations.

Gondola 纜車

The **gondola** (Lǎn Chē; fares NT30-50; ☽ 9am-10pm Mon-Fri, 8.30am-10pm Sat & Sun, public holidays) opened in July 2007. In short, on clear days or nights the views across Taipei and up the valley will be stupendous. On foggy days they will be dreamy.

The gondola ride begins at the Zoo station, just beside the Taipei Zoo MRT station, and goes through two stations before it gets to Maokong. You can alight and disembark at any station. Total travel time is 28 minutes. Travellers can use their Easy Card to pay for fares.

Zhinan Temple 指南宮

In days gone by, the only way up to this **temple** (Zhǐnán Gōng; Map p137) was by walking up 1200 steps. These days, the gondola system takes you to Zhinan Temple station and much closer to the temple than before.

Zhinan Temple sits high above Muzha and on a clear day you can see across Taipei to Yangmingshan. The temple is dedicated to Lu Tung Pin, one of the eight immortals of classic Chinese mythology. Himself a jilted lover, Lu often tries to break up couples who visit his temple before they are married. You'll find that many people still take this superstition very seriously.

As you head down from the gondola, be aware that the big multistorey edifice on the right is not the original 1891 temple. The real deal is further down and has three arches in the front.

GETTING THERE

In addition to the gondola, or your own two feet, you can take bus 15 (NT15) from MRT Taipei Zoo station or bus 10 (NT15) from Wanfang Community station. Buses run every hour on weekdays and every 30 minutes on weekends. Drivers know the teahouses so show them the script characters if you want to go somewhere specific. You can get on or off anywhere.

The Wild West

The extension of the blue line out past the suburb of Tucheng has made convenient neighbourhoods that a few years back would have been too much bother to visit from the city. Below are a few spots that we recommend highly.

MUSEUM OF WORLD RELIGIONS
世界宗教博物館

This beautiful and unique **museum** (Shìjiè Zōngjiào Bówùguǎn; Map pp82-3; ☎ 8231 6699; 7th fl, 236 Zhongshan Rd, sec.1, Yonghe City; www.mwr.org.tw; adult/concession/student NT150/120/80; ☽ 10am-5pm, closed Mon) incorporates symbols, art, ritual objects and ceremonies to illuminate 10 of the world's great religions. Though founded by a Buddhist order, the stated goal of the museum is not to promote Buddhism, but to build harmony by showing the communality of all religions. The museum was designed by the same designer as the Holocaust Museum in Washington, DC. Highlights include scale models of various religious holy sites throughout the world; the insides of most can be viewed via tiny cameras. There are also a number of excellent multimedia presentations, a meditation room and a beautiful gift shop.

Signage in English is mostly good and there's a recorded English audio tour available for NT50. Knowing the religious nature of the exhibits might prove a bit too solemn for the little ones, curators built a small but fun children's museum on the same floor called **Wonderland of Love** (NT100).

Located on the same floor as the museum, the **Tao Shine Vegetarian Restaurant** (Táoshān Sùshí Cāntīng; Map pp82-3; ☎ 8231 6668; 7th fl, 2 Baosheng Rd, Yonghe City; weekday/holiday buffet NT370/398, weekday/holiday tea NT218/250; ◷ 11am-9pm) is good for soul and stomach alike. Its desserts are so fine as to make even the most hardened agnostic see the light.

Take the MRT to Dingxi station and transfer to bus 51, 243, 297, 706 or orange bus 6. All bus fares are NT15. There's also a free shuttle that runs between the station and Pacific Department Store (beside the museum) every 15 minutes. Alternatively, it's about a 10-minute walk from the station.

TAIWAN NOUGAT MUSEUM 牛軋糖博物館
Not Taipei's biggest **museum** (Niúgátáng Bówùguǎn; ☎ 2268 7222; 31 Zihchang St; admission NT50; ◷ 9am-

5pm; MRT Yongning), nor its most well known, but one title that the Taiwan Nougat Museum surely wins hands down is that of 'sweetest museum'. The family that runs this museum and candy factory in Taipei's far-west suburb of Tucheng have been in the business of making nougat, a traditionally important confection for Taiwanese weddings, for over a century. After the family matriarch passed away, her son Chiu Yi-rong decided to transform parts of the newly expanded family factory into a place where families with children could come to learn about the history of nougat in Taiwan, watch sweets and wedding cakes being made, and even make the nougat themselves.

The 1st floor of the museum has nougat exhibits (including the world's biggest chunk of the stuff, covered in edible gold) and a larger showroom with a film in English and Chinese about the history of nougat in Taiwan. On the 2nd floor visitors can watch candy and cakes being made. Though the museum offers DIY candy-making classes for schoolchildren, this is usually reserved for classroom-sized groups as opposed to individual travellers. But a few members of the staff speak English and if you call in advance they'll try to steer you towards a time when individual travellers with kids can join up with a local class for some hands-on nougat making.

Northern Taiwan

If you don't have the time, or perhaps resources, to travel all over Taiwan, you can see much of the best it has to offer within a few hours of Taipei. The north has one of the best networks of hiking trails, an abundance of hot springs, a strong aboriginal presence and three towns devoted to traditional industries.

For something fresh, try swimming or river tracing in the jungle-lined rivers of Pinglin or Wulai. The opportunity to engage in such a splendid sport almost year-round has kept more than one expat happy with life in Taiwan.

The northern trail system begins right at the edge of Taipei and extends, with easy connections, as far as the North Cross-Island Hwy and the northeast coast. Most trails take you through thick forest or steamy jungle, but some run along coastal bluffs or grassy headlands or even across ridges so thin only one person can cross at a time.

The northern towns of Sanyi, Pinglin and Yingge still thrive as centres of traditional industry, producing fine wood carvings, tea and ceramics respectively. It's not uncommon for people to visit Pinglin for tea, then Yingge for a teapot set and finally Sanyi for a traditional table to display everything on handsomely.

Two weeks in the north would just begin to do it justice, while a month would not be too much. We have lived in this area for years and never tire of getting out to explore.

HIGHLIGHTS

- Explore the quaint mining villages of **Jiufen & Jinguashi** (p157)
- Hike and swim under a jungle canopy in **Wulai** (opposite)
- View the work of Taiwan's master carver at the **Juming Museum** (p156)
- Enjoy wild vistas and natural hot springs on the **North Cross-Island Highway** (p166)
- Cycle through tea fields in **Pinglin** (p148)
- Spend the night in a temple on the slopes of **Shitoushan** (p175)
- Soak in top-quality hot spring water in **Taian** (p176)**Jiaoshi** (p163)
- Wander the shops in **Sanyi** (p178), the woodcarving capital of Taiwan
- Tread carefully along the knife-edged ridge of Wuliao Jian in **Sansia** (p152)

National Parks & Forest Recreation Areas

The north has more than its fair share of parks and is a hikers' paradise. Sheipa National Park has the second highest mountain in Taiwan in its Wuling Forest Recreation Area (FRA). Guanwu FRA, on the northern side of Sheipa, was closed at the time of writing, while Syuejian FRA was just about to open. Neidong FRA has three beautiful waterfalls and is a popular birding destination. Manyueyuan FRA is home to a stand of 2000-year-old cedars and is connected to Dongyanshan FRA by a 16km-long trail. Mingchih FRA on the North Cross-Island Hwy makes a great base for exploring an area rich in natural hot springs and old forests.

Getting There & Around

There's good rail and bus transport along the coastlines (except the northern top, which only has bus services). Heading inland, bus routes dry up and you will really need your own transport to visit some places. Traffic is pretty light on weekdays.

The high-speed rail has stops in Taoyuan, Hsinchu and Miaoli, but these won't be of much use to the average traveller.

TAIPEI COUNTY

In many ways the county is the poor cousin of Taipei, but at least transportation is good, and there are some real treats for the nature and culture lover once you get away from the urban sprawl.

WULAI 烏來

☎ 02 / pop 7000

The little aboriginal village of Wulai (Wūlái) has long been touted as one of the top hot-springs resorts in Taiwan. But we advise against spending your money here as the town is pretty grubby (though many hotels are first rate inside) and the water is reportedly not very pure. As one local friend quipped, the only prosperous business in Wulai these days is selling water heaters.

That said, step outside the village and you're in a thickness of jungle that has impressed travellers for 200 years. You can hike, swim, river trace or just picnic by cool mountain streams. There are spectacular waterfalls in the area, some accessible just off the road, others known only to a few, and many excellent bird-watching venues. Even the tourist street in the village is not bad, especially for a hearty meal after a long day in the wilds.

If you're seeking a hot spring, you'll find endless choices and prices, including free ones by the river.

Orientation

Wulai is about 25km almost directly south of Taipei. The main tourist areas are Wulai Hot Springs Village and Wulai Waterfall, 2km from the village. There is a pedestrian-only street in the centre of the village lined with shops and hot-springs hotels.

Dangers & Annoyances

If you go river tracing, plan to be out of any river by 3pm or 4pm. Afternoon showers are a daily occurrence in late spring and summer, and rivers can become swollen very quickly. Also, be on the lookout for snakes. There are no water snakes in Taiwan, but many species sun themselves on the rocks, or hole up in nooks along canyon walls. Leeches are also a nuisance on many of the more overgrown trails.

Sights & Activities

WULAI WATERFALL 烏來瀑布

This 80m-high waterfall (Wūlái Pùbù) is a beauty and the fact that you can float past it on a **gondola** (adult/child NT220/150) is one more reason to come to Wulai. There's a **minitrain** (adult/child NT50/30; ☷ 8am-5pm) to the base, or you can walk the pedestrian route beside the train line.

SWIMMING & RIVER TRACING

Every weekend in the hot summer months river-tracing clubs or informal groups of friends flock to the rivers and streams around Wulai to practise river tracing (suòxī; see p331), which combines scrambling, swimming and hiking (and true technical climbing and rappelling at higher levels).

One popular venue is the **Jia Jiu Liao Stream** (加九寮溪; Jiā Jiǔ Liáo Xī), which features a jungle canopy worthy of a Tarzan film, an amazing natural rock slide and a deep pool large enough for a group to swim in. The stream has no steep inclines and flows relatively gently, so it's pretty easy going but still an absolute joy to trace up.

The best time to go is summer, though on weekend afternoons you may find yourself

NORTHERN TAIWAN

NORTHERN TAIWAN

40 km
20 miles

PACIFIC OCEAN

Foguei Cape
78 Lords Temple
Baishawan Beach
Chianshuiwan Beach
Junjing Museum
Shalun Beach
Bayen Hot Springs
Jinshan Beach
Jinshan
2nd Nuclear Power Plant
Yangmingshan NP
Yangmingshan
Bali
Danshui
Betou
Guanyinshan (616m)

Keelung Island
Green Island
Keelung
Rueifang
Jiufen
Pitou
Jingtong
106
Sandiaoling
Shihting
Pingsi
Maokong

Bitou Cape
Bitou Cape Trail
Longdong
Yenliao
Fulong Beach
Longmen Camp Site
Sandiao Cape
Fulong
Daxi (Miyuewan)
Dali
Wai-ao
Wushih Harbour
Toucheng
Turtle Island

TAIPEI
Banciao
Xindian
Feiciuei Reservoir
Xindian River
Wuliao Jian
Sansia
Dongyanshan
Fusing
Daxi
Shimen Reservoir
Window on China
Leofoo Village
Neiwan
Neiwan Small Rail Line (Temporarily Closed)

Wufengchi Waterfall
Neidong
Wulai
Xiao Wulai Waterfall
Manyuryuan
Fan Fan Hot Spring
Daguanshan (Lalashan; 2030m)
North Cross-Island Hwy
Baling
Cingcyuan Hot Springs

Caoling Historical Trail
Hsuehshan Tunnel
Ilan
Jiaoshi
Luodong
Suao

Renze
Chihlan
Mingchih
Sileng Hot Spring

Chilan
Taipingshan
Nanhutashan (3740m)
Chungyangchienshan

Wangyangshan (2050m)
Cuifeng Lake
Nanfang'ao
Wuta
Nanao

Taroko Gorge
Taroko NP
Tiensiang
Kuanyun
To Hualien (20km)
Chingshui

CKS International Airport
Taoyuan
Taoyuan
Jhongli
Hsinchu
Guofeng
Jhudong
Beipu

Shihtoushan (492m)
Nanzhuang
Touten

Jhunan
Miaoli
Miaoli
Mingde Dam
Talan

Dahajianshan (3492m)
Syueshan (Snow Mountain; 3884m)
Sheipa NP
Guanwu
Syuejian

Wuling
Deji Reservoir
Jishan
Tayuling
Guguan
Bashianshan
Dacunshan

Central Cross-Island Hwy (Permanently Closed)
Dongshih
Fengyuan
Dakeng Scenic Area
Houli
Sanyi

Tunghsiao Beach

TAIWAN STRAIT
TAIWAN STRAIT

sharing the river with organised groups. Follow one to find out where the rock slide is; the general location is about 100m downstream from the big pool. An average person can reach the pool in less than an hour, though it takes most organised groups about two.

To get to the Jia Jiu Liao Stream, take a bus to Wulai and get off just past the 11.5km mark at Cheng Gong Village (成功). Head down the side road for 1km to a large river. Cross the car bridge and then walk up and around until you come to another bridge. The stream that flows under this is the Jia Jiu Liao. Head up the path on the left and then make your way to the stream when the path veers off to the left. The first part of the stream is very crowded on a summer weekends, but after five minutes you will be alone.

HIKING

Taipei Day Trips II (see Hiking, p329) lists some interesting trails in the area that are too detailed for us to mention here. One clear simple path, about an hour long, follows the Nanshih River downstream from Wulai to the Jia Jiu Liao Stream. The path starts near the old tollgate at Wulai St Bridge.

CYCLING

Mountain bikers rave about the trail riding around Wulai, though you'll likely have to go with a local group to actually find the trails. Contact the guys at www.formosanfattire.com or post a message on www.forumosa.com.

One popular route you can do on your own follows the **Tonghou Stream**. From Wulai head east along (and soon high above) the river on the paved road. After a few kilometres you'll pass a police checkpoint. Register using your passport or Alien Resident Certificate (ARC) if you want to go further. The process is simple and costs NT10.

At the end of the road (15km to 20km from Wulai) you can continue on foot, or on mountain bike, along the **Tonghou Trail** (桶后越領古道; Tǒnghòu Yuèlǐng Gǔdào). This goes all the way to Jiaoshi on the east coast and it takes about three to four hours to walk one way. In 2006 the forestry bureau expanded, marked and signposted the trail making the way completely clear.

BIRD-WATCHING

Wulai is renowned for its bird-watching areas and there are two main routes birders take.

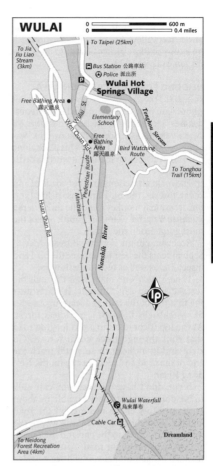

One follows the path to Neidong Forest Recreation Area (p144). The other follows the Tonghou Stream, starting from the parking lot in Wulai.

To begin, cross the first bridge and then take a left before Wulai St (the tourist street). Follow the road along the Tonghou Stream for a short distance, then turn right up a small road. The loop road/trail that eventually leads back to the road alongside the Tonghou Stream is said to be the best bird-watching area in Wulai. A word of warning though: the route is often littered with rubbish.

Among the birds you can see in Wulai are river kingfishers, collared owls, the yellow-throated minivet and the Indian black eagle. Winter is a particularly good viewing time

NORTHERN TAIWAN

as many mid-altitude species migrate to the lower river valleys. For more information pick up a copy of *Birdwatcher's Guide to the Taipei Region*, and see p328.

NEIDONG FOREST RECREATION AREA
内洞森林遊樂區

About 4km past Wulai Waterfall is this **recreation area** (Nèidòng Sēnlín Yóulè Qū; http://recreate.forest.gov .tw; adult/child NT80/40), popularly known as Wawagu, or 'Valley of the Frogs'. This place alone is wonderful enough to make it worth a dedicated trip.

The main attractions are the broadleaf and cedar forests, the bird and insect life (and the occasional monkey), and the three-tiered **Hsinhsian Waterfall** (Xìnxián Pùbù), one of the most gorgeous in the north.

According to the Forestry Bureau, May to September is the best time to see the bird and insect life, as well as blooming flowers.

There's only one main trail through the reserve so you can't miss it. It starts near the first tier of the falls and leads up a series of switchbacks through a broadleaf forest. At the top it connects to a dirt logging road that runs through thick cedar forests. Go right and in an hour or so you'll reach the end of the road and reconnect with the Neidong River.

If you don't have a vehicle you can walk to Neidong without much trouble in about an hour. Most of the route is off the road and flat. Take the pedestrian walkway or the minitrain in Wulai to the end and then make your way to the main road. After you pass through a small tunnel you will see a bridge on the left. Cross it and follow the abandoned road on the other side upstream all the way to Neidong.

Eating

Aboriginal cuisine is the standard fare in Wulai. A few mouth-watering selections that can be found at any number of shops along Wulai St include mountain vegetables and wild pig (not really wild any more in the Wulai area), *zhútǒng fàn* (竹桶飯; sticky rice steamed and served in bamboo tubes) and freshwater fish. Snacks and alcoholic drinks made from *xiǎomǐ* (小米; millet) can be found at many shops and stalls in the village.

Note that there is no food near Neidong.

Getting There & Away

Buses to Wulai (NT32, 40 minutes, every 30 minutes) run frequently from near the Taipei Xindian MRT station (the last stop on the line). When you get off the escalators, walk to the main road in front of the station and turn right. Walk two blocks to the bus stop just past the 7-Eleven. Buses are not numbered but they now have English signs.

PINGXI BRANCH RAIL LINE 平溪支線
☎ 02

Of the three small branch lines that have remained open for tourism, this 12km track (Píngxī Zhīxiàn) is the closest to Taipei, and our favourite by a long shot. For one thing, it's a highly scenic ride through a wild, wooded gorge. Furthermore, the stops are full of rewarding sights and activities, including thrilling hikes, high waterfalls, river pools to swim in, and the remains of what was once a thriving coal industry. Pingxi town itself is the site of the annual sky lantern release during Lantern Festival, an event not to be missed (see the boxed text, p149).

The Pingxi line branches off from the main east coast trunk line at Sandiaoling and ex-

---

DAY TRIPS FROM TAIPEI

All of the following can be reached by public transport from Taipei within an hour.

- The emerald tea fields and bike paths of **Pinglin** (p148)
- The swimming holes, hiking trails and hot springs of **Wulai** (p141)
- The old streets of **Sansia** (p152) and the nearby ceramic shops and museum of **Yingge** (p151)
- The sand and surf of **Fulong Beach** (p160) and **Baishawan Beach** (p156)
- The waterfalls, mines and craggy peaks along the **Pingxi Branch Rail Line** (above)
- The teahouses and gold mines of **Jiufen & Jinguashi** (p157)
- The six-hour **Bijia Shan Trail** (p150) ridge walk from Shihting to Maokong

Pick up a copy of *Taipei Day Trips* (see Hiking, p329) for many more ideas.

WALKING THE WALK WITH PROF HUANG *Robert Kelly*

I've been invited by a friend to join the TMITRAIL Association for a hike from Wulai to Jiaoshi along the historic Tonghou Trail. As I've wanted to do this hike for almost 10 years, and to meet the association and its founder, Professor Huang Wu-hsiung (黃武雄), since I first read about them in the local papers, I can't say no.

TMITRAIL Association, which stands roughly for 'a thousand kilometres of trails around the island', began as the vision of Professor Huang to rebuild Taiwanese people's relationship with nature through a network of walking and biking paths. 'We should be able to walk from village to village, as in the old days', Huang says, 'but we can't because the priority has been to make roads accessible for cars, not walkers'.

And yet, many of Taiwan's mountain roads are so seldom used that they do in fact form an extensive walking system already. To prove this I set out in autumn 2006 to walk from Taipei to Daxi on the east coast with my hiking partners Chris Nelson and Peter Widdle. In what turned out to be a classic example of ideas cross-fertilising, the TMITRAIL Association later learned about our walk and drew their own inspiration from it.

Now when I meet the association I am rather amused that everyone, including the media, know who I am. 'So who's the fellow who walked to Daxi?', I hear a reporter shout out, and before I realise it's me, all fingers are already pointing in my direction.

Professor Huang, the founder, is late arriving. When he does I can't help but notice he is dressed in a white cotton collared shirt and khaki pants. If he was part of my hiking club, I would have long ago introduced him to the wonders of quick-drying fabric. But his outfit is pretty standard for men of his generation, as is the old smooth stick he uses for a walking pole. In any case, he is as fast a walker as I am, and seems to sweat a lot less.

Professor Huang doesn't have a sad face, but he looks sad for most of the day. When I first get the chance to ask him why he started the association, he says wearily, 'Because I had to'. Taiwan needs civic groups to stand in opposition to politicians who focus solely on economic development. If Taiwan is ever to reach the living standards of Western countries, with their order, cleanliness and civic mindedness, it will have to come through bottom-up organisations such as TMITRAIL.

Huang is well aware he is preaching a new idea, but I soon see that he is serious about taking the message directly to the people. As we walk along a section of pitch, he stops to talk to two workers expanding the road. He explains to the men how their actions are making the road more prone to washouts, and also increasing people's ability to drive faster (thus making the road even more likely to be damaged, to say nothing of making it unsuitable for walking). At first I think the professor is preaching to the wrong people (what can these guys do?), but later I realise that this is the whole point of his mission: to get ordinary people thinking and involved in changes.

As we talk further, I realise that Professor Huang is actually not very sanguine about the future of Taiwan. Despite the widespread practice of recycling, and huge improvements in air and water quality, he feels the overall environmental situation has worsened in the past 10 years. I understand his point, but can't quite agree with his pessimism. I'm a bit Pollyanna-ish for sure, but these days I'm meeting more and more people, such as the professor, who are willing to do something concrete to improve this island. And this surely will make all the difference.

tends to Jingtong, about a 30-minute ride east of the Taipei Zoo. The most interesting stops are Sandiaoling, Shifen, Pingxi and Jingtong. The entire ride takes about 45 minutes.

At the Shifen Scenic Administration Office (☎ 2495 8409; 🕑 8am-5.30pm), near Shifen station, you can pick up English-language brochures and consult the large maps on the 1st floor.

Getting There & Around

If you are going to start at Sandiaoling, catch a direct train from Taipei, though note there are usually only two or three in the morning hours. If you are going to any other stop, first take a train to Ruifang (fast/slow train NT80/62, 40/50 minutes, every 30 minutes) and then transfer to the Pingxi line on the same platform. All-day train passes cost NT50

NORTHERN TAIWAN

and give you a discount on admission to the Shifen Waterfall.

Alternatively, you can catch a bus from Muzha MRT station. From the station walk south to the main road and cross the street to catch bus 16. At the time of writing the buses came by around 7.30am, 8.20am and 9.45am every day (NT45). For the return schedule check the bus stop signs in Pingxi. If you have three or four people in your group, consider taking a 30-minute taxi ride (approximately NT450) from Muzha MRT.

Every sight listed along the Pingxi Branch Rail Line can be reached easily on foot from the various stations. The track is only 12km long and trains only come by every hour or so, so it is possible to walk part or all of it. There are a few tunnels – be extremely careful going through these – but if you carry a torch and a schedule of the trains, you should be fine. If you do hear a train coming, note that there are special alcoves built into the tunnel walls for you to squeeze into.

Sandiaoling Waterfall Trail
三貂嶺瀑布步道

This wonderful trail (Sāndiāolǐng Pùbù Bǔdào) starts just a few minute's walk from the first stop along the Pingxi line and is a must-visit for any waterfall lover. In just a couple of hours you can see three of the highest and most beautiful falls in the north in their natural glory. The second waterfall even allows you to get right in behind it via a cave formed by the overhang: it's like something out of *The Last of the Mohicans*. If you have the afternoon or the whole day, you can see at least four more falls, and if you are willing to river trace a little, seven more after that.

To get to the trailhead, exit the station and follow the tracks south until they split. Cross over and follow the tracks to the right (the Pingxi line). After a few minutes you will see the wooden signpost (it's in English) for the trailhead. The trail is simple and clear to follow at least as far as the third fall (about an hour away). If you want to continue after this all the way to Shifen station (further down the Pingxi line) pick up a copy of *Taipei Day Trips II* (see Hiking, p329) or go with someone who knows the trail. It's not difficult, except for a couple of climbs up ladders, but it is a little tricky with the turns.

Shifen 十分

The upstream watersheds of the Keelung River receive more than 6000mm of rain a year and have more waterfalls than any other river system in Taiwan. One of the most spectacular is the 40m-wide **Shifen Waterfall** (十分瀑布; Shífēn Pùbù; adult/child NT180/100; 7.30am-6pm), the broadest waterfall in Taiwan.

A park has been built up around the falls, complete with coffee shops, lookouts and stone trails that allow you to get right beside the falls. It's outrageously expensive to get in, and we object to the walls the owners have set up along the tracks, blocking any view to the falls, but the falls are truly something to see after a heavy rain.

To reach the falls, turn right as you exit the train at Shifen station. Walk about 15 minutes until you come to a split in the road. Follow the lower road for another five minutes to the tourist office. The waterfall path begins behind this building and takes another 15 minutes of walking. Note: don't mistake (as many do) the first set of falls you encounter, called the Eyeglasses Waterfall, for the much larger Shifen Waterfall.

Back in town, a few minutes' walk in the direction of Taipei from Shifen station leads to the 40-hectare **Taiwan Coal Mine History & Culture Exhibition Hall** (台灣煤礦歷史文化陳列館; Táiwān Méikuàng Lìshǐ Wénhuà Chénlièguǎn; ☎ 2495 8680; 5 Tingliao Tsu; adult/child NT200/160; 8.30am-5.30pm). This was once a real coal-mining station and everything on display is authentic mining equipment: from the rotors to the motors, conveyor belts, coal washing machines, electric transport trains and mine tunnels. There's also a 1km electric-train ride to the main coal tunnel, and working jiggers with 100m of track to practise your pumping skills on. Most travellers can give this place a miss unless they have young children or a deep interest in coal history.

One of our favourite **day hikes** begins just behind the coal mine. Take the road to the left just before the entrance to the mine hall and follow it for about 1km. When it splits, take the road on the right down to the coal mine area. Swing round the mine to the left and you'll see the start of a trail. It's straight up for the first 40 minutes, but then levels out and runs along the top of a ridge until the peak of Wufenshan (五分山; Wǔfēnshān). The view from up here is perfect through 360 degrees, with the ocean to the east and mountain ranges in every other direction. Go on a clear day and give yourself around four hours for the return trip.

Around Shifen station you can sample traditional snacks such as *mìfānshǔ* (蜜蕃薯; sweet potatoes cooked in wheat sugar) and *zhēngyùtóu* (蒸芋頭; steamed taro).

Pingxi 平溪

Pingxi (Píngxī) is a bit grubby (though there were efforts at the time of writing to fix up the old village), but there are two reasons you should make a stop here: the Pingxi crags and the sky lanterns (see the Lantern Festival boxed text, p149).

If you've got a head for heights and like unusual hikes, don't miss out on the series of **crags** *(*慈母峰*; címǔfēng)* literally across the street from the train station. The highest crag is only 450m or so, but you must scramble up metal ladders and steps carved right into the rock face to reach the top. No technical skill is required, but it's an adrenalin rush nonetheless.

To reach the crags, head down to the road from the train station and look for an old map beside a set of stairs on the other side of the street. Follow the stairs up to a temple. Just beyond the temple is a dead-end road. The well-marked and easy-to-follow trails start here. It doesn't matter which crag you climb first, but we usually head right at the first junction and do a loop back to the road.

As if Pingxi wasn't enough fun already, there is a fantastic little **swimming hole** that has become sufficiently well known that we can let you in on it, but not so well known you won't want to go because of the crowds. The pool is 5m deep and has a small waterfall at the back you can stand under.

To reach the pools, walk to the main road from the train station and go right. Just past the spiffy-looking red-brick school you'll see a set of stairs to the left (if you cross the bridge over a small stream you've gone too far). Head up the stairs and continue along the flat. Veer right and stay on the flat trail at the second set of stairs. Walk 30m and look down into the ravine: you'll see the edge of the pools.

Note that if you head up the second set of stairs you will reach a rocky path that leads to an old mining area we call **Gollum's Lair**. It's an interesting place to explore.

Jingtong 菁桐

The coal mining industry in the Pingxi area operated for 100 years before finally closing in the mid-1980s. **Jingtong station** (菁桐站; Jīngtóng zhàn), the last station on the line, once served as a major centre for coal shipping. Today it has one of the best-preserved traditional station houses in Taiwan. With nearby coal carts, train engines, a **photo museum** (admission free; ☉ 9am-6pm) and an 'old street', it's a fun place to explore and take pictures. For more on the history of coal mining in Taiwan check out www.taipeitimes.com/News/feat/archives/2002/09/29/170075.

Another place to check out in town is **Prince's Guesthouse** (太子賓館; Tàizǐ Bīnguǎn; admission NT50; ☉ 10am-5pm Sat, Sun & holidays), a sprawling 10-room Japanese-style wooden house built in 1939 with wood from Alishan. Today, both the interior and exterior are in almost perfect condition, only in need of a little spit and polish (and paint) around the edges. On weekends you can tour inside the house and examine the old furniture, books and rooms.

The house sits on a little picturesque flat by the river. To reach it, exit Jingtong station, turn right and follow the 'old street' to the main road. Cross the street to the bridge and you'll see the house to the right in a cluster of trees. You can't miss it.

There's some great **hiking** around Jingtong and the excellent trails are never crowded, even on weekends. One favourite short hike is up to the pyramid-shaped **Shulong Point** (Shǔláng Jiān; 622m). It's the highest mountain in the area and you can see Taipei 101 from the top. We also highly recommend **Fengtou Point** (Fēngtóu Jiān), a tough but exhilarating ridge walk. For details on these and other hikes in the area pick up a copy of *Taipei Day Trips II* (see Hiking, p329).

For something to eat, try **Palace Restaurant** (皇宮咖啡簡餐; Huánggōng Kāfēi Jiǎncān; set meals NT220; ☉ 11am-9pm Tue-Sun). Set in a short row of Japanese-era houses, this restaurant has both an old-time wooden interior and good food. Guests can sit on the floor, Japanese style, or at tables. To reach the restaurant, cross the bridge by Prince's Guesthouse and turn right; it's 100m down the road. There are signs in Chinese.

Moca Cafe (紅寶精典咖啡餐坊; Hóngbǎo Jīngdiǎn Kāfēi Cānfāng; ☉ 9am-6pm) only serves drinks. Make sure you try the traditional and hearty *miànchá* (麵茶; sesame paste drink; NT30); it's great on a chilly day. When you exit the train station, turn right and follow the 'old street' 30m to this shop. You can't miss it as it has a blown-up photocopy of its Lonely Planet *Taiwan* entry plastered on the front with a caption about foreigners going crazy about their drinks (indulge them).

PINGLIN 坪林

☎ 02 / pop 7000

Pinglin (Pínglín), which means 'forest on level ground', is famous nationwide for its locally grown bao chung tea. Only an hour from Taipei by bus (about 24km east of Xindian), it is also well loved by day-trippers for its emerald mountain landscape, picture-perfect tea fields, scenic bike paths and clear, swimmable (and kayakable) rivers teeming with fish. The town also features the world's largest tea museum, where you can learn not only how tea is grown and processed, but also how to drink it.

Information & Orientation

The town is quite small and easy to navigate. You can walk from the tea museum to the end of the dykes in 40 minutes. Admission to the tea museum includes a large foldout map of the area. It's all in Chinese but the

photographs and intuitive symbols make it useful nonetheless.

Pinglin Township is large and encompasses endless mountains, rivers, campgrounds and hiking trails. We only scratch the surface of the area here, essentially concentrating on places you can get to if you don't have your own vehicle. If you do, the Sunriver Maps (see p331) give a great overview. Country Rd 42, heading east, is particularly rich in camping spots, hiking trails and places to swim in the rivers.

Sights & Activities

TEA MUSEUM 茶葉博物館

This place has everything you ever wanted to know about tea – and then some. The two floors of the classically designed **museum** (Cháyè Bówùguǎn; ☎ 2665 6035; fax 2665 7138; adult/child NT100/50; ☉ 9am-5pm Tue-Fri, 8am-9pm Sat & Sun) feature all manner of displays, dioramas, charts, equipment and, of course, tea in all its forms. There are sections on the history of tea production in Taiwan and China, the culture of tea drinking and tea-making methods over the centuries. All exhibits now have complete English translations.

NORTHERN TAIWAN

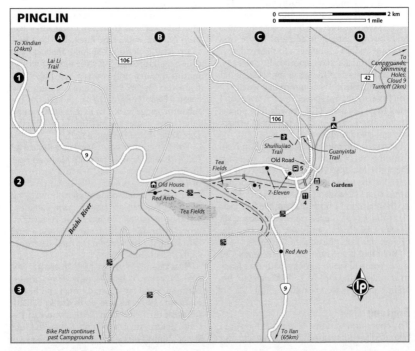

PINGLIN

0 —— 2 km
0 —— 1 mile

To Xindian (24km)
Lai Li Trail
106
To Campgrounds; Swimming Holes; Cloud 9 Turnoff (2km)
42
106
3
Shuiliujiao Trail
Guanyintai Trail
Tea Fields
Old Road
5
9
Old House
1
7-Eleven
Gardens
2
Red Arch
4
Tea Fields
Beishi River
Red Arch
9
To Ilan (65km)
Bike Path continues past Campgrounds

LANTERN FESTIVAL 元宵節

Lantern Festival (Yuánxiāo Jié) is quickly emerging as one of the most popular holiday events in Taiwan. And why not? Of all the ancient Chinese festivals, this one has best been reimagined for the modern age, with spectacular light shows, live concerts and giant glowing mechanical lanterns showing across the island. And yet, one of the best spectacles is still the simplest and most traditional: the sky lantern release in Pingxi.

A sky lantern (tiāndēng) is a large paper lantern with a combustible element attached to the underside. When the element is lit, hot air rises into the lantern sack and the lantern floats into the sky like a hot-air balloon.

In Pingxi people have been sending sky lanterns into the air for generations. Long ago, the remote mountainous villages were prone to attacks from bandits and marauders. Sky lanterns were used to signal to others, often women and children, to get packing and head into the high hills at the first sign of trouble. But today it's all about the sublime thrill of watching glowing colourful objects float up against a dark sky. Check out www.youtube.com for a teaser.

During the festival, which is spread out over two weekends, there are shuttle buses all day to the site. After dark, lanterns are released en masse every 20 minutes. Usually the participants in these events have been chosen beforehand, but if you hang around you may be asked to replace someone who didn't show up.

If you wish to light your own lantern, remember first to write some special wish on it. Then light the combustible element, wait till the paper sack has filled with hot air and made the skin taut and let your lantern go. As it floats away to the heavens repeat your wishes to yourself... and pray your lantern doesn't burn up prematurely and crash down into the crowds, or light a tent on fire, as occasionally happens.

See p337 for more information.

Sharing the grounds with the museum is a faux-classical style teahouse. There is a leaflet (in English) available to help as you follow the steps to make tea the proper way (around NT200 per person). Staff are also on hand to offer assistance.

CYCLING

After you've learned a little about how tea is grown and made, it's time to see it for yourself in the fields. Pinglin's **bike path** (jiǎotàchē zhuānyòng dào) runs for almost 20km through open tea fields and along an unspoiled river valley with deep pools loaded with fish (kudos to the town for really enforcing the ban on fishing). Take a rest in one of the tiny hamlets

along the way and you may see tea leaves spread on the ground drying, or even roasting in a tea oven.

No cars are permitted on the sections that run through the tea fields. From the 'old house', much of the route is on a raised footpath, making these areas safe for children to ride on. In any case, cars are few and far between even on the road sections, as the route finishes at a dead end.

You can rent bikes (per day NT250) at the He Huan Campground (see Sleeping, p150) any time of day. Helmets and locks are not provided. From the campground, ride back towards town and then follow Hwy 9 south for about 700m. Turn right at the big red arch and you are at the start of the bike route. Alternatively, you can follow the river and ride through the tea fields. Either way, signs denoting bike path guide the way.

It takes two leisurely hours to cycle to the end and about an hour to return.

SWIMMING

There are many sweet spots for a dip in the rivers around Pinglin. Head northeast on Country Rd 42 (the river here is very clean) or follow the bike path to the end.

HIKING

In the hills just back from town and along the rivers there are short paths suitable for families and strolling couples. To get to the trailhead for the **Guanyintai Trail** (Guānyīntái Bùdào), cross the bridge near the museum, turn right and walk about 200m. The stairs on the left take you up to the giant Guanyin statue that overlooks Pinglin.

At the end of the trail cross County Rds 42 and 106 and continue to the suspension bridge at the beginning of town. From here you can walk along the river back to the museum.

Children usually like watching the 'flashing fish' along the **Fish-Viewing Path** (Guānyú Bùdào). A return trip from the museum takes about 1½ hours.

If you have your own vehicle there are numerous, more challenging trails in the Pinglin area. Look for the trail signs (in English and Chinese) around town to point you in the right direction.

Sleeping

In addition to the **He Huan Campground** (Héhuān Lùyíng Dùjià Shānzhuāng; ☎ 2665 6424), there are numerous campgrounds heading south along the bike path and along Country Rd 42. Our favourite spot just off along the route is **Cloud 9** (☎ 0911-126 337; www.cloud9tw.com; Pinglin Township; camping per person NT200), run by a friendly South African family who've made Taiwan their home.

The campground sits on a shady grassy flat beside the Beishi River. It's in a prime spot with several deep but calm swimming holes just steps away, and numerous hiking and biking trails nearby. The owners are avid kayakers and offer lessons and rentals. They also offer two- to five-hour inner-tubing excursions down the Beishi River. A maximum of 30 people are permitted to camp at one time, which is a welcome change from the more-the-merrier (and louder-the-better) locally run sites. Meals are available (NT150 to NT200) and there are also kitchen and barbecue facilities.

Cloud 9 is a bit tricky to get to from central Pinglin, so call for a pick-up or consider taking a taxi from Taipei Main Station. The campground has a working relationship with a local driver and the fee is NT500 to NT600 (very reasonable if there are a few of you). You don't need your own transportation once you are here. Note that at the time of writing the campground was only open on weekends.

Eating

He Huan Restaurant (Héhuān Cháyàn Fēngwèi Cāntīng; ☎ 2665 7775; 5-1 Shuide Village; dishes NT200; ◷ 11am–6pm) The speciality here is food made with tea. Not every dish is successful in our opinion, but the *cháyè xiāngsū* (茶葉香酥; deep-fried tea leaves; NT150) are a hit with most people. The menu is in Chinese but there are pictures to aid selection.

For simple, cheap fare there are noodle shops along the main road and a 7-Eleven that sells sandwiches.

Shopping

On the main drag into town there's no end of stores selling tea and products made with tea. While tea jellies, Popsicles and *tǒngzǎi mǐgāo* (筒仔米糕; sticky rice) are inexpensive, a jar of good *bāo zhǒng chá* (包種茶; bao chung tea), the local speciality, can cost thousands of dollars. In our opinion, though, it is one of the most delicious teas in Taiwan and easily appreciated by the untrained palate.

Getting There & Away

Pinglin is a popular destination and it's simple to get there by public transport. In Taipei, take the MRT to Xindian station. Turn right on the main road in front of the station and walk to the 7-Eleven. Just past the 7-Eleven you'll see a bus stop. Buses to Pinglin run about every hour to 90 minutes (NT68).

The bus drops you off in the centre of Pinglin. It's a short walk from here to the museum. Note that the last bus to Taipei leaves Pinglin at 5pm.

SHIHTING (SHIDING) 石碇
☎ 02 / pop 300

The little town of Shihting (Shídìng) sits in the hills about 15km east of Maokong. There's not much to see in the town itself, though locals do commend the various tofu dishes you can get on the 'old street'. For the foreign traveller there are two excellent hikes that shouldn't be missed: Huangdi Dian (皇帝殿; Huángdì Diàn) and Bijia Shan (筆架山; Bìjià Shān). Huangdi Dian runs east of Shihting along a narrow ridge that in parts is no more than 20cm wide – with sheer drops on the right and left! There are ropes and guide poles in place in the more dangerous parts, but still, don't go if you haven't a head for heights.

The Bijia Shan trail runs west of Shihting all the way to Maokong and is a safer but still immensely satisfying hike along a wooded ridge. Give yourself about six hours for this trail, and four to six hours for Huangdi Dian.

Shihting can be reached by taking bus 666 (the bus of the beast as we call it; NT15, 20 minutes, frequent service in the morning) from Muzha MRT station. Exit the station, walk to the main road and cross to reach the bus stop.

Both trails have a few too many twists and turns (some to avoid) for us to give you safe directions in a few words. Pick up a copy of *Taipei Day Trips I & II* (see Hiking, p329) for a full description.

YINGGE 鶯歌
☎ 02 / pop 83,468

C is for Ceramics. C is for – Yingge? Well, not quite, but 'Yingge is for ceramics' is something almost any Taiwanese can chant. This little town (Yīnggē) in the very southern part of Taipei County lives by and for the production of high- and low-quality ceramic and pottery objects: everything from cupboard handles to Song-dynasty vases.

Pottery was introduced to Yingge in 1804, and a century later ceramics also began to be developed. Both industries flourished due to the excellent local clay and good local transport network, originally using the river and later rail. In recent years the town made the successful leap from manufacturing base to cultural venue. The opening in 1999 of the NT6-billion Yingge Ceramics Museum and the creation of the 'Old Street' solidified this crossover and put Yingge on the traveller's map for lovers of traditional crafts.

Yingge makes an enjoyable, long day trip from Taipei and fits in naturally with a stopover at nearby Sansia for a look at the masterfully restored Tzushr Temple and the nearby blocks of Qing- and Japanese-era buildings.

Orientation

At the train station, English signs direct you left or right to the Old Street and ceramics museum. Ignore the signs and exit on the right side of the station no matter where you want to go. Turn right when you're outside and walk down the road until you reach a big four-way intersection. To get to the Old Street, turn right, pass through the tunnel and then head towards the arches on the left. The Old Street begins here.

To reach the ceramics museum, turn left at the four-way and walk for another five minutes. Just past the petrol station you'll see the museum on the right.

The Old Street is pedestrian only (most of the time), but there are few footpaths in Yingge and a lot of traffic, which makes walking about unpleasant. If you're travelling with children consider taking a taxi (NT100 to the museum).

Sights & Activities
YINGGE CERAMICS MUSEUM
鶯歌陶瓷博物館

Most people think that pottery and ceramics are the same thing, but they are quite different. They use different types of clay and are fired at very different temperatures: pottery under 1250°C, ceramics above 1260°C. Humans have been making pottery for around 8000 years, but only mastered the ceramic process around 3000 years ago.

If you didn't know this (as we didn't), then it's time to head to the very stylish and terrifically informative **Yingge Ceramics Museum** (Yīnggē Táocí Bówùguǎn; ☎ 8677 2727; www.ceramics.tpc .gov.tw; 200 Wenhua Rd; adult/child NT100/70; ⏱ 9.30am-5pm Tue-Fri, to 6pm Sat & Sun). This is really one of our favourite museums in Taiwan, in part because of the exposed concrete and steel design. Exhibits cover everything from 'snake kilns' (see p224) to the various woods used in firing, and influences on Taiwanese ceramics from China, Japan and the Netherlands. Special exhibitions of local artists show the direction modern ceramics is taking, and the occasional humorous exhibit and flashy videos help to keep interest high as you move around the three floors.

Adults can make their own pots on weekends, while supervised children's workshops (for kids four to eight years old) are run every day (NT75 for materials). Instructions are in Chinese only, though it's common to have someone around who can speak English and help out. Call for times.

YINGGE OLD STREET 鶯歌老街

Dozens of pottery shops and stalls, large and small, compete for your business on the Old Street (Lǎo Jiē) and you could spend hours just browsing. Prices start at around NT30 for a cup or saucer, but these will most certainly be mass-produced in China. Quality handmade Yingge pieces can cost tens of thousands, though many of the best shops are not even on the Old Street.

The Old Street, although not really old at all is somewhat quaint, with its cobbled roads, traditional street lamps and a walk-in kiln. At the time of writing the street was getting a lot of added character in the form of red-brick façades and cleaned-up buildings. Most shops close between 6pm and 7pm.

Eating

On the Old Street there are plenty of vendors to help you line your stomach. Next to the museum you'll find a street filled with small restaurants and noodle shops.

Getting There & Away

Trains from Taipei (NT31, 30 minutes) run about every 30 minutes.

SANSIA (SANXIA) 三峽

☎ 02 / pop 86,958

Across National Hwy 3 from Yingge is this old town (Sānxiá), most noted for a temple that has been under reconstruction since 1947 and a couple of blocks of perfectly restored Qing- and Japanese-era buildings. In short, Sansia and Yingge go hand in hand, contrasting and complementing each other like peanut butter and chocolate.

Sights & Activities

TZUSHR TEMPLE 祖師廟

Originally constructed in 1769, this **temple** (Zǔshī Miào) has been rebuilt three times. The last involved the life's work of Professor Li Mei-shu, a Western-trained painter who supervised reconstruction with such fastidious care that today the temple is a showcase of carving, painting and temple reliefs. For example, while most temples have a couple of dragon pillars, this one has 156. There are also a number of features you'll not see in another temple in Taiwan, such as bronze doors, carvings of bears, turkeys and octopuses, and even Greek-style gargoyles. Pick up an English brochure at the temple for a very thorough introduction.

The temple is dedicated to the Divine Progenitor and is the centre of religious life in Sansia. It's liveliest on the deity's birthday, the sixth day after Chinese New Year.

If you plan to see only one temple in Taiwan, make it this one. It's often the first place

guests are taken to when they arrive in Taiwan, as it's on the way from the airport to Taipei. No one has failed to be impressed.

MINCHUAN OLD STREET 民權老街

Take a walk back in time on this old street (lǎo jiē), which features several blocks of red-brick shops dating from the end of the Qing dynasty to the early years of the Japanese colonial era. If you look closely you can see a diversity of styles in the shop façades as they incorporate traditional Chinese, Japanese and Western baroque elements. Note that the mortar used for the bricks is sticky rice and crushed seashells.

At the time of writing the street had just completed its renovations and was looking much as it must have 80 years ago. To reach the old street turn right as you exit the temple and walk up the alley to Minquan (Minchuan) St.

HIKING

There are some excellent hikes in the Sansia area, including many people's favourite in all the north: **Wuliao Jian** (五寮尖; Wǔliáo Jiān). The Wuliao Jian trail take about six hours to finish, but it doesn't cover much ground as most of it involves treading lightly along a knife-edge ridge. These days you'll find secure ropes and guide poles in place, and they really are necessary. On one section, for example, you must go up and along a bumpy narrow slice of rock that's exposed on all sides. Years ago, when we first hiked the route, there was only a thin rope attached to the flat of the ridge and you actually had to straddle the rock and shimmy across. It was insane then; now it's just a good thrill.

Needless to say, don't go unless you have a good head for heights and are in the mood for a challenge.

Like many hikes, this one has a few too many twists and turns for us to describe safely in a short space. Once again consult *Taipei Day Trips II* (see Hiking, p329) for full information, including transport. One transport option not included, however, is to take the MRT to Yongning Station (the last on the blue line) and then a taxi (NT300). It's worth it if your group numbers several people, as bus service is very infrequent to the trailhead. At the temple at the end of the hike you can ask for a taxi to come and pick you up.

Getting There & Away

From Yingge, the only sensible way to get to Sansia is by taxi (from ceramics museum to temple NT110).

MANYUEYUAN FOREST RECREATION AREA 滿月圓森林遊樂區

This **recreation area** (Mǎnyuèyuán Sēnlín Yóulè Qū; http://recreate.forest.gov.tw; adult/child NT100/75; ☻ 8am-5pm) is truly a park for all seasons, and all people. The first section has paved or cobbled paths, scenic pavilions and short walks to a number of gorgeous waterfalls. It's perfect for families or strolling couples.

Once you get past this section, however, you're on natural trails that take you through sweet-smelling cedar forests, up to mountain peaks and, further afield, to a stand of **giant ancient cedars** (神木; shénmù). The trail starts up a short incline to the right of the bathrooms at the end of the paved route to Manyueyuan Waterfall. It's broad and clear, takes about four hours to hike and has many side branches. The main route connects Manyueyuan with Dongyanshan Forest Recreation Area (p168), but note that there is no public transport to and from Dongyanshan. If you walk there you must walk back.

The trails to the old cedars, and to the higher mountains, are unfortunately not straightforward enough for us to write up in a short space. They are fairly popular trails though and anyone in decent shape can manage them. Get a copy of Taipei Day Trips II (see Hiking, p329) for clear directions.

Autumn is a nice time to visit the park as the gum and soap-nut trees are changing colours. Fireflies come out in the spring and summer, though we have seen them as late as October. You can often spot monkeys further into the park during the day. Be aware that the park has its own microclimate, and while it may be sunny and dry in Taipei, it could be cool and wet here.

To get to the park take an infrequent **Taipei Bus Company** (☎ 2671 1914; NT48) bus from the station on Dayung Rd (台北客運三峽站 大勇路) in Sansia to Lele Valley (樂樂谷; Lèlè Gǔ). From Lele Valley it's about a 30- to 40-minute walk to the park gates. If you can get a few people together, take a taxi (NT450) from Yongning MRT station to the park. You may be able to get a taxi back on a busy summer weekend, but don't count on it. Hitchhiking into Sansia is an option, as well as walking down to Lele Valley and catching the bus. The last bus leaves Lele Valley around 6pm (call the Taipei Bus Company to confirm).

KEELUNG TO DANSHUI

☎ 02

This pleasant route follows Provincial Hwy 2 as it winds along the top of the island. To one side, the blue ocean stretches to the horizon, while to the other, the lush dark-green hills of Yangmingshan National Park (see p132) rise up to dominate the sky. Public transport is limited to buses, but these are frequent and hit every place we mention.

There are a few good swimming beaches along the way, a couple of excellent hot-spring resorts and a great little sculpture museum. At the time of writing, Fuguei Cape, the most northerly point in Taiwan, was getting a new look, along the lines of Fisherman's Wharf in Danshui. Let us know how it turned out.

Most of this area falls under the auspices of the **North Coast & Guanyinshan Scenic Administration** (☎ 2636 4503; www.northguan-nsa.gov.tw/en/index.php; ☻ 8am-5pm). By the time you read this, its headquarters and visitor centre should have moved back to Baishawan Beach from its temporary home in Sanjhi.

KEELUNG (JILONG) 基隆

☎ 02 / pop 399,000

Keelung (Jīlóng) is a port city, the second largest in Taiwan, and has the rough-around-the-edges, devil-may-care vibe so common in places where mingling with sailors is common. Though a modern city today, in the markets and alleys you'll still catch a whiff of the city's long and storied history, which involves foreign invaders, pirates and intrigue by the barrel full.

Keelung is a quick trip from Taipei by either bus or train and offers a lot to the casual traveller who knows where to look. Thanks to its strategic importance over the centuries, the area has a number of old forts. Befitting a coastal town, you'll also find ocean parks, scenic lookouts and, perhaps most germane to the gourmand, copious amounts of excellent seafood.

Weatherwise, Taiwanese sometimes joke that Keelung is Taiwan's Seattle, with wet

NORTHERN TAIWAN

and drizzly winters and three other seasons in which it may well rain a bit on any given day. But something about the damp, mist-shrouded climate of Keelung suits its moody nautical feel to a T.

Orientation & Information

Keelung is a very wander-able town, with a small centre and plenty of winding alleyways that turn into quaint MC Escher-esque neighbourhoods (with houses built into the sides of hills and steep alleyways that become staircases). You can visit most of the sights outside of the city by bus within 30 minutes.

The bus and train stations are adjacent to each other at the northern end of the city. You can pick up good English maps at the **Keelung Tourist Service Centre** (☎ 2428 7664; www.klcg.gov.tw; ☺ 8am-5.30pm), right next to the train station.

Sights

KEELUNG MIAOKOU 基隆廟口夜市

It's still thought of as a **night market** but you're not going to go hungry at Miaokou (Jīlóng Miàokǒu) if you show up during the day. Encompassing several square blocks around the intersection of Ren 3rd Rd and Ai 3rd Rd, this area (famous throughout Taiwan) became known for its great food during the Japanese occupation, when a group of clever merchants started selling snacks at the mouth of the **Dianji Temple** ('Miaokou' means 'temple entrance' and also 'temple mouth', which is

a fine play on words if you ask us). After the war, more shops opened up in both directions. Nowadays, Miaokou is considered the best place in Taiwan for street snacks, especially seafood. Though some shops are open during the day, it's after dark when the place really comes to life.

For the benefit of all, stalls on the main street are all numbered and have signs in English, Japanese and Chinese explaining what's on the menu. If you can possibly make it past them all without falling over, the temple itself is worth visiting.

JUNGJENG PARK 中正公園

This park (Zhōngzhèng Gōngyuán) overlooks the city and the harbour. You can get here from the train station by bus 101, 103 or 105, but shouldn't you walk off that afternoon snack-fest at Miaokou? In any case, the park isn't hard to find. Let a Keelung icon, the bone-white 22m tall **Guanyin statue**, flanked by two gigantic golden lions, be your guide. Note that while there's a main road leading up from the south side of the hill, the stairs and alleyways from the west side have more character.

ERSHAWAN FORT 二沙灣

Also known as Haiman Tienxian, this first-class historical relic (Sea-gate Fort; Èrsháwān) was once used to defend Taiwan during the First Opium War. Its imposing main gate and five cannons, still tucked into their battery emplacements, are a dramatic sight.

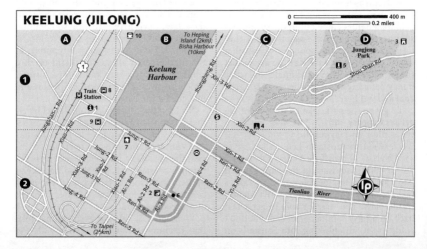

FOGUANGSHAN TEMPLE 佛光山寺

Just south of Jungjeng Park is this beautiful and subdued **Buddhist complex** (Fóguāngshān Sì) with an open meditation hall.

AROUND KEELUNG

If you have a bit more time to spend around Keelung, check out **Keelung Island** (基隆嶼; Jīlóng Yǔ), a tiny spot of land with an emerald peak and surprisingly high cliffs. Boats to Keelung Island (adult/child NT300/200) leave from **Bisha Harbour** (碧砂漁港; Bìshā Yúgǎng), 10km east of the island and itself worth visiting. The return trip takes about 90 minutes and includes time on the island. Boats leave when full; on weekdays and in winter months you may find yourself waiting for a while.

To get to Bisha Harbour take bus 103 from the train station. Buses are frequent and the trip takes about 20 minutes. Foreign travellers should bring their passport or ARC.

Bisha Harbour is also known as a great place for seafood.

Festivals

During the seventh lunar month, Keelung is host to one of Taiwan's most renowned **ghost festivals** *(zhōngyuán jié)*. The festival lasts the entire seventh lunar month (usually August), and each year a different Keelung clan is chosen to sponsor the events. Highlights include folk art performances, the opening of the Gates of Hell and the release of burning water lanterns.

Sleeping

Most people treat Keelung as a day trip. If you want to stay a night there are cheap hotels close to the harbour. In the midrange, **Harbourview Hotel** (Huáshuài Hǎijǐng Fàndiàn; ☎ 2422 3131; www.hhotel.com.tw/; 109 Xiao-2 Rd; 孝2路109號; s/d incl breakfast NT1950/2340) is a chic, smartly furnished place in between the train station and night market. For food, try the **vegetarian restaurant** (☎ 2423 1141; dishes NT80-150; 10am-8pm) beside the Foguanshan Temple. We recommend the wonton soup, a vegan rarity.

INFORMATION	
Keelung Tourist Service Centre 基隆遊客中心	1 A1
SIGHTS & ACTIVITIES	
Dianji Temple 奠濟宮	2 B2
Ershawan Fort 二沙灣	3 D1
Foguangshan Temple 佛光山寺	4 C1
Guanyin Statue 觀音佛像	5 D1
Keelung Miakou 廟口夜市	6 B2
SLEEPING	
Harbourview Hotel 華帥海景飯店	7 B2
TRANSPORT	
City Bus Hub 市公車站	8 A1
Keelung Bus Company Station 基隆客運公車站	9 A1
Matsu Ferries 基港大樓東二碼頭	(see 10)
Pier No 2	10 B1

Getting There & Around

Trains from Taipei to Keelung (NT43, 40 minutes, every 20 minutes) run till 11.30pm. Buses to local sights start at the city bus hub near the train station area and cost NT12 no matter the distance. Buses to sights along the north coast start from the **Keelung Bus Company** (☎ 2433 6111) station, which is also near the train station.

Though not always reliable, you can take an overnight boat from Keelung to Matsu Island. Boats leave from Keelung Harbour's Pier 2.

YELIU 野柳

Just a few kilometres northwest of Green Bay sits this **limestone cape** (Yěliǔ; adult/child NT50/25; 8am-5pm) that has long attracted people to its delightfully odd rock formations. Aeons of wind and sea erosion can be observed firsthand in hundreds of pitted and moulded rocks with quaint (but accurate) names such as Queen's Head (Nǚwáng Tóu) and Fairy's Shoe (Xiānnǚ Xié). It's a geologist's dreamland but also a fascinating place for the day-tripper.

The **visitor centre** (☎ 2492 2016; 8am-5pm) has an informative English brochure explaining the general conditions that created the cape and also the specific forces that formed different kinds of rock shapes, such as the mushroom rocks, marine potholes and honeycomb rocks. To get to the park, take a Kuo Kuang Hao bus heading to Jinshan from the Zhongxiao-Fuxing MRT station (the bus stop outside exit 2). Buses (NT83) run every 15 minutes.

JINSHAN (CHINSHAN) 金山

☎ 02 / pop 5000

Continuing northwest, not far past Yeliu and the nuclear power plant is Jinshan (Jīnshān), a small town hemmed in by the mountains of Yangmingshan to the west and the East China Sea to the east. With its good beach, scenic cape, grassy-banked river and abundant hot springs, Jinshan should be a great little summer getaway. And it may yet be.

At the time of writing, however, chaos seemed to rule on Jinshan's beaches. Too many swimmers, surfers, wannabe surfers and vendors were all trying to compete for the same stretch of sand. However, the situation may be very different by the time you read this if the North Coast & Guanyinshan Scenic Administration get control over the area as they are attempting to do.

Sights & Activities

Our favourite hot spring resort in the north, the five-star **Tienlai** (天籟; Tiānlài; ☎ 2408 0000; www.gio.gov.tw/taiwan-website/gogo/goen_32.htm; 1-7 Mingliu Rd; 金山鄉重和村名流路1-7號; unlimited use of public pools NT800) is just outside of Jinshan and the road into Yangmingshan National Park. The resort features over a dozen outdoor and indoor pools that can massage, soak, perfume, shower and even spin you right round. This is a place to take a loved one when you want to spoil them. Check out the website to see how lovely it all is. Tienlai is a 10- to 15-minute taxi ride from Jinshan.

Just down the road from the entrance to Tienlai is the start of a trail to the natural springs called **Bayen Hot Springs** (八煙溫泉; Bāyān Wēnquán). At the 5.5km mark, head down the side paved trail. Follow the signs or, on a weekend, ask other hikers. It's a well-known place, a bit too popular at times, but still lovely.

Not far from Jinshan, the **Juming Museum** (朱銘美術館; Zhūmíng Měishùguǎn; ☎ 2486 9940; www.juming.org.tw; adult/child NT250/220; ❂ 10am-6pm Tue-Sun May-Oct, to 5pm Nov-Apr) is a 15-hectare park built to display the creative works of internationally recognised sculptor Juming from Miaoli County, including works that have been displayed in Paris, Hong Kong and Tokyo. It's a 10-minute taxi ride (NT150 to NT200) to the museum from Jinshan. For more information, check out the museum's excellent website and see the boxed text on p53.

Getting There & Away

To get here, take a Kuo Kuang Hao bus heading to Jinshan from the Zhongxiao-Fuxing MRT station (the bus stop outside exit 2). Buses (NT83) run every 15 minutes.

18 LORDS TEMPLE 十八王公

People sometimes refer to this temple (Shíbā Wánggōng) as the 'dog temple'. According to one version of the legend, 17 fishermen went missing one day. One loyal dog pined for days for the return of his master until, unable to bear the suffering any longer, he leaped into the foaming sea and drowned himself. Local people were so impressed by this act of loyalty they built a temple in honour of the dog.

Years later, the Kuomintang (KMT) constructed the first nuclear power plant behind the temple. Both buildings are now just off Provincial Hwy 2.

The temple, we should warn, is not at all picturesque. In fact, you can barely see it for the ugly crowded shops and stalls. Still, the opportunity to be blessed by a dog should not be missed if you are driving through the area.

BAISHAWAN BEACH 白沙灣

The best beach on the north coast is found at this little bay (Báishāwān), the name of which translates as 'white sand bay' (though these days it is definitely more of a yellow colour). The **North Coast National Scenic Area Administration** (☎ 2363 4503; www.northguan-nsa.gov.tw/en/index.php; ❂ 8am-5pm) has helped to clean up the area and keep the vendors and shops organised. There's none of the chaos plaguing the nearby beaches at Jinshan, though there certainly are crowds on the weekend.

The entrance to the beach is down a road 100m or so off Hwy 2 (there are brown signs in English). Swimming is permitted during summer (June to September) and in recent years a surfing scene of sorts has taken off. You'll find no end of shops offering boards and wetsuits should you want to try your hand at the sport. And you'll also find no end of young Taiwanese paddling their boards in the shallows not daring or caring to actually get on the waves.

To get to the beach, take the MRT to Danshui, then catch a **Tamshui (Danshui) Bus Company** (☎ 2621 3340) bus heading east to Jinshan/Keelung (NT50, 20 minutes, every 30 minutes).

DANSHUI & BALI

There are two places worth seeing further up on the North Coast; the Taipei-river suburb of **Danshui** (see p126) and the charming seafront town of **Bali** (see p129) are both easy day trips best made out of Taipei. These towns are accessible via the MRT from Taipei and are popular as day trips with locals as well as tourists.

NORTHEAST COAST

We're using Keelung as our kicking off point again, but this time we're heading east, where the mountains rise straight from the sea. This is a great region for lovers of the outdoors; as there are swimming and surfing beaches and a number of excellent day hikes along the coastal bluffs. And, of course, this being Taiwan, you'll find hot springs.

For the history and culture buff there are two old mining towns from the Japanese era to explore. Interestingly, one of the most precious legacies of this era is an old street filled with teahouses. Further south, you'll find a fantastic private collection of stone lions and a centre devoted to the traditional arts.

Most of this area falls under the auspices of the **Northeast Coast Scenic Administration** (☎ 2499 1115; www.necoast-nsa.gov.tw). Its headquarters and visitor centre are in Fulong.

JIUFEN & JINGUASHI 金瓜石 九份
☎ 02 / pop 2000

Nestled against the mountains and hemmed in by the sea are the small villages of Jiufen (Jiǔfèn) and Jinguashi (Jīnguāshí), two of the quaintest stops along the northeast coast. Both villages were once centres of gold mining during the Japanese era. In the 1930s, Jiufen was so prosperous it was known as 'Little Shanghai'. Jinguashi later became notorious during WWII as the site of the prisoner of war camp Kinkaseki.

When the mining sources dried up, Jiufen and Jinguashi became backwaters just waiting to be rediscovered. Jiufen's discovery happened first. After the release of the 1989 film *City of Sadness*, set in Jiufen during the Japanese occupation, urban Taiwanese began to flock to the old village in search of a way of life that had been all but swept away in the rush to modernisation. The old town, rich in decorative old teahouses, Japanese-style homes and traditional narrow lanes gave them exactly what they were looking for.

Jinguashi hit the traveller's radar just recently and we have to say it has completely eclipsed its neighbour, except for as a place to sit and drink tea. Our recommended itinerary would be to spend the morning and early afternoon in Jinguashi enjoying the Gold Ecological Park and strolling through the verdant treeless hills, and the afternoon and early evening hanging out at one of the old teahouses on the hillsides of Jiufen before returning to Taipei.

Orientation & Information

Many of Jinguashi's sites are in what's called the Gold Ecological Park. The park is a showcase for just how well the Taiwanese government can design a new tourist area when they can start from scratch and own the rights to the land. The contrast between the orderliness of the park and its high quality facilities and infrastructure, and the chaos, grubbiness and piecemeal improvements in Jiufen is striking.

The park is free but a ticket allows you entry into the Crown Prince Chalet and the Museum of Gold. There's a **tourist office** (☎ 2496 2800; www.gep.tpc.gov.tw; ☯ 9am-5pm) at the start of the park, where you can pick up an English brochure that includes a good map and information on all the attractions, both inside the park and out.

As for Jiufen, there are really only two main streets to consider and they intersect: Jishan St, a narrow covered alley, and Shuchi Rd, a long set of stairs. On these two streets you'll find most of the teahouses, craft shops, galleries and food stalls Jiufen is famous for.

Jiufen Sights & Activities

JISHAN STREET 基山街

Narrow, covered Jishan St (Jīshān Jiē) often leaves lasting impressions. We were taken there and to a nearby teahouse during our first week in Taiwan, and have never forgotten it. Jishan is really just one long, narrow covered lane, but spending a few hours here browsing the knick-knack, curio and craft shops is a lot of fun.

One of the most popular activities on the street is snacking. Some distinctive snacks to look for include *yùyuǎn* (芋圓; taro balls), *yúwán* (魚丸; fish balls), *cǎozǐ gāo* (草仔糕; herbal cakes) and *hēitáng gāo* (黑糖糕; molasses cake).

TEAHOUSES

Apart from shopping, strolling and snacking, the main attraction in Jiufen is spending a few hours in a stylish traditional teahouse sipping fine tea. This isn't everyone's – well – cup of tea, but for those of us who love it,

Jiufen gets top marks as a place to indulge in a favourite pastime. The best shops, which are mostly on the stepped Shuchi Rd, are like folk art museums, filled with curios and antiques. Note that the teahouses don't have English signs outside.

The price for making your own tea (*pào chá*) is much the same everywhere: NT250 to NT400 for a packet of leaves and NT100 for your water fee. The following teahouses are among the best.

The owner claims his business, **Jiufen Teahouse** (Jiŭfèn Cháfāng; ☎ 2496 9056; 142 Jishan St; ☼ 10am-10pm), housed in a 90-year-old building, was the first teahouse in Jiufen. There is indoor and outdoor seating, and it's hard to decide which to choose, though we usually sit inside as the wood and brick design has such a charming old-world feel to it. The teahouse only serves tea and snacks, but if you want a meal they will direct you to their (almost) as-nice sister restaurant down the street.

Bafan Gold Site Teahouse (Bāfān Cháguǎn; ☎ 2496 0692; 300 Chingpien Rd; ☼ 10am-10pm) is a three-storey place that's well stocked with antique furnishings. Indoor and outdoor seating is available. The views from the decks are the perfect complement to Chinese tea brewed the classical way.

We're listing **City of Sadness** (Bēiqíng Chéngshì; ☎ 2496 9917; 35 Shuchi Rd; ☼ 10am-midnight) because of its fame, but have to say that it is not one of our favourite teahouses. The place is a little cramped and unfortunately placed on the end of the lane where trucks and other modern nuisances can too often be heard.

JILONGSHAN 雞籠山

You can't miss this emerald colossus for the way it dominates the skyline. At only 588m, Jilongshan (Jīlóngshān) may read like a rather puny giant, but it rises up so fast and steep, it's dizzying to stare at from below. You can climb the peak in about 40 minutes.

Jinguashi Sights & Activities

GOLD ECOLOGICAL PARK 黃金博物園區

We could, and did, spend hours just wandering this park (Huángjīn Bówùyuánqū), set high above the village in green, quiet

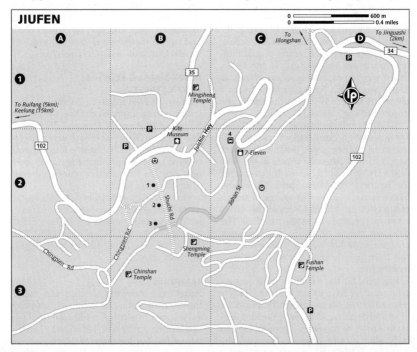

hillsides. In fact, the natural environment around Jinguashi should be as big a draw as the cultural attractions.

A couple of the highlights in the park include the **Crown Prince Chalet** (太子賓館; Tàizǐ Bīngguǎn), built as an official residence for the Japanese royal family to use when visiting Taiwan (alas, they never came). It's the best-preserved Japanese style wooden residence in Taiwan, and really quite a beauty. The ruins of the **Gold Temple** (黃金神社; Huángjīn Shénshè) sit high on the steep slopes above Jinguashi and look like something out of Greek mythology.

REMAINS OF THE 13 LEVELS 十三層

The remains are a massive **copper smelting refinery** (*shísāncéng*) that inspires such a heavy, dystopian industrial awe it has been used as a background for music videos. The remains are down from the park heading towards the sea. There are signs in English to direct you there from the park.

GOLDEN WATERFALL 黃金瀑布

Further towards the sea is this waterfall (Huángjīn Pùbù), so-called because its water has a yellow hue from the copper and iron deposits it picks up as it passes through Jinguashi's old mines.

Getting There & Around

The two towns are only 3km away from each other and are served by buses every 10 minutes or so. To get there, take a train from Taipei to Ruifang (fast/slow train NT80/38, 40/60 minutes, every 30 minutes). Pick up a ticket (NT100) to the Gold Ecological Park at the visitor centre in the train station and then cross the main road to catch the bus heading to Jiufen-Jinguashi (you'll pass Jiufen first). Your ticket allows you four rides on the bus.

The bus drops you off right at the start of the Gold Ecological Park in Jinguashi. Return to this spot when you want to go to Jiufen. Get off at the bus stop by the 7-Eleven. Jishan St begins just across the street.

SIGHTS & ACTIVITIES	
Bafan Gold Site Teahouse 八番茶館	**1** B2
City of Sadness 悲情城市餐廳	**2** B2
Jiufen Teahouse 九份茶坊	**3** B2
TRANSPORT	
Jiufen Bus Stop 九份站	**4** C2

BITOU CAPE 鼻頭角

One of three capes along the north coast, Bitou Cape (Bítóu Jiǎo) is of note for its beautiful sea-eroded cliffs, fantastic views along the coast, and the **Bitou Cape Trail** (鼻頭角步道; Bítóu Jiǎo Bùdào), which is like an easier version of the nearby and more majestic Caoling Historical Trail.

Interestingly, the rock formations at one part of the trail were formed six million years ago, while those at another, only 3km away, were formed 60 million years ago. For fun, make a bet with your companions to see who can tell which is which.

The trail starts near the bus stop before the tunnel and takes a couple of hours to walk. There is a map in English. To get here from Keelung, take a bus (NT65, 20 minutes, every hour) from the **Keelung Bus Company** (☎ 02-2433 6111) station.

LONGDONG 龍洞

Just through the tunnel past Bitou Cape is Longdong (Lóngdòng), a well known, but not particularly good, diving and snorkelling spot in the north. There are two sections of Longdong and they are connected by the very scenic **Longdong Cape Trail** (Lóngdòng Wānjiá Bùdào), which is around 7km long. The trail starts at the Longdong South Marina Ocean Paradise (Lóngdòng Nánkǒu Hǎiyáng Gōngyuán; the sign off the highway says Lungtungnankou), a few kilometres to the south of the Longteng Bay Park (Lóngdòngwān Gōngyuán).

Keelung Bus Company buses stop outside the park every hour or so (NT70, 20 minutes).

Within walking distance of the bay park is an area described as having the best **rock climbing** in northern Taiwan. Check out www .geocities.com/Yosemite/1976 for more information and contacts, and also pick up a copy of *Long Dong Trad Climbs* by Matt Robertson. The book is available at various mountain equipment shops around the Taipei Train Station.

YENLIAO 鹽寮

This is northern Taiwan's longest **beach** (Yánliáo; adult/child NT180/90; ☎ 8am-6pm) and we're always surprised that it doesn't get the same buzz as Fulong. Facilities at the beach include a garden area as you enter, a children's water park, a café, showers and changing rooms.

To get to Yenliao Beach, take a train to Fulong (fast/slow train NT132/85, 60/80 minutes, every 30 minutes), 5km to the south, and then a taxi. Alternatively, catch any bus heading up the coast.

FULONG BEACH 福隆海水浴場

The most popular **beach** (Fúlóng Hǎishǔi Yùchǎng; admission NT50; ☽ May–Oct) in northern Taiwan is also one of the best and easiest to get to. Fulong has a long sandy beach and clear waters suitable for sailing, windsurfing, surfing and other sports. In recent years the town of Fulong has seen some aesthetic improvements (some buildings have actually had a fresh coat of paint applied), and the beach area is getting new wooden boardwalks, pavilions, treed parks and open-air restaurants. All in all, the town is starting to shape up into a community that's on a par with its natural resources.

Note that there are two parts to the beach, divided by the Shuangshi River. The left beach, behind the visitor centre, is the pay area. If you head right and go through the YMCA grounds and continue towards a large temple on the end of a peninsula, you'll get to the free beach, which is a great place to swim or surf and is reasonably clean in summer.

Dangers & Annoyances

The beach is officially closed after October but people still go there to surf and swim. Note that the beach is usually pretty dirty at this time unless a crew has been in to clean it up recently.

The currents at Fulong can be treacherous in places, especially where the river flows into the sea. The beach is also constantly changing; it lost a lot of sand a few years back to a typhoon. Fortunately, it is coming back nicely.

The Environmental Protection Agency (EPA) recommends that people do not swim several days after a typhoon as many contaminants get washed into the sea from the land. During summer, the EPA makes regular announcements about the water quality here and at other beaches.

Festivals

Every July, Fulong is the host of the **Hohaiyan Music Festival**. Now in its eighth year, the festival has grown from a small indie event into the largest outdoor concert in Taiwan, attracting hundreds of thousands over a three-day period. The festival is free and features local and international bands (though so far nobody big). Being a long-weekend concert the exact date changes each year, and sudden cancellations or rescheduling may occur because of typhoons. The official website (www.alluni .com.tw/hahaiyan/) is all in Chinese, though this may change. In any case, the English-language newspapers always report on the festival, as does the Youth Travel in Taiwan website (http://youthtravel.tw/web/index .php).

Sleeping & Eating

Longmen Riverside Camping Resort (龍門露營區; Lóngmén Lùyín Qū; ☎ 02-2499 1791; 4-person site incl tent from NT800, 2-/4-person cabins NT2300/3500) This 37-hectare camp site by the Shuangshi River has accommodation for up to 1600 people. There are tent sites and A-frame log cabins. Camping is a bit pricey for sure, but two groups with their own small tents can rent one site for NT600. Note that there is an additional fee of NT70 per person to enter the camp site.

The site is well laid out and facilities are clean and modern. Bicycles, barbecues and rowboats are available for hire. To get to the camp site from Fulong train station, exit the station and turn left at the main road (the highway). Just past the visitor centre a dedicated lane runs along the highway to the campground, making it quite safe to walk. It takes about 10 minutes to walk to the campground from the station. There are plenty of restaurants, cafes, lunch-box shops and convenience stores around the train station. By the temple near the free beach are several good seafood places sharing an outdoor patio.

Getting There & Away

Trains from Taipei to Fulong (fast/slow train NT132/85, 60/80 minutes) leave every 30 minutes or so.

CAOLING (TSAOLING) HISTORIC TRAIL 草嶺古道

If you can only do one hike during your stay in Taiwan, make it this one, which runs along the rugged coastal mountains from Fulong to Daxi. The first sections of the trail take you through thick woodlands and scrub, which are pleasant enough, but it's the many, many kilometres along high grassy bluffs overlooking the Pacific that make this hike such a treasure. To top things off, there are wild grazing buffalo to observe and a few boulder-sized historical tablets.

In 1807 the government in Taiwan built the Caoling Trail (Cǎolǐng Gǔdào) to provide transport between Danshui and Ilan. The 8.5km section that remains today is one of the few historical roads left in Taiwan.

In recent years, a long addition was made to the trail called the **Taoyuan Valley Trail** (桃園谷步道; Táoyuángǔ Bùdào). Taoyuan Valley is not a valley but an emerald grassy bluff, kept trim by the water buffalo. It's stunningly beautiful up here and makes a prime spot for picnicking. With the addition of the Taoyuan Valley Trail section, the entire Caoling Trail is about 16km long and takes five to eight hours to complete.

The entire trail is broad and simple to follow, with signposts and maps, though it certainly is strenuous in places. There is not the slightest danger of getting lost, but do save the walk for the autumn, winter or spring months. You'll roast at the top during summer.

There are many ways to tackle this trail, so get a map from the Fulong visitor centre to plan which route is best for you. You need not do the entire trail, but if you do, we like starting at Daxi (the trailhead is clearly marked just north of the train station) and working our way back to Fulong. There are trains from Taipei to Daxi (NT104, 90 minutes, every two hours).

If you want to spend the night in the elaborate and sprawling **Tiengong Temple** (天公廟; Tiāngōng Miáo; ☎ 03-978 1075), stop in Dali (大里), about midway on the trail (though you must walk down to reach the temple). Room charge is by donation.

DAXI (MIYUEWAN) 大溪
☎ 03 / pop 500

There's not much to recommend in Daxi (Dàxī) itself, but just south of town is a popular surfing beach known as **Honeymoon Bay** (蜜月灣; Mìyuè Wān). The beach used to be a popular hang-out for foreign beach bums, but has become less so in recent times as the surfing scene has pretty much taken over and the quality of the beach itself deteriorates year after year. The waves are generally chest to head high, though during the summer typhoon months they can get much higher than that and conditions can become quite challenging.

Normally though, Honeymoon Bay is a fine location for beginner and intermediate surfers, though for more experienced surfers this means that during peak season you will be sharing the waters with a lot of people who don't know what they are doing. And we mean a lot, as surfing has really hit Taiwan big time in the past few years, and there isn't a lot of emphasis on skills and etiquette.

You can surf at Honeymoon Bay all year round, with only a swimsuit needed from April to November. Throughout the late spring and summer months (and now increasing into the autumn months too), you'll find a number of shops and kiosks on the beach renting surfing equipment (NT600 per day for boards), and selling things to eat and drink. Note that the boards for rent are pretty low quality.

To get to Daxi, take a train (NT104, 90 minutes, every two hours) from Taipei. When you get off at Daxi, cross the road and walk south about 600m along the seawall to reach the beach.

One place where English is spoken is the **Spider Surf Club** (☎ 978 1321; www.spidersurfing.com; 96 Binhai Rd, sec.5; 濱海路5段96號), which offers surfing lessons (including room and board NT3000) and dorm accommodation (NT300) on weekends. It also has showers (NT50) if you just want to rinse off after a day at the beach. When you exit the train station, the club is just to the left on the other side of the street.

If you wish to camp, you can use the grounds of the elementary school behind the beach on nonschool days. The school charges NT300 a site. Classrooms can also be rented for NT1000. Talk to the janitor.

WAI-AO 外澳

Wai-ao (Wài-ào) is a small village on the coast that has become a popular **surfing** venue in recent years. The surf is rough here and not really suitable for swimming or beginner surfers. Trains from Taipei (NT117, 100 minutes) leave every two hours or so.

LION'S KINGDOM MUSEUM & LEO RESORT 河東堂獅子博物館里歐海洋渡假中心

Despite the name making it sound like a Disney theme park, this **museum** (Hédōngtáng Shīzi Bówùguǎn; admission NT180) has a fantastic private collection of stone lions of every shape, size, colour and country of origin. Most are at least a hundred years old, and some are far, far older than that. The collection numbers around 6000 pieces and at least 500 are on display, in addition to some stone horses, turtles and old decorative window frames. This is really a must-see for anyone interested in Asian art.

The museum occupies two floors of the splendid seaside **Leo Resort** (Lǐōu Hǎiyáng Dùjià Zhōngxīn; ☎ 03-987 0782; 36 Binhai Rd, sec.4, Toucheng; 濱海路4段36號; d/tw from NT6300/9900, weekdays NT5600/8800), where we would gladly spend a major birthday or anniversary. Set off the road, next to a protected stretch of coastline, the five-storey hotel overlooks the ocean and includes a full view of Turtle Island from the dining room. Down by the seaside there's a lush green garden, a saltwater pool and various wooden decks overlooking the sea (but protected from the tide by high rocks). There are also hammocks in the trees, a nice, all-too-rare touch in Taiwan.

By the end of 2007 the hotel will offer genuine hot-spring water in both the rooms and the outdoor swimming pool. Room rates include admission to the museum, breakfast, afternoon coffee and dinner. The food is delicious and very fresh: the seafood, for example, is delivered daily from the nearby Wushih Fishing Harbour.

Note that nonguests can also stop by for a meal or just a coffee down by the sea.

If you are taking public transport, catch a train to Toucheng (fast/slow train NT189/122, 1½/two hours, every 30 minutes) and then a taxi, which should cost around NT150 to NT200 for the 10-minute drive.

TURTLE ISLAND (KUEISHAN ISLAND)
龜山島

This captivating volcanic islet (Gūishān Dǎo), 10km off the coast of Ilan, is less than 3km long yet rises up to 400m and supports 13 species of butterflies and 33 species of birds.

The island also has numerous quirky geological features. These include underwater hot springs that turn the offshore water into a bubbling cauldron, volcanic fumaroles that spout steam, and a 'turtle head' that faces right or left depending on where you stand on shore.

Turtle Island is open from March to October. You must apply at least two weeks in advance for a special permit if you wish to land on the island. (If you simply wish to sail around it you don't need a permit.) You can download a copy of the application form, but only from the Chinese section of the northeast coast's website (www.necoast-nsa.gov .tw). Once you get your permit, call a boat operator to make a reservation. Here's one to try: ☎ 978 0870.

Boats leave from Wushih Harbour (Wūshí Gǎng). It costs NT600 for a 1½-hour cruise to and around the island, and NT1000 for a three-hour tour that includes a stop on the island (though hopefully not as long as that more famous three-hour tour, Gilligan's Island). Combination tours involving stops on the island and whale-watching are also available (NT1400, 4½ hours).

To get to Wushih Harbour, take a train from Taipei to Toucheng (fast/slow train NT189/122, 1½/two hours, every 30 minutes) and then a short taxi ride.

Call the **English Tourist Hotline** (☎ 0800-011 765) or **Northeast Coast Scenic Administration** (☎ 02-2499 1115) for more information.

PEI KUAN CRAB MUSEUM
北關螃蟹博物館

After our respectful review of the Lion's Kingdom Museum (p161), you'd be forgiven for expecting this **crab museum** (Pángxiè Bówùguǎn; ☎ 03-977 2168; admission NT250; 🕙 9am-5pm) to be a slapstick afterthought. A crab museum? What's up with that?

Well, a lot actually. Two floors, in fact, devoted to the dozens of crab species found in Taiwan. The first floor exhibits whole crab exteriors, and the sheer range of colours, shapes and sizes is astonishing – and at times plain creepy. The horseshoe crab, for instance, has a dark slick cover that looks uncomfortably like the shell of the monster in *Alien*.

There are English signs for each category of crab though not for each species. Kids will love it here, as will anyone with even a mild interest in the natural world. The price is very steep because it includes access to the Pei Kuan Farm. Come during the spring months when fireflies light up the riverbeds and walkways.

The museum is up a side road a few kilometres off Hwy 2 south of the 131km mark. There are signs in English on the highway, though none on the way up, but just look for the crab pictures. It's best to have your own transport to get here.

JIAOSHI 礁溪

☎ 03 / pop 5000

Jiaoshi is a small town just off the coast well known for its three-layered waterfall, hot springs and related cuisine (they grow vegetables in hot spring water here). It's close enough to Taipei for a day trip, though with two dozen or so hot spring hotels, and countless restaurants and cafés, you can easily make it an overnighter or even stay a weekend.

Orientation & Information

Jiaoshi is fairly compact and you can walk around most of the hot-springs area in an hour. There's a helpful **visitor centre** (☎ 987 2403; 16 Gongyuan Rd; ⏰ 9am-5pm; 🖳) a 10-minute walk from the train station. Pick up some brochures, as there's a lot more in the area than we can cover, or check out the website for Ilan County (http://svr2.ilccb.gov.tw/ready ilan/e-sitemap.asp).

From the station, head up the road and take the first right. Walk a few blocks until the road joins Hwy 9. Cross and then take a quick left. The centre is just up the road. There is usually someone there who speaks English, but it's always good to call ahead to confirm this if you think you will need their services. There's free internet at the centre.

Sights & Activities

WUFENGCHI WATERFALL 五峰旗大瀑布

Almost directly in line with Turtle Island is the Wufengchi Waterfall (Wǔfēngchí Pùbù). There are three layers and each one is more impressive than the last.

The falls are 3.5km northwest of the Jiaoshi train station (礁溪火車站). There is no public transport to the falls so you must walk or catch a taxi (NT150).

HOT SPRINGS

Jiaoshi is one of the few hot-spring towns developed by the Japanese that has not been overdeveloped to the point where there simply isn't enough water for all the businesses that claim to use it. The springs produce salty, odourless water at 60°C, known to be good for countering nervousness and general feelings of malaise.

In general, we recommend the places west of Hwy 9 heading towards the mountains. An inexpensive option is the new stylish **public spring park** (湯圍溝公園; Tāngwéigōu Gōngyuán; ☎ 987 4882; admission NT80; ⏰ 10am-11pm) set up by the Jiaoshi government. There are free foot-soaking tubs outside, and very lovely wood and stone segregated pools inside (clothing optional). To get to the pools, head straight up the road from the train station. Turn left on Hwy 9 (the second road up) and then take the first right. The hot springs are on the left a few blocks up.

HIKING

The 6.5km historic **Paoma Gudao** (跑馬古道; Pǎomǎ Gǔdào), or Running Horse Historic Trail, trots over the grassy slopes high above Jiaoshi. The trailhead is 3km from the train station. It's best to take a taxi as the trail is one-way, and there's no point doing the road section twice. Paoma Gudao is wide, clear, smooth and simple to follow. On the way back just keep heading down and you will reach Jiaoshi and probably a hot-spring hotel will catchs your eye as a place to soak your tired bones.

Getting There & Around

Trains to Jiaoshi (Chiaoshi; fast/slow train NT205/132, 1½/2 hours) leave Taipei about every half hour.

You can rent scooters outside the train station (NT300 to NT600) with an International Driver's Licence.

LUODONG (LOTONG) 羅東

☎ 03 / pop 73,196

Not far south of Jiaoshi, this small town (Lódōng) has put itself on the map with its massively popular children's festival and a new centre dedicated to reviving traditional arts in Taiwan.

Every summer for four to five weeks in July and August, Ilan County plays host to the **Ilan International Children's Folklore & Folkgame Festival** (國際童玩藝術節; Guójì Tóngwàn Yìshù Jié; ☎ 931 0720; www.folkgame.org.tw; adult/child NT450/200), where top children's performers and performing troops are brought in from around the world. For families this is a must-see event. The festival is held in Chinshui Park (親水公園; Qīnshuǐ Gōngyuán), which has facilities for rowing, wading and getting wet and wild in summer.

The **National Centre of Traditional Arts** (國立傳統藝術中心; Guólì Chuántǒng Yìshù Zhōngxīn; ☎ 960 5230, ext 164; www.ncfta.gov.tw; admission free; ⏰ 9am-9pm; 🖳) occupies 24 hectares along the scenic Tongshan River, providing a venue for

NORTHERN TAIWAN

THE HSUEHSHAN TUNNEL 雪山隧道

At 12.9km, this tunnel (Xuěshān Sùidào) is the longest in Asia and the fourth longest in the world. It's also had one of the longest periods of construction – when it finally opened in June 2006, work on the tunnel had been underway since 1991.

The tunnel is the centrepiece of the 55km-long National Hwy 5 connecting Taipei with Ilan County. It was supposed to open up the east coast, but along the way it opened an ancient aquitard and the water just kept on pouring out. Boring machines were flooded and buried, work slowed to a halt for months on end, and at many points engineers wondered if they should consider giving up.

They persevered, but at the cost of US$1.8 billion and 25 lives. Was it worth it? Hwy 5 facilitates fast travel from Nangan in Taipei County to Suao in Ilan County. When it's not backed up (all the way from Nangan to Suao), the highway cuts travelling time down to a third of what it once was. While letting people rush to Jiaoshi in 30 minutes for an evening dip in a hot spring may seem a frivolous waste of money and life, the highway and tunnel will doubtless save lots of both in the future: the old tortuous route was the scene of countless fatal accidents.

If you decide to drive Hwy 5 and pass through the tunnel, avoid early mornings and evenings, especially on weekends and summer days. The best windows for smooth sailing are between 10am and 4pm and after 8pm.

---

the research and performance of folk music, opera, dance, toy making and even acrobatics. For visitors there is an exhibition hall, a learning centre, a temple especially built to help preserve temple-related arts, and a folk-arts street where you can browse for glassware, paper cuttings and glove puppets in a recreated traditional township atmosphere.

Trains to Luodong (fast/slow train NT243/157, 1½/2½ hours) leave Taipei about every half hour. Once in Luodong, it's a short taxi ride to the arts centre or water park. During festival times shuttle buses run between the train station and both sites.

SUAO TO HUALIEN

Just past Luodong, Hwy 9 rejoins the coast and begins what is known as the Suao–Hualien Hwy. The road stretches for 118km along the coastline and is literally carved into sheer cliff walls. One of the most breathtaking sections is called the Chingshui cliffs, where the highway twists its way around towering walls of marble and granite that loom over 1000m above the rocky seashore.

The beginnings of the route go back to 1874, when China's Qing government ordered a road to be built along the east coast, with the aim of alleviating some of the isolation of the region. The Japanese widened the road in 1920, battling with landslides and earthquakes the whole time. In fact,

the road didn't officially reopen for public use until 1932.

Most people drive the highway on their way to Hualien and only stop to look at the scenery. If you're a spring aficionado, consider a break in Suao for a cold spring, and then another in Nanao for a hot spring.

SUAO 蘇澳
☎ 03 / pop 44, 487

Suao is a grubby little port town noted only for the **Suao Cold Springs** (蘇澳冷泉; Sūaò Lěng Quán; ☎ 996 0645; admission NT70; ☼ 8am-10pm). The carbonated springs have an average temperature of 22°C and are completely odourless, making them a rare treasure in the world. The large outdoor facilities have been updated to look somewhat like a Roman bath. It gets pretty busy here in summer.

There are about 10 trains a day from Taipei (fast/slow NT273/176, two/2½ hours).

NANAO 南澳
☎ 03 / pop 500

The small coastal town of Nanao (Nánào) has a pretty crescent bay and dark sandy beach visible from the highway as you make your descent from the hills. It's a lovely beach for strolling along (though it's sometimes littered) and taking in the gorgeous coastal scenery. If you have time for more, Nanao has more, including hot springs, waterfalls, hikes and some quiet country roads for biking. Amazingly there is an English website in English (www.gmes.tpc.edu.tw/~2000/en/html/jyes/jyes3.htm) introducing the area. We guess the locals know they have a good thing going and want to share it.

Sights & Activities

JINYUE WATERFALL 金岳瀑布

The turnoff for the road to the falls (Jīnyuè Pùbù) is around the 133km mark on Hwy 9. After you cross the bridge you'll reach the school for the 200-soul aboriginal community of Jin-yue. Turn left and follow the road for a few kilometres. When you pass the second bridge, the road to the right leads to the falls in 10 minutes.

The main reason to come to this fall is to swim in the pool under it. You'll need river-

tracing boots as the trail takes you to the top of the falls and there's no way down. Instead you must walk back 100m or so and take a side trail down to the riverbed and then trace your way back upstream to the falls and the lovely pool under them, which is a simple enough matter with the proper shoes.

FOUR PARTS HOT SPRINGS 四區溫泉

These alkalescent carbonate hot springs (Sìqū Wēnquán) have water temperatures around 45°C. To get to them, follow the directions for Jinyue Waterfall, but when you reach the junction at the school, go right and follow the river up. Two or 3km later you'll see a sign in English for the springs. From the road, follow rough steps down to the river to find

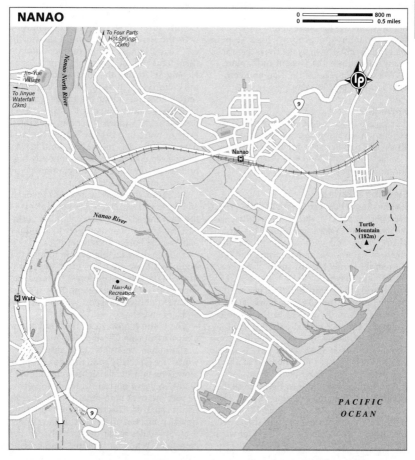

NANAO

three simple concrete pools under a simple roof. Though it would be nicer if the structure were a little more natural looking, it is still a pleasant place for a free soak and a great way to meet local people. Some people camp on the riverbank just behind the springs.

Afterwards, continue down to the end of the road and head down to the Nanao North River. When the grey muddy water is low (it's a grey colour as a result of quarrying far upstream) you can easily walk on the sandy banks and over the colourful boulders. The scenery is really splendid here, especially as the river takes a bend into a canyon whose walls rise up steeply for hundreds of metres.

CYCLING
Even if you have your own vehicle, Nanao is a great place for cycling. On both sides of the highway, towards the ocean or into the mountains, you'll find quiet country roads (especially midweek). Down by the rivers there are many rough dirt paths. Get out and explore.

You can rent bikes at the Nan-ao Recreation Farm for NT300 a day.

KAYAKING
The coastal waters here are known for excellent sea kayaking and the Nanao North River is a popular spot for river kayaking. Contact Andre at Cloud 9 in Pinglin (p150) for more information.

Sleeping & Eating
Nan-Ao Recreation Farm (南澳農場; Nánào Nóngchǎng; ☎ 988 1114; http://nanao-farm.e-land.gov .tw/html/link2.htm; tent sites from NT200) This large, clean, green and well-run camp site has showers, bathrooms, barbecue sites and lots of trees for shade. It's just south of the centre of Nanao town.

If driving south turn left after crossing the bridge, around the 134.5km mark. Follow the road down about 1km to the obvious camp site entrance (NT60 entrance fee).

If you are taking the train, note that you should get off at the station past Nanao, called Wuta. This is a little nothing of a station without even a ticket booth. Head downhill to the highway and turn right. Cross the bridge and follow the directions above. The distance from the station is about 2km.

There are many small noodle shops and restaurants in Nanao beside the highway. There's also a 7-Eleven, a small grocery store and a night market near the town square. Jin-yue Village also has simple places to eat.

Getting There & Away
There are five trains in the morning from Suao to Wuta Train Station (NT62, 45 minutes).

NORTH CROSS-ISLAND HIGHWAY

If you're looking for wild scenery but want a change of pace from coastal waters and rugged shorelines, try a journey down National Hwy 7, also known as the North Cross-Island Hwy (Běibù Héngguàn Gōnglù).

The highway starts in the old Taoyuan County town of Daxi (not to be confused with the Ilan County town on the northeast coast), famous for its excellent *dòugān* (firm tofu) and the Qing-dynasty façades on Heping St. At first the road winds through the countryside, passing flower farms and settlements, including the burial grounds of former leader Chiang Kai-shek. After passing above Shimen Reservoir, the largest body of water in northern Taiwan, the road narrows and starts to rise and wind its way along steep gorges, across precipitously high bridges and, in general, through some pretty fantastic mountain scenery.

At Chilan, the highway descends suddenly and an hour later enters the flood plains of the Lanyang River. It then continues northeast to Ilan, with spur routes to Luodong and Wuling Forest Recreation Area.

You can drive the highway in four or five hours, but there are many great stops leading to waterfalls, caves, forest reserves, hot springs and stands of ancient trees. It's best to have your own transport, as buses are few and far between.

The entire highway can literally become a car park during Chinese New Year and on hot summer weekends. Late autumn and winter are especially good times to go as the crowds are thin and the sights seem improved by the chill and mist in the air. If you drive, be very aware of both other drivers and the natural hazards. This road defines curvy and treacherous, and some part of the surface is always under repair due to typhoons and landslides. While much of the road is being widened these days, in some places there is only enough room for one car.

Information

The **Pei Herng Travel Service Centre** (Cihu Service Centre; ☎ 03-388 3552; ⏱ 8.30am-5pm), just off Hwy 7 at the back of a large car park, covers Taoyuan County and sights along the North Cross-Island Hwy. The centre is half a kilometre before the turn-off for the tomb of Chiang Kai-shek (to which you can walk from the centre). It really depends on who is working as to whether you'll get helpful information or not.

Taipei Day Trips II (see Hiking, p329) has an informative write-up about much of the highway, including a number of very interesting hikes that are too detailed for us to include.

Getting There & Around

To begin your journey by bus, you need to get to Daxi (大溪; Dàxī) first. Take the MRT to Ximen Station and take exit 2. Walk south to Guiyang St and turn left. Cross the road and just past Yanping Rd wait at the bus stop in front of Soochow University. Catch the Taipei–Daxi bus (NT104, one hour, every 30 minutes) to the **Taoyuan Bus Company** (桃園客運; ☎ 03-388 2002) station in Daxi. This is the last stop.

From here you can catch buses as far as Xiao Wulai, but be warned that there are fewer and fewer buses running these routes, so it's best to call the Taoyuan Bus Company to confirm the schedule. It's so much better to have your own vehicle. Consider renting a car in Taipei or a scooter in Jiaoshi.

CIHU 慈湖

Cihu (Cíhú; Lake Kindness) is a quiet, scenic park where the remains of Chiang Kai-shek's body are temporarily entombed. In the past we could hardly recommend people go here, but how time changes this country. Starting in 2006, Chiang statues have been shipped here as part of the DPP government's de-Chiangification of Taiwan. And there are *lots* of statues, as any dictator worth their salt creates a cult of personality through the constant repetition of their name and image.

Regardless of where you stand on the issue, Cihu is now a veritable wonderland of Chiang statues of all shapes, sizes and materials. Expect to take lots of pictures.

SHIMEN RESERVOIR 石門水庫

This **reservoir** (Shímén Shuǐkù; http://shihmenreservoir.wranb.gov.tw; adult/child NT80/40) is the largest body of fresh water in the north. In the past, when there were few areas for outdoor leisure in Taiwan, the dam was deservedly popular for the beauty of its dark green hills and green-blue water, its numerous scenic pavilions and well laid-out parks. There's no doubting its appeal, but today it's hardly a must-see destination, especially as it doesn't look as though it's had an update in the 11 years we have lived in Taiwan.

The **tourist service centre** (☎ 03-471 2000; ⏱ 8.30am-5pm) on the far western side of the lake has booklets in English about the dam, and there are large maps around the dam with clear directions to parks and trails.

FUSING (FUHSING, FUXING) 復興
☎ 03 / pop 1000

The aboriginal village of Fusing (Fùxīng), 18km down Hwy 7 from Daxi, makes for an excellent pit stop, or an even better base from which to explore the whole area. You can stay (or at least have a coffee) at the new Youth Activity Centre, the site of a former summer villa of Chiang Kai-shek. In town, you can get solid, aboriginal-style food, such as *tǔ jī* (土雞; free-range chicken), *zhútǒng fàn* (竹筒飯; rice steamed in bamboo tubes) and a variety of noodle dishes served with the mushrooms for which Fusing is famous.

The **Youth Activity Centre** (青年活動中心; Qīngnián Huódòng Zhōngxīn; ☎ 382 2276; d/tw incl breakfast NT2600/3200) sits in a pretty, landscaped park on a high ridge overlooking an arm of Shimen Reservoir. The land was formerly occupied by one of Chiang Kai-shek's summer villas (it burned down in 1992), which should clue you in to the fact that it's incredibly scenic here.

The centre has large, simply furnished rooms with balcony lookouts. Views from the rooms and the patio of the **coffee shop** (coffee & tea NT100; ⏱ 7am-10.30pm) are postcard perfect. Room 404 has one of the best views in the whole building. You can pick up a brochure in English at the centre that highlights attractions in the area.

On a small bluff to the right of the centre (head to the back of the parking lot and then down the wooden stairs) is **Senling Shui An** (森鄰水岸; Sēnlín Shuǐ Àn; ☎ 382 2108; coffee NT100; ⏱ 9am-9pm), a small wood-cabin coffee shop run by an aboriginal family. The view here is even more incredible than at the centre and the coffee is much better. The owner speaks English and used to be a pub singer. If there are enough people at the café, or he likes you, he will take out his guitar and play.

DONGYANSHAN FOREST RECREATION AREA 東眼山森林遊樂園

About 1km past Fusing is the turn-off for this 916-hectare **forest recreation area** (Dōngyǎnshān Sēnlín Yóulèyuán; http://recreate.forest.gov.tw). There are no buses, but if you have your own vehicle it's a pretty 13km drive up a good road to the **tourist centre** (☎ 03-382 1506; ☉ 8am-5pm), where you can buy simple meals and maps for the area.

The park's altitude ranges from 650m to 1200m, making it a perfect cool retreat in summer. There are many trails, some of which are nature interpretation walks suitable for families, while many others involve two- to three-hour hikes up small mountains. The longest hike is along a 16km trail that actually connects Dongyanshan with neighbouring Manyueyuan Forest Recreation Area (p153). All trails start near the tourist centre and are well marked and easy to follow.

XIAO WULAI WATERFALL 小烏來瀑布

Of the four big falls in northern Taiwan – Wufengchi, Shifen, Wulai and this one – we have to say that the 40m-high Xiao Wulai (Xiǎo Wūlái Pùbù) is our favourite. Like Wufengchi and Wulai, this fall is long and cascading, but unlike the other two you can view Xiao Wulai from a ridge almost half a kilometre away. The sweeping scene of steep mountain peaks and the long waterfall bears a remarkable likeness to the famous Song-dynasty landscape *Travellers in Mountains and Streams*.

If you are driving, the sign for the turn-off to the falls is just past the 20.5km mark. Two kilometres up County Rd 115 you'll run into a tollbooth charging entrance (NT50) into the waterfall scenic area. The ridge lookout and the start of the trails are just a few metres past the tollbooth. Further down the road are some nice swimming holes and a somewhat messy campground with hot springs.

UPPER BALING 上巴陵

☎ 03 / pop 300

This tiny aboriginal village (Shàng Bālíng) is famous for the **Lalashan Forest Reserve**

(拉拉山國有林自然保護區; Lālāshān Guóyǒ Lín Zìrán Bǎohùqū; ☎ 391 2761; ☉ 6am-5pm), which contains a stand of ancient cypress trees. The village is about an hour's drive from Fusing and can be disturbingly crowded on summer weekends and holidays. This is definitely a place to keep for a quiet winter weekday.

The way to the old tree area is clearly designated from Upper Baling. In the reserve itself, a 3.7km path winds through the forest and each tree is specially marked to indicate its age, species, height and diameter. There are over 100 old trees, the oldest reported to be 2800 years old!

To get to the reserve, exit Hwy 7 onto County Rd 116 at the village of (lower) Baling (巴陵; Bālíng). Pay your entrance fee (NT100) at the tollbooth, continue up a very steep road to Upper Baling and then go on to a parking lot at the end of the road (about 13km from the turn-off on Hwy 7). The trail starts here and there's a small **exhibition hall** (☉ 9am-6pm) where you can pick up maps and information. Note that there are no longer any buses to Baling.

From the reserve it is possible to hike all the way downhill to **Fushan** (福山; Fúshān; six hours) near Wulai on the Fu-Ba Trail (福八越領; Fú-bā Yuèlíng). This is part of the National Trail System (see Hiking, p329).

There are numerous B&Bs in the area should you want to stay the night. Note that the Baling area is famous for its peaches and pears, but don't buy them as high mountain fruit farming is a scourge on the environment.

MINGCHIH FOREST RECREATION AREA 明池森林遊憩區

This **reserve** (Míngchí Sēnlín Yóuqì Qū; ☎ 03-989 4104; adult/child NT150/75) makes for a great base for exploration, or a retreat from the relentless heat of summer in the city. Mingchih lies between 1000m and 1700m and so even in July the average temperature is only 20°C. If you want to get out and see the sites, there are a couple of wild hot springs nearby and a stand of ancient trees, and the old trees at Baling are only an hour's drive away, too.

Sights & Activities

MINGCHIH (LAKE MING) 明池

There's not much in the reserve itself except a pleasant little **pond** (Míngchí) across the highway that's very popular with ducks. Strolling around when you first wake up is a great way to start the day.

MA-KOU ECOLOGICAL PARK 馬告生態公園
If you continue down Hwy 7 past Mingchih, you'll see a gated road called No 100 Forest Rd. This leads into an ecological park (Mǎgào Shēntài Gōngyuán) with a stand of ancient red cypress trees. You need permits to enter the park, which essentially means you need to go with a tour organised by the forest reserve (room guest NT660, others NT869). The tours are in Chinese, but the majestic old growth forest speaks all languages. Inquire at the front desk for times and to make reservations.

HOT SPRINGS
There are numerous hot springs within a short drive of Mingchih. There are developed ones at **Renze** (仁澤溫泉), on the way up to Taipingshan, and at **Jiaoshi**, but there are also some natural ones. Here's are some good ones.

Sileng Hot Spring 四稜溫泉
What is it about the cross-island highways and their abundant hot springs? Whatever it is we are grateful. This particular natural spring (Sìléng Wēnquán) is down a steep ravine. The spring water pours and seeps down from the cliffs (stained a multitude of colours from the minerals) into a small rock pool set above a rushing river.

To get here, head west from Mingchih exactly 7.1km (to around the 59.5km mark). As you go right, round a sharp bend that juts out into the ravine, you'll see a small spot on the left to park. Park and then look for the faded signs for 'hot spring' (溫泉) on the cement barrier. When you see it cross the barrier; there's a trail starting on the other side. Follow the trail down for 40 minutes or so till you reach the river. The springs are obvious on the other side.

Note that as you hike down, the trail seems to run flat for quite a while. Note also that you must cross the river at the end, so don't go after heavy rain. River shoes will be helpful.

Fan Fan Hot Spring 梵梵溫泉
This spring (Fàn Fàn Wēnquán) is a lot easier to get to than Sileng, which means that on weekends you'll be sharing the place with the EQ-challenged who drive their 4WD vehicles up the river.

The spring is an alkali bicarbonate one, which is said to be good for the skin. The water is full of calcium and magnesium and you can drink it. To get to the springs from Mingchih,

follow Hwy 7 to the fork. Turn left and when you get to the village of Yingshi (英士) don't cross the bridge but take the side path to the right. Park and follow the river up a kilometre or so. The way up is flat and easy and the walk takes about 30 minutes.

Sleeping & Eating
Mingchih has cottages (from NT3200, 20% weekday discounts) set among tall cedar trees. Try to get a room away from the highway though, as trucks come by at all times of day or night and can disturb your sleep. An OK restaurant serves breakfast, lunch and dinner (average meal NT250).

Getting There & Away
Private buses to Mingchih (NT250, 1½ hours) leave from the back of the Ilan (Yilan) train station at 12pm daily (returning 5.30pm). You must call (☎ 03-989 4106) to make a reservation. Ilan is on the east coast just south of Jiaoshi.

If you want to rent a car in Ilan call **Shang Xin Car Rental** (☎ 03-935 7777). It does pick-ups from the train station and the staff speak English.

WULING FOREST RECREATION AREA (WULING FARM) 武陵農場
☎ 04
Most people feel that the North Cross-Island Hwy ends around Chilan, a small forest reserve, but it actually continues south to Lishan and north to Ilan. If you want to continue your exploration of Taiwan's rugged mountains, head north. Not far south down the road is the turnoff to **Taipingshan National Forest Recreation Area** (太平山國家森林遊樂區; Tàipíngshān Guójiā Sēnlín Yóulè Qū; http://recreate.forest.gov.tw/forest .php?init=05&char=en&forest=1; adult/child NT150/100), where you'll find hot springs, a small mountain train, a few trails and a pretty lake.

About 1½ hours further south down Hwy 7 itself is Wuling Forest Recreation Area, better known as **Wuling Farm** (Wǔlíng Nóngchǎng; admission NT160). The farm (elevation 1740m to 2200m) was originally established in 1963 as a fruit-growing area by retired soldiers. It became part of Sheipa National Park in 1992. By the time you read this there will be little farming left in the reserve as new land-use laws finally take effect.

Many travellers come to Wuling to climb Snow Mountain, Taiwan's second-highest mountain, and in the eyes of many, including ours, the most beautiful. But Wuling also makes for a nice weekend getaway, or a cool break from the heat of summer.

Orientation & Information

There's only one main road through the park, with an offshoot to the camping ground.

There's a **Travel Service Centre** (☎ 2590 1350; ⏰ 9am-4.30pm), but it doesn't have much information. The *Bunbury Map* available at the entrance gate (a treasure for fans of Oscar Wilde) is about as good as you'll get.

Online, check out the websites for the forest recreation area (http://recreate.forest.gov.tw), Sheipa National Park (www.spnp.gov.tw) and Wuling Farm (www.wuling-farm.com.tw).

Sights & Activities

SNOW MOUNTAIN 雪山主峰

Many hikers come to Wuling to tackle Snow Mountain (Xuě Shān; elevation 3884m). The trail takes two to three days to complete (three is best), and is broad, clear and well marked, with map boards every few kilometres and distance markers every 100m. Anyone in reasonably good shape can do it. There are two rough cabins to stay in on the way up with running water, toilets, solar lights and dorm bedding.

The best times of year to hike the mountain are autumn and spring. In late May/early June the alpine flowers bloom near the top, making this a particularly great time to go. From September to December, the weather is driest and most predictable, and your chances of having clear skies are best.

To climb the mountain you need a mountain permit and a park pass (see p330). Note that you must get your mountain permit stamped at the police station at Sheipa National Park Wuling Station before proceeding to the ranger station at the trailhead (where you show your park pass).

A basic itinerary involves driving from Taipei (four hours) to the trailhead ranger station and then hiking to Chika Cabin (1½

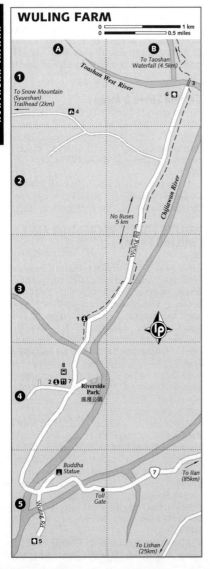

WULING FARM

0 — 1 km
0 — 0.5 miles

To Taoshan
Waterfall (4.5km)

Toashan West River

To Snow Mountain
(Syueshan)
Trailhead (2km)

Chijiawan River

No Buses
5 km

Wuling Rd

Riverside
Park
溪濱公園

Buddha
Statue

To Ilan
(85km)

Toll
Gate

Wuling Rd

To Lishan
(25km)

INFORMATION	
Police Station 檢查站	(see 1)
Sheipa National Park Wuling Station 雪霸國家公園武陵管理處	1 A3
Travel Service Centre 旅遊服務中心	2 A4

SIGHTS & ACTIVITIES	
Wuling Suspension Bridge 武陵吊橋	3 B1

SLEEPING	
Camping Ground 露營管理中心	4 A1
Wuling National Hostel 武陵賓館	5 A5
Wuling Villa 武陵山莊	6 B1

EATING	
Convenience Store 便利商店	7 A4

TRANSPORT	
Bus Stop 公車站	8 A4

to two hours). The second day involves hiking from Chika to 369 Cabin (five to six hours), and the third, hiking to the summit (three to four hours) and returning to 369 Cabin (two hours). Here, most people rest for a while then hike back to the ranger station and their car (four hours).

Maps of the hiking route, in Chinese, are available at the mountain equipment shops near the Taipei Main Train Station.

OTHER HIKING

For the average hiker the park offers short walks down by the **Riverside Park** (Xībīn Gōngyuán) or strolls along newly built paths beside the main road. The only longish hike is to **Taoshan Waterfall** (桃山瀑布; Táoshān Pùbù; elevation 2500m), 4.5km from the end of the road near the Wuling Mountain Hostel. The falls are 50m high and well worth the 90-minute hike.

SALMON

Wuling Farm is well known for its efforts to preserve the unique **Formosan Landlocked Salmon** (櫻花鉤吻鮭; Yīnghuā Gōuwěn Guī), also known as the masu salmon. Unlike other salmon, these never leave the cool freshwater rivers they were born in. At the time of writing about 1000 salmon lived in the waters of three rivers in Wuling. If conservation measures go as planned, around 5000 should exist in five years. They will then be introduced into three more rivers with the goal of having 10,000 or so in 10 years. At this point the population will be considered stable.

One place to try to see the salmon is below the **Wuling Suspension Bridge** (Wǔlíng Diàoqiáo).

Sleeping & Eating

Camping ground (Lùyíng guǎnlǐ zhōngxīn; ☎ 2590 1265; sites from NT400) This campground is set high on a gorgeous alpine meadow. There are clean, modern facilities (including showers and a convenience store), raised camping platforms and sites with parking included.

Wuling Villa (Wuling Mountain Hostel; Wǔlíngshān Zhuāng; dm/s/d NT480/2130/2280) Run by the Wuling National Hostel, rooms here have simple wooden interiors with a minimum of furniture. Breakfast (congee and salty eggs) is included.

Wuling National Hostel (Wǔlíng Bīnguǎn; ☎ 2590 1259; rooms & cabins from NT3420) A pleasant place

to stay, the cabins here offer decent comfort and nice scenery. Buffet-style meals (NT150 to NT350; breakfast, lunch and dinner) are available for guests and nonguests at the hostel's restaurant.

Besides the buffet meals at the National Hostel, there's a **convenience store** (🕙 9am-5pm) near the visitor centre for instant noodles and snack foods.

Getting There & Away

There are two Kuo Kuang Hao buses a day from Ilan to Wuling Forest Recreation Area (NT276, three hours, 7am and 12.40pm). From Wuling you can continue south to Lishan and transfer to a bus to Taichung. You could also consider renting a scooter in Jiaoshi (see p163), or a car in Ilan through **Shang Xin Car Rental** (☎ 03-935 7777).

HSINCHU TO SANYI

The Hsinchu Science Park is by far the most famous site in this region, but most travellers come for the high mountains or the rural countryside where the old traditions are still going strong in a few small towns. There's also a top-quality hot-spring resort out here and a small mist-shrouded mountain dotted with temples that you can spend the night in.

Hsinchu, Taoyuan and Miaoli Counties have a heavy concentration of Hakka people, and this is reflected in the food you'll find in many small towns. It's good to familiarise yourself with some of the staples before heading out (see p59).

Getting around this region is pretty easy. Trains run up and down the coast all day, and there is inland bus service to most places.

HSINCHU 新竹

☎ 03 / pop 386,950

The oldest city in northern Taiwan, and long a base for traditional industries such as glassmaking and noodles, Hsinchu (Xīnzhú) sprang into the modern era in 1980 with the establishment of the Science Park. The park has often been described as the Silicon Valley of Taiwan and is the centre of the semiconductor industry. Though it's the most famous landmark of the city, the park does not offer much to the average visitor. Nor, to be honest, does Hsinchu itself. We recommend a visit here mostly to see the rich collection of curios and antiquities at Guqifeng on the outskirts of town. A few other nearby sites help round out an afternoon.

Hsinchu is an hour from Taipei on the train, and it's best taken in as a day trip.

Orientation & Information

The town centre is small and most sights can be reached on foot. Hsinchu lacks good footpaths in many places, but the traffic is not bad during the day and the constant wind (this is the Windy City) keeps air pollution down.

Hsinchu roads use Hanyu Pinyin for their Romanisation scheme and almost all roads are signed. There are plenty of banks in the town centre, as well as ATMs in 7-Elevens and other convenience stores.

The **Hsinchu Cultural Bureau** (☎ 531 9756; www .hcccb.gov.tw/english/index.asp; 1 Lane 15, Dongda Rd, sec.2; ⏰ 9am-5pm Wed-Sun) acts as the city's tourist centre. The bureau's website now has good information in English about all the sites in the city, including a long list of historical relics and places to eat.

The tourism bureau's website (http://dep -tourism-en.hccg.gov.tw) is also an excellent guide to the city. Check out 'Theme Trips' for English maps, but be aware that many of the themes, especially the 17km of 'glorious coastline', are not quite ready for prime time (the middle third of the way is still a very messy, dirty construction zone).

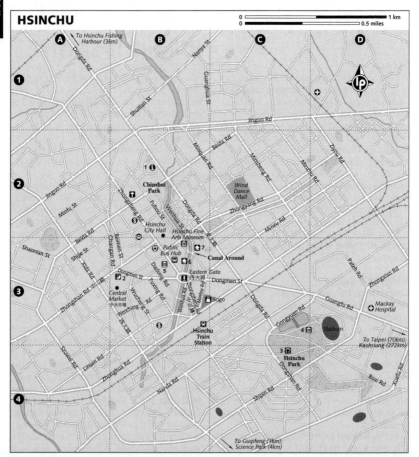

The science park has an **administration centre** (☎ 577 3311; http://eweb.sipa.gov.tw/en/index.jsp; 2 Shinan Rd, sec.2; ☒ 8am-6pm) where you can get maps and books about the park. The website is also very informative.

Sights & Activities

GUQIFENG (GUQI MOUNTAIN) 古奇峰

The Pu Tian Temple complex on the slopes of **Guqifeng** (Gǔqífēng; admission free) houses one of the most impressive private collections of artefacts and curios we have seen in Taiwan. A few standouts include a life-size Chinese bed made out of pure jade, a 6m-long panel of pure jade high relief, ferocious carved dragon heads whose mouths you could step into, several miniature villages carved from wood and a small taxidermy collection of rare Taiwanese mammals. The 40m-high statue of Kuang Kong that squats above the temple is quite a site too.

The Hsinchu government is interested in making Guqifeng a flagship attraction in years to come, and we hope they do, as this collection deserves a much better venue than it currently has. Note that the collection is only available for viewing on weekends, though the temple is always open.

There are no public buses to Guqifeng. A taxi will cost around NT200.

RELICS

Hsinchu was called Hsinchang by the early Chinese settlers who built a bamboo fence *(hsinchang)* around the city to protect themselves from Taiya, Saisha and Pingpu aborigines. In 1826 a solid brick wall was constructed around the city. Only one portion of the wall remains today, the **Eastern Gate** (Dōng Dàmén), but it is in fine shape and a great central landmark.

The second most famous landmark is the **City God Temple** (Chénghuáng Miào). Built in 1748, it has the highest rank of all the city god temples in Taiwan. It also has a lot of very finely carved statues and wall reliefs, whose quality doesn't take an expert to recognise. The temple is most lively during the seventh lunar month and on the 29th day of the 11th month, when the birthday of the temple god is celebrated. There's a lively and surprisingly well-organised market around the temple selling all manner of traditional foods.

For more information on these and other important relics, check out the websites listed earlier.

MUSEUMS

It is not well known, even by many Taiwanese, that Hsinchu has a long history of glassmaking, nor that in recent years several local artists have gained an international reputation. The **Municipal Glass Museum** (Bōlí Gōngyì Bówùguǎn; ☎ 562 6091; www.hcgm.gov.tw; 2 Dongda Rd, sec.1; adult/child NT20/10; ☒ 9am-5pm Wed-Sun) was designed in part to promote and display the active glass scene. Informative tours in English are available if you request them in advance (by phone or email).

The museum is situated in Hsinchu Park (Xīnzhú Gōngyuán), which also features a **Confucius Temple** (Kǒng Miào; ☒ 8.30am-4.30pm Wed-Sun) and zoo.

The **Municipal Image Museum** (Yǐnshàng Bówùguǎn; ☎ 528 5840; www.hmim.gov.tw; 65 Zhongzheng Rd; adult/child NT20/10; ☒ 9.30am-noon, 1.30-5pm & 6.30-9pm Wed-Sun) occupies a stylish old building that was once the first air-conditioned movie theatre in Hsinchu that now serves as a movie relics museum, educational centre and public movie theatre. Movies are shown around 7pm Wednesday to Friday and at 10am, 2pm and 7pm on Saturday and Sunday. Admission is a low NT20 unless a festival is on.

Sleeping

Hsinchu has plenty of hotels that mostly serve the people working at the Science Park.

Dong Cheng Hotel (Dōngchéng Dàlǚshè; ☎ 522 2648; 1 Lane 5, Fuhou St; 府後街5巷1號; d/tw NT800/1200) A nondescript budget hotel, this place has clean good-sized rooms that won't make you wish you'd brought a sleeping bag. It's one of the cheapest hotels in town, and bars, restaurants and cafés abound nearby.

Sol Downtown Hotel (Yíngxī Dàfàndiàn; ☎ 533 5276; fax 533 5750; 10 Wenhua St; 文化街10號; d/tw incl breakfast NT3800/4700; ☒) This is a solid mid-range business hotel, also suitable for visitors looking for softer beds, better bathrooms and a higher thread count in their sheets. Discounts of 30% to 40% are available every day.

Eating & Drinking

The train station area is chock-a-block full of places to eat, both on the streets and in the shopping malls. The area around the City God Temple holds a lively, though orderly market, where visitors can sample any number of local dishes. For information about some of these, from duck noodles to 'black cat steamed buns', check out the Cultural Bureau's website. Almost 50 restaurants and stalls are listed (including hours and addresses), with pictures, useful descriptions in English of the dishes and touching stories of the trials and triumphs of the owners of various establishments.

Hsinchu has scores of cafés and pubs, though not all of the latter are welcoming to strangers. One good area to try is Wenhua St alongside the canal.

Shopping

For high-quality glass products ask at the Glass Museum for the numbers and addresses of Hsinchu artisans.

Getting There & Around

Trains leave from Taipei (fast/slow train NT180/116, 60/90 minutes) and Taichung (fast/slow train NT198/128, 60/90 minutes) from 5am to 11pm.

The high-speed rail doesn't go directly to Hsinchu downtown from Taipei (NT290, 40 minutes), so you still need to catch a bus to complete your journey (NT31, 30 minutes, every 30 to 40 minutes). A taxi will cost about NT300 to the Hsinchu train station.

At the time of writing there were high-speed rail trains about every hour, though this will certainly increase as time goes on.

Roaming taxis are not that numerous in Hsinchu. Get your hotel to call before you head out or keep the number of the driver once you've found one.

BEIPU 北埔
☎ 03 / pop 10,400

'I'm a little bit Lukang, I'm a little bit Meinong, too.'

With all due respect to Donnie and Marie, that's Beipu (Běipǔ), a small Hsinchu County town that in recent years has, like the others, tried to pull in visitors with its Hakka cultural heritage. Lest our little jingle makes it sound like Beipu has not been successful, we have to note that it makes for an excellent day trip. There's a nice authentic feel to the place, and while it could be a little cleaner, the quality of its attractions (temples, teahouses, old houses and some speciality foods) is quite good. It's certainly one of the best places to try Hakka pounded tea.

Orientation

There are almost no signs in English around town, but it's very small and most of what you'll want to see is close together. The bus drops you off in the heart of things. Some teahouses have a Chinese map. The town's website is also in Chinese only (www.peipu.com.tw).

Sights

The following is written as a short tour from the bus stop on Jhong Jheng Rd (中正路), across from an OK convenience store.

From the bus stop head back towards the hill. In a minute or so you will see old buildings on either side of the road. On the right is **Tian Shui Hall** (天水堂; Tiān Shuǐ Táng), the largest private traditional three-sided compound in Beipu. You can look in over the walls, but you can't go in.

To the left is **Jinguangfu** (金廣福公館; Jīnguǎngfú Gōngguǎn), a heritage house from 1835 that unfortunately you also can't enter. If you continue up the narrow alley between the buildings you'll reach the very quaint teahouse The Well (see opposite).

Facing Tian Shui Hall, go right. Shortly you will pass **Jian Asin Mansion** (A-Hsin Jiang Residence; 姜阿新故居; Jiāngāxīn Gù Jū) on the left. This two-storey Western-styled house was built by a rich tea merchant who, not surprisingly, had a lot of Western clients. Entry is by prior reservation only.

From the mansion it's just a hop to our favourite site in Beipu, the **Zhitian (Citian) Temple** (慈天宮; Cítiān Gōng). You can enter this building and should to see the very beautiful pillars and the high relief on the walls.

To the left of the temple (as you face it) is a small passageway; walk to its curvy end. Notice a few loose stones? That's not an accident. In the wilder days of Taiwan's history the narrow passageways into Beipu were lined with the occasional loose stone so that intruders (who of course wouldn't know this) could be heard approaching.

As you exit the temple the street directly in front of you is **Beipu Street** (北埔街). There are a number of old buildings along the first few blocks and many pleasant snack shops, teahouses and cafés.

One block up, at the intersection with Nansing Rd (南興街), look right for an OK convenience store sign. This is where you got off the bus, and where you can catch it again back to Jhudong. Note that you catch the bus back on the opposite side of the road.

Eating & Drinking

Like Meinong in the south, Beipu (which means northern wild area) is over 90% Hakka. In almost every restaurant you'll find Hakka staples such as *bǎntiáo* (板條; flat rice noodles) and *lěi chá* (see the boxed text, below).

The Well (水井; Shuǐjǐng; ☎ 580 5122; set meals NT250, lei cha for 3 NT300; ☼ 10am-6pm) One of the best places to try *lei cha*, The Well is a rustic Hakka-style house that has just the perfect heritage character. It hasn't been gussied up for modern times, nor is it old and dirty. You can sit inside at tables, or on wooden floors, or even outside on a wooden deck under the plum trees. The food here is not bad, but most people come for the atmosphere and the chance to grind and make their own *lei cha*.

People don't linger in Beipu so expect most shops to close by early evening.

Getting There & Away

To get to Beipu from Hsinchu, take a **Hsinchu Bus Company** (☎ 03-596 2018) bus, which you'll find just to the left of the train station, heading to Xia Gong Guan (NT44, every 20 minutes). Forty minutes later get off at Jhudong (竹東) and then transfer to a bus to Beipu (NT23, 20 minutes, every 30 minutes). At the time of writing the first bus left Jhudong at 7am, and the first bus from Hsinchu to Xia Gong Guan left at 6.10am.

SHITOUSHAN 獅頭山

☎ 03 / elevation 492m

Shitoushan (Shītóushān) is a foothill on the border of Miaoli and Hsinchu Counties. Beautiful dense forests and rugged rock faces define the topography, but if you ask anyone it is the temples tucked into caves and hugging the slopes that have given the place its fame. Shitoushan is sacred ground for the island's Buddhists and draws big weekend crowds, with people coming to worship or simply enjoy the beauty and tranquillity of the mountain. Over the years, Shitoushan has been consistently described by Lonely Planet travellers as a highlight of their trip to Taiwan.

Yuanguang Temple (元光寺; Yuánguāng Sì) was the first temple to be constructed in the area (in 1894). Many more buildings were added over the years, including **Chuanhua Tang**

LEI CHA 擂茶

If you pronounce it incorrectly, *lei cha (lěi chá)* sounds like 'tired tea', but this hearty brew was designed to do anything but make you sleepy. It was a farmer's drink, rich and thick and full of nutrients and calories. In the old days, Hakka farmers would drink it both during and after work in the tobacco fields in order to fortify their bodies.

Or so the story goes.

Very likely, *lei cha* is a modern invention (like the Scottish tartan), or at best a family drink that has been cleverly promoted as an authentic part of Taiwan's Hakka heritage. In any case, it's everywhere now, and authentic or not, it's definitely part of the Taiwan experience.

Lei cha means pounded tea, and that's exactly what you must do before you can drink it. If you go to an authen…well, if you go to a shop that does it right, you will be given a wooden pestle and a large porcelain bowl with a small amount of green tea leaves, sesame seeds, nuts and grains in the bottom.

Then comes the 'pound' part of 'pounded tea'. Using the pestle, grind the ingredients in the bowl. Yes, we know we said this is *pounded* tea, but then your host also said this is an ancient recipe. So grind, atomise, pestle (it's a verb, too), pulverise and mix the ingredients to a fine mush. Your host will then add hot water and dole out the 'tea' in cups. At this moment, or perhaps earlier, you will be given a small bowl of puffed rice. Add the rice to the drink and consume before the kernels get soggy.

If this sounds like your cuppa (and really, it is delicious), head to any teahouse in Beipu, Meinong or Sanyi.

(勸化堂; Quànhuà Táng), which today also serves as a guesthouse, and the **main gate**, built in 1940 by the Japanese to celebrate the 2600th anniversary of their royal court (that's one ancient royal line!). There are 11 temples, five on the front side of the mountain, six on the back, as well as numerous smaller shrines, arches and pagodas. Shitoushan is a veritable temple wonderland and a great hit with photographers, nature lovers and temple aficionados. Give yourself at least three hours to explore the area or an overnight stay for the full effect.

On the other side of the mountain, connected by a walking trail, is the **Lion's Head Mountain Visitor Centre** (☎ 580 9296; ☷ 9am-5pm). The centre is a pleasant place to grab a meal or a map, should you wish to explore beyond Shitoushan itself.

Visitors (including non-Buddhists) are allowed to stay overnight at **Chuanhua Tang** (Chuanhua Hall; ☎ 822 020, 823 859; d/tw NT800/1100). Excellent vegetarian meals are NT60 each, but if that doesn't appeal to you there are stalls and shops lining the back parking lot and even a café on the way up the stairs to the hall. The old rules forbidding talk during meals or couples sleeping together are no longer enforced, but do be on your best behaviour.

From the car park it's a short walk up the stairs to Chuanhua Tang. The check-in counter is to the left, just before the temple. There's a large map (with some labels in English on it) on the right side of the car park to show you the way.

Getting There & Away

It's not easy to get to Shitoushan. The best way at present is to take a bus from the **Hsinchu Bus Company** (☎ 03-596 2018), just to the left of the Hsinchu train station, heading to Xia Gong Guan (NT44, every 20 minutes). Forty minutes later get off at Jhudong (竹東) and transfer to a bus heading to Shitoushan (NT50). Ask the driver to let you off at Shitoushan Old Hiking Trail Arch (獅頭山舊登山口牌樓). From here it's a 30-minute uphill walk through a dreamlike forest landscape to the parking lot. Note that there are few buses a day to Shitoushan, so call to check the schedule.

AROUND SHITOUSHAN

Not far from Shitoushan, down County Rd 124 (甲), is one of the most pleasant hot-spring resorts outside the Taipei area. **East River Spa Garden** (東江溫泉; Dōngjiāng Wēnquán; ☎ 03-825 285; www.eastriver.com.tw, Chinese only; public baths unlimited time adult/child NT350/150; ☷ 9am-10pm) is nestled in the bend of a fast flowing river in an area with no other development. The design makes use of traditional red bricks and lots of wood. It looks traditional, but there's no denying it's for urbanites who want *their* version of rural Taiwan, ie folksy but clean and comfortable.

If you are staying at Shitoushan you can get a taxi to the hot springs for about NT200. If you have your own car, make sure you explore the rural roads around the hot springs. The area is called **Nanzhuang** (南庄) and it's full of little surprises.

TAIAN HOT SPRINGS 泰安溫泉
☎ 037

There are hot springs all over Taiwan, and beautiful mountains for hiking, too, but we still think Taian (Tàiān Wēnquán) is special. For one thing, it has hot spring water so good the Japanese built an officers' club here to take advantage of it 90 years ago.

More recently, Taian has gone from largely unknown to the hot new hot-spring place (we never doubted it for a second, though now that it's happened, we aren't all that happy sharing). Weekdays are best if you want to avoid the crowds, but note that if you are going hiking, a warm weekend is not going to attract the hot springers. Whatever you do, avoid the hugely popular strawberry season in autumn. And avoid the strawberries: they are loaded with pesticides.

Orientation & Information

Taian is in a remote corner of southeastern Miaoli County, near Sheipa National Park (see p178). The area is not precisely defined on any map, but is more or less the region that County Rd 62 runs through. Beginning just outside the town of Wenshui, Country Rd 62 runs for 16km alongside the Wenshui River before ending in a car park just below the Japanese Police Officers' Club.

Most visitors stay within the last 3km stretch of Country Rd 62, in an area of Taian known as Jinshui Village (Jīnshǔi Cūn; population 200). A tourist map, in Chinese, is available at the Tenglong Hot Spring Resort.

Sheipa National Park Wenshui Visitor Centre (☎ 996 100; www.spnp.gov.tw; 100 Shuiweiping, Dahu; ☷ 9am-4.30pm Tue-Sun) sits at the start of Country Rd 62. It doesn't have any information on Taian, however.

Dangers & Annoyances

Taian suffers frequent landslides, which can wash out roads and change the course and look of riverbeds. Avoid the area after heavy rains or earthquakes.

Sights & Activities

HIKING

There are a number of trails marked on our map, but you should always check with locals about the conditions before heading out. This is a rough area. Try to finish higher trails before mid-afternoon, as fog can obscure the views and make it easy to get lost.

HOT SPRINGS 溫泉

Taian's springs produce alkaloid carbonic water at a temperature of about 47°C. The water is clear, tasteless and almost odourless and said to be good for treating skin problems and nervousness. The **Sunrise Hot Spring Hotel** (Rìchū Wēnquán Dùjià Fàndiàn; ☎ 941 988; public pool unlimited time adult/child NT350/150; ⏰ 8am-11pm) has excellent modern facilities to enjoy the waters. Both public outdoor pools and private tubs in rooms are designed to let you take in the mountain views as you bathe.

Sleeping

Tenglong Hot Spring Resort (Ténglóng Shānzhuāng; ☎ 941 002; www.tenglong.com.tw/; camp sites NT300, with tent & sleeping bags for up to 8 people NT1000, 2-person cabins NT3000; ⏰ 6.30am-10pm) Tenglong has a good, central location, near food stalls, restaurants and hiking trails. The campground is nothing special and you probably wouldn't want to go on a sunny weekend due to the noise and crowds. The cabins are pretty good value (weekday discount 25%) if you want a little more privacy. The public pools here cost NT200.

Sunrise Hot Spring Hotel (☎ 941 988; d/tw NT5500/7000, 20% weekday discount) Rooms here are stylish, but some are holding up better than others; make sure you check before paying.

Eating

Food is fresh and local, and we've never had a bad meal in many visits. There are numerous small restaurants and shops along the main road, and a collection of small **food stalls** (dishes NT100) open for lunch and dinner beside the suspension bridge into Tenglong. There's a convenience store in the village that also has good lunch boxes.

Mountain Legend Café (Shānzhōng Chuánqí; ☎ 941 380; 16 Qingan Village; dishes NT150; ⏰ 10am-10pm)

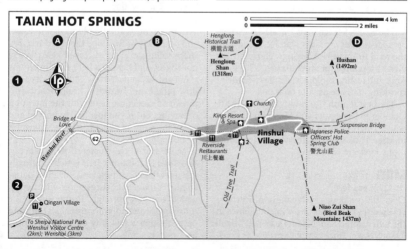

TAIAN HOT SPRINGS

Worth a special mention, this rustic Qingan Village establishment has been in the Peng family for three generations now, and while grandma is no longer cooking (a great shame), we can't really complain about the fare her daughter-in-law whips up. The menu features great fried tofu and Hakka-style food such as salty eggs, bitter melon and excellent mountain chicken. The café sits atop the Turtle Nest (Gūi Xuè), a large rock standing in the exact location where the three Miaoli County townships intersect. The most powerful feng shui in all of Taian is right here.

Getting There & Around

The one bus route that used to get you close to Taian is no longer running, so you will need your own transportation.

SHEIPA NATIONAL PARK
雪霸國家公園

Many rivers and one mountain range run through this 76,000-hectare national park (Xuěbà Guójiā Gōngyuán). Sheipa National Park is home to 51 mountain peaks over 3000m and is the primary source of drinking water for northern and central Taiwan.

The park was established in 1992 and much of it remains inaccessible, in fact prohibited. The three sections you are permitted to enter are the forest recreation areas of Wuling (see p169), Guanwu and Syuejian. Guanwu (觀霧森林遊樂區; Guānwù Sēnlín Yóulè Qū) was closed at the time of writing, while Syuejian (雪見森林遊樂區; Xuějiàn Sēnlín Yóulè Qū) was just about to open after a three-year delay.

The park's **headquarters** (☎ 037-996 100; www .spnp.gov.tw; Dahu; ⏰ 9am-4.30pm Tue-Sun) are on the road to Taian Hot Springs. Here you can pick up a number of brochures and check out some interesting ecological displays. English-speaking staff are usually on hand.

The best months for hiking in the park are October to December and March to April. In winter, high-altitude trails are often snowed in; after April, seasonal heavy rains, including monsoons, are common.

SANYI 三義
☎ 037 / pop 5000

Over 100 years ago, a Japanese officer discovered that camphor grew in abundance in the hills around Sanyi (Sānyì), a small Miaoli County town. Since camphor makes for excel-

lent wood products (it's aromatic, extremely heavy and can resist termites), the officer wisely established a wood business. Over time, Sanyi became *the* woodcarving region in Taiwan. Today, nearly half the population is engaged in the business in one way or another, with the other half probably wishing they were.

In addition to the wood products, Sanyi is worth visiting for its excellent museum, old train station village and You Tong trees. The You Tong (*Aleurites fordii*) is a hardwood whose oil was once used to waterproof wood products. It covers the mountainsides around Sanyi, and during the spring months its blossoming white flowers give the landscape the appearance of being dusted with snow.

Orientation

The sights in Sanyi are spread out and, now that the public shuttle bus service has been cancelled, it is not that easy to see everything in a day without your own transportation. If you're on foot, and starting at the Sanyi train station, walk out and up to Jungjeng Rd, the main thoroughfare in town, and turn left (everything you want to see is left). The turnoff for the old train station and village is about 1km down the road, though the station itself is another 5km away. The main commercial carving street and the wood museum are about 2km away, making them easy to walk to. There are signs in English about town.

Sights & Activities
WOODCARVING

Woodcarving is the lifeblood of the town, and on Jungjeng Rd alone there are over 200 shops selling an array of carved items. We're not talking dull signposts here, but 3m cypress statues of savage-faced folk gods, delicate window reliefs and beautiful traditional furniture. You can come here with the intention of buying, but if you just like to browse and enjoy the work of skilled artisans you won't be disappointed.

Most stores are clustered in two areas: Shueimei St (Shǔiměi Jiē), which is actually just a few blocks of Jungjeng Rd; and Guangsheng Village (Guǎngshēng Xīnchéng), which you pass through on the way to the museum. Stores in both areas close around 6pm, though a few stay open till 10pm or later on weekends.

MIAOLI WOOD SCULPTURE MUSEUM
苗栗木雕博物館

This **museum** (Miáolì Mùdiāo Bówùguǎn; ☎ 037-876 009; adult/child NT60/50; ☽ 9am-5pm Tue-Sun, closed holidays) opened in 1995 with the goal of promoting Taiwan's wood culture. Exhibits include informative displays on the origins of woodcarving in Sanyi, a knockout collection of Buddhas and Bodhisattvas, some gorgeous traditional household furniture and architectural features, and even a few pieces by Juming (see the boxed text, p53).

Other than the titles to these displays, there is no information in English at all, which is a shame. Some of the history of Sanyi is quite quirky, such as how the town became popular in the '50s with American Catholics who came to custom order hand-carved statues of the Virgin Mary.

The museum is just at the end of Guangsheng Village. You can't miss it for the two carved mastodons outside.

SHENG SHING TRAIN STATION 勝興火車站

Built during the Japanese era and without the use of nails, the charming Sheng Shing Train Station (Shèngxīng Huǒchēzhàn) is now a little too popular on the weekends with day trippers coming to explore the old grounds, walk through a 1km-long tunnel (bring a torch) or stroll along the abandoned railway tracks.

At 480m, the station used to be the highest stop along the whole Western Trunk Line. When it was closed in 1997, walkers soon discovered that the 12km of abandoned track made for a fine stroll through the countryside. A small tourist village soon popped up around the station, and, when not overrun with tourists, it is very pleasant here. The street is cobbled and lined with all manner of old-style teahouses, cafés and restaurants, many in charming old brick buildings with rustic decks made out of old railway ties. Evening time really brings out the charm of the place.

Four kilometres past the station stand the picturesque ruins of the **Long Deng Viaduct** (Lóngténg Duàn Qiáo). The viaduct was built in 1905 and destroyed in a 7.3 magnitude earthquake in 1930. The remains are fairly dramatic and rather interesting in that the terracotta brick arches are held together with mortar made of sticky rice and clam shell.

HIKING

In addition to the abandoned rail tracks, you can walk the **April Snow Trail** (四月雪步道; Sìyuè Xuě Bùdào). This begins just to the right of the museum and takes you through a beautiful forest of You Tong trees whose white blossoms in April and early May give the trail its name. The trail leads, in about 30 minutes, to a beautiful open tea field.

Tours

Taiwan Tour Bus (☎ 0800-011 765; tours NT1500) runs tours to Sanyi, which include a hot-springs stopover in nearby Taian.

Festivals & Events

Every May artists from around Taiwan are invited to display their best work and to create new works, in wood and ice, right on the street during the **Sanyi Woodcarving Festival** (三義木雕節; Sānyì Mùdiāo Jié). For visitors there are also opportunities to try your hand at woodcarving and to sample Hakka food.

The **Miaoli Mask Festival** (苗栗國際假面藝術節; Miáolì Guójì Jiǎ Miàn Yìshù Jié) has been getting rave reviews since the first one was held in 1999. Now held yearly in the **Shangri-La Paradise Theme Park** (香格里拉樂園; Xiānggélǐlā Lèyuán; ☎ 561 369), the event draws bigger and bigger crowds each year. In 2005, Central and South American masks and cultures were highlighted, though local mask makers, opera troupes and folk dance troupes were also showcased. The festival usually runs from late March through to the end of May.

Eating

There is no end of places to eat and drink traditional Hakka fare near Sheng Shing station and Shueimei St.

Getting There & Away

There's only one train in the morning from Taipei (NT193, 2½ hours, 8.53am), but many more from Taichung.

East Coast

For many travellers, a love affair with the east coast begins with a journey to Taroko Gorge. Wandering this bedazzling marble canyon, visitors often find a private paradise in the form of a deep waterfall-fed pool or rocky lookout. Such delight does this discovery give that most people fear losing the spot to the masses and try to keep it secret.

But fear not, there are places like this all over the east coast. This chapter will let you in on some of them, but if ever you should take our recommendation to get off the beaten track, this is the time and place to do it.

Two main highways run through the east; try to travel them both (one down and one up). Hwy 11 is the coastline route and offers stops for swimming, biking and visiting aboriginal and fishing villages. Hwy 9 runs through a wide valley, rich in hot springs and local flavour. This is also prime farmland and the vast fields of rice, backed up by dark green hills, are wonderfully photogenic.

Eastern Taiwan has the highest concentration of indigenous peoples in Taiwan and many tribal members maintain both their language and lifestyle. Visiting an aboriginal village or attending a traditional festival is a highlight for most travellers.

For years, people have been saying that the time to visit the east coast is now before its backwater charms are lost forever, but we see no danger of that happening for a while yet. In any case, if you happen to find one piece of this paradise has gotten too crowded, there's always the next valley over.

HIGHLIGHTS

- Hike ancient hunting trails in **Taroko Gorge** (p188)
- Raft the scenic **Hsiukuluan River** (p198)
- Cycle down the winding coastline on **Highway 11** (p192)
- Photograph colourful fields of orange day lilies on **Sixty Stone Mountain** (p200)
- Visit the wetland classroom of **Mataian** (p197)
- See monkeys and barking deer in a banyan forest in **Chihpen** (p205)
- Retrace history and nature-watch on the **Walami Trail** (p200)
- Check out the thriving local music scene at **Dulan Sugar Factory** (p194)

★ Taroko Gorge

Highway 14 ★

Mataian ★   ★ Highway 11

Walami Trail ★   ★ Hsiukuluan River

★ Sixty Stone Mountain

★ Dulan Sugar Factory

★ Chihpen

Culture & History

Because of its geographical isolation, the east coast was slow to develop. Before the 20th century there were few settlers apart from indigenous peoples such as the Ami, Atayal, Bunun, Puyuma and Yami.

But things began to change (albeit less dramatically than in other areas) under Japanese rule. In 1926 the Eastern Railway Line began operations and wood and sugar processing factories were established up and down the coast. These factories drew large numbers of workers from other parts of Taiwan, especially the Hakka, who over time became the largest ethnic group in Taitung County. When Taiwan was returned to Chinese rule, the east was opened further with the completion of the Central Cross-Island Hwy in 1961 and the South Cross-Island Hwy in 1972.

Today, the east coast is still a relatively undeveloped area. The real legacy of the 20th century is the diverse mix of ethnic groups and cultural traditions that is easily seen in towns across the region. The indigenous people, while not the majority, have one of the strongest influences, reflected in the large numbers of annual festivals held throughout the year and the food visitors will encounter.

Climate

It gets warmer and more tropical the further south you go and the vegetation becomes lusher; you can see, feel and smell the differ-ence. Hualien is always slightly cooler than Taitung, and anywhere in the mountains will be cooler than along the coast.

Unlike in the north, there are not afternoon showers every day in summer, which makes the area more suitable for outdoor activities. Mid-August to October is typhoon season and the east coast is frequently battered with severe storms. Winters are chilly and the pervasive dampness and overcast skies can make it seem much colder than the actual temperature. Don't go to the east coast looking to swim in winter; head to Kenting (p282) instead.

National Parks & Forest Reserves

The crown jewel of Taiwan's national park system is Taroko, with its marble canyons and ancient hiking paths. The Nanan section of Yushan National Park, no slouch itself, features the rugged Walami Trail. Chihpen, Fuyuan and Chihnan National Forest Recreation areas each have their highlights: Chihpen has a beautiful old banyan forest, Fuyuan a butterfly valley and camphor forests, and Chihnan highlights the history of the logging industry in Taiwan.

Getting There & Around

There is air and rail service to the east coast and bus service is available locally, but having your own transport is the most convenient way to see eastern Taiwan. There are simply too many places you can't get to without

---

EAST COAST EATING

Hualien and Taitung Counties have a diverse mix of aborigines, Hakka, Taiwanese and former mainland Chinese, all contributing to the culinary traditions of the area. One of the most influential cuisines in Hualien is that prepared by the Ami people. The cooking tends to be simple and emphasises the natural flavours of fruits, flowers, taro and wild vegetables. Dishes made from betel-nut flowers, sorghum and rattan are common and can be seen in night markets and restaurants around Hualien. For something unique, head to Mataian for hotpot made to boil with heated rocks.

Fruit grown in eastern Taiwan is often tastier and fresher than elsewhere. Pineapples, mangoes and watermelons can be seen growing (or for sale) along the sides of roads, and some orchards allow you to pick your own fruit and pay by weight. City markets have tables and carts heaped with a colourful assortment of common and exotic fruits, including star fruit, pomelos (the ones grown in Dulan are best), coconuts, durian, papaya and lychees. Taitung's custard apple, or Buddha head fruit (so-called because the bumpy ridges on the fruit resemble the head of the Sakyamuni Buddha), has even garnered its own festival; sad to say, it's pretty lame. The fruit is delicious though and really does have the consistency of custard.

Other delicacies to try include the dumplings in Hualien, the dried fish of Chengkung and the sticky rice of Taitung. Fresh seafood is available all along the coast; some of the best places to find it are Chengkung, Shihtiping and Fukang Harbour, north of Taitung.

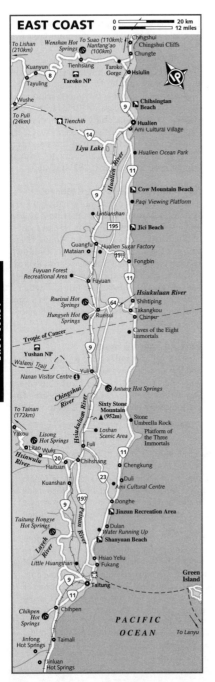

EAST COAST

your own wheels. That said, it's best to take the train, or fly, to Hualien as the twisting Suao–Hualien Hwy can be a bit unnerving.

Driving the highways between Hualien and Taitung (and the many splendid mountain roads connecting them) is a breeze, with light traffic on weekdays and plenty of places to pull off the road and explore.

Eastern Taiwan doesn't see as many cyclists as it deserves, which in part is why you should go. You can't ride the Suao–Hualien Hwy (and wouldn't want to anyway for safety reasons), so ship your bike down and begin at Hualien. Most riders travel on either Hwy 9 or 11, but there are numerous side routes (such as the highways connecting the 9 and 11) as well as county roads (such as the 195) that allow you to enjoy the same stunning scenery as drivers, but with far less traffic. The 11 is much more winding and steep than the 9.

There are numerous camp sites on the east coast, some overlooking the ocean, and a few that even have hot springs. If you are looking for B&Bs, you'll find them. In general you can set up a tent on most deserted beaches (just don't swim unless you know it's safe).

Past Taitung there is little of interest and in any case the truck traffic can be pretty bad. For more infomation, including some detailed routes, check out the website of a long-term Taiwan expat and avid biker (http://rank.blogspot .com/2006/05/great-taiwan-bike-rides-part -1-taidong.html).

HUALIEN 花蓮

☎ 03 / pop 109,324

Hualien (Huālián) is eastern Taiwan's largest city and the capital of Hualien County. It doesn't have many attractions of its own and most people can give it a miss or minimise their time here without worrying about whether they're losing out. It's best thought of as a base for visiting Taroko Gorge, Taiwan's most famous scenic spot, and other sites around the county.

Orientation

Hualien isn't a large place and it's easy to get around on foot. The city can be divided into three areas. The train station is where most travellers arrive and is surrounded by budget and midrange hotels. It's also where the bus stations are located for those wishing to go to Taitung or Taroko Gorge. The city centre features the most developed part of town, for what

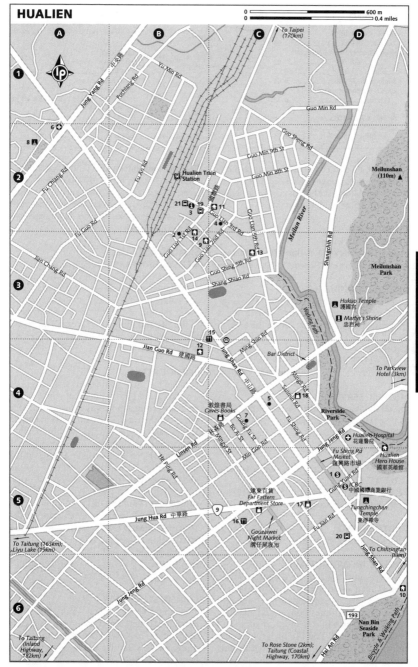

EAST COAST

it's worth. If you need a coffee at a nice shop, or a foreign-exchange bank, head here. In the third part of town, the harbour area, you'll find the fanciest hotels and restaurants.

Information

INTERNET ACCESS
Hualien City Library (170 Guo Lian 1st Rd; 10am-5pm Tue-Sun) Free internet access close to the train station.

INTERNET RESOURCES
Hualien County's tourist website (http://tour-hualien.hl.gov.tw/en/index.jsp) is a good introduction to the attractions in the area.

LAUNDRY
There's a DIY coin **laundromat** (46 Guo Lian 2nd Rd; 24hr) very close to Amigos hostel.

MEDICAL SERVICES
Tzu-chi Buddhist Hospital (Cíjì Yīyuàn; 856 1825; 707 Jung Yang Rd, sec.3) A hospital known for its excellent facilities.

MONEY
There are ATM machines all over town and in most 7-Elevens.
Bank of Taiwan (832 2151; 3 Gung Yuan Rd) Offers money changing in addition to ATM service.

PHOTO STUDIO
There's a studio at 306 Jung Shan Rd.

TOURIST INFORMATION
The free monthly English magazine *Highway 11* focuses on life on the east coast. It's a great source of information about restaurants, hotels, guesthouses and the like. Readers will also find it an informative and entertaining read. You can pick it up at the information centre and in many restaurants around town.

Hualien County Information Centre (Huālián Xiàng Lǚyóu Fúwù Zhōngxīn; 836 0634) An excellent visitor centre, on the right of the train station exit, with an abundance of information available in English: everything from bus schedules to tour prices and times. Staff are friendly and speak good English.

Sights & Activities

MEILUNSHAN PARK 美崙山公園
This **park** (Měilúnshān Gōngyuán) rises up behind the Hualien train station and has pleasant walking trails that lead up to the summit. From the top of the hill are excellent views of the city and the Pacific Ocean. The easiest way to get to the park is to follow Linsen Rd north across the bridge.

SEASIDE PARKS
Hualien has three seaside parks, all joined by a walking and bicycle path that continues to Chihsingtan Beach (passing the city garbage dump on the way). The path starts at **Nan Bin Seaside Park** (南濱海濱公園; Nán Bīn Hǎibīn Gōngyuán), the southernmost park, which is a pleasant place for a stroll or a snack at the night market. You are right next to the ocean and the sound of the surf is always with you.

CHINGSZU TEMPLE 靜思佛堂
The simple white and grey exterior of the 10-storey **Chingszu Temple** (Jìngsī Fó Táng; Chungyang Rd) is striking. Inside, a large exhibition hall showcases the Tzu Chi Buddhist organisation's activities around the world. Exhibits are in English and Chinese.

CHIHSINGTAN BEACH 七星潭
This pretty **beach** (Qīxīng Tán), about 3km north of Hualien, sits at the foot of a series of high cliffs. The water is too rough for swimming, but this doesn't stop crowds flocking here on weekends.

Tours

Calvin Cycle Outdoor Explore (Guānghé Zuò Yòng; ☎ 835 7992; www.outdoor-taiwan.com; 130 Guang Fu St; ☑ 10am-7pm) For outdoor adventure tours (cycling, rock-climbing, tree-climbing, kayaking, river tracing and hiking), check out this shop with a good local reputation. The owner and staff speak English.

Festivals & Events

One of Hualien's long-standing traditions is stone carving, which is not surprising considering the city's main export is marble. The **Hualien International Stone Sculpture Festival** (www.2007stone.com.tw/eng/home/home.asp), established in 1995, showcases the work of local artists and promotes Hualien to the international art world. The festival lasts for over a month starting October and takes place annually in towns around Hualien County.

For aboriginal festivals around Hualien County, see the boxed text on p195.

Sleeping

BUDGET

Most of the sub-NT1000 hotels in Hualien have become pretty awful of late. Competition from hostels and B&Bs is driving them out of business. For bare-bones budget travellers, hostels are the only option now, and thankfully Hualien has some very nice new ones.

Formosa Backpackers Hostel (Qīngnián Mínsù; ☎ 835 2515; 206 Jian Guo Rd; 建國路206號; dm adult/student NT400/350; ☑) You might as well toss a coin to decide whether to stay here or at Amigos. Both are run by young, well-travelled English-speaking Taiwanese women, and both offer great hostel value for money. Formosa has laundry service, a full kitchen, a small café, a 500-book English library and free pick-up from the train station. Each dorm room has its own bathroom, and if free shampoo and soap are what you need, you'll find it here. The hostel owner is a keen surfer and from May to September she works in conjunction with a Canadian surf instructor to provide lessons (NT1500 per day).

Amigos (Āměikè Guójì Qīngnián Guǎn; ☎ 836 2756; www.amigos68.com; 68 Guo Lian 2nd Rd; 國聯2路68號; dm incl breakfast NT450; ☑) This place has everything you could want in a hostel: it's bright, clean, inexpensive, run by a friendly, well-travelled local who speaks your language (English anyway), and it's just a five-minute walk from the train station. There's air-con in the dorms, a shared kitchen, free ADSL, clean sheets and enough showers for everyone. Amigos' owner can help with everything from scooter rentals to tours.

ODD THEME MUSEUMS IN TAIWAN

Taiwan has its share of themed museums, and more than its share of odd ones. Here are a few to keep in mind for a rainy day:

■ **Taiwan Salt Museum** (see p258) See the display of salt crystals from around the world.

■ **Taishan (Barbie) Doll Museum** (泰山芭比娃娃博物館; Tàishān Bābǐ Wáwa Bówùguǎn; ☎ 02-8531 1406; 26 Lane 26, Fengchiang Rd, Taishan, Taipei County; admission free) Mattel had Barbie dolls made in Taishan for 20 years. This is one attempt to relive the glory days.

■ **TaiPower North Visitor Centre** (核二場台電北部展示館; Héèrchǎng Táidiàn Běibù Zhǎnshì Guǎn; ☎ 2498 5112; 60 Badou, Yeliu Village; admission free; ☑ 9.30am-4.30pm) An exhibition hall for the second nuclear power plant just north of Yehliu on the Northeast Coast. *Excellent, Smithers.*

■ **Taiwan Nougat Museum** (p139) Come see the biggest piece of nougat in the world.

■ **Crab Museum** (p162) It's a lot more interesting than you would expect.

■ **Chunghwa Postal Museum** (郵政博物館; Yóuzhèng Bówùguǎn; ☎ 02-2394 5198; 45 Chongqing Rd) This museum in Taipei has stamps, uniforms and so, so much more for a token admission price.

■ **Coca Cola Museum** (可口可樂博物館; Kěkǒu Kělè Bówùguǎn; ☎ 03-364 8800; 46 Hsing Bo Rd, Taoyuan City, Taoyuan County; admission free; ☑ 10-11am & 2-3pm Fri) This museum, of course, is IT! Call before visiting.

■ **Chihsing Tan Katsuo** (七星柴魚博物館; Qīxīng Cháiyú Bówùguǎn; ☎ 03-823 6100; Chihsingtan Beach; admission free; ☑ 9am-5pm) This museum near Chihsingtan Beach is dedicated to dried bonito. All we can say is ???

EAST COAST

Reservations are recommended from July to September and on long weekends; you can book online. There are no lockers, but you can store things downstairs. Also, there's no laundry, but there's a laundromat just a block away.

Yongqi Hotel (Yǒngqí Dàfàndiàn; ☎ 835 6111; fax 835 5727; 139 Guo Lian 1st Rd; 國聯1路139號; d/tr NT1200/1500) This hotel is a good budget option and a popular place for travellers. The accommodation is simple but comfortable.

Ching Yeh Hotel (Qīng Yè Dàfàndiàn; ☎ 833 0186; fax 833 0188; 83 Guo Lian 1st Rd; 國聯1路83號; d from NT1500) The Ching Yeh is one of the best options by the train station. Rooms are small, simply furnished and very clean. Some have great views of the mountains.

MIDRANGE

Rose Stone (福園古厝客棧; Fúyuán Gǔcuò Kèzhàn; ☎ 854 2317; www.rosestone.com; 48 Hai Bin Rd; 海濱路 48號; d/tw NT2300/3800) It's a little bit out of the way, but this is our choice for accommodation in Hualien. The Rose is technically a B&B but it's set in one of the best preserved old courtyard buildings we have seen in Taiwan. Rooms are cosy, with tatami-style bedding and old furnishings. But it's the old-time atmosphere of the place that is the real draw. There's an elaborately decorated tearoom for tea and meals (NT250) and a large chamber filled with the family's collection of antiques.

To get to the Rose, drive south down Jung Shan Rd to the end and turn right onto 193 (the last road at the coast). Continue down the 193 (also Hai An and later Hai Bin Rd) until the 19km mark. The turnoff for the Rose is just past this on the left. Note that you really can't see the place until you are on top of it and the nearby area does not look promising. A taxi from the train station will cost about NT200. Room rates are discounted by 20% on weekdays.

Naluwan Hotel (Nàlǔwān Fàndiàn; ☎ 836 0103; fax 832 0409; 7-3 Guo Lian 5th Rd; 國聯5路7-3號; d/tw incl breakfast NT3300/4500) This is a nice looking place with touches of aboriginal décor. Rooms are spacious and feature comfortable beds, plasma TVs and attractive furnishings. Seasonal discounts of 20% to 50% are available.

Bu Lao Hai Yang Homestay (Bùlǎo Hǎiyáng Mínsù; ☎ 0928-299 567; fax 832 2129; 16 Hai Bin Rd; 海濱街 16號; r incl breakfast from NT3800; 🖳) Another excellent addition to the B&B scene in Hualien is this modern four-storey building offering a super-clean environment (the owner is a self-described clean freak) and romantic room designs. East facing rooms have clear ocean views and wide balconies for lounging. Walking and biking paths can be accessed through the back door, and free bike rentals are offered to guests. The B&B is just on the outskirts of town. A taxi will cost about NT150 from the train station. Weekday discounts of 30% are available.

TOP END

Many visitors complain about the top-end accommodation in Hualien. If the service isn't bad, then the rooms will have terrible sound insulation (a common complaint). If the rooms are good, the food will be lousy.

Parkview Hotel (美崙大飯店; Měilún Dàfàndiàn; ☎ 822 2111; www.parkview-hotel.com/pv_hotel_e/pv _1-1_e.htm; 1-1 Lin Yuan; 林園1-1號; r from NT5400) If you must stay in a five-star, try this place. The amenities include a golf course, tennis courts, restaurants, a swimming pool and everything else you can imagine.

Eating

Hualien cuisine is a mixture of typical Taiwanese cuisine (soups and noodles) and the food of the aboriginal tribes who for centuries have sustained themselves on fish, wild game and wild vegetables and flowers. The most enjoyable way to try the local food is to head to one of the many markets and sample what's on display. Central Hualien, along Fu Shing Rd, is a good place to start, as are the markets around Jung Jeng and Jung Shan Rds. Some things to sample include *dùn páigú* (燉排骨; stewed spareribs) and *kǔguā* (苦瓜; bitter gourd).

For the latest restaurants and cafés check out *Highway 11* magazine.

Ye Hsiang Shi Dian (Yè Xiāng Biānshí Diàn; 42 Shin Yi St; dishes NT40; ⏲ breakfast, lunch & dinner) This tiny place is a favourite of locals for its steaming bowls of pork and seafood dumplings. The restaurant has been around for over 70 years and is known all over Taiwan.

Buk Kut Ten (Ròugǔchá; ☎ 835 4499; 477-2 Jung Shan Rd; dishes NT60) The speciality at this little makeshift shop is southeast Asian–style wild-boar soup with herbal medicine. Other meat and noodle dishes are available, as is an English menu.

For seafood, go to Gouzaiwei Night Market (Gōuzǎiwěi Yèshì), the oldest market in town, sometimes nicknamed 'Seafood Street'. Here you'll find such treats as squid-on-a-stick and grilled clams. The market is near the intersection of Nanching and Po'ai Sts.

There's a small night market out at Nan Bin Seaside Park. Grab a snack here and then go for a stroll along the ocean front.

Drinking

Hualien has many trendy cafés and teahouses along its main streets. On Linsen Rd, east of Jung Shan Rd, you'll find a small bar district with at least six establishments to choose from. Also check out the seaside parks for bars with outdoor seating.

Shopping

Hualien's main export, marble, is all over the city. Numerous souvenir shops sell marble carvings, but be aware that the mining of marble is having a devastating effect on the local environment.

Hualien's delicious cakes and cookies are available at bakeries and gift shops around town.

Hui Pi Hsu Cake Shop (Huì Bǐ Xǔ; 65 Jung Hua Rd) This shop has been in business since 1899 and is well known for its delicious peanut and sesame cookies. Goodies are sold in bulk or in attractive tins that make good souvenirs.

Ya Chi Hsiao Fang (Yǎ Jí Xiǎo Fǎng; 84 Sanmin Rd) To find something with more lasting value, head to this government-certified antique shop.

Getting There & Away

AIR

Far Eastern Air Transport (☎ 826 5702), **Mandarin Airlines** (☎ 826 8785) and **Transasia Airways** (☎ 826 1365) have reservation counters at Hualien Airport (www.hulairport.gov.tw). There are flights from Hualien to Taipei, Taichung and Kaohsiung.

There's an **information desk** (☎ 821 0768; ⏰ 7am-9pm) on the airport's 2nd floor.

BUS

The bus situation along the east coast is rather confusing (even to locals), with multiple companies operating out of multiple stations. Thankfully, the information centre at the train station is up to date on all this and can advise you on the latest. You are well advised to seek their help to confirm times and departure points.

The **Hualien Bus Company** (☎ 832 3485) has a full station downtown at the end of Jung Shan Rd and a small kiosk to the right of the train station information centre (as you face the centre).

The **Dingdong Bus Company** (☎ 089-333 023; 138-6 Guo Lian 1st Rd) has no station, just a small bus stop sign to the left of the train station information centre as you face the centre.

Both companies run buses to Taitung via Hwy 11. Dingdong runs about four buses a day (NT479, three hours), while the Hualien Bus Company runs one every hour or so. However, most Hualien buses only go as far as Chengkung.

Between Hualien and Taitung, it's possible to get off the bus at certain spots, do some exploring and hop on the next bus when it comes by. This is a slow way to travel, but possible. Verify when the next bus is supposed to come to avoid being stranded.

The Hualien Bus Company also runs buses to Tienhsiang and the National Park Headquarters in Taroko Gorge.

TRAIN

There are frequent trains running between Taipei and Hualien (fast/slow NT455/343, 2½/four hours). They can be crowded, so make sure you buy tickets ahead of time to reserve a seat.

In early 2007, the Taiwan Railway Administration purchased a fleet of tilting trains from Japan that can cover the distance from Taipei to Hualien in less than two hours. They should be running by the time you read this.

Getting Around

TO/FROM THE AIRPORT

The Hualien Bus Company runs buses to the airport (NT25, every 20 minutes) from its downtown station.

CAR, MOTORCYCLE & SCOOTER

Vehicles are available for rent around the train station. For a scooter or motorcycle, rates are NT400 to NT500 a day and for a car NT1500 to NT2000, excluding petrol. Most scooter shops ask for a Taiwanese driver's licence. If you don't have one, go to **Pony Leasing & Rental Group** (☎ 826 2538), just to the left of the Ching Yeh Hotel. For some reason staff here will still rent scooters to foreign visitors with just an International Driver's Licence.

We have also heard of people having more luck renting scooters at Hsincheng, the closest train station to Taroko Gorge.

EAST COAST

TAXI

Hualien taxi drivers congregate around the train and bus stations, hustling passengers for tours around the city and to Taroko Gorge. If you are interested, a Taroko tour will cost up to NT3000 a day, depending on the time involved.

TAROKO GORGE 太魯閣

☎ 03

Just 15km north of Hualien, inside Taroko National Park, lies Taroko Gorge (Tàilǔgé), Taiwan's top tourist destination. With its marble-walled canyons, lush vegetation and cliffs so outsized they block out the sky, Taroko Gorge puts the 'Formosa' in *Ilha Formosa*.

Taroko contains almost half of all the animal species in Taiwan, including the Formosan black bear and wild boar. It's unlikely travellers will come across these larger animals but it's not hard to spot a Taiwan macaque or two. The park covers over 120,000 hectares and rises from sea level in the east to over 3700m further west. The blue-green Liwu River cuts through the centre, forging deep slitted valleys and ravines before emptying into the sea.

Some people get immense satisfaction just touring the park in a bus, car or taxi, while taking in the majestic scenery. For the more active, there are numerous hiking trails and some lovely spots for swimming and river tracing. (Just do these activities out of sight of regular tourists as many Taiwanese can't swim, but for some reason think water is safe when they see others in it. Summer drownings are in the hundreds every year as a result.)

You can visit the park any time of year, but be warned (with an extra stern look) that during weekends and holidays the place is a madhouse, especially on the road. Occasionally you may get stuck in traffic for a considerable length of time as two tour buses try to figure out a way to get past each other in some narrow, twisting tunnel. On the other hand, if you go on any of the longer trails, you will soon leave the crowds behind.

Quite a few visitors take a bus to Tienhsiang and walk the 19km back down to the National Park Headquarters. While this is a great way to take in all of the scenery, as increased traffic in the gorge has spoiled a once enjoyable walk. If you do walk, wear reflective clothing

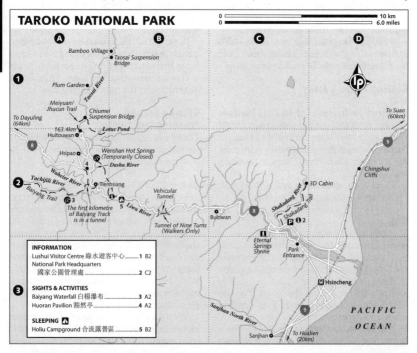

TAROKO NATIONAL PARK

0 _____ 10 km
0 _____ 6.0 miles

INFORMATION
Lushui Visitor Centre 綠水遊客中心..........1 B2
National Park Headquarters
　國家公園管理處.....................................2 C2

SIGHTS & ACTIVITIES
Baiyang Waterfall 白楊瀑布...................3 A2
Huoran Pavilion 豁然亭..........................4 A2

SLEEPING
Holiu Campground 合流露營區................5 B2

and bring a torch for the tunnels. Try leaving as early in the morning as possible to avoid traffic. Mid-morning, mid-week, mid-winter would be an ideal time to go.

Summer is obviously the best time to do any river tracing or swimming; unless a typhoon is coming, the weather is usually sunny. Winters are chilly and there's often drizzle, but that keeps the crowds away. May and June are the rainy season.

History

The original inhabitants of the park area were the Atayal people, known for their fine weaving skills, facial tattoos and headhunting. Most of the Atayal have now moved out of the park but a few families remain, supporting themselves by selling woven products to tourists. Many of the trails in the gorge now used by tourists were once Atayal hunting and trading routes. For example, the old Hohuan Trail (Héhuān Yuèlǐng Gǔdào), the precursor of the Central Cross-Island Hwy, was once used for crossing the island.

In 1914 the Japanese entered the gorge hoping to gain access to the forestry and mineral resources. The Atayal resisted but the Japanese crushed all opposition with brutal military force. They then began to cut roads and widen existing trails. A road was built as far as Tienhsiang, and Taroko became a popular hiking spot for Japanese tourists in the 1930s. Later, in the 1950s, the KMT extended the road as part of the first Cross-Central Hwy; not surprisingly, much of it followed the old Hohuan Trail.

Taroko National Park was officially established on 28 November 1986.

Orientation & Information

The **National Park Headquarters** (Guójiā Gōngyuán Guǎnlǐ Chù; ☎ 862 1100; www.taroko.gov.tw; ☯ 8.30am-4.45pm, closed 2nd Mon of month), at the entrance of the gorge, provides useful information on the status of trails and road conditions. It also has free maps and brochures of hiking trails and a bulletin board with bus schedules and notices to travellers. There's also a café and a souvenir shop with books for sale.

Tienhsiang (Tiānxiáng), the tiny resort area at the other end of the gorge, is where most of the accommodation is centred. You'll also find here a post office, a smaller visitor centre and a few small cafeterias (with awful food) next to the bus station.

Amazingly, there are still no ATMs in the park that accept international cards.

Sights

WENSHAN HOT SPRINGS 文山溫泉

How we miss this place. About 3km above Tienhsiang, these lovely secluded **springs** (Wénshān Wēnquán) once flowed into an open basin of solid marble beside the Dasha River (Dàshā Xī). In 2005, however, a rockslide killed and injured several tourists and the springs were closed. At the time of writing, they were still closed pending a final decision by the park's administration. We believe this decision will be in favour of opening the springs, though the water may be diverted to a safer location.

ETERNAL SPRINGS SHRINE 長春祠

This **shrine** (Cháng Chūn Cí) sits on a steep cliff overlooking the Liwu River and above a rushing waterfall fed by springs that never dry. It is dedicated to the 450 workers who lost their lives building the highway. It's a strangely beautiful site.

To reach the shrine, cross the suspension bridge and hike up the steps.

HSIANGTE TEMPLE 祥德寺

Just before Tienhsiang a suspension bridge leads to the **Hsiangte Temple** (Xiángdé Sì), which sits high on a cliff overlooking the valley. The temple is named after the Buddhist monk Kuangchin, who prayed for the safety of the workmen as they built the Central Cross-Island Hwy.

Activities

SHORT HIKES

For short hikes, pick up the free brochure at the National Park Headquarters. You can also easily find and follow most trails using our overview map. These hikes require little effort by the walker and many are done by tourists in silly shoes coming directly off a bus. The trails are all wide, clear, obvious, well marked, and safe unless they have been damaged by a typhoon or earthquake. Of course, this does not mean they are not still immensely scenic and enjoyable.

Note that the following lists do not exhaust the possibilities of hiking in the park.

The **Shakadang Trail** (砂卡礑步道; Shākǎdāng Bùdào), formerly the Mysterious Valley Trail, is a flat 4.4km hike (one hour one way). The route follows the crystal-clear Shakadang River, which winds through marble canyons and boulder-strewn flats that create massive pools of blueish-green water (tinted by limestone in the rocks). Many outdoors groups from Hualien come here in summer to swim and river trace, though the park's board members are not entirely happy about that.

Coming from the National Park Headquarters, the trailhead is to the right after emerging from the first tunnel. Follow the stairs down to the river to access the path. Note that you can only go as far as 3D Cabin without a permit.

The **Tunnel of Nine Turns** (九曲洞; Jiǔ Qū Dòng) is actually a 2km section of the original highway through the park. In the early '90s, the highway was diverted to leave this section – the most scenic in the entire gorge – open to walkers. Don't miss this one!

Our favourite short hike is along the **Baiyang Trail** (白楊步道; Báiyáng Bùdào), which runs high over a river valley, through a series of solar-power lit tunnels, to the high **Baiyang Waterfall** (Báiyáng Pùbù). The entire trek to the waterfall and back is 3.6km and takes two hours to complete. The trail starts about 500m up the road from Tienhsiang. Look for the tunnel on the left; you have to go through this to get to the trail on the other side. Bring a torch as it's 380m long!

Once part of the Hohuan Trail, the **Lushui– Holiu Trail** (綠水－合流步道; Lǜshuǐ–Héliú Bùdào) runs for 2km above the highway along a cliff, with fantastic views of the Liwu River. The trailhead is behind the Lushui Visitor Centre. Note that at the time of writing a new five-hour-long trail from Lushui to Wenshan (the site of the old hot springs) was about to open. You'll probably need a permit for this so inquire at the park headquarters.

The **Huoran Pavilion Trail** (豁然亭步道; Huòrán Tíng Bùdào) is short but steep, gaining 400m in elevation in 1.9km. The trail leads to **Huoran Pavilion**, which has fantastic views of the Liwu River and Tienhsiang. Note that the trail turns into a slippery mess when it rains and is best avoided at these times. Landslides occasionally close the area, so check with the National Park Headquarters before starting out. The trail starts off the road on the way up to the Youth Activity Centre.

LONGER HIKES

For longer hikes, pick up a copy of *Trails of Taroko Gorge and Su-Hua Areas* (NT220) at the National Park Headquarters. The book has a chapter on most of the hikes (long and short) in the park. Useful trail maps are included with clear information on length, times, conditions and things to observe along the way.

It's always good to confirm trail conditions with staff at the National Park Headquarters before setting out on any longer hike. It's important to follow only those trails that you find on the park's maps or in its books. It seems some readers (using very old *Taiwan* Lonely Planet guides) sometimes set out on trails that have been closed for years because of typhoon and earthquake damage. Several foreign visitors have lost their lives over the years most likely wandering off the beaten path. Don't add to the list.

The Shakadang Trail officially ends at 3D Cabin but if you have permits you can continue on the **Dali–Datung Trail** (大禮－大同步道; Dàlǐ–Dàtóng Bùdào), leading to Dali and Datung, two isolated Atayal villages. At the time of writing, the trails were getting new signs and being made more accessible and clear, and should be ready for hiking by the time you read this. Maps should be available at the park headquarters. Apply for permits at the police station by the park headquarters. The trail should take about seven to eight hours return.

About 6km north of the main road from Tienhsiang, at the 163.4km mark on a switchback, is the trailhead for the **Meiyuan/Jhucun Trail** (Bamboo Village/Plum Garden Trail; 梅園竹村步道; Méi Yuán/Zhúcūn Bùdào). This is a clear, level 9.2km-long trail (one way) that takes six hours return. It's an exciting trail in parts, especially where the path has been chiselled into the walls of a cliff, or where it crosses over high suspension bridges.

At the Jiumei (Chiumei) suspension bridge there is a 4.3km side trail to **Lotus Pond** (蓮花池步道; Liánhuā Chí Bùdào), a former farming area now reverting to its natural state. It is a three-hour return hike from the suspension bridge to Lotus Pond.

You can camp at Plum Garden and Bamboo Village, but make sure you ask the park for permission first.

RIVER TRACING

The Sanjhan North River (三棧北溪) flows through southern Taroko Park. A short 2km trail has been built along the river following a canal built by the US government in 1952 (clean, clear water still flows down the canal), but the real reason to come here is to river trace to an area called the **Golden Canyon** (黃金峽谷; Huángjīn Xiágǔ). Those who have done the trip rave about the beauty of the gorge, the numerous waterfalls and the deep swimming pools.

River-tracing outings are organised year-round by the local aborigines in Sanjhan from the community **activity centre** (三棧社區發展協會; Sānzhàn shèqū fāzhǎn xiéhuì; ☎ 826 9916, 0972-100 684; http://pratan.eyp.com.tw/eyp/front/bin/home.phtml). The cost is NT2000 per person including all rental equipment. Trips take about eight hours return and start from the activity centre, usually in the early morning. You should be able to just go and join a group.

Sanjhan is just south of Taroko Park on the way back to Hualien. Heading south, turn right off Hwy 9 at the sign for Sanjhan (San-chan; 三棧; Sānzhàn). When you cross the bridge into the village stay right along the river. The community centre is obvious, 150m on at the end of the road on the left.

Note that you are technically supposed to apply for a police permit to enter the village but there often may not always be someone on duty.

Tours

All travel agencies in Hualien and Taipei can arrange full- or half-day tours of the gorge. **Taiwan Tour Bus** (☎ 0800-011 765; half-/full-day tours NT600/988) leaves from beside the visitor centre at the Hualien train station. The staff at the visitor centre can help you purchase tickets.

Taking a tour is a convenient way to see Taroko but it doesn't leave enough time for exploring.

Festivals & Events

Since 2000, the park has been the venue for the autumn **Taroko International Marathon**. Organisers like to stress that it's 'the only canyon marathon in the world'. The event attracts runners from all over the world and there are 42.195km and 21km marathons. Contact the park for more information.

Sleeping
TIENHSIANG

Catholic Hostel (Tiānzhǔ Táng; ☎ 869 1122; dm NT250, d/tw NT1000/1200, s/d without shower NT350/600) The

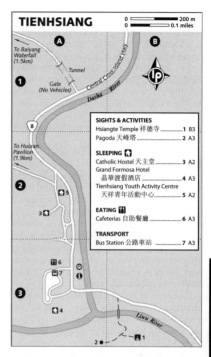

TIENHSIANG

0 ____ 200 m
0 ____ 0.1 miles

To Baiyang Waterfall (1.5km)

Tunnel

Gate (No Vehicles)

Central Cross-Island Hwy

Dasha River

To Huoran Pavilion (1.9km)

SIGHTS & ACTIVITIES
Hsiangte Temple 祥德寺 1 B3
Pagoda 天峰塔 2 A3

SLEEPING 🏠
Catholic Hostel 天主堂 3 A2
Grand Formosa Hotel
晶華渡假酒店 4 A3
Tienhsiang Youth Activity Centre
天祥青年活動中心 5 A2

EATING 🍴
Cafeterias 自助餐廳 6 A3

TRANSPORT
Bus Station 公路車站 7 A3

Liwu River

EAST COAST

Catholic Hostel has been the principal budget hostel in Tienhsiang for 50 years. The place is getting a bit long in the tooth but it still offers clean decent rooms and dorms at no-nonsense prices. The dorm rooms are a bit stark though, with old metal frame bunk beds and zero decorative touches.

Tienhsiang Youth Activity Centre (Tiānxiáng Qīngnián Huódòng Zhōngxīn; ☎ 869 1111; http://cyctsyac .myweb.hinet.net; dm NT450, r from NT1700) Up the hill from the Catholic Hostel, the Youth Activity Centre is the only other budget option in the gorge. Rooms are simple – try to get one that faces the canyon – and discounted by 15% midweek. Many travellers consider the dorms here better value than those at the Catholic Hostel.

Grand Formosa Hotel (Jīnghuá Dùjià Jiǔdiàn; ☎ 869 1155; www.grandformosa-taroko.com.tw; r from NT6000) This is the first building you'll see upon entering Tienhsiang. The five-star hotel is fairly generic, both inside and out, but rooms are comfortable and spacious, with fancy marble bathrooms. The hotel boasts a lounge, two restaurants, a café and a gift shop. Shuttle buses from Hualien airport or train station are available.

BULOWAN 布洛灣

Meaning 'echo' in Atayal, Bulowan (Bùluòwān) is a former Atayal mountain village. In the upper village, on a high meadow surrounded by postcard-perfect scenery, the **Leader Village Taroko** (利德布洛灣山月村; Lìdé Bùluòwān Shānyuè Cūn; ☎ 610 111; www.leaderhotels.com; 2-person cabins incl breakfast NT4500) rents out 36 quality wood cabins with old-time porches to let you relax and take in the views. This is by far the best place to stay in the park.

Thankfully, there is no KTV or loud entertainment permitted (though there are nightly aboriginal musical performances). Management encourages guests to be quiet and enjoy what nature has to offer, which includes a small trail behind the cabins where monkeys are sure to be seen, along with the occasional civet and deer. Our only complaint is the pricing system, which is highly misleading. Despite quoting prices per person, rooms are only rented at a double price, and the package deals usually offer no savings at all.

Bulowan is about 8km west of the park entrance. To get to the village, look for the English sign on the main road that indicates the turn-off. In the lower village a few aboriginal families sell and display good quality **arts & crafts** (⏰ 8.30am-4.30pm, closed 1st & 3rd Mon of month).

CAMPING

There is a free camp site in Holiu (合流) with wooden platforms and bathrooms with showers. It's a lovely spot on a flat spot overlooking the gorge, but there aren't that many tent sites so arrive early on a weekend.

Eating

Tienhsiang Youth Activity Centre (☎ 869 1111; breakfast NT100, lunch & dinner NT150) Meals are available to guests and nonguests here. Buy a ticket in advance. For breakfast, let the centre know before 9pm the night before.

Leader Village Taroko (lunch & dinner set meals NT400-600) This place in Bulowan serves excellent aboriginal food prepared by aboriginal chefs. Portions are large and every last bite is a delight. A typical set meal might include both barbecued wild pig and mountain chicken, soup, rice steamed in bamboo tubes, and exotic mountain vegetables. Menus are in English.

Grand Formosa Hotel (lunch/dinner buffet NT600/650) The breakfast buffet here is free for guests but NT400 for everyone else. The food in the Western restaurant is only mediocre; it's much better in the Chinese restaurant.

The cafeterias around the bus station in Tienhsiang deserve a sign above them reading 'Serving barely edible food since 1986'.

Getting There & Away

BUS

The Hualien Bus Company runs frequent buses every day from Hualien to the park headquarters at Taroko Gorge (NT77, one hour) from its train station branch. There are eight buses a day to Tienhsiang (NT155, 90 minutes). Check the visitor centre at the Hualien train station for the latest schedule. The earliest bus leaves Hualien at 5.30am, the last at 9.30pm. Note that not all buses go to the visitor centre.

TAXI

Taxi tours to the gorge are easy enough to arrange – cabbies will come looking for you, rather than the other way around. A return trip through the gorge with stops will cost around NT2500 from Hualien. Another option is to have your driver take you through the gorge and drop you off at Tienhsiang, which will cost about NT1500.

TRAIN

Hsincheng (Sincheng) Station (新城站; fast/slow train NT409/315, 2½/3½ hours from Taipei) is quite close to the park entrance and preferred by travellers who don't want to go to Hualien. All buses to Taroko NP stop here.

HIGHWAY 11

There are two routes to decide between when travelling south of Hualien: Hwys 9 and 11. Hwy 9 (see p196) cuts through the verdant East Rift Valley (Huādōng Zòng Gǔ), while Hwy 11 travels down the east coast, skirting some stunning coastal scenery. The coastal route allows you to visit small aboriginal villages, numerous beaches, the arts scene at Dulan, and Lanyu and Green Islands (see the Taiwan's Islands, p288). There are several places to camp along the way, and more and more guesthouses seem to spring up every year.

Much of Hwy 11 falls under the auspices of the East Coast National Scenic Area, whose

visitor centre (☎ 089-841 520; www.eastcoast-nsa.gov
.tw/en/index.php; 25 Shintsuen Rd, Chenggong; ☯ 9am-5pm)
is between Duli and Chengkung.

Getting Around

The Dingdong Bus Company runs several
buses daily from its Hualien train station bus
stop to Taitung (NT354, 3½ hours). Hualien
Bus Company runs buses about every hour
but most do not go all the way to Taitung,
only to Chinpu or Chengkung. See the visitor
centre outside the Hualien train station for the
latest schedule.

Your own scooter, car or bicycle is ideal for
travelling Hwy 11 unless you are just heading
out to one site.

HUALIEN OCEAN PARK 海洋公園

This **ocean park** (Hualien Far Glory Ocean Park; Huālián
Hǎiyáng Gōngyuán; www.hualienoceanpark.com.tw/e/page01
.htm; admission adult/child NT890/790; ☯ 9am-5pm) is
a large aquarium/amusement park south of
Hualien off Hwy 11. The facilities are first-
class and attractions include dolphin shows,
sea lion exhibits and a water fun park. Kids
love this place.

The easiest way to get here if you don't have
your own transportation is to take a **Taiwan
Tour Bus** (☎ 0800-011 765) from outside the visitor
centre in front of the Hualien train station.
The price is around NT1000 per person and
includes transport and tickets. Inquire at the
visitor centre for details.

COW MOUNTAIN BEACH 牛山

A short but wide stretch of sandy coastline
with rocky cliffs, Cow Mountain Beach
(Niúshān) is about 27km or so south of
Hualien. It's a lovely place to enjoy the surf
and escape the crowds of the more developed
beaches on the east coast. Note that there is no
swimming here, though, because of the rough
surf and a quick drop-off.

Apart from the quiet beachside atmosphere, travellers come here to stay in the **Huting Recreation Area** (呼庭休閒區; Hūtíng Xiūxián Qū;
☎ 03-860 1400; ☯ 10am-7pm), an old grazing area
(Cow Mountain is called Huting by the local
aborigines) developed by a friendly Ami
family into a rustic resort. The recreation
area is just back from the beach up a short
road. There's a café-restaurant serving Ami
food, a simple camp site (NT150 per person)
set up on the open grassy fields, and very
rustic driftwood cabins (double/twin with

shared bathroom NT1200/2200, with a 30%
discount from Sunday to Thursday).

The beach and recreation area are about
1.5km off the highway. Look for the sign
with the cow head on it for the turn-off.

JICI (CHICHI) BEACH 磯崎海濱遊憩區

This **beach** (Jīqí Hǎi Bīn Yóuqì Qū; admission NT60) is
one of only two you can swim at between
Hualien and Taitung so if you're looking
for a dip, a paddle, or a bit of surfing, don't
pass by – at least from May to September
between 9am and 6pm.

Erosion has sadly taken its toll in recent
years and body surfing is becoming a bit
more painful as a line of rough pebbles extends along the shoreline. But the beach is
still an excellent summer playground and
the almost completely undeveloped coastline is very scenic. There are some nice hikes
up to the bluffs to the south, and a waterfall walk about 20 minutes up the river on
the other side of the highway. Many people
trace up for a shower as a fun way to conclude their day.

The beach is developed to a degree, meaning you'll find showers, changing rooms and
rental equipment, as well as a **campground**
(☎ 03-871 1251; tent site/cabins NT500/1500). All Hualien and Dingdong buses pass by the beach
so you should never have to wait more than
an hour for a ride.

SHIHTIPING 石梯坪

Shihtiping (Shítīpíng) is a small fishing village halfway between Hualien and Taitung,
30km south of Jici Beach. Shihtiping means
'stone steps', referring to the volcanic rock
along the coastline that has slowly eroded
to form natural stone steps. It is this coastline that draws visitors in and a pleasant
park has been developed with paths down
and along the rocks. If you love exploring
rocky, rugged coastlines you'll be in your
element here.

There's a **camp site** (tent site NT250) with raised
platforms that face the sea, which is just 30m
away. It's a wonderful spot to camp out and
there are showers and barbecue pits.

CAVES OF THE EIGHT IMMORTALS 八仙洞

A mandatory stop for all tour buses going up
and down the east coast, the **Caves of the Eight**

Immortals (Bashian Cave; Bāxiān Dòng; ☯ 8.30am-noon & 1.30-5pm) are hardly worth your while. If you have the choice to pass them by, do so.

PLATFORM OF THE THREE IMMORTALS
三仙台

This series of **arched bridges** leading to a small coral island that was once a promontory joined to the mainland is also known as Sansiantai (Sānxiāntái). The island's three large stone formations have been likened to the three immortals of Chinese mythology – hence the name.

Sansiantai is a very pleasant spot to wander around for a couple of hours, though on holidays and weekends it is a bit of a madhouse with all the tour bus crowds.

CHENGKUNG 成功

To the south of the Platform of the Three Immortals is the fishing village of Chengkung (Chénggōng), the largest town between Hualien and Taitung. The town has a lively fish market and is a good place to sample local seafood. Every afternoon between 3pm and 4pm the daily catch is unloaded and goes on auction. All the noise and excitement makes the auction entertaining to watch. Around the harbour are plenty of small seafood restaurants worth checking out. Dried fish slices are a speciality of Chengkung; they make a very good, though smelly, snack.

Incredibly, Chengkung has an English website (www.changkang.gov.tw/) highlighting its history and a few pretty natural spots in the area.

AMI CULTURAL CENTRE
阿美族民俗中心

About 11km south of Chengkung is the **Ami Cultural Centre** (Ami Folk Centre; Āměi Zú Mínsú Zhōngxīn; ☎ 089-841 751; 25 Sinchuan Rd, Sinyi Borough, Chengkung; ☯ 9am-noon & 1.30-4pm Wed-Mon), which is highly recommended for its exhibits of Ami handicrafts and traditional architecture. The centre is on the grounds of the East Coast National Scenic Area office.

JINZUN RECREATION AREA
金樽遊憩區

Another 11km south on Hwy 11 is this recreation area (Jīnzūn Yóuqì Qū) centred on a beautiful 3km-long sand beach hemmed in by high cliffs. There's not much to do here other than head down the stairs to the beach,

stroll around and admire the view (and maybe have a picnic, get your feet wet in the surf, take some photos, paint a seascape, read a book, write a book etc, etc).

DULAN 都蘭
pop 500

The tiny town of Dulan (Dūlán) hardly merited a nod years ago as you passed by on the way south. But in recent years this has changed as a thriving local arts scene has taken off. There's live music on the weekends and a larger arts festival held in autumn. Dulan is also the site for many of the larger yearly aboriginal festivals (see opposite). Check the Taitung County Cultural Affairs Bureau website (www.ccl.ttct.edu.tw/) or the Taitung County website (www.taitung.gov.tw/index .htm) for dates and details.

The Dulan area has been inhabited for thousands of years, as is evidenced by archaeological ruins of the Beinan culture in the hills west of town. These days it has one of the largest Ami settlements along the east coast, and the aboriginal presence in the arts scene is strong.

The **Dulan Sugar Factory** (都蘭糖廠; Dūlán Tángchǎng; ☎ 089-530 060; 61 Dulan Village; 台東縣東河鄉都蘭村61號), a once-busy processing plant, was shut down in the 1990s. Local artisans and craftspeople began to use the abandoned warehouse space for makeshift studios and soon a genuine local arts scene developed, which continues to develop and gain in reputation. Every Saturday night there is live music on a driftwood-framed stage. Both Taiwanese and foreign musicians can be seen playing, and the event attracts people from all over the island. As you arrive in Dulan from the north it is easy to spot the factory on the right near the edge of town: it looks like a factory, with high walls and smokestacks, except for the incongruous driftwood stage and a small café.

Just south of Dulan, around the 152km mark, is a big stone with a sign for the road heading up to the trailhead for **Dulan Mountain** (都蘭山; Dūlán Shān), a sacred place for the Ami people. The sign says the trailhead is 2km away but it is actually 4km and they are four very steep kilometres. Small cars should not attempt to go up. In fact, you could just begin your hike here as there is little development the whole way up. The trail was just being finished at the time of research. From the trailhead to the top and back will probably take a few hours. The views should be fantastic as they certainly were from the viewing platform at the start of the trail.

Just south of Dulan is the geological oddity **Water Running Up** (水往上流; Shuǐ Wǎng Shàng Liú). Look for the English roadside sign that leads to a large ditch off the highway (or just follow the tour buses). The water in the ditch really appears to be flowing upwards for 100m or so. See if you can figure out why.

If you wish to spend the night in Dulan, inquire at the café at the sugar factory about guesthouse rooms. As for eating, there are many small shops along the highway (the main road through town) to grab a bite.

SHANYUAN BEACH 杉原海水浴場

Beautiful Shanyuan Beach (Shānyuán Hǎishuǐ Yùchǎng) is the closest beach to Taitung and the second swimmable beach between Hualien and Taitung. With its soft yellow sand, tropical blue water and stunning mountain backdrop, it's a fantastic place to enjoy the natural life.

Unfortunately, the beach has been officially closed for some time as a 'five-star' hotel is built, and built, and built. At the time of writing it was said to be another two years before the hotel would be completed. If the model plans are accurate, the hotel is going to look like a Taiwanese technical junior college (c 1975).

Currently, you can still enjoy the beach by simply entering it from the north end beside a temple.

HSIAO YELIU 小野柳

Just a few kilometres north of Taitung is Hsiao Yeliu (Siao Yeliou; Xiǎo Yěliǔ), a **coastal park** known for its bizarre rock and coral formations, formed over thousands of years by wind and water erosion. The landscape is truly unearthly here, with rocks curving and twisting into all manner of fantastic shapes.

EAST COAST

ABORIGINAL FESTIVALS ON THE EAST COAST

Dates for festivals are only roughly the same each year so it's important to find out the exact schedule before you go. Fortunately that is easy these days. Call the 24-hour tourist hotline (☎ 0800 011 765) or check out the events calendars on the websites for Hualien (http://tour -hualien.hl.gov.tw/en/index.jsp) and Taitung County (www.taitung.gov.tw/english/index.php). The Events page on the National Youth Commission's website (www.youthtravel.net.tw/web/index .php) is also a good source of information.

- **Ami Harvest Festival** This festival is the largest in Taiwan and takes place every July or August in various towns around Hualien and Taitung Counties. In June tribal chiefs choose the exact date.

- **Rukai Harvest Festival** One highlight of this harvest festival is watching tribal youths play on giant swings. The swings are built to allow guys to show their affection for the gals by sending them higher and higher into the air. The festival takes place every July or August.

- **Bunun Ear Shooting Festival and Millet Harvest Festival** The Ear Shooting Festival takes place around the end of April and is meant to honour the legendary hunting heroes of the tribe and to teach young boys how to use bows and arrows. The Millet Harvest Festival is held after the April millet harvest. Both festivals take place in towns throughout the East Rift Valley.

- **Paiwan Bamboo Pole Festival** The Paiwan tribe holds this festival every five years in October to honour its ancestors and to pray for a good harvest. The festival takes place in Daren township, Taitung. The next festival will take place in 2012.

- **Puyuma Tribe Annual Festival** This festival combines the old monkey and hunting rituals with the larger coming-of-age ceremony for young men. The festival is celebrated by tribal members in Beinan township, near Taitung, at the end of December.

- **Yami Flying Fish Festival** The Yami on Lanyu Island hold this festival every March to May during the beginning of the flying fish season. Like the Puyuma festival, this celebrates a young man's passage into adulthood. For more info, see p318.

A large park has been developed around the most interesting stretch of coastline and most nature lovers would have a happy time here exploring the rocks and tidal pools. It's also a fun spot for families with young children, as the area is compact but full of surprises. It's simple to get around and there are English signs. There's a good **camping ground** (per camp site NT350) at the back of the park, with wooden tent platforms facing the sea. Bring your own food. A **visitor centre** (☎ 089-280 093; ⌚ 9am-5pm) has English maps and information about the various rock formations.

HIGHWAY 9

The East Rift Valley is a long fertile strip of land between the Central Mountain and Coastal Mountain Ranges. It's great farming country and highly scenic. There are plenty of hiking and biking routes – and even a white-water rafting venue – to keep the outdoor enthusiast happy, and numerous hot springs exist for those who want to indulge themselves. A few quirky highlights include the fields of orange day lilies that bloom in late summer, and the wetlands in Mataian. Those interested in organic farming should check out the scene at Loshan.

Travelling by train, bus or your own vehicle is simple. The road is relatively flat and straight and there are English signs for most of the places we list. Cyclists can consider taking quiet alternative routes such as County Rds 64 and 195, and Hwys 23 and 197. Camp sites are available along the way and there are some lovely, lovely B&Bs.

LIYU LAKE 鯉魚潭

This very scenic 2km-long lake (Lǐyú Tán), shaped somewhat like a carp (lǐyú means 'carp' in Chinese), sits in the foothills of the Central Mountain Range about 19km southwest of Hualien. It's the largest natural inland lake in Taiwan, and has a splendid backdrop of lush green hills. It's also blessedly free of overdevelopment. There are pavilions and walking trails and even boat rental shops along the shores, but they are mostly of wood-and-stone construction and blend in nicely with the environment.

Families with small children who enjoy camping or picnicking will like it here. There are safe bike trails around the lake, and short

hikes in the nearby hills. There's also a forest recreation centre just 1km away that highlights the history of the logging industry in Taiwan. Most kids will get a kick out of the real locomotive engines on display and the old logging equipment.

Information

There's a **visitor centre** (☎ 03-864 1691; ⌚ 8.30am-5.30pm) at the lake with English maps of the area. At the time of writing there was no English sign for the centre; it's on the north side of the lake.

Sights & Activities
CYCLING

For the casual biker, there's a 4km **bike path** (Jiǎotàchē Zhuānyòngdào) around the lake itself, but for a real adventure consider heading out to **Hwy 14** (midweek is best). It's more like a backcountry road than a highway, and runs through a wild, rugged, marble-walled canyon that is like a smaller version of Taroko Gorge. The road is very narrow in parts, and goes through a series of long, dark winding tunnels, so headlights are essential.

To get to Hwy 14, head north along Hwy 9 from Liyu Lake. Cross the bridge heading back to Hualien and then turn left to follow the river upstream. Cross the next bridge and continue upstream (now on the left bank). Just past the power plant, stop and register with the police and pay NT10 (bring your passport).

The road goes on for 10km or so, ending at a dam. After that a very narrow farm road continues up a side canyon. This is the eastern portion of the Nenggao Cross Island Historic Trail (see p230).

There are **swimming holes** down a side road. After passing the police station continue for a few kilometres until you reach a large red bridge. Don't cross, but instead take the lower road to the left going upstream along the Chingshui River. After the first tunnel look down to the right. See the massive, marble-lined natural swimming hole with deep blueish-green crystal clear water? To get down, ride up to the second tunnel and look for the stairs to the right (before the tunnel entrance). Head down to the river and then river trace downstream to the swimming hole. Decent quality bikes can be rented on the west side of Liyu Lake for NT250 per day. Look for the building with the Giant bike sign on top.

HIKING

You can walk around the lake in about an hour, or do the **Liyu Mountain** (鯉魚山; Lǐyú Shān; 600m) circuit in three to four hours.

CHIHNAN NATIONAL FOREST RECREATION AREA 池南國家森林遊樂區

This small **forest reserve** (Chíhnán Guójiā Sēnlín Yóulèqū; ☎ 03-864 1594; http://recreate.forest.gov.tw; adult/child NT50/25; ☷ 8am-5pm) exists to preserve the history of Taiwan's logging industry. The old steam locomotive engines stole the show (for us anyway), though the museum of old logging equipment and the cable system are pretty interesting too. The visitor centre has an informative English brochure, which includes a simple map. Sometimes there are English-speaking tour guides available.

The reserve is just west of the lake. There are clear signs to it in English.

Sleeping & Eating

The **Liyu Lake Campground** (鯉魚潭露營區; Lǐyú Tán Lùyíngqū; camp sites with shelter NT500/800, wooden cabins NT1200) is just 1km south of the lake off Hwy 9. The modern campground has showers, barbecue areas, tent sites and small wooden cabins . There's a nice clean flowing river behind the campground to paddle in.

There's a string of simple restaurants and noodle shops on the main road across from the lake.

Getting There & Away

To get to Liyu Lake by bus, go to the Hualien Bus Company station (☎ 03-833 8146) on Jung Shan Rd and catch a bus heading to Shoufong (壽豐). Buses (NT52, 20 minutes) run about every two hours.

LINTIANSHAN (LIN TIEN SHAN)
林田山林業文化園區

Lintianshan (Líntiánshān) was once a Japanese logging village, with a population of over 2000. It's now a quaint ghost town (with a few remaining residents), which highlights a colonial heritage that involved stripping this island of most of its ancient forests. But it's worth a visit if you are in the area. The surrounding mountains are beautiful and there is a genuine historical atmosphere to the village, which is made entirely out of spruce. The atmosphere here grows on you.

A fire in 2001 destroyed a whole section of old houses but there is still plenty to see, and there are ongoing efforts continue to restore what was burned. There is even talk of opening up the old hot springs that once served the village.

When you visit, check out the nearby river. The water is a beautiful light blue-green colour. At first we thought it was pollution – it was so unreal looking – but it turned out to be the natural result of minerals washing into the water from the eastern mountains. You see some of this same blue colouring in Taroko Gorge, but it's never this bright.

The turnoff for Lintianshan is marked in English on Hwy 9. From Hualien, there are two trains in the early morning (NT41, 55 minutes) and one around 1pm. Get off at Wanrong Station and turn left down a short lane. Turn left again at the end of the lane and follow the road (Hwy 16) for about 2.5km to Lintianshan. There are English signs along the way.

HUALIEN SUGAR FACTORY光復糖廠

Despite the history here, there's no confusing this old **factory** (Guāngfù Tángchǎng; ☎ 03-870 5581; 9 Tangchang St, Dajin Village, Guangfu township ☷ 8am-8pm) with the Dulan Sugar Factory (p194), a genuine venue for local culture. This is a tourist trap, with gift shops galore, tacky music and a freak-show museum out the back. However, it is still worth a pit stop if you are driving down the highway for its ice cream (NT25). While you eat your cone or dish, wander around the factory grounds and check out the row of old Japanese-built wooden buildings. A bit of trivia for you: the large carp pools beside the ice cream shop are craters from the US bombing of Taiwan during WWII.

The sugar factory is just south of the town of Guangfu (光復) on Hwy 9. There are signs in English on the highway directing you there.

MATAIAN馬太鞍

☎ 03 / pop 500

On the west side of Hwy 9, very close to the Hualien Sugar Factory turnoff is the wetland area known as Mataian . It's an ideal place for farming and fishing and the Ami people have lived here for generations. Recent efforts by the Taiwanese government to protect wetlands have seen the Mataian area turned into a bit of an ecological classroom. Many come here at the end of June to see fields of blooming lotus flowers, or to cycle along the quiet country roads. Ecological tours are offered by local Ami residents, and if you are lucky enough to come in autumn or winter you can see glow-in-the-dark mushrooms in the nearby hills.

Information

The **Mataian Cultural Centre** (拉藍的家; Lālánde Jiā; ☎ 870 0015; 光復鄉大全村大全街42巷15號) acts as the region's visitor centre. Tours around the wetlands, which include demonstrations of traditional harvesting and fishing techniques (the fishing is like nothing you've seen before) can be arranged here (NT50 per person). We have been told there is someone who can do English tours but call ahead for this.

Sleeping & Eating

Shin-liu Farm (欣綠農園; Xīnlǜ Nóngyuán; ☎ 870 1861; www.shin-liu.com; 光復鄉大全村大全街55號; dorm per person NT450, dbl NT3000) This farm has two places to stay. One offers comfortable modern double rooms in a stone house, the other rustic dorm-style bedding in a structure that is actually a converted pig house. It's a fine place to stay, though rooms have shared bathrooms and thin walls. Check out the website for pictures. Shin-liu can also arrange eco-tours and has bicycles for rent.

The cultural centre also has rooms from NT1600. Both places offer good midweek discounts.

Cifadahan Cafe (Hóngwǎwū Wénhuà Měishí Cāntīng; 紅瓦屋文化美食餐廳; ☎ 870 4601; www.cifadahan.net; 光復鄉大全村大全街62巷16號; 9-course set meal NT250; ☉ 10am-9pm) Don't miss this place, run by a talented Ami artist who makes all the carvings, furniture and decorations you see in the café. The café serves traditional Ami food, including *shítóu huǒguō* (石頭火鍋; stone hot pot; NT500) made out of betel nut leaves and boiled by fire-heated stones. A favourite of ours is the salad made with 19 local vegetables.

The café is easy to find – once someone shows you where it is, that is. Inquire at the visitor centre or just drive around and show the characters to people. Everyone knows this place. By the time you go, there may even be signs up in English.

Getting There & Around

To get into the Mataian area, look for the signs (in Chinese at the time of writing) around the 251.7km mark. It's not far from the turn off for the Hualien Sugar Factory.

If you want to go there by train from Hualien, get off at Guangfu Station. There's about one train an hour (fast/slow NT100/77, 45 minutes/one hour). From the station walk to Hwy 9, turn right, then walk 1km south. Turn right at the sign for Mataian. Note that the whole area is a maze of unmarked country lanes so watch where you're going and ask people for directions.

FUYUAN FOREST RECREATIONAL AREA 富源國家森林遊樂區

This **recreational area** (Butterfly Valley Resort; Fùyuán Sēnlín Yóulèqū; ☎ 03-881 1514; http://recreate.forest.gov.tw; adult/child NT80/40; ☉ 8am-5pm) is a peaceful 235-hectare camphor forest with many good walking trails and waterfalls. It's a popular bird-watching venue, and there's also a valley famous for its butterflies, which swarm here from March to August. There used to be cheap cabins for rent here but they have been replaced with rooms starting at NT8000.

RUEISUI 瑞穗
☎ 03 / pop 5000

The small town of Rueisui (Ruìsuì) in the East Rift Valley is used as a base for white-water rafting trips down the Hsiukuluan River. It's also the site of the Rueisui (Juisui) Hot Springs, one of the oldest developed springs in Taiwan.

Sights & Activities
RUEISUI HOT SPRINGS 瑞穗溫泉

These springs (Ruìsuì Wēnquán) are the only carbonated hot springs in Taiwan. The first public baths were opened by the Japanese in 1919. The water is rich in iron and has a temperature of 48°C. Because of the heavy iron content, the water has a pale brown colour and a slightly salty, rusty flavour. People believe that frequent bathing in the spring water increases a woman's chance of bearing a male child.

The hot spring area is a few kilometres directly west of Rueisui town (on the other side of Hwy 9). As you drive down the highway there are English signs pointing to the area. From the train station head directly west.

RAFTING

A **raft trip** (泛舟; *fànzhōu*) down the Hsiukuluan (Siouguluan) River (Xiùgūluán Xī) is the main reason many people come to Rueisui, especially in the summer months. The river is the longest in eastern Taiwan and originates from the Hsiukuluan Mountain Range, eventually emptying into the sea at the aboriginal town of Takangkou. The rafting portion of the river, from Rueisui to Takangkou, is 24km long, twisting and turning its way through gorges and steep cliffs. It takes 3½ hours to complete the route but there are few rough spots. This is, for the most part, very leisurely rafting.

Rafting trips can be arranged in Rueisui at the **Rueisui Rafting Service Centre** (瑞穗泛舟服務中心; Ruìsuì Fànzhōu Fúwù Zhōngxīn; ☎ 887 5400; 215 Jhongshan Rd, sec.3; 中山路3段215號; ☷ 6am-3pm Jun-Aug, 8am-5pm Oct-Apr, 7am-4pm May & Sep), which is right at the start of the rafting route. Travel agents in Taipei and Hualien can also book for you. The standard fee is NT750, which includes transportation from and to Hualien, lunch, equipment and insurance. The cheapest option if you have your own wheels is to buy a ticket at any Family Mart convenience store (NT500).

To get to the centre from the Rueisui train station, head out the front exit and continue straight along Jhongshan Rd for about 4km to 5km. A taxi will cost around NT100.

Sleeping & Eating

In the Rueisui Hot Springs area there are many hot spring hotels and resorts offering rooms at varying degrees of quality and price.

Rueisui Hot Springs Hotel (瑞穗溫泉山莊; Ruìsuì Wēnquán Shān Zhuāng; ☎ 887 2170; 23 Hongye Village; r from NT1200) We can't say this is our favourite place for a soak, but interestingly it was the first public hotel in the area and is still open. The hotel is run by an eccentric local family who keep the atmosphere very local and, well, eccentric. This is the kind of place where the owners will keep breakfast for you if you get up late, but might not bother to heat it up for you. The rooms are OK, but it's a bit noisy. The hotel is up a small road off the main road through the hot springs area. There are English signs.

Hungye Hotsprings Hotel (紅葉溫泉旅社; Hóngyè Wēnquán Lǚshè; ☎ 887 2176; cabins from NT2500) This hotel, actually a row of nice wooden cabins, is the only one to use water from the Hungye Hot Springs. It has a pleasant setting on a flat grassy riverbank. To get to the hotel head directly west of the Rueisui Hot Springs and follow the road to the end.

There's a good **camping ground** (per camp site NT250) with raised wooden platforms and

showers on the grounds of the Rueisui Rafting Service Centre. There are also several B&Bs in the area. Inquire at the train station.

Most hot spring hotels have restaurants in them. Around the train station there are numerous small noodle stands and restaurants as well as convenience stores for snacks, sandwiches and drinks.

Getting There & Away

There are trains from Hualien to Rueisui (fast/slow train NT146/112, one/1½ hours) about every hour.

YULI 玉里
☎ 03 / pop 3000

The small rift valley town of Yuli (Yùlǐ) makes a good base for exploration. Within 30 minutes there are hot springs, mountains for viewing the lovely day lilies in late summer, a lush green valley dedicated to growing organic produce, and the eastern section of Yushan National Park (p243), which offers some of the best hiking along the east coast.

There are plenty of restaurants, noodle shops and convenience stores around town and a couple of cheap hotels across from the train station. A decent one to try is **Yu Chiling Hotel** (玉麒麟別莊; Yù Chílíng Biézhuāng; ☎ 888 3113; 210 Datong Rd; 大同路210號; s/d NT700/1200).

The place to stay in the Yuli area is **Wisdom Garden** (智嵐雅居; Zhìlán Yǎjū; ☎ 888 2488; http://home.kimo.com.tw/wisdom_garden; 玉里鎮大禹里酸柑98-1號; r from NT2400), just north of the train station off Hwy 9. Without doubt it's our favourite B&B in Taiwan. The house sits in an orchard high above the rift valley looking across to Chikha Mountain. Be sure to take your meals out on the front lawn. The owner, a Buddhist and former hotel manager, has made a true retreat here; it's both soothing and nurturing for the soul. Each room has its own character, and is flooded with light and green views. Furnishings are country quaint, bathrooms large and modern, and the owner's original paintings, watercolours and tie-dye works add a special decorative touch.

If you are driving, the turn-off for Wisdom Garden is at the 289.4km mark on Hwy 9. Just follow the English signs from here. If you make prior arrangements the owners will pick you up from Yuli train station.

There are frequent trains from Hualien to Yuli (fast/slow train NT193/149, 80 minutes/two hours). A bicycle is a good way to get

EAST COAST

around, as is a scooter. If you have a Taiwanese licence you can rent scooters (NT400 per day) from around the train station.

ANTUNG (ANTONG) HOT SPRINGS 安通溫泉

These hot springs (Āntōng Wēnquán) are about 8km south of the town of Yuli off Hwy 9, a little up a mountain road. The springs produce clear, odourless, sodium hydro-sulphate water at a temperature of 42°C. It's drinkable and very soothing on the throat, which may be why the hotels here use it to make delicious coffee (the only places in Taiwan we know of that do).

Hotels in the lower village seemed a little run-down when we visited. For something nicer, and with a scenic mountain view, try the **New Life Hot Springs Resort** (加賀屋溫泉山莊; Jiāhèwū Wēnquán Shānzhuāng; ☎ 03-888 2686; d/tr NT2100/3800). Rooms are small but comfortable with wooden interiors and stone tubs. The hotel has its own source of hot-spring water, which you can see if you take a short stroll up the road. So much water is produced that no-one seemed worried that the tanks were overflowing onto the footpath the day we visited. Unlimited use of the public pools costs NT200 for nonguests. Hotels guests have free access to the pools.

To get to the resort and Antung area, follow the signs on Hwy 9 south of Yuli. As you drive into Antung you will see a sign for the resort (in English) on the left. Don't forget to try the coffee.

WALAMI TRAIL 瓦拉米古道

A must-do hike, this trail (Wǎlāmǐ Gǔdào) begins about 15km southeast of Yuli in the Nanan section of Yushan National Park, at an altitude of 500m over the Nanan River. There are waterfalls along the way, suspension bridges, lookouts, sections of path cut straight into the cliff walls, and the constant sound (and occasionally sight) of monkeys crashing through the trees. It's a jungle out there, and one of the best preserved in Taiwan. The views down the valley and across the mountains are chillingly beautiful.

The trail hails from the Japanese era and was built to facilitate the opening of the east as well as to maintain a careful eye on aboriginal tribes. As such this is a walk through history as much as nature. The trail has been fortified (meaning barriers have been placed on the

sides of the trail where you can drop hundreds of metres to your death) and improved in recent years, making it safe for most people to travel on, especially the first couple of kilometres, which you can do without any permits.

The Walami Trail is actually part of the much longer Japanese Occupation Era Batongguan Traversing Route (see p245), which goes all the way to Donpu. But this is a seven- to 10-day journey. The 13km hike up to the Walami cabin takes about six to seven hours and is not a particularly difficult route for anyone in decent shape.

Hiking all the way to the cabin and spending the night is highly recommended. The cabin has rough bedding (bring your own sleeping bag), water and solar-powered lights. If you go midweek you can get your mountain permit on the day at the police station near the **Nanan Visitor Centre** (☎ 03-888 7560; 83-3, Choching; ☯ 9am-4.30pm, closed 2nd Tue of month or Wed if Tue is a national holiday). But first go to the visitor centre to pick up maps of the trail and book a bed in the cabin. The cabin only has 24 beds so if you are going on a weekend it is recommended that you arrange things ahead of time (see Mountaineering, p330).

If you don't have your own transport you can take a taxi from Yuli to the visitor centre (NT300), then walk the last 6km to the trailhead (after arranging permits). Along the way you'll pass **Nanan Waterfall** (南安瀑布; Nánān Pùbù). On a warm day stand under the falls for a natural spa treatment.

SIXTY STONE MOUNTAIN 六十石山

Once a typical rice growing area, Sixty Stone Mountain (Liùshí Dàn Shān; 952m) became a centre for growing day (tiger) lilies (金針; jīnzhēn) a few decades ago. Day lilies are popular with Taiwanese consumers who eat them fresh or dried in tea drinks and a host of other products. Every August to early September, around harvest time, the mountainsides become carpeted with the orange flowers of the blooming lilies, attracting hordes of visitors (see boxed text on opposite).

There's no public transportation to the area, though that may change. For now, consider a tour bus, or take a train and rent a taxi (probably a couple of thousand for a few hours) from Fuli (富里). If you have your own transport there are English signs on Hwy 9 (Sixty Stone Mountain Recreation Area) as you head south of Yuli. You can't miss it.

STOPPING TO SMELL THE FLOWERS

Tourism is a funny thing. It often makes people look twice at their surroundings. Take the folk who work on Sixty Stone Mountain in the Rift Valley. For decades they had been planting day lilies to sell for use in tea and soups but no-one really stopped to consider just how beautiful the green hills became when tinted with the blooming orange flowers in late summer. But nowadays, thanks to promotion from the tourism board, those same indifferent farmers run guesthouses and organised tours catering to a steady flow of visitors.

In the north, blooming You Tong trees (see Sanyi, p178) have been painting mountainsides white for centuries, but again, no-one ever paid them much mind. All the glory went to the cherry blossom, which in Taiwan is a spindly dwarf compared with the You Tong. But five years ago, talk about a tall sturdy hardwood with pretty white petals that looked like snow when they fell to the ground began to spread. Towns began to hold You Tong festivals as part of a revival of local Hakka culture and soon everyone had their own little favourite place to go and see the trees in April.

If flowers are really your thing, Baihe has a two-month-long summer festival devoted to the lotus (see p258), while Yangmingshan (p132) holds minor festivals from February to April for cherry blossoms, rhododendrons, peaches, azaleas and calla lilies.

In April and November look out for a white trumpet-like flower called the Formosan lily. It blooms everywhere in the wild and the smell is intoxicating.

LOSHAN (LUOSHAN) SCENIC AREA
羅山風景區

Just north of Fuli, in an area called the rice barn of Taiwan, lies this **valley** (Lóshān), which has become the centre of the organic industry in Hualien. But it's also one of the most scenically splendid valleys along all of the east coast. Some highlights include the 120m-long **Luoshan Waterfall** (羅山瀑布; Lóshān Pùbù) and a number of small bubbling mud volcanoes.

At the time of writing the valley had a campground, but the ownership and maintenance of it was being argued over by the local government and the Rift Valley Scenic Administration. Hopefully this will get sorted out as it would make for a wonderful base. Guesthouse accommodation is available in Loshan Village. Inquire at the **visitor centre** (☎ 882 1991; ☷ 8am-6.40pm), which is a block north of the entrance into the scenic area, down a side road to the right.

KUANSHAN (GUANSHAN) 關山
pop 2000

Kuanshan (Guānshān) is a small farming community 50km north of Taitung. It's positioned right at the end of the East Rift Valley on Hwy 9. The main reason to come here is to take advantage of the bicycle paths set up in the town's large **riverside park** (admission NT50; ☷ 7am-5.30pm), which pleasantly wind their way through colourful rice paddies and fields of colza and sugar cane. The paths are pretty flat, and all in all total only 10km, so they won't appeal to serious cyclists – unless they happen to be birders as well. Another path leading from the park follows the river and is a great place for bird-watching, with viewing platforms set up at various points. For a longer ride, cross the river and head up County Rd 197 in either direction.

To get to the park, turn left as you exit the train station at Kuanshan, then take the first left and walk up the road about 1km. You can rent bicycles (NT150 to NT500) at any number of shops on your way. There are trains to Kuanshan from Hualien (fast/slow train NT287/221, two/three hours) about every two hours.

TAITUNG HONGYE (HUNGYE) HOT SPRINGS 台東紅葉溫泉

Don't confuse these **hot springs** (Hóngyè Wēnquán) with the Hungye Hot Springs near Rueisui. This is a new open-air place with a large tiled pool set high in the mountains of Bunun country. Facilities include showers, changing rooms and even a camping ground with raised wooden platforms. It's a really quaint little place to stay, especially on a quiet weekday, or just drop in on your way down the highway for a quick soak. Somebody should be around to take your money, but not always.

You need your own transport to get to Hongye. Since it's not so far off the highway it makes an excellent stop if you are cycling. Look for the signs (in English) as you head south of Kuanshan.

It's worth exploring further up past the springs if you have time. There's a quaint little **Bunun village** (head right when the road forks after the hot springs) and a beautiful **gorge** (turn left at the fork).

TAITUNG 台東
☎ 089 / pop 110,192

There aren't a lot of reasons for the short-term visitor to make a long stop in Taitung (Táidōng) city itself. Taitung's charms reveal themselves slowly as you get to know the locals, discover the treasures in the surrounding hills and coastline, and learn how to move with, not against, the rhythms of southern life. But if you don't have time for that, we suggest either giving the place a complete miss (there are other places nearby to use as a base) or just spend some time in transit.

Orientation & Information
There are enough pinyin roads signs around for you to orientate yourself fairly easily.

Visitor centres at the **Railway Art Village** (☎ 359 085), the **new train station** (☎ 238 231) and the **airport** (☎ 362 476) are open from 9am to 5pm daily, but except for the volunteers, the staff's English ability tends to be weak. However, there is written English information on buses and trains, as well as some useful brochures.

Taitung County has two useful websites: http://tour.taitung.gov.tw/english/index .asp and www.taitung.gov.tw/english/Tour _information.php.

In addition to 7-Elevens for ATM service, the **Bank of Taiwan** (☎ 324 210; 313 Chungshan Rd) will exchange foreign currency and has an ATM that takes international debit cards.

Sights & Activities
The two most touted sites of Taitung, the **National Museum of Prehistory** (Guólì Shǐqián Bówùguǎn; adult/child NT80/50) and the associated **Peinan Culture Park** (Bēinán Wénhuà Gōngyuán; admission free) are disappointing. The museum's exhibits are mostly pictures and dioramas with write-ups. There are some artefacts, but far fewer than at other places, such as the Indigenous People's Cultural Park in Sandimen (see p279).

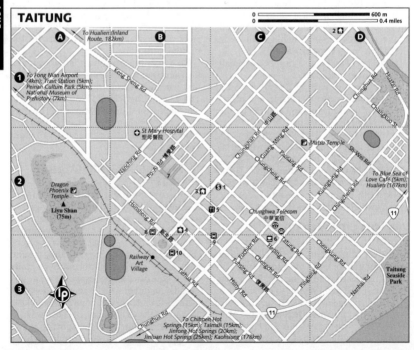

Taitung's culture park is the site of the largest prehistoric settlement found in Taiwan. Unfortunately, almost all the artefacts have been shipped to Taipei for storage, and the site has been reburied (except for one tiny area) to protect it from looting.

If you're interested in **surfing** around the Taitung area, talk to Dave at KASA (see p204).

Festivals & Events

The **Festival of Austronesian Cultures** is held annually in August at the National Museum of Prehistory and Forest Park. The festival is a great opportunity to see traditional aboriginal handicrafts, musical instruments and wood carvings, as well as to try a smorgasbord of local foods. Festival participants include not only Taiwan's aboriginals, but also aboriginal groups from several South Pacific nations who are believed to share a common ancestry with Taiwan's indigenous people.

The **Ami Harvest Festival** is another large festival in the region that takes place in July or August every year in towns around Taitung County. It's a boisterous event, with plenty of singing and dancing.

Bombing Master Handan is an old festival (well, from the '50s) that is getting a new lease on life as Lantern Festival activities get bigger and bigger each year. During the festival, volunteers dress as Handanyeh, the Money god, and are carried through the streets. Since the god reportedly hates the cold, people shell him with exploding firecrackers to warm him up and thus win his favour. The festival takes place on the 15th and 16th day of the Lunar

New Year. Every year volunteers appear on TV a few days earlier to remind the public that the god doesn't like firecrackers thrown directly at his face.

Sleeping

Accommodation is pretty basic in town, with few worthwhile midrange options. If you have a vehicle consider spending the night outside of town in Chihpen Hot Springs, Jinluan Hot Springs, Dulan or at the camping grounds at Hsiao Yeliu and Hongye Hot Springs.

Fuhyuan (Fuhtuan) Hotel (Fúyuán Dàfàndiàn; ☎ 331 1369; 72 Wenhua St; 文化街72號; d/tr NT700/1000) This pleasant budget hotel is centrally located in a busy market area. The owners don't speak any English but they have had so many foreign guests over the years they have written down a wealth of bilingual travel information. The hotel is right on the bus route from the airport, which is good if you are carrying a heavy bag.

Hotel Hsin Fu Chih (Xīnfúzhì Dà Lǚshè; ☎ 331 101; 417 Chungshan Rd; 中山路417號; d/tw NT700/1000) The rooms at the Hsin Fu Chih are old but clean and pretty comfortable. It's no more nor less than a decent budget hotel.

Aboriginal Cultural Centre (Yuán Zùmín Wénhuà Huìguǎn; ☎ 340 605; fax 341 416; 10 Chungshan Rd; 中山路10號; d/tr NT1150/1450) The Cultural Centre has clean, spacious rooms with just a couple of chips and smudges here and there. There are a couple of traditional Yami canoes outside. The staff are very friendly

Hugo Farm (雍雅居民宿; Yōngyǎjū Mínsù; ☎ 237 781; fax 238 990; 利吉路86號; r from NT6000, cash only) This is our choice for a top-end place to stay in the Taitung area. The farm, about an acre in size, is like a landscaped garden. From the back it looks onto Little Huangshan (小黃山), a very scenic stretch of craggy mountains along the Beinan River. The farm's guesthouses are modern and stylish. Rooms are huge and feature cool stone bathtubs (the only off feature are the plastic shower curtains). The slightly fizzy tap water comes from a nearby spring and is said to improve skin tone.

One thing to note about the price is that it never goes down, nor up, not even during summer or Chinese New Year. When you consider that during holiday times even bland midranges can charge NT4000 a night, the farm, which includes delicious multicourse breakfasts and dinners (with wine, coffee and dessert) in its rates is a solid deal.

EAST COAST

Hugo is about a 15-minute drive out of Taitung. Head west on Hwy 11甲 and turn right up County Rd 45 after you cross a long bridge. Hugo is about 2km up the road on the left. There is an English sign out the front and the owner speaks good English.

Eating & Drinking

Chungshan Rd and Chunghua Rd are chock-a-block full of cheap eateries and cafés. Some local delicacies to try are *tǒngzǎi mǐgāo* (筒仔米糕; sticky rice) and *zhū xiè tāng* (豬血湯; pork blood soup), a Puyuma dish.

Beikang Xiao Chi Pu (Běigǎng Xiǎo Chī Bù; 212 Guang-Ming Rd; sticky rice NT25-40; ☺ 8am-7pm) The Beikang is an unassuming little place that has been around for over 20 years. The sticky rice here is some of the best in town. Try it with some *ròu gēng* (thick meat soup).

KASA (☎ 0921-548 769; www.wretch.cc/blog/kasa taitung; 102 Heping Rd; drinks NT100; ☺ 11am-midnight) KASA has been around Taitung for many years in various manifestations. The latest, off Heping Rd, is a rustic little café made out of driftwood and recycled yellow cedar. It's got a great laid-back atmosphere and a friendly crowd of regulars, both Taiwanese and foreign. Come here for a good brunch or sandwich in the afternoon, or a drink or two in the evening.

Entertainment

Every Saturday night there is live music at the Dulan Sugar Factory (see p194). On Friday nights, music is a little closer to town in Fukang, just a couple of kilometres north of Taitung.

Blue Sea of Love Cafe (藍色愛情海; Lánsè Àiqíng Hǎi; ☎ 089-281 755) This little café made out of driftwood is right, and we mean right, on the ocean. It's a bit tricky to get to, but as you head into Fukang look for a blue painted alley on the right about 100m before the 7-Eleven. Head down the alley for 100m or so. It's a bit junky here but the café has a great view.

Shopping

Taitung has some of the freshest and most delicious fruit in Taiwan. In central Taitung, between Po'ai and Chungshan Rds, there's a lively fruit street (*shuǐguǒ jiē*) selling a colourful assortment of fruit, including pineapples, coconuts, bananas, mangoes, dragon fruit and papayas. There's also Taitung's most famous fruit, the delicious custard apple, nicknamed

'Buddha's fruit' (釋迦; *shìjiā*) because its shape resembles the head of the curly haired Sakyamuni Buddha.

Aboriginal arts and crafts are on sale at the gift shops of the National Museum of Prehistory and the Peinan Culture Park.

Getting There & Away

AIR

The following airlines have booking counters at Taitung's **Fong Nian Airport** (☎ 362 530; www.rcfn .gov.tw/en/en1.asp): **Far Eastern Transport** (☎ 362 677), **Mandarin Airlines** (☎ 362 699), **Uni Air** (☎ 362 626) and **Daily Air Corporation** (☎ 362 489).

There are flights to Taipei, Taichung and Lanyu and Green Islands. The airport has a nice tropical feel to it, and is a pleasant way to enter the south. There's a **visitor centre** (☺ 9am-5pm) to help you out.

BUS

Taitung has four bus stations and finding which bus goes where can be confusing. Ask at any visitor centre for the latest. Listed below are the three most likely to be used by travellers.

The **Dingdong Bus Station** (☎ 333 343), near the Railway Art Village, runs about four buses a day to Hualien (NT479, three hours) along Hwy 11.

The **Kuo Kuang Hao Bus Company** (☎ 322 027) runs about five buses a day to Kaohsiung (NT455, 4½ hours). Buses to Tienchih (NT351, 4½ hours) on the South Cross-Island Hwy leave daily at 7.10am (but always confirm this time as some schedules still say they leave at 6.40am). There are no direct buses to Kenting.

The **Dingdong Inland Bus Station** (☎ 333 433) has about 10 buses a day to Chihpen Hot Springs (NT40, 40 minutes). There are also frequent buses to the new train station (NT22).

TRAIN

There are about 15 trains a day between Hualien and Taitung (fast/slow train NT355/273, 2½/3½ hours). The train follows the inland route through the East Rift Valley.

If taking a taxi to the train station, be clear with your driver that you mean the new station. From central Taitung it will cost around NT200. Buses for the new train station (NT22) leave from the Dingdong Inland Bus Station about every hour.

Getting Around
TO/FROM THE AIRPORT
A taxi to or from the airport will cost about NT300. Buses (NT22) leave about every hour from the Dingdong Inland Bus Station. Check at any visitor centre if you need to know the exact schedule.

SCOOTER
Rentals are available around the new train station and typically cost NT400 to NT500 a day. Most rental agencies are now refusing to rent scooters to customers who don't have a Taiwanese licence.

SOUTH OF TAITUNG

Not many travel further south than Taitung, but there are a few interesting little stops where you can enjoy quiet hot springs, beach combing, camping and a fascinating banyan forest.

CHIHPEN (ZHIBEN) 知本
☎ 089 / pop 3000

The town of Chihpen is famous for the Chihpen Hot Springs (Zhīběn Wēnquán), one of Taiwan's oldest hot spring resorts. The sodium bicarbonate water is colourless and tasteless and has a temperature of 32°C.

As with Wulai in the north, today's Chihpen is an overcrowded weekend playground with far too many hotels of all shapes, sizes and prices. There's no doubting the beauty of the natural surroundings, set in a canyon at the foot of a mountain range, but it's a tourist town and an unpleasantly aggressive one at that. Touts wait at every corner to rush out and stuff brochures in your face when you stop at red lights. Some will even drive beside you on a scooter waving their hotel's business card!

With so many hotels, we (and many knowledgeable locals) question the purity of the hot spring water and so would never pay top dollar to stay here, though we know many who have, and gladly, because of the beautiful surroundings at some of the better hotels. We've used the public facilities at a few places and enjoyed the experience though, especially after exploring the beautiful forest recreation area at the end of the road.

Sights & Activities
HOT SPRINGS
Most hotels have hot-spring facilities open to nonguests. We liked the large, multilayered, multipooled complex run by the **Dongtai Hotel** (東台溫泉飯店; Dōngtái Wēnquán Fàndiàn; ☎ 089-512 290; 147 Longchuan Rd; 龍泉路 147號; adult/child NT250/150), near the end of the road towards the forest recreation area. The views from the upper deck over the river valley and mountains are excellent. This is worth a visit (and soak).

For the swankiest hot spring pools, head to the **Hotel Royal Chihpen** (老爺飯店; Lǎoyé Dàjiǔdiàn; ☎ 089-510 666; Lane 23, 113 Longchuan Rd; 龍泉路23巷113號; adult/child NT350/200), the finest hotel in town.

CHINGCHUEH TEMPLE 清覺寺
This temple (Qīngjué Sì) sits incongruously next to the Hotel Royal Chihpen. It's home to a beautiful white-jade Buddha from Myanmar and a bronze Buddha from Thailand; they're worth dropping in to see if you are already in the area.

CHIHPEN (ZHIBEN) FOREST RECREATION AREA 知本森林遊樂區
At the far end of the canyon is this **recreation area** (Zhīběn Sēnlín Yóulèqū; ☎ 510 961; http://recreate .forest.gov.tw; admission NT100; ☺ 7am-5pm), a lovely forested region with hiking trails, rivers and waterfalls. It is worth coming to Chihpen just to wander the trails, especially along the upper slopes where there's a wonderful old banyan forest that reminds us of the Ent world in *Lord of the Rings*. In this area you can hear Taiwan macaques crashing around in the trees overhead and may be lucky enough to see, or more likely hear, the tiny Reeves muntjac, which makes a strange barking sound like a dog.

To get to the forest recreation area, either catch a bus from Taitung or simply follow the signs to Chihpen Hot Springs and drive through the hotel wonderland to the end of the road. The recreation area is obvious to the right. Cross a short bridge to the visitor centre where you can get English maps.

Eating
The main road through Chihpen (Longchuan Rd) has plenty of small restaurants and noodle stands selling decent local food at regular prices.

EAST COAST

Getting There & Away

The Dingdong Bus Company has about 10 buses a day to Chihpen (NT40, 40 minutes) from its Inland Bus Station in Taitung. According to the company, all buses drop you off near the end of the valley road a few hundred metres from the forest recreation area.

TAIMALI 太麻里

It sounds like a Mexican dish, but Taimali (Tàimálǐ) is a little nothing town south of Chihpen. Ah, but there is one thing here: a beach. A long, beautiful palm-studded beach that stretches on and on. There's no swimming (it's far too rough), but the crashing surf, wide soft-sand beach, green mountains rising to the west, and long coastline sweeping out to the north make this an absolutely fabulous place for a couple of hours' strolling. There's also plenty of driftwood should you want to build a fire, and no-one would object if you set up a tent and camped out.

Interestingly, the BBC chose this beach as one of the 60 best places in the world to watch the sunrise of the new millennium on the eve of 1 January 2000.

It's best to have your own transport to get here.

JINFONG (JINFENG) HOT SPRINGS 金峰溫泉

pop 500

Just south of Taimali are these rather odd little hot springs (Jīnfēng Wēnquán) set up by the local community. While most community hot springs are makeshift affairs – heavy on concrete, light on aesthetics – these ones have two large, open, tiled pools, a lovely little camping ground with covered wooden tent platforms, changing rooms and showers, in addition to the beautiful natural setting (a large grassy field in the mountains beside a flowing river). At the time of writing it was only open on weekends and till 5pm, but it should be truly open by the time you read this. The spot is ideal for cyclists heading down the coast.

The springs are simple to get to. As you drive down Hwy 9 you'll see the English sign for the Jinfong Hot Springs. Turn right onto County Rd 64 and drive a short distance until you see a police station on the right. Stop and tell the officer inside where you are going, fill out the forms and pay the NT10 fee (make sure you have your passport). Then drive a couple more kilometres, following the river,

until you see a strange stone chimney on the left in a wide clearing, belching out steam like a locomotive engine. This is the hot spring area, but you can't always make out the pools from the road so use the steam stack as your reference. Take the next left down to the camping ground/hot spring area.

JINLUAN HOT SPRINGS 金崙溫泉

pop 500

Just south of Jinfong on Route 66 is yet another hot springs (Jīnluán Wēnquán) village. Here you have both wild and developed options to choose from, as well as an interesting little museum devoted to the local Ruiki and Paiwan tribes.

Sights & Activities

HOT SPRINGS

Most of the hot spring hotels are small local establishments with very basic facilities. For something much, much nicer try the **East Sun Spa Spring Hotel** (東太陽溫泉會館; Dōngtàiyáng Wēnquán Huìguǎn; www.east-spa.com.tw; d/tw NT2800/4200, weekdays NT2000/3000). The hotel has a simple modern design, with rooms taking advantage of clear ocean views. Six outdoor pools (unlimited time NT200) sit on a bluff with views over the river valley and the Pacific Ocean. Yes, it's nice up here.

To get to the hotel, drive about a kilometre or so west down Route 66. The hotel is 500m up a steep hill on the right. The sign for the turnoff has English on it so you can't miss it.

Locals tell us there is a great natural hot spring about two hours' walk up the **Jinlun River** (金崙溪). Inquire at the Dawu Mountain Education Centre for a local guide.

DAWU MOUNTAIN EDUCATION CENTRE 大武山自然教育中心

In such a remote part of Taiwan, you hardly expect a little **museum** (Dàwǔshān Zìrán Jiàoyù Zhōngxīn; ☎ 089-771 957; admission free; ◷ 9am-5pm Tue-Sun, closed 1-5 Jun & 1-5 Dec) such as this one to have such good displays and to be completely bilingual But it's here, and if you're in the area it's worth a stop to learn about the local Ruiki and Paiwan tribes of Taiwan, and the indigenous flora and fauna. Staff are very knowledgeable and helpful, though they do only speak Chinese.

To get to the museum, drive or walk west along Route 66 about 2.5km from the highway turnoff. The museum is to the left, just past a bridge, and looks like a nice hotel with a grey stone exterior.

Eating

There are plenty of restaurants and noodle shops and even a 7-Eleven in Jinluan village. The East Sun Spa Spring Hotel also has a restaurant serving local aboriginal food.

Getting There & Away

If you are driving, the turn-off for Route 66 is at the 414km mark on Hwy 9 and is marked with an English sign. Trains from Taitung run every few hours (fast/slow train NT62/38, 35/40 minutes). When you exit Jinluan station, head west uphill to Hwy 9. Turn left and you'll quickly see the sign for the turn-off to Route 66 and the springs. The first train leaves just after 7am.

EAST COAST

Western Taiwan

If you want contrasts, head to western Taiwan and start at the coastline, continue through rich farmland and end in the high mountains of the central range. In fact, for a study in contrasts, just head to the Alishan National Scenic Area. Here you can travel through three biogeographical zones – tropical, subtropical and temperate – in just three hours (a rare old single-track alpine railway is your carriage).

But unless you have unlimited time, the west's contrasts will demand you choose from among them. Should you explore Taiwan's southern Chinese heritage (which includes a great collection of temples) or its aboriginal culture? Should you join a pilgrimage for the goddess of the sea or learn to meditate at a Buddhist temple? Should you climb one of the highest mountains in East Asia or cycle easy bike lanes through the countryside?

Of all the regions in Taiwan, this is one we suggest you follow our advice for most carefully (which includes letting you know those areas you don't need to follow our advice). While there are some real treasures out there, there's also a lot of dismal wasteland. In general, the cities can be given a miss except as jumping-off points. For smaller towns, don't miss Lukang, Puli and, to a lesser extent, Changhua, even if your time is tight. Forget the miles of coastline unless you like Styrofoam, cables, plastic and – you get the picture. Look to the rice fields, the mountains and Sun Moon Lake, the largest body of water in Taiwan, for your scenic fix.

WESTERN TAIWAN

HIGHLIGHTS

- Climb Yushan, one of East Asia's highest mountains, in **Yushan National Park** (p243)
- Get a primer in Buddhism at the **Chung Tai Chan Temple** (p226) in Puli
- See mountainsides light up with fireflies in **Rueili** (p237)
- Ride a rare alpine railway to **Alishan** (p241)
- Swim the rivers in remote **Fengshan** (p239)
- Bird-watch at **Aowanda** (p230)
- Cycle, boat and stroll at **Sun Moon Lake** (p222)
- Become a pilgrim for Matsu in **Dajia** (p216)
- Cross the island on the **Nenggao Cross-Island Historic Trail** (p230)
- Wander the old merchant streets of **Lukang** (p216)

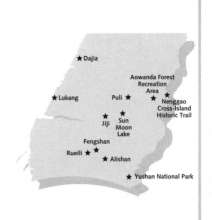

National Parks & Forest Recreation Areas

Western Taiwan is one of the most pristine parts of the country and offers endless opportunities for long hikes, including several week-long ones. Yushan National Park is home of 3952m Yushan (Jade Mountain). Tame Alishan Forest Recreation Area is the polar opposite, with an old alpine train and cherry blossom trees being the draw. Aowanda Forest Recreation Area is one of the best bird-watching sites in the country. Rugged Hehuanshan Forest Recreation Area offers scenic hikes above the tree line.

Getting There & Around

Regular trains run frequently down the coast, connecting all major and minor cities, and there are decent bus services to most smaller towns. The High-Speed Rail (HSR) is now running, but stations are quite far from downtown. Taichung has one airport for both international and domestic services. A small-gauge alpine train (one of only three in the world) does the route from Chiayi to Alishan. In most cities you'll find scooter and car rental.

The only areas where public transportation is inconvenient are Yushan National Park, the more remote parts of the Alishan National Scenic Area, and Hwy 14 past Puli.

TAICHUNG 台中市

☎ 04 / pop 1,021,292

Taichung (Táizhōng), the third-largest city in Taiwan, is hardly a must-see for the short-term visitor, though many long-term expats do enjoy it as a weekend getaway. The city has several pleasant tea and restaurant streets, an excellent science museum and a very good art museum, which includes a top-of-the-line storybook fantasyland library for children. Taichung is also a bright ray of sunshine (literally) on a dreary winter day for those living in the capital. Taipei and Taichung have very similar average temperatures but Taichung is much drier, receiving around 1700mm of rain a year compared with Taipei's 2170mm.

Orientation

The area around the train station is called Central Taichung but, in reality, the focus of the city is shifting westward all the time. Note

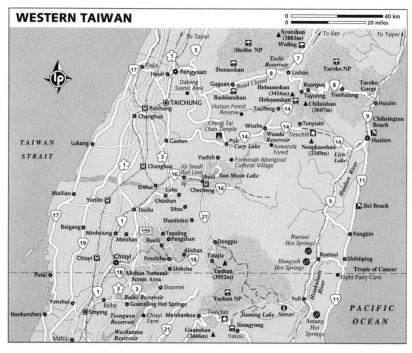

WESTERN TAIWAN

that Zhongzheng Rd, which starts at the train station, runs northwest through the heart of the city and later turns into Taizhonggang Rd and then Hwy 12.

The city government has officially chosen Hanyu Pinyin for its road signs, but at the time of writing many signs had not made the switch. Be aware that some odd spellings may still exist, and sometimes both old and new signs may appear on the same street.

Information

There are plenty of banks and 7-Elevens with ATMs around the train station, and further up along Zhongzheng Rd and Taizhonggang Rd.

Internet places come and go frequently. Ask at the visitor centre. The websites given here are useful and list some obscure sights and activities.

Bank of Taiwan (144 Zhongzheng Rd) Offers money-changing facilities in addition to an ATM.

Compass Magazine (www.taiwanfun.com) This locally produced magazine is available free at the tourist office and many restaurants and shops around town. It's an excellent source of information about the city and you can download the latest copy of the magazine from the website.

Taichung County Government (www.taichung.gov.tw) The county's official website.

Visitor Information Centre (☎ 2221 2126; ⊙ 9am-6pm) Right in the train station. Staff speak English and have an abundance of useful information including bus schedules (and prices), hotel prices and travel brochures.

Welcome to Taichung (http://english.tccg.gov.tw/) The city government's website.

TAICHUNG

Map of Taichung showing streets and numbered sights including Wenhsin Jade Market, Botanical Gardens, People's Park, Taichung Municipal Cultural Centre, Fengle Sculpture Park, and the Restaurant & Bar District.

Sights

TEA STREETS

ChingMing (Jingming) 1st Street (Jīngmíng Yījiē) has a range of modern and traditional-style (or a mix of the two) cafés and restaurants. The area looks best when visited at night. To get there by bus take Taichung Bus 88 or 103, both of which run along Taizhonggang Rd. Get off around Jingcheng Rd and walk down.

Fengle Sculpture Park & Lakeside Tea & Shopping Street (Fēnglè Diāosù Gōngyuán) has a nicely landscaped environment and some decent statues and is also best experienced at night. Around the park is an area of teashops, restaurants, and craft shops that open around noon and close about 10pm (most are closed on Mondays). To get to the park take UBus 73.

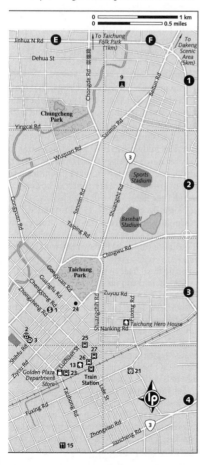

TAIWAN MUSEUM OF ART 台灣省立美術館

The **museum** (Táiwān Shěnglì Měishùguǎn; ☎ 2372 3552; 2 Wuquan W Rd; admission free; ☑ 9am-5pm, closed Mon) is one of the best in Taiwan, and appeals to both kids and parents. The open modern design is visually sophisticated (though not pretentious), and there are high-quality exhibits of both Taiwanese and foreign artists. Exhibits change often, though unfortunately there is almost no signage in English.

For children there is a wonderful hands-on play area and a fantasyland library that includes an igloo, castle and rainforest area (and of course loads of children's books). One expat father we know described it as the best children's library he has ever seen.

To get to the museum take UBus 75.

NATIONAL MUSEUM OF NATURAL SCIENCE 自然科學博物館

This was Taiwan's first **museum of science** (Zìrán Kēxué Bówùguǎn; ☎ 2322 6940; www.nmns.edu.tw; 1 Guanqian Rd; admission exhibition hall adult/child NT100/50, botanic garden NT20/10, space theatre NT100/50, IMAX 3D theatre NT 70/30; ☑ 9am-5pm, closed Mon) and though lacking explanations in English (except for display titles) it's still worth visiting for the visually interesting dioramas, models and exhibitions. Children usually thoroughly enjoy themselves here, especially when they see the life-size dinosaur skeletons and the moving (and roaring) dinosaur automatons. The museum is divided into various buildings, or centres, most of which have their own entrance charges. The Byzantine fee structure is explained in English at the ticket window. To get to the museum take Taichung Bus Company buses 88, 103 or 106.

PAOCHUEH TEMPLE 寶覺寺

This **Buddhist temple** (Bǎojué Sì; 140 Jianxing St; admission free; ☑ 8am-5pm) features one of the largest and fattest Milefo (laughing) Buddhas in Taiwan. The 30m-high statue sits against a backdrop of old apartments, which unfortunately mar photos. There was a lot of work going on around the statue at the time of writing and it looks like some modern structures will soon block out the old ugly ones. It's best to take a taxi to get to the temple.

TAICHUNG FOLK PARK 台中民俗公園

The **park** (Mínsú Gōngyuán; ☎ 2245 1310; 73 Lu Shun Rd, sec.2; adult/child NT50/20; ☑ 9am-5pm Tue-Fri, to 7pm Sat & Sun) is divided into several sections but most of the interesting material is to the far right as you enter (to the left are cheap souvenir stalls). Don't miss the collections of folk artefacts (everything from ceramic pillows to farming implements). It's one of the best we have seen in Taiwan. The park is north of the city centre. To get there, take Taichung Bus 14 or 131 from the stops up on Luchuan St.

ART STREET 藝術街

Another road chock-a-block full of cafés, restaurants and shops – **Art St** (Yìshù Jiē) has the atmosphere of an alternative city-centre neighbourhood and is northwest of the city. To get there, take Taichung Bus 88 or 103 and get off at Tunghai University. Spend a little time walking around the nicely landscaped campus and then walk up the hill a few blocks until you come to a big intersection with an overpass. Turn right and walk a few more blocks until you see a 7-Eleven. Turn left and you are on Art St.

DAKENG 大坑

To the east of the city is a hilly area known as Dakeng (Dàkēng). If you are going to spend any time in the city, Dakeng is worth exploring, as there are pleasant hiking trails and even a few hot springs. You can pick up a detailed brochure (with map) of the area at the visitor centre.

Taichung For Children

In addition to obvious sights such as the science and art museums (p211 and p211), the big Buddha (see p211) appeals to many kids. Dakeng (above) has some nice outdoor hot spring and pool facilities for families. The

buildings of the folk park (p211) are complex enough to be fun for kids to explore on their own. The collection of curios can be very interesting if you highlight the right stuff (such as the – oh my neck – ceramic pillows).

Sleeping

The main problem with Taichung is that most of the budget hotels are right around the train station, which is a thoroughly unpleasant area, or far out of town. It's really a land that time (and the sanitation department) forgot. In fact, the budget traveller would do better to stay somewhere else (Changhua or Taipei) and just come in for the day. If you have to stay overnight, there are plenty of options.

Fuh Chun Hotel (Fùchūn Dàfàdiàn; ☎ 2228 3181; fax 2228 3187; 1 Zhongshan Rd; 中山路1號; r from NT530) This place, just across from the train station, has long been popular with foreign travellers and Taiwanese students. The women who run the place are exceptionally nice and make a point of offering fresh fruit to their guests every day.

Athens Taichung Hotel (Yǎdiàn Shāngyè Lǚguǎn; ☎ 2305 2370; fax 2305 2378; 3 Da He Rd; 大和路3號; r from NT1400; 🖥) This hotel is one of the few budget options in a modern upscale part of town. Staff are very friendly and rooms are a good size and value for money. The hotel is just far enough off Taizhonggang Rd that you won't be bothered by the noise of traffic. There is a 20% weekday discount.

Ful Won Hotel (Fùwáng Dàfàdiàn; ☎ 2326 5436; 636 Wenxin Rd; 文心路636號; s/d/tw incl breakfast NT2350/2900/3200; 🖥) This bright, professionally run hotel sits directly across from the Jade Market. There is a 30% discount on rooms every day except public holidays, which makes staying here a great deal if you are looking for a higher level of comfort.

Evergreen Laurel Hotel (Chángróng Guìguàn Jiǔdiàn; ☎ 2313 9988; www.evergreen-hotels.com; 6 Taizhonggang Rd, sec.2; 台中港路2段6號; d/tw/ste NT6400/7600/9800; ▣ ⊠) Close to the business district and airport, the Evergreen Laurel has a spacious and relaxed atmosphere. Facilities are top-notch and include a business centre, a number of excellent restaurants and cafés and a health club with squash courts. Book online for the best deals, which are often 50% off the rack rate.

Eating

Taichung has a great assortment of restaurants serving a wide range of Asian and Western cuisines. A few popular areas for restaurant dining are Art St, the streets south of the Art Museum (for lunch and dinner only) and the Chingming District. Check out Compass magazine for the latest offerings as places come and go quickly.

There are dozens of cheap noodle, Japanese fast-food and pizza places clustered around the train-station area.

Chunghsiao Night Market (Zhōngxiào Yèshì) Behind the train station; well known for its good, traditional, cheap food.

Shantung Dumplings & Beef Noodles (Shāndōng Jiǎozi Niúròu Miànguǎn; ☎ 2321 5955; 96 Gongyi Rd, sec.1; dishes NT90; � 11am-9pm) Serves tasty traditional home cooking with a Shantung province flavour.

Finga's Base Camp (Fēnggé Cānting; ☎ 2327 7750; 61 Zhongming S Rd; � 7am-10pm) A deli, restaurant, butchery and bakery all in one.

Drinking

For tea or coffee, head to one of the 'tea streets' (p211). There are a dozen or more places to sit and relax (some with outdoor seating) in both locations. For beer or cocktails, head to the restaurant and bar district labelled on our map.

Wu Wei Tsao Tang Teahouse (Wúwéicǎotáng; ☎ 2329 6707; 106 Gongyi Rd, sec.2; � 10am-1am) This classical wooden teahouse invites guests to relax and drink tea the old-fashioned way. Soft Chinese music, thick willow trees and the swish of water from the carp pool keep the outside traffic noise to a minimum. A package of tea leaves costs NT400 and the 'water fee' is NT120 per person.

Smooth Bar & Grill (☎ 2329 3468; 5-7 Lane 50, Jingcheng Rd; drinks from NT150; � 3pm-1am) One long-running place to try. The bar is well stocked

and has a big-screen TV for watching sports. There's also an international menu offering curries, steaks, pastas, goulash and more.

Londoner (☎ 2314 6919; www.londoner.com.tw; 143 HuaMei West St, sec.1; beer NT120; � 7pm until late, noon-late Sat) Another veteran of sorts is this sports bar with a lively vibe and a great menu.

Entertainment

Vie Show Cinemas (www.warnervillage.com.tw) Tiger City Mall (4-6F, 120-1 Henan Rd, sec.3) Taichung Central Mall (4F, 186 Fuxing Rd, sec.4) You can book tickets in advance on the Warner Village website.

Shopping

Roman (☎ 093-123 1905; romantatoo@yahoo.ca; 56 Art St) Canadian-born Roman McNamara has found his niche on Art St with this funky little shop selling one-of-a-kind, handmade leather goods. The shop is on the 2nd level at the back of the small square about half way up the street. Since the last edition of this book, Roman has gone from part-time to full-time work, a testimony to the quality of his products.

Ceramic Art (Héxuān Táoyì Gōngfāng; 321-12 Wenxin S 5th Rd; � 1-11pm) Near the Lakeside Sculpture Park, this small studio is run by well-known ceramic artist Hong Chi-shuen.

Getting There & Away

AIR

Taichung's new **Cing Cyuan Gang Airport** (☎ 2615 5206; www.tca.gov.tw/English/Introduction.htm) mostly serves the domestic market though there are flights to Hong Kong. In the future more international flights are expected.

UNI Air (☎ 2615 5188) and **Mandarin Airlines** (☎ 2615 5080) have ticket counters at the airport. There are flights to Taipei, Penghu, Matsu, Kinmen, Hualien and Taitung.

There's a **visitor centre** (☎ 2615 5029; � 8am-5pm) to help you with your travel questions.

BUS

Taichung Bus Company (☎ 2225 5561) runs frequent buses to Puli (NT150, one hour). **Renyou Bus Company** (☎ 2225 5166) has four buses a day to Sun Moon Lake (NT190, 90 minutes) leaving from their office at 110 Luchuan St. The first bus leaves at 8am.

Kuo Kuang Hao Bus Company (☎ 2226 6168) runs frequent buses to Taipei (NT260, 3 hours). **Fengyuan Bus Company** (☎ 2222 3454), near the train station, run buses once a day

WESTERN TAIWAN

(8am departure) to Hehuanshan, Lishan and Wuling Farm.

TRAIN

There are frequent trains to/from Taipei (fast/slow train NT375/241, two/three hours) and Kaohsiung (fast/slow train NT470/303, 2½/three hours) from early morning until almost midnight.

High-Speed Rail (HSR)

You can take a HSR train to Taichung (or to nearby New Wurih) from Taipei (NT700, one hour) but you may not save much time over the regular fast train and it will cost you nearly twice as much (see p236). At the time of writing there were trains running about every hour, though this freqency will certainly increase as time goes on. Below the station you can catch a regular train to Taichung station (NT15, 10 minutes, every 20 min).

Getting Around

Bus 115 (NT53) runs frequently between the airport and a stop on Zhongzheng Rd a couple blocks up from the train station.

For car hire call **Central Auto** (☎ 2254 7000; www.rentalcar.com.tw).

There are three bus companies serving the Taichung City area, which is confusing, but fortunately the visitor centre at the train station has information on them all. Renyou Bus Company buses have a red stripe at the front while Taichung Bus Company buses have a green stripe. **UBus** (☎ 2226 3034) buses are completely green. The usual fare for a single journey within the city is NT22.

Taichung Bus Company runs its buses from a station directly across from the train station and also from stops along Luchuan St, a block north of the train station. Renyou buses also run from stops along Luchuan St and the company has its office at 110 Luchuan St. The UBus station is across the street from the Kuo Kuang Hao station.

CHANGHUA 彰化市

☎ 04 / pop 234,308

Changhua City (Zhānghuà Shì), the capital and political heart of Changhua County, is usually been considered a gateway to the old town of Lukang, but there are some treats in the town itself, including an old Dutch-built well and a giant Buddha on a hilltop. Birders should note that Changhua is on the migratory route of the grey-faced buzzard and that the hilltop with the giant Buddha gives a 360-degree panoramic view.

Orientation & Information

Changhua is not a compact city, but you needn't wander too far from the train station during your stay. Even the Great Buddha Statue is only a couple of kilometres to the east. Road signs around the town are large, bright and green with easily read pinyin on them. We wish every town were set up so well.

You can change money at **Bank of Taiwan** (90 Zhonghua Rd).

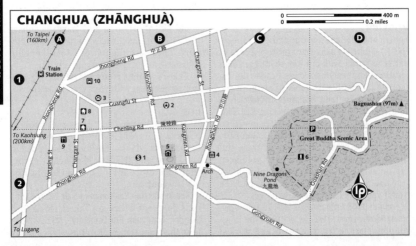

CHANGHUA (ZHĀNGHUÀ)

A valuable source of travel information is the county's website in English (http://tourism .chcg.gov.tw) and the city's website (www .changhua.gov.tw). There is a **visitor centre** (☎ 728 5750; ◷ 8.30am-5pm) in the train station.

Sights & Activities

CHANGHUA ARTS MUSEUM & HONGMAO WELL 彰化藝術館 紅毛井

The **museum** (Zhānghuà Yìshùguǎn; ☎ 728 7243; 542 Jhongshan Rd, sec.2; ◷ 9am-9pm, closed Mon & holidays) sits in Jungshan Hall, a lovely heritage building that we are happy to see has received a new life since the last edition. It now once again serves as a performance theatre, lecture hall and art gallery.

On the grounds of the museum is the 300-year-old **Hongmao Well** (Hóngmáo Jǐng), the last of the original Dutch-built wells (hence the name Hongmao, meaning 'red hair') in central Taiwan. Incredibly, the well still produces drinkable water, though you should boil it first.

CONFUCIUS TEMPLE 孔廟

This 1726 beauty is one of the oldest **Confucius temples** (Kǒng Miào; 6 Kongmen Rd) in Taiwan and a first-class historical relic. There's an inscribed plaque in the ancestral hall donated by the Qing-dynasty emperor Chien Long. It's a must vist if you are in Changhua. On Confucius' birthday every year (28 September) there is a colourful dawn ceremony.

BAGUASHAN 八卦山

Changhua is best known for the 22m-high **Great Buddha Statue** (Dà Fó Xiàng) that sits atop **Baguashan** (Bāguàshān) and looks out over the city. Visitors are permitted to walk in and up the statue. Admission is free. Dioramas at each level depict major events in the Buddha's life. In addition to the Buddha a new and very spacious park has been built on the mountaintop with wooden walkways, pavilions, and playground areas for children. It makes for pleasant strolling.

You can easily walk up to Baguashan from the train station area. Just look for the signs in English to the Great Buddha Scenic Area.

Baguashan is a prime **bird-watching** area. During March and April grey-faced buzzards and sparrow hawks appear in great numbers. Contact the **Changhua County Wild Bird Society** (☎ 728 3006) for information.

Sleeping

Rich Royal Hotel (Fùhuáng Dàfàndiàn; ☎ 723 7117; 97 Changan St; 長安街97號; r from NT800; Ⓟ) This place feels like a love hotel when you walk down the long garage (where you can park) to the check-in counter but it is, in fact, popular with families. Rooms are slightly frilly in design, and aging a bit, but it's probably your best value for money in town.

Ing Shan Hotel (Yíngshān Dàfàndiàn; ☎ 722 9211; 129 Changan St; 長安街129號; d/tw NT900/1500) The hotel has received some renovations (new mattresses and a paint job) and you now have a choice of soft or hard mattresses and tiled or carpeted floors. Overall it's a good budget choice and the owners are friendly.

Eating & Drinking

Changhua is famous for its *ròu yuán* (肉圓; meatballs) and you'll find many places to try them out on Chenling St. For more local foods, check out the city's website. For cheap eats and cafés, there are plenty of places around the train station and on Guangfu Rd. For a beer, head up Chengling St past Heping. There are a few bars in the area, some more respectable looking than others.

Cat Mouse Noodle (Māoshǔmiàn; ☎ 726 8376; 233 Chenglin St; noodles NT50; ◷ 9am-8.30pm) The Changhua tourist website claims this shop's special noodle dish is one of the three culinary treasures of the city. It's a stretch, but the tangy flavoured noodles are pretty tasty. The shop's odd name arose because the owner's nickname sounds like 'cat mouse' in Taiwanese and not because of anything you'll find in the food.

THE MATSU PILGRIMAGE

It's the 23rd day of the 3rd lunar month, and you arrive early in Dajia, Taichung County, to visit the Chenlan Temple (鎮瀾宮). You've read that today a week-long pilgrimage in honour of Matsu, the goddess of the sea, is going to begin around 10pm. All around you spirits are high as masses of people flow from one chamber of the temple to another, bowing, and prostrating themselves to a host of deities. In the corner of one incense-filled room you see the costumes of a god with a large happy pink face piled on display in a neat row. He intrigues you and you want to ask someone his name. But outside there are performances of ear-shattering opera, puppetry and folk dances, and you head out to catch a few moments of each.

The goddess Matsu remains hidden in the temple, housed in a glass case. But soon she will be taken out in a heavenly sedan chair and carried 280km around the island. If past years are any indication, you know that tens of thousands of worshippers will follow her.

Matsu is the most popular folk deity in Taiwan, with over 500 temples dedicated to her around the island. Legends about her origins vary but most agree that she was once a real person named Lin Mo, who was born into a fisherman's family on Meizhou Island, Fujian, China, sometime in the 10th century.

Stories are told about how the intelligent and gifted Lin Mo loved the sea and would often stand on the rocks of the harbour mouth dressed in red to direct ships in safely during storms. After her ascension into heaven, Matsu began to appear frequently to distressed sailors. Soon temples were being built along the coast of mainland China in her honour. The first Chinese settlers (all fishermen) to Taiwan brought statues with them and established rough temples. The site of the present Chenlan Temple in Dajia was founded in 1781.

Statues usually depict the goddess with black skin, a beaded veil and a red cape (which she wore to guide ships to harbour). Standing next to her are her loyal attendants, Eyes that See a Thousand Miles and Ears that Hear upon the Wind.

Preparations for the pilgrimage begin much earlier than the day you arrive, but the final steps are the most interesting. Everything must proceed according to custom and at times ordained by divination. As you wait, local men come out periodically to light off firecrackers to bless the earth that Matsu will be carried over. Drums beat, gongs are stuck and folk gods dance about, including the pink-faced god you saw earlier. He's the god of wealth, the woman beside you says.

And then, just before Matsu is paraded out on her heavenly sedan, three cannon blasts ring the air.

The official procession that starts carrying Matsu is relatively small but soon looks to be over a kilometre long. Lay people jostle to touch the sedan chair while the most devout actually kneel down on the road and allow the goddess to be carried over them.

Over the next week the goddess will be carried through over 50 towns, in three different counties. Over a million people will see her pass their homes. Many devotees will follow Matsu the entire way, though most, like you, will only walk with her a short distance. But it's enough and this exotic and exuberant parade of folk worship and ritual is something you will never forget.

For information on the dates and events of each year's pilgrimage, check out the website http://mazu.taichung.gov.tw/English/index.htm. If you wish to participate in the pilgrimage the best way is to contact the National Youth Commission (see Youth Travel in Taiwan, p328).

To get to Dajia take a train from Taipei. Chenlan Temple is a few blocks straight ahead as you exit the front of the train station.

Getting There & Away

There are frequent trains from morning till late at night to/from Taipei (fast/slow train NT416/268, 2½/three hours) and Kaohsiung (fast/slow train NT432/333, two/three hours).

Buses to Lukang (NT44, 30 minutes) leave frequently from the **Changhua Bus Company**

(☎ 722 4603; 563 Jhongjeng Rd) station near the train station.

LUKANG (LUGANG) 鹿港
☎ 04 / pop 84,767

Ninety percent of Lukang (Lùgǎng) is as nondescript as most small towns in Taiwan. But then there is that other 10%. Comprising some of the oldest and most gorgeous temples in the country, and featuring curiously curved streets, art museums in heritage buildings, and dusty old shops where equally dusty old masters create colourful fans, lanterns and tin pieces, it is this small part of Lukang that justifiably brings in the crowds.

People call Lukang a 'living museum' and this is true as much for the food as it is for the buildings and streets. Traditional dishes are cheap and readily available near all of the major sights. Look for the enticingly named phoenix eye cake, dragon whiskers and shrimp monkeys, among many other dishes.

On the central coast and just half an hour from Changhua by bus, Lukang is easily reached from anywhere on the west coast.

History

Lukang translates as 'deer harbour', and earlier large herds of deer gathered here in the lush meadows adjacent to one of the best natural harbours on the west coast. In the 17th century the Dutch came to hunt and trade pelts (which they sold to the Japanese to make samurai armour) and venison. Trade continued into the 18th century and Lukang became one of the most thriving commercial cities and ports in Taiwan. Over the years settlers from different provinces and ethnic groups in China made their home here and, almost as a gift to the future, left a legacy of temples and buildings in varying regional styles.

In the 19th century, silt deposits began to block the harbour and in 1895 the Japanese closed it to all large ships. The city began to decline. To make matters worse, conservative elements in Lukang refused in the early 20th century to allow trains and modern highways to be built near their city. Lukang became a backwater, only to be reborn decades later when modern Taiwanese began to search for a living connection with the past.

Orientation & Information

You can cover the sights on foot in one long day, but be aware that Lukang has few signs in English pointing to sights and few roads with pinyin on them: use our map.

The new **visitor centre** (☎ 784 1263; Fusing Rd; ⊙ 9am-5.30 Mon-Fri, to 6pm Sat & Sun) is easy to spot in a large field/parking lot across from the Changhua Bus Station. Pick up a brochure in English for more sights than we can cover here. Also check out the town's website (www.lukang.gov.tw). It's an informative introduction to the history and sights.

Sights

LONGSHAN TEMPLE 龍山寺

Though originally a rather small temple (and the first Buddhist temple in Taiwan), the present-day **Longshan Temple** (Lóngshān Sì) covers an area of more than 1000 sq metres. It's considered the best-preserved Qing-dynasty temple in Taiwan and really is a beautiful sight. At the time of writing restoration work was almost completed and you could wander around most of the temple grounds including the long inaccessible back courtyard, which used to hold theatrical performances. Some tourist offices still have an old copy or two of a brochure explaining the history and architectural features of this temple. Keep your eye out for it.

CASTING STONES, THE LUKANG WAY

Surely one of the most unusual customs of old Taiwan had to be the rock fight held in Lukang every spring. In *Lukang: Commerce and Community in a Chinese City*, a mostly serious academic study, Donald R DeGlopper describes this very odd event in rather humorous detail. During the fight, men from the three principal families in Lukang lined up in a field and threw rocks: Shih at Huang, Huang at Hsu, Hsu at Shih, and so on.

According to DeGlopper, the atmosphere was not one of aggression and hostility but of festivity. Children and women stood on the sides and cheered, and vendors, who seem to have been as ubiquitous back then as they are today, sold snacks and drinks.

The Japanese did their best to suppress the festival during their time on Taiwan, but to no avail. Unfortunately, it just seemed to die out on its own a few years before WWII. Later, when participants were asked why they joined in such bloody sport, some explained that it was 'tradition', while others noted that if blood was not spilled in the spring, disaster could not be averted in the coming year. As one reviewer of DeGlopper's book noted, however, the explanation is probably much simpler: the families just didn't like each other very much.

WESTERN TAIWAN

MATSU TEMPLE 天后宮

Another large and really splendid structure, the **Matsu Temple** (Tiānhòu Gōng) was renovated in 1936 and is completely accessible today. It is said that the Matsu statue in this temple was brought to Taiwan by a Qing-dynasty general. The statue is now called 'The Black-Faced Matsu', as decades of incense smoke have discoloured her original complexion. Check out the front of the temple for a cool display of old weapons.

The area around the temple is pedestrian-only and great crowds gather here on weekends, though the atmosphere feels festive and not touristy. Vendors and the surrounding stores sell a variety of traditional snacks, sweets and drinks.

FOLK ARTS MUSEUM 民俗文物館

The **Folk Arts Museum** (Mínsú Wénwùguǎn; ☎ 777 2019; 152 Zhongshan Rd; adult/child NT130/70; ⏰ 9am-5pm, no entry after 4.30pm, closed Mon) has always been one of our favourite heritage sights in Lukang. Built in the Japanese era and originally the residence of a wealthy local family, the museum houses a large collection of daily-life artefacts from a bygone age.

The museum is behind Zhongshan Rd and can now be access via the **Din Family Old House** (Dīngjiā Jìnshì Gǔcuò; 132 Zhongshan Rd; admission free; ⏰ 9am-5pm), another lovely heritage building recently restored and opened to the public. The building was once the home of a top imperial scholar and is the last remaining house of its kind in Lukang.

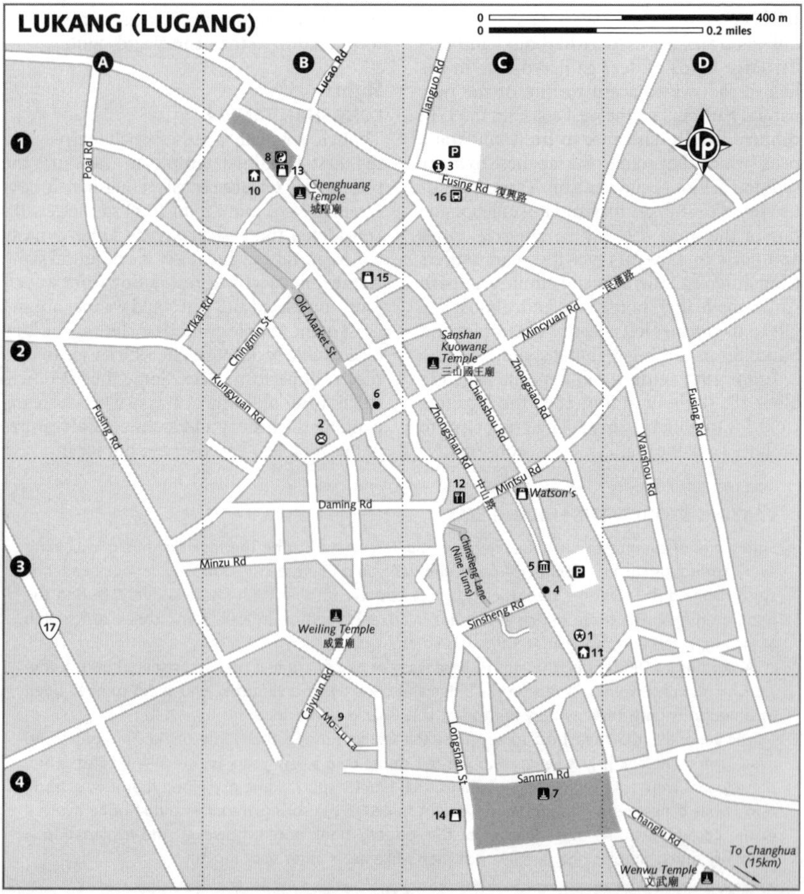

LUKANG (LUGANG)

OLD MARKET STREET 古市街

The merchant streets of old Lukang are well represented (if you skip the first shop with Pachinko machines) by the shops lining both sides of the curved, red-tiled lanes of what is now called the **Old Market Street** (Gǔshì Jiē). Almost all the shop fronts have been restored and the interiors decorated with antiques. You can shop for traditional items here or just enjoy a stroll through history.

Not everyone likes it, but to us the **half-sided well** (Bànbiān Jǐn) is something we always look forward to seeing. The well, aptly named because you can only see half of it, was built to share: the rich family inside the complex used the interior half, while the poor and passers-by were permitted to use the outer half.

BREAST TOUCHING LANE (MO-LU LANE) 摸乳巷

This old **alley** (Mōlǔshàng), also called Gentleman's Lane, gets its label from the fact that a man could not pass a woman down the extremely narrow inner passageway without her breasts brushing against him. (While we suppose she and he could always have turned their backs, Bum Touching Alley just doesn't have the same ring to it.) The true gentleman then, would always wait for a lady to pass through first. Take a stroll through the lane with someone you love – or hope to.

Tours

Taiwan Tour Bus (☎ 0800 011 765; http://taiwan.net .tw) has day tours of Lukang (NT1500) leaving from major hotels in Taichung and the Changhua train station.

Festivals & Events

Every year Lukang hosts a four-day **folk-arts festival** that begins three days before the Dragon Boat Festival (p337). This is a crowded but rewarding time to come. Matsu's birthday, the 23rd day of the third lunar month (usually in April; see boxed text, p216), is also cause for intense celebration at the Matsu Temple.

Sleeping

Quanzhong Hotel (Quánzhōng Lǔshè; ☎ 777 2640; 104 Zhongshan Rd; 中山路104號; d/tw NT650/850) This hotel is getting old but at least it isn't raising its prices – and the location is good. Rooms are small, cheaply furnished and a little musty, but clean enough for a night's stay.

Matsu Temple Believer's Hotel (Lùgǎng Tiānhòugōng Xiāngkè Dàlóu; ☎ 775 2508; 475 Zhongshan Rd; 中山路 475號; d/tw NT950/1790) You don't have to be a believer to stay here, though it might help you to ignore how bland (hospital-room bareness comes to mind) the rooms are. Note that the entire hotel may be booked out months in advance of Matsu's birthday and other important festivals.

Eating

Since the pedestrian-only zone was opened around Matsu Temple, the area has become a lively market of food stalls and small restaurants. Some famous local dishes to try are *xī xià* (溪蝦; shrimp monkeys), *é ā jiān* (蚵仔煎; oyster omelettes), *ròu yuán* (肉圓; meatballs) and sweet treats such as *níushé bǐng* (牛舌餅; cow-tongue crackers) and *lóngshū táng* (龍鬚糖; dragon whiskers).

Yu Chen Chai (Yùzhēnzhāi Shípǐn Yǒuxiàn Gōngsī; 168 Minzu Rd; ☻ 8am-11pm) This fifth-generation shop sells pastries based on original Qing-dynasty recipes. Try the *fèngyǎn gāo* (鳳眼糕; phoenix eye cake) or the *lǜdòu gāo* (綠豆糕; green bean cake).

Shopping

Lukang offers great shopping (or just browsing) if you're in the market for original crafts. Several shop owners have received 'Living Heritage' awards for their skill and dedication in preserving old crafts.

WESTERN TAIWAN

Wan Neng Tinware (Wànnéng Xípù; ☎ 777 7847; 84 Longshan St) The master here is a fourth-generation tinsmith. His elaborate dragon boats and expressive masks cost thousands but are worth the price for their beauty and craftsmanship.

Mr Chen's Fan Shop (Chéncháozōng Shǒugōngshàn; ☎ 777 5629; 400 Zhongshan Rd) The shop is just on the right before you enter the pedestrian-only area near Matsu Temple. Fans range from a few hundred dollars to many thousands for the larger creations. Mr Chen has been making fans since he was 16.

Wu Tun-Hou Lantern Shop (Wúdūnhòu Dēnglóngpù; ☎ 777 6680; 312 Zhongshan Rd) Mr Wu has been making lanterns for about 70 years and has collectors from all over the world come to make purchases. Lanterns start at a few hundred dollars but the really creative works cost thousands.

Getting There & Away

Buses to Changhua (NT44, 30 minutes) leave frequently from the **Changhua Bus Company station** (Fusing Rd).

JIJI SMALL RAIL LINE
集集小火車線
☎ 049

Like the Pingxi, Alishan and Neiwan lines (the latter closed at the time of writing), the 19km narrow-gauge Jiji Small Rail Line (Jíjí Xiǎo Huǒchē) once served an important industrial purpose. In the Jiji line's case it was assisting in the construction of power plants. But these days the line remains open to boost local tourism.

The 45-minute train ride begins south of Changhua in the wide, fertile plains of Ershui. It then proceeds into the forested hills around Jiji and ends at Checheng, a vehicle yard surrounded by high mountains in Nantou County.

While the train ride is short, the list of things to see and do in this area is long: you can cycle, hike, bird- and monkey-watch, as well as visit temples, museums and historic buildings. You can visit any time of year, but don't bother on a summer weekend when crowds really make the place unpleasant and miniscooters roar up and down the bike paths. Winter weekdays are lovely and quiet and the weather is usually dry and in the mid-20s. If you plan on staying in the area, a hotel in Jiji is your

best choice. Accommodation in Shuili and Ershui is pretty dreary.

ORIENTATION & INFORMATION
There are six stations along the way, the most visited of which are Ershui, Jiji, Shuili and Checheng. There is much work being done around the Chechen station at the time of writing and it definitely looks like it will be a nice place to stop in for a stroll by the time this book comes out.

You can sometimes get a map at the train stations but in Chinese only. Most of the towns have 7-Elevens with ATMs.

GETTING THERE & AROUND
You can get to Ershui, the start of the Jiji line, from anywhere along the West Coast Line, but note that not every train stops there. From Changhua (NT47) it's about a 30-minute journey. At Ershui station, alight and transfer to the Jiji Small Rail Line (there are signs in English telling you where to stand on the platform). You can buy your ticket on the train. It's NT44 from Ershui to Checheng and you are allowed to alight and reboard once along the way without buying another ticket. There are eight trains a day in either direction, about one every two hours. You can pick up a schedule at any station or go to the Taiwan Railway website (http://new.twtraffic.com.tw/TWRail_en/index.aspx; note that Jiji is spelt Chi-Chi).

Ershui 二水站
pop 3000

A good way to see Ershui is by the cycling-only **bike path** (jiǎotàchē zhuānyòngdào) which intersects with quiet country roads that are also bikable. To reach the path, turn right when you exit the train station. Go 100m and then turn right to cross the train tracks. You will see the bike path on your right. Give yourself at least three hours to explore.

The countryside is picturesque, with lush fields, and temples, shrines, traditional brick villas and pagodas popping up in unexpected places. Just to the north stands Songbo Ridge, a holy spot for Taiwan's Taoists. With its thick forests and crumbling cliff faces, the ridge helps to break up the flat landscape along the bike path.

You can rent bikes outside the train station, though mid-week, mid-winter you may be out of luck. In such a case, you can always walk the paths or continue on to Jiji.

Jiji (Chi Chi) 集集
pop 3000
The fifth stop down the line, Jiji (Jíjí) offers the most tourist facilities, though some attempts at town improvement, such as the creation of a fake old street, have failed miserably. In general though, it's a pleasant place when the crowds are low, and it has a real country charm about it with, fields of banana and betel nut trees, grape vines, and dragon fruit plants lining the roads.

SIGHTS & ACTIVITIES
Wuchang Temple 武昌宮
This is one of the oddest sites billed as an attraction you're likely to come across in Taiwan. Previously unknown to outsiders, the **temple** (Wǔchāng Gōng) made its name after the 921 Earthquake (21 September 1999; measuring 7.3 on the Richter scale) collapsed its lower floors leaving the roof to lie in ruins on the ground. Very photogenic in its state of disrepair, the temple is now one of the first things people rush to see when they come to town.

To get to the temple turn right as you leave the train station and walk about 10 minutes to Ba Zhang St (八張街). Turn left and walk another 10 minutes. You can also reach the temple on the bike path.

Cycling
Jiji's 10km **bike path** (jiǎotàchē zhuānyòngdào) is for the most part scenic and easy to follow, with distance markers and clear turning signs. There are now signs in English to the major sights along the path such as the Endemic Species Research Institute (see below). Note that when you get down near the weir the bike path takes you back to town, but it's fun to explore this area as well.

You can rent bikes (NT100 per hour) at numerous locations around the train station.

Endemic Species Research Institute
特有生物保育中心
The **institute** (Tèyǒu Shēngwù Bǎoyù Zhōngxīn; ☎ 276 1331; www.tesri.gov.tw; 1 Minsheng East Rd; adult/child NT80/50; ⌚ 9am-4.30pm) functions as a research

centre and natural history museum for plant and animal species endemic to Taiwan. There's a very strong conservation message promoted throughout, which we found very refreshing. Displays are highly informative and now feature full text in English.

Don't miss the little pond in the back for observing fish, insect and bird life. It's not quite Walden, and we wouldn't spend two years, two months and two days here, but we would like to have stayed a lot longer than we had time for.

The institute is about 1km east of the train station on the bike route.

Jiji Station
The original Jiji Station was levelled in the big earthquake of 1999. As part of a plan to boost tourism in the area, the station was rebuilt to the standards of the simple Japanese-era original and has since become extremely popular with Taiwanese tourists looking for a photo op on the weekend.

SLEEPING & EATING
Jiji Vacation Village (集集渡假村; Jíjí Dùjiàcūn; ☎ 276 2988; fax 276 2986; 205 Chenggong Rd; 成功路 205號; d/tw NT2200/3000; 🏊) Rooms are bright, clean, simply furnished and have large comfy beds. A buffet breakfast (7am to 9.30am) and use of the swimming pool (fed with mountain water), steam room and spa are included (summer only). To reach the hotel, go north from the train station to Cheng Gong Rd and turn right. The peach-coloured hotel, which looks like an apartment building, is on the right. Thiry percent discounts are usual.

Train Head Original Food Restaurant (火車頭 集集原味廚房; Huǒchētóu Jíjí Yuánwèi Chúfáng; 299 Minquan Rd; dishes NT120-180; ⌚ lunch, lunch & dinner Sat & Sun, closed Wed) This popular Chinese-style restaurant has a motto: 'locally grown foods cooked in the traditional way'. Downstairs, the restaurant sells various local agricultural speciality items. The restaurant is across the road from the station and to the right.

Shuili 水里
pop 1000
The penultimate stop on the Jiji Line (the last stop is the quaint station at Checheng) is Shuili (Shuǐlǐ), a bland little town set among lovely mountain scenery.

Go to **Yushan National Park Headquarters** (☎ 277 3121; www.ysnp.gov.tw; 300 Jungshan Rd, sec.1; ⌚ 9.30am-

4.30pm) for English-language brochures and films about the park, as well as the latest road and trail information. To reach the headquarters from Shuili train station, walk straight down Minsheng Rd about 1km until you reach the river. Turn right and walk another 1km to where the road connects with Hwy 16. Turn left and cross the bridge. The park headquarters is in the white building on the right. Usually someone working can speak English.

From Shuili you can catch buses to Sun Moon Lake (NT49, 30 minutes, hourly), and Dongpu (NT112, 80 minutes, eight buses a day). There are two bus stations in Shuili. **Yuanlin Bus Company** (員林客運; ☎ 277 0041), which runs buses to Dongpu, and **Fengrong Bus Company** (豐榮客運; ☎ 277 4609), which runs buses to Sun Moon Lake (and on to Puli). Note that buses to these places run during daylight hours only (6am to 5pm or so).

To reach the Yuanlin Bus Company, exit the train station and turn left on Minquan Rd. The station is on the opposite side of the road from the 7-Eleven and just past the food stalls. The Fengrong Bus Company is further down the road on the same side.

Highway 16

To explore a relatively remote part of the country keep heading down Hwy 16 east of Shuili. Soon the road runs alongside a wide river valley that looks perfect for inner tubing down when the water level is low.

At the time of writing the highway ended at a washed-out bridge. You could, however, cross on a suspension bridge and continue on foot up what is called the **Danda Logging Road** (丹大林道; Dāndà Líndào), which gets you into some real back country. You're advised to get local reports on the condition of the road before you head up on a bike or on foot.

SUN MOON LAKE 日月潭
☎ 049

Sun Moon Lake (Rìyuè Tán) is the largest body of freshwater in Taiwan and has one of the island's loveliest natural landscapes. In his blue period, Picasso would have had no end of inspiration. At an altitude of 762m, the lake is backed by high-forested mountains and boasts good weather year-round. Boating is popular, both touring in large craft and in DIY rowing boats, as is hiking and biking. By the time you read this there will be a hotel offering hot springs.

Orientation

Sun Moon Lake is part of the 9000-hectare Sun Moon Lake National Scenic Area, under the control of the central government. The scenic area stretches north to include the Formosan Aboriginal Cultural Village, south to the snake kiln in Shuili and the old train station at Checheng, west to Great Jiji Mountain, and east to Mt Shueishe. It's also close to Puli (15km) and makes for a nice base from which to explore that town (as accommodation in Puli is poor). Note that you can get to all these places from the lake by public transport.

Accommodation is more than plentiful, with the majority of hotels centred in Shueishe Village, on the northwestern corner of the lake. Most first-time visitors stay here, though increasingly people are taking advantage of the quieter atmosphere at Itashao on the other side of the lake.

Information

There are no banks but the 7-Eleven on the main road up from the village has an ATM.

Sun Moon Lake National Scenic Area (www.sunmoon lake.gov.tw) Excellent resource now with full bus information for both getting there and around.

Visitor Information Centre (☎ 285 5668; 163 Jhongshan Rd, Shueishe Village; ☻ 9am-5pm) Now in a large modern building off the main road just before the turn-off for the village. English-speaking staff are on hand to help with all your needs. If you see a kind elderly gentleman called Hsu Ting-fa (Tim), thank him for all the great work he has done to make Sun Moon Lake easy for English-speaking tourists to get around. Generous retirees like him are truly a national treasure.

Sights & Activities

Swimming is banned in the lake except during the Annual Across the Lake Swim (see below).

SHUIESHE VILLAGE 水社村

People often refer to Shueishe Village (Shuǐshè Cūn) as Sun Moon Lake Village. The cobbled main road, Minsheng Rd, is supposed to be pedestrian-only but this rule is not being enforced very strictly. The area by the **Shueishe Pier** (Shuǐshè Mǎtóu), which was being rebuilt at the time of writing, is particularly attractive and a great place to hang out day and night. Most of the hotels have added new façades to their sides facing the water and built decks with food and beverage service.

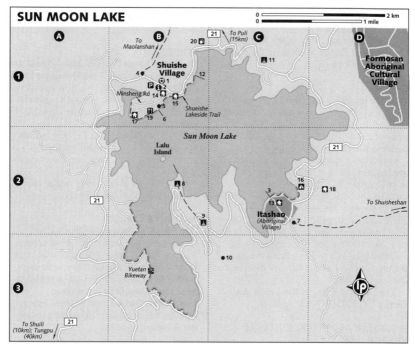

SUN MOON LAKE

The **Meihe Garden** (Méihé Yuán) is a heavenly spot to hang out on a sunny day (and the night view is pretty charming too).

BOATING

Boat tours are a popular way to take in the scenery and leave at 9am and 4pm daily (NT300 per person) and other times when there is demand. Tours stop at all four piers. You can hire private boats at Shueishe and Itashao Piers. A trip to Lalu Island costs around NT300 per person. You can also rent small rowing boats for NT200 per hour and take yourself out on the water.

HIKING

Sun Moon Lake offers some very pleasant hiking, and on the longer trails you are sure to leave the tour groups behind. The trails to **Maolanshan** (Māolánshān; two hours return) and **Shueisheshan** (Shuǐshèshān; seven to eight hours return) are the longest, if you don't include the bike paths, which can, of course, be walked too. Signs in English mark the trailheads for all routes. The trail (which is really a road) to Maolanshan begins near Shueishe

WESTERN TAIWAN

Village, while the one to Shueisheshan begins at the far end of Itashao.

Other walks are listed in the tourist brochures. Most can be reached by the round-the-lake public bus.

CYCLING

We hope increased tour buses won't ruin the lake for cycling. For now it is quiet enough midweek to cycle around the lake (30km or so) without much hassle. Give yourself four to five hours so you can stop and enjoy the sites.

One shorter route to try, and one that will minimize exposure to traffic, is to go left (east) from Shueishe Village and follow the road by the lake. In about 30 minutes you will see the sign to the 8km **Yuetan Bikeway** (月潭自行車道; Yuètán Zìxíngchē Dào). This is a very lovely wide path that runs right beside the lake. No cars or scooters are allowed here.

Other bike-only routes around the lake are planned so check at the tourist office for the latest information.

You can rent bikes at the Youth Activity Centre (NT120/270 per hour/day).

FORMOSAN ABORIGINAL CULTURAL VILLAGE 九族文化村

It's an unlikely business model, a cultural showpiece combined with amusement park rides, but the **village** (Jiǔzú Wénhuà Cūn; ☎ 289 5361; www.nine.com.tw; adult/child NT650/350; ☒ 8am-5.30pm) comes highly recommended. You can get to the village on a Fengrong bus (NT22, 20 minutes) from in front of the Visitor Information Centre. There are only four buses a day so see the Visitor Information Centre for the latest schedule.

After summer 2008 a cable car should run to the village from the Youth Activity Centre.

SHUILI SNAKE KILN 水里 蛇窯

Snake kilns were first developed in China during the late Ming dynasty. The name comes from the long, narrow, snake-like appearance of the kiln. The **Shuili Snake Kiln** (Shuǐlǐ Shéyáo; ☎ 277 0967; adult/child NT120/60; ☒ 8am-5.30pm), for example, is more than 30m long. Within the kiln grounds are a gallery, museum, exhibition hall and a pottery shop selling good quality pieces.

The kiln is part of the Sun Moon Lake Scenic Area but is about 10km south of the lake itself. To get there take a Fengrong bus heading to Shuili from in front of the

Visitor Information Centre (NT49, 20 to 30 minutes, hourly).

OTHER SIGHTS

The **Wenwu Temple** (Wénwǔ Miào), **Syuentzang Temple** (Xuánzhuàng Sì) and **Syuenguang Temple** (Xuánguāng Sì) are all worth a visit if you have time. Syuenguang Temple is said to hold the remains of the monk immortalised in the novel *Journey to the West*.

Stately **Tsen Pagoda** (Ciēn Tǎ), built by Chiang Kai-shek in honour of his mother, is also worth visiting, as the views are about as good as it gets.

Note that all of the above can be reached by the public round-the-lake bus.

Festivals & Events

Thao Tribe Annual Harvest Festival Held every summer (during the eighth month of the lunar calendar). Visitors can watch all aspects of the festival, which include fortune-telling, mortar pounding to summon the people, as well as the sacrifice of wild animals. Festivities last for several days and take place in Itashao Village.

Annual across the Lake Swim Held every September to promote the lake and physical fitness, this is the only time swimming is permitted.

Sleeping

All hotels at the lake offer discounts during the week and often on the weekend, too. These can be up to 50%. Rooms that face the lake are always the most expensive. For homestays (double NT1000 to NT1500, ask at the Visitor Information Centre or just wander down the main road from the Visitor Information Centre toward the village (around the 7-Eleven).

Sun Moon Bay Campsite (Rìyuèwān Lùyíng Nóngchǎng; ☎ 285 0559; www.rock-camp.com.tw; per site NT500) The camp site is set beside the lake and has clean grounds with some trees for shade. Showers and bathrooms are on site. To reach the site, take a round-the-lake bus to the Youth Activity Centre. Continue on foot just a little further and turn right onto a small road heading down to the lake.

Teachers Hostel (Jiàoshī Huìguǎn; ☎ 285 5991; with Youth Guesthouse pass dm Sun-Thu NT500) This is a hotel, not a hostel, but travellers with a Youth Guesthouse Network Card (see p328) can stay here fairly cheaply. The hotel is a 10-minute walk up the hill from the village. Single female travellers without transport should be aware that parts of the walk are isolated and dark at night.

Youth Activity Centre (Rìyuètán Qīngnián Huódòng Zhōngxīn; ☎ 285 0071; Ru-Uei Village; d/tw 1800/3830). It's a 20-minute ride or so from Shueishe Village (the round-the-lake bus also stops here) but the centre has its own restaurant and store and large grounds for hanging out. You can also rent bikes here (see opposite). There's a 15% weekday discount on accommodation.

Full House Resort Hotel (Fùháoqún Dùjiǎ Mínsù; ☎ 285 0307; www.fhsml.idv.tw; 8 Shueishe St; d/tw NT2800/4500) The hotel, really a B&B, is set in a two-storey wooden house behind a small garden in Itashao. The lobby and restaurant are filled with quirky *objets d'art* that reflect the individualistic taste of the owner, a painter whose works adorn the lobby and rooms. Rooms are large (one has a second-storey loft for children to sleep in) and feature all-wood interiors, solid wood furniture, and antique decorations. In the last edition we mentioned that travellers bored with the same-old same-old of Taiwanese hotels would do well to stay here – and it appears from the photos the proud owner showed us that many of you have taken our advice. The hotel runs a 24-hour café and restaurant (set meals NT200).

Harbour Resort Hotel (Mǎtóu Xiūxián Dàfàndiàn; ☎ 285 5143; 11 Minsheng Rd; d/tw NT3000/4500) The last hotel on Minsheng before the dock, it's lakeside rooms are bright and airy and have a modern décor that includes plasma TVs. Though the room windows are small there are excellent lake views from the balconies. There is a simple spa in the basement for guests.

Spa Home (☎ 285 5166; fax 285 5577; 95 Jungshan Rd; r from NT6500) The cosy rooms are all doubles with an extra sofa for lounging, and rates include two breakfasts, night tea on the café balcony, and a 1½-hour massage for one person.

Eating & Drinking

If you are on a budget, there's a 7-Eleven in town for noodles and sandwiches, and cheap stir-fries and filling set meals are available from the nearby restaurants usually for around NT200. If you're a vegetarian try the Full House Resort Hotel. Along the waterfront, both in Shueishe Village and Itashao, many hotels runs cafés where you can take in the lake views from your table.

Min Hu Old Restaurant (Mínghú Lǎo Cāntīng; 15 Minsheng Rd; dishes NT150; ⊙ 9am-9pm) This bland-looking restaurant in Shueishe Village has what most agree is the best Chinese food at the lake.

The five-star **Lalu** (Hánbìlóu; ☎ 285 5311; 142 Jhongsing Rd) resort (which is overpriced in our opinion as a sleeping option) has several lovely restaurants open to nonguests, including the Oriental Brassiere (dishes NT200-500; ⊙ 7am-9pm daily). The brassiere is on level seven and is divided into two sections: one serving contemporary Western cuisine, and the other Eastern. The lake-view balcony tables outside are very popular at lunchtime.

Getting There & Away

From Taichung, catch a Renyou bus to Sun Moon Lake (NT212, two hours). There are at least two buses a day (at 8am and 3pm). From Taipei, **Kuo Kuang Hao** (☎ 02-2311 9893) runs buses directly to Sun Moon Lake (NT465, 4½ hours). Buses end their journey in the large car park behind the village.

From Taichung, you can also catch one of the frequent Fengyuan buses to Puli (NT150, one hour) and then transfer to a Fengrong bus to Sun Moon Lake (NT54, 30 minutes, every hour).

From Shuili, Fengrong buses run to Sun Moon Lake (NT49, 30 minutes, hourly). Buses from Puli or Shuili drop you off on the main road by the Visitor Information Centre.

Getting Around

The scenic area administration runs a round-the-lake bus (all day pass NT80) from about 6.45am to 6pm. Buses leave from in front of the Visitor Information Centre and do not quite go around the lake but turn back at Syuenguang Temple (there isn't much to see after this anyway). Buses run about once an hour and there is a full schedule in English available at the Visitor Information Centre.

You can rent scooters (NT800 per day) with an international driving licence at shops along the main road, left of the 7-Eleven.

HIGHWAY 14

Though it starts just south of Taichung in the bland town of Caotun, Hwy 14 makes up for a poor start in no time. After Puli, which is worth stopping in to visit the marvellous Chung Tai Chan Temple, the elevation rises and one turn after another brings stunning mountain views. Along the way you can stop for hot springs, sightseeing and even some hiking if you are up for it (one trails takes you down all the way to the east coast).

Hwy 14 ends at Tayuling, just north of the forest recreation area of Hehuanshan (at 3300m), and from here you can go east to Taroko Gorge or north to Wuling Farm and Ilan. Public transport is not great, or even good, along the highway. Only Puli has anything like regular bus service from Taichung. However, there is one bus a day from Taichung all the way to Lishan, with a stop at Hehuanshan. Driving and not stopping often, you could cover the route in four to five hours, but give yourself at least two days.

PULI 埔里

☎ 049 / pop 87,069

Most people in Taiwan know Puli (Pǔlǐ) as being the town hardest hit by the 921 earthquake. Puli has rebuilt itself since then, though perhaps not to the satisfaction of Japanese retirees (see p228), and today there is little evidence that it was once the epicentre of a massive 6.9 magnitude quake.

Puli is a 90-minute drive from Taichung, and is the first stop of note on a journey down Hwy 14.

Orientation & Information

Central Puli is small and it's not hard to figure your way around. Note that some sights, however, are a way out of town and will require a taxi ride. Taxis are not that common in Puli so it's best to have your hotel call one before you head out.

The tallest and most distinctive building in town is not what it seems, ie a department store. Rather it's the Pu Tian Community Centre (Pǔ Tián Jīn Shè), built by the Chung Tai Chan Buddhists. The centre is open to the public and has a children's library, movie room, meditation hall and gallery.

Sights & Activities

CHUNG TAI CHAN TEMPLE 中台禪寺

Completed in 2001, the 43-storey **Chung Tai Chan Temple** (Zhōng Tái Chánsì; ☎ 293 0215; www .chungtai.org in Chinese but has some interesting pictures) is more than just another massive modern temple – it's an international centre of Buddhist academic research, culture and the arts.

If that sounds intimidating, rest assured. In large part, the temple exists for those who

desire to learn about Buddhism, no matter what their current level of understanding. Several of the resident nuns speak English, and it is their duty to help visitors to understand what they see to as well as to explain the basic tenets of Buddhism.

The temple has embraced modern technology and the lighting and design are innovative and pleasing to the eye. The artwork is superb. Highlights include the 15m-high carved pillars of the guards of the four directions in the entrance hall, the pure-jade relief of the 18 lohans, the hand-painted chamber ceilings, the seven-storey (indoor) pure-teak pagoda and the massive Buddha statues that dominate each level.

There is no accommodation at the temple for the casual visitor, but there are meditation classes and week-long retreats where practitioners are permitted to stay at the temple.

To get to the temple, drive north on Jungjeng Rd out of Puli and then follow the signs. The temple is about 6km north of Renai Park. A taxi should cost around NT300.

For information about tours or to prearrange one, email or call the monastery.

MUHSHENG MUSEUM OF ENTOMOLOGY
木生昆蟲博物館

Taiwan has more than 400 species of butterflies, 350 of which can be seen around Puli, so it's no surprise that there is a **museum** (Mùshēng Kūnchóng Bówùguǎn; ☎ 291 3311; 622 Nan Cun Rd; adult/child NT120/100; ☯ 8am-5.30pm) dedicated to the winged insect here.

The museum features a live butterfly compound (which is just OK) and a display centre. On the 1st floor there are live beetles, stick insects and scorpions. On the 2nd floor hundreds and hundreds of preserved specimens are presented behind glass. There is a bizarre Thai 'face' butterfly, an 'owl faced' butterfly, a butterfly with wings that look like leaves, and the very odd hermaphrodite butterfly (the male half is dark, the female light).

It's best to take a taxi to the museum.

KUANHSING PAPER FACTORY 廣興紙寮

Really more cottage industry than factory, **Kuanhsing** (Guǎnxīng Zhǐ Liáo; ☎ 291 3037; 310 Tiehshan Rd; admission free; ☯ 8am-5.30pm) is dedicated to preserving the craft of handmade paper. You can watch paper being made by hand and even

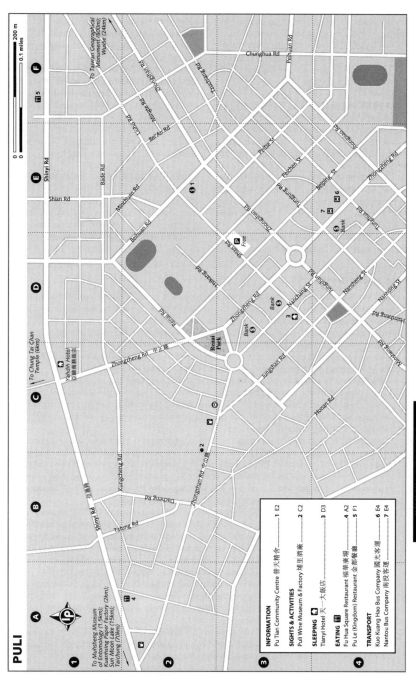

PULI

WESTERN TAIWAN

try it yourself. Though this place is set up for visitors it has a very authentic atmosphere.

You'll definitely need to take a taxi to get to the factory. Drivers will ask for NT200 but NT150 is fair. Kuanhsing is a popular destination for school field trips.

PULI WINE MUSEUM & FACTORY 埔里酒廠

Puli is famous for its Shaohsing wine (Shàoxīng jiǔ), made from glutinous rice and wheat. It has a kick and a bite, and while the wine is rarely appreciated by the Western palate, the jugs are very attractive and make for nice gifts.

The **museum** (Pǔlǐ Jiǔchǎng; ☎ 298 4006; 219 Zhongshan Rd, sec.3; admission free; ☷ 8am-5pm) was undergoing renovations at the time of writing, with no word on when it will open or what it will present.

Across the street, in any case, is the wine-tasting area and **factory** (☎ 8am-4pm Mon-Fri,

8.30am-5pm Sat & Sun). There are a dozen or more 'wines' to sample, including some delicious fruit liqueurs. You'll also find tasty wine-flavoured ice blocks and cakes.

Do visit the 2nd floor, as you'll find an exhibit area of old posters, household items and, interestingly, Taiwan Beer bottles and cigarette packages from throughout the ages. The 'Great Men' series of cigarettes (featuring Winston Churchill and Chiang Kai-shek among others on the packaging) are some of the funniest artefacts we have seen in a long time.

TAIWAN GEOGRAPHICAL MONUMENT
台灣地理中心

If you follow Zhongshan Rd to the edge of town (where it turns into Hwy 14), you'll see a giant menhirlike stone with Chinese characters reading **Taiwan Geographical Monument** (台灣地理中心; Táiwān Dìlǐ Zhōngxīn). Though many

---

55 POOPS IN PULI

I pull into Puli on a sunny spring afternoon and there he is: going about his business as brazen as any streetwalker. Only this streetwalker has four legs, a furry coat and his business is pooping on the sidewalk of this small town in central Taiwan.

Odd as it may sound, I sit in my car to see what will happen next. The dog is a stray so I'm not expecting an owner show up and lay claim to the prize, but I am expecting the 'Puli Poop Patrol' or some-such entity to come and clean up the mess. When they don't, after a considerable wait, I leave in disgust, much like the old Japanese Nakamura couple did a year previously.

The Nakamuras arrived in Puli in 2006 as part of a pilot long-term stay program for Japanese retirees. The first of the Japanese baby boomers have just begun to retire and the total value of their pension funds could exceed US$44 billion. Around the world, countries, cities, counties, you name it, are vying for a piece of that pie. Puli, which yes, does sound like 'poo village' ('li' is village in Chinese), is one of these cities.

Unfortunately, Puli's dog poop problem was not to the liking of the fastidious Japanese couple. And they weren't shy about venting their frustration. The you-know-what hit the fan, and the couple soon found themselves hiding out in a police station as an angry mob hunted for the slanderers (for as everyone knows, Puli is the jewel of Taiwan). In the end, however, most people slowly came to admit that the Japanese couple were right; like too many other small Taiwanese towns, Puli was butt ugly, dirty, polluted, and strewn with dog faeces.

Such admission could not help but translate into robust government action. Puli declared the 10th of every month clean-up day. The Environmental Protection Agency (EPA), not to be outdone, calculated the number of stray dogs in the country, divided that by the number of towns, divided that further by three (as one-third of dogs are reported to do their business wherever they like) and determined that no town should have more than 55 pieces of poop on the streets at any time. Any more and the town risked losing government funding.

How effective has the program been? Well, a few months later another couple, by coincidence also called Nakamura, arrived in Puli and their first impression was 'very good'. Mrs Nakamura went so far as to say the town had the best living environment and quality of life in the world. Mrs. Nakamura is Taiwanese, by the way.

Truly in Puli's defense, however, I did only see the one dog get away with leaving his lunch remains behind. And there really wasn't that much poop anywhere else. If progress continues like this, there may come a day the town will have to consider changing its name.

GHOSTS IN THE MACHINE

Like the Japanese, Taiwanese are quick and eager to adopt new technology. Even temples have gotten into the spirit. At the Chung Tai Chan temple in Puli, for example, a special Windows program and a 2m-wide LCD screen help members locate their donation plaques among the thousands on the walls of a vast chamber. In other temples around the country, it's quite common to see sales of virtual candles, online fortune telling, and even online booking for special religious services (to be held at a real temple), such as blessings to rid one of bad fortune during inauspicious years.

For years the EPA has been trying to get Taiwanese to go virtual in their burning of ghost paper. During Tomb Sweeping Day and Ghost Month, over 100,000 tonnes of thick paper pads are burnt as offerings to the spirits, sending the pm12 and CO_2 ratings to the heavens. To mitigate the effects of the bonfires on air quality, the EPA has tried both central sites (with some success) and online temple sites, where people can make virtual offerings of ghost money (with less success).

It's always an uphill battle when tradition comes up against the environment. But we honestly suspect it won't be that long before virtual ghost-money burning catches on. After all, it's so much more convenient to burn online, and in a country that has the highest per capita ratio of 7-Elevens in the world, nothing sells like convenience.

---

people get their picture taken here, this is just a park sign. The plaque on the top of **Mt Hutoushan** (虎頭山; Hǔtóushān) officially marks the geographical centre of Taiwan. To reach the plaque, walk up the stairs located 50m or so to the right of the menhir and follow the trail up. Past the plaque, the trail continues to Carp Lake. It's about a one-hour walk.

CARP LAKE鯉魚潭

Just on the outskirts of Puli lies **Carp Lake** (Lǐyú Tán), a very pretty, willow-lined pond with a lush green mountain backdrop. Around the lake itself you'll find pavilions, restaurants and cafés overlooking the water (but not so many to spoil things). In recent years a couple good hotels have opened up, one offering hot springs. Come mid-week as the place is small and you don't want to share it with too many others.

SOLAS RESORT 天泉溫泉會館

This **resort** (Tiānquán Wēnquán Huìguǎn; ☎ 298 8187; www.solasresort.com; hot springs NT250; ⏰ 2pm-10pm) has attractive modern outdoor public pools, and facilities that include a unique wrap-around jet contraption, and a long trench with picnic tables and swings built inside. The general public can also use the hot springs, but you need to bring your own towels.

Sleeping

Accommodation in Puli is a little dreary: prices are going up as quality is going down.

This is unlikely to change as investment is going to Carp Lake or Sun Moon Lake. If you have your own vehicle, or even not, consider staying at Sun Moon Lake as it's only 15km away. You can also stay at Carp Lake or 15 to 20 minutes further east down Hwy 14 at one of several small, midrange hot-spring resorts.

Tianyi Hotel (Tiānyī Dàfàndiàn; ☎ 998 100, ext 2; 299 Shian Rd; 西安路299號; d/tw NT1600/1700, weekdays NT1000/1200) The hotel is in downtown Puli. Rooms are basic, but clean. The weekend price is far too high.

Lakeside Resort (天水蓮大飯店; Tiānshuǐlián Dàfàndiàn; ☎ 290 3411; www.lakeresort.com.tw; r from NT4000) Overlooking Carp Lake (actually built right over it) is this smart little hotel with comfortably furnished rooms. Those with lakeside views cost NT600 more. There are 25% weekday discounts, and room rates include free use of the hot springs at Solas Resort (left) across the lake.

Eating & Drinking

There are plenty of cheap noodle stands, simple restaurants and cafés around Puli, especially on Zhongzheng Rd south of Renai Park. For something fancier, or just more scenic, head to Carp Lake.

Carp Lake Restaurant On Water (台揚水上餐廳; Táiyáng Shuǐshàng Cāntíng; ☎ 298 5445; http://tai-young.myweb.hinet.net; dishes from NT80; ⏰ 9am-8pm). This vegetarian restaurant sits above the lake and features authentic hand-puppet theatre around 8pm on evenings when groups have booked a show (usually on weekends).

Fu Hua Square Restaurant (Fúhuá Guǎngchǎng; ☎ 291 4788; 1099 Shinyi Rd; average dish NT150) The vegetarian dim sum here is a favourite with the monks and nuns from Chung Tai Chan Temple, and for good reason. It's not often you get Cantonese vegetarian-style cooking in Taiwan (especially with a real Cantonese chef). The restaurant is just off Shinyi Rd in a small square with an arched entrance.

Pu Le (Kingdom) Restaurant (Jīndù Cāntīng; ☎ 299 5096; 236 Shinyi Rd; per person NT300) Nantou County (of which Puli is a part) is the biggest flower-growing region in Taiwan. At Pu Le Restaurant, gorgeous-looking and tasting dishes are decorated and even cooked with fresh flowers. It's best to come with as many people as possible so you can try a number of dishes.

Getting There & Away

A visit to Puli could be part of an extended visit to the Sun Moon Lake region or a weekend getaway from Taichung. From Taichung, the Taichung Bus Company runs frequent buses to Puli (NT150, 1 hour). To Sun Moon Lake, catch a bus (NT54, 30 minutes, every hour) with the **Nantou Bus Company** (☎ 298 4031; 342 Zhongzheng Rd).

AOWANDA NATIONAL FOREST RECREATION AREA
奧萬大國家森林遊樂區

As you drive along Hwy 14 east of Puli, you reach the mountain community of **Wushe** (霧社) in less than an hour. It's very scenic up here and if you are interested in Taiwanese history there is a monument (just up the main road on the left) to the Wushe Incident, the last large-scale revolt against the Japanese, which led to a massacre of Atayal aborigines.

Half an hour or so south, down a long and winding road, is the forest recreation area of **Aowanda** (Àowàndà; http://awdonline-eng.forest.gov.tw/stop.php; adult/child NT200/150). It's well worth a stop here, or even an overnight stay in the quaint wooden cabins (NT1500) surrounded by plum and maple trees. Aowanda has a **visitor centre** (☎ 049-297 4511; ⏰ 8.30am-5pm) with maps and brochures in English.

The park ranges in altitude from 1100m to 2600m, making it a cool retreat from the heat in summer. On the developed trails you can walk from one end of the reserve to the other

in about two hours. All signs are bilingual and trails are simple to follow.

Aowanda is famous around Taiwan for its **maple trees** (fēngshù). November to late January when the leaves change colours is a busy time for the park. **Bird-watching** is also popular here and a visit to Aowanda is usually on the itinerary for tours from Western countries. In all, 120 species of bird live in the park, and of the 15 endemic species of birds in Taiwan, 10 can be found here, including Swinhoe's pheasant and the Taiwan partridge. The park has even set up a **bird-watching platform** (shǎngniǎotái) and benches, one of which bears an amusing dedication to Jo Ann McKenzie, a Canadian twitcher who has been to Aowanda many times.

From Taichung, catch a **Nantou Bus Company** (☎ 2225 6418; 35-8 Shuangshi Rd) bus (NT270, 2½ hours) on weekends or holidays from November to February. The bus leaves at 7.30am.

NENGGAO (NENG-GAO/NENGKAO) CROSS-ISLAND TRAIL
能高越領國家步道

This 200-year-old high mountain **trail** (Nénggāo Yuèlǐng Guójiā Bùdào; http://trail.forest.gov.tw/NationalTrailSystem_En/TR_H_02.htm) was first used by the Taiya to help them ply the trade between Puli and Hualien. During the Japanese occupation it was expanded and used, ironically, to police aboriginal tribes. During the latter half of the 20th century, the path was expanded further by Taipower, which used it when laying high-voltage powerlines. (Hence you will sometimes also hear the trail called the 'Nenggao Powerline Trail').

Today the path offers a fantastically scenic hike for those really looking to get into the heart of the central mountains. Depending on how you tackle the trail, it is for the most part not terribly demanding for anyone in decent shape. From the trailhead at **Tunyuan** (屯原) most people spend the first day walking to **Tienchi** (天池; 2860m). The elevation gain is 800m and it takes the average hiker about five or six hours to walk (allow three hours for the downhill return). Tienchi has a cabin where you'll find beds, a kitchen and water. You can also camp.

Many hikers use Tienchi as a from which-base to climb nearby peaks including **Chilai South Peak** (奇萊主山南峰; 3358m) and **Nenggaoshan North Peak** (能高北峰; 3184m). The trails to these peaks are not as well marked or as wide as the cross-island trail and are more demanding, but they can be done together on one long day with a return to Tienchi cabin. There's also a beautiful high waterfall, just a few hundred metres from the cabin, that's worth visiting.

On the second or third day most people return to Tunyuan to conclude their hike, but it's also possible to continue on to Liyu Lake in Hualien County. The way is clear and takes about two days from Tienchi. Note that the second day from Tienchi you will be on paved surface the whole time. Fortunately, the way is downhill and there is almost no traffic. If you need them, there are buses at Liyu Lake to take you to Hualien city.

Information

The Nenggao Cross-Island Trail is part of the National Trail System (p329). Only a mountain permit is needed to hike and one can be picked up at the **police station** (☎ 049-280 2520) in Wushe or at the **Ministry of the Interior** (Map p88; ☎ 02-2321 9011; 7 Zhongxiao E Rd, sec.1, Taipei). For information about the cabin at Tienchi, contact the **Nantou Forestry Bureau** (☎ 049-236 5226; http://nantou.forest.gov.tw/e6-1.asp).

Getting There & Away

It's best to do this hike with your own vehicle or with arrangements for someone to drop you off and pick you up (either at the Tunyuan trailhead or over on the Hualien County side). To get to the Tunyuan trailhead drive along Hwy 14 to the 94km mark. You'll see a sign in English directing you to turn right to the trail. Follow the road to the end and park. The trail begins here.

Past Wushe, Hwy 14 splits into Hwy 14甲, which heads north, and Hwy 14, which heads east to the trail. Note also that a side road later splits off Hwy 14 east to Lushan Hot Springs, a grubby, overdeveloped hot-spring resort.

HEHUANSHAN (HOHUANSHAN) FOREST RECREATION AREA
合歡山森林遊樂區

The last interesting stop on Hwy 14甲 before the descent into Taroko Gorge is **Hehuanshan** (Héhuānshān Sēnlín Yóulè Qū; http://recreate.forest.gov.tw; ☎ 049-280 2732). At over 3000m, the recreation area sits mostly above the tree line, and the bright, grassy green hills of the Mt Hehuan Range roll on and on, often disappearing into the fog or a spectacular sea of clouds.

Hwy 14甲 passes right through the park and at Wuling saddle (not to be confused with the forest recreation area called Wuling) it reaches the highest elevation of any road in Taiwan at 3275m. It snows up here in winter and when it does the road becomes a skating rink, parking lot and playground for the Taiwanese so expect crowds then.

Summer is delightfully cool, and highly scenic as different alpine flowers bloom from May to September. Autumn and spring are excellent times for hiking. In the autumn the 'sea of clouds' formations are at their best.

Despite its chilly temperatures (12°C average) Hehuanshan has a remarkable amount of plant and animal life to admire. It's even considered a good spot for birding. Check out the website for details.

Activities

There are a number of short hikes starting close to Ho-huan Cottage. Most have signs in English at the trailhead but you are advised to still get a proper map of the area (see p331). Be aware that fog or rain can come in suddenly in the mountains so always be prepared with warm clothing and some kind of rain protection. Be aware also that if you have driven straight up from lower altitudes your body may take time to get used to exercising at 3000m plus.

The trail to **Hehuanshan East Peak** (合歡山東峰; Héhuānshān DōngFēng; 3421m) starts across the road from the cottage. It's about an hour to the top.

The marked trailhead to **Hehuanshan North Peak** (合歡山北峰; Héhuānshān Běifēng; 3422m) starts a few kilometres north of the cottage off the highway. It's three to four hours return.

The trailhead for **Shimenshan** (石門山; Shíménshān; 3237m) is just north of the cottage on the east/left side of the road. It's a short walk to the top and people often go here to watch the sunrise.

The paved path up to **Hehuanshan Main Peak** (合歡山主峰; Héhuānshān Zhǔfēng; 3417m) starts just before Wuling and takes about two hours return.

The trail up to **Hehuan Jian Shan** (合歡尖山; Héhuānjiānshān; 3217m) starts just behind the cottage. It takes about 15 minutes to reach the top.

For longer, overnight hikes check out the website.

Sleeping & Eating

You can stay overnight in the very spartan **Ho-huan Cottage** (合歡山莊; Héhuānshānzhuāng; ☎ 049-280 2732; dm/tr with bathroom incl breakfast & dinner NT480/2650). The cottage has a simple overview map of the area and trails. You're advised to book ahead in winter and on weekends. There's a 30% discount from Sunday to Thursday. Bring a sleeping bag, towel, your own toiletries and some food. Simple dishes can also be picked up from vendors at Wuling.

Getting There & Away

There is one Fengyuan Bus Company bus a day (8am, NT393, 4½ hours) to Hehuanshan from Taichung. You could rent a scooter in Jiaoshi but it's a long ride. Consider a car.

If you want to continue north from Hehuanshan, catch the Fengyuan bus as it passes Hehuanshan heading north to Lishan (around 12.30pm daily, NT149, 2½ hours). The bus arrives in Lishan around 3pm. There's little to keep you here these days so take the 4pm bus to beautiful Wuling Recreation Area (NT62, one hour). From here you can continue to Ilan and Taipei.

ALISHAN NATIONAL SCENIC AREA

☎ 05

The Alishan National Scenic Area covers a region of over 37,000 hectares. From a starting altitude of 300m in the west at Chukou, the land quickly rises to heights of more than 2600m. As a result, the variety of plant and animal life is nothing short of amazing. One of the best ways to appreciate this variety is on the narrow-gauge Alishan forest train, which, in the space of 3½ hours (71km), takes you through three vegetative zones.

Don't confuse the Alishan National Scenic Area with the popular Alishan Forest Recreation Area, which is where the small train takes you. The forest recreation area is but one part of the national scenic area. Other areas include tea-growing communities such as Rueili and Fengshan, and aboriginal villages such as Shanmei, where the Zhou are trying to keep their culture and environment as healthy as possible.

Alishan can be as safe or as challenging as you want it to be. You can sip tea or swim in rivers. Your meals can come from a hotel kitchen or a rough barbecue pit. The forest recreation area offers a cool, relaxing, well-developed mountain retreat, while smaller towns offer homestays and a more traditional way of life.

The whole region is also perfect for just cruising around on a scooter. The roads are in good shape, signs in English are ubiquitous, and you're never really that far from a place to eat or sleep.

You can visit Alishan any time of year, though be careful in summer as rains can and do wash roads out. Do not go up during or after a typhoon or earthquake. Be aware that the higher up you go the colder it gets, and even in summer it can be pretty chilly at night in Alishan Village.

Check out the official website (www.ali .org.tw) before you go. There's information on accommodation, eating, transport and activities, as well as the history and culture of almost every village and town.

CHIAYI 嘉義

☎ 05 / pop 270,341

While Chiayi (Jiāyì) is not part of the Alishan National Scenic Area, almost every traveller will have to pass through here on the way in. The narrow-gauge train to the Alishan Forest Recreation Area leaves from Chiayi train station, as do buses and taxis. There are a few better-than-OK sights to recommend in Chiayi so plan to spend a half-day or so before moving on.

Orientation

Chiayi lies directly on the tropic of Cancer, which nearly cuts Taiwan in two. Central Chiayi is small enough to walk across in 30 minutes, though air pollution often makes it unpleasant to do so. Most road signs have pinyin on them. Taxis are plentiful except in the area west of the train tracks.

Information

For information about the restaurant and entertainment scene, pick up a copy of the excellent monthly *FYI South Magazine*, which includes a pull-out map that is updated regularly. Copies are available at the visitor centre, many bars and restaurants in town, or you can download the content at the website www

.taiwanfun.com. There are usually internet cafés around the train station. They come and go, so ask at the visitor centre for the latest.

Chiayi City Government (www.chiayi.gov.tw/newweb /index_english.htm) Good for general information about the city, including sights and activities for tourists.

First Commercial Bank (307 Jhongshan Rd) ATMs and currency exchange. There are also numerous banks and ATMs on Renai Rd near the train station.

Laundromat (701 Jhongjheng Rd; 24hr) This DIY place is just up the road from the Jiaxin Hotel.

St Martin De Porres Hospital (275 6000; 565 Daya Rd, sec.2)

Visitor Information Centre (225 6649; 8.30-5pm) The centre, inside Chiayi train station, provides brochures and travel information in English about Chiayi, Alishan and pretty much anywhere else you want to go. Staff speak English.

Sights

COCHIN CERAMIC MUSEUM 交趾陶館

This **museum** (Jiāozhǐ Guǎn; 278 8225; 275 Jungshiau Rd; admission free; 9am-noon & 1.30-5pm Wed-Sun) is one of the best small museums dedicated to a single folk art in Taiwan. Cochin (*zhāo zhǐ tǎo*) is a low-fired, bright-coloured-glaze style

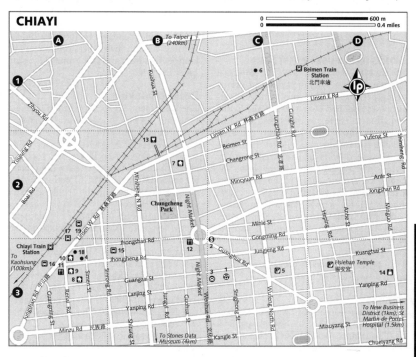

WESTERN TAIWAN

of ceramic and is often used to make figurines and wall decorations. You've probably seen cheap work in tourist shops around the island. But much of the work here, especially that of Master Yeh (1826–91), is outstanding. For example, the set of figurines with lively faces performing what look like different martial arts gestures: you'd swear they had muscles and bone under their robes, so realistic is the motion captured by the artist.

Cochin artists have been working in the Chiayi area since the Qing dynasty and have won praise from as far afield as Japan and France. The museum is in the basement of the **Chiayi Cultural Centre** (Jiāyìshì Wénhuà Zhōngxīn), across from the Beimen train station.

STONES DATA MUSEUM 石頭資料庫

The **museum** (Shítóu Zīliàokù; ☎ 235 5333; 366 Huzihnei Rd; admission free; ☯ 8.30am-5.30pm) is an astonishing personal collection of strangely coloured and shaped stones, minerals, fossils and statues. There are rocks that look like craggy mountain ranges; brightly coloured mineral specimens from all over the world; meteorites; dozens of oversized monkey statues; and a fossil collection that also contains great reproductions of the skeleton of a prehistoric elk (3.4m in length), several dinosaur heads, a mastodon with full tusks, and human skulls from the australopithecenes (Lucy) up to modern *Homo sapiens*. And this just starts to describe the collection. Kids will love it here.

To get to the museum take a taxi or drive south down Minsheng S Rd.

TEMPLES

Chiayi has a number of beautiful temples scattered around the city. **Chenghuang Temple** (Chénghuáng Miào), also known as City God Temple, is particularly fascinating for the array of elaborately carved and dressed statues of demons and guards.

Sleeping

There are many cheap hotels scattered around the train-station area. Those with a Youth Travel Pass (see p328) can stay in the Chiayi City Labour Recreation Centre but note it's quite a distance from the train station and no cheaper than the hotels listed below.

Yixing Hotel (Yìxīng Lǚguǎn; ☎ 227 9344; fax 227 9345; 730 Jhongjheng Rd; 中正路730號; s/d/tw NT450/600/850)

This is probably the cheapest place in town that's reasonably clean and comfortable. There are only two single rooms.

Jiaxin Hotel (Jiāxīn Dàfàndiàn; ☎ 222 2280; 687 Jhongjheng Rd; 中正路687號; d/tw from NT700/1200; 💻) Rooms are clean, not too small, and overall offer good value for money. Some rooms have ADSL (for NT100 more).

Country Hotel (Guóyuán Dàfàdiàn; ☎ 223 6336; fax 223 6345; 678 Guangzal St; 光彩街678號; d/tw NT1260/2300; 🅿) This place is more expensive than the others but offers a car park next door. Usual weekday rates for a double are NT950.

Chinatrust Hotel (Zhōngxìn Dàfàndiàn; ☎ 229 2233; 257 Wenhua Rd; 文化路257號; d/tw NT3600/4000; 💻) One of the top hotels in town, offering a 30% discount on weekdays. Facilities include a business centre, small fitness room and VIP lounge, restaurant and café. Some of the staff speak English.

Eating & Drinking

There are many inexpensive generic restaurants and cafés on Jhongshan and Renai Rds and around Chungcheng Park. The **night market** (Wenhua Rd; ☯ 5pm-2am), between Mincyuan and Chuei Yang Rds, is also good for cheap food. For fancier fare try the **Cantonese restaurant** (☎ 229 2233; 257 Wenhua Rd; dishes NT100; ☯ lunch & dinner) on the 3rd floor of the Chinatrust Hotel.

If you head east on Minzu Rd a kilometre or two beyond the boundaries of our map (the road turns into Daya Rd) you'll hit the new business area of town. Many nice cafés and restaurants have opened up recently.

Pen Shui Turkey Rice (Pēnshuǐ Huǒjīfàn; 325 Jhongshan Rd; dishes NT40; ☯ 8.30am-10pm) Everyone in Taiwan knows that Chiayi is famous for its turkey rice dish (huǒ jīròu fàn). This is the place that started it all over 60 years ago.

Gongbing Vegetarian Restaurant (Gōngbīn Dàzìrán Sùshíguǎn; ☎ 227 3461; 457 Renai Rd; meals around NT100; ☯ breakfast, lunch & dinner) Offers buffet-style vegetarian food.

Calgary Pub (Kǎjiālǐ Měishì Cānyǐndiàn; ☎ 227 1626; 19 Lane 351, Guohua St; beer NT150; ☯ 6pm-2am) This long-running Western-style pub is busy most nights. The crowd is a mix of expats and locals. Western-style dishes (NT150) such as hamburgers and pizza are staples on the menu. Even though the address says Guohua St, approach from Linsen W Rd (coming from the train-station area) and turn left down the alley just before Guohua St.

Shopping

Original En Dian Cookie Shop (Ēndiǎnsū Chuàngshǐ-diàn; ☎ 238 7898; 123 Minguo Rd) Chiayi is famous for square cookies (ēndiǎn sū) and this is the store that invented them. The cookies taste a lot like Graham Crackers and cost only NT50 for a box.

Getting There & Away

Chiayi is the gateway to the Alishan National Scenic Area. To get there you can take a train, bus or (our favourite) hired scooter.

TRAIN

If you are taking the small train to Alishan, note that you can board at Beimen station, northeast of the main station. This station is less crowded and has a few sights nearby, such as the Cochin Ceramic Museum and a Japanese-era station just across the tracks, to help you pass the time while waiting for the train.

There are two trains a day to Alishan (NT399, 3½ hours, 9am and 1.30pm). The earlier train is recommended as afternoon fog in the mountains can obscure views. If you catch the train at Beimen station the schedule is slightly later. During Chinese New Year and other holidays there are more trains scheduled each day. It is advisable to reserve tickets (☎ 276 8094, up to two months in advance) beforehand as travel agents and hotels tend to buy them up. You can make online reservations in Chinese only (https://forestrailway .forest.gov.tw).

Trains to/from Taipei (fast/slow NT600/462, three/4½ hours) and Kaohsiung (fast/slow NT248/160, one/two hours) run from morning till late at night.

High-Speed Rail

The HSR station is pretty far from downtown Chiayi but there is a shuttle bus (NT42, 40 minutes, every 20 min) between the two. The stop in Chiayi is behind the train station. Look for the BRT (bus rapid transit) signpost. At the time of writing there were trains (NT1080, 90 minutes) about every hour to/from Taipei.

BOAT

The *Tomorrow Star* runs between Putai (near Chiayi) and Penghu's Makung (NT650, 70 minutes). For inquiries call **Makung Tomorrow Star** (☎ 926 0666).

BUS

Buses to Alishan (NT214, 2½ hours) usually leave every two hours from early morning to late afternoon from the **Chiayi County Bus Company** (☎ 224 3140) station to the right of the train station as you exit. The full schedule (in English) is available at the visitor centre or at the bus station itself.

There are Kuo Kuang Hao buses (NT368, three hours) to/from Taipei every hour.

Getting Around

You can hire scooters (NT200 per day) from several shops across from the train station with an international driving licence. Travelling on a scooter up to the Alishan National Scenic Area is highly recommended. Take the old narrow Hwy 159 for less traffic and a pure mountain experience.

FENCHIHU–RUEILI HISTORIC TRAIL
奮瑞古道

Fenchihu (奮起湖; Fènqǐhú) is a tiny village (estimated population 200) at the halfway point on the narrow-gauge Alishan railway. Just a few years ago the place had a great remote outpost feel to it and we highly recommended a stop here. But those days have gone. The 'old street' now has a shiny 7-Eleven on it, completely ruining the atmosphere, and the merchants have traded their rural friendliness for indifference – unless you want to buy something. It's also on the tour bus route and even midweek you'll get packs of silly-shoed urbanites treading through the cedar forests making noise and leaving garbage.

Is there a reason to stop here now? Yes, and it's even better than the old one. An old walking trail, called the Fenchihu–Rueili Historic Trail (Fèn–Ruì Gǔdào) was recently opened up from, you guessed it, Fenchihu all the way to Rueili. The trail is long (7km) and steep enough to discourage the tourists, but it's not so long and steep that anyone in average shape should miss out on it. An average walker will take four hours, though longer with a heavy pack. Much of the trail runs through bamboo forests that look like something out of a wushu film, though some of it is along narrow farm roads.

From Fenchihu train station it's about a five-minute walk to the trailhead. Just cross the train tracks after you get off, and head up. You'll pass through an interesting grove of square bamboo (四方竹; *sìfāng zhú*) and within minutes reach the road. Turn left and walk for another few minutes until the road takes a sharp bend to the right. Head into the parking lot to the left and you'll see the map board and start of the trail. The map is in English and along the clear trail you'll see markers and posts and maps at every junction. With these in place, and our map to guide you, there's little danger of getting lost, though a compass is still useful as some of the map boards are placed backwards (see p331).

In Rueili the trail ends (or begins) on the main road into town, close to hotels and restaurants. A short side route at the end takes you to the visitor centre.

It's cool in this part of the country so come prepared. Fenchihu has an average temperature of 19°C in summer and 12°C in winter.

RUEILI (JUILI) 瑞里
☎ 05 / pop 970 / elevation 1000m
Rueili (Ruìlǐ) is a small, quiet, temperate-mountain community that thrives on tourism and tea growing. It's always been one of our favourite places in the Alishan region and the fact that we can now walk there from the Fenchihu train station makes it all that more special. Rueili excels in eye candy

for the nature-lover. There are panoramic mountain scenes, bamboo forests, caves, waterfalls and historic walking trails. Come midweek (especially late autumn or winter) and it's practically yours alone.

One distinctive local feature that's highly commendable is that Rueili people have long been working to preserve the environment. As a result, the region is not only clean, green and pesticide-free, but it's one of the best places in the country for watching fireflies.

You can visit any time of year, though with the altitude winter nights can be chilly so bring warm clothing. Most hotel rooms aren't heated.

Information
Rueitai Tourist Centre (☎ 250 1070; 1-1 Rueili Village; ◷ 8.30am-5pm) offers brochures (in English) and a very knowledgeable, friendly staff of locals. These people really love their land and want to share its treasures with you. The centre covers not only Rueili but nearby (and even more remote) Taihe (太和, Tàihé) and Rueifong (瑞峰, Ruìfēng). The centre has internet access (for checking email). Note that there are various maps of Rueili around, but ours is the most accurate according to the staff at the tourist centre (who have helped us develop it over the years).

TAIWAN'S HIGH-SPEED RAIL: BRINGING THE BOONDOCKS TO YOU

It's a slick system, with state-of-the-art Shinkansen technology from Japan, and it gets you from one city in Taiwan to the next in record time.

Or does it? If you look at the map you'll see that many High-Speed Rail (HSR) stations in Taiwan are literally in the sticks. When you factor in time spent on shuttle services from the HSR to urban centres, the reported savings start to look pretty meagre. On one test run from Taipei it us took a total of two hours, 40 minutes to get to Taichung on the HSR (this included getting to the station from home and all wait times). Return time on the regular fast train: two hours, 45 minutes.

Now friends complained that this test was not really fair as we could have taken a taxi from the HSR station to Taichung (yes, at an even greater cost), and in any case we did miss the first connecting shuttle train to Taichung getting a burger (OK, so subtract 15 minutes). But still, this is just not what we expected from high-speed rail.

The problem is that in many ways the system was built for a Taiwan that doesn't exist yet. Take Chiayi's station, for example. Eventually, it will be surrounded by a modern community of wide streets, green parks, sewage lines and building codes. Nearby will be, among other things, the southern branch of the National Palace Museum and a bus hub with direct links to Alishan. Visitors to Taiwan will be able to fly into Taoyuan Airport, catch the HSR to Chiayi station, see some great local sites, and return home all without having to deal with the traffic, noise, pollution and appalling architecture of Chiayi (or any other small city in Taiwan, for that matter).

It will be a powerful boost to tourism for sure, and we look forward to the day the system all starts to come together. In the meantime, look carefully at the true times of your journey on the HSR, and decide whether those few minutes saved really are worth the extra money.

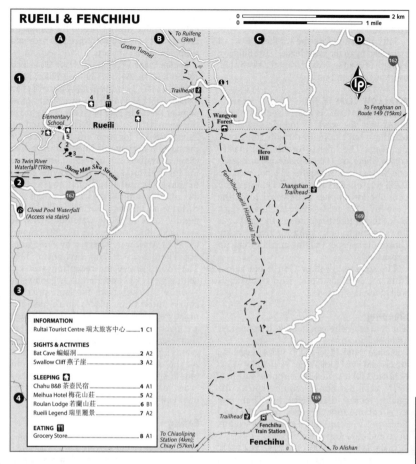

RUEILI & FENCHIHU

To Ruifeng (3km)

Green Tunnel

Trailhead

Wangyou Forest

Elementary School

Rueili

To Twin River Waterfall (1km)

Sheng Mao Shu Stream

Cloud Pool Waterfall (Access via stairs)

Hero Hill

Zhangshan Trailhead

To Fengshan on Route 149 (15km)

Fenchihu-Rueili Historical Trail

Trailhead

Fenchihu Train Station

To Chiaoliping Station (4km); Chiayi (57km)

Fenchihu

To Alishan

INFORMATION
Rultai Tourist Centre 瑞太旅客中心 **1** C1

SIGHTS & ACTIVITIES
Bat Cave 蝙蝠洞 **2** A2
Swallow Cliff 燕子崖 **3** A2

SLEEPING 🏠
Chahu B&B 茶壺民宿 **4** A1
Meihua Hotel 梅花山莊 **5** A2
Roulan Lodge 若蘭山莊 **6** B1
Rueili Legend 瑞里麗景 **7** A1

EATING 🍴
Grocery Store **8** A1

Sights & Activities

FIREFLIES 螢火蟲

Rueili is one of the best places in Taiwan to see these amazing little creatures (*yínghuǒchóng*) show off their bioluminescent skills. From March to June the mountainsides literally sparkle as countless fireflies turn each other on throughout the night. Try to get a copy of *The Love Light: A Guide to the Great Alishan Fireflies*, a free brochure highlighting the different types of fireflies in the area.

WATERFALLS

Rueili's most impressive fall is the **Cloud Pool Waterfall** (Yúntán Pùbù), which can be reached by a series of steep stairs. The return walk from the car park, which is just past the

22km mark on County Rd 122, takes about 45 minutes.

There is also the **Twin River Waterfall** (Shuāngxī Pùbù), which can visited as part of a trip to Swallow Cliff (p238)

RUITAI OLD TRAIL 瑞太古道

This **hiking trail** (Ruìtài Gúdào) was once used for travel between Rueili and Taihe. Now it's a very enjoyable two- or three-hour walk through bamboo forests that look like they came from a movie set. The trailhead starts about 1km or so west of the visitor centre (there's also an access point right across from the centre) and is well marked with signs and map boards in English. Note that this trail is part of the overall system that connects

Fenchihu to Rueili via the Fenchihu–Rueili Historic Trail (see p235).

Fifty metres before the trailhead a set of stairs lead up to the **Green Tunnel** (Lǜsè Sùidào), a length of road sealed off from the sky by tall, overhanging bamboo.

SWALLOW CLIFF 燕子崖

The **cliff** (yànzǐyái) is a large rock overhang pitted with the work of countless swallows who have built nests in the soft stone over the years. The hike is for the Stairmaster crowd (there are 1600 stone steps) and takes one hour return. Along the way you pass the 1000-year-old **Bat Cave** (Biǎnfú Dòng). If you continue for another hour you'll reach the Twin River Waterfall (Shuāngxī Pùbù), which is not that interesting, though the canyon it flows through looks good for river tracing (suòxī; the sport of walking and climbing up a riverbed).

The steps to Swallow Cliff begin across from the Meihua Hotel. The trailhead is well marked.

Sleeping

The tourist centre can help with homestays and hotel bookings.

Meihua Hotel (梅花山莊; Méihuā Shānzhuāng; ☎ 250 1668; 103-1 Rueili Village; 瑞里村103-1號; d/tw NT1500/2000) It's tiled-floor rooms are spotlessly clean but nondescript except for the quaint mosaic-tiled bathtubs. There are excellent mountains views from the 2nd floor and weekend and weekday discounts of 20 and 40% respectively so ask.

Chahu B&B (茶壺民宿; Cháhú Mínsù; ☎ 250 1806; http://052501349.travel-web.com.tw in Mandarin but with pictures; 100-6 Rueili Village; 瑞里村100-6號; d/tw NT2000/3000) Set in a spanking-new modern building, this cosy place offers rooms with soft beds, high ceilings and excellent views. On the 2nd floor there is a large balcony and a common area for reading or watching DVDs. Breakfast is served at the restaurant next door. There are weekday discounts of 20%.

Rueili Legend (瑞里麗景景觀民宿; Ruìlì Lìjǐng; ☎ 250 2288; http://052502288.travel-web.com.tw in Mandarin but with pictures; 105 Rueili Village; 瑞里村105號; d/tw 2800/3200, weekdays NT2000/2400) Another new kid on the block, boasting about the best views you can find here from their patio deck. In the late afternoon you can witness a 'sea of clouds' fill up the deep valley below and the

sun setting over the distant mountains (the patio faces due west). Oh, and the rooms are pretty good here too with nice soft beds and simple modern comforts.

Roulan Lodge (若蘭山莊; Ruòlán Shānzhuāng; ☎ 250 1210; fax 250 1555; 10 Rueili Village; 瑞里村幼葉林10之1號; d/tw NT1800/2400, cabins from NT3200) This has long been one of the most popular places to stay in Rueili. Every night the owners, who have often appeared on Taiwanese TV for their efforts to preserve the natural heritage of Rueili, show a film (English available) to introduce fireflies and the local history. They then invite guests to make tea and traditional snacks in a quaint old room filled with farm tools and curios from the past. During firefly season, nightly tours to prime watching areas are arranged. But book early: in 2007, rooms for all of April were reserved by early January. There is a weekend discount of 30%. The rooms above the reception area are getting pretty old and are not as good value as other places in town for same price (of course those other places don't have the nightly entertainment). The cabins though are lovely and range from aging but full of character to sleek and modern. The lower cabins are prime spots for watching fireflies. As the owner says, you must keep your mouth shut down here, not even whisper a 'wow!' or the fireflies (which are so numerous) will fly into your mouth.

Eating

Most hotels have their own restaurants though there are scattered places around town as well. Most are open for breakfast, lunch and dinner, but don't try to eat too late midweek. An average set meal will cost NT100 to NT200. There's a small grocery store in town selling instant noodles, canned goods, eggs, fruit and veggies, and drinks.

Getting There & Around

If you aren't hiking from Fenchihu, take a Chiayi County Bus Company bus (NT189, two hours) from Chiayi. At the time of writing the schedule was 9.30am and 4.30pm.

You can also take the Alishan train to Chiaoliping (交力坪; Jiāolìpíng; NT174) and then call a hotel in Rueili to pick you up. If there are enough of you, the hotel probably won't charge anything. Otherwise, the pick-up fee will be around NT300.

FENGSHAN 豐山

☎ 05 / pop363 / elevation 750m

In the strongly aboriginal Alishan National Scenic Area, Fengshan (Fēngshān) is a bit of an anomaly in that it is exclusively ethnic Chinese. This doesn't make it any less interesting a place to visit and if you are tired of the tame resort atmosphere at Alishan Village, a scooter ride to this remote corner of Taiwan will reward you on so many levels.

First of all, there's an appealing ruggedness to the place. Stratified canyons rise up sharply from stony riverbeds, and dark green mountains fill up half the sky. The village and the pesticide-free fields of tea, sugar cane and mountain vegetables seem as if they remain there only by the grace of God. And in many ways they do, as typhoons and landslides (and the occasional earthquake) ravage the area almost yearly.

Outside of the little village there is precious little development and few good roads (though road reconstruction is ubiquitous). In fact, without a 4WD vehicle you will probably have to walk to most sights, though a scooter can probably make it if you are careful.

You can visit all year round. Summer is a great time to visit for swimming and river tracing. The weather is more stable than in the north, and there are no daily afternoon showers to dampen your plans. Be careful when typhoons come, as rivers become dangerously swollen and roads get washed out. It's always best to call ahead to check on road conditions before you head out.

Autumn and winter are dry and warm and a good time for hiking and exploring canyons.

Orientation & Information

Fengshan village is pretty much in the centre of the three sights we list in the next section. There's a basic map of the area available in local B&Bs. Bring a compass to help orientate yourself.

Sights & Activities

The various natural sights around Fengshan include **Jiaolong Waterfall** (蛟龍瀑布; Jiǎolóng Pùbù), which at around 1000m is the highest waterfall in Taiwan. It's bone dry in winter but has a magnificent flow in summer. The fall is southeast of the village, about an hour's walk.

We've never seen so many deep valleys cut into a picturesque landscape as in Fengshan. One of them, **Shimeng Valley** (石夢谷; Shímèng Gǔ), a rough canyon west of the village, is a must-visit in summer as it has one deep **swimming hole** after another. It takes about an hour to walk to the area with the swimming holes and three hours to the valley itself. The trail is actually a very rough road almost impassable even with a jeep.

Shipan Valley (石盤峭谷; Shípán Qiàogǔ) used to have six waterfalls along its hour-long path but several of them have been destroyed over the years by earthquakes and typhoons. It's still a scenic place to explore, and during summer the remaining falls have a heavy flow. There's an interesting rock-climbing area at the end of the trail. The valley is about a 40-minute walk north of the village.

Sleeping & Eating

There are a few local eateries around the village and the B&Bs have their own restaurants.

Fengye Shan Zhuang B&B (楓葉山莊; Fēngyè Shānzhuāng; ☎ 266 1197; fongshan123@yahoo.com.tw; d/tw NT1800/2500, weekdays NT1500/2200) Has simple rooms in a guesthouse with spacious grounds located down a quiet rural lane. The owner is a very friendly, helpful local who really knows the land. To get to the B&B, keep going down the main road after crossing the bridge, and turn left at the corner just past an orange house on the right. Take the second left and the B&B is prominent on the right.

Shopping

You usually can't buy tea in Fengshan as it's mostly grown for individual consumption, but you can purchase unusual coloured teapots (NT1500) made from calcified limestone. The teapots have a light sandy colour (they look like you could eat them) and sparkle as if loaded with fool's gold. Calcified limestone is in fact sometimes called 'gold-plated stone'.

Getting There & Around

Fengshan is about a 40-minute drive (15km) from Rueili. As you drive up county road 149甲 (169 on some maps) you'll see the sign for Fengshan on the right. Turn and cross the new bridge (it should be ready by the time this book is out) and follow the road right as it heads into the village.

You'll need your own transport to get to Fengshan. Once there it's best to walk.

ALISHAN FOREST RECREATION AREA
阿里山
☎ 05

The high mountain resort of **Alishan** (Ālǐshān; adult/child NT150/100, during holidays NT200/100) has long been one of Taiwan's top tourist attractions. While many other spots around the island are as scenically splendid, Alishan has a peerless draw in the wonderful old narrow-gauge railway (one of only three in the world) that still runs the route up from Chiayi. Alishan is also one of the best places to see the sunrise, the sunset, and the glorious 'sea of clouds' phenomenon.

You can visit Alishan at any time of year, but weekdays are best as the crowds are thinner. The climate is cool even in summer (at least compared to lower altitudes). In spring and summer late-afternoon thunderstorms are common. During winter the mountaintops may get a light dusting of snow. Summer temperatures average from 13°C to 24°C, while those in winter are 5°C to 16°C. You should bring a coat or sweater and an umbrella or raincoat, no matter what time of year you visit.

Orientation

Despite its size, it's simple to get your bearings in Alishan. Most people stay in what is technically Zhongzheng Village, though most just refer to it as Alishan Village. The village comprises a car park, post office, police station, bus station, visitor centre and most of the hotels and restaurants.

WESTERN TAIWAN

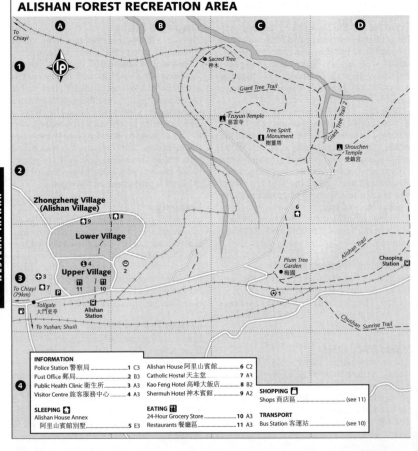

ALISHAN FOREST RECREATION AREA

INFORMATION				EATING 🍴		SHOPPING 🛍	
Police Station 警察局	1 C3	Alishan House 阿里山賓館	6 C2	24-Hour Grocery Store	10 A3	Shops 商店區	(see 11)
Post Office 郵局	2 B3	Catholic Hostel 天主堂	7 A3	Restaurants 餐廳區	11 A3		
Public Health Clinic 衛生所	3 A3	Kao Feng Hotel 高峰大飯店	8 B2			TRANSPORT	
Visitor Centre 旅客服務中心	4 A3	Shermuh Hotel 神木賓館	9 A2			Bus Station 客運站	(see 10)
SLEEPING 🛏							
Alishan House Annex 阿里山賓館別墅	5 E3						

Paths around the park are broad and attractions are usually marked with signs in English. Traffic is not permitted in the park, so you can walk on roads as well as trails without concern. With our basiç map of the area you will have no trouble finding your way around.

Information

For information about train and bus schedules, hotels, attractions and weather, check out the official website (www.ali.org.tw/en-index .php). There's an ATM in the village post office on the Cirrus network but you'd be advised to bring some cash with you.

Public health clinic (Wèishēngsuǒ ; ☎ 267 9806) The clinic has irregular hours, but is always open in the mornings and usually the afternoons. The clinic is just down the road from the Catholic Hostel, near the entrance gate to the park.

Visitor Centre (☎ 267 9917; ☺ 8am-5pm) Maps and brochures in English are available, though you can find the same ones in visitor centres in Taipei and other urban centres.

Sights & Activities
ALISHAN FOREST TRAIN

For many people, taking the train up to Alishan is the peak experience of their entire trip. For this is no ordinary train and certainly no ordinary ride. The Alishan Forest Train runs on narrow-gauge track (762mm) and begins at 30m, ascending to above 2200m in 3½ hours. The total length of track is 71km and includes 49 tunnels and 77 bridges. Along the way it passes through three climatic zones: tropical, subtropical and temperate.

Yes, there's a lot to take in; it really is as exciting as it sounds and the train ride is probably a must-do. Suffice to say the ride offers a very pleasant trip on a very special small train up very scenic landscape.

For more check out the forestry bureau's website on the train (http://railway.forest.gov.tw/ index-eng.asp).

SUNRISE

We're not big fans of sunrise viewings but it's *de rigueur* here. When you check into a hotel you will inevitably hear the question, '*Yàobúyào kàn rìchū?*', which means, 'Do you want to see the sunrise?' Say no, and you'll get a funny look as if you just committed a huge cultural faux pas.

Assuming you do go, there are two main viewing venues: the summit of **Chushan** (Zhùshān; 2489m) and **Tatajia** (Tǎtǎjiā), a mountain pass 2610m above sea level in nearby Yushan National Park.

To reach Chushan you can either take the train from Chaoping station (one way/round trip NT100/150, departure time varies according to the season), or hike up along the **Chushan Sunrise Trail** (Zhùshān Guānrìchū Bùdào). The train takes about 25 minutes, while hiking can take up to 1½ hours if you start in the village.

If you wish to see the sunrise at Tatajia, pay for a seat on one of the sunrise-tour minibuses (NT300, three hours). Every hotel can arrange it for you. Buses come directly to your hotel.

The minibus has several advantages over the train in that it stops at numerous scenic locations, such as the monkey-viewing area

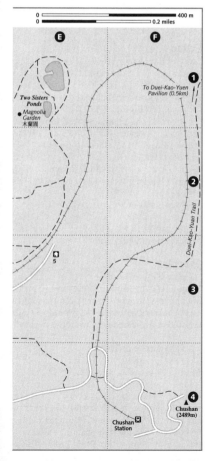

Two Sisters Ponds

Magnolia Garden 木蘭園

To Duei-Kao-Yuen Pavilion (0.5km)

Duei-Kao-Yuen Trail

Chushan (2489m)

Chushan Station

WESTERN TAIWAN

and the site of a few ancient trees on the way back from the sunrise viewing.

HIKING

There are many trails in the park, ranging from strolls around flower gardens to hikes up mountaintops requiring several hours or more to complete. On the **Giant Tree Trail** you'll find majestic old cypresses that are up to two thousand years old. For a bit of peace and quiet and a few hours workout on a natural path, the **Duei-Kao-Yueh Trail** (對高岳步道; Duìgāoyuè Bùdào) is just the ticket. The Chushan Sunrise Trail and the viewing platform, so busy at dawn, empty of people by the late morning.

For more information, including times and distances for trails, pick up the brochure at the visitor centre.

Festivals & Events

The **Cherry Blossom Festival** runs in March or April for two weeks while the trees are in bloom. This is an extremely busy time for the park. To our eyes though, Taiwanese cherry trees look spindly.

Sleeping

Alishan has more than a dozen hotels, but on weekends, during Chinese New Year, or the Cherry Blossom Festival, when more than 10,000 people a day visit the park, you could find yourself without a room if you didn't book in advance. The majority of hotels are in the village, behind and down from the car park. This is a convenient place to stay as there are a dozen or more places to eat, but it does feel as if you are staying in a big car park.

Most hotels offer weekday and low-season discounts, which can be up to 50%. Though heating in rooms was not standard a few years ago, it does seem to be now and there is usually no extra charge for it in winter.

Catholic Hostel (Tiānzhǔtáng; ☎ 267 9602; dm/d/tw NT250/1000/2000) The hostel is not always open (especially on weekdays) so call before you go.

Shermuh Hotel (Shénmù Bīnguǎn; ☎ 267 9511; fax 267 9667; s/d/tw NT1000/3200/4000) This newish hotel has clean, simply furnished rooms. For single travellers there are a limited number of tiny single-bed rooms that go for NT600 midweek.

Kao Feng (KF) Hotel (Gāofēng Dàfàndiàn; ☎ 267 9411; www.kaofeng.net.tw/kaofeng/kf-2_e.htm; d/tw NT3600/4800) Rooms at this new hotel with a modern look have comfy beds, wooden floors and a fairly spacious design.

Alishan House Annex (Ālǐshān Bīnguǎn Biéshù; ☎ 267 9811; 6-/8-person cabins NT5060/7700) Part of the Alishan House group, these charming cabins are set back among flowers and shrubs. Beatrix Potter would be right at home here. Note that the six-person cabins have a single open room, while the eight-person have sleeping and living quarters.

Alishan House (Ālǐshān Bīnguǎn; ☎ 267 9811, ext 6; r from NT6000) Set in a remodelled Japanese-era building, this is Alishan's top hotel. We love the new patio in the back, with its expansive mountain views, but feel some of the old-world charm has gone out of the place. But if you get a room on the west side you can see just how good the original design was: your chaise lounge by the window lets in mountain views during the day, sunsets in the evening, and moonlight during the night.

Eating

Most of the restaurants in Alishan are clustered around the car park and serve similar decent fare at similar prices: hotpots, stir-fries and local vegetables and meat dishes for around NT100 to NT200. Most are open for breakfast, lunch and dinner, though occasionally places close for one shift. Menus are starting to be available in English.

Note that while the Alishan House used to have a lovely old-fashioned dining room, it has been remodelled into a soulless banquet hall.

There is a 24-hour grocery shop in the car-park area. Instant noodles and hot and cold drinks are available. The shop has a microwave for heating up food.

Shopping

Alishan High Mountain Tea (Ālǐshān Gāo Shān Chá), dried plums, cherries, fruit liqueurs, tǒngzǎi mǐgāo (sticky rice) in almost every conceivable flavour and aboriginal crafts are sold in the shops back from the car lot.

Getting There & Away

BUS

From Chiayi buses to Alishan (NT214, 2½ hours) leave from the Chiayi County Bus Company station about every two hours from early morning to late afternoon. You can find the full schedule (in English) at the visitor centre in the train station at Chiayi or posted at the bus station itself. From Alishan to Chiayi buses leave from outside the 24-hour grocery store. The return schedule is posted in English.

TRAIN

There are three train stations in Alishan: the main Alishan station in Zhongzheng Village (this station was being rebuilt at the time of writing but we have been assured it will be ready by the time you read this). This is close to the main hotel area and most passengers disembark here. Chaoping is a few minutes away up the track. Chushan station, 25 minutes away, is where the train takes passengers in the morning to watch the sunrise.

The Alishan Forest Railway leaves Chiayi station (NT399, 3½ hours) daily at 9am and 1.30pm. Return times are 1.18pm and 1.40pm. During Chinese New Year and holidays extra trains are scheduled.

DANAYIGU ECOLOGICAL PARK
達那伊谷自然生態保育公園

If you have your own vehicle, plan on a side trip to Shanmei to see this remarkable **park** (Dánàyī Gǔ Zìrán Shēngtài Bǎoyù Gōngyuán; ☎ 05-258 6994; adult/child NT100/60, weekday NT80/40, parking scooter/car NT20/50; ⊗ 8am-5pm).

From 1989 to 1999 the Zhou people closed off the dying 18km Danayigu Creek to all outsiders. The plan was to clean up the river and protect and restock the dwindling fish population. The success of the project amazed everyone. Today, in certain natural river pools, literally hundreds of fish squirm and wiggle in as little as one shallow square metre of water. The concentration of fish is more akin to a healthy coral reef than a mountain stream (though some speculate that the Zhou stock the stream).

The surrounding parkland is a model of ecological diversity. Zhou tribesmen give tours of the park and while they speak only Mandarin, it can still be worthwhile to join in if only because you will be forced to stop every few feet to discover yet another species of plant life.

Food is available at several rustic shops. The barbecued wild boar and sausages are lean and delicious. At the time of writing a new walkway was being built around the park and you could not access the more interesting pools. Everything should be back to normal by the time you read this.

To reach the park, take Hwy 18 east of Chiayi towards Alishan. At Lungmei (龍美;

Lóngměi) you will see a sign directing you to Shanmei and Danayigu (Tanayiko) Ecological Park via County Rd 129 south. The trip from Chiayi takes about an hour by car. There is no public transport.

YUSHAN NATIONAL PARK
玉山國家公園

As hiking enthusiasts, Yushan National Park (Yùshān Guójiā Gōngyuán) gets our heart beating faster every time we hear its name or, better yet, pore over its borders on a map. The park takes its name from one of the highest mountains in East Asia. Yushan, which means Jade Mountain, attracts climbers from all over the world. The route up to the 3952m peak is surprisingly straightforward and is completely doable for anyone in decent shape.

In recent years a number of old trails throughout the park have been repaired and opened for the general public. Some of these trails cross the entire park and take a week or more to complete.

There's never been a better time for foreign visitors to come to Taiwan to climb its high mountains or just traverse across its alpine ridges. Why? The routes are in good shape, with well-located huts or camping grounds, and water sources in strategic locations. Trails are marked with distance posts and map boards. Good maps are available of the routes (though in Chinese only), and the restrictive Class A permit system has been altered so that local guides are no longer needed and you do not have to travel in large groups. A pair of foreign travellers, with the proper equipment, can now head out to explore some of the most pristine and beautiful parts of Taiwan.

Yushan covers over 100,000 hectares, or 3% of the landmass of Taiwan. It's the largest and most undeveloped of all the parks in Taiwan. It is also the grandest. There are 30 peaks over 3000m and six vegetative zones harbouring 50% of the endemic plant species in the country. The landscape is strikingly rugged, with deep valleys and high mountains. In general, the park tends to be wet in summer and dry in winter.

Yushan is not part of the Alishan National Scenic Area, but it is so close that many people come here on a day trip to admire the clear alpine views and perhaps do a few short hikes around the Tatajia area.

Orientation

Yushan National Park covers areas of Chiayi, Nantou, Kaohsiung and Hualien counties. A 20km drive west will take you to the Alishan Forest Recreation Area, while a drive from Tainan to Taitung on Hwy 20, the South Cross-Island Hwy (see Map p247), takes you through the southern portion of the park. From Yuli in the east, you can reach the Nanan section of the park, with its fantastic Walami Trail.

MAPS

Climbers can pick up maps of the area and hiking routes at the park headquarters in Shuili and outdoor shops, including those around the train station in Taipei. The maps give detailed daily itineraries including how long (in hours) each section takes to hike and the distances covered. They are in Chinese only but on the national park's website you can get general itineraries.

If you can get someone to translate the itinerary and pertinent places on the maps (cabins, peaks, water sources etc) you can use them in conjunction with the large park map (in English) that you can pick up at the national park visitor centres, or download from the website (www.ysnp.gov.tw; note you should go to Site Map first, then Downloads, then Mountain Hiking Route Map.)

At most visitor centres you can pick up a brochure called *Yushan National Park: Ecotourism Guide*, which has a map of the main peak trail with useful warnings and notices: safe here, foggy here, landslides common here, and so on.

Information

Other than in Meishankou and Tienchih in the south, and Dongpu just outside the park boundaries in the north, there is no accommodation. The park has a very informative website (http://english.ysnp.com.tw). For information on permits see p330. Note that the Yushan Main Peak Trail is a very popular route and only 150 hikers a day are allowed on it. You have almost no chance of getting a permit on the weekend. If this is your only available time, contact a hiking club (p330). Other routes through the park are less popular.

For information on hiking routes, as well as current trail, road and weather conditions, and details of the plant and animal life in the park, check out www.ysnp.gov.tw.

There are four visitor centres for the park: Meishankou (p263); Nanan (p200); the park headquarters at Shuili (p221), an hour north of the actual park; and **Tatajia** (☎ 049-270 2200; 🕙 9am-4.30pm, closed 2nd & 4th Tue of every month. If these are national holidays, closed Wed), which is the visitor centre closest to the trailhead for the main peak. All can provide maps (in English), brochures and information on current trail conditions.

Hiking

On the trails, signs are usually in English and Chinese, and there are distance posts every 500m. Cabins are simple and have rough bedding, and some have running water and solar lights. If you are doing the Yushan peaks trails you will have no worries about water, but for other areas confirm with the national park that the water sources on the maps are stable (according to the authorities we spoke to at the time of writing they are, but please confirm before you head out). Before beginning any hike make sure you drop into the local police squad and park office to have your mountain permit checked. For the main Yushan peak you do this right at the start of the trail at Tatajia. If you are starting in Dongpu, carry your papers with you.

The best time to hike in the park is in the autumn and early spring (October to December and March to April). May has monsoon rains, and typhoons are a problem from June to September, though if there is no typhoon you can certainly hike (though the sun is awfully fierce). In winter the peaks are covered with snow.

Note that there is nowhere to buy supplies in the area. Be aware that fog can come in anytime and bring your hike to a halt. Have everything you need for overnighting when you head out.

Note also that Yushan peak is usually closed for almost two months every winter to give the environment a rest.

YUSHAN MAIN PEAK 玉山主峰

The trail to the **main peak** (Yùshān Zhǔfēng) starts in **Tatajia** (塔塔加; Tǎtǎjiā) a mountain pass where people often go to watch the sunrise on an excursion from Alishan. It's about 8.5km or a five- to six-hour hike to the **Paiyun Cabin** (排雲山莊; Páiyún Shānzhuāng), where hikers can spend the night. The next day, a 2.4km climb (about three hours) leads to the summit

(3952m). After resting, climbers then return to Paiyun Cabin (1½ hours), gather their gear and hike back to Tatajia (four hours).

It is also possible to climb Yushan starting in Dongpu in the north, or starting in Tatajia and then continuing on to Dongpu (this is a good option for people without transport). This is a longer route and takes three days to complete but many people consider it to be the more scenic way.

To do all five peaks of Yushan (main, north, south, east and west) takes about five days.

JAPANESE OCCUPATION ERA BATONGGUAN TRAVERSING ROUTE 八通關日據越道線

This 90km-long trail (Bātōngguān Rìjù Yuèdào Xiàn) was constructed during the time of the Japanese occupation to facilitate a policy of carefully managing aboriginal groups in remote mountainous regions. The trail is remote, and for years it was in rough shape, with washed-out bridges and barely passable sections of trail. After three years of reconstruction it was opened to the general public in late 2005.

The trail starts in Dongpu and ends in Nanan, near Yuli on the east coast. It takes seven to 10 days to complete. There are cabins, camping grounds and water sources along the way. The area is still prone to landslides and washouts, so always check on conditions before heading out.

SOUTH CROSS-ISLAND HIGHWAY SECTION 2 TRAIL 南二段線

This seven-day trail (Nán Èrduàn Xiàn) runs from Dongpu to the South-Cross Island Hwy. Though a long hike it is considered easier than the Japanese Occupation Era Batongguan Traversing Trail and can be accomplished by most hikers who are fit and carrying the proper equipment. There are cabins, camping grounds and water sources along the length of this incredible trail.

One notable section of the trail passes **Jiaming Lake** (嘉明湖; Jiāmíng Hú), which was formed by a meteorite strike 4000 years ago. You can camp out here, and enjoy one of the most inspiring alpine scenes in all Taiwan.

Other hikes include Walami Trail (p200) and Guanshan (p263).

Tours

The park organizes hikes to Yushan main peak (around NT5000) twice a month from October to December. Call one of the visitor centres for reservations. If you are looking for a hike where English is spoken, contact Freshtreks (www.freshtreks.com) or 523 Mountaineering Association (www.523.org .tw/English/index). The latter can help with hiring drivers.

Getting There & Away

Public transport is limited but most trails can be done this way (for information on hiring a driver, see p330). Hikers can reach the trailhead to Yushan main peak by taking a sunrise shuttle bus from Alishan. Since there is no transport back from Tatajia they should continue on to Dongpu as there are buses from this location.

DONGPU (TUNGPU) 東埔

pop 500

Just over the northern tip of Yushan National Park, or directly south of Sun Moon Lake, sits the hot-spring village of Dongpu (Dōngpǔ; elevation 1200m). The village is a popular destination for hikers looking for a good workout, good weather, remarkable scenery and the chance to soak in a nice tub at the end of it all. Of course, lovers of hot springs are fond of the place, too. The spring is a carbon-acid hot spring, delivering clear and odour-free water with an average temperature of 50°C that's considered to be of quite a high quality.

For hikes through Yushan National Park see the previous section. If you just want to hike for the day you can go along the trail to Yushan for a few hours without the need for a permit. Make sure you are well prepared for all hikes to higher elevations and always ask about conditions before you head out.

There are plenty of hot-spring hotels in Dongpu. For an inexpensive option, try the **Youth Activity Centre** (青年活動中心; Qīngnián Huódòng Zhōngxīn; ☎ 049-270 1515; 64 Dongpu Village; r from NT700) at the high end of town.

You can take a Yuanlin bus (NT112, 80 minutes) between Dongpu and Shuili. They run approximately every hour between 6am and 5pm.

Southern Taiwan

In the south, people's ties to rural folk culture are strongest. Local gods are more fervently worshipped, traditions more respected, and a clannish regard for kith and kin more obvious. And in a land of hospitable people, southerners shine as the most hospitable of all.

Outside of Taipei, the only cities really worth visiting are in the south: ie Tainan and Kaohsiung. Tainan has a temple heritage second to none, and a great array of local foods to sample. Kaohsiung is a harbour city on a mad drive to make up for decades of lost development time. Ten years ago we could hardly stand to drive past it. But these days you can feel the buzz (much like Taipei a decade ago) and couple of days here soaking it in would be well spent.

For some of the best mountain scenery in the country head to the South Cross-Island Hwy. This route literally crosses the island, and can be used as a walking path, with side trips up to 3000m-plus mountains and down to beautiful natural hot springs in the river valleys.

In fact, the south pretty much has it wrapped up for the nature-lover. There are two butterfly valleys – one of which (in Maolin) has recently been put on equal footing with the Monarch Butterfly Valley in Mexico – and a winter resting ground for the rare black-faced spoonbill. The southern landscape also varies from coastal mud flats, to grassy headlands, to majestic cypress forests.

Weatherwise, the south is hot and sticky in summer and warm and dry in winter. If you want to swim in January, head south.

HIGHLIGHTS

- Hike ancient forests and soak in natural hot springs along the **South Cross-Island Hwy** (p260)

- Bike through lush fields, eat traditional foods and shop at **Meinong** (p274)

- Explore Taiwan's temple heritage in the old capital of **Tainan** (p248)

- Swim or surf year-round in **Kenting National Park** (p282)

- Visit the winter resting grounds of the purple butterfly in **Maolin** (p277)

- Cross the southern tip of Taiwan on the **Jin-Shui Ying Old Trail** (p280), a steamy jungle route once used by the Qing dynasty military

- Get rained on with fireworks at **Yenshui** (p259)

- Scooter and snorkel around Taiwan's only coral island, **Little Liuchiu Island** (p281)

- Watch a ceremonial boat burn to the ground in **Donggang** (p280)

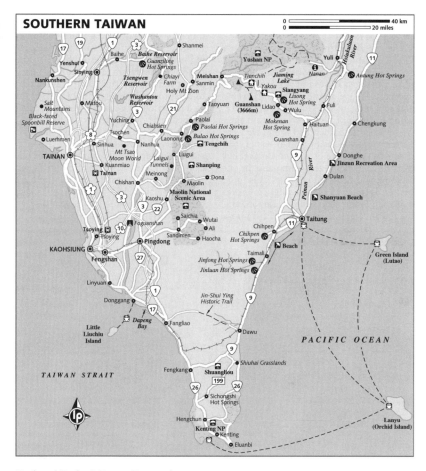

National Parks & Forest Recreation Areas

There are three national parks in the south. Beautiful, remote Maolin is a stronghold for aboriginal culture but also holds an important winter resting ground for the purple butterfly. The South Cross-Island Hwy runs through the southern end of Yushan National Park and there's some excellent hiking to be done there. Kenting National Park is a beach playground, though there are also some interesting protected areas few people venture into. Siangyang Forest Recreation Area is an excellent bird-watching venue. Shuangliou Forest Recreation Area has a gorgeous waterfall, while much of Tengchih Forest Recreation Area boasts intact virgin forest. Shanping Forest Recreation Area offers peaceful trails, abundant plant life, and excellent bird-watching. There's something for everyone in this part of Taiwan.

Getting There & Around

It's easy to get to and around the major urban centres by public transportation. The High-Speed Rail (HSR) is convenient for travel to Kaohsiung but not Tainan (the station is 40 minutes walk from downtown). Scooters and cars can be hired in the cities and are recommended for travel into the countryside where public transportation is poor, such as in Meinong, Maolin and along the South Cross-Island Hwy.

TAINAN CITY 台南市

☎ 06 / pop 754,917

We've always been very fond of Tainan (Táinán), and always impressed with its array of temples and historical relics. But we often wondered if we simply needed to get out more. So one day we travelled to Beijing and saw some of the greatest architectural wonders of the Chinese world. And then we returned to Tainan and found we were no less impressed with it than before. No, it couldn't compare directly to Beijing, but then travel is not a zero sum game in our opinion, and the wonderful deserves to be praised as much as the amazing.

Tainan is the oldest city in Taiwan, and the fourth largest. It was here that Taiwan's modern history began and it is here that much of its traditional culture continues to thrive. Outside Dutch-built forts, lively night markets sell dishes exclusive to the region. Inside hundreds-of-years-old temples, people *bobui* (toss divination sticks) to determine the best course of action, just as their ancestors did when the temple first opened. The only difference is that today, people then jump into their cars and head to air-conditioned homes.

But no-one seems worried by the dichotomy. Modernity is embraced in Tainan as much as the past is respected. There are shopping malls, luxury hotels, sharp-looking cafés and trendy bars. But there is also an approved NT3-billion-dollar budget for re-

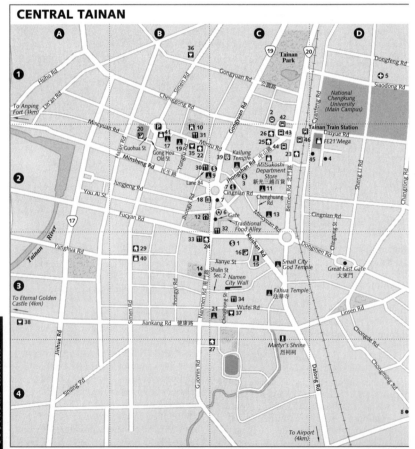

CENTRAL TAINAN

viving and restoring the old harbour area of Anping and its trove of historical sights. Tainan has industries producing metals, textiles and machinery, a few old masters working on traditional crafts, as well as a new science park that promises to bring the city into the avant-garde of Taiwan's hi-tech revolution.

You can visit Tainan any time of year, though we love winter when it's warm (in the high twenties on average) and dry, and few tourists are about (try and find all those conditions in Beijing). Traditional festival days are of course a great time to come, as are the birthdays of temple gods. Give yourself at least a couple of days here to see the sights and observe the local culture.

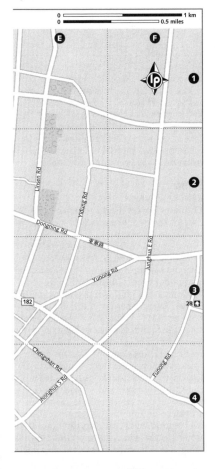

History

The Chinese first settled in the Tainan area in 1590. Not long after, the Dutch arrived. After colonising the island, the Dutch used Tainan as a base for their trade with Japan and China. The Dutch ruled from 1624 until 1662, the year they were expelled by the Ming loyalist Koxinga.

Koxinga established his central government in Tainan and built up the city. In 1683, when the Qing dynasty regained control of Taiwan and turned it into an official province, Tainan was chosen as the capital. Tainan remained the political, cultural and economic centre of the island until 1885, when the capital moved to Taipei. If you have a discerning eye, Tainan's pedigree is apparent by the stately quality of the city's temples and historical sights.

Orientation

Almost all the sights in Tainan are concentrated around the city centre (west of the train station) and the Anping District. Both areas are compact enough to get around on foot, though you may want a taxi or bus to take you from one area to the other.

Please note the English spelling on road signs in Tainan has changed since the last edition. It may change again before the shelf life of this one expires.

Information

Tainan is probably the most English-friendly city in Taiwan after Taipei. Nearly every sight worth seeing has English interpretation signs around it. Large map boards guide you along a walking-tour route similar to ours, though not identical (ours was first).

CULTURAL CENTRES

Tainan Municipal Cultural Centre (Map pp248-9; ☎ 269 2864; 332 Jhonghua E Rd, sec.3; ☼ 9am-5pm)

INTERNET ACCESS

National Museum of Taiwanese Literature (Map pp248-9; ☎ 221 7201; www.nmtl.gov.tw; 1 Jhongjheng Rd; ☼ 8am-5pm, closed Mon) You can get free internet access in the library here.

INTERNET RESOURCES

Tainan City Government (www.tncg.gov.tw) A good resource, especially for anyone staying in Tainan long term. It can be a bit tricky to navigate but there is a wealth of information (and pictures) on everything there is to see, do and consume in the city.

LAUNDRY
Laundromat (Map pp248–9; 111-1 Yu Le St; 24hr)
Behind the train station, to the right of the FE21' Mega department store, is DIY laundry.

MEDICAL SERVICES
National Cheng Kung University Hospital (Map pp248–9; 235 3535; 138 Sheng Li Rd)

MONEY
There are ATMs in most 7-Elevens (which are everywhere) in Tainan. You can use the ATMs or change money at the following:
Bank of Taiwan (Map pp248–9; 155 Fucyan Rd, sec.1)
International Commercial Bank of China (ICBC; Map pp248–9; 90 Jhongshan Rd)

PHOTO STUDIO
Fuji photo shop (Map pp248–9; 5 Nanmen Rd)

POST
GPO (Map pp248–9) Near the North Bus Station.

TOURIST INFORMATION
FYI South Magazine (www.taiwanfun.com) A free monthly entertainment magazine. You can pick up a copy at the information centre or many restaurants across town. You can also download it at the website. The magazine's

pull-out map is especially useful as it's completely bilingual and up to date with the changes to the English spellings on road signs.
Visitor Information Centre (Map pp248–9; 229 0082; 8.30am-5.30pm Mon-Fri, 8am-6pm Sat & Sun) There are two centres in Tainan but the most convenient one for travellers is right in the train station. Staff speak English and have all the information you could need.

Sights
CENTRAL TAINAN
Chikan Towers (Fort Proventia) 赤崁樓
One of the best preserved, or perhaps we should say reconstructed, historical sights in Tainan is this old **fort** (Chikǎn Lóu; Map pp248–9; 212 Minzu Rd; adult/child NT50/25; 8.30am-9pm). It's a splendid place to roam around, or even enjoy an outdoor concert on the weekends.

Chihkan has gone through many masters (Ming, Qing, Japanese and the Kuomingtang or KMT, China's Nationalist party) since the foundations were first laid by the Dutch in 1653. At that time the seashore reached the fort's outer walls. Our favourite features are the nine stone turtles with tablets on their backs. These steles hail from the Qing dynasty and if you check the backs you can see where the carver made a mistake on one and, rather than starting over with a fresh slab, simply turned the stone around and redid everything on the other side. The craftsmanship is amazing.

There are English explanations around the site as well as a brochure you can pick up when you enter. At night the whole area around the fort is filled with shops and vendors selling traditional foods.

Official God of War Temple (Sacrificial Rites Temple) 祀典武廟

This is the oldest and most impressive **temple** (Sì Diǎn Wǔ Miào; Map pp248-9; 229 Yongfu Rd, sec.2) in Taiwan dedicated to Kuan Kung, a Han dynasty general deified as the war god.

The temple's overall size and structure were established in 1690, though much splendid artwork and many historically valuable objects have been added over the years. The long deep rose-colored walls of this temple have always been one of its highlights for us. Other interesting features to note are the beggar seats built into the doorframe (so that the poor could beg alms from every visitor), the high threshold at the entrance (originally designed to keep women out!), and the bamboo-shaped poem on a scroll at the back, which contains words said to have been written by Kuan Kung himself.

Matsu Temple 大天后宮

This lively **temple** (Dà Tiānhòu Gōng; Map pp248-9; 18 Lane 227, Yongfu Rd, sec.2) once served as the palace of Ning Jin, the last king of the Ming dynasty. If you wish to confirm visually that a king's status is lower than an emperor's, count the steps to the shrine. There are only seven; an emperor would have nine.

Matsu is the most popular folk deity in Taiwan, with over 500 temples dedicated to her around the island. For more on Matsu see p216.

Some features to note (besides the elaborate carvings and paintings) include the 300-year-old Matsu statue, and the shrine in the back to Matsu's parents in an area that used to be King Ning Jin's bedroom. Look up and you'll see the roof beam where the king's concubines hanged themselves so many years ago (see Wufei Temple, p252).

For fun, check out the eyes and feet of the door guards. Notice something odd?

Altar of Heaven 天壇

Have you had a run of bad luck lately? Then visit this **temple** (Tiāntán; Map pp248-9; 16 Lane 84, Jhongyi Rd, sec.2) and pray to the supreme Taoist entity, the Jade Emperor (or Lord of Heaven),

to help you out. Tainan families have been doing this for generations on the 1st and 15th of every month.

The temple is noteworthy for two things. First, it has no statue of the god. The original temple was established as a temporary measure – 300 years ago! Second, there's a famous *Yī* (One) inscription over the altar. *Yī* signifies that for heaven and earth there is only one true way: humanity and righteousness.

National Museum of Taiwanese Literature 國家台灣文學館

The building that houses the new **museum** (Guó Jiā Táiwān Wénxué Guǎn; Map pp248-9; ☎ 221 7201; www .nmtl.gov.tw; 1 Jhongjheng Rd; admission free; ☯ 8am-5pm, closed Mon) was once the Tainan District Hall. Built in 1916 by the Japanese, it's a gorgeous example of colonial architecture. Even if literature is not your greatest interest, it's worth coming here just to wander the halls and relax in the foyer.

The museum highlights the development of Taiwanese literature from pre-Han aboriginals through the colonial periods up to the modern era. All exhibits and displays have English signs.

Confucius Temple 孔廟

You expect a **Confucius Temple** (Kǒng Miào; Map pp248-9; http://confucius.cca.gov.tw/; 2 Nanmen Rd; adult/ child NT50/25; ☯ 8.30am-9pm) to exude the calm, grace and dignified beauty of traditional Chinese culture, and this, the first Confucian temple in Taiwan, doesn't disappoint. Nor do the grounds, which contain one of the largest and most beautiful banyan trees in all of Taiwan.

The temple grounds are free (and nice to sit in at night), but you must pay to enter the palace area. The receipt comes with an excellent short brochure and map of the temple. One thing to look for that is not on the

---

SIGHT PASS

If you plan to visit all the major sights, buy a pass (NT150, good for one year) at any of the following: Confucius Temple, Chihkan Towers, Koxinga Shrine, Anping Fort, Eternal Golden Castle, and the Former Tait & Co Merchant House.

Unless otherwise noted, temples are free and open from 9am till 5pm.

brochure is the stone tablet on the right as you enter the Edification Hall. The words on the tablet explain the school rules (the site was once a centre for Confucian studies), such as prohibitions against gambling, drinking and cheating.

At the time of writing there was a lot of work being done to the grounds beside the temple. Expect new walkways, ponds and a museum.

Across the street from the temple entrance is a **stone arch** built in 1777. It's now the gateway to a pedestrian street filled with cafés and small eateries.

Great South Gate 大南門城

The garrison commander in you will love the martial feel of this old **city gate** (Dà Nánmén Chéng; Map pp248-9; Lane 34, Nanmen Rd; admission free; ☾ 8.30am-5.30pm), the only one in Tainan that still has much of its defensive wall intact. The inner grounds feature several cannons and a section of the old wall marvellously overgrown with thick roots. As with the Confucius Temple, the trees here are an attraction in themselves.

Koxinga's Shrine 延平郡王祠

When the Ming dynasty was overthrown by the Manchus in 1661, Koxinga (Cheng Cheng-kung) led his army to Taiwan with plans to restock supplies and then retake the mainland. He found the Dutch already here, but after nine months battle they surrendered and departed Taiwan.

Koxinga did much to improve conditions on the island. But, like the KMT of modern times, he did not live to see the Mainland retaken. He died after only a year in Taiwan, and his grandson surrendered to the Manchus in 1683.

There's a certain atmosphere of dignity surrounding the **Koxinga Shrine** (Yánpíng Jùnwáng Cí; Map pp248-9; 152 Kaishan Rd; adult/child NT50/25; ☾ 8.30am-5.30pm), even though most of it is of rather recent origin: the original southern-style temple was rebuilt in a northern style by the KMT government in the '60s. Many of the artefacts are historical, however, including the boxes in the shrine that hold the original imperial edict from 1874 permitting the shrine to be built.

Beside the shrine there's an interesting **museum** featuring displays of traditional puppets and clothing.

Lady Linshui's Temple (Chen Ching Gu Temple) 臨水夫人媽廟

This elaborately designed and excessively ornamental **temple** (Línshǔi Fūrén Mǎ Miào; Map pp248-9; 1 Jianye St) is dedicated to a woman – in this case, the goddess Lady Linshui.

For generations now, women have come to this temple to ask Lady Linshui to protect their children. This is demanding work and the goddess employs 36 assistants (three for each month), whose statuettes can be seen in little glass vaults around the inside walls of the temple.

In addition to offerings of incense, you'll often see flowers, face powder and make-up left at the temple.

Wufei Temple 五妃廟

When Koxinga's grandson surrendered to the Manchus in 1683, all hope of restoring the Ming dynasty ended. King Ning Jin, the last contender for the Ming throne, knew his time was up. Before he committed suicide, however, he urged his concubines to 'get thee to a nunnery'. The concubines refused, claiming their honour was as important as the king's, and hanged themselves on a roof beam in the bedroom of his palace. The palace is now the shrine to Matsu's parents at the Matsu Temple (p251) and the beam is still in place.

This dainty **temple** (Wǔfēi Miào; Map pp248–9), off Wufei Rd, was constructed in the concubines' honour and now sits in a 2000-sq-metre garden park. Note that the real tombs of the concubines are behind Koxinga's shrine and are covered with cement.

Dongyue Temple 東嶽殿

People often come to this **temple** (Dōngyuè Diàn; Map pp248-9; 110 Mincyuan Rd) to communicate with the dead through spiritual mediums. It's a fascinating place to catch a glimpse of Taiwanese folk culture.

The first chamber of the temple holds the city god, Chenghuang; the second, Zizang Wang, the Buddhist king of the underworld; the last, a number of demon gods who rule the underworld.

The disturbing yet fascinatingly grim murals on the walls of the second chamber are as graphic as the depictions of hell by Hieronymus Bosch: there are disembowelments, eye gougings, stabbings, boilings and so much more.

City God Temple 城隍廟

The city god tallies our good and bad deeds in this life, after we die. Hence it is not unusual that his image appears in the Dongyue Temple, dedicated to underworld, nor that these two temples are very close to each other.

When you enter the **City God Temple** (Chénghuáng Miào; Map pp248-9; 28 Guosheng Rd) you'll see two large abacuses. These are used to calculate if you have done more good than bad in life. Overhead is large sign with a gold inscription that translates roughly as 'You've come at last'.

The pink slips of paper you often see on the altar are from students asking for help to pass an exam. Yep, school is hell everywhere.

ANPING 安平區

After central Tainan, the western Anping (Ānpíng) District has the most interesting concentration of relics and temples. In recent years the area has undergone a dramatic face-lift as part of a NT3 billion plan to revive, restore and recreate the historical district. As in central Tainan, almost all sights have English signs and there are map boards everywhere.

From Chihkan Towers it's only 2km to the start of the canal leading directly to Anping. But if you don't feel like walking, take city bus 2 or weekend tour bus 88 or 99 from the North or South Bus Station.

Anping Fort (Fort Zeelandia) 安平古堡

In 1624 the Dutch seized the area known as Anping to establish a military and commercial base in Taiwan. This **fort** (Ānpíng Gǔbǎo; Map p253; adult/child NT50/25; 8.30am-5.30pm) was a stronghold of Dutch power until captured by Koxinga in 1661. Though most of the fort has been reconstructed, it's still an impressive site.

Anping Matsu Temple 安平天后宮

The Matsu Temple (Ānpíng Tiānhòu Gōng; Map p253) in Anping is yet another of the 'first' Matsu temples in Taiwan. But it does genuinely feature what many believe to be the oldest Matsu statue. It's not the one you think (the biggest one in the back shrine), however, but the middle one in the second row of smaller Matsu statues.

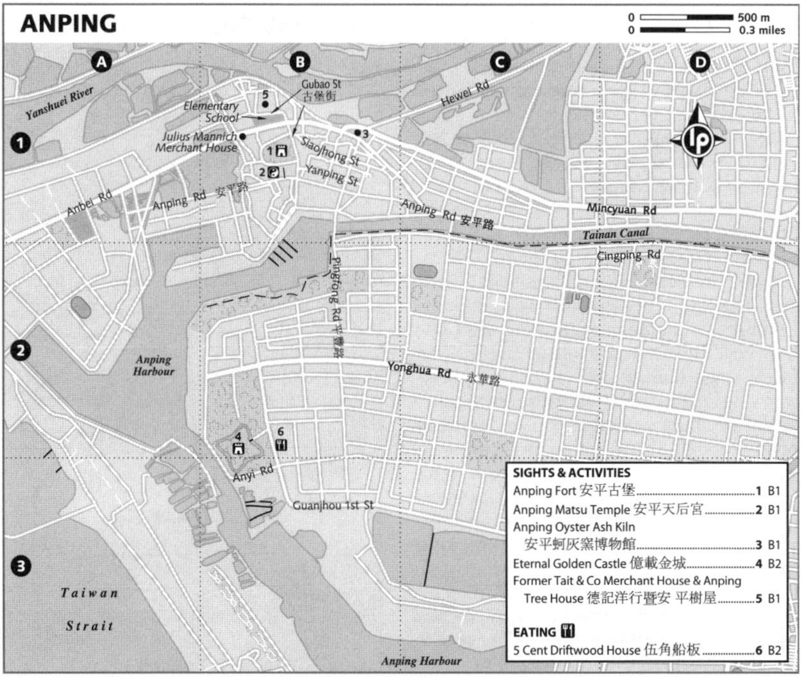
ANPING
0 500 m
0 0.3 miles
A
B
C
D
1
2
3
Yanshuei River
Elementary School
Gubao St 古堡街
Julius Mannich Merchant House
Hewei Rd
Siaojhong St
Yanping St
Anbei Rd
Anping Rd 安平路
Mincyuan Rd
Tainan Canal
Cingping Rd
Pingfong Rd 平豐路
Anping Harbour
Yonghua Rd 永華路
Anyi Rd
Guanjhou 1st St
Taiwan Strait
Anping Harbour
SIGHTS & ACTIVITIES
Anping Fort 安平古堡 1 B1
Anping Matsu Temple 安平天后宮 2 B1
Anping Oyster Ash Kiln 安平蚵灰窯博物館 3 B1
Eternal Golden Castle 億載金城 4 B2
Former Tait & Co Merchant House & Anping Tree House 德記洋行暨安 平樹屋 5 B1
EATING
5 Cent Driftwood House 伍角船板 6 B2

Near the altar you can pick up a little packet of 'safe rice' to take home. The packets are designed to keep you and your family safe.

The Former Tait & Co Merchant House and Anping Tree House
德記洋行暨安平樹屋

The **merchant house** (Déjì Yángháng; Map p253; Gubao St; adult/child NT50/25; 8.30am-5pm) was built by the British in 1867 and now holds a permanent exhibit of household artefacts from the 17th century (donated by the Dutch government). Through a series of decorated rooms, the exhibit highlights the lifestyle of Dutch, Chinese and aboriginal families.

Anping Tree House (Ānpíng Shùwū), on the same grounds as the merchant house, stands out with the large banyan growing in the gutted centre.

Anping Oyster Ash Kiln
安平蚵灰窯博物館

It's generally believed that the Dutch taught the Taiwanese to make a durable brick mortar using crushed oyster shells mixed with sugar water and sticky rice. At one time, oyster-shell kilns (which produced the ground-oyster ash) were a common sight in Tainan. The ruins of this **kiln** (Ānpíng Kē Huīyáo Bówùguǎn; Map p253; Anbei Rd; admission free; 9.30am-5pm, closed Mon) represent the last of its kind.

The kiln is nothing special to look at but it's still worth a visit to learn more about this little-known industry.

Eternal Golden Castle 億載金城

Like many famous sights around Tainan, this **fort** (Yìzǎi Jīn Chéng; Map p253; adult/child NT50/25; 8.30am-5pm) goes by different names: Erkunshen Cannon Fort, Anping Big Cannon Fort and Eternal Golden Castle. The fortress was built in 1876 to shore up Taiwan's defences against the Japanese threat.

Not much remains of the original fortress; oddly, though, the intact arched front gate was built with bricks pilfered from Anping Fort. The reconstructed fort and the cannons make for good photo ops. It's possible now, and recommended, to walk to the castle from the other sights in Anping.

If you are heading to the castle directly from the train station you can catch city bus 14, or tour bus 88 or 99 on the weekend, from the North or South Bus Station.

Walking Tour

The following walking tour covers all of the major temples and sights in central Tainan. You'll have plenty of opportunity to sample local snacks and drinks along the way, so it's best to go on a light or empty stomach. Some people have told us they prefer to do the tour backwards so they can end around the quiet Confucius Temple instead of the busy Chihkan Towers area.

After you've taken in your fill of history and fine writing at the **National Museum of Taiwanese Literature** (**1**; p251), head south a block to the peaceful **Confucius Temple** (**2**; p251) on Nanmen Rd. A few blocks south on Nanmen you'll find the martial **Great South Gate** (**3**; p252) and just east on Shulin a large section of the **old wall** (**4**; p252) that used to connect with the gate.

WALK FACTS

Start National Taiwan Museum of Literature
Finish Matsu Temple
Distance 6km
Duration Four to six hours

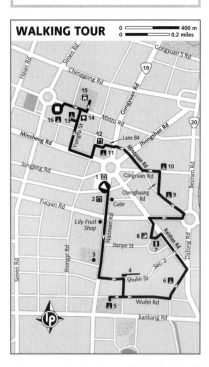

SOUTHERN TAIWAN

On Shulin St, take the first right and head down a quiet lane filled with quaint cafés and teahouses. When you reach Wufei St, check out the dainty **Wufei Temple** (**5**; p252), built to honour the concubines of the last contender for the Ming throne.

Now look for building No 76 on the left as you head east down Wufei St. When you see the number, turn left onto a small lane. Fifty metres on the left you'll see the grounds of the 300-year-old **Fahua Temple** (**6**). When the temple was first built, the ocean reached the edge of the outer wall.

Continue up the alley until you reach a large intersection. Head north up Kaishan Rd until you see **Koxinga's Shrine** (**7**; p252) on the left. When you leave the compound, take the back right gate to visit **Lady Linshui's Temple** (**8**; p252). You'll mostly see women at this elaborate temple, asking for protection for their children from Lady Linshui and her 36 helpers.

Now get back on Kaishan Rd and turn right at the intersection. Head east down Fucyan Rd and then turn left at the big intersection onto Mincyuan Rd. At the **Dongyue Temple** (**9**; p252) check out the terrifying visions of hell painted on the walls.

Continue up Mincyuan to Chenghuang Rd and turn right. At the end of this short street you'll see the **City God Temple** (**10**; p253) across the road.

Now head west down Cingnian and then turn right up Mincyuan. Cross Gongyuan and turn left. You'll see a bank and then a small alley. Turn right into the alley to get to the **Altar of Heaven** (**11**; p251). If you're hungry, consider the seafood at **A Xia Restaurant** (**12**; p256).

When you leave the alley, it's a quick left and then a right onto Minsheng. A block later, turn right up Yongfu St. Two blocks ahead you'll see the beautiful deep rose-coloured walls of the **Official God of War Temple** (**13**; p251) on the left and **A Chuan Melon Drink** and **Tainan Kuang Tsai Embroidery Shop** (**14**; p257 and p257) on the right. Don't miss a gander at the fantabulous works of one of the last masters of embroidery in Tainan.

Now continue to the end of Yongfu St to the **Chihkan Towers** (**15**; p250). Legend has it that the old well here leads all the way to Anping Fort!

On the opposite side of the street, a tiny alley leads to the **Matsu Temple** (**16**; p251). Don't forget to check out the door guards and the roof beam! If you're hungry head back to Chihkan Towers and get something to eat at the nearby stalls.

Festivals & Events

Traditional Chinese holidays such as the Dragon Boat Festival, Lunar New Year and the Lantern Festival are celebrated in a big way in Tainan. See p337 for more about each of these. In addition, the birthdays of the various temple deities – Matsu (the 23rd day of the 3rd lunar month), Confucius (28 September), Lady Linshui – usually feature colourful and lively events at the respective temples.

Sleeping

BUDGET

Tainan City Labour Recreation Centre (Táinánshì Láogōng Yùlèzhōngxīn; Map pp248-9; ☎ 215 0174, ext 6; fax 215 0177; 261 Nanmen Rd; 南門路261號; s/d/tw NT470/570/700) Part of the Youth Guesthouse Network (p328) but anyone can stay here. Rooms are ageing and sheets are threadbare, but it's clean and central and an OK price. There's laundry on the 3rd floor. To get to the centre, take bus 2 from the North or South Bus Station.

Cheng Kuang Hotel (Chéng Guāng Bīnguǎn; Map pp248-9; ☎ 222 1188; 294 Beimen Rd; 北門路294號; d/tw NT650/1000) Rooms are small, simply furnished but well maintained, except for some bathrooms that have mould going black. If this bothers you, ask for another room. This hotel is conveniently close to the train station.

Hann Gong Hotel (Hànggōng Dàfàndiàn; Map pp248-9; ☎ 226 9115; 199 Jhongshan Rd; 中山路199號; d/tw from NT700/1300) Rooms are nondescript but clean, and the location, near the train station, is good.

Tainan Student Hostel (Táinán Xuéyuàn; Map pp248-9; ☎ 267 0526; cyctnsh@ma15.hinet.net; 1 Lane 300, Funong St, sec.1; 富農街一段300巷1號; d/tw NT1000/1450) The double and twin rooms are pretty plain, and the hostel is a bit out of central Tainan, but it's a good place to stay if you're a young traveller and want to meet young Taiwanese. There's a 15% weekday discount. To get to the hostel it's best to take a taxi first then figure out the bus route back.

MIDRANGE

Confucius Inn (Jiànqiáo Nánshāng Wénwù Huìguǎn; Map pp248-9; 4 Nanmen Rd; 南門路4號; ☎ 214 0033; fax 213 2277; r from NT1800, weekday NT1200, incl breakfast;

🖳) Our favourite midrange hotel in Tainan by a Confucian mile. This professionally run hotel, directly south of the Confucius Temple, could easily charge much more. Rooms have a spiffy modern décor, with large comfy beds. Extras like ADSL and laundry service are available, and the hearty Western breakfast is fantastic for a midrange hotel (think fried eggs, bacon wraps, wheat toast, cereal and fruit).

Cambridge Hotel (Jiànqiáo Dàfàndiàn; Map pp248-9; ☎ 221 9966; 269 Minzu Rd, sec.2; 民族路2段269號; d/ tw NT2400/2800; 🖳) Run by the same company as the Confucius Inn, the Cambridge is well positioned in the business district and just a stone's throw away from the Chihkan Towers. Facilities include underground parking, a business centre, ADSL in every room and direct service to the Tainan Science Park. Rooms are nicely furnished with modern conveniences and have passed all the latest fire-safety regulations.

Hotel Tainan (Táinán Dàfàndiàn; Map pp248-9; ☎ 228 9101; www.hotel-tainan.com.tw; 1 Chenggong Rd; 成功路1號; d/tw/ste NT3200/3600/4800; 🖳) For service and comfort this deserves to be in the top end but we're putting it here to let you know what a good deal it is, especially weekdays when a standard room goes for as low as NT2200. The hotel is a stone's throw from the train station, and about the only negative thing we have to say is that the outside does not do the inside justice. Rooms are comfortably furnished in a modern style and are regularly updated. Rooms also have ADSL. The hotel includes a business centre and health club. The buffet meals at the Jade Room Restaurant (meals NT290 to NT680; open breakfast, lunch and dinner) come highly recommended.

TOP END

Taiyih Landis (Dàyìlìzhì Jiǔdiàn; Map pp248-9; ☎ 213 5555; www.tayihlandis.com.tw; 600 Simen Rd, sec.1; 西門路1段 600號; d/tw/ste incl buffet breakfast NT5800/6200/8800; 🖳 🍴) The Landis is the only five-star place in town and one of the few hotels in the south deserving of the label. Rooms have an elegant modern décor, with plasma TVs and workstations. The hotel is close to the new upmarket Shin Kong Mitsukoshi Department Store, as well as a number of cultural attractions, and has its own top-notch food and beverage outlets. Package deals for two usually run at NT4000 a night.

Eating

For simple inexpensive noodle, rice and Japanese fast-food outlets, check out the area around Vie Show Cinemas, or behind the train station (the student area). For traditional food you can't beat the area around Chihkan Towers in the evenings. Look for *dànzǐ miàn* (擔仔 麵; noodles with a tangy meat sauce), *guāncái bǎn* (棺材板; coffin cake), and *hǎixiān zhōu* (海鮮粥; seafood congee).

The old street directly east of the Confucius Temple (through the gate) has turned into a pleasant pedestrian-only area with a dozen or more cafés and small restaurants. If you're hungry, you'll find something here.

CENTRAL TAINAN

Chi Kin Dandanman (Chì Kàn Dāndānmiàn; Map pp248-9; 180 Minzu St, sec.2; dishes NT40; ⏰ 24hr) This is a fun place to try traditional *dànzǐ miàn* as the restaurant is set in a Japanese-era merchant's house. *Dànzǐ miàn* means 'two baskets and a stick' and refers to the baskets used to carry the noodles around for sale. The dish is a simple, refreshing mix of noodles with a tangy meat sauce. This shop uses no MSG.

Lily Fruit Shop (Map pp248-9; ☎ 213 7522; 199 Fucyan Rd, sec.2; ⏰ 11am-11pm, closed 2 Mondays per month) Across from the Confucius Temple is this well-known shop, serving delicious *bào bīng* (刨冰; shaved iced and fruit; NT50) and fruit drinks.

Yu Shen Restaurant (Yòuxiàn Sùshí Xīcān; Map pp248-9; ☎ 214 1180; Chingjhong St; dishes NT120-200; ⏰ 11am-10pm) A popular vegetarian restaurant serving à la carte dishes. On a street with many quaint teahouses and cafés.

Green House (Map pp248-9; ☎ 224 4474; 3F, 21 Lane 196, Fucyan Rd, sec.1; dishes from NT150; ⏰ 10am-10pm) A long-running Western restaurant with a casual vibe, especially on the rooftop. Dishes include pasta, hamburgers and Mexican, and there are large, filling sandwiches (NT90 takeaway).

A Xia Restaurant (Ā Xiá Fàndiàn; Map pp248-9; ☎ 221 9873; 7 Lane 84, Jhongyi Rd, sec.2; dishes NT500-700) A popular seafood restaurant serving the freshest seafood in Tainan, now sporting a modern look. It's popular for weddings and other celebrations.

ANPING

The area close to Fort Anping is also well known for its local foods. It's fine during the day but we find the night market rather grubby and messy. Some snacks to look out for include *xiājuǎn* (蝦捲; shrimp rolls) and *yúwán tāng* (魚丸湯; fish ball soup).

5 Cent Driftwood House (WǔJiǎo Chuánbǎn; Map p253; ☎ 2999 3321; 88 Guangjhou Rd; 9-course set meal NT500-700) This is one place that you should at least have a gander at. It's across from the Eternal Golden Castle. Designed by an artist from Tainan County, who had no previous background in architecture, the house will strike you as either daring, original and awesome, or proof that people should stick to their field of expertise. The house is made from driftwood, railway ties, brick, stone, glass and other natural materials. It's massive inside, with an open interior fed with natural light. The outside is indescribable, though if we had to describe it we'd say it looks like a castle battling cancer. If this sounds harsh it isn't meant to be. The restaurant is a quirky, idiosyncratic work of love and we quite like it just the way it is.

Drinking

There are cafés and teahouses all around Tainan. One street with many pleasant options to try is Chingjhong St (慶中街), just south of the Nanmen City Wall on the way to Wufei Temple. For the latest pubs and cafés check out the *FYI South Magazine* listings.

A Chuan Melon Drink (Ā Chuān Dōngguāchá; Map pp248-9; 212 Yongfu Rd, sec.2; drinks from NT15; 9am-10pm) This well-known melon-drink stand is just across from the God of War Temple and often has people lining up for a beverage.

A few staples of the bar scene include **Armory Pub** (Map pp248-9; ☎ 226 9520; http://armorypub .net; 82 Gongyuan S Rd; drinks from NT120; 8pm-5am) and **Willy's Second Base** (Wēilì Èrlěi Jiǔbā; Map pp248-9; ☎ 291 1050; 321 Jiankang Rd, sec.3; drinks from NT120; 6.30pm-late, closed Mon). Note that both places serve meals and the Armory has a decent range of vegetarian options.

Entertainment

Vie Show Cinemas (Huánà Wēixiù Yǐngchéng; Map pp248-9; ☎ 600 5566; www.warnervillage.com.tw in Chinese; 8th fl, 60 Gongyuan Rd; adult/child NT240/240) You can book tickets online in English.

Shopping

Shin Kong Mitsukoshi Department Store (Táinán Xīntiāndì Xīnguāng Sānyuè; Map pp248-9; 658 Simen Rd, sec.1) Most older locals remember the days

when this location housed a prison and execution room, and not an upscale mall.

Shuang Chun Chang Shoes (Shuāng Quán Cháng Xiéháng; Map pp248-9; 316 Simen Rd, sec.2; 9am-10.30pm) For something traditional, check out the cute *mùjī* (wood slippers) at this old shop near the Matsu Temple.

Tainan Kuang Tsai Embroidery Shop (Guāngcǎi Shòu Zhuāng; Map pp248-9; ☎ 227 1253; 186-3 Yongfu Rd, sec.2) Across from one treasure of Tainan, the War God Temple, is this other; Mr Lin, one of the last remaining embroidery masters in Tainan. Mr Lin has been working at his craft since he was 16 (he's in his late 60s now) and in recent years has taken embroidery to a new, modern level. All his pieces have the light touch and expressiveness of a craftsman truly at the peak of his skills. The most famous and expensive samples of his work are the long Eight Immortals panels, which used to be popular at weddings and other special occasions. Such panels cost tens of thousands of Taiwanese dollars but this doesn't stop buyers from all over the world coming to the shop. For the less extravagant, smaller pieces can be purchased for a few thousand, and even browsers are more than welcome, as the sign outside the shop reads.

Getting There & Away

AIR

There are flights from Tainan to Taipei and Kinmen. **Far Eastern Air Transport** (☎ 260 1271), **Uni Air** (☎ 260 3683) and **Transasia Airways** (☎ 260 1273) have reservation counters in **Tainan Airport** (www.tna.gov.tw). There's a **visitor centre** (☎ 335 9209; 8.30am-5.30pm) at the airport with English-speaking staff who can help you with all your needs. There's also an ATM at the airport and a car-hire agency.

BUS

Buses to Taipei (NT500, five to six hours, every hour) leave from the **UBus Station** (Map pp248-9; ☎ 226 8108; 2 Beinan Rd) to the left of the train station. Buses also leave from a host of other bus stations to the right down Beinan Rd. Note that if you catch the UBus between midnight and 6am the fare is only NT260.

TRAIN

Tainan is a major stop on the Western Line. Trains to/from Taipei (fast/slow train

NT741/476, four/5½ hours) and Kaohsiung (fast/slow train NT107/50, 30 minutes/one hour) run every half hour from 5am to midnight.

The High-Speed Rail (HSR; NT1450, two hours) runs trains about every hour between Taipei to Tainan. Note the station is about 30 to 40 minutes south of the city centre.

Getting Around

TO/FROM THE AIRPORT & HIGH-SPEED RAIL (HSR)

Bus 5 to the airport leaves from the South Bus Station (NT18, 20 minutes, every hour). Buses to the HSR leave from the North Bus Station (NT40, 40 minutes, every hour).

BUS

City Bus

Tainan's city bus system (http://ebus.tncg .gov.tw) is pretty good and covers a wide area. Basic fares are NT18 and most buses run every 15 to 30 minutes. Note that the hub is across from the train station and there are two stations: North Bus Station and South Bus Station. Most city buses stop at either station, as do the tourist buses.

Tourist Bus

On the weekends, two tour buses (day pass NT60, every 30 minutes from 8.30am to 6pm) run to all the major sights. Bus 88 covers the cultural sights while bus 99 covers natural attractions including the Black-faced Spoonbill Reserve (right). Go to the train station visitor centre to purchase a ticket and a map of all the stops (it's in Chinese but the staff can help translate it).

SCOOTER

With an international driving licence you can rent scooters from several shops behind the train station for NT200 per day.

AROUND TAINAN

Taiwan Salt Museum (台灣鹽博物館; Taíwān Yén Bówùguǎn; 69 Yencheng Village, Cigu Township; adult/child NT100/80; 9am-5pm, closed 3rd Wed every month) is not a must-see, but if you are in the area do drop by. The 1st floor has English signs, and there are several movies to watch, including one about the back-faced spoonbill (see right). The 2nd-floor display of salt crystals from around the world is fascinating. We had no idea there was so much variety. Next

to the museum are several **salt mountains** (admission NT50; 9am-6pm Mon-Fri, to 8pm Sat & Sun) that look just like giant mounds of snow (there is a Santa and reindeer on display). Kids can climb and even slide down in places (where the salt has not hardened). To get to the museum and mountain head north up Hwy 17 from Tainan and look for the English signs.

The **Black-Faced Spoonbill Reserve** (黑面琵鷺野生動物保護區; Hēimiàn Pílù Yěshēng Dòngwù Bǎohùqū; ☎ 06-786 1000; Cigu Township) is a small section of wetlands on the west coast of Tainan County dedicated to protecting the extremely rare black-faced spoonbill. The bird, which gets its name from its comically long black bill, spends summer (May to September) in Korea and northern China and migrates to Tainan County for the winter. Once down to just a few hundred, the species now has closer to two thousand, though this is still tiny and the bird's future is by no means assured. If you visit the reserve you won't be able to see the birds up close but there are high-powered binoculars you can use for free. To get to the reserve drive north up Hwy 17 from Tainan or take tourist shuttle bus 99 from the hub across from the Tainan train station. For more information check out the website of the **Black-faced Spoonbill Conservation Association** (http://mail.tnssh.tn.edu.tw/~bfsa/en /index.html).

The majority of people in Tainan County worship Wang Yeh, who is both a Taoist god and a brother of the first emperor. **Nankunshen Temple** (南鯤身代天府; Nánkūnshēn Dàitiān Fǔ) is the oldest (established 1662) and most important Wang Yeh temple in the county. It's also a beautiful structure and larger than anything you'll find in Tainan City. On most Sundays the temple atmosphere explodes with exuberant displays of ritual devotion: there are fireworks, parades, chanting and, occasionally, self-mutilation. If possible, try to visit during the **Welcoming Festival for Wang Yeh** (20 April, lunar calendar) or the **Birthday of Wu-tzu-yeh** (10 September, lunar calendar). Buses to Nankunshen (NT121, 40 minutes, every hour) leave Tainan City from the Hsingnan bus station on Jhongshan Rd.

The **Baihe Lotus Festival** (白河蓮花季; Báihé Liánhuā Jì), in northern Tainan County, celebrates the blooming of the lotus flower. The two-month-long festival includes cycling tours through lotus fields, seed-shucking con-

---

YENSHUI FIREWORKS FESTIVAL 鹽水蜂炮

There may be nothing stranger in this land than the annual **Yenshui Fireworks Festival** (Yénshǔi Fēngpào) – or battle, or blowout – in which thousands of people place themselves willingly in the melee of exploding fireworks. Officially, the festival re-enacts the time when the people of Yenshui turned to Kuan Kong, the god of war and righteousness, to save them from a terrible epidemic.

It was 1875, and cholera was killing off the town; nothing known to man was helping. In desperation, people began to parade their gods through the town and set off noisy and smoky firecrackers to scare away evil disease-spreading spirits.

For the older generation, the current Yenshui festival still honours the old event, but for the younger crowd it's an opportunity to live life on the edge. Crowds of 100,000 or more can gather. It's hot, smoky, and tense, very tense. When a nearby 'beehive' is set off, thousands of bottle rockets fly at you and over you (though hopefully not through you). The noise deafens, the smoke blinds, and the rockets sting.

Some people travel from overseas every year to be part of the excitement. Tens of thousands more come in from all parts of Taiwan. Accidents, burns and lost eyes are all common, though most try to mitigate damage by wearing protective clothing. A motorcycle helmet is considered mandatory, as is thick, nonflammable clothing and earplugs. Many people also wrap a towel around their neck to prevent fireworks from flying up under their helmet.

If you're injured you should be able to find medical help nearby, but don't expect any sympathy. And certainly don't expect any compensation. You participate at your own risk.

The festival is getting bigger and bigger each year and more activities are being added to draw in the crowds. In 2007 a 14km-long chain of firecrackers was lit, breaking the Guinness record by 2km. The chain took 45 minutes to completely burn up.

Yenshui is in the north of Tainan County. You can reach the town by taking an express train to nearby Sinying and then a taxi. Be prepared to be out all night if you go, and take care of your valuables. The festival happens every year during Lantern Festival, two weeks after Chinese New Year.

For more information, and some fantastic footage, check out the website of an amateur New York filmmaker who was doing a documentary of the event at the time of writing (http://homepage .mac.com/glchin).

---

tests and photographic competitions. This is your chance to see what a country fair is like, Taiwanese style. The festival is held in July and August. The place to stay here is **Ama's Scenic Guesthouse** (阿嬤的家; ☎ 06-687 6899; fax 687 6531; Baihe Town; d/tw 2000/2400, with Youth Guesthouse card NT1500), but you better book early if you want a room. The guesthouse is set in the middle of lotus fields and every morning visitors are taken out on bikes to watch the lotus blossoms unfold. Note that except for during the festival times there is little reason to come to the area.

GUANZILING (KUANZILING) 關子嶺
☎ 06 / pop 2000

This small hot-spring village (Guānzǐlǐng) in northern Tainan County is famous for an old temple (now finally repaired and open to the public) and two geological oddities. The first oddity concerns the hot-spring water itself, which is a light grey 'mud' colour owing to the heavy mineral content. The second oddity is a cave where natural-gas flames burn continuously on top of a small pool of spring water. Either is a good reason to plan a day trip from Tainan or Chiayi.

Orientation & Information

The Guanziling area is essentially one long dip off County Rd 172 on County Rd 96. The village, on the eastern end of the dip, is divided into lower and upper sections. There's a big, new park with stone steps at the back joining the two sections. Buses to Guanziling pull in here to turn around. The lower village is the older part of town. It's not that pleasant through here as many of the buildings are shabby and the hot-spring owners send touts to drive you into their establishment as if you are cattle. There's an ATM in the 7-Eleven in the lower village.

Sights & Activities

WATER & FIRE MIX 水火同源

In a small **grotto** (Shǔihuǒ Tóng Yuán; admission free; 24hr), west of the hot-spring area, fire and water really do mix as natural gas from far underground bubbles up through a pool of water and ignites as it hits the surface air. The result is a surreal dance of flames atop pure water. The grotto is in a small park across from a car park. It's a popular sight in Guanziling so it would be hard to miss it.

The flames are not as high as they were when we wrote the last edition, though then they were higher than the previous edition so it seems the intensity of the natural gas flow varies from year to year. Still, we have never seen the flames less than a metre high. If possible, try to visit the area at night.

BIYUN TEMPLE 碧雲寺

This Ming-dynasty-era temple (Bìyún Sì) is dedicated to Guanyin, the goddess of mercy. It's a small affair, but rich in excellent wall relief, and colourful Chochin-style carvings.

HOT SPRINGS

Guanziling's mud hot springs were opened during the Japanese era, and have always been considered therapeutic. The town is now catching up on the hot-spring craze, and more and more hotels are being built. Most of these are attractive modern-style hotels with excellent facilities, but we do hope that the place can resist overdevelopment.

Maple Hot Spring Cottage (紅葉溫泉度假山莊; Hóngyè Wēnquán Dùjià Shānzhuāng; ☎ 682 2821; unlimited use of public pools adult/child NT450/200; 10am-10pm) has modern outdoor public pools set in a valley off the main road. To get here, walk up from the park where the bus turns around (the park between the upper and lower sections of the village). On the right you'll see a café perched on the side of the hill. You can buy tickets here for the pools below.

There are also pleasant cottages (doubles from NT2880) across from the outdoor pools on the side of a hill.

King's Garden Villa (景大渡假莊園; Jǐngdà Dùjià Zhuāngyuán; ☎ 682 2500; www.myspa.com.tw in Chinese; unlimited use of public pools adult/child NT450/200; 9am-10pm) is another modern hot-spring resort, with 15 distinctive pools in the spa. There's a range of accommodation styles, from cottages with their own walled-in compound and outdoor springs (NT7600) to rooms (from NT4200) with hot-spring tubs inside. Though these looked great on the surface we found a few rooms had pretty shoddy construction (eg sinking floors).

Eating & Drinking

There are plenty of cafés and restaurants around Guanziling. Across from the bus stop sit a row of barbecue stalls, though these usually serve group-size portions. Most of the hotels have restaurants and decent set meals can be had for around NT200.

Getting There & Around

It's best to take your own transport here (scooters are only NT200 per day in nearby Chiayi) but if you can't, take a bus (NT79, one hour, every 30 minutes) from the Chiayi Bus Company station in Chiayi. Buses stop at Biyun Temple first, then continue to Guanziling. Get off the bus in the new park.

SOUTH CROSS-ISLAND HWY 南部橫貫公路

A friend once said that the South Cross-Island Hwy (南部橫貫公路; Nánbù Héngguàn Gōnglù) perfectly illustrates the principle that 'sometimes the journey matters more than the destination'. With all due respect, we think he needs to get out of his car more often.

The highway bisects southern Taiwan, running from Tainan in the west to Taitung in the east. It passes through the southern section of the Central Mountain Range, skirting the bottom of Yushan National Park. The area is sparsely developed, scenically grand, and blessed with easily accessible old forests, aboriginal villages, fantastic hikes both long and short, and numerous hot springs, including Lisong, which many consider the most beautiful natural spring in Taiwan.

Be aware that, as with all mountain routes in Taiwan, parts of the high, narrow road are frequently washed away during landslides, and falling rocks are all too common. Don't go after heavy rains or earthquakes. The safest time to visit is in winter, during the dry season. Afternoon fog is a hazard year-round, especially around Yakou: plan to be off the road, or trail, by 3pm or so. Hiking conditions are best October to

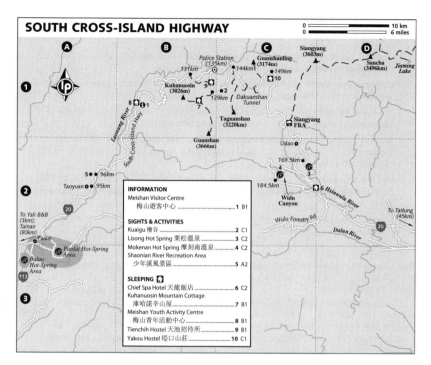

SOUTH CROSS-ISLAND HIGHWAY

INFORMATION
Meishan Visitor Centre
梅山遊客中心 1 B1

SIGHTS & ACTIVITIES
Kuaigu 檜谷 2 C1
Lisong Hot Spring 栗松溫泉 3 C2
Mokenan Hot Spring 摩刻南溫泉 4 C2
Shaonian River Recreation Area
少年溪風景區 5 A2

SLEEPING 🏠
Chief Spa Hotel 天龍飯店 6 C2
Kuhanuosin Mountain Cottage
庫哈諾辛山屋 7 B1
Meishan Youth Activity Centre
梅山青年活動中心 8 B1
Tienchih Hostel 天池招待所 9 B1
Yakou Hostel 埡口山莊 10 C1

March when it's cool, even cold, but dry. Traffic is very light during this time too, especially midweek.

Information

There's a Yushan National Park **visitor centre** (☎ 07-686 6181; ⏰ 9am-4.30pm, closed Mon following 2nd & 4th Sun of every month, if these are national holidays, closed Tue) in Meishankou for maps and general information on most of the eastern section of the highway. Hikers who wish to climb Guanshan can apply for permits here for a climb the same day.

Getting There & Around

You can of course start the highway from either end but if you are riding a bike, or walking, west to east is best. With a car or scooter it doesn't matter, though west to east just seems the better route. The long, scenic drive downhill through the Wulu gorge and out into the rift valley is a very satisfying conclusion. Similarly, if you are hiring scooters, Tainan is your best option as hire shops accept international driving licences while those in Taitung do not.

With public transportation it's a different story. The **Hsingnan Motor Transport Company** (☎ 06-265 3121) runs four buses daily from Tainan to Meishankou (NT319, six hours, first bus 7am). In Taitung, the **Kuo Kuang Hao Bus Company** (☎ 089-322 027) runs one bus a day to Tienchih (NT351, 4½ hours). It leaves at 7.10am, but always confirm this time as some schedules (even the one at the bus station) still say it leaves at 6.40am.

Unfortunately this means that the 27km stretch between Meishankou and Tienchih has no public transportation. It's possible to hire someone in Meishankou to give you a ride, but it won't be cheap. You could walk, but if you don't have so many days take the bus from Taitung to Tienchih and start your journey east from here. Meishankou has little of interest anyway and you can always see Paolai and Taoyuan when you visit Maolin.

PAOLAI 寶來
☎ 07 / pop 600
The town of Paolai (Bǎolái) is considered the gateway to the South Cross-Island Hwy, which is appropriate because right here, at

---

WALKING THE SOUTH CROSS-ISLAND HIGHWAY

- Day one: take the bus from **Taitung** (p202) to the **Guanshan** (opposite) trailhead. Climb to **Kuhanuosin Mountain Cottage** (opposite) and stay the night.

- Day two: complete the hike to the Guanshan summit, then return to the highway and walk 3km north to spend the night at **Tienchih Hostel** (opposite).

- Day three: walk 13km along the highway to **Yakou** (opposite), with a possible side trip up **Taguanshan** (opposite). Spend the night in **Yakou Hostel** (p264).

- Day four: hike up **Guanshanling Mountain** (opposite), then take the afternoon bus to **Motian** (p264). Hike down the side road to **Lisong Hot Spring** (p264) and spend the night camped by the river.

- Day five: hike back up to the highway and walk 10km to **Lidao** (p264), then 7km to 8km or catch the afternoon bus to **Wulu** (p264). Spend the night in the Chief Spa Hotel or camped out in the hills.

- Day six: explore **Wulu Canyon** (p264) and wild **Mokenan Hot Spring** (p265). Take the afternoon bus down to Taitung.

---

the start, are hot springs and the opportunity for adventure in the form of rafting down the Laonong River.

The **Laonong River** (荖濃溪; Lǎonóng Xī) begins on the slopes of Yushan and the rafting *(fànzhōu)* traverses 20km of rough water (much rougher than the Siougukluan River in Taitung) from Paolai to Sinfa. A trip costs about NT800 including lunch and transportation. For more information, and online reservations, check out www.rafting.com .tw/index1-1.htm. Or contact the **Laonong Whitewater Rafting Company** (105 Jhongjheng Rd, Paolai Village, ☎ 07-688 2996; fax 07-688 2997).

Paolai has bicarbonate water, with a pH of about 7.5, and temperature about 60°C. If you have your own vehicle, and love hot springs and scenic landscapes, it is worth exploring this area for a day or two. About 6km south of Paolai on county road 133 is the **Bulao Hot Spring** (不老溫泉; Bùlǎo Wēnquán), a low-alkaline carbonic-acid spring. There are some lovely hotels along the road, many with great open views over the Laonong River valley.

Hot-spring hotels are reasonably priced in the Paolai area (NT2500 to NT4000 a night with good midweek discounts) and if you just want a soak it will cost around NT300 per person.

For something a little homier we recommend a little aboriginal family-run place a few kilometres before Paolai called **Yali B&B** (亞力民宿; Yǎlì Mínsù; ☎ 688 2042; www .travel-web.com.tw in Chinese; with Youth Guesthouse card

s/d/tw NT600/1500/2400). The family are very kind-hearted, and the mother is simply a wacky riot at times. Rooms (each one is named after a member of the family) are simple but good value for money and are decorated with little handmade articles. ('No money,' the mother kept repeating when we were there, 'so we have to make our own decorations.') Guests can learn how to make bamboo chopsticks, and also enjoy a swim in a natural spring-fed pool (not a hot spring) next door. If you plan to stay a night, bring your own towels and toiletries. There is a 20% weekday discount. To get to the guesthouse turn left just past the 77km mark on Hwy 20 into **Jianshan Village** (建山村; estimated population 100) and head up the road 1km. If you are taking the bus from Tainan the stop is just before the turn-off for Jianshan Village.

TAOYUAN TOWNSHIP

North of Paolai, the Taoyuan township area has an abundance of undeveloped hot springs (we only touch on a couple) and rivers for swimming.

At the 96km mark on the highway you'll see a sign for the **Shaonian River Recreation Area** (Xiàonián Xī FōngJǐng Qū). There's an interesting waterfall here and free hot-spring pools set up by the local community. The falls are visible across the river from the parking lot and can be reached by crossing the suspension bridge. To get to the hot springs, turn right after the suspension bridge and follow the road up and then left, over the falls. It's about a 20-minute walk and the way is pretty obvious. You can camp in the recreation area.

MEISHANKOU (MEISHAN) 梅山口
☎ 07 / pop 200

The next stop on the road is the tiny village of Meishan (Meishankou usually refers to the visitor centre area), home of the Bunun aboriginal tribe. Note that this is the last stop on the bus from Tainan, and the last gas station for 100km is just up the road. There's a **visitor centre** (☎ 07-686 6181; ⊙ 9am-4.30pm, closed Mon following 2nd & 4th Sun of every month, if these are national holidays, closed Tue) just off the highway to the right.

The **Meishankou Youth Activity Centre** (Méishān Qīngnián Huódòng Zhōngxīn; ☎ 686 6166; d incl breakfast NT2400, 4-person tatami r incl breakfast NT3200) is the only hotel in town. It's a very quiet, relaxing place, and makes for a good base if you are exploring the area with your own transportation. Lunch and dinner are extra.

TIENCHIH 天池

The 27km no-man's (or no-bus's) land from Meishankou to Tienchih (Tiānchí; elevation 2280m) is blessed with dramatic mountain vistas, and if you have to walk it, you certainly won't hurt for things to look at.

Note that Tienchih is not a town, or even village, but a forestry department outpost with a police station just up the road. The only place to stay is at the minimalist **Tienchih Hostel** (Tiānchí Zhāodàisuǒ; ☎ 07-678 0006; dm NT300). There are no meals available, though there is a kitchen, so bring supplies with you.

Activities

Tienchih is a great starting point for a number of hikes and is an ideal spot for beginning a multiday journey (walking or otherwise) down the highway.

HIKING
Jhongjhiguan 中之關

The trail (Zhōngzhīguān), also known as the Guanshan Historic Trail, begins a few kilometres west of Tienchih at the 131km mark on the highway, and ends just up from the hostel at the 136km mark. The trail was built by the Japanese to control the Bunun tribe, and the 3.5km section that is open to the public now takes two or three hours to complete one way. Most people who hike it take the trail one way and the road the other.

Guanshan 關山

The clearly marked trailhead for Guanshan (Guānshān; 3666m) is at the 139km mark, or just 3km south of Tienchih. Permits are needed to climb the mountain and can be applied for in Meishankou at the visitor centre. The Yushan National Park's board considers Guanshan a very basic climb, despite being over 3000m, so applying in advance is usually unnecessary. However, if you plan to go on a weekend you should apply in advance (see p329) as there are limited beds in the cabin.

The hike takes two days (though really fit people can climb up and down in a day). It's a few hours climb to **Kuhanuosin Mountain Cottage** (Kùhānuòxīn Shānwū), a rough cabin at 3026m where you can leave your heavy bag and tackle nearby **Kuhanuosin Mountain** (elevation 3206m). The next morning, climb to the summit of Guanshan, return to the cabin, and head back to Tienchih. Note that there is a stream for water at the trailhead to Guanshan, and tanks that hold rainwater at the cabin (but confirm the latter before you head out).

The next day (or any day for that matter), it is possible to walk 13km to Yakou, the next pit stop with food and accommodation. Along the way the highway passes through an area called **Kuaigu** (Cypress Valley; Kuàigǔ), a gorgeous stretch of giant ancient trees that is worth taking in at a leisurely pace. At the 144km mark is the clearly marked trailhead for **Taguanshan** (Daguanshan; 大關山; Dàguānshān). The steep trail takes a few hours to complete and takes you through an enchanting old-growth forest. Much of this forest is within the first 15 minutes of the hike, so do explore the trail a bit even if you can't do it all.

YAKOU 埡口

Yakou (Yǎkǒu) is the halfway point along the highway. The scenery is dominated by high mountain ridges and sharp valleys (that is if you can see any of it through the thick fog). Right before Yakou is the 600m **Dakuanshan Tunnel** (大關山隧道; Dàguānshān Suìdào), the dividing line between Taitung and Kaohsiung Counties.

Just east of the Dakuanshan Tunnel is the trail to **Guanshanling Mountain** (關山嶺山; Guānshānlǐng Shān). It's three to four hours return with excellent views from the flat top if the weather is clear (go early morning for best results).

Travellers can stay in the **Yakou Hostel** (Yǎkǒu Shānzhuāng; dm NT600, 4-person tatami r NT2400) just off the highway down a side road at the 149km mark. It's cold up here and the rooms have no heat but it's much more comfortable than at Tienchih. Fairly decent meals (NT120) are prepared by the hostel but must be ordered in advance . The front desk has a small selection of snacks and drinks for sale. Note that rooms must be booked through the **Meishan Youth Activity Centre** (☎ 07-686 6166).

SIANGYANG FOREST RECREATION AREA
向陽森林遊樂區

From Yakou you can continue walking on the highway 8km to this new forest recreation area (Xiàngyáng Sēnlín Yóulè Qū) with several short trails through beautiful cypress and pine forests. There's a **visitor centre** (☎ 089-345 493; http://taitung.forest.gov.tw; 8.30am-4.30pm) at the start of the reserve just off the highway. Note it does not sell any food or drinks.

Siangyang is starting to become known as a prime bird-watching area and is also the start of the three-day round-trip trek to **Jiaming Lake** (嘉明湖; Jiāmíng Hú), a tiny alpine lake that resulted from an asteroid collision ages ago. Those who have done the route rave that the scenery is about the best in Taiwan. The Jiaming Lake trail is part of the National Trail System (p329). Only a police permit is required to hike it.

LISONG HOT SPRING 栗松溫泉

Arguably the most beautiful natural hot springs in Taiwan, Lisong (Lìsōng Wēnquán) is a must-visit for any lover of the sublime in nature. At the base of a deep river valley, eons of mineral deposits have painted a small limestone grotto shades of deep green, white, red and black. Steam rises from the rocks, and hot-spring water bubbles, spits and streams from fissures and cracks in the canyon walls. Stand in the right place and you are in a hot-spring shower. It really is as good as it sounds.

If Lisong wasn't already well known among Taiwanese hot spring fans, we'd probably keep it a secret. Fortunately, the remoteness of the spring and the very steep trail down keep it from being wrecked by crowds. In fact, on a weekday you likely won't see another soul. We never have.

To get to Lisong look for a metal shack around the 169.5km mark, near the village of **Motian** (摩天). Take the farm road behind the shack down about 1.5km to the end. (You can drive it but it's pretty rough and steep.) Turn right across a farmer's field and look for the trailhead on the other side. It's pretty much straight down from here and there are many sections where you must use ropes (already in place) to assist you. When you reach the river, cross and head up the bank 30m then cross back using the rope in place. Scramble up the bank to the now obvious springs. People have made a small pool out of rocks and you can dip into the deep pools of the Lidao River when you get too hot.

If you walk in from the highway, it will take 1½ to two hours to reach the springs. Since the turn-off for the springs is about 20km from Yakou, you could easily walk from there and camp overnight by the river.

LITAO 利稻
pop 300

From Lisong Hot Spring it's about 8km to 9km to the small aboriginal village of Litao (Lìdào), where you can get food and drinks and catch the afternoon bus to Wulu or onwards to Taitung.

The Litao Hotel, run by the Meishan Youth Activity Centre, has closed but there are numerous inexpensive homestays. These tend to go in and out of business, not to mention up and down in quality, so ask around or show the characters for *mínsù* (民宿).

If you are looking for a bit more comfort, continue another 7km to 8km (about two hours' walk) to Wulu.

WULU 霧鹿
pop 100

The last real stop on the highway, Wulu (Wùlù), like Paolai, the first, offers hot springs galore (both wild and developed), bird-watching, hiking and a rushing river. There's no rafting here but you can enjoy the beautiful Wulu Gorge as you walk or drive along the road.

Sights & Activities
WULU GORGE

This deep, twisting **canyon** (Wùlù Xiágǔ) runs beside the highway for the last stretch before opening out into the East Rift Valley. It's scenic enough on its own, but there are also about a dozen wild hot springs to explore along the canyon floor. It's tough getting down to the bottom, though, so watch out for paths or temporary access roads built by road crews. There are also a few suspension bridges if you want a good viewpoint for photos.

HOT SPRINGS

There are dozens of natural hot springs along the South Cross-Island Hwy, some requiring half a day to hike into. Around Wulu, however, there are several that can be reached fairly easily. One of the most wild is the **Mokenan Hot Spring** (Mókènán Wēnquán). In this large open area of steamy fumaroles, and long cliff faces stained with colourful mineral deposits, hot-spring water spits dribbles and boils out from cracks in the canyon walls.

To get here, look for a clearing wide enough to park a car or two on the left side of the highway just before the 184.5km mark as you head down (east). You should see a tag on the bushes. Look for a trail on the right side of the clearing. It's steep, very steep, going down, so take care. Wear river-tracing, or rock-climbing, shoes for better grip.

At the bottom, scramble down the final rocks and cross the river. (Don't attempt when the water is high after heavy rain.) Then, explore.

Wulu's water has a pH of about 7.5 and is odourless and silky to the touch. It is, in fact, almost identical to the water at Taian, our favourite hot spring in Taiwan. We've seen pictures of people soaking in contrived pools at Mokenan but you'd better make sure you mix the hot spring water with cooler river water first.

For something a little more refined, check out the nearby **Chief Spa Hotel** (Tiānlóng Fàndiàn; ☎ 089-935 075; www.chiefspa.com.tw). If the hotel is not busy, nonguests can use the outdoor pools (NT300) that look out onto the canyon. Comfortable rooms (single/double NT3000/3600) with piped-in hot spring water are also available, and there's a 30% discount Sunday to Friday. Audrey, the manager, speaks fluent English and is a great source of local information.

HIKING

Behind the Chief Spa Hotel, the **Heavenly Dragon Bridge** (Tiānlóng Diào Qiáo) spans the gorge. It's the longest suspension bridge in the east of Taiwan and an obligatory visit for most tour buses.

On the other side of the bridge, a clear **trail** allows for a pleasant 1½-hour walk through lush forests, with expansive views over the canyon.

BIRD-WATCHING

Organized tours from North America and Europe have in recent years started coming to the Wulu area for bird-watching, especially on the lookout for endemic species like the Taiwan partridge, mikado pheasant and rusty laughing thrush. While the trail on the other side of the Heavenly Dragon Bridge seemed to our eyes to team with birds, it is a nearby forestry road that is the real draw.

The **Wulu Forestry Road** (霧鹿林道) starts a few kilometres east of the Chief Spa Hotel but you need to drive up about 15km to the best bird-watching spots. And for this you really need a 4WD vehicle.

Eating

Across from the Chief Spa Hotel sits a little **Sichuan restaurant** (Sìchuān Fàndiàn; dishes NT60), where you can fill up on fried noodles and tofu with chilli at any time of the day. The Chief Spa Hotel has excellent aboriginal food prepared by Bunun cooks.

KAOHSIUNG TO KENTING

KAOHSIUNG CITY 高雄市

☎ 07 / pop 1,512,677

In the last edition of the Taiwan guidebook, we called Kaohsiung not a must-see, but a city to keep your eye on. Well, no-one is more surprised than we are at how quickly the change has come.

In some ways of course this is because Kaohsiung, Taiwan's second-largest city, and largest port (the fourth- or fifth-largest in the world), was so sorely and long neglected. Like the double-digit growth of many developing countries, Kaohsiung's transformation seems astonishing in part because it has so much catching-up to do.

We wouldn't be thrilled about the change if Kaohsiung didn't have something worth transforming. But it does. The harbour, the beaches, the Love River, the historical sights, and the 1000 hectares of almost-pristine forest have of course always been there. It finally took someone with a good vision to see their true worth.

The visionary in many ways was former Mayor Frank Hsieh. He saw the Love River cleaned up, and its banks turned into lovely promenades. He also saw the city get potable water for the first time, oversaw the start of an extensive MRT system (though he was tainted with a scandal on that matter), the opening of the harbour to tourism, and even scored the 2009 World Games. The city is proud to be hosting the games, the second-largest sporting event after the Olympics. And like many Olympic-bid-winning cities, Kaohsiung is using

the honour to push through even more urban renewal projects.

Orientation

Kaohsiung is a large city but most of what you want to see is clustered in a few areas: the Love River, especially in the section between Jianguo-3rd and Wufu-3rd Rd; the Tsoying District in the north; the harbour and Cijin Island; and the Sun Yat-sen University grounds.

Most travellers will have to spend at least some time around the train station, if only when catching a bus. It's still a grubby part of town, but at least it's not all torn up anymore with MRT construction. If you wish to cross the tracks behind the station, use

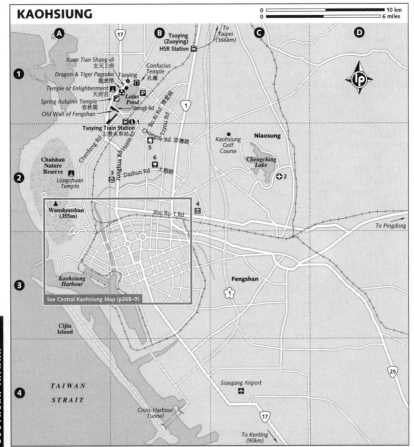

SOUTHERN TAIWAN

the tunnel starting in the train station. The fee is NT6 and you can purchase tickets in the train station.

One great change is the bilingual signage, not only for roads, but major attractions. And no more hiding street names behind coconut palms for this town.

Information

CULTURAL CENTRES

Chiang Kai-shek Cultural Centre (Zhōngzhèng Wénhuà Zhōngxīn; Map pp268-9; ☎ 222 5136, ext 237; 67 Wufu-1st Rd; ☺ 9am-5pm, closed Mon) The centre has lecture and concert halls, galleries and a library. To get there, catch bus 50 or 51. Note that the name of the centre may change as part of the de-Chiangification of Taiwan.

INTERNET ACCESS

There are many internet cafés around the Bo Ai Rd/Cisian-2nd Rd area (Map pp268–9). For free internet at Access Kaohsiung see below.

INTERNET RESOURCES

Kaohsiung City (www.kaohsiung.gov.tw) One of the best city tourism websites in Taiwan.

MEDICAL SERVICES

Chung-Ho Memorial Hospital, Kaohsiung Medical University (☎ 312 1101; www.kmuh.org.tw; 100 Zihyou 1st Rd)

MONEY

There are banks and ATMs everywhere, including most 7-Elevens. You can change money at the following:

Bank of Taiwan (Map pp268-9; 264 Jhongjheng-4th Rd)

ICBC (Map pp268-9; 308 Jhongjheng-4th Rd)

TOURIST INFORMATION

Kaohsiung is not lacking in places to help you find the information you need. Look for the booklet *Fun Kaohsiung* for an excellent overview.

Access Kaohsiung (Map p266; ☎ 342 2101, ext 811 or 0917-119 930 ask for Melissa; http://accesskaohsiung .blogspot.com; 801 Chongde Rd, Tsoying District; ☺ 9am-5pm Mon-Fri) Largely the brainchild of Canadian expat Mellisa Wriston, Access Kaohsiung (part of the Bureau of Human Resources) exists to help foreigners travel or get set up in Kaohsiung. In its little office, you'll find free internet, books, tons of English information including bus schedules and many guides and brochures that are hard to find elsewhere. You can take a 301 bus (2 zones) to the centre or walk from Lotus Lake.

FYI South Magazine (www.taiwanfun.com) This free bilingual monthly focuses on the south of Taiwan. You can pick it up at tourist centres and at many restaurants and entertainment venues across town. You can also download it.

Tourist Office (Map pp268-9; ☎ 281 1513; 5F, 235 Jhongjheng-4th Rd; ☺ 9am-5pm Mon-Fri) Good for brochures and such, though staff speak limited English.

Train Station Visitor Centre (☺ 9am-7pm) Staff speak English and are a good source of information, especially for buses, as the city hub is right outside the train station.

Sights

LOTUS POND 蓮池潭

The pond (Liánchí Tán; Map p266) has been a popular destination since the Qing dynasty and is well known for the 20 or so temples dotting the shoreline and nearby area. In recent years much money and effort has gone into returning the lake and its cultural and natural heritage to its former glory. There's now a path right around the lake, and efforts are underway to restore the wetlands on the west side. At night coloured lights give the lake a very festive and modern appearance.

Two long sections of the impressive **Old Wall of Fengshan** (Fèngshān Jiùcháng; Map p266), built in 1826, lie to the southeast of the lake. The best section is along Chenfong Rd about 100m up Shengli Rd from the train station.

If you are going to the pond, get your hands on a copy of the free booklet *Lotus Pond: Tourism Guide*. This is a highly informative and useful guide to all the temples and sights around the lake, including places to try traditional food. Tourist offices don't always have copies; try Access Kaohsiung.

To get to the lake, take a train to Tsoying station (Zuǒyíng; Map p266). Exit the station and walk straight ahead two blocks up Shengli Rd. The lake is unmissable on the right. You can also catch bus 301.

CIJIN ISLAND 旗津

Cijin island (Qíjīn; Map pp268–9) makes for a pleasant half-day trip from the mainland. Attractions include the **seafood street** (*hǎichān jiē*), a centuries-old **Matsu Temple** (Tiānhoù Gōng) with excellent relief and pillar carvings, and an old **lighthouse** (Qíjīn Dēngtǎ; admission free; ☼ 9am-4.30pm) with fantastic views over the ocean and harbour. There's also a long strip of sandy beach where you can swim in summer (there are free public changing rooms and showers) and stroll in winter (the city keeps it clean all year round, quite a rarity in Taiwan).

To reach the island, take bus 248 to the ferry terminal. The ferry (NT10, five minutes) runs every five minutes.

BRITISH CONSULATE AT TAKOU (DAGOU) 打狗英國領事館

Kaohsiung has a large number of well-preserved relics scattered around the city. The handsome redbrick **consulate** (Dǎgǒu Yīnguó Lǐngshì Guǎn; Map pp268-9; ☎ 531 2560; 18 Linhai Rd; admission free; ☼ 9am-midnight), built in 1865 by a British trading company, has recently become one of our favourite hang-out spots. The consulate sits about 70m or so above the mouth of Kaohsiung harbour, and it's a great location for watching the giant container ships sail through the tiny mouth of the harbour.

Recently the old dining and tearooms were reopened. With their Victorian British design, and arched windows letting in the

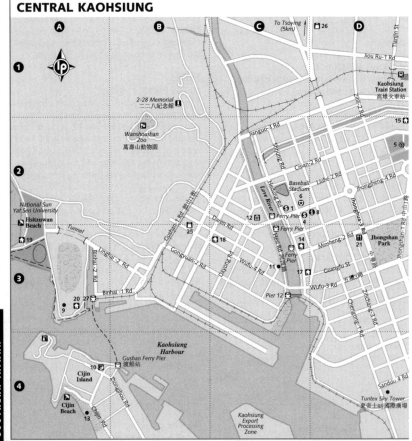

CENTRAL KAOHSIUNG

sea views and breezes, they are top spots for enjoying a meal or drink (open from 10am to midnight).

While you're in the area check out a tiny **temple** to the left of the larger temple beside the consulate. There are two gods within the shrine, and if you ask most Taiwanese people they would not be able to identify them. And that's because these gods are not Chinese, but Dutch!

During the 17th century many Taiwanese revered the Dutch for their military and technical prowess. This temple, the only one of its kind in Taiwan, went so far as to deify two naval commanders, much as old Chinese generals have been deified over the centuries.

To get to the consulate, take bus 99 to the consulate stop and walk up the stairs. Or, take bus 248 to Binghai-2nd Rd (the harbour) then walk along the new paths around the cape to the stairs.

MUSEUMS

The **Kaohsiung Museum of Fine Arts** (Gāoxióng Měishùguǎn; Map p266; ☎ 555 0331; http://english.kmfa .gov.tw; 20 Meishuguan Rd; admission free; ☺ 9am-5pm, closed Mon; bus 205) has a stylish interior and highlights the art of southern Taiwan. The level of work on display is impressive.

The **National Science & Technology Museum** (Kēxué Gōngyì Bówùguǎn; Map p266; ☎ 316 0331; www .nstm.gov.tw; 720 Jiou Ru-1st Rd; adult/senior/child NT100/ free/70, foreigner with passport NT50, IMAX adult/child

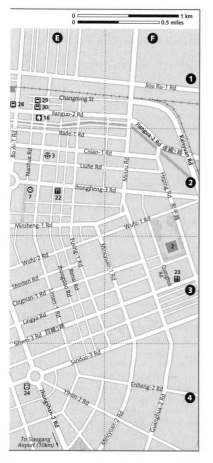

NT150/100; 9am-5pm, closed Mon & Chinese New Year) features an hourly IMAX show and high-quality hands-on science exhibits designed for children. Most of the IMAX shows and displays are in Chinese only. The exhibit on the Industrial History of Taiwan, however, has full English displays and is so informative it alone is worth the price of admission. You can take bus 60 to the museum.

LOVE RIVER 愛河

About five years ago, the **Love River** (Ài Hé; Map pp268–9) began to be cleaned up after years of neglect, if not outright abuse. As the waters flowed clear again, the banks were turned into strips of lovely parkland featuring walkways, benches, shady trees, outdoor cafés and stages. And it just keeps getting better year after year. These days it has become the focal point of the renewed pride Kaohsiung citizens feel for their city. One of the most popular activities now is cruising along the river at night. There are four piers from where you can catch a boat for a 20-minute ride (NT50) from 4pm to 11.30pm every day. Boats leave often and are usually full on weekends.

Just back from the river is the wonderful **Municipal Film Archives** (Diànyǐng Túshūguǎn; Map pp268-9; ☎ 551 1211; 10 Hesi Rd; admission free; 1.30-9.30pm, closed Mon), where you can enjoy on-site private and public viewings of the Archives' films. It's just a shame they won't sell the movie posters in the lobby.

A few blocks north of the Archives, also beside the river, is the lovely **Museum of History** (Lìshǐ Bówùguǎn; Map pp268-9; ☎ 531 2560; http://w5.kcg.gov.tw/khm; 272 Jhongjheng-4th Rd; admission free; 9am-5pm, closed Mon), formerly the city government building during Japanese times. Inside are a number of photographic exhibits, furniture displays and special seasonal exhibits. But we just like to walk up and down the cool marble staircase. Bus 248 stops by the Museum of History, putting you in the centre of the Love River area.

KAOHSIUNG HARBOUR

The harbour (gǎngkǒu; Map pp268–9) itself has recently become an attraction as more and more of it is opened up to the public. Down by Pier 12 and the Gushan Ferry Pier you'll find walkways and cafés where you can sit by

---

THE BETEL NUT BEAUTY   Robert Kelly

It's said in advertising that sex sells, as do small cute animals and children. Leave it to the Taiwanese to find a way to conflate all three ideals into one. They did and they call it the Betel Nut Beauty (Bīnláng Xīshī).

The beauty is a young woman, or teenage girl, often extremely pretty, who sits in a glass booth on the side of provincial highways and county roads, wearing as little as possible to attract customers. Her ware is the betel nut (bīnláng), the seed of the betel palm, a tree that grows throughout Asia. As for the cute animal angle, well (and yes this is a bit of a stretch, I admit), very often a little dog accompanies her in the booth, or at the very least a shelf full of Hello Kitty products.

In any case, betel nut is a US$1 billion dollar industry in Taiwan. To make it fit for consumption, the nut is usually slit down the middle, mixed with lime, and wrapped in a leaf. The effects on the mind and body are comparable to nicotine and caffeine. It's extremely popular, though it does lead to oral cancer, and growing the nut tree is a scourge on the environment.

While many countries have betel nut, only Taiwan has the Betel Nut Beauty, named after Xi Shi, a legendary paragon of Chinese beauty. The phenomenon started in the 1990s and grew quickly, through competition and one-upmanship, to the point where literally nothing was being worn by the girls but see-through skirts and blouses. Many locals took a strange pride in this and an even stranger joy in exposing foreign guests to the, well, exposed charms of the local beauties.

But all good things must end, and by the time everyone could admit the empresses really had no clothes on, the politicians had gotten involved. 'No exposure of breasts, belly buttons or buttocks', they declared, and somehow or other this ban has managed to stay enforced. It's true we do see the occasional flash of defiance in our travels around the country, but by all accounts the glory days of the Betel Nut Beauty are behind us. For one last glimpse of what has been lost, do a search for 'Betel Nut Girls Taiwan' on Youtube.com to see a trailer for South African Tobie Openshaw's upcoming documentary.

the water and enjoy the ships sailing in and being loaded and unloaded. No, we're not talking about a scene of shirtless coolies hauling bamboo crates off a four-masted barque – these are massive container ships, and the modern port is fully outfitted with cranes and lifts to unload the cargo. (And it's no less enjoyable for that.)

Harbour cruises leave from Pier 12 several times a day (NT150, 90 minutes). Check at the visitor centre for the current schedule.

BEACHES

Kaohsiung is lucky to have two decent beaches right within the city borders. The beach on **Cijin Island** (Map pp268-9; admission free) is just a five-minute ferry ride (and another five-minute walk). There are showers and changing rooms but be aware that there are serious rip tides along the more open parts of the beach.

Hsitzuwan (Sizi Bay; Xīzǐwān; Map pp268-9; winter/summer admission NT50/70) is smaller than Cijin, but it's a calmer swimming beach and is also an excellent place for hanging out and watching the sunset. We prefer it to Cijin, as it has a cool tropical feel and a lovely mountain backdrop. The beach is on the grounds of Sun Yat-sen University so the whole environment on and around the beach is clean and well maintained. To get to the beach, take bus 224 to the Sun Yat-sen University stop and then walk through the tunnel. You'll see signs for the beach on the other side. There are changing rooms and showers here too, as well as a café.

Both beaches are open all year round, and kept clean all year round, though swimming is only from May to October.

Activities

HIKING

Within Kaohsiung City there is good hiking in the 1000-hectare **Chaishan Nature Reserve** (Cháishān Zìrán Gōngyuán; Map p266), which has been preserved since Japanese times. There's a decent brochure and map of the area at the tourist office. The Chaishan reserve is famous for its macaque population, so don't carry food into the area and watch out that the monkeys don't steal your camera!

On weekends and holidays you can take the Chaishan Line bus to the reserve from the train station. On weekdays take bus 248 to Yancheng Station (鹽埕站) then change to bus 219 to Longcyuan Temple (龍泉寺). The trails start behind the temple.

Just walking around the university (Map pp268-9)) and getting lost in the hills is pleasant too. Some trails will take you up to the zoo, and also up to the nature reserve.

VOLUNTEERING

Animal-lovers can make Kaohsiung a better place for our four-legged friends by helping out at **BARK** (www.atkaohsiung.org). BARK was started in 2006 by expats in Kaohsiung and since has grown quickly to become a registered nonprofit organization (NPO) with plenty of both Taiwanese and Western volunteers. BARK is involved in rehoming, catch-neuter-release (CNR) programmes, and rescues, in addition to raising awareness of the huge problem of stray animals in Taiwan. Not only is helping out a great thing to do, but you'll meet a lot of kind, generous folk. (For more information, see p343).

2009 WORLD GAMES

The World Games are the second-largest international sporting event after the Olympics. The 2009 events will take place in Kaohsiung from 16–26 July. Over 3000 athletes are expected to attend and the whole spectacle will certainly be a huge boost for the city's international image.

Festivals & Events

As befitting a port city, there is a quirky **International Container Arts Festival** (Guójì Huòguì Yìshù Jié) in November, during which containers are used as art material.

There are also praise-worthy shows during Chinese New Year at the Chiang Kai-shek Cultural Centre and the colourful (and often hi-tech) lantern displays along the Love River during Lantern Festival.

Sleeping

BUDGET

Budget accommodation took a turn for the better in 2007 as two new hostels opened up. Both are run by English-speaking expats and, best of all, one is in the southern part of the city beside the Love River, while the other is up by Lotus Pond.

Kaohsiung 202 (Map pp268-9; ☎ 0938-020 304; www.kaohsiung-taiwan.com/202/; 202 Guangfu-3rd St;

光復3街202號; dm/s/d with shared bathroom NT280/350/500; 🖳) Taipei has its 101, and now Kaohsiung has its…202? It's a little smaller but it does the trick for the independent traveller coming for a visit or looking for a place to stay while he or she gets set up. Bright colours and liberal use of wood give the hostel a welcoming atmosphere, and the rooftop views over the harbour make it comfortable for hanging out. Other perks include an English-speaking manager, free use of a computer with ADSL, and the location: close to the harbour and right by the Love River.

International Friendship House (Map p266; ☎ 0971-119 930; accesskaohsiung@yahoo.com; 83 Lane 129, Wun Tze Rd, Tsoying; 左營文自路129巷83號; per person NT400; 🖳) The house is a modern five-storey apartment 1km from Lotus Pond. Run by a member of Access Kaohsiung, it features a homey atmosphere with all the fixings: wireless internet, full shared kitchen, TV, stereo etc. There are two rooms per floor (for two to four people each) and each floor has its own bathroom. Towels and toiletries are provided should you need them. Laundry was being set up at the time of writing. The house is down a quiet lane but there are plenty of cheap eats (and fancy eats, too) nearby. Long- and short-term stays are accepted. In either case, you should call or email Melissa before heading out. Don't just show up.

Hotel Skoal (Shìguó Dàfàndiàn; Map pp268-9; ☎ 287 6151; fax 288 6020; 64 Min Zhu Heng Rd; 民主橫路64號; d/tw NT780/1600; 🅿) Rooms are small and a little dark, but kept very clean. There's a car park across from the hotel.

Hwa Hung Hotel (Huá Hóng Dàfàndiàn; Map pp268-9; ☎ 237 5523; 243 Jianguo-2nd Rd; 建國2路243號; d/tw NT950/1500; 🖳) This place has two things going for it: it's right by the train station, and it's got a fresh, funky interior that looks like it was taken out of a comic book. In fact we were completely unprepared for the interiors, with their bright tropical colours, and decent furnishings. And all for a sub-thousand dollar price! Ask for the rooms with wood floors.

MIDRANGE

Kaohsiung hotels offer good value for the midrange dollar and good locations.

Kingship Hotel (Hànwáng Dàfàndiàn; Map pp268-9; ☎ 531 3131, ext 60; fax 531 3140; 98 Cisian-3rd Rd; 七賢3路98號; s/d/tw NT2100/2300/3500; 🖳) With its fresh, modern design (we are so happy the flower prints are gone), proximity to the Love River and the bars and restaurants along Wufu-4th Rd, and good price (10% weekday discount), the Kingship makes for a solid midrange option.

Uni Resort (Tōngyí Dùjiàcūn; Map pp268-9; ☎ 533 6680; 14 Shaochuan St; 哨船街14號; d/tw NT4000/5500; 🖳) An excellent place to stay if you want both a comfy environment and lots of room to move around. The hotel is right on the waterfront, with walking paths to the ferry and the university right on your doorstep. There's a small spa in the basement. There's a discount of 45% in winter, 20% in summer.

Sunset Beach Resort & Spa (Xīzǐwān Shātān Huìguǎn; Map pp268-9; ☎ 525 0005; hsizuwan@yahoo.com.tw; 51 Lianhai Rd; 蓮海路51號; d/tw NT6000/6800; 🖳) The rooms are a good size and feature soft beds, good bedding and other midrange comforts. But it's the location that really sells the place. It is literally on the beach, and the hotel has its own private entrance. It's also right within the university grounds, giving you access to tennis courts, jogging tracks, hiking trails and lots of greenery. The hotel has a restaurant and café on the premises. There are discounts of 30% to 50% in winter, 30% to 40% in summer.

TOP END

Ambassador Hotel (Guóbīn Fàndiàn; Map pp268-9; ☎ 211 5211; fax 281 1115; 202 Minsheng-2nd Rd; 民生2路202號; s/d/tw NT4500/5500/5500; 🖳 🖳) Part of a group of luxury hotels in Taiwan, the Ambassador is rated one of Kaohsiung's best. Facilities include business centre, outdoor pool, health club and a host of food and beverage options.

Eating

There's food everywhere in Kaohsiung, at all times of day and night.

Shou-Yu Vegetarian Buffet (Xiùyǔ Sùshí; Map pp268-9; 274 Jhongsiao-1st Rd; dishes NT120) Shou-Yu has branches in most major Taiwanese cities and is popular for the light, fresh taste of its food. It's old looking, but the food is good.

Wudu Organic House (Wúdúde Jiā Yǒujī Jiànkāng Shíjiè; Map pp268-9; ☎ 556 1178; 114 Sihwei-2nd Rd; dishes NT120-200; 🕙 10am-9pm) The health conscious can head to this place, an organic restaurant and shop.

The train-station area, especially as you head down Jhongshan Rd, is filled with inexpensive cafés and restaurants. Nearby **Liuhe Night Market** (Liùhé Yèshì; Map pp268-9; 🕙 6pm-2am) is famous island-wide for its hundred-plus food stalls. You can eat well here for NT100 to NT200. (It's also very clean, as there is literally one rubbish can every 10m.) Other places to try traditional foods include the Lotus Pond area, especially on Shengli Rd.

For fresh seafood head over to Cijin Island's seafood street. Or try the locally recommend **Lai Lai Seafood Barbecue Restaurant** (Lái Lái Tànkǎo Hǎixiān Cāntīng; Map pp268–9; ☎ 215 6966; 53 Minsheng-2nd Rd; ⊙ 10am-3pm & 5pm-3am). It's the kind of place you go to eat good seafood, drink cheap beer, and be loud. Just tell the staff how much you want to spend and they will arrange dishes for you. Be sure to tell them anything you don't eat (like fish head perhaps?).

Drinking

The area around Jhongshan Park (Map pp268–9) houses an assortment of modern cafés, and there's even one in the park itself. Along the Love River the many small cafés stay open late into the evening. For a beer or meal at a pub, head to one of the joints along Wufu-4th Rd.

A new area to check out for tea or coffee, or even a beer, is the harbour. At the time of writing there were a few cafés at Gushan Ferry Pier with open decks facing the water. More will doubtless open as the harbour continues to be developed for tourism. And of course there is the British Consulate (p268), which overlooks the harbour and has to be one of the nicest settings in the south for a meal or drink .

Lighthouse Bar & Grill (Dēngtǎ Měishì Jiǔguǎn; Map p266; ☎ 559 2614; 239 Fuguo-1st Rd; beer NT100; ⊙ 6pm-late) is a popular hang-out in the Tsoying District with good service, seasonal activities and live sports.

Entertainment

Clubs come and go quickly, so ask around or check out *FYI South* magazine.

Vie Show Cinemas (Huánà Wēixiù Yǐngchéng; Map pp268–9; ☎ 337 1234; www.warnervillage.com.tw in Chinese; 13-14F, 21 Sanduo-4th Rd; adult/child NT230/210) In the FE21' Mega Department Store. You can book tickets online in English.

Shopping

Bamboo Street (Lǎozhú Jiē; Map pp268–9) At the end of Wufu-4th Rd you'll find wares from the past, including traditional hats, raincoats and household articles made from bamboo.

Jade Market (Yù Shìchǎng; Map pp268–9; cnr Shihcuan-2nd Rd and Zihli Rd; ⊙ 10.30am-late afternoon Wed & Thu) Bargain hard and, if possible, bring someone along who knows something about jade. Of course it's also fun just to browse.

Getting There & Away

AIR

Kaohsiung's Siaogang Airport, located south of the city centre, serves both international and domestic flights.

UNI Air (☎ 801 0189), **TransAsia Airways** (☎ 803 0599), **Mandarin Airlines** (☎ 805 7900), **Daily Air Corporation** (☎ 806 9397) and **Far Eastern Transport** (☎ 801 2311) have counters in Kaohsiung's **Siaogang Domestic Airport Terminal** (Map p266; www .kia.gov.tw). There are flights from Kaohsiung to Taipei, Hualien, Kinmen, Matsu and Penghu. **EVA** (☎ 536 9301) and **China Airlines** (☎ 282 6141) have counters in the international terminal. There are flights to Hong Kong, Japan, Macau, Singapore and Korea.

There are two **visitor centres** (☎ 805 7888; ⊙ 9am-12.30am) in the airport, one in each terminal. Both can help with hotels, tours, buses, car hire and so on. Staff speak good English.

The domestic and international terminals are joined and you can quickly walk from one to the other. There are money-changing facilities available in the international terminal till 10pm (cash only, no travellers cheques). There's a post office in the domestic terminal. All airport signs are bilingual.

BOAT

The **Taiwan Hangye Company** (☎ 561 3866; www .taiwanline.com.tw/table.htm in Chinese) operates *Taiwanline*, which has services to Makung, Penghu. Boats (NT600 to NT1300) leave from Kaohsiung's Pier 1 (Map pp268–9), near the ferry to Cijin Island, from mid-March into September. The schedule changes every three months and boats are limited in winter. Schedules are posted online (in Chinese only).

BUS

Buses to Foguangshan (NT77, 30 minutes, every 40 minutes), Kenting (two-hour ride NT342, three-hour ride NT298, every hour, 24 hours per day) and Meinong (NT121, 1½ hours, every hour) leave from the **Kaohsiung Bus Company station** (Map pp268–9; ☎ 746 2141; 245 Nanhua St). Don't confuse this with the **Kuo Kuang Hao Bus Company station** (Map pp268–9; ☎ 236 0962; 306 Jianguo Rd), which is just in front and has buses to Taipei (weekday/weekend NT400/500, 5½ hours, every 30 minutes, 24 hours per day).

TRAIN
Kaohsiung is the terminus for most west coast trains. Trains to and from Taipei (fast/slow NT845/544, 4½/seven hours) run frequently from early morning till almost midnight. To Taichung (fast/slow NT470/363, 2½/three hours), trains run about every two hours.

High-Speed Rail (HSR)
At the time of writing there was HSR service (NT1490, two hours) between Taipei and Tsoying (Zuoying) Station (Map p266) about every hour.

Getting Around
TO/FROM THE AIRPORT & HIGH-SPEED RAIL
Bus 301 goes to both the airport (NT12, every 15 minutes) and the HSR, and leaves from the bus hub in front of the train station. Note that the two destinations are in opposite directions so make sure you get the bus going in the right direction or you will make a big and time-consuming loop. Taxis to the airport or HSR should cost around NT200 from the city centre.

BUS
Buses in Kaohsiung usually have English signs at the front and electronic English signs inside indicating the next stop. The city bus hub (Map pp268–9) is directly in front of the train station. The fare for a one-zone trip is NT12. Pick up a copy of the very useful English *Kaohsiung Bus Guide* at a visitor centre or Access Kaohsiung.

CAR
For car hire call **IWS** (☎ 0800 009 414), **Hertz** (☎ 0800 015 168) or **Central Auto** (☎ 802 0800; www .rentalcar.com.tw). All have English-speaking staff and do pick-ups.

MASS RAPID TRANSIT
Kaohsiung's MRT system was behind schedule at the time of writing but may be ready by the end of 2008. When the KMRT (underground railway) opens there will be a line to both the airport and HSR station.

FOGUANGSHAN 佛光山
☎ 07
The Light of Buddha Mountain or Foguangshan (Fóguāngshān; www.fgs.org.tw), is a 52-acre temple complex about a 30-minute drive from Kaohsiung. The complex serves as

monastery, university and meditation centre. It is considered *the* centre of Buddhism in southern Taiwan.

The most famous feature here is the **Great Buddha Land** (大佛城; Dàfóchéng), where a towering 36m Amitabha Buddha stands over a garden of 480 smaller Buddha statues. For many, though, the Disneyland-like **Pure Land Cave** (淨土洞窟; Jìngtǔ Dòngkū), with its animated figures and light show, is the more interesting sight.

Tours in English of up to a half-day can be arranged with the nuns at **reception** (信徒中心; xìntú zhōngxīn; ☎ 656 1921, ext 6203-6205). Temple tours stress the ceremonial aspects of Buddhism and you will be requested to bow, kowtow and otherwise observe all forms of respect and devotion. Wear appropriate clothing and do not carry any food or drinks. In return, you will be instructed in Buddhist thought, history and iconography and may receive advice and blessed trinkets.

The **Pilgrim's Lodge** (Jáushān Huìguǎn; d NT2000) invites devotees and tourists to spend the night. The accommodation is surprisingly good. The meditation centres host frequent retreats for beginners and experienced practitioners. Check the website for details, and more on the history and mission of the temple. Arrangements for meditation classes or an overnight temple stay can be made in advance.

To get to the temple, take a bus (NT77, 30 to 60 minutes, hourly) from the Kaohsiung Bus Company station in Kaohsiung.

MEINONG 美濃
☎ 07 / pop 45,187
Northeast of Foguangshan, rural Meinong (Méinóng), once the centre of a thriving tobacco industry, has now refashioned itself as a rural retreat. Fortunately, its popularity hasn't yet ruined the very reasons people want to come here. The countryside is still covered with fields of bananas, tobacco and rice, people still smile at strangers from their front porches, and everyone wants to know your story.

Meinong was settled about 200 years ago by Hakka (Kèjiā rén) immigrants. While the Hakka make up about 10% to 15% of the population of Taiwan, in Meinong the percentage goes up to 95%. The Hakka are traditionally seen as a hard-working people, who value education, and little Meinong can count a disproportionate amount of PhDs (and in the past, imperial scholars) among its population.

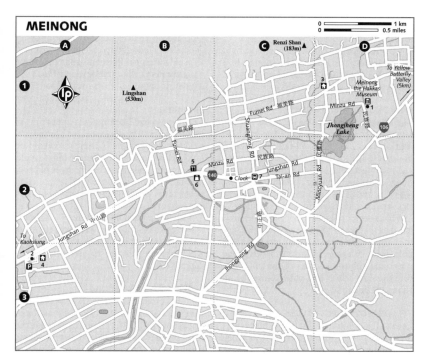

In recent years a number of B&Bs and even a camping ground have opened in Meinong. It's well worth your while to while away a few days here. Winter is our favourite time to go, as the weather is perfect – warm and dry – and the tourists are few. And, around Chinese New Year farmers plant colourful cosmos flowers in the fallow fields to help restock the soil before the next growing season. It's a lovely sight.

Information

Road signs in Meinong are usually bilingual. With our map you should have no problem getting around.

For more history on the Hakka people check out http://en.ihakka.net and see p45.

The Kaohsiung County tourism website (http://cultural.kscg.gov.tw) has a good overview of the sights at Meinong, including many we don't have the space to list.

Sights & Activities
CYCLING

One of the most pleasant things to do in Meinong is to get into the countryside on a bike. The town of Meinong is not particularly atractive, but the countryside is lush and dotted with tobacco sheds and three-sided Fujian-style houses.

Some of the best cycling is off the main road towards the ridge. Another enjoyable route is to ride out of town on County Rd 140 east towards Liugui and then head left into the fields. There are colour-coded bike routes across Meinong but at the time of writing the

SOUTHERN TAIWAN

lines on the road were fading, and in any case, maps were in Chinese only.

On weekends you can hire bikes to the right of the Meinong the Hakkas Museum on 40-3 Minzu Rd. The Shui Lian Tian Campground also rents bikes, as do most B&Bs.

MEINONG FOLK VILLAGE 美濃民俗村

The **village** (Měinóng Mínsú Cūn; ☎ 681 0072; 80 Lane 421, Jungshan Rd, sec.2; admission free; ◷ 8am-8pm) is an artificial recreation of an old-fashioned neighbourhood. It is definitely touristy but worth visiting nonetheless, as you can watch traditional crafts being made and sample *léi chá* (擂茶; pounded tea), an assortment of sticky-rice snacks, and tasty traditional noodles.

Village stores sell well-made paper umbrellas, fans and bamboo baskets. At the back of the village, outside the last shop, are two metal pots filled with water. Dip your hands in the water and rub the handles of the pots. The sound is like a hundred wine glasses being rubbed at one time.

YELLOW BUTTERFLY VALLEY 黃蝶翠谷

Locals have told us that the butterflies are coming back in numbers to the valley (Huángdié Cuìgǔ) and recent seasons have been the best in years. The butterflies flock to the valley in June and July and are best seen in the morning when the sun rises (and rouses the butterflies from sleep).

Sleeping

Jhong Jheng Hu B&B (Zhōng Zhèng Hú Shānzhuāng Mínsù; ☎ 681 2736; fax 681 7783; 30 Fumei Rd; 福美路30號; dm with Youth Guesthouse card NT300, r from 1500) The owner of this pleasant B&B is a local tour guide. She doesn't speak English but her son helps out. Stay in the newer building for the larger windows overlooking the fields and perfect sunset views over palm trees and low mountains. Bikes are free for guests.

Shui Lian Tian Campground (Shuǐ Lián Tiān; ☎ 0911-735 589; 80-1 Lane 421, Jungshan Rd, sec.2; camp sites NT500) A family-run camping ground with a quaint old wooden restaurant and teahouse on the grounds, with traditional foods and tea. The camping ground is just to the left of the folk village from the back parking lot. Bike rental is free for guests and NT100 per day for nonguests.

Eating

Meinong Traditional Hakka Restaurant (美濃古老客家菜; Měinóng Gǔlǎo Kèjiācài; ☎ 681 1156; 362-5

Jungshan Rd, sec.1; dishes NT120-200; ◷ 9am-2pm & 5-9pm) One of many places around Meinong to try good Hakka food. The restaurant is decorated with old farming implements and other rustic daily use items. A simple bowl of *bǎntiáo* (板條; flat rice noodles) costs only NT35.

Shopping

Craftsmen have been making umbrellas in Meinong for 80 years, ever since a local businessman bought up a Chinese master's shop (and all his suppliers) and forced him to move to Meinong. The umbrellas are made of paper and bamboo, hand-painted and lacquered to make them durable and waterproof. They make great decorations and gifts.

Guan De Xin Paper Umbrella Shop (Guǎng Dé Xīn Zhǐsǎn; ☎ 681 0451; 361 Jungshan Rd sec.1) If you're looking to buy, this is one of the best places. An umbrella here costs between NT600 and NT1200.

Getting There & Around

You can catch a bus directly into Meinong from the Kaohsiung Bus Company station in Kaohsiung (NT121, 1½ hours, every hour).

Meinong is quite small but the surrounding countryside is expansive and you'll need a vehicle or bicycle (which you can hire) to get around. If you stay at a B&B the owners can likely help you hire a scooter.

SANMIN 三民

pop 500

Not many foreign travellers make it as far as remote Sanmin (Sānmín), north of Meinong on Hwy 21. But with your own transport, especially a scooter, you can explore rugged canyons, high mountains, small aboriginal villages, and long winding country roads dotted with palms and yellow and red poinsettias (at least in winter).

Be prepared though for a lot of attention. At one breakfast shop, we got three marriage proposals in the first 10 minutes (and a fourth a little after that). Don't leave your sense of humour at home for this trip.

The best way to approach Sanmin is just to go. There are three small villages with shops, restaurants and B&Bs (民宿) so you won't go hungry or lack a place to stay. A few shops even serve exotic fare such as squirrel and cricket. There are English road signs to waterfalls, natural-gas fires and deep gorges, so you won't just wander around lost (not that that isn't fun).

One local sight that deserves a mention is **Holy Mt Zion** (錫安山; Xīānān Shān; admission free; 6.30am-5pm). The mount is the home of the New Testament Church, a fundamentalist group founded by Hong Kong movie actress Kong Duen-yee in 1963. It's an odd, odd place, with loudspeakers blasting out Hallelujahs, and posters on walls depicting the end of the world, and sporting such slogans as 'Diplomas are the tool of Satan' (which of course they are, but to actually say it!). And yes, that reads diplomas!

The members welcome visitors to the mountain, however, and you can wander around freely. Quality organic produce is available for sale. For a good overview of the history of Mount Zion check out www.taiwanho.com /print.php?sid=209.

It takes about two hours to drive to Sanmin from Meinong. If you continue north you can reach Danayigu in the Alishan National Scenic Area on a narrow county road. There's hardly any traffic along this route and the scenery is superb.

MEINONG TO MAOLIN

The cross-island highways get all the glory, but for sheer diversity of landscape and activity don't miss this stretch of road through the interior of Kaohsiung County.

The drive begins outside Meinong on Provincial Hwy 28. The first attractions of note are the **Liugui Tunnels** (六龜隧道; Liùgūi Sùidào), a series of seven long mountain tunnels opened recently for people to walk through. (Note that some of the tunnels were closed at the time of writing.)

Just past the tunnels, the **18 Lohan Mountains** (十八羅漢山; Shíbā Lóhàn Shān) begin to appear. The exotic beauty of these crags, jutting up like the rows of armour on a dinosaur's back, had us jumping out of our car every minute for a photo.

Next you'll reach the town of **Liugui** (六龜; Liùgūi), famous for bell fruit and mangoes. If you're interested in **river rafting** continue up to Paolai (p261).

A few kilometres south of Liugui are roads leading into two forest recreation areas: **Tengchih** (藤枝森林遊樂區; Téngzhī Sēnlín Yóulè Qū; http://recreate.forest.gov.tw) and **Shanping** (扇平森林生態科學園區; Shànpíng Sēnlín Shēngtài Kēxué Yuán Qū).

Tengchih is said to have one of the best-preserved natural forests in Taiwan, while little-visited Shanping offers peaceful trails and excellent bird-watching.

The last stretch of the trip takes you down Hwy 27 to Maolin. Interestingly, the landscape looks completely different on this side even though you are just retracing your route down on the opposite bank of the river.

MAOLIN RECREATION AREA
茂林遊憩區
☎ 07

The recreation area (Màolín Yóuqì Qū), part of the much larger Maolin National Scenic Area, covers a protected region from Maolin (estimated population 200) to Dona (estimated population 200) Village. Here you'll find pristine mountain landscapes, vertiginously high suspension bridges, waterfalls, natural swimming pools and even free outdoor hot springs. Rukai aboriginal culture is strong in this part of the country and Dona Village is one of the best places to see tradition stone slab houses.

But Maolin's greatest hit is the Purple Butterfly Valley. Considered one of the two most important butterfly migratory resting grounds in the world (the other is the Monarch Butterfly Valley around Mexico City), the valley gifts Taiwan in the winter with a daily show of hundreds, or even thousands, of butterflies dancing in the air as the first rays of the morning sun tip over the mountains.

Orientation & Information

It's simple to get around the scenic area. There is only one main road, County Rd 132, connecting the two villages. It's 15km from the Maolin administration office to Dona.

The **Maolin National Scenic Area Administration Office** (Màolín Guójiā Fēngjǐng Qū Guǎnlǐ Chù; ☎ 680 1488; www.maulin-nsa.gov.tw; 9am-5pm) is just past the **tollgate** (admission NT70; 6am-10pm) to the scenic area. The staff speak no English, but the exhibits are usually bilingual and includes an excellent introduction to the purple butterfly.

For information about the Rukai people see www.sinica.edu.tw/tit/scenery/0296_Maolin .html.

Sights & Activities
PURPLE BUTTERFLY VALLEY 紫蝶幽谷
The valley is not just one geographic location so there are several good places to see the insects. Just to the left of Maolin Village, **Maolin Park** (Màolín Gōngyuán) has a few hectares of

butterfly-protection area. The park maintains a small display shelter but it's more fascinating to see the butterflies on the trails around the park. Though the good spots seem to change every year, at the time of writing the best location could be found by following the park trail up to where it connects with a small road and by following the road down to the right. Eventually the road crosses a bridge before returning to the small road that leads back to the park. Around the bridge we saw a thousand or more butterflies fluttering in the air.

Just up the road from the administration office is another butterfly viewing area on the left. You can't miss this one as there are usually crowds of people and buses and even a vendor or two.

The best time to watch the butterflies is between 9am and 11am, when the sun first comes over the mountains and rouses the insects from sleep. It's possible to arrange a tour, but we usually just follow one in progress.

WATERFALLS

You can drive up to the first of the five levels of the **Qingren Valley Waterfall** (Qíngrén Gǔ Pùbù). It's then a 10-minute walk to the second level.

The next waterfall in the park is the **Maolin Gorge Waterfall** (Màolín Gǔ Pùbù). As you drive down into Maolin Gorge (Valley) there is a sign and map for the waterfall just before you cross the river. Follow the road until it forks at the end and go right. There's a parking area 1.5km up the road. The trail runs beside the river for 2km. You can swim in the waterfall pool but be careful as it's a slippery descent.

Further up the main road through Maolin is the turn-off for the picturesque **Meiyagu Waterfall** (Měiyǎgǔ Pùbù). From the car park it's about a 15-minute walk on a smooth stone path.

ROAD TO DONA

County Rd 132 from Maolin Village to Dona features a number of roadside attractions, including the **Dona High Suspension Bridge** (Dōnà Gāudiàoqiáo), and the **Snake Head mountain** (Shétóu Shān) and **Dragon Head mountain** (Lóngtóu Shān), which are actually odd-shaped mounds in the middle of the river valley.

Dona (Dōnà) is a stronghold for Rukai aboriginal culture, and stonework, including traditional shale houses, which are visible everywhere (though there is quite a bit of ugly modern development as well).

HOT SPRINGS

The free outdoor **Dona Hot Springs** (Dōnà Wēnquán) have been, well not quite ruined, but made a lot less attractive recently. Instead of small pools in the rocks, there is now a concrete platform with two long concrete pools. Many people ignore this now and head upstream. There is a small wild spring pool not far up on the left and a canyon just made for exploring.

You can reach the springs by a trail that begins at the end of Dona Village, or by

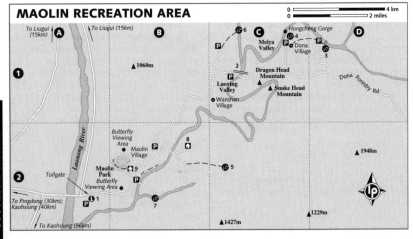

MAOLIN RECREATION AREA

To Liugui (15km)

To Liugui (15km)

Hongcheng Gorge

Meiya Valley

Dona Village

▲1060m

Dragon Head Mountain

Laoying Valley

▲ Snake Head Mountain

Dona Forestry Rd

Wanshan Village

Butterfly Viewing Area

Maolin Village

Leonong River

▲1948m

Maolin Park

Tollgate

Maolin Butterfly Viewing Area

To Pingdong (30km); Kaohsiung (40km)

To Kaohsiung (56km)

▲1427m

▲1229m

0   4 km
0   2 miles

driving on County Rd 132 past the village a few kilometres.

A new set of springs (we think they are free, though it wasn't clear) have opened up recently in the **Hongcheng Gorge** (Hóngchén Xiágǔ). Again they are pumped into cement pools, but the setting is very scenic as you overlook the river valley from tub level. Even if you don't visit the hot springs you can park here and use the location as a base for exploring the river.

Sleeping

There are half a dozen guesthouses in Dona charging around NT1500 a night for a double. Just walk around and you will see them.

De En Gorge Guesthouse (Dé Ēn Gǔ Mínsù; ☎ 0955-055 132; dm/camp sites/2-person cabins NT300/500/2000) Set high above the river on a grassy meadow, and run by an exceptionally friendly couple, this should be your default accommodation in Maolin. Camping is permitted. The Indigenous People's Culture Park on the grass bluff and the cabins, made of grey stone, are a great stylish option. Dorm rooms have two single beds per room so if you're a couple you can get your own room and bathroom. To get to the guesthouse head down to Maolin Valley and cross the bridge. When the road ends at a fork, head left and up about a kilometre or so. The first building you see is the guesthouse.

Fungshan Agricultural Activity Centre (Fèngshānshì Nónghuì Màolín Huìyuán Huódòng Zhōngxīn; ☎ 680 1115; d/tw NT1500/3200) Rooms are large and clean but very spartan. There's a restaurant in the hotel but it's for groups only.

Eating

Your options are very limited and most dishes have MSG in them (even asking for barbecued

corn to be made without it just elicits blank stares). Little stalls are set up on the main road in Maolin (often in what looks to be people's ramshackle living rooms), but be aware that these places close early (by 6pm or 7pm) on weekdays. Don't wait to eat!

On weekends, large barbecue pits are set up in Dona, but these are not suitable for a single person unless you can eat a whole chicken. Around Dona Hot Springs a number of small shops sell pretty good barbecued meats, soups and stir-fried mountain vegetables (average dish NT100). Some places claim to be open 24 hours a day.

Just before the tollgate there are a few other shops, including a good fruit-shake stand, but these also close by 6pm. Down Provincial Hwy 27 a short distance there's a small grocery store on the right.

Getting There & Away

There are buses from Pingdong, but Maolin is just too large an area to explore without your own vehicle unless you have a lot of time. Consider renting a scooter in Tainan (per day NT200) and riding there.

PINGDONG 屏東

☎ 08 / pop 216,777

Though Pingdong (Píngdōng) is actually not a bad-looking little town, there is little here for the traveller. If you need to spend the night there are a couple of obvious places across from the train station where you can get a room for less than NT1000 a night.

Trains between Kaohsiung and Pingdong (NT31, 25 minutes) run about every 15 minutes.

The **Pingdong Bus Company station** (☎ 723 7131) is a block left of the train station as you exit. You can't miss it. Buses to Donggang (NT72, 40 minutes) run every 20 minutes. There are also buses to the Indigenous People's Culture Park (below).

SANDIMEN 三地門

☎ 08 / pop 2000

This small aboriginal community (Sāndìmén), an hour east of Pingdong, is well known for the **Indigenous People's Cultural Park** (台灣山地 文化園區; Táiwān Shāndì Wénhuà Yuánqū; ☎ 799 1219; www.tacp.gov.tw; 104 Fongjin, Peiyei Village, Majia; adult/child NT150/80; ☯ 8.30am-5pm, closed Mon). The park, set in forested mountains, covers a large area and is an excellent introduction to aboriginal

---

THE BURNING OF THE WANG YEH BOATS *Robert Kelly*

In the old fishing town of **Donggang** (Dōnggǎng), Wang Yeh worship runs deep. Wang Yeh, a Tang dynasty scholar, is said to watch over the waters of southern China. To the Taiwanese, who largely descend from southern Chinese fisherman, his importance is eclipsed only by Matsu, the goddess of the sea, and protector of fishermen.

At the resplendent Donglong Temple (Dōnglóng Gòng) in Donggang, a very odd festival is held in Wang Yeh's honour every three years. It's a little like Burning Man, only with a boat.

The last **Boat Burning Festival** (王船祭; Wángchuánjì), or the Burning of the Wang Yeh Boats as it's often called, was held in 2006, and a few friends and I were fortunate enough to see the final event. The whole festival runs over an eight-day period. During this time, a 20m-long wooden boat (that had taken local craftsmen more than a year to build) is filled with replicas of houses, clothing, cars, horses and electrical appliances, as well as sacrificial offerings of food. On the final day, or rather, morning, the entire model is dragged to the beach through the main streets of Donggang, then hundreds of kilos of ghost paper are piled round. During a slow, elaborate ceremony that goes on for hours, local gods are called onto the boat. Sometimes the gods are reluctant and have to be persuaded to get aboard. (Can't say I blame them.)

During the 2006 festival, it took till almost 4am for all the gods to board the vessel. And then, as per tradition, the boat was set on fire.

Looking back, the time spent waiting for this moment was worthwhile, but at the time it was agonisingly tedious. It's a good idea to bring along a folding chair if you go, and maybe a book.

It's surprising how long the boat takes to really start burning once it has been lit. For the first 30 minutes you can stand pretty close. Afterwards the heat and smoke keep the crowds back, but this is also the time to get the best photos as it's easy to push your way to the front for a clear shot.

By dawn, most people have usually had enough and begin to set out, leaving the now gutted but still glowing hull behind. They also leave behind an unceremonious amount of garbage, which can now be seen clearly in the morning light. As my Taiwanese friend Kitty said upon witnessing the aftermath, 'It's a little like waking up, rolling over and thinking, "Wow! You looked a whole lot better last night!"'

The next boat burning is scheduled for autumn 2009. To get to Donggang take a Pingdong Bus Company bus (NT72, 40 minutes, every 20 minutes) from Pingdong.

---

culture in Taiwan. A useful English-language brochure (with map and events schedule) can be picked up at the reception area. The park's website is worth a look before you go.

Separate areas have been established to highlight the nine indigenous tribes. Each area features authentic, life-size displays of traditional houses and communal structures. You can walk around each area if you give yourself several hours, or you can ride the free shuttle buses that cruise the park every 10 minutes or so. The park also houses several interesting exhibitions and there are daily performances of aboriginal dancing, though the ones we saw were slightly tacky.

From Pingdong, buses to the park (NT65, one hour) run only on weekends. The first bus leaves at 8.40am. On weekdays take a bus to Sandimen (NT58) and then walk to the park (15 minutes) or take a taxi if you can find one.

From Sandimen it is possible to get further into the mountains to very remote aboriginal villages in the Maolin National Scenic Area (www.maolin-nsa.gov.tw).

JIN-SHUI YING OLD TRAIL
浸水營古道

Part of the National Trail System (p329), this Qing dynasty path (Jìnshuǐ Yín Gǔ Dào) used to cross the entire southern part of the island. Today it still covers about half and takes a full six to seven hours of downhill walking to reach the end of the trail near Dawu on the east coast (it would be another two hours of walking to reach Dawu and the sea on back-country roads). Along the way you pass the remains of a Qing dynasty army camp and various other historical sights.

The trail runs along the point where the summer and winter monsoon airstreams meet, and receives the second-highest rain-fall in Taiwan (bring an umbrella). It's a jungle here and the relative remoteness of the trail and its long history means you have a good chance of spotting local wild-life, including the Formosan macaque, the Reeves muntjac, wild boar and over 80 species of bird.

To hike the trail you need a police permit (NT10). Contact the **Pintung Forestry Bureau** (☎ 08-733 8835) for information, including hot to arrange a van in **Fangliao** (枋寮) to take you to the trailhead and pick you up on the other side. You can catch a train to Fangliao from Kaohsiung (fast/slow train NT109/66, one/1½ hours) every hour or so.

LITTLE LIUCHIU ISLAND (HSIAO LIUCHIU ISLAND)小琉球

☎ 08 / pop 13,000

This pretty coral island (Xiǎo Liúqiú Yǔ), no more than 5km long, offers more than enough sea vistas, convoluted caves, sandy beaches and odd rock formations to keep you happy for a long, long day. Best of all, it's simple to get to and around.

Winter is a great time to visit as the weather is still in the mid-20°C range but the place is practically deserted (at least midweek).

Information

There's a new **visitor information centre** (☎ 861 4615; ⏱ 9am-5pm) just above Lingshan Temple on the cliff. Very little English is spoken but the view is good up here.

Little Liuchiu Island is part of the Dapeng Bay National Scenic Area; check out the website (www.tbnsa.gov.tw) for more information.

Sights & Activities

You can ride around the island on a scooter in about 30 minutes but give yourself at least half a day. This island was made for exploring.

Some attractions to look out for are **Vase Rock** (Huāpíng Yán), a giant eroded coral with a thin base and large head, **Black Ghost Cave** (Wūguǐ Dòng; admission NT120; ☎ 8am-5pm) and **Beauty Cave** (Měirén Dòng; admission NT120; ☎ 8am-5pm). For the bloody stories behind these names check out www.sinica.edu.tw/tit /scenery/0496_Hsiao.html.

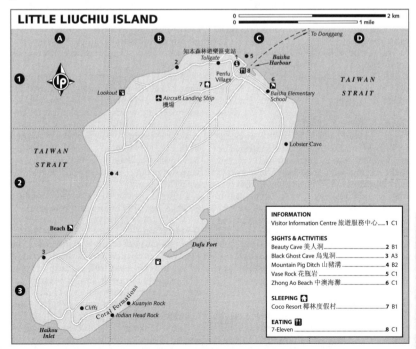

LITTLE LIUCHIU ISLAND

To Donggang

知本森林遊樂區東站
Tollgate
Penfu Village
Baisha Harbour
Lookout
Aircraft Landing Strip 機場
Baisha Elementary School
TAIWAN STRAIT
TAIWAN STRAIT
Lobster Cave
Beach
Dafu Port
Coral Formations
Cliffs
Kuanyin Rock
Indian Head Rock
Haikou Inlet

INFORMATION	
Visitor Information Centre 旅遊服務中心	1 C1
SIGHTS & ACTIVITIES	
Beauty Cave 美人洞	2 B1
Black Ghost Cave 烏鬼洞	3 A3
Mountain Pig Ditch 山豬溝	4 B2
Vase Rock 花瓶岩	5 C1
Zhong Ao Beach 中澳海灘	6 C1
SLEEPING	
Coco Resort 椰林度假村	7 B1
EATING	
7-Eleven	8 C1

SOUTHERN TAIWAN

Other must-sees include the narrow, twisting, root-strangled coral passageways at **Mountain Pig Ditch** (Shān Zhū Gōu) and **Lingshan Temple** (Língshān Sì), just up from the pier. The temple offers, like several others around the island, fine clear views across Taiwan Strait.

The best place for a swim is at **Zhong Ao Beach** (Zhōng Ào Hǎitān). The beach at Vase Rock is nice for wading as you search for sea life, and the tiny but picturesque stretch of shell-sand beach before Black Ghost Cave makes for a sweet picnic spot. You can go for a dip here as well, but only up to your knees. Be sure to wear something on your feet if you go in the water as the coral rocks can really cut you up. Also, don't go more than 20m to 30m from shore unless you are wearing fins. There is a nasty undertow around the island.

Sleeping & Eating

There are several inexpensive hotels around the village at Baisha Harbour (Báishā Mǎtóu) with rooms for NT1000 or less should you decide to stay a night. For something a little nicer, try the quaint **Coco Resort** (Yělín Dùjiàcūn; ☎ 861 4368; 20-38 Minzu Rd; 2-/4-person cabins NT2200/3200), a minute's scooter ride up a quiet lane.

The village at Baisha Harbour has many small restaurants. You can eat expensive fresh seafood or simple stir-fries for less than NT100. There is also a 7-Eleven in the village where you can buy sandwiches and drinks.

Getting There & Away

From Pingdong, catch a bus to Donggang (NT72, 40 minutes, every 20 minutes). The bus will first stop in town and then proceed to the harbour ferry terminals. There are two ferry terminals on the right before the fish market and both offer trips to Little Liuchiu Island. The first terminal is the one we recommend. Boats to Baisha Harbour on Little Liuchiu Island (return NT410, 30 minutes) leave every hour in the morning (first ferry at 7am) and every 1½ hours in the afternoon. The last boat back to Donggang leaves at 5pm or 6pm, depending on the season.

Getting Around

The island is only 9km around so you could easily walk it in a day. Scooters (half/full day NT150/300) can be rented as soon as

you get off the ferry at the spiffy new dock or even before you get on the boat at Donggang from the local touts. Don't worry, they are legitimate.

KENTING NATIONAL PARK
墾丁國家公園
☎ 08

It's the end of the road down here, but there's nothing remote or isolated at all about Kenting National Park (Kěndīng Guójiā Gōngyuán). Over 5 million visitors a year flock here to swim, surf, snorkel, dive, visit museums, hike, visit hot springs, eat good food and enjoy a little nightlife. And they do so all year round. The average January temperature is 21°C (many days are much warmer). Unless a cold front has hit the island, you can usually swim even year round. In July it can get to a scorching 38°C.

The park occupies the entire southern tip of Taiwan, an area known as the Hengchun Peninsula. Low mountains and hilly terraces prevail over much of the land, along with, in a few places, rugged high cliffs and sandy deserts. The swimming beaches won't stun you with their beauty like those in Thailand, but they are lovely nonetheless, with yellow sands and turquoise waters. All in all, the topography is wonderfully suited for recreation, in particular cruising around sightseeing on a scooter.

In many ways, the park gets better every year, but also worse. You can no longer just pitch a tent anywhere, but now fireworks are banned on the beaches. There's a greater emphasis on cleanliness but with more and more travellers visiting, some places are trashed during the busy season (summer and Chinese New Year). The main street in Kenting Village is looking better, but there's still no plan for a pavement.

Suffice to say, some love it here for what there is, while some do not for what there isn't.

Orientation

The national park covers a large area (18,000 hectares) but as there are few major roads it is easy to get around with our map in hand. The majority of people stay in Kenting Village. There are literally dozens of hotels here as well as scores of restaurants, bars and assorted shops.

Those looking for a quieter atmosphere should consider staying further down the

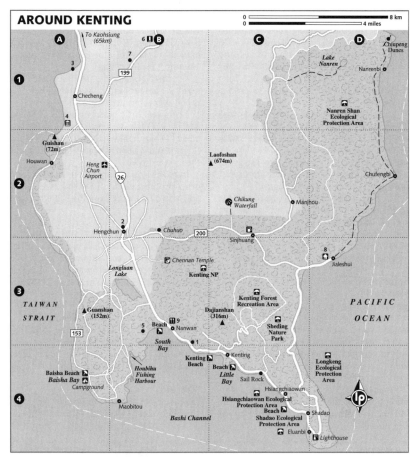

AROUND KENTING

peninsula at Sail Rock or Eluanbi. Surfers and beach bums will probably like Nanwan or Jialeshui.

Information

There's free wireless internet at the National Park Headquarters and the McDonald's on Kenting Rd. There are ATMs in the 7-Elevens in Kenting Village on the main road.

Kenting National Park (www.ktnp.gov.tw) The official website is more than thorough in its introduction to the park.

National Park Headquarters (Map p283; ☎ 886 1321; 946 No 596, Kenting Rd; ☯ 8.30am-5pm) You'll find English-speaking staff and several useful English brochures and maps. The centre is a few kilometres north of Kenting so you'll probably need to check into your hotel and rent a scooter before visiting.

Sights

Must-sees include **Kenting Forest Recreation Area** (Kěndīng Sēnlín Yóulè Qū; Map p283; admission NT100; 🕙 8am-5pm), with its limestone caves and botanical gardens, and **Jialeshui** (Jiālèshuǐ; Map p283; admission NT100; 🕙 8am-5pm), a 2.5km-long stretch of coral coastline with rocks eroded into the shapes of animals.

The **National Museum of Marine Biology** (Guólì Hǎiyáng Shēngwù Bówùguǎn; Map p283; ☎ 882 5001; www2.nmmba.gov.tw; 2 Houwan Rd, Checheng; adult/child NT300/200; 🕙 9am-6pm Mon-Fri, 8am-6pm Sat & Sun, 8am-7pm Jul & Aug) is also rated highly for the live displays of colourful and exotic sea life that are professionally and imaginatively designed.

The park maintains strict access controls to ecologically sensitive regions, such as the area around **Lake Nanren** (Nánrén Hú; Map p283) and the fine shell beach at **Shadao** (Shādǎo; Map p283). You can apply for permits on the park's website to enter these areas ahead of time.

Activities

SWIMMING

Taiwan is a volcanic island, which means the land rises steeply from the sea and the ocean begins to drop not far offshore. As a result, the waters just offshore have treacherous currents and undertows. Some sound advice from a long-term expat is not to go out much further than you can stand.

Kenting Beach (Map p284), the longest swimming beach in the area, is now free to the public. You can enter via the campsite off Dawan Rd.

The beach across from the Caesar Park Hotel is smaller but set in picture-perfect **Little Bay** (Xiǎo Wān; Map p284). There's a beach bar and showers (free for Caesar Park guests, a nominal fee for others).

Nanwan (Nánwān; Map p283) sees a few too many jet skis for our liking, though there is a roped-off swimming-only area now.

The sweet little crescent beach at **Baisha Bay** (Báishā Wān; Map p283) is a little further afield but worth taking the extra time to visit. It is not as unvisited as years ago, but it is still the least crowded.

In recent years, jumping off the chin (and other protuberances) of **Sail Rock** (Chuánfān Shí; Map p283), aka Nixon Rock, has become quite popular.

SURFING, SNORKELLING & SCUBA DIVING

The waters around **Jialeshui** (Jiālèshuǐ; Map p283; admission NT100; 🕙 8am-5pm) and the nuclear power plant (Map p283) at **Nanwan** have the best surfing waves. You can rent boards (NT500 to NT800 per day) in Jialeshui at Winson House (opposite), in Nanwan at Beach House (p286) or at numerous shops along Kenting Rd.

For snorkelling, check out the coral formations near **Sail Rock**. You can rent gear across the road. If you want to scuba dive, check out one of the shops in Nanwan.

BOATING

There are sea tours from **Houbihu** (後壁湖; Hòubìhú; Map p283) for NT400 for two hours. No reservations are required and there are no

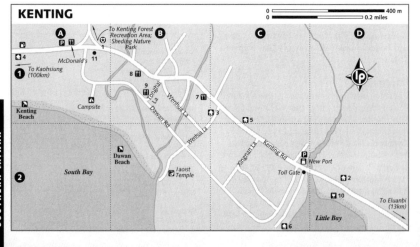

KENTING

0 _____ 400 m
0 _____ 0.2 miles

To Kenting Forest Recreation Area; Sheding Nature Park

McDonald's

To Kaohsiung (100km)

Kenting Beach

Campsite

Haipin La

Wenhua La

Dawan Rd

Dawan Beach

South Bay

Taoist Temple

Xingnan La

Kenting Rd

New Port

Toll Gate

To Eluanbi (13km)

Little Bay

SOUTHERN TAIWAN

fixed schedules. Just show up during spring or summer days.

BIRD-WATCHING

With its grasslands, forests, lakes and coastline, Kenting is a prime bird-watching area, and the National Park Headquarters has several good brochures on the species you may encounter. For the casual birder, **Longluan Lake**, **Eluanbi**, **Sheding Nature Park** and **Manjhou** (all Map p283) are considered prime spots.

Among the more famous birds to sail the Kenting skies are the migratory goshawks and grey-faced buzzards. Early to mid September the goshawks start arriving on their journey south to Indochina. The best time to see them is morning in Sheding Nature Park. As many as 200,000 fly by in 20 days.

Around October 10 (National Day) about 20,000 grey-faced buzzards pass through the park also on their way to Indochina. The best place to see them is Manjhou between 3pm and 6pm. Sadly, as many as 2000 buzzards are poached every season for food.

Festivals & Events

Indie music fans should definitely try to time their Taiwan visit for April when **Spring Scream** (www.springscream.com) takes over Kenting. It's the longest-running music festival in the country, now in its midteens. The multistaged musical event brings together names big and small in Taiwan's indie music scene, along with a few imported bands. In 2007 there was a change of venue from the old Liou Fu Campground, so check out the website for the location of future events.

Sleeping

Bookings are advisable if there's a particular hotel you wish to stay at. Otherwise, it's possible, even during Chinese New Year, to just show up and find accommodation. Kenting Rd and Dawan Rd are filled with budget and midrange accommodation.

At Sail Rock you'll find a number of small, nondescript hotels and a few restaurants across the street from the water. Prices are similar to Kenting Village.

Summer (approximately May to September), Chinese New Year and other public holidays are considered the high season. Discounts of 40% or more for midrange and top-end hotels are standard on weekdays and during the low season.

BUDGET

At the time of writing there were two camping grounds (*lùyíngqū*) at Baisha beach on either end of the bay. By the time you read this, however, the park have bought the land they stood on and started building its own camp sites. In Kenting Village, a camping ground just back from the beach off Dawan Rd was being reconstructed at the time of writing. It looked to be an ideal place to stay.

Winson House (Map p283; ☎ 880 1053; www.tbay .com.tw; 244 Chashan Rd; 滿州鄉茶山路244號; dm/s/d NT300/800/1200) Just 100m before the entrance to Jialeshui is this B&B-style place run by Winson, a well-known local surfer. Lessons (NT2000 a day) and equipment rental (board NT800 a day) are available. The surfing beach, which is considered the best in the Kenting area, is literally just down the hill from the house.

Catholic Hostel (Tiānzhǔjiào Huódòng Zhōngxīn; Map p284; ☎ 886 1540; fax 886 1352; 2 Wenhua Lane; 文化路2號; d/tw NT1200/2000) The hostel is immaculately clean and a close walk to the swimming beaches. There's a dorm, but only for groups.

MIDRANGE

Hotel California (Jiāzhōu Lüdiàn; Map p284; ☎ 886 1588; www.hotelca.idv.tw; 40 Kenting Rd; 墾丁路40號; d NT2000; 🖵) With its brightly coloured rooms, and surf-shop décor (it's run by a local surfer), the California is a good place to stay if you want a bit of character. Dorm rooms for four to eight people (NT3000/5000) are also available.

Kenting Youth Activity Centre (Kěndīng Qīngnián Huódòng Zhōngxīn; Map p284; ☎ 886 1221; 17 Kenting Rd;

墾丁路17號; d/tw from NT2500/3000) The centre occupies 25 hectares of land and features a reproduced traditional Fujian-style courtyard dwelling for guests to sleep in. The centre will appeal to families, not only for the rather fun design (kids just love playing around the old-style buildings) but because it's on its own secluded road.

Beach House (Hǎibiān; Map p283; ☎ 888 0440; www .beach.idv.tw; 230 Nanwan Rd, Nanwan; 南灣 南灣路 230號; d/tw 3200/4000) Also run by local surfers. Rooms are small but brightly painted and the upper-floor rooms have excellent views over the ocean. Nice friendly vibe here and suitable even for older travellers.

TOP END

While there's no doubt the top-end hotels in Kenting have lovely rooms and excellent facilities, we do find them overpriced considering the level of the rest of Kenting (that place that exists outside the hotel) is fair to middling.

Chateau Beach Resort (Xiàdū Shātān Jiǔdiàn; Map p284; ☎ 886 2345; 451 Kenting Rd; 墾丁路451號; r from NT6100; 🏊) There's a light, breezy, whimsical feel to the pastel-coloured Chateau, making it a nice contrast to the posh Caesar. The Chateau sits right on the beach and you pay for this access – overall the rooms are nothing special. A new wing was opening at the time of writing and the rooms here promised higher standards (and considerably higher prices). In the off season 40% discounts usually apply.

Caesar Park Hotel (Kǎisà Dà Fàndiàn; Map p284; ☎ 886 1888; fax 886 1818; 6 Kenting Rd; 墾丁路6號; d/tw NT10,560/12,980; 🖥 🏊) The Caesar has a swanky new Southeast Asian design and a new price tag to go with it. Hotel features include a spa, business centre and a fine new supervised children's play area (with storytelling at night). If you want a room in summer you'd better book at least two months in advance. In winter, weekday rates go as low as NT4600 per night.

DON'T EAT THE FISH!

The national park administration asks that visitors refrain from eating coral fish because fishing is damaging the reefs. You can recognise coral fish easily by their bright colours.

Eating

Kenting is a tourist town and there is no shortage of food, including Thai, Chinese, Yunan, Italian and even South African. Most places are open late.

There are a couple of breakfast shops and fruit-drink stands along Kenting Rd. The breakfasts at the Caesar Park Hotel (NT462) have long been popular.

Warung Didi (Dídí Xiǎochī; Map p284; ☎ 886 1835; 176 Dawan Rd; dishes NT200; 🕙 5.30pm-1am, closed Tue) The service can be spotty, and the place can be costly (NT300 for a curry and the rice is extra?) but Didi draws in the crowds every night with the promise of Thai and Malay curries, good music, beer and a lively beach-hut atmosphere. Reservations are recommended on weekends.

Amy's Cucina (Nánxīng Dàfàndiàn; Map p284; ☎ 197 7131, ext 1; 131-1 Kenting Rd; dishes NT200; 🕙 10am-midnight Oct-May, 10am-2am Jun-Sep) This was the first place in Kenting to serve pizza and it's still got some of the best Italian food in the park. The casual redbrick- and wood-design makes it suitable for hanging out and enjoying a nice meal.

Waves Kitchen (Bōlàng Cāntīng; Map p283; ☎ 888 3399; 212 Nanwan Rd; dishes NT200; 🕙 noon-10pm, later on Sat) A stylish new restaurant off Nanwan beach, with a decent menu serving well-prepared seafood, pasta and sandwiches.

Lu Nan Seafood (Lǔ Nán Huó Hǎixiān; Map p284; ☎ 886 1036; 193 Kenting Rd; dishes NT500-1000; 🕙 noon-10pm). Recommended by locals for its fresh, delicious seafood. The place has all the atmosphere of an airplane hanger but that's not why people come here.

Drinking

Many restaurants, such as Warung Didi, Amy's Cucina and The Waves Kitchen also serve as bars (beer from NT120), often with good music played loudly in the evenings. The Caesar Hotel runs an **outdoor bar-café** (Map p284; beer from NT90; 🕙 9am-6pm weekday, 9am-10pm weekends, later in summer) on Little Bay beach (seperate from the hotel premises).

Getting There & Away

AIR

TransAsia Airways (☎ 02-2972 4599), **Mandarin Airlines** (☎ 02-2717 1188) and **Uni Air** (☎ 07-801 0189) all have flights to **Heng Chun Airport** (Map p283; www.hca.gov.tw/english/default.htm) from Taipei. While Heng Chun is much closer to Kenting than Kaohsiung (a 20- to 30-minute drive), you will still need to catch a bus or taxi to complete your journey. Note there are no shuttle buses between the airport and Kenting. You have to walk out onto the main road and wait for a Kenting Express Bus to come by.

BUS
From Kaohsiung catch the 'Kenting Express' (two-hour ride NT342, three-hour ride NT298, every hour) from the Kaohsiung Bus Company station or the airport.

FERRY
Ferries are said to leave from Houbihu Harbour for Lanyu during the summer months.

Getting Around
The only way to get around Kenting is with your own transport. There are no buses of any kind except those coming in from Kaohsiung and Heng Chun. Any hotel can arrange car, jeep or scooter hire. Most travellers use scooters and as you enter town there are scooter-hire shops (NT400 to NT500 per day) to the right.

SICHONGSI HOT SPRINGS
四重溪溫泉
☎ 08
One of the pleasures of a trip to Kenting is the sheer variety of things to see and do. Outside the park boundaries, but still accessible by car or scooter, is the hot-spring village of Sichongsi (Sìchóngxī). While you may not want to visit hot springs during the summer months, a soak in an outdoor pool with a clear starry sky above on a cool winter evening is a real treat. There are numerous hotels, many with modern facilities, including differ-ent temperature pools, spa jets and showers. You can stay overnight but most people just come for a few hours.

Recommended by Kenting locals is **Dashan Hot Spring Spa** (Dàshān Wēnquán Nóngchǎng; Map p283; ☎ 882 5725; 60-1 Tamei Rd, Wenquan Village; unlimited time NT200; ☻ 6am-11pm). The spa is at the far end of the village. Drive until you are almost out of town and turn left 30m or so before the strange castlelike building. Follow the road about 1km and then turn onto a dirt road marked with a sign in Chinese for the hotel.

To get to Sichongsi, follow Hwy 26 almost as far as Checheng (車城; Chēchéng) and turn right onto County Rd 199. Sichongsi is a few kilometres down the highway and is the first real settlement you pass through. It's about 32km to Sichongsi from Kenting.

SHUANGLIOU FOREST RECREATION AREA 雙流森林遊樂區
It's well worth continuing down County Rd 199 east of Sichongsi. Along the way, you will pass the **Shihmen Historical Battlefield** (Shímén Gǔzhàn Cháng; Map p283) and be rewarded with a varying landscape of ponds, aboriginal villages, mountains and open fields.

Just before the coast, you have the choice of taking Spur Route 199 to the photo-genic **grasslands** and **hot springs** around Shiu-hai (Xùhǎi), or continuing up the 199 to Hwy 9 and turning left to reach **Shuangliou Forest Recreation Area** (Shuāng Liú Sēnlín Yóulè Qū; ☎ 08-870 1394; http://recreate.forest.gov.tw; adult/child NT100/50; ☻ 8am-5pm).

The park has two main walking trails, one to the gorgeous **Shuangliuo Waterfall** (雙流瀑布; Shuāngliú Pùbù; two hours return) and the other to 630m **Mautzu Mountain** (帽子山; Màuzi Shān; three hours return). Both trails begin near the visitor centre and are marked with English signs.

Taiwan's Islands

Beautiful, well off the beaten path for most Western travellers and as chock-full of culture and history per square kilometre as you're likely to find in East Asia, Taiwan's outer islands abound with opportunities for those intrepid enough to make the trip.

Kinmen and Matsu, both in the Taiwan Strait, have remained out of the travel spotlight until very recently. Situated between mainland China and Taiwan, these islands have been a source of tension, war and fierce political debate for more than half a century. Because of their location and history, they offer a superb window into Taiwan's turbulent military past and also the rich cultural heritage of coastal Fujian. As trade and travel relations between Taiwan and mainland China develop, these islands are being transformed from barriers into gateways.

Penghu, the most visited of the Strait Islands, is a popular resort destination that attracts beachgoers – both local and foreign – who flock here in summer for the fine-sand beaches and water sports. As autumn sets in and the winds pick up, the archipelago attracts sailors and windsurfers, drawn by its combination of excellent water and high winds. Off Taiwan's Pacific coast lie Green Island, with beautiful hot springs and pristine coral reefs, and Lanyu, Taiwan's furthest outpost in geographical and cultural terms.

The outer islands are still a well-kept secret among travellers, but as Taiwan seeks to promote the beauty of its farthest-flung counties both nationally and abroad, more and more people are finding a side trip to the outer islands a highlight of their Taiwan experience.

HIGHLIGHTS

- Sleep in a traditional Fujian-style home on **Matsu** (opposite)
- Soak in a sea-water hot spring on **Green Island** (p320)
- Spend a few days living in a Yami family home on **Lanyu Island** (p319)
- Bird-watch at Kinmen's **Shuangli Wetlands Area Centre** (p304)
- Temple-hop and windsurf in **Penghu** (p306)

★ Matsu

CHINA

★ Kinmen

Penghu ★

TAIWAN (ROC)

Green Island ★

Lanyu Island ★

National Parks & Forest Recreation Areas

Though you'll find higher mountains and larger stretches of green in Taiwan proper, the outer islands have things well covered when it comes to park land. Reforested Kinmen itself is a national park (quite fitting, we think, as the whole area was once totally deforested by Ming dynasty general Koxinga to build a sailing fleet), and there's talk of turning Green Island into a national park in the next few years. Except for a few small towns, mountainous Lanyu is almost entirely covered by forests, and its indigenous Yami inhabitants are quite militant about fighting any improper development. Spreading across the whole archipelago, the Matsu Island Bird Sanctuary provides a protected home to 30 avian species (mostly gulls and terns). Most of the Penghu archipelago are desert islands and are covered with low-lying cacti and other succulents. Trees in Penghu's Lintou and Chitou parks tend to all grow at a pronounced angle thanks to the persistent wind.

MATSU 馬祖

☎ 0836 / pop 9000

If you're looking for an 'off the beaten path' experience, look no further; you can't get much farther from Taiwan on an ROC visa than here. Matsu (Mǎzǔ) lies directly off the coast of mainland China's Fujian province, and its people – though nominally schooled in Mandarin – speak a dialect mostly unintelligible to speakers of Taiwanese. And politically, though Matsu is a part of the ROC (with a serious troop presence to prove it), most Matsu folk identify with their kin across the narrow Straits separating them; people who, for over a generation, they could only watch through binoculars.

Matsu, like Kinmen, still retains much of its feel as a place perpetually on the military defensive. However, while both are still considered military posts, we find the Matsu vibe a bit more martial; for one thing, half the people you run into on Matsu are in uniform. For another, while Kinmen has a number of fine war museums, you're unlikely to be serenaded by live-ammo drilling, a regular occurrence on Matsu (and on that note, mind where you wander there!).

History

The development of Matsu began in the 1400s with the arrival of Fujianese mainlanders escaping political turmoil in their homeland. Later, the migrant waves of the 1600s from mainland China to Taiwan saw an increase in Matsu's population as boatloads of Fujianese fishermen arrived on the island. They brought with them the language, food, architecture and religious beliefs of their ancestors, much of which is still around today.

Throughout the 1700s and 1800s piracy plagued the islands, causing residents at various times to temporarily abandon their homes

Island(s)	...in ten words or less?	Who should go?	Best time to visit	Page
Matsu	Ancient nautical culture, beautifully preserved	Temple-lovers, traditional-architecture buffs, war historians and people who want to get seriously off the beaten path	summer, autumn	above
Kinmen	Front-line military outpost transformed into national park	Military enthusiasts and bird-watchers	summer, autumn	p296
Penghu	Spectacular beaches and more temples than you'd ever think possible	Windsurfers, beachcombers, spiritual travellers	spring, summer, autumn (winter if you like high winds)	p306
Green Island	Yesterday's prison, today's paradise	Political-history enthusiasts, snorkellers, divers and hot-spring lovers	Year round (crowded in summer)	p320
Lanyu	Tribal island with otherworldly feel	Hikers, bird-watchers, those interested in authentic aboriginal culture	spring, summer, autumn	p316

to seek shelter elsewhere. Matsu was largely politically insignificant until the Nationalists fled to Taiwan in 1949 and established Matsu, along with Kinmen, as a front-line defense against the communists. Matsu residents saw their quiet islands transformed into battle-fields and had to adjust to the constant threat of war. The Mainland bombed Matsu intermit-tently until the deployment of the US 7th Fleet in 1958 prevented any further escalation.

Martial law was lifted from Matsu in 1992, a number of years after it was lifted over in 'mainland' Taiwan. In 2001, Matsu (along with Kinmen) became an early stepping stone in cross-Strait travel when the 'Three Small Links' policy was instituted, permit-ting limited trade and limited travel between ROC- and PRC-controlled territory. Today, people in Matsu are permitted to travel freely between their islands and ports in Fujian, and many Taiwanese businesspeople use Matsu as a way station between Taiwan and the Mainland (though not as many go through Kinmen, which has better infrastructure and is close to Xiamen).

Orientation

Of all of Taiwan's outer islands and archipela-gos, Matsu is the trickiest to get around. Eight-een islands (many of which are still off limits to tourism) make up the area collectively known as Matsu. These islands are grouped into townships with the main ones being Nan-gan, Beigan, Jyuguang and Dongyin. Nangan and Beigan are the largest islands, the closest

together and, rather inconveniently for those wishing to tour the other islands, the only ones with airports. Jyuguang is 45 minutes by ferry south of Nangan, and the boat from Nangan to Dongyin takes about two hours.

Dangers & Annoyances

Travellers in Matsu, especially Nangan, should be mindful of the fact that live-firing exercises are conducted regularly. Warning signs should be obeyed and straying too far off marked roads is a bad idea

NANGAN 南竿
Orientation

Shaped like a poorly baked croissant, Nangan (Nángān, Nankan) is Matsu's largest island. Compared to the rest of Matsu, it's a veritable hotbed of activity. The largest settlement on Nangan is **Jieshou Village** (also spelled Chieh-shou), which is where you'll find places to rent scooters and the island's only bank. The walk to Jieshou from the airport takes about 20 minutes, and is quite pretty. Ferries to outly-ing islands leave from Fu'ao harbour (Fúaò Gǎng), just a few kilometres from Jieshou. The central bus station is in Jieshou Village, at the end of the main road leading to the harbour. Tour buses and public buses depart from here too.

Information

Taiwan's tourism department has information booths in the airport and ferry terminal, both of which are stocked with English travel infor-mation. There's also a good English map of Matsu in the park in front of Jieshou's public vegetable garden.

Bank of Taiwan (Táiwān Yínháng; Map p291; ☎ 25400; 257 Jieshou Village) The only place in Matsu to change money.

Military Post Office (Jūn Yóujú; Map p291; ☎ 22050; 258 Jieshou Village) For all your mailing needs.

Sights & Activities
DISTILLERY TOURS

Like booze but don't like paying for it? Well, friend, a tour of Fùxīng Cūn's **Matsu Distillery** (Mǎzǔ Jiǔchǎng; Map p291; ☎ 22820; 208 Fuhsing Village; ad-mission free; ☑ 8.30-11.30am & 2-5pm Mon-Fri, 3-5pm holi-days) may well be for you. This factory is where two of Matsu's best-loved products are made: *Gāoliáng jiǔ* (Kaoliang liquor), made from sorghum, and *làojiǔ* (medicinal rice wine). Try to tag along with a Chinese-language tour to

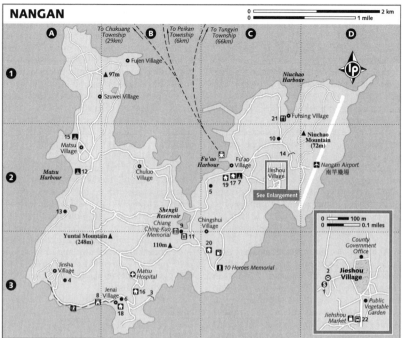

NANGAN

partake of the samples that are given out liberally at the end of each session. Don't worry about not finding the place – you'll smell it before you see it.

MILITARY HISTORY

Matsu is replete with forts, tunnels and other sights connected with the islands' important position in the struggles between communist and Chinese Nationalist forces. While some of these sites are open for tourism, others are still active military bases. Telling the two apart is sometimes tricky; if there are armed soldiers eyeing you suspiciously, assume you're at the gates of the latter. We've gone ahead and listed a couple of our favourite tourist sites.

Most impressive is the abandoned **Iron Fort** (Tiě Bǎo; Map p291), really a rocky strip of granite jutting out over the sea and hollowed out to house Matsu's amphibious forces. Visitors are allowed to enter and have a look at the spartan living quarters of the soldiers who once lived there. Be sure to look out over the ocean through sniper slots. Gruesome stories are told by Matsu residents of how Mainland frogmen would sneak inside the fort at night, slit the throats of the Taiwanese guards on duty and carry back an ear to show their comrades.

Close to Fu'ao harbour is the **Fushan Illuminated Wall** (Zhěngē Dāidàn; Map p291). Facing mainland China, the bright-red characters warn communist forces across the water to 'sleep on spears', Chiang Kai-shek's way of reiterating his intention to one day invade despite his temporary setbacks.

The 700m **Beihai Tunnel** (Běihǎi Kēngdào; Map p291; admission free; 9am-5pm Mon-Fri) was carved out of a sheer rock face by soldiers using only simple hand tools. Begun in 1968, the project took more than three years and many young men lost their lives in the process. The tunnel was used as a hiding place for military boats and is supposedly large enough to hide 120 small vessels inside its cavernous interior in case of attack.

At the top of 248m **Yuntai Mountain** (Yúntái Shān), Nangan's highest peak, sits a **military museum**. Though the museum is normally closed to the public, tour groups are sometimes let in. It's worth the trip in any event, both because the peak offers a lovely panoramic view of the Chinese coast and the surrounding islands, and because the front of the structure bears a metal plaque showing Chiang Kai-shek urging his soldiers to fight diligently. The last time we visited, Chiang's image seemed to have been recently pelted with one or more eggs.

TEMPLES & VILLAGES

The **Matsu Temple** (Mǎzǔ Tiānhòu Gōng; Map p291) is adjacent to Matsu harbour (Mǎzǔ Gǎng) in Matsu Village (Mǎzǔ Cūn). It's the oldest temple on the Matsu Islands and is considered one of the most sacred temples dedicated to popular folk deity Matsu in Taiwan. (Locals say the bones of Matsu were once stored here.) Show up on Matsu's birthday (p216) to check out a serious festival.

The **Huakuang Tati Temple** (Huáguāng Dàdì Miào; Map p291) in Fu'ao Village is named after the god of fire. Legend has it that during the Ming dynasty a Fu'ao villager dreamt that the god of fire came to him and told him about an incense burner made of sandalwood that was buried somewhere in Fu'ao. The man woke up, searched for the burner and discovered it where the god had said it would be. Later the villagers built this temple in the god's honour.

The **White Horse God Temple** (Bái Mǎ Wén Wǔ Tiān Wáng Miào; Map p291) is a small temple devoted to the worship of a deified general who once defended Fujian. The story is told that during the Qing dynasty two bodies washed up onto Matsu's shores and the locals buried them. Supposedly, the spirit of the general spoke through a spirit medium, asking the villagers to build a temple in his name, which they did. Now, whenever a storm approaches, locals say a light can be seen moving across the water, guiding ships to the harbour.

A collection of old Fujian-style stone homes perched on a hill overlooking the sea, **Jinsha Village** is well worth a visit. In the centre of town is a lovely 200-year-old temple with ornate paintings on stone walls depicting gods and legends playing *Xiàngqí* (Chinese chess). One tiny stone building has been transformed into something of an unmanned museum; over its door is painted the phrase 'What inspires you? Being playful and finding the unexpected beautiful.'

We think this sentiment sums up the charm of Matsu nicely.

Sleeping

BUDGET

Fuhua Hotel (Fúhúa Lǚdiàn; Map p291; ☎ 22990; Fu'ao Village; 福澳村; r NT700) A bit dumpy, but cheap. Its proximity to the harbour makes it a good place to stay if you need to catch an early-morning ferry.

Kaixiang Hotel (Kǎixiáng Kèzhàn; Map p291; ☎ 22652; Fu'ao Village; 福澳村; r NT1000) Just up the street from the Fuhua Hotel, this place is marginally nicer.

MIDRANGE

Hailanghua Hotel (Hǎilànghuā Kèzhàn; Map p291; ☎ 22569; Jenai Village; 仁愛村; r from NT1200) Clean, modern rooms, friendly management and ocean views from the coffee-shop patio make the Hailanghua Hotel a good midrange choice. Popular with tour groups in the high season, so book ahead.

Shennung Hotel (Shénnóng Shānzhuāng; Map p291; ☎ 26333; Chingshui Village; 清水村; r from NT1800) With Yuntai Mountain on one side and the ocean on the other, this five-storey hotel offers some beautiful views. The manager, Mr Lin, will ply you with excellent tea and, if you speak Chinese, regale you with tales of his travels into the wilds of China.

TOP END

Coast Hotel (Rìguāng Hǎi'àn Hǎijǐng Lǚguǎn; Map p291; ☎ 26666; fax 25638; Jenai Village; 仁愛村; r/ste incl breakfast NT2000/3000) Definitely the prettiest place to stay in Nangan, this small seaside hotel boasts fabulous ocean views and an excellent restaurant and coffee shop. There are only 10 rooms, all tastefully furnished, most with Japanese soaker tubs. Well recommended.

Eating

There are a number of Taiwan-style restaurants along the main streets in the villages of Jieshou, Matsu and Fu'ao.

Banrixiang (Bànrìxiáng; Map p291; 140 Fuhsing Village; dishes from NT150; ⓨ 10am-2pm & 5-10pm) This lovely little restaurant is operated by a local artist, and the décor definitely shows its artistic sensibilities through hand-crafted glass-topped tables surrounded by scrolls, paintings and other works of art on the walls. Banrixiang serves a good mix of dishes, from seafood hotpot utilising locally caught ingredients to Western-style sandwiches on home-baked bread. The village itself (just over the hill from Jieshou) is picturesque and well worth the visit. The loft space is the owner's private art studio and you can check it out if you take your shoes off.

Getting There & Away

Uni Air has three flights daily from Taipei (55 minutes) to Nangan airport (Nángān jīchǎng).

During spring and summer boats run between Nangan and the outlying islands of Matsu. Schedules are cut back in autumn and winter because of bad weather. Between Nangan and Beigan, boats leave hourly from Fu'ao harbour (NT100, 10 minutes).

Getting Around

TO/FROM THE AIRPORT

Nangan's small size means that the airport is close to many of the main sights. Taxi and motorcycle touts hang around outside and are more than happy to offer their services. If you're travelling light, it's only a 20-minute walk to Jieshou or Fuhsing Villages.

CAR, MOTORCYCLE & MICROBUS

Motorcycles can be rented for NT500 per day, excluding petrol. If you want to get around the island in style, cars are available for NT1500 to NT2000 per day. If you're travelling with a group of people, you can rent a microbus with driver for NT4500 per day, excluding petrol. The information counter at the airport can help you book vehicle rentals.

PUBLIC TRANSPORT

Buses run hourly around the island (NT15 per trip), and schedules and routes are printed in English. Oddly enough, most soldiers we've met can speak a bit of English and are usually glad for a chance to help foreign tourists find their way around.

During summer, tours leave frequently from the central bus station. Most of the time it's possible to buy a ticket as you board. The tours will be conducted in Chinese but it's still a good way see the island. Prices for the half-day tour vary, but average roughly NT100.

TAXI

The flat on-call taxi rate to anywhere in Nangan is NT100. Drivers will rarely use the meter. Taxis in line-ups are usually NT200. Your taxi driver might offer to take you on a tour around the island. For this service expect to pay NT500 to NT600 an hour.

BEIGAN 北竿

Nangan too boisterous for you? A quick ferry brings you to Beigan (Běigān, Peikan), which boasts spectacular coastal scenery, fine beaches and wonderfully preserved Fujian

---

FLYING TO THE ISLANDS

During holidays and the summer months it's often difficult to book plane tickets to Taiwan's outer islands (especially on the weekends), so we recommend you book in advance. However, one peculiarity of Taiwan's aviation industry is that it allows passengers to book seats over the phone with neither prepayment nor penalty for not showing up. As a result of this, 'fully booked' flights often wind up having a good number of spaces for wait-listed passengers. If you're travelling in a small group and aren't on too tight a schedule, chances of just showing up at the airport and getting on a 'fully booked' flight to Kinmen, Penghu or Matsu are better than average. However, you'll have less luck on the 12- and 24-seat planes that go to Lanyu and Green Island.

architecture that you do more than visit, you can actually live there.

Orientation

Ferries to Beigan dock in Baisha harbour. The island's largest village is **Tangci** (Tángqí Cūn, Tangchi). The road is windy and steep in places, but the scenery is lovely. Beigan is a small island, so you can see the whole place in a day on foot, or even an afternoon with a scooter; and you could tour the village of Tangci in an hour.

Sights & Activities

VILLAGES

What makes sleepy Beigan really worth the visit is its architecture. Buildings are unique, well preserved, and unlike anything you're likely to find in Taiwan proper. Chief among the preserved villages of Beigan is **Cinbi Village** (Qínbì Cūn), comprising low-lying interconnected one- and two-storey homes built into the side of Bi Mountain, overlooking Turtle Island. The houses are built from slabs of granite and feature high, narrow windows to protect the inhabitants from wind and pi-

rates. Roofs have bright-red or black tiles. About half of the homes in the small village have been transformed into guest houses, and spending the night in one of these should be one of the highlights of your trip to Matsu.

A walk of a kilometre or so up the coastal road takes you to the foot of Leishan (Thunder Mountain), where you'll find **Ciaozai Village** (Qiáozǎi Cūn). The village has some beautifully restored temples devoted to the thunder god. Nowadays the village is mostly empty save for a few elderly residents who maintain the temples (the gods in the temples outnumber villagers now, or so they say). Outside of the odd grandchild, about the youngest person you'll find in the village is the woman who runs the **Ciaozai Village Folk Museum** (Map p294; admission free; 8am-6pm), a cool little museum with various articles from Matsu's nautical past (no English signage, though).

Although Tangci Village is modern and not terribly remarkable, it is home to a couple of temples with Fujian-style architecture: boxy buildings nearly square in shape, made of grey stone, with curved roofs and octagonal windows. If you're leaving Matsu

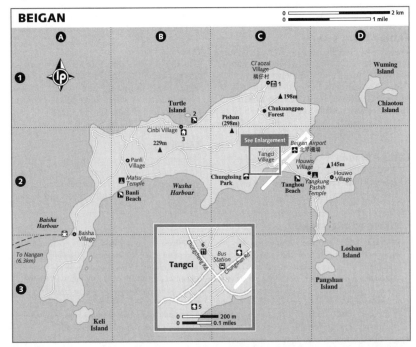

from Beigan airport, leave a couple of hours to wander around town, finding the unexpected beautiful.

SWIMMING

Tanghou Beach (Tánghòu Shātān) is a thin strip of sand, divided by a road, which connects the villages of Tangci and Houwo (Hòuwò Cūn). Before the road was built, locals had to wade through water during high tide to travel between the two villages. Some locals that we've spoken to pine for the preroad days.

Banli Beach (Bǎnlǐ Hǎitān) is a pretty little beach just up the road from where boats dock. There's a military base nearby, and also a rather attractive pink-and-yellow temple dedicated (naturally) to the goddess Matsu.

Cinbi Village overlooks a nice little patch of beach facing a small cluster of rounded rocks that looks like a turtle. Naturally this is known as **Turtle Island Beach** (Guīdǎo Shā), and it's a lovely place to swim most of the year. It's also known as Cinbi Beach.

Sleeping

Spending a night in the old Fujian-style stone houses in Cinbi Village is a big part of the reason people visit Beigan. Currently there are two groups managing guesthouses in the town; they're both next to each other, and in our eyes, fairly interchangeable. They are traditional Fujianese homes, complete with pleasant, breezy rooms, wooden-shuttered windows and ocean views, and are locally owned and operated. Interclan rivalry? Hard to say. On the day we visited both owners were having tea together on the veranda of the Cafe Cinbi. We've included the numbers for both, as you'll want to make reservations during the high season.

Cinbi Village Homestay (Qínbì Mínsù Cūn; ☎ 55456; 49 Cinbi Village; dm/d NT700/1200) is run out of the Cafe Cinbi and has nice four-bed dorms and decent double rooms.

Di Zhonghai Homestay (Dì Zhōnghǎi Mínsù; ☎ 56611; 54 Cinbi Village; dm/d NT860/1300) is run out of the Di Zhonghai Restaurant, and seems a tad newer than the Cinbi. Di Zhonghai also offers breakfast and free pick-up from the airport or ferry pier.

If staying in a stone building that's more than 200 years old doesn't do it for you (to be fair, they are on the drafty side), there are a number of hotels in Tangci Village.

Hongrui Hotel (Hóngruì Dà Fàndiàn; s & d NT800) Right on the main drag as you come into town, the Hongrui is run by a nice family, and the rooms are clean and well maintained.

Golden Dragon Holiday Villa (Lóngfú Shānzhuāng; ☎ 55066; www.matsu-play.com.tw; s/d NT1700/2500; 🖥) A newly opened hotel (right across from the airport) with lovely wooden furniture and ocean views. Also the only place in town (to our knowledge) with wi-fi, for laptop-toters.

Eating

Hong Xing Ping Seafood Restaurant (Hóng Xīng Píng Hǎixiān Lóu; Tangchi Village, 242 Chungcheng Rd; dishes from NT120; 🕙 10am-2pm & 5-8pm) This is a good place to meet the locals and try some of Beigan's seafood. The *yú miàn* (fish noodles) and *tángcù huángyú* (sweet-and-sour yellow croaker) are terrific.

Cafe Cinbi (Qínbì Rénwén Kāfēi Guǎn; 49 Cinbi Village; coffee from NT100, snacks from NT50, dishes from NT120; 🕙 10am-9pm) With a terrace and a view of Turtle Island this is the perfect place to linger for an hour or two over coffee and Matsu pastry on a sunny day.

Di Zhonghai Restaurant (Dì Zhōnghǎi Cāntīng; 54 Cinbi Village; dishes from NT120; 🕙 10am-9pm) Connected to the homestay of the same name, this place serves good seafood, hotpots and other local fare.

Getting There & Away

Uni Air has three flights daily from Taipei (NT2110, 55 minutes) to Beigan airport (Běigān Jīchǎng). Be prepared for last-minute cancellations and delays because of Matsu's volatile weather, especially in spring and winter.

Getting Around

TO/FROM THE AIRPORT

Beigan airport is at the end of Tangci Village's one main street. Were the runway any closer, it would be Tangci's one main street.

CAR, MOTORCYCLE & MICROBUS

Motorcycles can be rented for NT500 per day, excluding petrol. If you want to get around the island in style, cars are available for NT1500 to NT2000 per day, excluding petrol. If you're travelling with a group of people, you can rent a microbus with driver for NT4500 per day, excluding petrol. The information counter at the airport can help you book vehicle rentals.

PUBLIC TRANSPORT

Buses run hourly around the island (NT15), though there's less English signage than in Nangan.

TAXI

The flat on-call taxi rate to anywhere in Beigan is NT100. Drivers will rarely use the meter. Taxis in line-ups are usually NT200. Your taxi driver might offer to take you on a tour around the island. For this service expect to pay NT500 to NT600 an hour.

MATSU'S OUTER ISLANDS

Most casual travellers only make it to Beigan and Nangan, but if you're serious about heading way off the beaten path, the islands of **Dongyin** (Dōngyǐn, Tongyin), **Dongjyu** (Dōngjǔ, Tongchu) and **Hsijyu** (Xījǔ, Hsichu) await.

North of Beigan, Dongyin is the largest of the three outer islands, and thought to be the most beautiful section of the archipelago. Dongyin's landscape consists of steep cliffs, grassy hills and wave-eroded coastline. The main township is also called Dongyin, and it's here you'll find hotels and restaurants. Dongyin's most famous landmark is the **Dongyung Lighthouse** (Dōngyǒng Dēngtǎ), a simple white structure on a grassy hill overlooking the ocean. The lighthouse was built by the British in 1904 and remains an important part of Taiwan's coastal defence system.

Dongjyu and Hsijyu are the most southerly of Matsu's Islands. Both are remote and sparsely inhabited, poor in actual tourist sights but rich in friendly locals, pretty scenery and excellent food. The commercial centre of Dongjyu is **Taping Village** (Dàpíng Cūn). The **Dongjyu Lighthouse** (Dōngjǔ Dēngtǎ) sits high on a hill at the northeast tip of the island. Built by the British in 1872, the white-granite building aided the navigation of merchant ships during the Opium Wars.

The other main attraction of Dongjyu is the **Tapu Stone Engraving** (Dàpǔ Shíkē), on the south side of the island. The memorial is dedicated to a general from the Ming dynasty who successfully drove pirates off the island without losing a single one of his soldiers.

Hsijyu is rowdier than its sister island, but not by much. This small island was once a busy seaport, though there's little evidence of that now. During the Korean War, American companies set themselves up in **Chingfan Village** (Qīngfán Cūn) and nicknamed it 'Little Hong Kong'. Chingfan is still the centre of activity on the island, though most of the hotels are in the nearby village of **Tienwo** (Tiánwò Cūn).

The **Shinwa Boat Company** (Keelung ☎ 02-2424 6868; Nangan ☎ 22395) runs a night boat that leaves from Keelung around 9pm and gets to Matsu around dawn. The boat alternates, going directly to Nangan one night and to Nangan via Dongyin the next. In theory, this would make for a great travel tool, as visitors would be able to tour Dongyin for a day before taking a ferry to Nangan and points beyond. In practice, however, we've found Shinwa to be unreliable, cancelling trips without notice and leaving passengers stranded in Keelung. If you'd like to reserve a ticket, you'll need to do so three days in advance.

From Nangan to Dongyin (two hours), there is one boat a day from Fu'ao harbour. Boats to the two southern islands run two to three times a day, stopping first at Dongjyu before heading to Hsijyu. You'll need to check at Fu'ao harbour for current schedules and ticket prices as these seem to fluctuate with the seasons.

KINMEN 金門

☎ 082 / pop 45,000

Along with Matsu, Kinmen (Jīnmén; formerly known as Quemoy) occupies a unique place in modern history. It's a small chunk of Fujian province occupied by ROC forces and administered from Taiwan. Lying only 2km off the coast of mainland China, Kinmen is an odd remnant from the bitter civil war between communist and Nationalist forces, and this struggle (particularly the losing side's tenacious hold on the islands) is a major part of Kinmen's own history. And though war history supplies a big chunk of

Kinmen's appeal to tourists, there's plenty here to attract those with interests other than military history.

As a result of its strategic position, Kinmen is fairly well developed. Roads are wide and well cared for (so they can double as runways, just in case) and Kincheng has several internet cafés, where you'll often find off-duty soldiers practising their combat skills playing video games. There are ATMs, a not-bad pizza joint and plenty of English signage to make your trip fairly hassle-free. Though the environment is relaxed, don't lose sight of the fact that Kinmen is still a military outpost with restricted areas and a few beachfront properties bearing land-mine warnings.

History

Settlers began arriving on Kinmen as early as the Tang dynasty (AD 618–907), changing the original name of the island from Wuzhou to Kinmen, literally meaning 'Golden Gate' after the hopefully impenetrable gates that were put up to defend the island from pirate attacks. During the Ming (AD 1368–1644) and Qing (AD 1644–1912) dynasties, increasing numbers of Chinese migrants settled on Kinmen's shores. The Ming loyalist Koxinga, also known as Cheng Cheng-kung, used Kinmen as a base to liberate Kinmen and Penghu from the Dutch. In the process, he chopped down all of Kinmen's trees for his navy, something the residents still grumble about. Koxinga's massive deforestation project made Kinmen vulnerable to the devastating soil-eroding winds that commonly sweep across the Strait.

Kinmen was a fairly peaceful place until 1949, when Chiang Kai-shek transformed the island into a rear-guard defensive position against the communist forces that had driven his own Nationalist army off the Mainland. Though his original plan was to have his soldiers recuperate on the island for a short period before launching a full-fledged attack on Mao Zedong's armies, this never quite happened. Instead, martial law was declared on Kinmen as the island became the final flashpoint of the Chinese civil war. As a result, Kinmen was subject to incessant bombing from the Mainland throughout the 1950s and '60s.

Martial law was lifted in 1993 and Kinmen residents are now allowed to travel freely to

and from Taiwan. In 1995, Taiwan established Kinmen as the ROC's sixth national park, starting a massive reforestation project with the hopes of turning the once off-limits military zone into a tourist destination. Soldiers have been put to good use planting trees, maintaining roads and restoring the island's old houses, many built during the Ming and Qing dynasties.

In 2001, the so-called 'Three Small Links' were established between Taiwan and China, allowing legal (though limited) trade and travel between the two countries, via the Straits Islands – for the first time in more than half a century. This further opened Kinmen up to the outside world, and made it a vital channel for Taiwanese businessmen looking to travel to the Mainland more cheaply. Although there is some talk of opening these links further, the Xiamen–Kinmen route is not yet open to foreigners. Nonetheless, with all of its natural beauty and history, Kinmen is well worth a visit.

Orientation

Kinmen consists of 15 islands and islets at the junction of the mouth of the Chiulung River and Xiamen of mainland China. The largest islands (and the only two open to tourism) are Kinmen and Little Kinmen (Liehyu). The other islets are tiny, with three being controlled by mainland China and the rest by the ROC. There are a number of spots on Kinmen and Liehyu from which you can check out the PRC-controlled islands and have a gander at how 'the other side lives'. The main island of Kinmen is divided into Kincheng, Kinhu, Kinning and Kinsha Districts (you could say they share a 'kinship').

Getting There & Away

Kinmen Airport (☎ 322 381; Map pp298-9; www .kma.gov.tw/index-e.htm) is about 8km east of Kincheng city, and has a counter providing English information.

In spring, Kinmen is often fogged in, leading to cancelled flights. Book a return ticket, because flights are often fully booked as business people use Kinmen as a transit point to head into the Mainland.

Uni Air (☎ 324 881), **TransAsia Airways** (☎ 321 501) and **Far Eastern Air Transport** (☎ 327 339) all have offices at Kinmen airport and fly directly to Kinmen from Taipei, Chiayi, Taichung, Tainan and Kaohsiung.

TAIWAN'S ISLANDS

Getting Around

TO/FROM THE AIRPORT

Bus 3 travels hourly between Kincheng, Shanwai and the airport for NT15. From the Kinmen airport to Kincheng or Shanwai, taxi drivers charge a flat NT250. Coming from the opposite direction, the fare should be around NT200.

CAR, MOTORCYCLE & SCOOTER

Cars, motorbikes and scooters can easily be rented in Kincheng. Scooter rental is generally NT300 to NT500 a day, depending on the number of days rented. Cars can be rented for about NT1300 a day, excluding petrol. Kinmen has very little traffic and driving or riding a scooter is the easiest way to see the island.

PUBLIC TRANSPORT

Kinmen has bus stations in Kincheng, Shanwai and Shamei. Though buses run regularly, you'll have less flexibility if you decide to see Kinmen by public transport. Buses run every one or two hours between 6am and 5pm, with a few buses offering services into the evenings. Bus schedules are posted in the bus stations in Chinese but people are pretty willing to help if you know where you're going.

Buses 1 and 2 travel between Kincheng and Shanwai, and buses 5 and 18 go to Shamei. Buses run hourly and cost NT15.

TAXI

Most taxi drivers in Kinmen prefer to ask for a flat fare rather than use the meter. If you think

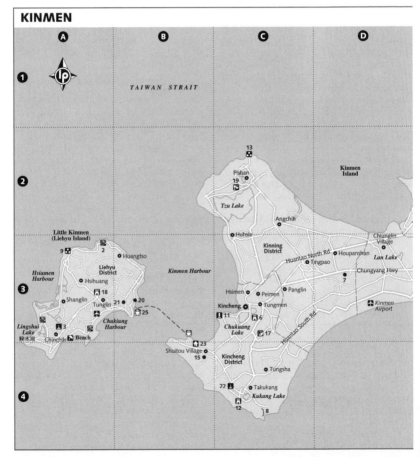

KINMEN

your trip will be cheaper with the meter on (probably so), then by all means insist on this method. Rides to and from the airport and for taxis waiting in taxi stands are flat fares that range from NT200 to NT300.

Taxi tours will cost around NT2000 to NT2500 a day and it's unlikely your driver will speak English. Most hotels can arrange discounted tours, as can the **Youth Activity Centre** (☎ 325 772).

BOAT

There is a frequent ferry service between Shuitou harbour in Kinmen and Chiukang harbour (NT20, around 15 minutes) on Little Kinmen (Liehyu) Island. During winter, the ferry service can be suspended if the water is too choppy. There's also a boat to Fujian, but at the time of writing, only ROC nationals with the proper paperwork can board it.

KINCHENG 金城

The Kincheng District (金城鎮, Jīnchéng Zhèn) is in the southwest region of Kinmen Island. This is where most of the hotels are. Kincheng City (Jīnchéng) is the busiest town on the island, with sights and restaurants all pretty much within walking distance of each other.

Information

The Bank of Taiwan has an international ATM on the west side of Minsheng Rd, south of the King Ring Hotel. The beautiful **Kinmen County Cultural Centre** (Jīnmén Xiàn Wénhuà Zhōngxīn; ☎ 325 643; 66 Huandao North Rd, Kincheng; ⏰ 8am-noon & 1.30-5pm) is a bit on the outskirts of the city. There's a café out the back where you can pick up a copy of the excellent and informative *Kinmen Sightseeing Guide*.

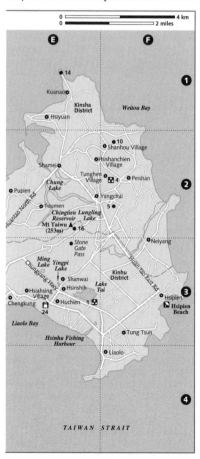

SIGHTS & ACTIVITIES	
August 23 Artillery War Museum 八二三戰史紀念館	**1** E3
Banyan Garden 榕園	(see 1)
Bike Path	**2** A3
Chaste Maiden Temple 烈女廟	**3** A3
Chen Chien Ancient Tomb 陳健墓	**4** F2
Chen Chien Memorial Arch 陳禎恩榮坊	**5** F2
Chiang Chingkuo Memorial Hall 經國先生紀念館	(see 7)
Chiang Kai-shek Memorial Forest 中正紀念林	(see 1)
Chukuang Tower 莒光樓	**6** C3
Chungshan Memorial Forest 中山紀念林	**7** D3
Dishan Tunnels 翟山坑道	**8** C4
Hsuchianghsiao Ancient Inscription 虛江嘯臥碣	(see 22)
Huchingtou War Museum 湖井頭戰史館	**9** A3
Kinmen County Cultural Centre 金門縣文化中心	**10** F2
Koxinga Shrine 延平郡王祠	**11** C3
Kukang Tower 古崗樓	**12** C4
Kuningtou Battlefield 古寧頭戰場	**13** C2
Kuningtou War Museum 古寧頭戰史館	(see 13)
Mashan Observatory 馬山觀測	**14** E1
Moon Grasping Tower 得月樓	**15** B4
Mt Taiwu Cemetery 太武公墓	**16** E2
Mr Yu Tawei Museum 俞大維先生紀念館	(see 13)
Mumahou Shrine 牧馬候祠	**17** C3
Pata Memorial 八達樓子	**18** A3
Shuangli Wetlands Area Centre 雙鯉溼地自然中心	**19** C2
Siwei Tunnel 四維坑道	**20** B3
Victory Gate 勝利門	**21** B3
Wentai Pagoda 文臺寶塔	**22** C4
Youtong Villa	(see 15)
SLEEPING 🏠	
West Sea International Hotel 西海國際大旅店	**23** B4
SHOPPING 🛍	
Kinmen Ceramics Factory 金門陶瓷場	**24** E3
TRANSPORT	
Chiukung Pier 九宮碼頭	**25** B3

Sights

Filled with winding alleys, brick-paved market streets, temples and interesting architecture, Kincheng is a great place to explore on foot; all of the sights listed here are free except where noted, and most are open from dawn to dusk.

Mofan St (Mófàn Jiē; Map p300) is a five-minute southeasterly walk from the Kincheng bus station. Built in 1924, the buildings on this charming little street have brick exteriors and arched door fronts modelled after both the Japanese and Western architecture that was in fashion back in the day. The street has a small but hip café district, so come back for cocktails.

Further east takes you into a busy brick-paved market area, in the middle of which you'll see Memorial Arch to Qiu Liang-Kung's Mother (Qiū Liánggōng Mǔ Jiéxiào Fǎng; Map p300). You'll be hard pressed to find a better example of Han Chinese-influenced filial devotion. Qiu Liang-kung, a native of Kinmen who became governor of China's Zhejiang province, had the arch built in 1812 to honour his mother who refused to remarry after her husband died. His mother instead chose to live 28 more years as a widow. The market is a great place to buy candy, dried seafood, knives and a wide variety of local knick-knacks.

Heading east through narrow alleyways, make your way to Chupu South Rd, where you'll find the cool little **Kuei Pavilion** (Kuí Gé; Map p300). This two-storey pavilion was built in 1836 to worship the god of literature, and it's here that aspiring scholars would come

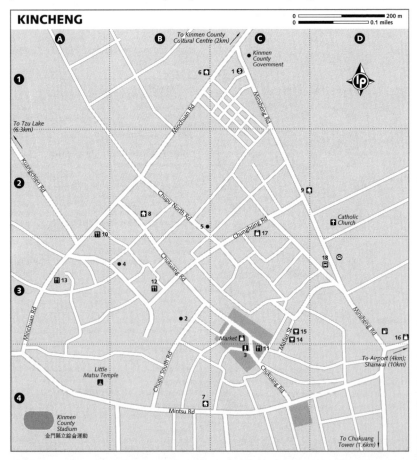

KINCHENG

to pray for success in the civil-service examinations. You can saunter northward to **Wú Jiāng Shū Yuàn** (Map p300), a walled complex constructed in the ancient Ming style. In the 1800s, the central building was a library and it was here we presume that aspiring scholars would come to study after receiving the spiritual message to 'hit the books' from the god of literature at the Kuei Pavilion. The most arresting thing about the complex is its deep, almost bloodlike red colour.

From here you can wind back west and check out the **Wu River Academy** (Map p300), a walled complex built in 1780 that once housed one of Kinmen's ancient schools. You won't find classes going on inside, but you will find the **Chutzu Shrine** (Zhūzǐ Cí), which honours the neo-Confucian scholar Chu Hsi, who sought a revival of Confucian values during the Sung dynasty.

Sleeping

BUDGET

Kinmen Hotel (Jīnmén Lǚguǎn; Map p300; ☎ 321 567; 169 Mintsu Rd; 金城 民族路169號; d from NT1000; 🖳 🖵) A quick walk from the bustle of Mofan St and Kincheng's main market, the Kinmen Hotel offers clean rooms, cable TV, and free ADSL for those toting their own laptops.

Six Brothers Hotel (Liù Guì Fàndiàn; Map p300; ☎ 372 888; 166 Chukuang Rd; 金城 莒光路166號; s/d/tr/q NT1000/1200/1500/1800) Down a side street off Minchuan Rd, this small quiet hotel has some lovely antique furniture in the lobby and rather friendly management. Rooms are clean and a bargain for the price.

MIDRANGE

Ta Chen Hotel (Dà Chéng Dà Fàndiàn; Map p300; ☎ 324 851; 16 Mingsheng Rd; 金城民生路16號; s & d from NT1200; 🖵) This hotel is right in the thick of things, just down the road from the Kincheng bus station. Rooms are shabby but clean and the décor is a bit on the eccentric side with mismatched antique furniture and other curios. The hotel also has wi-fi.

King Ring Hotel (Jīnruì Dà Fàndiàn; Map p300; ☎ 323 777; 166 Minchuan Rd; 金城 民權路166號; d/tr NT1680/1995, q from NT2310) The King Ring enjoys a good reputation among travellers and tour groups, meaning it's often fully booked. The hotel is just close enough to the town centre to be convenient, but just enough on the edge to be quiet as well.

West Sea International Hotel (Xīhǎi Guójì Dàlùdiàn; Map pp298-9; ☎ 322 992; 9 Xihai Rd; 金城 西海路9號; s/d NT1200/1500) Located outside Kincheng City, the West Sea is right next to the ferry that goes to Little Kinmen, making it a good place to stay if you're planning to spend the day exploring Liehyu. Rooms are comfortable, and pretty big for the price.

Eating

Central Kincheng, with its busy market streets and winding alleys, is a foodie's paradise. The area around Mofan St is chock-a-block with small stands and restaurants selling a variety of Kincheng snacks and sweets. Some of Kinmen's specialities include *gòng táng* (hard candy), *miàn xiàn* (sticky-rice noodles) and *chǎo shāchóng* (fried sandworms). Come to the market in the early morning or evening to get the best of what's on offer.

Shou Ji Kuangtung Zhou (Shòují Guǎngdōng Zhōu; Map p300; 50-1 Chukuang Rd, Sec 1; dishes from NT30; 🕑 6.30am-12.30pm) This restaurant, more than 80 years old, serves up steaming bowls of Cantonese-style congee. Locals favour the *zhū dù* (pig-stomach) congee but there are other varieties available.

Wen Ji Mian (Wénjì Miàn Xiàn Hú; Map p300; 37 Chunghsing Shihchang; dishes from NT30; ☯ 5am–noon) Here you can find Kinmen's famous sticky-rice noodle soup, served with fresh oysters. The noodles are a popular dish for breakfast, though they can be found around town at other times of the day, too.

Lao Liu Hsiao Kuan (Lǎo Liù Xiǎo Guǎn; Map p300; 65 Minchuan Rd; dishes from NT100; ☯ lunch & dinner) This restaurant serves great seafood, including locally caught whole steamed fish.

Xin Damiaokou (Xīn Dàmiàokǒu; Map p300; Minchuan Rd; dishes from NT100; ☯ lunch & dinner) Right next to a small temple on the west side of Kincheng, this restaurant serves up some mighty fine seafood. Weather permitting, management sets up tables so guests can sit outside and feast next to the temple.

Drinking

Pa Sa (Bāsà Shāokǎo Diàn; Map p300; 13 Mofan St; coffee from NT100, alcohol NT120, dishes from NT100; ☯ 11am–11pm) The Pa Sa is a chic bar-café selling a range of rice and noodle dishes as well as fruity drinks and coffees.

Hung Lou (Hóng Lóu; Map p300; 24 Mofan St; coffee from NT150, alcohol NT120; ☯ 10am–11pm) Across the street from Pa Sa, this place is extremely funky, with walls covered in political art representing both sides of the cross-Strait conflict. There's also lots of graffiti and guests are encouraged to add their own.

Shopping

Visitors to Kinmen generally leave with two of the island's most famous products: a potent liquor made from sorghum; and

extremely sharp knives constructed from spent shell casings lobbed over from the Mainland. Booze and weaponry: always a potent combination.

First the liquor. At 58% proof, Kaoliang liquor is sold all over the island; try a few shots at a local bar before purchasing any serious quantities to take home. 'Blinding' is an adjective often used to describe the liquor's effects. As for the knives, these unusual souvenir items are said to be made from melted-down artillery shells left over from the Mainland bombardments. The knives are available all over Kinmen and come in a variety of shapes and sizes, but the most fun place to shop for them is at the **Chin Ho Li Steel Knife Factory** (Jīnhélì Gāngdāo; Map p300; www.5657.com.tw/maestrowu/index .htm; 236 Bóyù Rd, Sec 1; ☯ 8.30am-6.30pm) just outside the city, where you can watch Maestro Wu as he crafts high-quality knives. Prices start at around NT800, and if you want to watch yours being made, don't come between noon and 2pm; that's when Maestro Wu rests. And of course, don't forget to pack your knives (or meat cleavers, swords or axes) in your checked baggage before trying to board the plane.

A wonderful little curio shop in central Kincheng is the **Kinmen Minsu Wenwu Chih Jia** (Jīnmén Mínsú Wénwù Zhī Jiā; Map p300; Lane 1, 124 Chunghsing Rd), where you can find all sorts of ceramic knick-knacks, dishes and one-of-a-kind items to take home.

Another popular item is Kinmen's tasty hard candy, called kung (gòng) or 'tribute' candy because it was once used to pay tribute when visiting the imperial court. The candy comes in a variety of flavours, with

---

WATCHING THE MAESTRO AT WORK

Living under bombardment has taught the people of Kinmen to make the best of things, and the island has done a good job transforming war history into tourist trade. One place where you can see this done with unique aplomb is at the Chin Ho Li Steel Knife Factory (see above), otherwise known as the factory of Maestro Wu. It's here where spent shell casings are transformed into one-of-a-kind knives. What makes a Maestro Wu knife so unique is what they're made from: old propaganda-laden shells lobbed by the communist Chinese in the '50s. These are shaped into beautiful steel blades of various sizes, intended for functions as varied as kitchen use and war souvenirs.

The current Maestro Wu is a wiry middle-aged fellow named Wu Tsong-shan, who studied smithing and weapon crafting under the tutelage of his father (another Maestro Wu, as the title is passed down). Wu says that the countless tons of shells that were lobbed over are ideal for making knives for both kitchen and ornamental use. Unlike regular shells, which were designed to shatter into killing fragments, propaganda shells are made of high grade steel, designed to split neatly open and demoralise the opponent.

WIND LIONS

Travelling around Kinmen, you'll no doubt notice an abundance of stone lions. These are Kinmen's Wind Lions, traditional totems said to have the power to control the winds and keep the land fertile. According to locals, these totems began appearing after Kinmen was deforested to build Koxinga's navy. The locals, forced to turn to supernatural aid as the denuded soil of their island ceased bearing crops, began placing the lions around the island. While the island has since been reforested, the Wind Lions can still be found in almost every village around the island. Replicas are a popular tourist item and a good place to pick them up is the **Kinmen Ceramics Factory** (Jīnmén Táocí Chǎng; Map pp298-9; ☿ 8am-noon & 1-5pm), said to produce some of the finest ceramics in Taiwan. The factory sells various pottery items made from the highly prized *gaoling* clay, found in abundance all over the island. Unlike other souvenirs (such as knives), ceramic Wind Lion statues can be packed in your carry-on luggage.

---

peanut being the most common. You'll see it being sold in barrels along the streets or in boxes in more upscale gift shops. If you have a sweet tooth, the candy is a must-buy item.

AROUND KINCHENG

Twelve kilometres long and roughly bow-tie shaped, Kinmen is easy to get around by scooter. The island is full of ancient towns, battlefield monuments and great parks (technically speaking, the whole island is a national park). The Kinmen County government puts out the excellent *Kinmen Sightseeing Guidebook* that you can get both at the airport and at the Kinmen County Cultural Centre (p299); the government also maintains a bilingual website with pictures, maps and plenty of useful information at www.kinmen.gov.tw. We recommend you spend at least two days on the island if you want to check out all the sites listed here.

Battle history & War museums

Just south of the city lies **Chukuang Tower** (Jǔguāng Lóu; Map pp298-9; admission free; ☿ 8am-noon & 2-5pm, closed Mon), a three-storey tower constructed in the style of a classical Chinese palace. It was built in 1952 as a memorial to the fallen soldiers of Kinmen. There's an excellent museum inside with bilingual exhibits that give a good introduction to the history and culture of the region. Buses 3 and 6 go here.

On the southern end of the Kincheng District sit the **Dishan Tunnels** (Díshān Kēngdào; Map pp298-9; admission free; ☿ 8.30am-5pm). Blasted out of solid granite in the early 1960s by soldiers, these tunnels stretch 357m to the ocean and were designed to protect boats from bombs during wars. Tourists are allowed to walk

through the spooky interior or follow a bridge over the entrance that leads to the piers.

Located in Kinning District (Jīnníng Xiāng), north of Kincheng, is the site of some ferocious battles between the communist Chinese and Taiwan. The **Kuningtou War Museum** (Gǔníngtóu Zhànshǐ Guǎn; Map pp298-9; admission free; ☿ 8.30am-5pm) sits on the site of the Kuningtou Battlefield and provides an excellent look into one of Kinmen's most gruesome conflicts, where 15,000 soldiers from both sides lost their lives in a battle lasting more than 56 hours. Buses 10, 11 and 26 stop at the museum.

The Kinhu District takes up the southeastern portion of Kinmen. Shanwai is the biggest town here, so you can eat here. Just south of town is the **August 23 Artillery War Museum** (Bā Èr Sān Zhànshǐ Guǎn; Map pp298-9; admission free; ☿ 8.30am-5pm). The museum documents the horrific battle that occurred on 23 August 1958, when the communists launched an artillery attack against Kinmen that lasted for 44 days and pummelled the island with more than 474,000 shells. Outside are fighter planes, tanks and cannons used during the siege. Adjacent to the museum is the **Mr Yu Tawei Museum** (Yú Dàwéi Xiānshēng Jìniàn Guǎn; admission free; ☿ 8.30am-5pm), dedicated to the ROC's first minister of defence.

On the farthest northeast tip of Kinmen, in the Kinsha District lies the **Mashan Observatory** (Mǎshān Guàn Cèzhàn), a fortified observation station that looks out at the Mainland (a mere 2km away). A dark, winding tunnel leads to a pillbox where you can peer through high-powered binoculars at villagers in Fujian. Though once this was a strictly controlled area, nowadays you'll find people trekking here to save money on their mobile-phone bills by making calls to the Mainland using Chinese-bought phones (from this close, mobile phones automatically latch into Fujian networks, as they do from much of Liehyu).

Temples & Shrines

To the southwest of Kincheng sits the **Koxinga Shrine** (Yánpíng Jùnwáng Cí; Map pp298–9), built in memory of the Ming general Koxinga who fought against the Dutch occupation (see p33). The shrine seems to be most popular with Taiwanese tourists – locals haven't quite forgiven him for cutting down all their trees. Not too far away is the **Mumahou Shrine** (Mùmǎ Hóu Cí; Map pp298–9). Bus 7 stops close by.

In the southern end of the Kincheng District you'll find **Kukang Lake** (Jǔgāng Hú; Map pp298–9) and **Kukang Tower** (Jǔgāng Lóu; Map pp298–9), just north of which sits the 14th-century **Wentai Pagoda** (Wéntái Bǎotǎ; Map pp298–9), considered one of the oldest constructions in Taiwan. The five-level hexagonal pagoda was originally built for the Ming emperor Hungwu as a place to honour the stars and celestial deities. Sitting on top of a giant boulder within the pagoda is the **Hsuchianghsiao Ancient Inscription** (Xūjiāng Xiào Wò Jié; Map pp298–9), carved by the Ming general Hsuchiang. The general, they say, used to come here to look at the sea. The inscription reads 'Hsuchiang is shouting and lying here'. There's a stand next to the pagoda that sells eggs fermented in Kaoliang liquor if you feel like you need something to make you shout and/or lie down. Bus 6 stops here.

In Kinsha District, check out the **Chen Chien Ancient Tomb** (Chén Jiàn Gǔ Mù; Map pp298–9), which commemorates an important official of the Ming dynasty. More impressive than the tomb (which doesn't contain the official's earthly remains, just his hat and gown) is the **Chen Chien Memorial Arch** (Chén Zhēn Ēn Róng Fǎng; Map pp298–9), dedicated to Chen Chien's father. It's considered one of the best-preserved Ming arches in Taiwan.

Parks & Nature Preserves

With its beautiful lakes, forests and bird sanctuaries, Kinmen truly is, as locals say, 'a garden built upon a fortress'. So much so that the island attracts visitors with no interest in military history.

North of Kincheng is **Tzu Lake** (Cí Hú), one of the most scenic spots on Kinmen and a habitat for migratory birds. The saltwater lake opens to the ocean and is on the migratory paths of a number of bird species not normally found in Taiwan. Ducks, kingfishers, herons and geese make their homes on the lake year round, and cormorants nest here in winter. Just north of the lake itself is the **Shuangli Wetlands Area Centre** (Shuānglì Shidì Zìrán Zhōngxīn; Map pp298–9; ☯ 8.30am-5pm), a research facility devoted to wetlands preservation. Some English information is available, and the 1st floor has a multimedia room, café and bird-viewing area. Buses 9, 10 and 11 stop here.

East of the city is the **Chungshan Memorial Forest** (Zhōngshān Jìniàn Lín; Map pp298–9), Kinmen's largest forest area. It was with the creation of this area that the government really showed its dedication to reforesting an island that had been stripped bare. Bus 1 passes by.

Just south of Shanwei is **Lake Tai** (Tài Hú), a 5m-deep lake that was dug entirely by hand in the 1960s. It's a popular picnic spot for locals and also a feeding ground for cormorants and ospreys. These species are best seen in the early morning. Check out the **Banyan Garden** (Róng Yuán; Map pp298–9), just south of the lake and inside the **Chiang Kai-shek Memorial Forest** (Zhōngzhèng Gōngyuán; Map pp298–9).

The highest mountain on Kinmen is **Mt Taiwu** (Tàiwǔ Shān) at 253m. On the west side of Mt Taiwu is the **Mt Taiwu Cemetery** (Tàiwǔ Shān Gōng Mù; Map pp298–9), built in 1952 to honour the ROC soldiers who died in battle. Though solemn, the grounds are peaceful as well. If you take the time to read the inscriptions on the flat grave markers, you'll note that officers are buried to one side, and enlisted men in the centre. The walk up the path takes about an hour and takes you past a number of small temples and shrines, and even an inscription of one of Chiang Kai-shek's favourite one liners, 'Wú Wàng Zài Jǔ Lèshì' or 'don't forget the days in chu' (in reference to a doomed battle that was saved at the last moment).

Ancient Villages

Kinmen has some fascinating examples of old Fujianese architecture the likes of which aren't found elsewhere (certainly not as well preserved). Old villages in Kinmen differ from those in Matsu both in building style and in layout as Kinmen is flat and Matsu mountainous. You'll come across such villages every few kilometres (another reason to ditch the bus and rent a scooter). One of our favourites is **Shuitou Village** (Shuǐtóu Cūn; Map pp298–9) in the Kincheng District. It's an old fishing community with ancient Fujian-style houses built by a wealthy merchant clan named Huang during the Qing dynasty. The **Youtang Villa** (Yǒu Táng Biéyè) is an excellent example of southern-style Qing architecture. Shuitou is also the home of the **11m-high Moon Grasping Tower** (Déyuè Lóu).

Chiunglin Village (Qiónglín Cūn) in Kinhu is famous for having more shrines than any other village on Kinmen. The most famous is the **Tsai Family Shrine** (Cài Shì Cí), which sits in the centre of the village. The characters on the main wall read 'loyalty and filial piety' and 'honesty and thriftiness'.

Probably the most well-maintained of Kinmen's ancient townships is in S**hanhou Village** in the Kinsha District. The **Kinmen Folk Cultural Village** (Jīnmén Mínsú Wénhuà Cūn; Map pp298–9) is a grouping of 18 Fujian-style houses, all interconnected, with narrow alleys and bricked walls. The roofs sport the 'horseback ridges' and 'swallow tails' common to southern Fujian architecture but unique in Taiwan. Buses 25 and 31 service the area.

LITTLE KINMEN 小金門

Little Kinmen (Xiǎo Jīnmén) is the common name for Liehyu Island (Lièyǔ Xiāng), a small 2-sq-km patch of land west of the main island. If Kinmen is an outpost, than Little Kinmen is the outpost of an outpost, a chunk of ROC territory so close to the PRC that cell phones automatically switch to Fujian-based networks (mind those roaming charges!). Pretty and windswept, Little Kinmen is basically an island park that just happens to sit atop of the 1958 war's last front lines.

Sights & attractions

A point of interest on Little Kinmen is the **Victory Gate** (Shènglì Mén; Map pp298–9), which stands in perpetual greeting to visitors coming off the ferry.

The **Pata Memorial** (Bādá Loúzi; Map pp298–9) is a replica of one of the towers on the Great Wall of China. This was built in 1963 by the Kinmen-stationed troops to

commemorate seven soldiers who died in a 1933 battle against Japan. On the top of the tower stand stone soldiers, arms perpetually cocked flinging grenades.

The **Chaste Maiden Temple** (Liè Nǚ Miào; Map pp298–9) is dedicated to Wang Yu-lan, a woman who, legend has it, fought against communist soldiers. She chose to swim out to the ocean to avoid being molested by the soldiers. The temple is built on the spot where she was buried after her body floated back to shore.

Huchingtou War Museum (Hújǐngtóu Zhànshǐ Guǎn; Map pp298–9) contains war memorabilia and an observation room with pay binoculars from which you can see Xiamen on a clear day.

The **Siwei Tunnel** (Sìwéi Kēngdào; Map pp298-9; 8.30am-5pm), on southeastern Liehyu, is an underground tunnel blasted through a granite reef. It's 790m in length, twice as large as the Dishan Tunnel on Kinmen, and is the top tourist attraction on the island. It's also home to Liehyu's only coffee shop. The Liehyu visitor centre is right next to the tunnel entrance.

Activities

Bicycling is the best way to see Little Kinmen and the price can't be beat. In an effort to increase tourism, the Kinmen tourism department actually loans visitors mountain bikes... free! Just head to the Siwei Tunnel when you get off the boat from Kinmen and pick one up at the visitor centre. Liehyu's perimeter is ringed by a bike path passing through lovely coastal scenery including Lingshui Lake, an artificial salt-water lake that's home to a number of species of waterbirds native to Fujian province. There are a couple of small stores that sell local specialities such as deep-fried oyster cake, in addition to groceries.

The beaches along the west side of the island are no good for swimming because of antiamphibious landing defences in the water (not to mention potential mines). There is a long, swimmable beach (though we've yet to find shower facilities) along the southeastern coast. There are also a few interesting sights: a decommissioned tank being slowly covered by flowering vines; small shrines surrounded by semiwild gardens; and a (sadly, poorly maintained) climbing wall. Liehyu has an hourly bus service travelling north and south around the island. As it's such a tiny place, it's probably faster to walk than wait for a bus.

PENGHU 澎湖

☎ 06 / pop 90,000

Penghu (Pénghú), also known as the Pescadores, is famous for its beautiful beaches, glorious temples and a plethora of traditional Chinese-style homes which are surrounded by walls made from coral. Penghu is famous for another thing as well; though the weather in the summer is hot and beautiful, in winter and spring the archipelago is quite possibly the windiest place in the northern hemisphere. Wind not a tourist draw, you say? Tell that to the droves of windsurfers who consider Penghu a sporting mecca and the Canary Islands of the Orient.

A flat, dry place covered mostly with low bush and grasslands, Penghu is quite a change from the mountainous subtropical environment. The wind- and water-eroded coastlines of the islands feature stunning basalt cliffs, reefs and, without question, some of the finest beaches in Taiwan.

History

Windswept Penghu has served for centuries as a strategic connection point between Taiwan, mainland China, Japan and Southeast Asia. But its strategic position proved both a blessing and curse, and over the centuries Penghu was grabbed by various colonisers from Asia and Europe looking to have a toehold in the Taiwan Straits.

The Dutch were the first to take the islands in 1622 but they moved to the Taiwanese mainland when they learned that the Ming imperial court had plans to remove them from Penghu by force. In 1662 the Ming loyalist Koxinga was sent to oust the Dutch from Taiwan for good. Penghu was a convenient place to station his troops as he drew up his battle plans. Some troops stayed in Penghu after the Dutch were gone and set up their own regime, which was short lived, however, because the Qing court threw them out in 1683. The French were the next to arrive in 1884, followed in 1895 by the Japanese, who settled down and stayed for the next 50 years, only to be replaced by the Nationalists in 1945.

Penghu is rich with historical relics, evidence of its long colonial history. Martial law lifted from the islands in 1979 and mainland Taiwanese were finally able to visit the island. To capitalise on Penghu's history and boost a drooping economy, the islands were transformed into a beach mecca for local and foreign visitors. The Penghu Archipelago has been designated a national scenic area and the islands have been given a makeover for the visitors that crowd Penghu's shores each summer.

Orientation

Penghu County includes 64 islands (only a third of which are inhabited). There's plenty to see and do on the main archipelago, four interconnected islands that collectively form a horseshoe containing the townships of Makung, Huhsi, Paisha and Siyu. Ferries run daily during high season between Makung and the two largest outer islands, Chimei and Wang'an, and tours are available to bring you to some of the smaller islands as well. Makung (on Penghu Island) is the only city, and though you can find whatever you need here, by Taiwanese standards Makung is more like a large town.

Getting There & Away

AIR

Makung is well connected to Taiwan's major cities, and flights leave daily from Taipei, Taichung, Tainan, Kaohsiung and Chiayi. Flights also leave regularly going to nearby Chimei and Wang'an Islands. Travel agencies around Chungcheng Rd can help arrange tickets. The following airlines have offices in Makung airport.

Fuhsing Airlines (☎ 922 8866)
Mandarin Airlines (☎ 922 8688)
TransAsia Airways (☎ 922 8888)
Uni Air (☎ 922 8999)

BOAT

The **Taiwan Hangye Company** (Kaohsiung ☎ 07-561 3866; 5 Chiehhsing-1st St; Makung Map pp308-9 ☎ 926 4087; Makung Harbour Terminal Bldg) operates *Taiwanline,* a boat that travels between Kaohsiung and Makung (NT800 to NT1300, 3½ hours) from mid-March into September. The schedule changes every three months and boats are limited in winter.

The *Tomorrow Star* runs between Putai (near Chiayi) and Makung (NT812, 90 minutes). To inquire call **Makung Tomorrow Star** (☎ 926 0666; Makung Harbour Terminal Bldg; Map pp308-9).

Getting Around
TO/FROM THE AIRPORT
An airport shuttle bus makes hourly rounds to Makung between 7.20am and 6.50pm. A taxi to and from Makung airport costs around NT300. If you're not too heavily weighed down, consider walking to the main road from the airport and hailing a cab there; you'll save around NT100 doing it that way.

CAR, MOTORCYCLE & SCOOTER
Car, motorcycle and scooter rental places are on and around Chungcheng Rd in Makung. Rates for motorcycles and scooters are generally NT350 to NT400 a day, excluding petrol. Small cars can be rented for NT1300 a day. Most rental agencies require an international or Taiwan licence for cars, but some will let the requirement slide for scooters.

PUBLIC TRANSPORT
There are two bus lines that traverse the archipelago, but they only run about once an hour from the **main bus station** (Chēzhàn; Map pp308–9) in Makung. Enough Penghu folk will stop for foreign tourists to make hitchhiking viable.

TAXI
Taxi drivers prefer flat rates to using the meter. A trip to just about anywhere on Penghu will

PENGHU ISLANDS

0 ___ 10 km
0 ___ 6 miles

TAIWAN STRAIT

Mutou Island

Chipei Village

Chipei Island

Kupo Island
Tiechen Island
Hsiao Paisha Island
Hsienchiao Island
Chihkan
Niao Island
Hsiaomen Island
Paisha Township
Yuanpei Island
Hsiyu Township
Chishan Island
Tingkou Island
Hsiyu Island
Tatsang Island
Penghu Bay
Huhsi Township
Makung
Makung Airport
Hsi Island Lighthouse
Sokang
Penghu Island
Tongpan Island
Huching Island

Chimei Island
Same Scale as Main Map
Chimei Airport
Nanhu
Tientaishan
Chiangchun Island
Wang'an Island
Wang'an Airport

TAIWAN STRAIT

Hsiyuping Island
Tungyuping Island
Lighthouse

To Chimei Island
(2.5km; see inset)
Hsichi Island
Tungchi Island

SIGHTS & ACTIVITIES		
Aimen Beach 隘門沙灘	1	B3
Chihli Beach 蒔裡沙灘	2	A3
Chipei Sand Beach 吉貝沙灘	3	B1
Chungshe Old Dwellings 中社古厝	4	A4
Dutch Fort 風櫃尾紅毛城遺址	5	A3
Erkan Old Residences 二崁古厝	6	A2
Fengkuei Cave 風櫃洞	7	A3
Green Mossback Turtle Sightseeing and Preservation Centre 綠蠵龜觀光保育中心	8	A4
Hsiaomen Geology Museum 小門地質博物館	9	A2
Lintou Park 林投公園	10	B3
Peichi Temple 北極殿	11	B3
Penghu Aquarium 澎湖水族館	12	B2
Shanshui Beach 山水沙灘	13	B3
Sokang Pagodas 鎮港子午賣塔	14	B3
Ta-yi Temple 大義宮	15	A2
Tomb of the Seven Virtuous Beauties 七美人塚	16	B4
Trans-Ocean Bridge 跨海大橋	17	A2
Tungliang Banyan Tree 通梁古榕	18	A2
Two Hearts Stone Weir 雙心石滬	19	B4
West Fortress 西台	20	A3
Whale Cave 鯨魚洞	21	A2

SLEEPING 🛏		
Chipei Sea Paradise Resort 吉貝海上樂園	22	B1
Fupeng Inn 福鵬旅社	23	B3
Penghu Sunrise B&B 澎湖民宿菓葉觀日樓	24	B3
Yuyue Yuli Harbour Camping Area 魚月魚里港露營區	25	B4

EATING 🍴		
Dongwei Homestyle 東未海濱客家餐廳	26	B3

TRANSPORT		
North Sea Tourist Service Centre 北海遊客服務中心	27	B2

cost NT200 to NT300. Taxi tours can be had for about NT2500 to NT3000 a day.

MAKUNG 馬公

Makung (Mǎgōng, Magong, Makong) is a pretty seaside town with a history stretching back to the 14th century. Though it's thoroughly modern (there's even a McDonalds, something which Makung people seem unusually proud of), you won't have to look far to find remnants of bygone dynasties. The Japanese have also left their mark in Makung with a number of Japanese-style administrative buildings around town. It's definitely worth spending a day exploring Makung before heading out to see the rest of the Archipelago or any of the outer Penghu islands.

Summer is prime time in Makung, with streets full of tourists and hotel prices rising like the temperature. In winter, when the howling of the wind sometimes becomes deafening, the town is markedly more subdued. Autumn and spring, however, can be perfectly lovely, with the weather warm enough to swim, cheaper accommodation, and low-to-no crowds.

Information

Visit http://tour.penghu.gov.tw/English for general info about the Penghu Islands.

Bank of Taiwan (Map pp308-9; ☎ 927 9935; 24 Jenai Rd) Foreign currency exchange and reliable cross-culturally-attuned ATMs.

Penghu Tourist Service Centre (Pénghú Yóukè Fúwù Zhōngxin; ☎ 921 6445; 171 Kuanghua Lane; ☼ 8am-

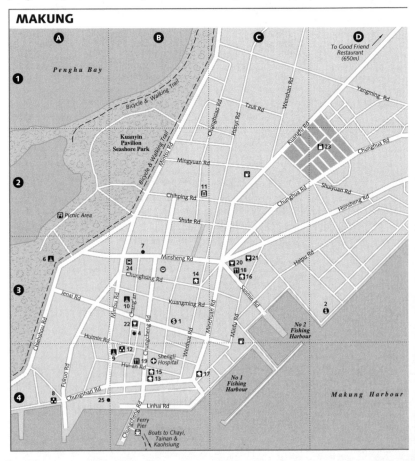

MAKUNG

5pm) Penghu pamphlets, magazines and books in English aplenty. The drawback? Bad location, halfway between the airport and Makung. Try to pick up your travel guides in the airport if possible.

South Seas Tourist Service Centre (Nánhǎi Yóukè Fúwù Zhōngxīn; Map pp308–9; ☎ 926 4738; Makung Harbour Third Fishing Dock; ☺ 8am-5pm) This centre provides information about Chimei, Wang'an and Tongpan Islands, as well as boat tickets. They also provide a free left-luggage service.

Sights

Makung is great to explore by foot or bicycle. Its old buildings, narrow cobblestone alleys, temples and remnants of the old city wall are waiting to be checked out. Chungcheng Rd is basically the main drag and it's here where

you'll find more coffee shops than you'd think a small Taiwanese city could ever support.

Probably the best place to start your exploration is down by the harbour at the end of Chungcheng Rd (this is where the boat from Taiwan leaves you). A quick walk west along Chungsan Rd takes you to **Shuncheng Gate** (Shùnchéng Mén; Map pp308–9) and a section of the **Makung Old Wall** (Mǎgōng Gǔ Chéng; Map pp308–9). City walls were constructed around Makung as a defensive measure. After the occupying French left the city in 1885, the walls were mostly knocked down by the Japanese. Parts of the wall are in the process of being overrun by cacti and aloe plants the size of ponies. The old neighbourhood around the wall is dilapidated, providing an interesting counterpoint to the renovated 'old' town sections.

A few blocks to the northeast is one of Penghu's most celebrated spots, the **Matsu Temple** (Māzǔ Tiānhòu Gōng; Map pp308–9; Hui-an Rd; 5am-8.30pm). It was constructed in the late 16th century, and locals say it's the oldest temple in Taiwan. Sailors have been coming here for centuries to pray to the goddess Matsu (see p216) for a safe voyage. The temple was originally built without using a single nail and though it has been refurbished several times over the years, the craftsmanship remains superb. Unlike many temples in Penghu, this temple still looks and feels ancient.

Behind the temple are a series of winding brick-paved pedestrian lanes that are home to a number of interesting sights such as the **Shihkung Ancestral Shrine** (Shīgōng Cí; Map pp308–9) and **Well of a Thousand Soldiers** (Wàn Jūn Jǐng; Map pp308–9), where in 1682 the goddess Matsu was said to have bequeathed a magical well to Ming soldiers massing for an invasion of Taiwan. Also in this warren of old streets and eclectically built homes of 1920s Western and Fujian buildings is the **Chienyi Tang Chinese Traditional Medicine Store** (Qiányì Táng Zhōngyào Háng; Map pp308–9; 42 Chungyang St; 7am-9.30pm); though the proprietor speaks no English it's a fun place to shop for traditional Chinese remedies.

From here, you can head back east and wander through Makung, checking out some of the town's unique architecture and abundance of smaller temples and shrines. including **Peichen Temple** (Běichén Gōng; Map pp308–9).

Alternatively, if you're in the mood to swim or just chill out in the sea breeze, head over to Makung's western shoreline, where you'll find the city's fabulous waterfront park, which has a great enclosed bay great for swimming. The park is named for the 300-year-old **Kuanyin Pavilion** (Guānyīn Tíng; Map pp308–9; 5am-8pm), dedicated to Kuanyin, goddess of mercy. This is one of the most important places for Buddhist worship around, which says a lot, as there are a great many places for Buddhist worship in Penghu. The most important artefact in the temple is the old bell, which dates back to 1696.

To the northeast of the park is the **Penghu Reclamation Hall** (Pénghú Kāi Tuò Guǎn; Map pp308–9; 30 Chihping Rd; admission NT30; 10am-10pm, closed Mon & last day of each month). This building was built by the Japanese, its architecture displaying an elegant mix of Japanese and Western styles. Inside are displays about Penghu culture and history as well as a small library (all in Chinese). From here you can continue to walk northeast and check out the Peichen market, a cool traditional wet market with a heavy fishing vibe; try the sea urchin, or some snails. There are also some stalls selling all manner of cooked foods around the market.

Though it's a bit of a hike from the centre of town, on the eastern edge of Makung you'll find the very grand Confucius Temple (Kǒng Miào; Map pp308–9). The temple was formerly the Wenshi College, built in 1766 and an important centre of learning during the Qing dynasty. The name of the college was changed to the Confucius Temple during the Japanese occupation to take advantage of the Japanese respect for Confucius, in the hope that the college wouldn't be torn down.

Also on the outskirts of Makung lies the **Penghu County Cultural Area** (Pénghú Xiàn Wénhuà Yuánqū; Map pp308–9; 230 Chunghua Rd), which has several museums and an art gallery worth visiting. On the grounds is the cultural bureau, a library, **Penghu Marine Exhibition Hall** (Pénghú Hǎiyáng Zīyuán Guǎn; admission NT20; 9am-noon & 2-5pm Wed-Sun) and the **Penghu County Science Hall** (Pénghú Xiàn Kēxuéguǎn; admission free; 9am-noon & 2-5pm Wed-Sun). Both the marine hall and the science hall have changing exhibitions devoted to Penghu's ecology and natural resources. Most of the information is in Chinese but the displays are interesting enough to make a visit worthwhile. Kids, in particular, will enjoy the dinosaur fossils housed in the science hall. Art enthusiasts might want to check out the nearby **Chao Ertai Art Museum** (Zhào Èrdài Yìguǎn; 240 Chunghua Rd; Map pp308–9; admission free; 9am-noon & 2-5pm Wed-Sun), a gallery displaying the works of Chao Ertai, a multitalented artist who is considered the Picasso of Penghu.

Activities & Festivals

Though the **Lantern Festival** (yuánxiāojié) is a sight to behold anywhere in Taiwan, Penghu's festival is truly a unique celebration. It takes place on the 15th day of the first lunar month (about 15 days after the first day of Chinese New Year, which begins anywhere from mid-January to mid-February, depending on the year). Penghu's celebrations include a bacchanalian parade with dancers, and fireworks through the streets and past the many temples of Makung. One twist unique to Penghu is the parading of gigantic golden turtle effigies through the streets. In the days before the festival most bakeries in town devote half their oven space to the production of turtle cakes, which are given away and eaten during the course of the festival.

Penghu is fast becoming Asia's premier spot for windsurfing. The **Penghu Pro-Am Windsurfing Festival** happens every November, attracting sailboard enthusiasts from all over the world. For more information on the festival check out www.penghu windsurf.idv.tw. Windsurfing lessons and equipment rental are available at both the Penghu Sunrise B&B (right) in Guoyeh, and in Makung at **Liquid Sport** (Map pp308-9; ☎ 926 0361; 36 Minsheng Rd). The first lesson is NT1500, including equipment, and Liquid Sport owner Alex Mowday says he can teach most beginners to windsurf in 'about two hours'.

Sleeping

During summer, hotel prices in Makung rise dramatically, and rooms are hard to come by on weekends and holidays. In high season book ahead or sleep on the beach. October and November are considered low season, and though windier than in the summer, the weather is usually still hot. The prices listed here are summer rates; in winter (October to March) sizable discounts can be had at even the most expensive of hotels.

BUDGET

Chunghsin Hotel (Zhōngxìn Dà Lǚshè; Map pp308-9; ☎ 927 2151; 22 Chunghsing Rd; 中興路22號; r from NT700) A good budget choice. It's in a convenient location, walking distance to all the Makung sights and shopping. The 21 rooms here fill up quickly in summer so book ahead.

Donghai Hotel (Dōnghǎi Lǚshè; Map pp308-9; ☎ 927 2367; 38 Sanmin Rd; 三民路38號; r from NT500) Near the fish market, this place is cheap but run down and dingy, and should only be considered if all the other hotels are full. There are a couple of other cheap hotels on the same block.

MIDRANGE & TOP-END

Hwa Shin Palace Hotel (Huáxīn Dà Fàndiàn; Map pp308-9; ☎ 926 4911; 40 Sanmin Rd; 三民40號; r from NT1680) The rooms here are well-maintained and comfortable, and the hotel is in a central part

of town and offers free airport pickup. During our last visit, management said the hotel would undergo renovation in mid-2007, so prices may be more expensive by the time you read this. However, there are similar quality hotels on the same block.

Mongfun Hotel (Htiàn Dà Fàndiàn; Map pp308-9; ☎ 926 2936; www.069263936.com.tw; 2 Minchuan Rd; 民權路2號; r from NT2800; ⌨) One of the newest hotels in Makung, the Mongfun has a very cool boutique feel to it, from the Art-Deco lobby to the 9th-floor Zen tea shop. Rooms are definitely comfy, and some have sea views. The whole place is wireless equipped, and management speaks English. There 30% discounts in the off-season.

Jih Lih Hotel (Rìlì Dà Fàndiàn; Map pp308-9; ☎ 926 5898; 25 Huimin 1st Rd; 惠民一路25號; d NT2200-8800) The Jih Lih has large, very pleasant rooms and offers deep discounts in winter. The hotel is a one-minute walk to Chungcheng Rd, the main shopping street of Makung, and close to the Peichen Temple.

Hotel Ever Spring (Chángchūn Dà Fàndiàn; Map pp308-9; ☎ 927 4881; www.everspring-hotel.com.tw; 6 Chungcheng Rd; 中正路6號; r incl breakfast NT1800-3800; ⌨) This is a nice place located very close to Makung harbour, with free internet access and breakfast. Some rooms have ocean views and there's even a 'Captain's Suite'.

Boha Hotel (Bǎohuá Dà Fàndiàn; Map pp308-9; ☎ 927 4881; 2 Chungcheng Rd; 中正路2號; d incl breakfast NT1750) Adjacent to Makung harbour, the Boha offers spotless rooms, some with ocean views. The 2nd-floor restaurant serves surprisingly good Western food, a rarity in Penghu.

Penghu Sunrise B&B (Pénghú Mínsù Guòyè Guānrílóu; Map p307; ☎ 992 0818; 129-3 Guoyeh village; 菓葉村129-3號; d incl breakfast NT2000) Run by Jan and Sylvia, a Taiwanese couple who decided to swap the rat race for windsurfing and sunshine, the Sunrise is a bona fide B&B with ocean views, fresh morning coffee and English-speaking hosts. Rooms are bright, airy and comfortably furnished, and there's a great communal lounge area with a panoramic view of the ocean. The B&B is in Guoyeh, 12km west of Makung, close to some great beaches. Scooter, bicycle, windsurfing and sea-kayaking equipment are available for rent and airport pickup is free of charge.

Eating

First and foremost, Makung is a seafood-lover's paradise; there are some other local specialties, such as *jīnguā mǐfěn* (pumpkin rice-noodles), *xián bǐng* (salty biscuits) and *shāo ròu fàn* (grilled meat with rice), but it's the seafood that keeps people coming back. Raw *lóng xiā* (lobster) and fried *wǔ xiāng cìhétún* ('five-flavour' balloonfish) are favourites. The one item that no Taiwanese visitor leaves without is Penghu's famed *hēi táng gāo* (brown-sugar sponge cakes); you can buy these all over Makung.

There are restaurants all over town and you'll find street food cooking in front of just about any temple, especially during high season. We've recommended just a few places that you might not otherwise find on your own.

Starfish (Hǎixīng Degùxiāng; Map pp308-9; ☎ 926 1406; 22 Hui-an Rd; dishes from NT150; ☽ lunch & dinner) A bit kitsch but fun, with swing-bench seating and seashell-covered walls. Meals are mostly seafood (naturally), curries and casseroles, and the place is in the pedestrian maze behind Matsu Temple.

Jingwang Vegetarian (Jíngwáng Sùshí; Map pp308-9; 46 Sanmin Rd; dishes from NT40; ☽ lunch & dinner) Vegetarians will want to know about this little storefront eatery with five tables. Though they only serve a handful of dishes (that are on display all the time, so just point), it's all good.

Dongwei Homestyle (Dōngwèi Hǎibīn Kèjiācāncūn; Map p307; ☎ 921 7688; 6-1 Dongwei Village; dishes from NT100; ☽ lunch & dinner) This generic-looking restaurant is adjacent to a hotel called the Dong Wei and a bit out of the city. Nonetheless it's worth the trip. It serves excellent Hakka food. Manager Kevin speaks enough English to help those not familiar with Hakka-style food to pick out some dishes.

Good Friend (Hǎopéngyǒu; ☎ 926 1158; 320 Sanduo Rd; dishes from NT100; ☽ lunch & dinner) Though it's on Makung's northern edge, we had to tell you about this primarily vegetarian restaurant which makes the best Taiwanese *niúròu tāngmiàn* (beef noodle soup) we've ever eaten. Quite the paradox, eh?

Drinking

Sunny Colony Bar (Yángguāng Zhí Míndì; Map pp308-9; Lane 3-6 Chungcheng Rd; drinks NT150-180; ☽ 6pm-2am) This bar is a trendy place to spend the evening. Speciality drinks include Penghu *xiánrénzhǎng zhī* (cactus juice) mixed with alcohol.

Freud Pub (Fúluòyīdé; Map pp308-9; 2-1 Hsinsheng Rd; drinks from NT90; ☽ 11-2am) This sports bar is where visiting windsurfers hang out. The house special is the potent cocktail 'Absolutely Drunk', made with six kinds of alcohol.

KEEPING UP WITH THE JONSES, PENGHU STYLE

For an archipelago of 90,000 people, Penghu has a lot of temples. We aren't talking small roadside shrines here (though there are plenty of these), we mean full-blown three- to five-storey temples with stone columns depicting legendary scenes, ornate hand-carved doors, boisterously painted interiors and exteriors and enough statues and devotional artwork to make even the most casual tourist wish they'd bought a larger memory card for their digicam. A scooter trip through the main islands looks something like this:

'…Flat bushland on one side, ocean on the other…small one-grocery store hamlet…massively grandiose three-storey Taoist temple…'

'…Pretty farms surrounded by coral walls…beautiful beach with scattered windmills…blindingly ostentatious six-storey temple dedicated to Matsu…'

'…Water buffalo grazing in field…7-Eleven…three-tiered temple complex surrounded by half a dozen stone deities re-enacting events of cosmic significance…'

During the high season, you'll generally see tourists in these palatial temples. In the low season, perhaps a monk or two. Or you might have the place to yourself. Though some are built by religious organisations, we understand that many of these grand temples were built with the private funds of locals who've left the island to seek their fortunes on Taiwan or abroad. The reason behind the temple construction? As near as we can tell, the ever-increasing grandeur is as simple as keeping up with the Joneses (or Huangs, or Zhuangs).

'The Hong family spent 10 million to build a temple in Ting-wan? We'll spend 15 to build ours in Tung-shih!'

In any event, it makes the island a magnificent place for shutterbugs. Invest in that 2-gigabyte memory card, you'll fill it up quickly.

Sha Ai Chuang (Shǎ Ài Zhuāng; Map pp308-9; 14 Hsinsheng Rd; cocktails from NT150; ☻ 10am-midnight) Loosely translated as 'foolish love pub', this place was once the home of Penghu's first county chief. It has been transformed into a colourful bar with great ambience. The fruit-juice cocktails are especially good on a warm night.

Shopping

Makung is full of shops selling all kinds of Penghu speciality items such as pink and black coral, shells and veined stones. We recommend against buying coral items as it only hastens the destruction of coral reefs and the decline of the marine creatures that live within them. If you need to bring home a nonedible souvenir, why not go for some nautically themed jewellery or perhaps a wind-chime set?

Edible items are especially popular with Taiwanese tourists, and stores selling squid jerky, smoked fish and dried seafood in general (but thankfully not shark's fin) can be found all over Makung. And of course, you can buy just about anything edible, from freshly caught fish and oysters to local vegetables and cooked snacks at the bustling **Peichen Market** (Běichén Shìchǎng; Map pp308-9) in central Makung. Snacking is best here before 1pm.

AROUND PENGHU ARCHIPELAGO

Though it's actually four islands, most locals simply refer to the horseshoe-shaped archipelago as the main island, or simply Penghu. The U-shaped route 203 shoots north from Makung on the west side of the main island, passing through the Paisha township before heading on to Hsiyu Island via the Great Bridge. Hsiyu is a long, narrow island, and 203 continues to the Western Fortress and lighthouse on its southern tip. The total distance of the one-way trip is just under 37km, so you can spend a full day exploring the sights along that road on a scooter and still make it back to Makung before dark. Good English-language travel information is available on http://tour.penghu.gov.tw/English, a fine site with maps. We've listed our favourites, along with some lesser-known spots.

Ancient Towns & Temples

Some call Penghu the Hawaii of Asia, but how many temples does Hawaii have? We frankly lost count of how many we saw in Penghu, but we think the person-to-temple ratio is

---

HIDDEN BUDDHIST DELIGHTS

While riding on Paisha island keep your eyes towards the west just before you get to the area of the **Penghu Aquarium** (Pénghú Shuǐzúguǎn; Map p307). When you see a large seated Buddha off in the distance, turn down that road to find a small Buddhist temple surrounded by several dozen astounding statues.

---

10 to one. Travelling around Penghu you'll undoubtedly stumble across some. On the wide, flat plains the huge, colourful complexes are a bit hard to miss.

Just southwest of Makung lie the **Sokang Pagodas** (Soǔgǎng Zǐwǔ Bǎotǎ; Map p307). These are two north- and south-facing stone towers that have been blessed by a Taoist priest and are reputed to contain supernatural powers that ward off evil and protect residents from natural disasters. So far they're working.

Not too far from the pagodas is the **Peichi Temple** (Běijí Diàn; Map p307), where you'll find a large gold turtle that represents longevity. This temple is a hub of activity during the Lantern Festival (see p149). The ruins of the **Dutch Fort** (Fēngguìwěi Hóngmáochéng Yízhǐ; Map p307), abandoned by the Dutch when they were driven out of Penghu by the Ming army in 1624, is at the end of the peninsula.

Paisha, north of Penghu Island, has a number of wonderful temples that will appeal to earth-worshippers. In Chiangmei you'll come across the Lungte temple, built around a large and ancient banyan tree. But don't get too impressed. In Tungliang Village, just south of the **Trans-Ocean Bridge** (Kuàhǎi Dàqiáo; Map p307) is the 300-year-old **Tungliang Banyan Tree** (Tōngliáng Gǔróng; Map p307) which dwarfs the Lungte banyan. A beautiful temple complex has been built there, and the two are now inseparable. It's said that during the Qing dynasty, a ship sunk off the coast of Penghu and a small seedling floated to shore and was planted by locals. There's a little snack shop next to this temple that sells cactus-fruit sorbet, something you'll only find in Penghu. Well worth trying.

On Hsiyu Island, the 200-year-old **Ta-yi Temple** (Dàyì Gōng; Map p307) is dedicated to Kuanyu, the god of war. Some say that when the French tried to attack Penghu, mysterious forces kept them away from the temple.

Just south of the temple is where you'll find the **Erkan Old Residences** (Èrkǎn Gǔ Cuò; Map p307; admission NT30; 8am-7pm). It's a group of houses dating back a century. These homes are built in a melange of southern Fujian, Western and Japanese styles. There's a small (but often noisy) temple over on one end of town with elaborately carved beams and columns. Though a tourist attraction, the village is inhabited and some of the people living there keep their front gates open and invite visitors to check out their unique homes.

On the southern tip of Hsiyu sits the **West Fortress** (Xī Tái; Map p307; admission NT30; 7.30am-6.30pm summer & 8am-5.30pm winter). It was built in 1887, following the Sino-French War, and 5000 soldiers were once stationed in this fortress. Interestingly, it's constructed with mud and sticky-rice pulp. It's possible to go inside and wander around.

BEACHES & COASTAL SCENERY

South of Makung, **Shanshui Beach** (Shānshuǐ Shātān; Map p307) has smooth white sand and breaking waves, and is a great place to relax. On the weekends, the beach is fairly crowded with sun worshippers from Taiwan, but during the week you may well wind up sharing the beach with a handful of other bathers. The beach is popular with Penghu's surf set when the waves are up.

Chihli Beach (Zhìlì Shātān; Map p307) is up the coast to the northwest. The shell-sand beach stretches for over 1km and is popular with beach-sport enthusiasts and sunbathers. This stretch of coast is known for its bizarre rock formations, formed thousands of years ago by cooling basalt magma. Sea erosion has created many unusual gullies and crevices that have taken the imagination of Penghu residents and tourists. Not far is **Fengkuei Cave** (Fēngguì Dòng; Map p307), on Penghu's south shore, a sea-eroded gully that reportedly makes a peculiar sound when the wind rushes through it during high tide.

The green expanse of pines in **Lintou Park** (Líntóu Gōngyuán; Map p307; NT30) is a rare sight in dry, windswept Penghu. The one-hectare forest borders a white-sand beach, a superb spot for a picnic. **Aimen Beach** (Àimén Shātān; Map p307) is a favourite among locals for all kinds of water sports and beach activities. It's possi-

ble to camp out here, though in summer it can be quite crowded. Both of these are around 20 minutes by scooter from Makung.

The western coast of Hsiyu is quite dramatic, full of steep cliffs and gullies. **Whale Cave** (Jīngyú Dòng; Map p307) is a hole in a rock that kinda-sorta looks like a whale; locals say the hole was created by a gigantic whale crashing into the rock, but we kinda-sorta doubt that. Checking it out gives you a fine excuse to ride over the Trans-Ocean Bridge, of which Penghu folks are quite proud.

MUSEUMS & AQUARIUMS

The **Penghu Aquarium** (Pénghú Shuǐzú Guǎn; 58 Chitou Village; admission NT200; 9am-5pm Mon-Wed & Fri-Sun) is on Paisha island and is one of the best little aquariums in Taiwan. The two-storey marine exhibition centre provides information on all the aquatic creatures swimming around Penghu. Kids and adults alike will have a great time communing with the sea turtles. The highlight of the aquarium is the 14m glass tunnel, allowing visitors and fish to meet eye-to-eye. There's also a petting tank where the little ones can touch starfish on the second floor.

On the northern tip of Hsiyu island is the **Hsiaomen Geology Museum** (Xiǎomén Dìzhì Bówùguǎn; 11-12 Xiaomen Village; admission NT20; 8am-5pm), with exhibits explaining the natural history of the Penghu Archipelago.

OUTER ISLANDS

The two largest of Penghu's outer islands are Chimei and Wang'an. Both are south of the main island and have boat and air service to Makung. Third largest is Chipei, north of Paisha, which has some great beaches.

Wang'an 望安鄉

About 30 minutes by boat from Makung harbour, Wang'an (Wàng'ān) is a must visit for those interested in aquatic wildlife. It's home to the **Green Mossback Turtle Sightseeing and Preservation Centre** (Lǜ Xiguī Guānguāng Bǎo Yù Zhōngxīn; Map p307; admission free; 9am-5pm), one of the few wild-turtle reserves in Taiwan. Inside are bilingual exhibits about the state of sea turtles in Taiwan and around the world. There's also information on wildlife preservation efforts in the Strait Islands and in Taiwan proper.

The **Chungshe Old Dwellings** (Zhōngshè Gǔ Cuò; Map p307) are a group of abandoned but

---

LOCAL VOICES: THE ORIGINAL FLAVOUR OF PENGHU *Jessica Du*

When people ask me about the island of Penghu – where I was brought up – I usually say that Penghu is to Taiwan what Hawaii is to the USA. This group of small islands is tranquil and simple. It is my home. After travelling around for a few years, I decided to come back to teach. There is a Taiwanese saying that goes, 'Always pray to the trees when you eat fruit; and always think of the origin when you drink spring water.' By returning to the place where I grew up, I feel that I am returning to my origins, to my source.

Growing up in Penghu gave me both an enthusiastic nature and a strong sense of contentment, characteristics common to Penghu people. Though many young people are leaving Penghu to make their fortunes in the Taiwanese mainland, I feel that I should return to give something back to the islands of my birth.

As a teacher, I will bring what I have learnt, what I have seen and what I know back to the next generation. I will tell them we should be proud of being 'Penghu Ren', which means Penghu people, and that we should keep our 'original flavour' no matter where we find ourselves in life.

---

well-preserved houses in Chungshe Village (Zhōngshè Cūn). The highest point on the island is Tientai Mountain (Tiāntái Shan), actually a grassy hill with some cows. The footprint of Li Tungbin, one of China's Eight Immortals, is impressed on a rock here; his other footprint is on one of the smaller of Penghu's Islands.

Chimei 七美鄉

Chimei (Qīmĕi) is located south of Wang'an; its name means 'Seven Beauties' and refers to a legend (a somewhat common one in Chinese culture) involving seven women who, in the Ming dynasty, threw themselves into a well rather than lose their chastity to Japanese pirates. After the well was turned into a tomb, seven trees sprung up to surround it, and the resulting **Tomb of the Seven Virtuous Beauties** (Qīmĕi Rén Zhŏng; Map p307; adult/child NT30/15) is a well-visited spot on Chimei Island. Another pretty Chimei spot quickly becoming a Penghu icon is the **Two Hearts Stone Weir** (Shuāng Xīn Shí Hù; Map p307), a heart-shaped ring of stones designed to catch fish during low tide.

There are several seafood restaurants by Nanhu harbour as well as a couple of small inns and homestays. We recommend the **Fupeng Inn** (Fúpéng Lǚshè; Map p307; ☎ 997 1043; 10 Nankang Village; r NT700-1200), a small and homey inn run by the Gong family. Though they speak no English, they'll come down to the harbour to get you if you can have someone communicate for you.

If you're carrying your own camping gear, there are some fine, flat expanses of grassland with great ocean views for camping out. Try the **Yuyue Yuli Harbour Camping Area** (Yúyuè Yúlǐgăng Lùyíngqū; Map p307).

Chipei 吉貝

With its lovely sand-shell beaches, Chipei (Jíbèi), north of Paisha, buzzes with tourists in summer but shuts down almost completely in winter.

Chipei Sand Beach (Jíbèi Shātān; Map p307) is the most popular beach on the island. This long strip of golden sand juts out into the water, its size changing with the coming and going of the tides. During summer, windsurfing, boating and even parasailing are popular activities here. Equipment is available for rent at the beach resort or in the small shops around the beach. During winter, you'll have the whole place to yourself. You can stay right on the beach at the **Chipei Sea Paradise Resort** (Jíbèi Hăishàng Lèyuán; Map p307; ☎ 991 1311; 187 Chipei Village; cabins from NT1500), which rents out small beachfront shacks whose great location more than makes up for their spartan nature. The beach is popular with speedboaters and sailors, and a wide variety of water toys are for rent. Chipei Village also has an assortment of homestays and small hotels.

Getting There & Away
Mandarin Airlines (Kaohsiung ☎ 07 802 6868; Makung ☎ 921 6966) has flights between Kaohsiung and Chimei (35 minutes) and Chimei and Makung (15 minutes); flight prices vary, but are under NT1000 each way.

Boats to Chimei and Wang'an leave from the **South Seas Tourist Service Centre** (Nánhăi Yóukè Fúwù Zhōngxīn; Map pp308-9-00; ☎ 926 4738; Makung

Harbour Third Fishing Dock; ☉ 8am-5pm) in Makung. In the high season you can often find boats that go to both before returning in the evening, often stopping on Tongan (Tǒngpán) and Huching (Hǔjǐng), two of the smaller islands on the way. A full-day trip that hits four islands with one- and two-hour stops at Wang'an and Chimei (and brief stops at the other two) costs around NT500, depending on the operators. Schedules are posted in the tourist service centre.

Boats leave for Chipei from the **North Sea Tourist Service Centre** (Běi Hǎi Yóukè Fúwù Zhōngxīn; Map p307) in Chihkan, in northeast Paisha, daily. Schedules vary, and some boats will go to Chipei as part of an overall tour to many of the smaller islands north of Paisha.

Getting Around

Rental scooters are available in Chimei, Wang'an and Chipei for NT400 to NT500 a day. Walking is another possibility, if you have the time and energy.

LANYU 蘭嶼

☎ 089 / pop 3000

The Yami people call their island home 'Pongso No Tao' or 'Island of the People' in their native tongue. The Taiwanese call it Lanyu (Lányǔ, Orchid Island), naming it after the flowers that have almost been picked to near extinction. A volcanic, mountainous island covered with a carpet of tropical rainforest, Lanyu lies about 65km southeast of the city of Taitung, making it the southernmost outpost of the Republic of China.

Lanyu's status as a far-flung outpost isn't merely geographical, but cultural as well, as the island is by far the least Chinese part of the Republic of China. The Yami people are of Australasian descent, speak their own distinct language and have a culture well removed from that of the people 'on the mainland' (as they sometime refer to the Taiwanese).

Coral reefs, perhaps the least spoiled in Taiwan, surround the rocky coastline, and at first glance the island appears a tropical paradise. In many ways it is. But to its inhabitants, the island is a sacred land, one mistreated for decades by a larger colonising neighbour and there are certain frictions between natives and outsiders. The opening of the island to tourism in the 1960s, coupled with controversial government policies, have forced the Yami to struggle particularly to retain their culture in the face of increasing outside influence. The Yami are well aware that most Taiwanese visitors view them as an oddity, so Western visitors to Lanyu should tread especially lightly.

HISTORY

For centuries the Yami were the only tribal group on their island and it wasn't until the 20th century that their way of life began to be seriously disturbed by outsiders.

During the Japanese occupation, the Japanese were fascinated by the local customs of the Yami and did little to interfere with their way of life. Things changed drastically after the KMT came to power and attempted to introduce Chinese language and culture to the Yami. Boatloads of mainland Chinese were shipped to the island in the hope that interracial marriages would Sinicise the Yami population. The Yami resisted this encroachment and years of fighting with the mainlanders ensued. In the late 1960s the government ordered that the traditional underground homes of the Yami be torn down and new cement structures built in their place. The houses were poorly made and couldn't hold up to the typhoons that whip through the island every year. At about the same time the housing law was passed, the island was opened to tourism and Taiwanese tourists began to arrive in droves. Christian missionaries also arrived, converting a large percentage of the population who are, to this day, primarily Christian.

Hardly based on mutual respect, the relationship between the Taiwanese government and the Yami took a turn for the worse when the government decided that the island would be a good place to dump nuclear waste. Long Men (Dragon Gate), at the southern tip of the island, was selected as a temporary storage facility for mid- and low-level nuclear waste. The site, which government representatives told locals was 'a fish cannery', became depository for up to 100,000 barrels of nuclear waste in 1982. When islanders discovered the truth from Taiwanese news reports they raised a furious outcry, protesting both on Lanyu and in front of the various government buildings in Taipei. Despite government promises that the dump would be removed, the barrels remain and there is evidence that approximately 20%

of the original barrels are beginning to leak and the concrete trenches they are buried in are cracking. Soil samples from the south end of the island show higher than normal levels of radioactivity and the possibility of health problems resulting from long-term contamination is of great concern to Yami people.

The Yami are doing their best to preserve their culture in the face of various social issues not uncommon in aboriginal communities. Alcoholism is a problem on the island, as is the overall brain drain caused by so many young people leaving to find greater economic prosperity in Taiwan. Even so, Yami traditions on Lanyu remain alive and one of the benefits that tourism has brought to the island has been to encourage the younger generation to learn more about their heritage before heading off to Taiwan to seek their fortunes. Visitors to Lanyu are generally made to feel welcome as long as they behave respectfully. Ask people before taking their photograph and don't wander into anyone's home or garden without getting permission first.

And no matter how cute they are, don't pick up the baby goats.

ORIENTATION

Lanyu Island is made up of two steep, jungle-covered mountains surrounded by a thin strip of coastal land. The 45km road circling both mountains can be driven in about 90 minutes, and a shorter, twisting road winds between both mountains from just south of the town of Hungtou on the west coast to the village of Yeyin on the east. This road also branches off to reach the weather observation centre at the top of Hongtoushan (Red Head Mountain). There are six villages located on the narrow flat strip of land wedged between the mountains and the sea, and the island's only petrol station is just north of the town of Yeyou.

INFORMATION

Summer is high season on Lanyu, and plane tickets are hard to get and accommodations scarce and more expensive. After mid-September, however, Taiwanese visitors are few and far between (especially during the week), despite the fact that the weather still leans towards the idyllic end of the scale. Consider visiting Lanyu between mid-September and mid-November, as long as there are no typhoons on the horizon.

There are no international ATMs on Lanyu, though the one in the post office accepts Taiwanese cards. Since high winds and rough weather (common around these parts, especially during low season) cancels flights and boats, coming prepared with money for a few unplanned days is a wise idea.

Teresa (☎ 0937 608 814; tbunnyteresa@yahoo.com) is one of the few people on Lanyu fully fluent in English. Though employed as a nurse at the island's health clinic, Teresa also acts as a guide for those interested in Yami culture, as well as an interpreter for Westerners

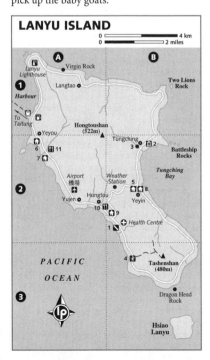

LANYU ISLAND

0 —————— 4 km
0 —————— 2 miles

looking for hotels, homestays or activities on Lanyu. Rates for her guide service are quite reasonable, but she asks that visitors contact her in advance. Teresa is keen on promoting both responsible travel and the culture of her people and will generally knows the dates of various village's Flying Fish Festivals.

SIGHTS & ACTIVITIES
Rock Formations
Visiting Lanyu is an otherworldly experience indeed and one of the features that gives Lanyu a vaguely Lovecraftian vibe is the twisted, jagged volcanic rocks jutting dramatically out of the ground and out to sea off the coast. Naturally, some of these strange geological formations have been named. Taiwanese tourists like to pose before formations with imaginative monikers such as **Dragon Head Rock** (Lóngtóu Yán) and **Two Lions Rock**. On the north coast of the island one rock has been dubbed **Virgin Rock** (Yùnǚ Yán); this is likely because the elliptical rock is hollow, save for a stalactite-like formation in the middle that gives the whole affair an appearance reminiscent of…well, you get the picture. Come see for yourself. In any event, the rocks' monikers have been assigned by the Taiwanese and not the Yami themselves (who generally find the names somewhat silly).

Hiking
The narrow island road winding past craggy cliffs, waterfalls, deep caves and the occasional village is really the only part of Lanyu level enough to be settled. This leaves the interior open for some magnificent hiking. One of the best hikes on Lanyu leads up to **Tienchi** (Tiānchí; Map p317), or Heaven Lake, a pond formed inside of a volcanic crater on the top of Tasenshan (Tashen Mountain). The hike to the lake and back is fairly easy, though one section requires hikers to navigate their way through a large, rocky ravine. The trailhead begins inauspiciously enough, across from the island's landfill, but you'll soon find yourself climbing into higher jungle elevations with beautiful views and amazing opportunities for both bird and butterfly watching. Allow three to four hours to do the round-trip hike.

Diving & Snorkelling
Because of heavy currents and an overall dearth of sandy beaches, Lanyu's shores are best suited for strong swimmers or the suicidally inclined. Snorkelling, however, is another matter and Lanyu offers some of Taiwan's most unspoiled coral reefs. **Badaiwan Diving** (Bādàiwān Qiǎnshuǐ; Map p317; ☎ 0921 729 313; 126 Hungtou Village) is run by a Lanyu native called Shaman, who charges NT400 for a half-day's snorkelling (including equipment and guide). Shaman is also a qualified diving guide but currently lacks rental equipment. His wife Teresa is a local guide, speaks excellent English, and will translate for him.

Traditional Crafts
Yami craftsmanship is quite unique. One of the most important cultural traditions is the building of elaborately carved wooden canoes, made from 27 individual pieces of wood, ingeniously held together without nails. However, buying such a canoe is unfeasible unless you intend to row it home (not advisable). However, the **Si Kang Chai Art Studio** (Shì Gāng Cài; Map p317; 38 Tungching Village) has an eclectic assortment of more portable sculptures and paintings on display. Close by is **Three Sisters** (Sān Jiě Mèi; Map p317; 23 Tungching Village), which sells woven bracelets, woodcarvings and paintings.

Festivals
The Flying Fish Festival is a traditional coming-of-age ceremony for young men whose societal standing was based on how many fish they could catch. The spring festival is a very localised affair and each of the villages holds theirs on a different day chosen by the elders of the village. During the festival, the men of the village wear traditional Yami loincloths, silver helmets and breastplates, and smear the blood of a freshly killed chicken on the rocks by the sea, all the while chanting 'return flying fish' in unison before heading out to sea in their canoes. According to custom, women are not allowed to view the festival, but most villages will make exceptions for visitors.

SLEEPING
Hotels
The few large hotels on Lanyu are concrete-block buildings run by Taiwanese and are generally cosy but nothing to write home about. Rooms are mostly doubles and rates vary by season.

Lanyu Hotel (Lányǔ Biéguǎn; Map p317; ☎ 342 226; d NT1200-1800) Popular with Taiwanese tourist groups, the Lanyu Hotel has reasonably clean double rooms, some with ocean views. During the high season this place fills up quickly, so advance booking is a good idea.

Hai Yang Kuo Chi Hotel (Hǎiyáng Guójì Fàndiàn; Map p317; ☎ 732 166; d/tw NT1620/1800) This Lanyu stalwart is within walking distance of the harbour and in the centre of the action in Yeyou village (for what that's worth). Rooms are a bit musty, but some have ocean views.

Homestays

Travellers looking for a more interesting, not to mention easier on the budget, experience should consider a homestay. Though the families running the homestays have limited to zero English ability, they're generally pleased by Western guests. Note that most homestays charge by person, not by room, and that charges are higher during the high season.

Enhui Mingsu Zijia (Ēnhuì Mínsù Zhìjiā; Map p317; ☎ 732 979; per person incl dinner NT300/400) Staying in the home of husband-and-wife team Li Ge and Li Sao is a great way to get to know both Lanyu and the Yami. Their home, located on a hill in Yeyin on the east side of the island, is spotless and has four doubles and a large dorm on the upper floor. Li Ge is an excellent guide, highly knowledgeable about both culture and botany, and Li Sao is a fine cook. For an extra NT100 per person, she'll cook up a suppertime feast of fish, pork and traditional Yami vegetables.

Lansya Mingsu (Lánxiáng Mínsù; Map p317; ☎ 732 236; per person NT500) This homestay, run by the Fu family of Yeyou, is clean, comfortable and convenient to both the airport and harbour. The Fus have both doubles and dorms. They also have a small gift shop where they sell arts and craft items.

Lanyu Guesthouse (Lányǔ Fēngwèiwū; Map p317; ☎ 732 891; per person from NT400) This guesthouse is run by a hip young Yami who digs Western rock music and speaks basic English. The guestroom is one large room and beds are priced dependent on group size. It's NT400 per person if you've got a group of three or more and NT600 per person with two or less. The room can fit eight, so naturally the place is popular with students.

EATING

The Yami diet consists primarily of fish and locally grown vegetables with a bit of pork and mutton (goats wander freely all over the is-

land) on special occasions. Given a few hours' notice most homestay owners are happy to cook up a feast for their visitors. The east side of the island lacks restaurants but there's an open-air market on the weekends in Tungching and a couple of grocery stores in Yeyin. The island's few restaurants are centred in Hongtou and Yeyou.

Kai Yuan Restaurant (Kāi Yuán; Map p317; 16 Yeyou village; dishes NT60-NT120; ☉ lunch & dinner) This is a decent little noodle shop with a good selection of seafood, meat and vegetable dishes. They'll also cook up meat-free dishes for vegetarians.

Breakfast (Zǎocān; Map p317; 9 Renai jie, Hungtou village; dishes NT25-NT50; ☉ breakfast) The name says it all, and the open doors of Breakfast will be a welcome sight for those getting an early start on the day and looking for a filling Taiwanese breakfast. Expect homemade soymilk and instant coffee from 6.30am.

GETTING THERE & AWAY
Air

Daily Air Corporation (☎ 362 489) has a counter in the Lanyu and Taitung airports, and flies six planes daily between the two places. The flight costs NT1405 each way and takes 20 hair-rising minutes. During summer, the 19-seat planes fill up quickly so you'll want to book both ways as far ahead as possible. In the winter months, flights in and out of Lanyu are erratic due to the volatile weather. Should the weather turn rough during your stay, you'll be stuck on Lanyu, so carry enough cash and clean clothes with you to wait out the storm.

Boat

Taking a boat to and from Lanyu is a distinct option, as several boat companies operate small vessels from Fukang harbour, outside of Taitung, to Lanyu. We've also heard that one company plans to begin service to Lanyu from Kenting soon, though as of writing schedules and prices haven't been made available. Our experience with trying to boat it to Lanyu has been a bit sketchy; schedules are dependent both on weather and the number of passengers, making booking further than a day in advance an iffy proposition (especially in the low season). We hear the three-hour trip can be quite an ordeal, even for the strongest of stomachs, which is probably the main reason that visitors and locals alike prefer to take the more expensive

TAIWAN'S ISLANDS

but infinitely more comfortable plane ride. If you're still set on taking the boat, verify with a travel agency in Taitung or at the harbour what boats are running and when. And bring those motion-sickness pills!

GETTING AROUND
To/From the Airport
Hotels will provide transport to and from the airport if they're notified in advance, as will most of the homestays. If a ride isn't available, it's about a 20-minute walk to Hungtou village, twice that to Yeyou. There are also a few taxis on the island; most of these hang out at the airport when planes come in and will take you anywhere on the island for around NT250.

Bus
A bus circles the island four times a day, stopping at various points. Locals just flag the bus down, so you should too. Due to its relative infrequency, the bus really isn't an ideal way of getting around the island unless you're absolutely committed to going with the flow completely. If you've got anything even vaguely resembling a schedule, you're better off renting a scooter. Hitch-hiking is also an option.

Car & Motorcycle
There's a vehicle rental shop next to the Lanyu Hotel. Motorcycles cost NT500 a day and cars NT1500 a day, excluding petrol. In winter, renting a car might be safer and more comfortable than a motorcycle because of the slippery road conditions.

Walking
If you have the time, walking is a fine way to see Lanyu and its people. As long as you stick to the main road (which, except for the road that cuts across the mountain, is also the

only road) you shouldn't get lost. Don't be surprised if locals stop you for a chat and offer you betel nut. The six villages of Lanyu aren't exactly evenly spaced, so don't forget to bring along water and snacks. Waterproof gear and a walking stick would be handy.

GREEN ISLAND 綠島

☎ 089 / pop 3000

Beautiful and lush, boasting good beaches and one of only three seawater hot springs in the world, Green Island (Lǜdǎo) is a popular resort destination for Taiwanese looking for rest and recreation. But in the not too distant past, the phrase 'off to Green Island' didn't conjure up visions of leisure pursuits in the Taiwanese psyche; quite the opposite, in fact, for once upon a time the very name of this tiny volcanic island, 30km east of Taitung, was synonymous with repression. It was where, under martial law, political opponents of the regime were sent to languish at the island's notorious prison camp, sardonically referred to as 'Green Island Lodge'.

Today, the prison's metal doors have been flung open and this once potent place of repression has been transformed into a museum and human-rights memorial. To a new generation of Taiwanese the island is thought of not primarily for its infamous past, but as a place to come to see pristine coral reefs and gorgeous tropical fish through glass-bottom boats and hang out on the beach and soak in the hot spring under the night sky.

ORIENTATION
Smaller than Lanyu, Green Island is ringed by a 17km road that you can get around on a scooter in 30 minutes. With one main road hugging the shore and another leading

---

GREEN ISLAND TRAVEL QUOTA
So popular has Green Island become as a travel destination that a quota system is currently being established for the high season that will keep daily visitors at an environmentally sustainable level. As of this writing the number had yet to be set, but locals in the tourist business suggest it will be around 3500 to 4000 per day. What this means for the independent traveller is the possibility of being turned away at the dock or airport if the daily quota has already been filled.

For this reason, we recommend making reservations well in advance during the high season (summer, Lunar New Year and most three-day weekends), either with one of the hotels or with **Green Island Adventures** (☎ 0972 065 479; www.greenislandadventures.com). There is also talk of turning Green Island into a national park, which would further limit development on the island.

up to Huoshao Mountain (great for hiking), getting lost is pretty difficult. Though you could spend a three-day weekend here easily, plenty of visitors fly to Green Island for a day of swimming and exploring and fly back to Taitung in the evening (a shame in our opinion, as the hot springs are best experienced under the stars).

INFORMATION

Green Island Tourist Information Centre (Lǜdǎo Yóukè Zhōngxīn; ☎ 672 027; 298 Nanliao Village; ☼ 8am-5pm) Near the airport, the centre can help with maps and information about the island. Staff can also arrange diving trips and make reservations for the camp site in the south of the island. During summer there are daily multimedia presentations about the island.

SIGHTS

Standing forlorn on a windswept coast, its back to a sheer cliff, sits the notorious **Green Island Lodge** (Lǜdǎo Shānzhuāng, Oasis Village; Map p322). It's now empty except for one wing which has been turned into a Human Rights Memorial Hall (Rén Chuán Jìniàn Yuán Qū) to document both life in the prison and during Taiwan's 'White Terror' period. It was during this period when dissidents, activists and others considered 'hooligans' by the Kuomintang (KMT) were sent here to languish. Visitors are welcome to walk around the halls of the prison itself, now open to the public, and inspect the cells where former prisoners like current vice president Annette Lu and Taiwanese writer Bo Yang (author of *The Ugly Chinaman*) once spent years. It's a sombre place, of course, so visit here first and devote the rest of the trip to more cheerful pursuits.

The 33m-high **Green Island Lighthouse** (Lǜdǎo Dēngtǎ; Map p322) stands in the northwestern corner of the island. It was built in 1937 under the Japanese after the American ship *President Hoover* struck a reef off the coast of Green Island and sunk. The KMT refurbished the lighthouse and changed the original gas lantern to an electric light.

Further down the coast is the **Kuanyin Cave** (Guānyīn Dòng; Map p322), an underground cavern with a stalagmite in a red cape. Locals have draped a red blanket around the rock as a sign of respect. Legend has it that during the Qing dynasty, a fisherman became lost at sea and a fiery red light came down from the sky and led him to safety in the cave. The fisherman believed the light to be the goddess Kuanyin and the stalagmite in the cape to resemble the form of the goddess. The cave was designated a sacred spot on the island and people come here from all over Taiwan to pay their respects.

Close to Kuanyin Cave is the **Yutzu Lake Ancient Dwellings** (Yòuzǐ Hú). This was the site of the first village on the island and some old stone houses still remain. Nearby is a sea-eroded cave that is worth a look.

Green Island has some intriguing volcanic-rock formations scattered around the coast, leading some Taiwanese to give the rocks curious names. The **Sleeping Beauty Rock** (Shuì Měi Rén), off the east coast of the island, is supposed to resemble the figure of a sleeping woman. You may need to use your imagination for this one. Near Sleeping Beauty is the **Hsiao Changcheng** (Xiǎo Chángchéng; Map p322), a rock that some believe resembles the Great Wall in China (only not quite so great).

Pahsien (Bā Xiān Dòng; Map p322) and **Lunghsia Caves** (Lóngxiā Dòng; Map p322), both offer great exploration opportunities.

ACTIVITIES
Hot Springs

History and strange rock formations aside, what brings people to Green Island is the sea; not just in the form of beaches, but also the **Chaojih Hot Springs** (Zhāorì Wēnquán; Map p322; admission NT150; ☼ 5am-11pm). One of only three of the planet's known sea-water hot springs, we think these hot springs are best visited during the low season. In the summer, the unshaded hot baths are a bit too intense during the day, and at night they're always crowded. Under an evening sky in autumn or winter, a soak in the hot pools followed by a quick dip in the sea is positively blissful. There are two sets of pools to choose from, the older circular stone hot-spring pits down by the beach and the modern tile pools in the better-lit part of the complex. The latter set features pools of varying temperatures, from just above freezing to just below scalding, artfully shaped artificial privacy grottos and a good number of massage showers (overhead pipes jetting down spring water at jackhammer frequencies).

Hiking

Huoshao Mountain (Huǒshāoshān), translated as 'fire mountain' and actually an extinct

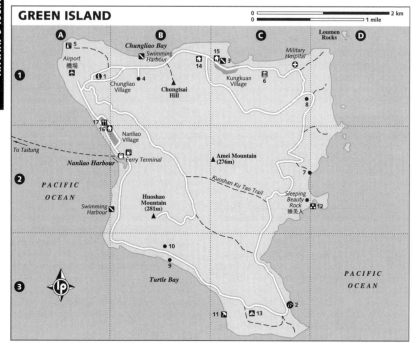

GREEN ISLAND

volcano, stands a towering 281m. Hiking trails go around the mountain, but you can't get to the summit (there's a military post there). The Kuoshan Ku Tao (Guòshān Gǔ Dào) trail, is another lovely and secluded hiking path, stretching 1.8km from behind Nanliao Village to the east coast of the island.

Diving & snorkelling

One of the main reasons people come to Green Island is to take advantage of the island's excellent coral reefs, some of Taiwan's most well preserved. Tourist authorities report that Green Island has over 176 types of coral and over 602 types of fish swimming around the coast. The waters surrounding the island are filled with tropical fish, possibly thanks to nutrients deposited in the water by the hot spring on the southern tip, and the government has gone to considerable lengths to protect the remaining reefs. Green Island is also popular with divers, who come from all over Asia and beyond to dive. In 2005 the island hosted Taiwan's first ever underwater wedding ceremony, with vows written out on waterproof cards!

Most hotels on the island arranges snorkelling and diving trips. Equipment can be rented at shops in Nanliao Village and around the harbour. Rates depend on how many people you have in your group and the type of equipment you'll need to rent.

Tapaisha Beach (Dàbáishā; Map p322) has fine white coral sand and is known for its stunning coral reefs, making it a good spot for snorkelling as is the small stretch of beach east of the Green Island Lighthouse.

One reputable place is the **Chufu Diving Centre** (Jūfú Qiánshuǐ; Map p322; ☎ 672 238; 78-3 Kungkuan Village). Run by diving enthusiast Mr Tsai, the centre offers diving and snorkelling tours, equipment rental, and summer trips aboard a glass-bottomed boat (NT350). The boat is a particularly good way to see the coral reefs and marine life within without leaving an ecological footprint. Hire boats depart from Nanliao harbour.

TOURS

For trips to and around Green Island, **Green Island Adventures** (GIA; ☎ 0972 065 479; www.green islandadventures.com) comes highly recommended.

Though the company's tour-guide brief has expanded to include Taiwan's outer islands and central Taiwan, Green Island is where they cut their teeth (professionally speaking). GIA founder Eddie Viljoen arranges year-round transport to the island, accommodations, and tailor-built tour packages including snorkelling, scuba diving, hiking, and, of course, hot springing. He can also arrange the use of a glass-bottom-boat for tours around the island's fabulous coral reefs.

SLEEPING

There are accommodations all over Green Island, mostly in Nanliao Village close to the harbour, but other places are scattered around the island. Green Island is a popular place in summer for Taiwanese tourists, which means that most hotels will be booked solid on weekends. With the new quota system looming, it seems that the days of just showing up at the dock will be a thing of the past, at least in the high season. During the low season (or even weekdays in summer), you'll likely be met by people at the boat offering to bring you to their hotels and guesthouses. In the low season, most hotels offer discounted prices, though this may change as Green Island becomes more difficult to visit.

Lijing Hostel (Lìjìng Shānzhuāng; Map p322; ☎ 672 000; Kungkuan Village; dm NT500, d/tr NT2500/4500) A friendly place run by local Mrs Tien, the Lijing offers dorm accommodations, doubles and triples. Mrs. Tien can also arrange motorcycle rentals.

Par Far Hotel (Shuāng Fā Píngjià; Map p322; ☎ 672 552; Nanliao Village; r NT1200) The Par Far is a true bargain and highly recommended. Rooms are immaculate and very spacious. Hoteliers Mr and Mrs Wong are nice folk and during the off season are willing to negotiate room prices.

Green Island Star Hotel (Lùdǎo Zìxīng Lǚguǎn; Map p322; ☎ 671 355; d NT2800) One of the newer and pricier hotels on the island, this tall yellow building seems a bit out of place on otherwise low-slung Green Island. But rooms are comfortable, and during the off season discounts of up to 40% can be negotiated.

Camping Ground (Lùyíng Qū; Map p322; camping on grass NT300, on wooden platform NT350) This camping site is in the south of the island near Tapaisha Beach. The tourist information centre takes all reservations for the camp sites and rents out equipment. We've heard that rental equipment can be a bit shoddy, and as the campsite is popular with mosquitos, we recommend those intent on roughing it at least bring their own gear. And bug repellent.

THE GREEN ISLAND VOMIT BARGE *Joshua Samuel Brown*

Green Island is among Taiwan's loveliest offerings, and as a traveller and writer I recommend a visit highly. However, a word on the boat: I am an islander, of sorts (Staten Island, New York, where the ferry to and from Manhattan, though hardly a strenuous voyage, was a daily routine for a decade). I've travelled extensively by ship and ferry around Taiwan, by riverboat through China's Pearl River Delta and Southeast Asia, and by a host of seagoing vessels large and small around Maritime Canada and in the Pacific Northwest.

Only twice in my extensive travels have I found myself, face pressed against a rolling floor, stinking of my own vomit, begging for the sweet, sweet release of death.

The first time was on the boat to Green Island while researching the chapter you're currently reading. The second was on the boat back. Consider yourselves warned.

EATING

Nanliao Village has quite a few seafood restaurants. Local dishes include *hǎi xiānggū* (sea mushrooms) and *suàn xiāng zhāngyú* (garlic octopus).

Chi Tang You Yu (Chí Táng Yǒu Yú; Map p322; 150 Nanliao Village; dishes NT100; ⏲ lunch & dinner) A congenial atmosphere and wonderful outdoor patio makes this a great place to have a beer and relax after a long day of diving. The garlic octopus is especially delectable.

GETTING THERE & AWAY
Air

Mandarin Airlines (☎ 672 585) has three flights a day between Taitung and Green Island (NT1028, 15 minutes) on small 19-seat propeller planes. During winter, flights are often cancelled due to bad weather. In summer it's hard to get on a flight unless you've booked your seat several weeks ahead. Mandarin Airlines has a reservation counter in the Green Island airport.

Boat

During summer, boats travel frequently between Taitung and Green Island (one-way/return NT420/800, 50 minutes). Boats also travel from Fukang harbour, north of Taitung, to Green Island. The boat schedule fluctuates so check with a travel agency or at one of the harbours for the exact times of departure. You can buy your ticket as you board the boat, but once the quota system comes into play we recommend that you book in advance.

During winter, boats run infrequently, if at all, due to choppy water. If you dare to take a boat during winter, prepare your stomach in advance and brace yourself for a very rough ride. Definitely not for the faint of heart.

GETTING AROUND
Bus

There is a bus that circuits the island several times daily; things are pretty casual on Green Island, so you can just flag it down. The fare is NT15 for the circuit, but schedules do not appear to be consistent so you may be better off taking a taxi if you're in a hurry (or walking if you're not).

Scooter

Scooters are the best way to get around Green Island; just remember that wandering cattle always have right of way. You'll find plenty of people willing to rent you a vehicle at the harbour and the airport. Rates are generally NT400 to NT500 a day, excluding petrol.

Taxi

Taking a taxi around the island costs around NT600 for a quick trip, more if you want to stop and do some exploring. Negotiate fares in advance.

Walking

Walking around the island is a totally viable option, but bring plenty of water (and sunscreen); outside of the towns there are few stores.

Directory

CONTENTS

ACCOMMODATION

Taiwan provides the full range of lodgings, from basic hostels to world-class hotels and resorts, and air-con is standard. Quality, however, can really vary, even at the same price range; a newly remodelled hotel may charge only slightly more than the decaying establishment beside it. In addition, many hotels are really a star or even two below their advertised rating. Few hotels really deserve the five-star rating as facilities and service are rarely top notch. Many continue to charge as if they do, however, which exasperates even the tourism board.

Unlike in many other countries, accommodation is generally priced per room (or number of beds per room) and not per guest. What's called a 'single' room in other countries (one single bed) is rare; a 'single' in Taiwanese hotel lingo usually means a room with one queen-sized bed, which most couples find spacious enough. 'Double' generally means a double bed, while 'twin' denotes two beds per room. The lesson here: couples travel cheaper per person.

Discounts off the rack rate are the norm except for a very few hotels (mostly strictly budget) that always charge the same price. Sometimes you must ask, but mostly discounts are given automatically (often they are even written on the hotel's price list). Discounts range from 20% to 50%. If you're heading to a resort, the most common time to find discounts is on weekdays, while business hotels most often have weekend discounts.

The tourist information booths at airports and high-speed rail stations can make hotel reservations for you. Many hotels offer shuttle services.

See the glossary (p371) for accommodation terms.

Camping

Camping is a real option now. Along the east coast you can set up a tent on pretty much any beach but there are some excellent public camping grounds as well. Remember that while camping in the hotter months on the beach sounds good, at sunrise the inside of your tent will become as hot as a pizza oven. Always look for shade.

A freestanding tent is useful as many camping grounds have wooden platforms

---

BOOK ACCOMMODATION ONLINE

For more accommodation reviews and recommendations by Lonely Planet authors, check out the online booking service at www.lonelyplanet.com. You'll find the true, insider lowdown on the best places to stay. Reviews are thorough and independent. Best of all, you can book online.

for setting tents on. You can pick up a tent cheaply in Taiwan for under NT1000. Grass camp-site spots cost on average NT200 per person per night, while a wooden platform with an eight-person tent already set up may go for NT800 (negotiable if there is just one of you and you have a tent). Most camping grounds offer bathrooms (with showers), barbecue areas and a small convenience store. Some unfortunately also have karaoke. You can camp in some national parks (Kenting, Sheipa and Taroko, and also Yushan if you are hiking on the trails) but not usually in forest recreation areas.

Remember to prepare for the elements. Higher elevations can get chilly at night and below freezing in winter, but it's important to monitor the weather carefully whatever time of year. See p333 for general weather conditions. And remember to bring bug repellent if you're going to stay by the beach.

Homestays/B&Bs

Mínsù (民宿; homestays) offer travellers a way to meet local people in a setting that can often lead to friendship. There's been an explosion of new homestays in the past few years, and most are well run and offer good accommodation at a fair price. Some are positively charming with rooms full of old furniture and mountain or sea views.

The tourism board puts out a booklet (also on its website: www.taiwan.net.tw) listing the 40 best homestays in the country. We checked out about two-thirds for our research and none were wanting. Most charge in the NT2000 to NT3000 range, with off-season and midweek rates dropping considerably. If you have a Youth Guesthouse Network card (see p328), you can stay in the Top 40 for NT1200 to NT1500 a night, sometimes less if they have a dorm room.

Signs for homestays are everywhere, with a big concentration down the east coast. Ask local people or look for the English signs that say B&B.

Hostels

The great news is that more and more excellent hostels are being opened, and by well-travelled, English-speaking young Taiwanese. A basic dorm bed starts at NT250, though the better places charge NT400 to NT500 per night. Private rooms, when available, are usually tiny and start at NT500. You can often arrange for weekly or monthly rates as well, as the owners are aware that many people come to Taiwan looking for work.

While some Taiwanese hostels are affiliated with Hostelling International (HI); and offer discounts accordingly for cardholders, most are not. Some are also technically illegal, though there is nothing dodgy about them otherwise.

Hostels generally have laundry, simple cooking facilities, a TV, computer hook-up with ADSL and a room for socialising. Note that many Taipei hostels are dingy and old, having catered to a different era. Choose carefully in the capital.

Hotels

There's a great range of options among hotels (*fàndiàn* or *dàfàndiàn*). Starting at about NT550 per night, you can have a private room in a very basic budget hotel. For that price you're likely to find threadbare accommodation and occasional mouldy odours, but private bathroom (no shower curtain), TV and phone are generally included. Don't count on being able to make yourself understood in English. At a slightly higher price, NT800 to NT1600, quality varies greatly. Usually above NT1200 rooms are good enough that you wouldn't feel embarrassed putting family up. ADSL, either in rooms or at a small central computer station, is common at this price range.

At midrange hotels (NT1600 to NT4000 per night), you're likely to find a fancy lobby, one or more restaurants on site, ADSL and possibly plasma TVs. Private bathrooms include shower (or bathtub with shower) and shower curtain. Décor can range from a little dated to very modern. Unless you're looking for a luxury experience, most travellers will feel comfortable here. In the big cities usually at least one or two staff members speak some English. Elsewhere you'll be able to muddle your way to a room.

The big cities abound with international-standard top-end hotels. Typical amenities include business centres, English-speaking staff, concierge services, spa and/or fitness centre, massage services and a sense of style. In this book, 'top end' starts at NT4000 per night, though rack rates at big-city hotels can easily be double that.

Don't forget that hot-spring hotels are also for those just looking for accommodation

PRACTICALITIES

Newspapers

The first three daily English-language papers have weekend entertainment listings and can be purchased at bookshops, hotels, convenience stores and kiosks.

▪ *Taipei Times* (www.taipeitimes.com)

▪ *China Post* (www.chinapost.com.tw)

▪ *Taiwan News* (www.etaiwannews.com)

▪ *International Herald Tribune* (www.iht.com) has worldwide circulation, and is available at hotels and news dealers.

Magazines

▪ *Taiwan Panorama* (formerly *Sinorama;* www.sinorama.com.tw) is an intelligent look at Taiwanese language and culture, sports, finance, history, travel and more. Available in Chinese-English versions.

▪ *Commonwealth Magazine* (www.cw.com.tw/english) is the Taiwanese *Economist.* Now available online in English.

▪ *Travel in Taiwan* (www.sinica.edu.tw/tit) is an excellent resource for all things cultural and touristy, with calendars of events and colourful coverage.

Also look for regionally published magazines for local listings and coverage of local topics. These include: *Taiwan Fun, FYI South, Highway 11, Journey East, 24/7, Xpat Magazine* and *Taiwanease.*

Radio & TV

▪ International Community Radio Taipei (ICRT) broadcasts nationwide in English 24 hours a day at 100MHz (FM) with a mix of music, news and information.

▪ Taiwan has three broadcast networks: CTS, CTV and TTV, with shows in Chinese, including dubbed foreign shows. Cable TV is available throughout Taiwan, with the usual options on the international circuit – movie channels, news channels and the like. Some of these are available in English. The exact selection changes from venue to venue and it's common around New Years for channels to suddenly switch numbers (if CNN was 47, for example, it may now become 102).

Electricity

▪ Taiwan uses the same electrical standard as the USA and Canada: 110V, 60Hz AC. Electrical sockets have two vertical slots. If you bring appliances from Europe, Australia or Southeast Asia, you'll need an adaptor or transformer. Some buildings have outlets for 220V plugs, which are intended for air conditioners.

Weights & Measures

▪ Taiwan uses the metric system (see the conversion chart on the inside front cover) alongside ancient Chinese weights and measures. When Taiwanese measure floor space, for example, the unit of measure is the *píng* (approximately 4 sq metres). Fruit and vegetables are likely to be sold by the catty (*jīn,* 600g), while teas and herbal medicines are sold by the tael (*liǎng,* 37.5g).

(and not hot springs) and cater to most budgets. Prices range from NT2000 to NT8000 a night. At the higher end it's not uncommon to have other services, such as massage, food and beverage, or spa treatments.

Note that if you're phoning someone at a hotel and do not speak Chinese, you may run into trouble at all but the high-end hotels as staff may not recognise the guest's name. Hint: speak clearly, and if the last name does not work, try the first name. A room number is best.

Rental Accommodation

If you're going to be in Taiwan for an extended period, getting your own place makes sense. Your employer may be able to help you set something up.

English-language newspapers carry rental listings, though these are usually luxury accommodation catering to expats on expense accounts. If you're looking for an upscale or even good midrange apartment, it's useful to hire an agent. Look in the papers for numbers. Usually the agent charges a fee of half a month's rent.

For less expensive accommodation, check out websites catering to the foreign community (see p23) or enlist the help of a Chinese-speaking friend to peruse the Chinese-language papers. You might also just choose an area where you'd like to live and look for signs tacked up on telephone poles and outside apartments. You can usually ask building guards if there are apartments for rent. The excellent **Tsui Mama website** (www.tmm.org.tw) provides listings of mid- to low-range accommodation by area and price in Taipei.

Bland studio apartments (no kitchen) in Taipei range from NT5000 to NT10,000 per month, while a small three-bedroom place might go for NT20,000. In a good neighbourhood, rents can easily be double that. Outside of Taipei, even in the cities, rents are much cheaper: a decent three-bedroom apartment could cost as little as NT7000. Negotiations are usually possible. One good approach is to say that you really like the place but can only afford (however much) right now.

Temple Stays

Here are three temples we know of that offer overnight stays: Shitoushan (p175), Foguangshan (p274) and Tiengong (p161). The accommodation at the temples is surprisingly good and the vegetarian meals delicious.

Youth Guesthouse Network

The **network** (www.youthguesthouse.org.tw) offers 15-to-35-year-old travellers basic accommodation around the country for NT300 to NT500 a night (usually only weekdays, however). Many are in old police hostels, hero houses (for soldiers) or labour recreation centres that previously were off limits to the public. Quality really varies and sometimes the hostels are quite far from a bus or train station. Still, the programme offers yet another budget option. It also offers good discounts on the 40 best B&Bs (see p326). See the boxed text, below for information on picking up a Youth Travel Card.

ACTIVITIES

Although Taiwan ranks among the world's most densely populated areas, opportunities for outdoor activities abound. About 40% of the land is mountainous and sparsely inhabited, and being an island, there is a long coastline.

Bird-Watching

Who knew Taiwan was a top spot for birding? We sure didn't until very recently. But the island has 15 endemic bird species and more than 60 endemic subspecies. Birders from around the world are now paying thousands for organized tours to see them.

We're not going to pretend we can give you the same for free, but we know most of the places they go and have included

---

YOUTH TRAVEL IN TAIWAN

In 2005 the National Youth Commission was asked to develop a programme to encourage international youth (backpackers, students etc) aged 15 to 35 to visit Taiwan. In addition to a guesthouse network (above), the programme offers discounts on train and bus tickets and museums, as well as free mobile phones called the Digital Tour Buddy (with Chinese-English dictionaries built in as well as access to special hotlines). The youth commission also works with local nonprofit organizations (NPOs) to offer cultural exchanges. These might involve a week-long stay in an aboriginal village, a few days walking on the Matsu pilgrimage (see p216) or visits to local artists. Check out the website (www.youthtravel.net.tw) for more information including registering for a cultural programme and applying to get the Digital Tour Buddy. You can pick up a Youth Travel Card (and the mobile phone) at the airport visitor centres.

D
I
R
E
C
T
O
R
Y

some in this edition. These include Kenting (p285), Wulai (p141), Wulu (p264), Aowanda (p230) and Taiwan's islands (p304).

See the website of the **International Taiwan Birding Association** (www.birdingintaiwan.com/index .htm) for more, and check out Kate Rogers' *The Swallow's Return*. See also the boxed text, p71.

Cycling

Taipei and Taipei County have over 100km of connected bike-only routes (p102) along the rivers. For short day trips, head to Pinglin (p149). You'll find a good 25km of dedicated bike routes, and lots of back roads as well. The stops along the Jiji Small Rail Line (p220) offer some pleasant wheeling through the countryside, as does the route in Kuanshan (p201). At Sun Moon Lake (p222) you'll find scenic paths alongside the lake.

For longer rides, try Hwy 11 (p192) from Hualien to Taitung, or the South Cross-Island Hwy (p260). And check out May and June 2006 archives on this biking blog (http://rank.blogspot.com) and the forum pages of www.formosafattire.com.

HIRE

You can hire bikes for around NT50 to NT100 an hour. A full day might cost NT150 to NT300. Sometimes you are asked to leave a deposit, sometimes not. In Taipei you can rent at one location and leave at another. You can also take bikes on the Mass Rapid Transit (MRT) during certain posted hours.

PURCHASE

A mountain-bike lookalike can be had for NT3000 to NT5000. These are fine for riding on paved paths, or on relatively flat stretches of grass or dirt. High-end models for real off-road riding can cost NT20,000 and up. It's usually possible to resell.

Folding bikes are a great option for travelling in Taiwan. You can't take an ordinary bike with you on a train (they must be sent a day ahead) but with a folder any little stop outside the congested urban areas is yours to explore.

Diving & Snorkelling

Taiwan's ocean conditions pose a serious challenge to the diver. Strong currents exist just offshore and exits are hard. In the north there

are good spots near Fulong (p160) but you'll need to go with local divers to find them. The tourism board recommends Longdong (p159), but no-one else seems to. Green and Lanyu Islands (p322 and p318), however, are considered fantastic venues by everyone.

For snorkelling, head to Fulong, Green Island, Kenting (p284) and Little Liuchiu Island (p281).

Check out the Leisure – Sports category of www.forumosa.com for the SCUBA thread: a group of expat diving enthusiasts post here regularly.

Golf

Golf driving ranges are everywhere, even in small towns, and all major cities have golf courses, though they are often in the suburbs as land is expensive. A lot of golf courses are illegally built and controversial due to run-off from pesticides and fertilizers. Call the official **Chinese Taipei Golf Association** (☎ 02-516 5611; Taipei) for information.

Hiking

It's not well known, but Taiwan is a paradise for hikers. One of the tallest peaks in East Asia is here (Yushan, 3952m), and there are dozens more peaks above 3000m. Most require fitness and basic equipment, but no technical skills.

There's also a vast network of trails at lower altitudes. These trails run through subtropical and tropical jungles and broadleaf forests, and along coastal bluffs. Some are just a few hours long while others go on for days. All three major cities – Taipei, Kaohsiung and Taichung – have mountains and trails either within the city limits or just outside.

A lot of time and money is going into developing a **National Trail System** (http://trail.forest .gov.tw/index.asp). At the time of writing, six of the longer national trails had been restored, including the Nenggao Cross Island Trail (p230), the Jin-Shui Ying Old Trail (p280), and the trail up to Jiaming Lake (p264). All national trails are clear and marked with distance markers and map boards. Good maps are also available (see p330). No advanced permits are necessary to hike. Just apply for a *dēng shān zhèng* (登山證; mountain permit) at a local police station, or secure this before you head out at the **Ministry of the Interior** (Map p88; ☎ 02-2321 9011; 7 Zhongxiao E Rd, sec.1, Taipei).

Regional trails (usually shorter) are being repaired and signposted and by the time you read this a booklet (in Chinese only) will be available listing about 70 of these. If you drive around you can also see signs for many trails in English and Chinese.

BOOKS & MAPS
For the north, pick up either volume of *Taipei Day Trips* by Richard Saunders or his new *Yangmingshan, the Guide*. These books are very detailed, with transportation information included, and we've been using them to good ends for years.

Taiwan Jiaotong Press (台北縣市近郊山圖) publishes a series of 14 maps at a scale of 1:25,000. These only cover the north (from Sansia/Wulai up) and you can pick them up at mountain equipment stores around the Taipei train station. Be aware that not every trail on these maps will be walkable when you get to them. Trails get washed out and overgrown all the time.

The forestry bureau puts out a useful four-volume set of books, called *Taiwan Forest Vacation Guide,* which cover 21 forest recreation areas around the country.

For the six national trails (see p329), you can pick up good waterproof foldable maps with a 1:25,000 scale at equipment shops or San Min bookstores (三民網路書店). These maps include itineraries, though the information is in Chinese only.

See also p334 for important safety notes.

CLUBS
Richard Saunders (richard0428@yahoo.com), author of *Taipei Day Trips,* runs a free weekend hiking club. Also check out the Events thread on www.forumosa.com for hikes organized by yours truly. **523 Mountaineering Association** (www.523.org.tw/English/index) runs a couple of free hikes a month as well as longer hikes that charge a reasonable fee.

Hot Springs
The diversity of Taiwan's hot springs is so amazing we wrote a special chapter for this edition (see p75).

Kayaking
We're told there are some good rivers for kayaking in Taiwan, and Nanao (p166) has a fantastic coastline for sea kayaking. Contact Andre at **Cloud 9** (0911-126 337; www.cloud9tw.com) in Pinglin about lessons or just advice on where to go and how to contact local clubs.

Martial Arts
You'll find the full range of martial-arts schools in Taipei, from Wing Chun to Brazilian Jiu-jitsu. Check out the expat websites (see p23) for recommendations from people who live for this kind of stuff.

Mountaineering
Great news! First, Taiwan has some fabulous climbs and anyone in decent shape can conquer most of them. Second, the routes have all been improved in recent years, with map boards and distance markers added along the way; good route maps are also available. Third, the old Class A permit system that required hikers to travel in groups with a 'qualified' guide is gone (in part because of the improvement mentioned above). Anyone can now climb the high mountains in Taiwan, though for safety reasons we include in this book only those hikes that we feel a pair of properly equipped travellers, with some mountain experience, can tackle on their own. Fortunately, these are some of the highest and most beautiful mountains, such as Snow Mountain (p170) and Yushan (p243).

Permits are still needed to climb, and possibly by the time you read this a new streamlined application form will be in place. The easiest way to apply, however, is to contact the folk at **523 Mountaineering Association** (www.523.org.tw/English/index). This association is a registered nonprofit organization (NPO) with a mandate to help introduce the foreign community to Taiwan's mountains. For a nominal fee it will get you your permits. It can also help arrange for a driver for private transportation to the mountains. The staff at 523 speak English, though it's best to email Doris Juan (doris@523.org.tw).

The best time to climb is always the autumn, when weather conditions are dry and stable. Spring is good if you get a patch of steady clear weather. Summer can be fine as long as there are no typhoons. Be aware of the ferocity of the sun, though, in the thinner mountain air. Winter hikes to the high mountains should not be attempted unless you have proper experience and equipment. If you have to ask whether you have these, then you don't.

EQUIPMENT
Most high mountain routes have cabins, though a tent is needed on some of the longer

hikes through Yushan National Park. Since the weather is extremely changeable, always be prepared with a Gortex jacket and pants (a climber died recently for want of these). A good sleeping bag, warm socks with reinforced toes and heels, quick drying shirts, comfortable pants, fleece jacket, thermal underwear, gloves and an all-weather hat are also necessary. Other useful items include a compass, stove (and something to cook in) and water filter.

It can be warm enough to wear shorts during the day but it can get close to 0°C at night even in autumn. We don't need to tell you to take out your rubbish but consider an extra bag to carry away the waste of the less enlightened.

See also p334 for natural dangers.

MAPS

Sunriver (上河文化) publishes maps of most of the main high mountains. The maps give detailed daily itineraries, including how long (in hours) each section takes to hike and the distances covered. They are in Chinese but if you get someone to translate the itinerary and pertinent places on the maps (cabins, peaks, water sources etc) you should be fine. Most national parks have basic maps (in English) of the climbing routes on their websites to give you a general overview.

Swimming & River Tracing

Suòxī (river tracing) is the sport of walking and climbing up a riverbed. At the beginning stages it involves merely walking on slippery rocks. At advanced stages it can involve climbing up and down waterfalls. Taiwan is fantastically suited for the sport: there are hundreds of good streams and rivers to trace, no dangerous animals in the water (though beware of snakes on the rocks), and the terrain is so thick and jungly in places you feel like a kid in a Tarzan movie. Summer is a great time to trace as it's too hot for regular hiking; in and above the water the temperature is mild.

Basic equipment includes a life jacket, helmet and a waterproof bag. You can buy dry bags for your regular knapsack but there are also specially made dry-bag knapsacks. Some people wear Neoprene to keep warm. Even in summer it can get chilly in some streams, especially when you've been wet all day.

The most important piece of equipment, though, is the felt-bottomed shoes that allow you to grip the rock and walk normally. You need to try these to believe how well they work. Don't bother with rubber-soled boots (no matter what your local equipment shop says). These will not grip the rocks in Taiwan. You can pick up shoes for NT300 to NT400 in the equipment shops near the Taipei train station.

Unfortunately there are no local river-tracing groups we can recommend. The ones that charge money don't impress us. We have literally seen leaders unable to swim across river pools with mild currents we were playing in.

Around Wulai (p141) and Pinglin (p148) you can safely trace with a couple of friends in the smaller streams.

Surfing & Windsurfing

Taiwan has some good surfing beaches, though it's become a little too trendy up in the north in the last few years. Real surfers will be frustrated with the hoards of floaters obstructing their path, and the general lack of surfing etiquette. Honeymoon Bay at Daxi (p161) has gotten particularly crowded but it's still popular with experienced surfers.

MIXED-UP MAPS

Be aware that many map boards in Taiwan are the mirror image of what they should be. To understand what this means, consider this example: you are walking north and come to a four-way split in the trail with a map in front of you. On the map, you see the trail to your destination heads to the right. Easy, you think. I should go right at this fork (heading west).

Wrong. If you look at the compass points on the map you'll see that the trail that actually points west in reality is pointing east on the map. Yes, this is nonsense and anyone but the supremely spatially intelligent will get a headache trying to flip the map over in their head.

To solve the problem ignore your immediate environment. Look at the map and discover what direction you should be going in. Then take out your compass and figure out where that direction lies. North and south are usually hard to mix up. East and west are easy to confuse.

Some places to get away from the crowds include Jialeshui in Kenting (p284) and various points along Hwy 11 (p192).

You can also surf the Penghu Islands (p306) – and windsurfing in autumn and winter is the tops. Makung (p310) holds international windsurfing competitions in November.

White-Water Rafting

See Rueisui, p198, for information on rafting along the Hsiukuluan River. See p262 for information on rafting the rougher Laonong River.

Contact Andre at **Cloud 9** (0911-126 337; www .cloud9tw.com) in Pinglin for inner-tubing down the Beishi River.

BUSINESS HOURS

Standard hours are as follows. Reviews won't list business hours unless they differ from these standards.

Banks (9.30am-3.30pm Mon-Fri)
Convenience stores (24hr)
Department stores (11am-9.30pm)
Government offices (8.30am-noon & 1.30-5.30pm)
Museums (9am-5pm, closed Mon)
Night markets (6pm-2am)
Offices (9am-5pm Mon-Fri)
Post offices (8am-5pm Mon-Fri)
Restaurants (11.30am-2pm & 5-9pm)
Shops (10am-9pm)
Supermarkets (to at least 8pm, sometimes 24hr)

CHILDREN

The Taiwanese are very welcoming, and doubly so when it comes to children. If you're travelling with kids, they will probably attract a lot of positive attention.

The website www.parentpages.net has all kinds of Taiwanese children-related forums. You'll be able to find information from birthing and midwifery to raising kids to keeping them amused. The Parenting forum on www .forumosa.com is also helpful. The **Community Services Centre** (Map p100; 2836 8134; www .community.com.tw; 25 Lane 290, Zhongshan N Rd, sec.6, Tianmu) in Taipei has lots of information for families relocating to Taiwan.

Lonely Planet's *Travel with Children* is a useful book that prepares you for the joys and pitfalls of travelling with the little ones. Also check out the Kids to Go branch of the Thorntree forum (http://thorntree.lonely planet.com).

Practicalities

You're not likely to find high chairs or booster seats for kids at lower-end restaurants, but you may well find them at more expensive places. Upper-end restaurants may have set menus for families, or even kids' menus. You can generally find Western baby formula and baby foods at supermarkets.

If you're travelling by car, note that children under four years of age and weighing less than 18kg must be in car safety seats. Parents who ignore the law can be fined NT1500 to NT3000. This law does not apply to taxis, and don't expect taxis to have child safety seats.

If you need a nanny, be aware it's not legal to hire an overseas one despite what agents may tell you. For a Taiwanese nanny in Taipei (NT15,000 to NT20,000 a month), call 2726 0735.

Taiwanese love children, and strangers may often want to touch or even handle your babies. Some people use a sling to help minimize contact and interruptions as they move about their daily business. You can also tell people your child has a cold. If you can't speak Chinese a little sign language will do.

See also p65 for information on dining out with children in Taiwan.

Sights & Activities

In general Taiwan is a great place for active families. The cities offer indoor adventure playgrounds, museums, water parks and hiking trails, and courses on martial arts, painting, yo-yoing, opera and dance. The gondola out to Maokong (p138) is a fun ride for kids of all ages.

Here are some suggestions for sights around the island that children will enjoy.

Hwy 11 (p192) Sleep in driftwood huts, camp on the beach, explore bizarre rock formations and see water run uphill.
Jiji Small Rail Line (p220) Cycling and light walking.
Kenting (p282) Beach activities, aquatic museum and forest parks.
Northeast Coast (p157) Sea-life displays, a stone lion museum and a crab museum, and sandy beaches perfect for kids.
Pinglin (p148) Cycling, swimming, camping, tree climbing and nature observation.
Pingxi Branch Rail Line (p144) Little kids can sit right up the front of the train, and play with real trains and self-propelled trolleys at the stations.
Sanyi (p178) Touch and feel giant wood statues, walk along abandoned rail tracks and go through 1km-long tunnels.
Yingge (p151) Hands-on pottery making.

CLIMATE CHARTS

For such a small place, Taiwan has a great variety of climates. Plus, as the island sits at the confluence of various trade winds, weather is known to change frequently, especially in late autumn and winter.

The island can be divided into essentially three climate zones: the north and east coasts (including Taipei), the central mountains and the southwest coast.

Daily temperatures in Taipei can be about 35°C in summer but rarely go below 12°C in winter. Very cold weather and snow are a function of elevation: temperatures can drop precipitously as you move from sea level to 2000m, and above 3000m you're likely to find snow in winter.

Taiwan's most agreeable weather is in autumn, specifically October and November. Winter in the north and on the east coast tends to be overcast and occasionally chilly with frequent drizzle – although more rain actually falls in the summer, it may not feel like it! Spring is warm and mild, but it is known for frequent rain (the locals poetically call it the 'plum rain'). Spring is also notorious for the sandstorms that blow in from China. These foul the air and people are advised to stay indoors.

Summers are hot and humid with frequent afternoon thunderstorms in the north. The mountains are the island's rainiest region, particularly in summer when rains fall in short thundershowers, especially in the mid-afternoon. In winter, the west side of the mountains tends to be drier than the east side. Southern winters are the best: warm and dry.

If you're travelling to Kinmen or Matsu in winter, be prepared for cold, and don't be surprised if your flight or ferry is cancelled because of inclement weather. Winter winds in the Penghu Islands can be severe. See p21 for information on the best times to travel.

COURSES

In addition to the following, contact the **Community Services Centre** (Map p100; ☎ 2836 8134; www.community.com.tw; 25 Lane 290, Zhongshan N Rd, sec.6, Tianmu) in Taipei for updates on various courses available for visitors and expats.

Studying Chinese

There are programmes at universities and private cram schools. Most are two to four hours a day, five days a week. Costs vary greatly from NT5000 a month at a private cram school to over US$1000 a month at a top programme.

To obtain a study visa at the time of writing, you had to enrol at a Ministry of Education–approved school (http://english.ctu.edu.tw/ct.asp?xItem=677&CtNode=417&mp=1). Some of the better-known programmes include **ICLP** (http://homepage.ntu.edu.tw/~iclp/) at National Taiwan University and the **Mandarin Training Program** (www.mtc.ntnu.edu.tw/indexe.html) at National Taiwan Normal University. Both are in Taipei but there are programmes around the country.

You can apply for a programme in your own country. Once you've been accepted, apply for a multi-entry extendable visitor visa (for study) at a local trade office or Republic of China (ROC) mission. You must start classes within the first month upon arrival and after four months of good standing you can apply for a resident visa at the **Bureau of Consular Affairs** (BOCA; ☎ 0800 085 078; www.boca.gov.tw; Hualien ☎ 03-833 1041; 6th fl, 371 Jungshan Rd; Kaohsiung ☎ 07-211 0605; 2nd fl, 436 Chenggung-1st Rd; Taichung ☎ 04-2251 0799; 1st fl, 503 Liming Rd, sec.2; Taipei ☎ 02-2343 2888; 3rd-5th fl, 2-2 Jinan Rd, sec.1). This then allows you to apply for an ARC (Alien Resident Card) at the **National Immigration Agency** (www.immigration.gov.tw), formerly the Foreign Affairs Police. An ARC should be good for up to two years, though you must renew it each year. Note that your school will not usually do anything to help you through the process.

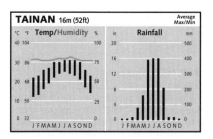

TAINAN 16m (52ft) — Average Max/Min — Temp/Humidity — Rainfall

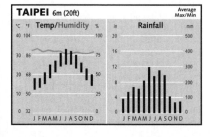

TAIPEI 6m (20ft) — Average Max/Min — Temp/Humidity — Rainfall

DIRECTORY

Check out the ever-informative www
.forumosa.com for the latest from people in
the know.

Calligraphy

Chinese-language schools (private and university) often have courses on calligraphy,
painting and other Chinese arts. Inquire at
the schools or check one of the foreigner chat
sites (www.forumosa.com or www.tealit.com)
for recommendations. You can also post ads
on these websites if you are looking for a
private teacher.

Meditation

There are four main Buddhist associations
in Taiwan: Tzu Chi, Foguangshan, Dharma
Drum and Chung Tai Chan. **Dharma Drum** (www
.dharmadrum.org) offers meditation classes in Taipei and Jinshan; click on Chan Meditation
on their website for more information. **Chung
Tai Chan** (ctworld@ms16.hinet.net) offers weekend
classes in its temple in Puli (see p226). **Foguangshan** (www.fgs.org.tw) has courses at its main
temple near Kaohsiung (see p274). All three
offer classes in English.

In addition, the **Taiwan Vipassana Centre** (www
.udaya.dhamma.org), in the mountains west of Taichung, offers a 10-day meditation course in
English: the course is the same as that taught
at its centres throughout the world.

Taichi

There are many schools in the cities offering
courses on taichi. Again, it is best to go to one
of the expat websites or Chinese schools and
ask for recommendations.

Yoga

Yoga classes are booming, in Taipei anyway.
For classes, check out gyms and other fitness
centres, as well as English newspapers and
expat websites.

CUSTOMS

Customs laws allow passengers 20 years and
older the duty-free importation of 200 cigarettes, 25 cigars or 450g of tobacco, one bottle
of liquor (up to 1L) and goods valued at up
to NT20,000 (not including personal effects).
Up to US$10,000 in foreign currency may also
be brought in.

And to quote a sign at Taoyuan International Airport: 'Drug trafficking is punishable
by death'.

DANGERS & ANNOYANCES

The following government websites offer
travel advisories and information on current
hot spots.
Australian Department of Foreign Affairs
(☎ 1300 139 281; www.smarttraveller.gov.au)
British Foreign Office (☎ 0845-850-2829; www.fco
.gov.uk/countryadvice)
Canadian Department of Foreign Affairs (☎ 800-
267 6788; www.dfait-maeci.gc.ca)
US State Department (☎ 888-407 4747; http://travel
.state.gov)

Dodgy Dealings

A barber's pole outside a shop with tinted
windows almost always indicates a brothel.

Food & Drink

Travellers are advised not to drink water
poured directly from the tap (though it's fine
to brush your teeth with). In most places you
will be served water that has been boiled,
which is fine to drink, and tea and bottled
drinks, including water, are widely available.
In general, look for plastic seal wraps, as water
can sometimes be contaminated in shipping.
We use the brands YES and More water.

Avoid cafeteria-style restaurants after the
lunch or dinner rush. Food can go bad if it
has been sitting for a while.

Stay away from brightly coloured local
snacks (including dried fruit) as they are often
bleached and full of preservatives. If you're
concerned about your health, speciality stores
and many supermarkets sell organic produce.
The most reputable is the small chain called
Cottonfields (p116).

Natural Dangers

When hiking in the mountains be aware of the
following. Afternoon fogs are common, as are
thundershowers, which can leave you soaked
and chilled. There are numerous species of
poisonous snake around the island (though
these are not usually a problem in the high
mountains), a poison ivy–like plant at around
1000m to 2000m, and wasps in summer. One
reader scoffed at this last warning but these
dangerous insects kill and put people in the
hospital every year. In the areas where they
are a danger you will often see warning signs,
though not always, so inquire locally.

Although the island is small, it is easy to get
lost. The forest is extremely thick in places,
and trails are quickly overgrown. Never leave

the trail and don't hike trails you don't know unless they are wide and clear. Prepare rain gear if you are going to be out for a few hours, and carry an umbrella, food, mobile phone and lots of water.

Earthquakes are common all over the island, and are especially strong along the east coast. If you are here for a few months you will likely experience one. Typhoons affect the island from summer to late autumn. Do not go outside when they are raging, and avoid going to the mountains in the few days after as landslides and swollen rivers can wash out roads and trails.

Many foreigners at first dismiss concerns about swimming too far from shore. But note there is no continental shelf here, meaning that the deep blue sea is just offshore, and dangerous undercurrents and riptides flow around the island. General advice: do not go out further than you can stand on your tiptoes and don't swim at a beach unless you know for certain it is safe.

Nightlife

Foreign men should be careful at bars and clubs. Taiwanese men can be very protective of any female in their group, even if there's no romantic relationship. Be careful about approaching a woman who is with a guy (or accepting her advances). Gangsters hang out in clubs, though they are usually not a problem unless threatened or forced to lose face. When that happens you are in serious trouble. Contrary to Western customs, Taiwanese don't fight alone. It's a sign of one's personal power and influence to be able to call 20 guys at the drop of a hat to come and beat the hell out of you. In general it's a good idea to get recommendations for bars and clubs, especially in the south.

Street Crime & Theft

In terms of street crime, Taiwan is one of the safer places in Asia, although residential burglaries do happen and pickpocketing is common where crowds gather. (We almost had our pockets picked at a religious festival.) If you're staying in a youth hostel or camping ground, be sure to lock up your belongings securely as most of these facilities are open to the public.

Most midrange and top-end hotels have safes or other facilities to guard your valuables. And if you're concerned about theft of your money, use travellers cheques.

Foreign victims of crime often don't get much help from the police, though we have to say that in many cases we have seen of this the foreigners made it easy for the police to ignore them. You can mitigate cultural misunderstandings by bringing along a Taiwanese person (someone respectable looking) and acting respectful yourself.

See also p344 for more advice to women travellers.

DISCOUNT CARDS

Student cards are widely used for public transport as well as museums, parks, (some) movie tickets and performances at public theatres. However, foreign student cards are not likely to be accepted. Foreigners studying Chinese can get student cards from their school, and these will be accepted.

Children's discounts usually go by height rather than age (eg discounts for children under 110cm). Seniors (65 years and older) are usually given the same discounts as children. Seniors over 70 often get in free.

EMBASSIES & CONSULATES

Because of the 'One China Policy' adopted by the Mainland (the idea that mainland China and Taiwan are both part of one country: People's Republic of China), only about 15 countries (the number keeps dropping) and the Holy See have full diplomatic relations with Taiwan. Most likely your country is represented not by an embassy but by an office calling itself something to do with trade and/or culture. 'Institute' figures in the name of many of these offices.

Overseas, Taiwan is represented by consular, information and trade offices. Both Taiwanese legations abroad and foreign legations in Taiwan serve the same functions as embassies or consulates would elsewhere: services to their own nationals, visa processing, trade promotion and cultural programmes.

For a complete list of embassies and trade offices (both Taiwanese overseas and foreign offices in Taiwan), visit the **Ministry of Foreign Affairs** (www.mofa.gov.tw) site.

Foreign Legations in Taiwan

All addresses are in Taipei unless otherwise indicated.

Australia (Australia Commerce & Industry Office; ☎ 02-8725 4100; www.australia.org.tw; The Presidential International Tower, 27-28th fl, 9-11 Song Gao Rd)

Canada (Canadian Trade Office in Taipei; ☎ 02-2544 3000; www.canada.org.tw; 13th fl, 365 Fuxing N Rd)

France (French Institute; Institut Français de Taipei; ☎ 02-3518 5151; www.fi-taipei.org; 10th fl, 205 Dunhua N Rd)

Germany (German Institute; Deutsches Institut; ☎ 02-2501 6188; 4th fl, 2 Minsheng E Rd, sec.3)

India (India-Taipei Association; ☎ 02-2757 6112; Room 2010, 20th fl, 333 Keelung Rd, sec.1)

Ireland (The Institute for Trade & Investment of Ireland; ☎ 02-2725 1691; 7B-09, Taiwan World Trade Centre Bldg, 5 Xinyi Rd, sec.5)

Japan (Interchange Association; ☎ 02-2713 8000; www .japan-taipei.org.tw; 28 Ching Cheng St)

Netherlands (Netherlands Trade & Investment Office; ☎ 02-2713 5760; www.ntio.org.tw; 5th fl, 133 Minsheng E Rd, sec.3)

New Zealand (New Zealand Commerce & Industry Office; ☎ 02-2757 6725; Room 2501 25th fl, 333 Keelung Rd, sec.1)

South Africa (Liaison Office of South Africa; ☎ 02-2715 3250; Suite 1301, 13th fl, 205 Dunhua N Rd)

South Korea (Korean Mission in Taipei; ☎ 02-2758 8320; Room 1506, 333 Keelung Rd, sec.1)

Thailand (Thailand Trade & Economic Office; ☎ 02-2581 1979; 12th fl, 168 Song Jiang Rd)

UK (British Trade & Cultural Office; Kaohsiung ☎ 07-238 7744; Suite D, 7th fl, 95 Mintzu 2nd-Rd; Taipei ☎ 02-2192 7000; 9th fl, 99 Renai Rd, sec.2)

USA (American Institute in Taiwan; www.ait.org.tw; Kaohsiung ☎ 07-238 7744; 3rd fl, 2 Chungcheng Rd, sec.3; Taipei ☎ 02-2162 2000; 7 Lane 134, Xinyi Rd, sec.3)

FESTIVALS & EVENTS

Dates vary, so we've listed them here by month.

FEBRUARY
Lantern Festival (opposite)

APRIL-MAY
Birth of Matsu The birth of the Goddess of the Sea and protector of fishermen is commemorated at temples island-wide on the 23rd day of the 3rd lunar month. A week-long pilgrimage begins at the temple in Dajia (see p216).

MAY
Sanyi Woodcarving Festival (p179) In Taiwan's wood-carving capital. Highlights include on-the-spot carving contests, Hakka food tasting and ice-sculpting.

JUNE
Dragon Boat Festival (opposite)

JULY-AUGUST
Ilan International Children's Folklore & Folkgame Festival (p163) Top children's performers and performing troupes are brought in to Luodong from around the world. In addition, there are exhibits of toys and games, and sales of exotic toys.

AUGUST
Festival of Austronesian Cultures (p203) In Taitung County, a stronghold for aboriginal culture in Taiwan. Good for purchasing native handicrafts.

Keelung Ghost Festival (Zhōngyuán Jié; p155) Each year a different Keelung clan is chosen to sponsor the events. Highlights include folk-art performances, the opening of the gates of hell and the release of burning water lanterns. Lasts the entire seventh lunar month.

OCTOBER
Hualien International Stone Sculpture Festival (p185) Features the stonework of local and international artists, as well as folk performances.

FOOD

This book classifies budget meals as under NT150, midrange NT150 to NT400 and top end NT400 and up. See the Food & Drink chapter (p58) and local listings for more on Taiwan's excellent local food and eating scene.

GAY & LESBIAN TRAVELLERS

In Taiwan's family-oriented society, where the propagation of children is considered a duty, there is a stigma attached to homosexuality. Taiwanese gays and lesbians, however, have made great strides towards openness and equality, particularly since the end of martial law. The island's big cities have some of the best gay life in the Chinese-speaking world. The Chinese-speaking world's first gay-pride parade was held in Taipei in 2003 and the community has never looked back. In 2006, then Taipei mayor and now presidential hopeful, Ma Ying-jeou, presided over the opening of the city's annual Gay, Lesbian, Bisexual and Transgender Festival – the first event of its kind to be sponsored by a local government in Taiwan.

Unlike in other East Asian countries, gay and lesbian visitors will likely find their Taiwanese hosts friendly and welcoming. Taipei in particular has a number of bars and clubs, as well as shopping, salons, saunas and other gay-friendly venues. You'll find similar venues, though in far smaller numbers, in other cities as well. One good website with updated information is www.utopia-asia.com/tipstaiw .htm. See also the boxed text, p118.

Taiwan's official stance towards gays and lesbians may be considered among the most progressive in East Asia, though police harassment in various forms is still too common. There is no sodomy law to penalise homosexuality, in 2002 the military lifted its ban on homosexuals and in 2003 the ROC government announced plans to legalise same-sex marriage (though the bill has gone nowhere since).

HOLIDAYS

Taiwanese holidays are set according to either the Western calendar or the Chinese lunar calendar. Holidays in the lunar calendar fall at different times each year in the Western calendar. Bad times to travel are Chinese New Year, winter holidays for students (three weeks around Chinese New Year), Tomb Sweep Day, Dragon Boat Festival, summer weekends (July to August) and Moon Festival.

Western Calendar Holidays

JANUARY

Founding Day (Yuándàn) 1 January. Commemorates the founding of the ROC back in 1911. Businesses and schools close, and many remain closed on 2 January. In recent years huge sponsored events have been held on December 31 to celebrate the countdown. Many people are now using 1 January to nurse their hangovers.

FEBRUARY

2-28 (Èrèrbā) 28 February. This holiday recollects events of 28 February 1947, when political dissent led to the massacre of thousands of Taiwanese. Instituted in 1997 at the behest of the Democratic Progressive Party (DPP), but without universal public support.

APRIL

Tomb Sweep Day (Qīng Míng Jié) 5 April or 4 April on leap years. Families return to the graves of their ancestors to clean them as a gesture of respect. Expect to see lots of ghost money being burned around the island. Bank holiday.

SEPTEMBER

Teachers' Day (Jiàoshī Jié) 28 September. Originally honouring the birthday of Confucius, this holiday now honours all teachers. Confucian temples around the country stage elaborate ceremonies all day and while people don't get the day off, the ceremonies are worth taking a holiday to see. Get your tickets well in advance.

OCTOBER

National Day (Shuāngshí Jié) 10 October. Sometimes called 'Double 10th Day' after its date, this day is marked by military parades, fireworks and beach parties. Bank holiday.

DECEMBER

Constitution Day (Guāngfù Jié) 25 December. Although it was a holiday in Taiwan long before Christmas was a significant presence here, you can guess which holiday has taken over the national psyche. Although it's not a national day off anymore, the night of the 24th can be party time.

Lunar Year Holidays

JANUARY–FEBRUARY

Chinese (Lunar) New Year (Chūn Jié) Lunar date: first day of the first month. The year's most important festival is marked by special banquets and family gatherings, red envelopes of money are given as gifts and it's common for people to wear new clothes. Visitors might consider staying away since many businesses and sights close for extended periods.

FEBRUARY

Lantern Festival (Yuánxiāo Jié) Lunar date: 15th day of the first month. This is fast becoming one of the most popular holidays in Taiwan. Festivities vary from fireworks displays to art shows to activities that combine tradition and technology. All draw large crowds. One highlight in the north is the release of thousands of sky lanterns into the air around Pingxi (see the boxed text, p149).

JUNE

Dragon Boat Festival (Duānwǔ Jié) Lunar date: fifth day of the fifth month. One of the most important Chinese holidays and very photogenic and colourful (though many find it dull and slow). The highlight is the dragon-boat races in which long, sleek boats, decorated like dragons, compete in remembrance of the suicide drowning of the poet Chu Yuan. Some of the best places to see them include Lukang (p216; where Dragon Boat Festival is part of a four-day folk festival), Keelung (p153), Kaohsiung (p270) and Sansia (p152). *Zòngzi* (粽子; sticky-rice dumplings wrapped in leaves) are a culinary treat not to miss. A national holiday.

SEPTEMBER–OCTOBER

Moon Festival (Zhōngqiū Jié) Lunar date: 15th day of the eight month. Also known as Mid-Autumn Festival, this traditional Chinese holiday celebrated the end of the harvest and was a time of plenty. These days it's a time for family and friends to get together, barbecue and eat moon cakes and pomelos. The moon is supposed to be the year's brightest and fullest, though it is often obscured by clouds in the north. The festival usually marks the beginning of cooler weather after the scorching summer.

INSURANCE

A travel-insurance policy to cover theft, loss and medical problems is a good idea. There are a wide variety of policies available, so check the small print. Some things to watch out for:

- Some policies specifically exclude 'dangerous activities', which can include scuba diving, motorcycling and even trekking.
- A locally acquired motorcycle licence is not valid under some policies.
- Some policies pay doctors or hospitals directly rather than you having to pay on the spot and claim later. If you have to claim later, make sure you keep all documentation.
- Some policies ask you to call (reverse charges) a centre in your home country where an immediate assessment of your problem is made.
- Check whether the policy covers ambulances or an emergency flight home.

For health insurance advice, see p354. For details on car insurance, see p350. Worldwide travel insurance is available at www.lonelyplanet.com/travel_services. You can buy, extend and claim online anytime – even if you're already on the road.

INTERNET ACCESS

Taiwan is among the most cyber-savvy places on the planet, and if you've got your own laptop you shouldn't have any problem getting online. In Taipei at least, most coffee shops have wireless access: some servers are free, others are accessible by buying a *wúxiàn wǎng kǎ* (pay-for-time card) with a name and password at 7-Eleven or most other convenience stores. You'll know if you need a card because when you try to access the web you'll be redirected towards a login page, most of which will have English instructions as well.

Many midrange and top-end hotels – especially in the big cities – offer in-room ADSL high-speed internet connections for laptops. Some of these carry hefty charges (up to NT300 per day), but more and more include the service in the room rate. If you don't have your own laptop, look for a hotel with a business centre. At smaller hotels this could be a single computer at a desk. This book denotes all forms of internet access with the icon 🖳.

All cities and towns have cyber cafés (though these aren't as common as they once were, as most Taiwanese own their own computers) or gaming parlours where you can go online. Libraries usually have free internet access, though you may have to sign up for a specific time slot. Tourist offices will sometimes let you use their computers.

For information about Taiwan on the web, see p23 and p342.

LEGAL MATTERS

Don't even think of messing with illegal drugs in Taiwan; this includes marijuana. Smuggling can carry the death penalty and even possession can get you busted.

If you are caught working illegally, you'll get a fine, a visa suspension and an order to leave the country. You may not ever be allowed back.

Under Taiwanese law, knowingly transmitting HIV to another person is punishable by up to seven years in prison. This law also allows for mandatory testing of members of high-risk groups, namely sexual partners of HIV carriers and intravenous drug users, as well as foreigners who come to work certain jobs and require an ARC. Oddly enough, adultery is also a crime.

If you're detained by the police, you should get in touch with your country's legation in Taiwan. Even if it can't provide any direct aid, it can at least offer legal advice and notify your family.

If you are arrested, you have the right to remain silent and to request an attorney, although authorities are under no obligation to provide an attorney. You also have the right to refuse to sign any document. In most cases, a suspect cannot be detained for more than 24 hours without a warrant from a judge – notable exceptions are those with visa violations.

Taipei City offers *pro bono* legal service at most district offices.

LEGAL AGE

- Voting: 20
- Driving: 18
- Military conscription: 18, but most do it after their university studies
- Consumption of alcohol: 18
- Consensual sex (heterosexual or homosexual): 16

MAPS

The best road map (in Chinese) is *Formosa Complete Road Atlas* by Sunriver (two volumes, about NT2000 each). You can pick up a good four-part collection of bilingual maps called *Taiwan Tourist Map* from tourist offices. These should suffice for most purposes. City and county maps are also available at tourist offices.

Eslite, Caves and other bookshops that sell English-language material have English maps of Taiwan and the major cities. See local listings for useful local maps.

A compass can be useful if you're going to be travelling on country roads; sometimes you may not see a road sign for kilometres.

For hiking maps see p330.

MONEY

Taiwan's currency is the New Taiwanese Dollar (NT). Bills come in denominations of NT50, NT100, NT200, NT500, NT1000 and NT2000, while coins come in units of NT1, NT5, NT10 and NT50. See the inside front cover for exchange rates with key currencies.

Unlike some other countries in Asia, Taiwan uses the local currency exclusively.

Foreigners can open Taiwanese bank accounts even without an ARC if they get a identification number at the local police office.

See p21 for information on costs.

ATMs

ATMs are the easiest way to withdraw cash from your home account, and 7-Elevens are usually our first choice as they are always on the international Plus or Cirrus network and have English-language options; and 7-Elevens are literally everywhere in the country (there are around 4000 of them).

Many ATMs at banks around the country are also on the Plus and Cirrus networks, and as sometimes on Accel, Interlink and Star. networks. Keep in mind that there may be limits on the amount of cash that can be withdrawn per transaction or per day, and that your home financial institution may charge a fee on withdrawals from other banks. Banks islandwide charge a NT7 fee per withdrawal for all but their own customers.

Cash

Nothing beats cash for convenience – or for risk if it's lost or stolen. For peace of mind, keep any extra cash in the safe deposit box at your hotel. If you're carrying foreign cash to exchange, the most widely accepted currency is US dollars.

Credit Cards

Credit cards are widely accepted. The bottom-of-the-barrel budget hotels won't take them, but if your room costs more than NT1000 a night, the place will most often be set up for credit cards. Most homestays, however, do not accept them.

Small stalls or small food joints never take credit cards. Most midrange to top-end restaurants do but always check before you decide to eat. We've been caught without cash a few times, but the staff have never had a problem with us leaving to withdraw money.

Moneychangers

Private moneychangers do not proliferate in Taiwan like they do elsewhere. Hotels will change money for their guests, but banks are the most common option.

Tipping

Tipping is not customary in restaurants or taxis (but is still appreciated). However, if a porter carries your bag at a hotel or the airport, a tip of NT100 is considered courteous. Also, many foreigners tip at better bars and clubs, especially those run by expats, and so staff may expect this. Note that the 10% service charge added to the bill at many restaurants is not actually a tip to be shared with the staff.

Travellers Cheques

As with cash, it's best if your travellers cheques are in US dollars. You get a slightly better rate on exchange, but that can be cancelled out by commissions so check carefully before you change money.

PHOTOGRAPHY

Taiwan is a technologically up-to-date place and every city has scores of photo studios where you can download digital pictures onto a CD, or print them out. Look for Fuji or Konica signs if you can't read Chinese.

POST

Taiwan's postal system is efficient and fast. Domestic letters generally arrive within two days, and take about seven to 10 days to destinations in North America and Europe; fewer to Hong Kong or Japan. Stamps can be purchased at post offices and convenience stores or even online now.

Main post offices in the big cities have poste restante services. Mail should be addressed to GPO Poste Restante, with the city name. Generally, mail must be claimed within two months or it will be returned to sender.

For general inquiries, visit www.post.gov .tw, or phone ☎ 02-2321 4311 or toll free ☎ 0800 099 246.

Basic mailing rates	Postcard	Letter
within Taiwan	NT2.5	NT5
China/Hong Kong	NT6	NT9
elsewhere in Asia/Australia	NT10	NT13
USA/Canada	NT11	NT15
elsewhere	NT12	NT17

SHOPPING

Taiwan is a shopper's paradise.

Night markets are a highlight of any trip to Taiwan. While the specialities vary from market to market, you can generally expect to find cheap clothing (though occasionally cheap in both senses), toys, home wares and trinkets. They're also among the best places to find snack food – some night markets specialise in food only.

Other good buys include jade and aboriginal crafts. See the Lukang (p219), Yingge (p151), Sanyi (p178), Meinong (p276), Kinmen (p302) and Taipei (p122) sections for buying traditional crafts.

Electronics are widely available, including some Taiwanese brands and many international brands. However, prices may not be any better than in your own country. If there's something you've been looking for, price it before leaving home and don't be disappointed if you leave Taiwan without it. Also, make sure that the current of any item you buy is compatible with the one at home.

The Guanghua Market (p122) in Taipei specialises in computers, peripherals and components. Knowledgeable buyers can try shops that will assemble a computer to specifications for about half what you would pay back home. See right for information on VAT refunds.

Bargaining

At chain stores, convenience stores and department stores you pay the marked price. At pretty much any market or privately owned shop, you can certainly bargain (though don't bargain for your fruits and vegetables or a pen and notebook). Discounts range from 10% to 20%, so if you aren't comfortable bargaining, you're usually not losing much.

Convenience Stores

There are around 7000 convenience stores nationwide, the highest concentration in the world. In addition to newspapers, drinks, snacks and sundries, you can usually find daily-made sandwiches, sushi triangles, fresh fruit (at 7-Elevens only) and bread. You can also buy beer, wine and fine cognac, and withdraw money at ATMs (most of which are capable of handling international cards).

The ubiquitous 7-Eleven chain has the greatest range of services, from faxing and copying to bill payments (phone, water, electricity, parking) for residents. By the time you read this you may even be able to purchase train tickets. In the countryside, 7-Elevens act as rest stops, with public bathrooms inside and picnic tables outside. Other chains include Family Mart, Hi-Life and Nico Mart.

SOLO TRAVELLERS

Larger Chinese restaurants tend to serve portions meant for groups and may not know what to do with a solo traveller. Smaller restaurants are generally no problem. Night-market vendors always cater to the single customer.

Simple tea or coffee shops often have set meals (meal and drink) for less than NT150. Noodle stands and breakfast shops are always cheap. Be wary around barbecues as often the portions are set for a table or half-table.

Solo female travellers should have no problems in Taiwan if they use common sense. Make ATM withdrawals during the day, stick to brightly lit areas by night in cities and towns, and avoid obviously seedy hotels and hitchhiking.

If a problem arises, you'll probably find the Taiwanese very helpful.

TAXES
Residents

If you're a working resident of Taiwan, you are responsible for paying Taiwanese taxes. You can find complete information in English on the website of the **National Tax Administration** (www.ntat.gov.tw).

Value Added Tax Refunds

Visitors with foreign passports and others with certain ROC documents are eligible to receive refunds of Taiwan's 5% value added tax (VAT). There are catches, however. First, just a small number of shops are registered as Tax Refund Shopping (TRS) stores: mostly large department stores and shopping malls in major cities. Second, you must make a minimum purchase of NT3000 in a single day at a single store. Third, when you leave Taiwan you must present your items with your passport, plus an original copy of the uniform invoice to the 'Foreign Passenger VAT Refund Service Counter' at the airport or seaport. You may claim your refund at Taoyuan International Airport (either terminal), Keelung Harbour, Hualien (airport or harbour) or Kaohsiung (airport or harbour).

For further information, contact the visitor centre at the airport or seaport when you arrive.

TELEPHONE & FAX

The country code for Taiwan is ☎ 886.

Taiwan's telephone carrier for domestic and international calls is **Chunghwa Telecom** (www.cht.com.tw). For detailed information on rates and services, visit the website.

Area Codes

Area codes throughout Taiwan are shown below. Note that you do not dial the area code when calling within an area code.

The number of digits in telephone numbers varies with the locality, from eight in bustling Taipei to five in the remote Matsu Islands.

Domestic Calls

From public telephones, local calls cost NT2 per two minutes and local long-distance calls are NT3 per minute. From private phones it's NT1.6 every three minutes for a local call and NT.035 per second for a local long-distance call. Calls to mobile phones (beginning with ☎ 09) vary from NT0.05 to NT0.11 per second depending on the provider and the time of day. Rates are discounted from 11pm to 8am Monday to Friday, from noon on Saturday and all day Sunday.

Fax

Most hotels offer fax services – but you'll probably pay through the nose for them. However, at 7-Eleven stores, local black-and-white faxes cost NT15 per page; local long-distance faxes are NT20 per page; and international faxes are NT85 per page.

International Calls

For overseas direct-dial calls, dial ☎ 009 or ☎ 002 before the country code and number. Chunghwa Telecom's E-call cards are sold in denominations of NT200, NT300 and NT500 and entitle users to a 30% discount on standard rates, although the quality of connection is somewhat lower. E-call cards can be purchased at Chunghwa Telecom locations and 7-Eleven stores. To use, dial the access number on the back of the card and then follow the instructions (English option available).

Overseas calls are charged per six-second unit, as follows:

Country	Direct dial	E-call
Australia	NT1.30	NT0.96
Canada	NT0.59	NT0.40
China	NT1.22	NT0.77
France	NT1.60	NT1.04
Germany	NT1.60	NT1.04
Japan	NT1.30	NT0.96
Netherlands	NT2.00	NT1.10
New Zealand	NT1.30	NT0.96
UK	NT1.40	NT0.96
USA	NT0.59	NT0.40

There is a discount of approximately 5% on calls made during off-peak hours. You can dial via an overseas operator (☎ 100), but this will cost a bundle. For directory assistance in English, dial ☎ 106 (NT3 per call).

If you have your own phone line in Taiwan, note that there are always specials going on. See Chunghwa's website for details. The absolute cheapest way to stay in contact with people around the world is through **Skype** (www.skype.com), a peer-to-peer internet telephoney

TELEPHONE AREA CODES

0836	Matsu Island
0826	Wuchiu Island
082	Kinmen Island

02 Taipei
03 Taoyuan
03 Hsinchu
03 Ilan
037 Miaoli
04 Taichung
04 Changhua
049 Nantou
03 Hualien
05 Yunlin
05 Chiayi
06 Penghu Islands
06 Tainan
07 Kaohsiung
089 Taitung
08 Pingtung
089 Green Island
08 Liuchiu Island
089 Orchid Island

network. Rates are just a couple of US dollars an hour to most countries, and completely free if the person you are calling is also set up with Skype on a computer.

Mobile Phones

These are often called *dàgēdà* or just cell phone. There are many options. Chunghwa Telecom and **FarEastone** (www.fareastone.com.tw) are two big carriers. Costs of handsets can vary widely, from NT1000 to NT25,000. In general, expect to pay about NT1 a minute for outgoing domestic calls. Some packages charge more but give you a number of free minutes, while others offer a low monthly fee and fewer or no free minutes. Check locally or on the web for the latest options.

You can usually bring your phone from home and buy a SIM card from a local carrier and a prepaid phonecard (there are desks right at the airport arrival terminals). If you have an ARC you can apply for a mobile phone in Taiwan.

All mobile phones in Taiwan start with the prefix ☎ 09XX, followed by six digits. Note that when calling within an area code, you still have to use the area code. A Taipei call then would look like this: 02-XXXX XXXX.

Public Phones & Phonecards

Calls from public phones cost NT2 for local calls of up to two minutes, NT3 per minute for local long-distance, and NT6 per minute for calls to mobile phones. Note that with the proliferation of cell phones, public phones are not as numerous as they once were.

In addition to coin-operated telephones, there are two types of card-operated phone. Ordinary phonecards cost NT100, while IC cards cost NT200. Cards are available at convenience stores. When your card is about to run out, the display will flash: press the 'change card' button to insert your new card. For international calls with prepaid cards see p341.

TIME

Taiwan is eight hours ahead of GMT; the same time zone as Beijing, Hong Kong, Singapore and Perth. This means that when it's noon in Taiwan, it's 2pm in Sydney, 1pm in Japan, 4am in London, 11pm the previous day in New York and 8pm the previous day in Los Angeles.

Taiwan does not observe daylight-saving time. During daylight-saving time, add one hour to the local times listed here for locations outside Taiwan (eg 5am in London).

TOILETS

Western-style toilets are standard in apartments and hotels. Restaurants and cafés can have either Western or squat toilets (fewer and fewer of the latter), while public facilities are likely to have squat toilets, except for a handicapped stall. Most businesses have their own toilets on site. Some toilets have toilet paper, but it's always good to be prepared with your own (pocket packs of tissues are common giveaways on streets in the big cities). Many places ask you not to flush the toilet paper down the toilet but put it in the wastebasket beside the toilet. There's a lot of controversy about whether this is truly necessary. The claim is that old pipes and septic systems just cannot handle toilet paper. It's best to comply when asked.

It's also handy to remember the characters for 'male' (男; *nán*) and 'female' (女; *nǚ*)

TOURIST INFORMATION

In addition to Taiwan's main tourism website (www.taiwan.net.tw), look for information on specific counties, national parks and national scenic areas on the following websites:

Alishan National Scenic Area (www.ali.org.tw)
East Coast National Scenic Area (www.eastcoast-nsa.gov.tw)
East Rift Valley National Scenic Area (www.erv-nsa.gov.tw)
Forest Recreation Areas (http://recreate.forest.gov.tw)
Hualien County (www.taitung.gov.tw/english/index.php)
Ilan County (http://enwww.e-land.gov.tw/default.asp)
Kaohsiung County (http://english.kscg.gov.tw)
Kenting National Park (www.ktnp.gov.tw)
Maolin National Scenic Area (www.maolin-nsa.gov.tw)
Matsu National Scenic Area (http://www.matzu-nsa.gov.tw/)
North Coast & Guanyinshan National Scenic Area (www.northguan-nsa.gov.tw)
Northeast Coast National Scenic Area (www.necoast-nsa.gov.tw)
Penghu National Scenic Area (www.penghu-nsa.gov.tw)
Sheipa National Park (www.spnp.gov.tw)
Sun Moon Lake National Scenic Area (www.sunmoonlake.gov.tw)
Taitung County (http://tour-hualien.hl.gov.tw)
Tri-Mountain National Scenic Area (www.trimt-nsa.gov.tw)

HELPING OUR FOUR-LEGGED FRIENDS IN TAIWAN

Like many Westerners in Taiwan, Sean McCormack couldn't stand the sight of so many homeless dogs and cats. But unlike most of us here, he did more than just feel sad and hopeless. In 2005 he started an animal-rescue association that is now making a major impact on the stray population in this country.

Sean has always worked with animals in one way or another (even when he was a pub manager in Folkstone, England, he says). When he first came to Taiwan he began to take in strays, pay for their medical care and seek families for adoption. But his work may never have gone any further had it not been for Jane Goodall. Yes, that Jane Goodall.

Goodall has an institute in Taiwan and visits often. On one such visit, she asked a local friend to introduce her to people who were trying to make a difference in Taiwan. And with that, Sean found himself one day in a hotel room in downtown Taipei, listening to the greatest living animal-rights activist tell him that he should start an association of like-minded people. Unable to convince himself he couldn't do it, Sean founded AnimalsTaiwan.

At first, AT had only a handful of members but they cleverly garnered support by asking people for help for 'planned' activities, as opposed to helping plan activities. (They knew that people would be more willing to join an activity when they thought the ball was already rolling – even if in truth these people were the ones really pushing it.) Soon AT was getting free vet care from local clinics, coverage on Taiwanese TV and funds from drives, doggie biscuit bake sales and generous patrons. In 2006 AT moved operations from Sean's apartment near the Taipei Zoo to a large holding facility out in Shilin.

Around the same time, Goodall returned to Taiwan and Sean was able to meet her again. In fact, he marched with her on parade through the streets of Taipei holding her hand while dressed as a gorilla. It was one of the happiest days of his life and Goodall's genuine enthusiasm for AT was just what he and the others needed to reinvigorate themselves after two very long years.

Sean's work has inspired other foreigners around Taiwan to start their own animal rescue branches. One of the most successful has been in Kaohsiung. Called BARK, it was founded by Canadians Chris Leroux and his wife Natasha Hodela, who like Sean began as small team just trying to make a difference.

Both groups are now registered nonprofit organizations (NPOs) and are helping hundreds of animals to a better life. Their long-term goal, however, is to reduce the stray population to manageable levels (manageable because if cities reduce it altogether then other, less desirable, animals will move in). For this they are employing a counterintuitive, but very successful and humane method called CNR (catch-neuter-release). CNR is endorsed by the World Trade Organisation and has been used to great effect in India in recent years to reduce the stray cat population.

If you're in Taiwan, for a year, a month, or even a week, give the fine folk at AnimalsTaiwan or BARK a shout (for more details see p344). They can always use the help. Or rather, the animals can.

Yushan National Park (http://english.ysnp.com.tw)
The following websites, while not specifically aimed at tourists, are helpful resources:
Forumosa.com (www.forumosa.com)
Information for Foreigners (http://iff.immigration.gov.tw)
Taiwan Fun (www.taiwanfun.com)

And don't forget the 24-hour English/Japanese/Chinese tourism hotline: ☎ 0800 011 765.

TRAVELLERS WITH DISABILITIES

While Taipei is slowly modernising its facilities for the disabled (new buildings must now meet a building code), disabled travellers may be dismayed to find footpaths are uneven, kerbs are steep, and public transport, other than the MRT, is not well equipped with wheelchair access.

On the other hand, disabled parking is usually available and respected.

Committed to ensuring that those with disabilities can enjoy all Taiwan has to offer, the **Eden Social Welfare Foundation** (http://engweb .eden.org.tw) provides advice and assistance to disabled travellers.

VISAS

At the time of writing citizens of the following countries could enter Taiwan without a visa and stay for 30 days (this period cannot be extended under any circumstances): Australia, Austria, Belgium, Canada, Costa Rica, Denmark, Finland, France, Germany, Greece, Iceland, Ireland, Italy, Japan, Liechtenstein, Luxembourg, Malaysia, Malta, Monaco, Netherlands, New Zealand, Norway, Portugal, Republic of Korea, Singapore, Spain, Sweden, Switzerland, UK and USA.

Those coming to Taiwan to study (see p333), work or visit relatives for an extended period of time should apply at an overseas mission of the ROC for a visitor visa good for 60 to 90 days. These can be extended up to six months under certain circumstances at the **Bureau of Consular Affairs** (BOCA; ☎ 0800 085 078; www.boca.gov.tw; Hualien ☎ 03-833 1041; 6th fl, 371 Jungshan Rd; Kaohsiung ☎ 07-211 0605; 2nd fl, 436 Chenggung-1st Rd; Taichung ☎ 04-2251 0799; 1st fl, 503 Liming Rd, sec.2; Taipei ☎ 02-2343 2888; 3rd-5th fl, 2-2 Jinan Rd, sec.1).

BOCA requires anyone entering Taiwan to have a passport valid for at least six months, a ticket and/or seat reservation for departure from Taiwan and no criminal record.

Citizens of countries not listed here can find information on various visa requirements via the mission in their country or on the bureau's website. The website also contains advice on procedures and requirements for changing visa status, for example from student to resident.

If you're planning to stay longer than three months and work in Taiwan, the law requires you to have an ARC. However, if you're an Australian or New Zealander aged 18 to 30, you may obtain a working holiday visa, which enables you to undertake short-term, part-time work in Taiwan for one year. This scheme was introduced in 2004 though we have not heard many positive things about it.

VOLUNTEERING

There are few opportunities for foreigners to volunteer in Taiwan, often because it is technically illegal. One area where you can help out, and where help is truly needed, is with animal welfare. Contact **AnimalsTaiwan** (☎ 02-2833 8820; www.animalstaiwan.org) in Taipei and **BARK** (☎ 07-

348 7444; www.barktaiwan.org) in Kaohsiung. See also the boxed text, p343.

WOMEN TRAVELLERS

Taiwan is a safe country, but women should take care and be wary of walking through underground tunnels alone at night; there's a danger of getting felt up on crowded buses and the MRT, or occasionally of being stalked. If you have to take a taxi home at night alone, ask a friend to call as there will be a record. For additional safety let the driver see the friend write down the taxi licence-plate number. If the driver can also see that you have a mobile phone, trouble is less likely.

Women travelling to Taiwan for business should dress modestly and conservatively (as should men). Also, although drinking and smoking are a part of Taiwanese business culture, Taiwanese women tend to smoke and drink less than Taiwanese men, though this is changing fast among the younger generation.

Apart from the attention normally given to foreign travellers, women travellers should not expect any special attention.

WORK

If you're going to Taiwan to do a business deal, it helps to have an introduction through a government office or some other contact that does business with the other party. At least for the first meeting, modest, conservative dress is in order. This typically means dark wool suits and ties despite the country being tropical. Short sleeves are acceptable in summer.

There has been an attempt to introduce island wear (bright floral shirts) as acceptable business attire in summer but this has by no means caught on with everyone.

You don't need us to tell you that Taiwan is a popular place to teach English. The market is no longer a seller's, and wages have stagnated for 10 years (while the NT has lost 20% value) but you can still make a good living here and save money to pay off loans or travel. To find out the latest on visas, regulations, costs, salaries and so on, check out the local expat sites www.forumosa.com and www.tealit.com.

Transport

CONTENTS

GETTING THERE & AWAY

ENTERING THE COUNTRY

Most visitors enter through Taiwan Taoyuan International Airport, where the immigration procedures pose few hassles. Guards are basically efficient.

For visa information, see p343.

AIR
Airports & Airlines

Taiwan's main international airport is **Taiwan Taoyuan International Airport** (TPE; www.taoyuanairport .gov.tw/) in Dayuan, 50km (40 minutes) west of central Taipei. It was formerly called Chiang Kai-shek and may still be referred to as CKS Airport. Taiwan's other international airports are **Siaogang Airport** (KHH; www.kia.gov.tw) in Kaohsiung and **Cing Cyuan Gang Airport** (RMQ; www .tca.gov.tw/English/Introduction.htm) in Taichung. TPE handles traffic from around the world, while most of the international traffic into and out of Siaogang Airport and Cing Cyuan Gang Airport comes from Hong Kong and Southeast Asia. At the time of writing there were still no direct flights between China and Taiwan.

TPE airport has two terminals connected by a small skytrain. Terminal 2 is newer and by far the more attractive of the two. Both terminals have signs in English for every service and facility. There is also a tourist information booth in each. You can contact the booth in Terminal 1 on ☎ 03-383 2790, or Terminal 2 on ☎ 03-398 3341. Both are open from 7am to 11.30pm and can help with hotel bookings and bus information, as well as with getting a Youth Travel Card (see p328).

Other facilities include showers, free wireless internet, a post office, several banks for currency exchange and ATM withdrawals, mobile-phone service desks (for buying prepaid SIM cards, renting phones etc) and **Lost & Found** (☎ 03-398 2538).

Getting to/from TPE is simple. Several bus companies run the route (average fare NT125, 60 minutes) every 15 minutes from the airport to the main train station in Taipei from 4am to midnight. Some buses also go to the domestic airport, Songshan (see p347). You can buy bus tickets in the arrival areas of both terminals. Look for the 'Express Bus' signs in Terminal 2 and 'Bus Stop' (Station) signs in Terminal 1. If you want to get dropped off at a particular hotel let the staff at the ticket counters know, as there are different routes.

Buses also connect with the High-Speed Rail (HSR) station in Taoyuan, which can then whiz you off to Taipei in 25 minutes. From Taipei to Taoyuan station the HSR fare is NT160. From the airport to the station by bus costs NT20. Buses run every 20 minutes. However, because trains were not that frequent at the time of writing, this was not the best way to travel to Taipei except during rush hour when buses were slowed by traffic.

Taxis from the airport to downtown Taipei will cost around NT1200, and NT1000 going the opposite direction.

See p274 and p214 for details on transport to/from the airports at Kaohsiung and Taichung.

Note that the domestic terminal is nowhere near the international. If you want to fly within Taiwan you need to go to Songshan Airport in Taipei (see p347), about an hour away by bus.

INSURANCE

Please see p337 for guidelines on purchasing travel insurance.

AIRLINES FLYING TO & FROM TAIWAN

If the names of the airlines listed below sound familiar but not quite right, there's a reason. Owing to agreements with China, many large international carriers operate flights to Taiwan under different names. For example, All Nippon Airways becomes Air Nippon.

Taiwan has two major international airlines: China Airlines and Eva Air. While Eva Air started operation in 1991 and has had no fatalities to date, the same cannot be said of China Airlines, which is somewhat infamous for its safety record. However, incidents so far this decade have been far fewer than in the '90s; officials credit this to new training practices (with pilots training at US flight schools) and a new corporate culture.

Air Macau (NX; ☎ Taipei 02-2717 0377, Kaohsiung 07-251 0860, TPE airport 03-398 3121; www.airmacau.com.tw/default.asp; hub Macau)

Air New Zealand (NZ; ☎ Taipei 02-2567 8950, TPE airport 03-398 3018; www.airnz.co.nz; hub Auckland)

Air Nippon (EL; ☎ Taipei 02-2501 7299, Kaohsiung 07-330 9019, TPE airport 03-351 6805; www.ana.co.jp; hub Tokyo)

Ankor Airways (G6; ☎ Taipei 02-2504 6522, TPE airport 03-398 3968; www.angkorairways.com; hub Phnom Penh)

Asiana Airlines (OZ; ☎ Taipei 02-2581 4000, TPE airport 03-398 6010; www.flyasiana.com; hub Seoul)

Cathay Pacific Airways (CX; ☎ Taipei 02-2715 2333, TPE airport 03-398 2501; www.cathaypacific.com; hub Hong Kong)

China Airlines (CI; ☎ Taipei 02-2715 1212, Kaohsiung 07-282 6141, TPE airport 03-398 8888; www.china-airlines.com; hub Taipei)

Continental Airlines (CO; ☎ Taipei 02-2719 5947, TPE airport 03-398 2404; www.continental.com; hubs Newark, Houston)

Dragon Airlines (KA; ☎ Taipei 02-2518 2700, Kaohsiung 07-201 3166, TPE airport 03-351 6805; www.dragonair.com; hub Hong Kong)

Eva Air (BR; ☎ Taipei 02-2501 1999, Kaohsiung 07-337 1199, CKS airport 03-351 6805; www.evaair.com; hub Taipei)

Far Eastern Air Transport (EF; ☎ Taipei 02-4066 6789, Kaohsiung 07-801 2311, TPE airport 03-398 3170; www.fat.com.tw; hub Taipei)

Japan Asia Airways (EG; ☎ 0800-065 151, TPE airport 03-398 2282, Kaohsiung 07-237 4101; www.jal.co.jp; hub Tokyo)

Jetstar Asia Airways (3K; ☎ Taipei 02-8176 2288, TPE airport 03-398 8888; www.jetstar.com/sg/index.html; hub Singapore)

KLM Royal Dutch Airlines (KL; ☎ Taipei 02-2711 4055, TPE airport 03-398 2769; www.klm.com; hub Amsterdam)

Korean Air (KE; ☎ Taipei 02-2518 2000, TPE airport 03-383 3248; www.koreanair.com; hub Seoul)

Malaysia Airlines (MH; ☎ Taipei 02-2514 7888, TPE airport 03-398 2521; www.malaysiaairlines.com; hub Kuala Lumpur)

Mandarin Airlines (AE; ☎ Taipei 02-2717 1230, TPE airport 03-398 2620; www.mandarin-airlines.com; hub Taipei)

Northwest Airlines (NW; ☎ Taipei 02-2772 2188, TPE airport 03-398 2471; www.nwa.com; hub Detroit)

Pacific Airlines (BL; ☎ Taipei 02-2543 1860, Kaohsiung 07-338 1183, TPE airport 03-398 2404; www.pacificairlines.com.vn; hub Ho Chi Minh City)

Palau Trans Pacific Airlines (GP; ☎ Taipei 02-3393 5388, TPE airport 03-398 3170; hub Koror, Palau)

Philippine Airlines (PR; ☎ Taipei 02-2506 7255, TPE airport 03-398 2419; www.philippineairlines.com; hub Manila)

Qantas Airways Limited (QF; ☎ Taipei 02-2559 0508, Kaohsiung 07-566 6516; www.qantas.com.au/international/tw/index.html; hub Sydney)

Singapore Airlines (SQ; ☎ Taipei 02-2551 6655, TPE airport 03-398 3988; www.singaporeair.com; hub Singapore)

Thai Airways (TG; ☎ Taipei 02-2509 6800, Kaohsiung 07-215 5871, TPE airport 03-383 4131; www.thaiair.com; hub Bangkok)

TransAsia Airways (GE; ☎ Taipei 02-449 8123, Kaohsiung 07-805 7861, TPE airport 03-398 2404; www.tna.com.tw; hub Taipei)

UNI Airways (B7; ☎ Taipei 02-2518 2626, Kaohsiung 07-791 7977, TPE airport 03-351 6805; www.uniair.com.tw; hub Taipei)

United Airlines (UA; ☎ Taipei 02-2325 8868, Kaohsiung 07-273 5544, TPE airport 03-398 2781; www.united.com; hub Chicago)

Vietnam Airlines (VN; ☎ Taipei 02-2517 7177, Kaohsiung 07-227 0209, TPE airport 03-398 3026; www.vietnamair.com; hubs Hanoi, Ho Chi Minh City)

Baggage Transport

If you don't feel like dragging your luggage between TPE airport and central Taipei, **Pinoy Express** (☎ Taipei 02-2591 0888, TPE airport 03-

---

THINGS CHANGE...

The information in this chapter is particularly vulnerable to change. Check directly with the airline or a travel agent to make sure you understand how a fare (and ticket you may buy) works and be aware of the security requirements for international travel. Shop carefully. The details given in this chapter should be regarded as pointers and are not a substitute for your own careful, up-to-date research.

398 3652; 294-2 Chungqing N Rd, Taipei; ☻ 6am-11.30pm) can transport it for you. Same-day service is available if the bags arrive before 10pm at the Pinoy Express counter (in the arrival hall of each terminal). To arrange pick-up of luggage from your hotel or residence in Taipei, ring Pinoy Express one day in advance.

One-way rates to/from central Taipei are NT340 for the first bag (up to 20kg) and NT300 for each additional bag. Cash only.

GETTING AROUND

AIR

TPE airport is for international flights only, so passengers flying into Taipei and transferring elsewhere within Taiwan will have to travel to **Songshan Airport** (TSA; www.tsa.gov.tw). It's north of central Taipei, but the city has pretty much engulfed it in recent decades.

Considering that Taiwan is such a small island, Songshan Airport is a very busy place. Four domestic-based carriers cover the country from about 7am until 10pm, with an average of about one takeoff or landing every three minutes. Destinations served include Hualien, Kaohsiung, Kinmen, Penghu, Taichung, Tainan and Taitung.

Songshan Airport facilities include a bank (with foreign currency exchange), a post office, food shops and restaurants, free wireless and a **tourist information counter** (☎ 02-2546 4741; ☻ 8am-8pm). Small/large coin-operated lockers cost NT80/120 per 24 hours and have a six-day limit.

From Taipei's main train station take bus 275 or 262. A taxi will cost around NT200.

AIRLINES IN TAIWAN

Daily Air Corporation (☎ 02-2712 3995; www.dailyair.com.tw)

Far Eastern Air Transport (☎ 02-2715 1921; www.fat.com.tw)

Mandarin Airlines (☎ 02-2717 1230; www .mandarin-airlines.com) China Airlines affiliate.

TransAsia Airways (☎ 02-2972 4599; www .tna.com.tw)

UNI Air (☎ 07-801 0189; www.uniair.com.tw) Eva Air affiliate.

DOMESTIC AIR FARES

Map shows major routes with one-way economy air fares in NT. Note that these air fares are subject to change.

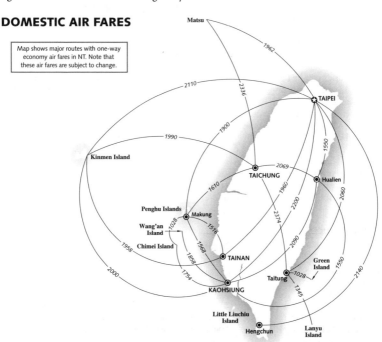

TRANSPORT

CLIMATE CHANGE & TRAVEL

Climate change is a serious threat to the ecosystems that humans rely upon, and air travel is the fastest-growing contributor to the problem. Lonely Planet regards travel, overall, as a global benefit, but believes we all have a responsibility to limit our personal impact on global warming.

Flying & climate change

Pretty much every form of motorised travel generates CO2 (the main cause of human-induced climate change) but planes are far and away the worst offenders, not just because of the sheer distances they allow us to travel, but because they release greenhouse gases high into the atmosphere. The statistics are frightening: two people taking a return flight between Europe and the US will contribute as much to climate change as an average household's gas and electricity consumption over a whole year.

Carbon offset schemes

Climatecare.org and other websites use 'carbon calculators' that allow travellers to offset the level of greenhouse gases they are responsible for with financial contributions to sustainable travel schemes that reduce global warming – including projects in India, Honduras, Kazakhstan and Uganda.

Lonely Planet, together with Rough Guides and other concerned partners in the travel industry, support the carbon offset scheme run by climatecare.org. Lonely Planet offsets all of its staff and author travel.

For more information check out our website: www.lonelyplanet.com.

Several buses an hour make the run to/from TPE airport (average fare NT125, 60 minutes).

Although Songshan is the hub and most other destinations on the island are the spokes, the airports at Taichung, Tainan and particularly Kaohsiung also serve multiple destinations. Because of weather, flights to Taiwan's islands can be hair-raising.

At smaller airports around Taiwan you'll usually find a visitor centre or information desk (sometimes with English speaking staff), banking or ATM services, and a post office or DIY postal service.

BICYCLE

We don't recommend biking as your usual means of transportation. Traffic in the cities is too intense and the air quality at road level is not good. Biking is recommended down the east coast of Hualien and also in other rural areas. See p329 for more.

BOAT

There is regular ferry service between Taiwan and its outlying islands (although in recent years air transport has become more popular). It's a cheaper way to travel but some routes could make a Navy SEAL vomit. And if the weather doesn't cooperate, forget it: you're not going anywhere.

See the regional chapters for details of schedules and prices. See also the 'Ferry Services' boxed text (below).

BUS

While Taiwan has a long-established system of private bus companies, competition in recent

---

FERRY SERVICES

Route	Operator	Contact
Fugang (Taitung)–Lanyu & Green Islands	Jiou-Xin Ferry	☎ 089-320 413, various others
Kaohsiung–Kinmen	Kaohsiung Harbour	☎ 07-521 6206
Kinmen		☎ 082-329 988
Kaohsiung–Makung	Taiwan Hangye Company	☎ 07-561 3866 (Kaohsiung)
		☎ 06-926 4087 (Makung)
Putai (near Chiayi)–Makung	Makung Tomorrow Star	☎ 06-926 0666 (Makung)
Donggang–Little Liuchiu Island	Donggang–Liuchiu Route Ferry	☎ 07-551 1373

BUS COMPANIES

Company	Contact
Aloha Bus	☎ 02-2550 8488; www.aloha168.com.tw
Kuo Kuang Hao	☎ 02-2311 9893; www.kingbus.com.tw
UBus	☎ 0800-241 560; www.ubus.com.tw

Sample bus costs and journey times from Taipei on Kuo Kuang Hao:

Destination	Price (NT) & Frequency	Duration (Hr)
Taichung	230 Mon-Fri, 260 Sat & Sun	2½
Tainan	310 Mon-Fri, 450 Sat & Sun	4
Kaohsiung	370 Mon-Fri, 450 Sat & Sun	5
Sun Moon Lake	390 Mon-Fri, 465 Sat & Sun	4½
Alishan	620 daily	6

years from trains, planes and automobiles has brought down the number of people using them, especially on rural routes. Between major cities you'll never have to wait more than an hour for a bus, but congestion is a problem on the highways, and that five-hour trip to Kaohsiung could easily become seven hours, or even 10. On the positive side, buses are smoke-free and quite comfortable. The more pricey intercity buses have airplane-like seats and show movies. Buses along rural routes are more basic.

The main transit points are Taipei, Taichung and Kaohsiung. See regional chapters for individual routes and schedules and the contact numbers for local bus companies. For intercity travel we recommend Aloha, UBus and Kuo Kuang Hao. See also the 'Bus Companies' boxed text (above).

Reservations are advisable for weekend travel and especially during holidays. Note that some buses run 24 hours a day and fares can drop considerably from midnight to 6am.

CAR, MOTORCYCLE & SCOOTER

To reach certain choice areas and to get around once you're there, your own transport is advisable, and sometimes absolutely necessary: we've noted where in relevant chapters. Driving a car is not terribly difficult outside of the cities, especially on weekdays. Scooters are cheap to rent (average NT400 per day, but some as low as NT200), but not every place will let you rent one without a local licence. At the time of writing, you could rent scooters with just an International Driver's Licence in Hualien, Kenting, Chiayi, Tainan, Sun Moon Lake and Jiaoshi.

Wikipedia (http://en.wikipedia.org) has an excellent overview of Taiwan's road and highway system, which includes explanations of the numbering system. Go to the website and type 'highway system in Taiwan'.

Driving Licence

An International Driver's Licence (IDL; available in your home country) is valid in Taiwan for up to 30 days. After that you can apply for an IDL permit from a local Motor Vehicles Office. This is a simple procedure and validates the IDL for as long as it is valid (up to one year). You can do this every year if you can get someone back home to apply for a new IDL. This is much easier than going through the Taiwanese driver's test, which requires you, among other nonsensical manoeuvres, to go backwards in an S-shape.

If your country has a reciprocal agreement with Taiwan, you may be able to obtain a Taiwanese licence just by showing your home licence and passport. If not, and you really want a local licence you will have to take a written test as well as the 'practical' test on a closed course. Driving licences are issued by county. For an idea of what to expect, see the Taipei government's Motor Vehicles Office website (www.tcmvd.gov.tw).

Fuel & Spare Parts

Petrol stations are everywhere, as are garages to get parts and repairs for scooters and cars. Check out www.forumosa.com for a thread on reliable and trustworthy mechanics.

Hire

Car rental fees typically run between NT800 and NT1500 for a half day, or NT1500 and

TRANSPORT

ROAD DISTANCES (KM)

	Chiayi	Hsinchu	Hualien	Ilan	Kaohsiung	Keelung	Kenting	Taichung	Tainan	Taipei	Taitung	Taoyuan
Chiayi	---											
Hsinchu	169	---										
Hualien	339	240	---									
Ilan	270	101	139	---								
Kaohsiung	103	272	337	373	---							
Keelung	264	95	185	46	367	---						
Kenting	203	372	306	473	100	467	---					
Taichung	86	83	253	184	189	178	289	---				
Tainan	63	232	373	333	40	327	140	149	---			
Taipei	239	70	170	31	342	25	442	153	302	---		
Taitung	272	407	167	306	170	352	132	348	210	337	---	
Taoyuan	215	46	194	55	318	49	418	129	278	24	361	---

NT2800 for a full day, depending on the type of vehicle and rental company. Typical long-term discounts are 10% for three to seven days, 20% for eight to 20 days and 30% for longer. Ask if there is a limit to the number of kilometres you can drive. All airports have car rental agencies (or else they do free delivery), as do most of the High-Speed Rail stations. You can also check with local tourist information offices for rental agencies in your area. The following are two possibilities:

Central Auto (☎ 02-2828 0033; www.rentalcar.com.tw) Long-running foreign-managed rental company with Taipei, Taichung and Kaohsiung branches. Good reputation.
Hertz (☎ 02-2731 0377; www.hertz.com) Many branches islandwide.

Insurance
Insurance laws were modified in 2007 but at the time of writing it wasn't clear how this would play out in rental businesses. Many agency staff members seemed unaware of any changes. At the time of writing, the best deal we could find was decent third-party liability insurance and the option of buying comprehensive insurance with a NT10,000 deduction for damages. In the case of theft or loss, the renter would also be charged 10% of the value of the car. Not the best, but much better than years ago when you essentially were uninsured despite what rental companies might have told you.

Road Conditions
It's not advisable to drive in Taipei or any other large or medium-sized city until you get used to the way people drive. In the countryside, it's not much different from driving in the West, but be on the lookout for drunk drivers at night. Seriously consider renting a car or scooter (or even a bicycle) when you visit, as you'll really be missing out on a lot of the best this country has to offer if you rely exclusively on public transportation.

Road Rules
By the standards of your home country, driving in Taiwan might seem just a little out of hand. The Taiwanese drive on the right-hand side of the road, although at times you'd be hard-pressed to tell! Taipei drivers are the best of the lot, Taichung are probably the worst.

As for the rules, right turns on red lights are not allowed. Passengers in the back seats must buckle up and children under four (and 18kg) must be secured in safety seats. Violators face fines of NT1500 (NT3000 to NT6000 on highways). Front-seat passengers are also required to wear seat belts.

HITCHING

Hitching is never entirely safe in any country in the world, and we don't recommend it. Travellers who do decide to hitch should understand that they are taking a small but potentially serious risk. If you do choose to hitch you will be safer if you travel in pairs and let someone know where you are planning to go.

LOCAL TRANSPORT

Bus

Outside of Taipei, buses are the only public transport option in the big cities. It used to be difficult to catch a bus outside Taipei, but now most buses have signs in English at the front. You can usually find complete bus schedule information at the visitor centre in town (often right inside the train station). Take advantage of this. In smaller towns it's easier just to walk than bother with sporadic bus services.

It doesn't usually matter whether you enter at the front or the back, but be aware that sometimes you pay when you get on and sometimes when you get off (and if you cross a zone you pay when you get on and again later when you get off). Just follow the passengers ahead of you or look for the characters 上 or 下 on the screen to the left of the driver. 上 means pay when you get on (pretend the character points up to tell you to pay when you step up on the bus). 下 means pay when you get off (pretend the character points down to tell you to pay when you get down off the bus). If you make a mistake the driver will let you know.

Fares vary by city. The fare within a single zone in Taipei is NT15, in Kaohsiung NT12. The fare for riding within two zones is always double the one-zone fare.

Metro

Taipei's MRT (Mass Rapid Transit) has made a huge difference to the city's environment, traffic, cleanliness and general culture (see p124). Kaohsiung's system should be ready by the end of 2008.

Taxi

In the large cities, taxi rates are NT70 for the first 1.5km or portion thereof. After that, it's NT5 per 300m, or per two minutes of waiting time (for example, at traffic lights or if you're caught in traffic). The waiting time is cumulative – taxi meters are fitted with timers. Fares are surcharged approximately 20% after midnight. Surcharges may also apply for things such as luggage and reserving a cab (as opposed to hailing one).

In the big cities, taxis are everywhere and you hardly need to bother calling for one except for safety concerns (all calls are recorded and saved for one month). In smaller cities it's a good idea to get your hotel to call first, then keep the driver's number for subsequent rides. In Taipei, call the taxi hotline on ☎ 0800-055 850 to find a particular company or call ☎ 02-2799 4818 for English-, Japanese-, Cantonese- and even Spanish-speaking drivers.

TOURS

Taiwan Tour Bus (☎ 0800-011 765; www.taiwantourbus.com.tw/) is organised by the tourism bureau and has easy-to-understand half-day and full-day itineraries. Buses depart from train stations, airports and major hotels. See the website or pick up the booklet *Taiwan Tour Bus: Route Handbook* at any visitor centre. Tours range in price from NT600 to NT2000.

Green Island Adventures (☎ 0972-065 479; www.greenislandadventures.com) has tours to Taiwan's outer islands and the mainland.

Taipei-based **Fresh Treks** (☎ 02-2700 6988; www.freshtreks.com) offers adventure tours around the island, including mountain climbing, river tracing and laser tag. Few tours are open to the public these days, however.

Edison Travel Service (☎ 02-2563 5313; www.edison.com.tw) has been around for a long time and can handle tours, flights, hotels and car rental.

WHICH WEB BROWSER TO USE?

As with many Taiwanese government websites, you may have problems using the interactive pages of the train website with a Firefox-based browser (such as Netscape). Opera and Microsoft Internet Explorer work fine for this and every other site we have tried.

TRAIN

The Taiwan Railway Administration (TRA) operates trains on two main lines. Major stops on the Western Line include Pingdong, Kaohsiung, Taichung, Taipei and Keelung, while the Eastern Line runs from Shulin via Taipei and Hualien to Taitung. The Southern Link connects Kaohsiung and Taitung. There are also several small branch lines maintained for tourist purposes, including Pingxi (p144), Alishan (p241), Jiji (p220) and Neiwan (closed at the time of writing for the next several years). For detailed timetable and fare information, you can pick up the *Taiwan Railway Passenger Train Timetable* at train station info centres, kiosks or 7-Eleven stores, or visit http://new.twtraffic .com.tw/TWRail_en/index.aspx.

Express trains are reasonably comfortable and they all offer reserved seating and carts coming through the aisles offering boxed meals (such as they are). Snacks are available on platforms at many stations, and there are always shops and convenience stores nearby.

Most major cities now have visitor information centres inside or just outside the train station with English-speaking staff. They are usually open from 9am to 6pm and are a blessing for getting local bus, food and accommodation information.

Classes

There are different classes of service: Tze-Chiang (*Zìqiáng*) is the fastest and most comfortable; Chu-kuang (*jǔguāng*) and Fu-hsing (*fùxīng*) are slower and more ordinary. There are also the very cheap DRC and Ordinary Express trains that stop at all stations, have no reserved seating and usually no air-conditioning. Sometimes it's fun to take one of these along the east coast just to watch the scenery go by so slowly.

Reservations & Fares

For the fast trains, especially on weekends or holidays, it is advisable to buy your tickets up to two weeks in advance. You can book online but many people report problems with this on the English-language pages. By the time you read this you may be able to book at 7-Elevens.

HIGH-SPEED RAIL

Taiwan's **high-speed rail** (HSR or THSR; www.thsrc.com .tw) system started operations on 5 January 2007. At their fastest, trains reach speeds of 330km/h and can cover the 345km distance between Taipei and Kaohsiung in 90 minutes (though most trains take two hours with stops). The trains are beautiful works of engineering, and the ride itself is smooth, quiet and comfortable. The total cost of the project has been estimated at US$15 billion, most of which came from the public purse despite the HSR being billed as a BOT (build-operate-transfer; a form of financing for public projects in which a private company finances, designs and builds a project and is then allowed to operate it for profit for a certain number of years before it is returned to the public sector) project. Essentially, the government has paid for most of the project but still doesn't have ownership.

At the time of writing, eight stations had opened and there were trains about every hour. A regular ticket from Taipei Main Station (in the same building as the regular train station) to Kaohsiung (actually, to Zuoying station, as the final stop in downtown Kaohsiung hasn't opened yet) costs NT1490. Taipei to Taichung costs NT700. See the website for all fares.

You can buy tickets at the stations, either at machines or counters. The machines have had glitches since the beginning, so we tended to prefer the counters. By the time you read

TRAIN SERVICES

From	To	Duration (Hr)/Fare (NT, Tze-Chiang)	Duration (Hr)/Fare (NT, Fu-hsing)
Taipei	Hualien	2½/445	3½/343 (Chu-kuang)
Taipei	Kaohsiung	4½/845	7/544
Taipei	Tainan	3½/741	5¾/476
Kaohsiung	Taichung	2½/470	3/241
Hualien	Taitung	2½/355	3¼/273 (Chu-kuang)
Taichung	Taipei	2/375	3/241

this, the online booking system should be up and running.

At every station you'll find a visitor centre and English-speaking staff to help with transfers, hotel information and the like. You'll also find car rental and taxi services, hotel shuttles and buses or commuter trains to take you downtown when the station is outside the city centre. It's a really easy and convenient system and it's going to revolutionise travel in Taiwan (see the boxed text, p236).

For a personal take on the system, here's an article by one of the authors of this book: www.thingsasian.com/stories-photos/21126.

Health Dr Trish Batchelor

CONTENTS

Health issues and the quality of medical care vary significantly depending on whether you stay in Taipei or venture into rural areas.

Travellers tend to worry about contracting infectious diseases, but infections are a rare cause of serious illness or death while overseas. Pre-existing medical conditions, such as heart disease, and accidental injury (especially traffic accidents) account for most life-threatening problems. Becoming ill in some way, however, is relatively common. Fortunately most common illnesses can either be prevented with sensible behaviour or be treated easily with a well-stocked traveller's medical kit.

The following advice is a general guide only and does not replace the advice of a doctor trained in travel medicine.

BEFORE YOU GO

Pack medications in their original, clearly labelled containers. A signed and dated letter from your physician describing your medical conditions and regular medications (use generic names) is also a good idea. When carrying syringes or needles, be sure to have a physician's letter documenting their medical necessity. If you have a heart condition bring a copy of your ECG taken just prior to travelling.

If you take any regular medication bring double your needs in case of loss or theft. In Taiwan it may be difficult to find some of the newer drugs, particularly the latest antidepressant drugs, blood-pressure medications and contraceptive pills.

INSURANCE

Even if you are fit and healthy, don't travel without health insurance – accidents do happen. Declare any existing medical conditions you have – the insurance company *will* check if your problem is pre-existing and will not cover you if it is undeclared. You may require extra cover for adventure activities. If your health insurance doesn't cover you for medical expenses abroad, consider getting extra insurance – check lonelyplanet.com) for more information. If you're uninsured, emergency evacuation is expensive; bills of over US$100,000 are not uncommon.

Find out in advance if your insurance plan will make payments directly to providers or reimburse you later for overseas health expenditures. Note that doctors in Taiwan expect payment in cash. Some policies offer lower and higher medical-expense options; the higher ones are chiefly for countries that have extremely high medical costs. These include places such as the USA. You may prefer a policy that pays doctors or hospitals directly rather than you having to pay on the spot and claim later. If you have to claim later, make sure you keep all documentation and receipts. Some policies require you to call (reverse charges) a centre in your home country where an immediate assessment of your problem is made.

RECOMMENDED VACCINATIONS

Specialised travel-medicine clinics are your best source of information: they stock all available vaccines and will be able to give specific recommendations for you and your trip. The doctors will take into account factors such as past vaccination history, the length of your trip, activities you may be undertaking and underlying medical conditions, such as pregnancy.

Most vaccines don't produce immunity until at least two weeks after they're given, so visit a doctor four to eight weeks before departure. Ask for an International Certificate of Vaccination (otherwise known as the yellow booklet), which will list all the vaccinations you've received.

MEDICAL CHECKLIST

Recommended items for a personal medical kit:

- Antifungal cream (eg Clotrimazole)
- Antibacterial cream (eg Muciprocin)
- Antibiotics if you are visiting rural areas; one for skin infections (eg Amoxicillin/Clavulanate or Cephalexin) and another for diarrhoea (eg Norfloxacin or Ciprofloxacin)
- Antihistamine – there are many options (eg Cetrizine for daytime and Promethazine for night)
- Antiseptic (eg Betadine)*
- Antispasmodic for stomach cramps (eg Buscopan)
- Contraceptive method
- Decongestant (eg Pseudoephedrine)*
- DEET-based insect repellent
- Diarrhoea – consider an oral rehydration solution (eg Gastrolyte), diarrhoea 'stopper' (eg Loperamide) and an antinausea medication (eg Prochlorperazine)*
- First-aid items such as scissors, elastoplasts, bandages, gauze, thermometer (but not mercury), sterile needles and syringes, safety pins and tweezers*
- Anti-inflammatory (eg Ibuprofen)
- Indigestion tablets (eg Quick Eze or Mylanta)
- Iodine tablets (unless you are pregnant or have a thyroid problem) to purify water
- Laxative (eg Coloxyl)
- Migraine medicine – sufferers should take their personal medicine
- Paracetamol*
- Permethrin to impregnate clothing and mosquito nets
- Steroid cream for allergic/itchy rashes (eg 1% to 2% hydrocortisone)
- Sunscreen and a hat
- Throat lozenges*
- Thrush (vaginal yeast infection) treatment (eg Clotrimazole pessaries or Diflucan tablet)
- Ural or an equivalent if prone to urine infections

* Indicates most commonly used items by travellers.

INTERNET RESOURCES

There is a wealth of travel health advice available on the Internet. For further information, **Lonely Planet** (www.lonelyplanet.com) is a good place to visit for starters. The **World Health Organization** (WHO; www.who.int/ith) publishes a superb book called *International Travel & Health,* which is revised annually and is available online at no cost. Another website of general interest for up-to-the minute information is **MD Travel Health** (www.mdtravelhealth.com), which provides complete travel-health recommendations for every country and is revised daily. The **Centers for Disease Control and Prevention** (CDC; www.cdc.gov) website also has good general information.

FURTHER READING

To begin with, pick up a copy of Lonely Planet's *Healthy Travel Asia & India.* Other recommended references include *Traveller's Health* by Dr Richard Dawood and *Travelling Well* by Dr Deborah Mills – have a look at the website (www.travellingwell.com.au).

IN TRANSIT

DEEP VEIN THROMBOSIS (DVT)

Deep vein thrombosis (DVT) occurs when blood clots form in the legs during plane flights, chiefly because of prolonged immobility. The longer the flight, the greater the risk. Though most of the time these blood clots are reabsorbed uneventfully, it is possible for some to break off and travel through the blood vessels to the lungs, where they may cause life-threatening complications.

The chief symptom of deep vein thrombosis is swelling or pain of the foot, ankle or calf. This usually (but not always) occurs on just one side of the body. When a blood clot travels to the lungs, it may cause chest pain and breathing difficulties. Travellers with any of these symptoms should seek medical attention as soon as possible. To prevent the development of DVT on long flights you should make sure you walk around the cabin, perform isometric compressions of the leg muscles (ie contract and relax the leg muscles while sitting), drink plenty of fluids and avoid alcohol and tobacco.

HEALTH

JET LAG & MOTION SICKNESS

Jet lag is most common when crossing more than five time zones; it results in insomnia, fatigue, malaise or nausea. To avoid jet lag try drinking plenty of fluids (nonalcoholic) and eating only light meals. Once you have arrived at your destination, seek exposure to natural sunlight and readjust your schedule (for meals, sleep etc) as soon as possible.

Antihistamines such as dimenhydrinate (Dramamine), prochlorperazine (Phenergan) and meclizine (Antivert, Bonine) are usually the first choice for the treatment of motion sickness. Their main side effect is drowsiness. A herbal alternative is ginger, which works like a charm for some people.

IN TAIWAN

AVAILABILITY & COST OF HEALTH CARE

Taiwan is a relatively well-developed country and the quality of medical care reflects this. In Taipei the quality is high, however in rural areas you cannot expect to find Western standards of care.

A recommended hospital in Taipei is the **Adventist Hospital** (Map p96; ☎ 2771 8151; 424 Bade Rd, sec.2); it has English-speaking staff.

INFECTIOUS DISEASES
Dengue Fever

This mosquito-borne disease is becomingly increasingly problematic in Taiwan in both cities and rural areas. It can only be prevented by avoiding mosquito bites – there is no vaccine. The mosquito that carries dengue bites day and night, so try to avoid bites at all times Symptoms include high fever, severe headache and body ache (previously Dengue was known as 'break bone fever'). Some people develop a rash and diarrhoea. There is no specific treatment, just rest and paracetamol. Do not

take aspirin, and see a doctor to be diagnosed and monitored.

Hepatitis A

A problem throughout the country, this food- and water-borne virus infects the liver, causing jaundice (yellow skin and eyes), nausea and lethargy. There is no specific treatment for hepatitis A; you just need to allow time for the liver to heal. All travellers to Taiwan should be vaccinated against hepatitis A.

Hepatitis B

The only sexually transmitted disease that can be prevented by vaccination, hepatitis B is spread by body fluids, including sexual contact. People who have hepatitis B usually are unaware they are carriers. The long-term consequences can include liver cancer and cirrhosis.

HIV

HIV is also spread by body fluids. Avoid unsafe sex, sharing needles, invasive cosmetic procedures such as tattooing and needles that have not been sterilised in a medical setting. HIV rates in Taiwan remain low by Asian standards, although infection via contaminated-needle use is increasing. However, transmission is mainly via sexual contact in Taiwan.

Influenza

Influenza is transmitted between November and April. Symptoms include high fever, muscle aches, runny nose, cough and sore throat. It can be very severe in people over the age of 65 or in those with underlying medical conditions such as heart disease or diabetes – vaccination is recommended for these individuals. There is no specific treatment, just rest and paracetamol.

Japanese B Encephalitis

This viral disease is transmitted by mosquitoes, but is rare in travellers. The transmission season runs from June to October. Risk exists in all areas except the central mountains. Vaccination is recommended for travellers spending more than one month outside of cities. There is no treatment, and a third of infected people will die, while another third will suffer permanent brain damage. However, as mentioned earlier, this is a rare disease.

HEALTH ADVISORIES

It's usually a good idea to consult your government's travel-health website before departure, if one is available.
Australia (www.dfat.gov.au/travel)
Canada (www.travelhealth.gc.ca)
New Zealand (www.mfat.govt.nz/travel)
UK (www.doh.gov.uk/traveladvice)
USA (www.cdc.gov/travel)

REQUIRED VACCINATIONS

Yellow Fever Proof of vaccination is required if entering Taiwan within six days of visiting an infected country. If you are travelling to Taiwan from Africa or South America check with a travel-medicine clinic whether you need the vaccine.

RECOMMENDED VACCINATIONS

The World Health Organization (WHO) recommends the following vaccinations for travellers to Taiwan.

Adult diphtheria & tetanus Single booster recommended every 10 years. Side effects include sore arm and fever.

Hepatitis A Provides almost 100% protection for up to a year, a booster after 12 months provides at least another 20 years protection. Mild side effects such as headache and sore arm occur in 5% to 10% of people.

Hepatitis B Now considered routine for most travellers. Given as three shots over six months. A rapid schedule is also available, as is a combined vaccination with Hepatitis A. Side effects are mild and uncommon, usually headache and sore arm. In 95% of people three shots results in lifetime protection.

Measles, mumps & rubella Two doses of MMR required unless you have had the diseases. Occasionally a rash and flu-like illness can occur a week after receiving the vaccine. Many young adults require a booster.

Typhoid Recommended unless your trip is less than two weeks and only in Taipei. The vaccine offers around 70% protection, lasts for two to three years and comes as a single shot. Tablets are also available, however the injection is usually recommended as it has fewer side effects. Sore arm and fever may occur. Travellers should get vaccinated before they get to Taiwan.

Varicella If you haven't had chickenpox, discuss this vaccination with your doctor.

The following immunisations are recommended for long-term travellers (more than one month) or those at special risk.

Influenza A single injection lasts for two months. Recommended for all travellers over 65 years of age and those with underlying medical conditions such as heart disease, lung disease, diabetes or a compromised immune system.

Japanese B encephalitis Three injections in all. Booster recommended after two years. Sore arm and headache are the most common side effects. Occasionally an allergic reaction comprising hives and swelling can occur up to 10 days after any of the three doses.

Pneumonia A single injection lasts five years. Recommended as per the flu vaccine.

Tuberculosis A complex issue. Adult long-term travellers are usually recommended to have a TB skin test before and after travel, rather than vaccination. Only one vaccine given in a lifetime.

Lyme Disease

This tick-borne disease occurs in summer. Symptoms include an early rash and general viral symptoms, followed weeks to months later by joint, heart or neurological problems. Prevent this disease by using general insect-avoidance measures and checking yourself for ticks after walking in forest areas. Treatment is with Doxycycline.

SARS

In mid-March 2003 the world's attention was drawn to the outbreak of an apparently new and serious respiratory illness that subsequently became known as SARS. At the time of writing SARS appears to have been brought under control. Since the outbreak commenced, 8500 cases were confirmed, resulting in 800 deaths. The peak of disease activity was in early May 2003, when over 200 new cases were being reported daily in Asia. Taiwan had a significant number of cases of SARS.

STDs

Sexually transmitted diseases are common throughout the world, and the most common include herpes, warts, syphilis, gonorrhoea and chlamydia. People carrying these diseases often have no signs of infection. Condoms will prevent gonorrhoea and chlamydia but not warts or herpes. If after a sexual encounter you develop any rash, lumps, discharge or pain when passing urine seek immediate medical attention. If you have been sexually active during your travels, have an STD check on your return home.

Tuberculosis

Taiwan has a high rate of tuberculosis (TB) infection. While rare in travellers, precautions should be taken by medical and aid workers and long-term travellers who have significant contact with the local population. Vaccination is usually only given to children under the age of five, but adults at risk are recommended

---

DRINKING WATER

- Never drink tap water.
- Bottled water is generally safe – check the seal is intact at purchase.
- Avoid ice.
- Avoid fresh juices – they may have been watered down.
- Boiling water is the most efficient method of purifying it.
- The best chemical purifier is iodine. However, it should not be used by pregnant women or those with thyroid problems.
- Water filters should also filter out viruses. Ensure your filter has a chemical barrier such as iodine and a small pore size (less than four microns).

---

pre- and post-travel TB testing. The main symptoms are fever, cough, weight loss, night sweats and tiredness.

Typhoid

This bacterial infection is spread via food and water. It gives a high and slowly worsening fever and headache, and may be accompanied by a dry cough and stomach pain. It is diagnosed by blood tests and treated with antibiotics. Though contracting typhoid is rare, vaccination is recommended for all travellers spending more than two weeks in Taiwan and travelling outside of Taipei. Be aware that vaccination is not 100% effective so you must still be careful with what you eat and drink.

TRAVELLER'S DIARRHOEA

Traveller's diarrhoea is the most common problem affecting travellers – between 10% and 30% of people visiting Taiwan will suffer from it. In the majority of cases, traveller's diarrhoea is caused by a bacteria (there are numerous potential culprits), and therefore responds promptly to treatment with antibiotics. Treatment with antibiotics will depend on your situation – how sick you are, how quickly you need to get better, where you are etc.

Traveller's diarrhoea is defined as the passage of more than three watery bowel-actions within 24 hours, plus at least one other symptom such as fever, cramps, nausea, vomiting or feeling generally unwell.

Treatment consists of staying well hydrated: rehydration solutions such as Gastrolyte are the best for this. Antibiotics such as Norfloxacin, Ciprofloxacin or Azithromycin will kill the bacteria quickly.

Loperamide is just a 'stopper' and doesn't get to the cause of the problem. It can be helpful, for example, if you have to go on a long bus ride. Don't take Loperamide if you have a fever or blood in your stools. Seek medical attention quickly if you do not respond to an appropriate antibiotic.

Eating in restaurants is the biggest risk factor for contracting traveller's diarrhoea. Eat only freshly cooked food and avoid shellfish and food that has been sitting around in buffets. Peel all fruit, cook vegetables and soak salads in iodine water for at least 20 minutes. Eat in busy restaurants with a high turnover of customers.

Giardiasis

Giardia is a common parasite in travellers. Symptoms include nausea, bloating, excess gas, 'eggy' burps, fatigue and intermittent diarrhoea. The parasite will eventually go away if left untreated but this can take months. The treatment of choice is Tinidazole, with Metronidazole being a second-line option. Giardia is not common in Taiwan.

ENVIRONMENTAL HAZARDS
Air Pollution

Air pollution, particularly vehicle pollution, is a severe problem in Taipei. If you have severe respiratory problems speak with your doctor before travelling to any heavily polluted urban centres. This pollution also causes minor respiratory problems such as sinusitis, dry throat and irritated eyes. If you are troubled by the pollution, avoid downtown during busy hours and visit the suburbs instead. The air is much better in the early morning and at night.

Insect Bites & Stings

Insects are not a major issue in Taiwan, though there are some insect-borne diseases present.

Ticks can be contracted from walking in rural areas. They are commonly found behind the ears, on the belly and in armpits. If you have had a tick bite and experience symptoms such as a rash at the site of the bite or elsewhere, or fever or muscle aches, you should see a doctor. Doxycycline prevents and treats tick-borne diseases.

Bee and wasp stings mainly cause problems for people who are allergic to them. Anyone with a serious bee or wasp allergy should carry an injection of adrenaline (eg an Epipen) for emergency treatment. For other people, pain is the main problem; apply ice to the sting and take painkillers if necessary. There are warning signs over problem areas. Please heed them as some wasps in Taiwan are known to be deadly.

Parasites

There are a number of flukes (liver, lung and intestinal) that can be contracted by eating raw or undercooked seafood, meat and vegetables in Taiwan. Such dishes should be avoided unless eating in a top-class restaurant.

Skin Problems

Cuts and scratches can become easily infected when travelling. Take meticulous care of any cuts and scratches to prevent complications such as abscesses. Immediately wash all wounds in clean water and apply antiseptic. If you develop signs of infection (increasing pain and redness) see a doctor.

Rashes can often be very difficult to diagnose, even for doctors. If you develop a rash you should seek medical advice as soon as possible.

WOMEN'S HEALTH

In most well-developed areas of Taiwan, supplies of sanitary products are readily available. Birth-control options may be limited so bring supplies of your own contraception.

Heat, humidity and antibiotics can all contribute to thrush. Treatment is with antifungal creams and pessaries such as Clotrimazole. A practical alternative is a single tablet of fluconazole (Diflucan). Urinary tract infections can be precipitated by dehydration or long bus journeys without toilet stops: it's best to bring suitable antibiotics.

Pregnant women should receive specialised advice before travelling. The ideal time to travel is in the second trimester (between 16 and 28 weeks), when the risk of pregnancy-related problems are at their lowest and pregnant women generally feel at their best. During the first trimester there is a risk of miscarriage and in the third trimester complications such as premature labour and high blood pressure are possible. It's wise to travel with a companion. Always carry a list of quality medical facilities available at your destination and ensure you continue your standard antenatal care at these facilities. Avoid rural travel in areas with poor medical facilities and transport. Most of all, ensure travel insurance covers all pregnancy-related possibilities, including premature labour.

Traveller's diarrhoea can quickly lead to dehydration and result in inadequate blood flow to the placenta. Many of the drugs used to treat various diarrhoea bugs are not recommended in pregnancy. However azithromycin is considered safe.

TRADITIONAL & FOLK MEDICINE

Traditional Chinese Medicine (TCM) remains very popular in Taiwan. TCM views the human body as an energy system in which the basic substances of *chi* (*qì*; vital energy), *jing* (essence), blood (the body's nourishing fluids)

INSECT AVOIDANCE

Travellers are advised to prevent mosquito bites at all times by following these suggestions:

■ Use a DEET-containing insect repellent on exposed skin. Wash this off at night as long as you are sleeping under a mosquito net. Natural repellents such as citronella can be effective, but must be applied more frequently.

■ Sleep under a mosquito net that has been impregnated with permethrin.

■ Accommodation should have screens and fans if not air-conditioned.

■ Impregnate clothing with permethrin in high-risk areas.

■ Wear light-coloured long sleeves and pants.

■ Use mosquito coils.

■ Spray your room with insect repellent before going out for your evening meal.

and body fluids (other organic fluids) function. The concept of yin and yang is fundamental to the system. Disharmony between yin and yang or within the basic substances may be a result of internal causes (emotions), external causes (climatic conditions) or miscellaneous causes (work, exercise, sex etc). Treatment modalities include acupuncture, massage, herbs, dietary modification and *qijong* (the skill of attracting positive energy) and aim to bring these elements back into balance. These therapies are particularly useful for treating chronic diseases and are gaining interest and respect in the Western medical system. Conditions that can be particularly suitable for traditional methods include chronic fatigue, arthritis, irritable bowel syndrome and some chronic skin conditions.

Be aware that 'natural' doesn't always mean 'safe', and there can be drug interactions between herbal medicines and Western medicines. If you are using both systems, ensure you inform both practitioners what the other has prescribed.

Language

CONTENTS

After the Kuomintang (KMT; Nationalist Party) fled China for Taiwan in the late 1940s, it promoted Mandarin Chinese as the official language for the island. At the time, however, few Taiwanese could speak it. The main languages of Taiwan then were Hokkien, usually referred to as 'Taiwanese' (also called *Minnanhua*, a name that emphasises its roots in southeastern China, where it is also spoken), and Japanese. Hakka, another Chinese language, is also spoken in some areas, and Taiwan's aboriginal tribes have their own languages, which belong to a completely separate language family to Chinese.

Although Taiwanese is often referred to as a 'dialect' of Mandarin, the two are in fact separate languages and are not mutually intelligible. Relatively little has been written in Taiwanese beyond Christian religious material, due in part to the efforts by the authorities during the Japanese colonial era (1895–1945), and later by the KMT, to suppress the language. Despite these years of suppression, the Taiwanese language has endured, and today at least half the population prefers to speak Taiwanese at home, especially in the south and in rural areas. It's too soon to know whether the government's recent creation of a Hakka-language TV station will succeed in helping revive the use of Hakka.

Travellers to Taiwan can get by without having to even attempt any Taiwanese. Virtually all young and middle-aged people speak Mandarin. Many older people also know Japanese as a result of the 50-year Japanese occupation of Taiwan.

Although Taiwan's students are required to study English, few actually learn to speak it. As a result they tend to read and write English much better than they can speak it so if you need to communicate in English try writing your message down. The reason for this is that students learn English from textbooks, without any opportunity for conversation. Introductory English now begins in junior, rather than secondary school, and classes have begun to focus more on the spoken language. This shift is too recent to have had any noticeable effect on the proliferation of spoken English.

MANDARIN

TONES

Mandarin, Taiwanese and Hakka are all tonal languages – by altering the voice's pitch within a syllable, the meaning of a word is completely changed. Getting your tones wrong can have embarrassing consequences – *wǒ gǎnmào*, for example, means 'I've caught a cold', while *wǒ gàn māo* means 'I copulate with cats'! Mandarin has four tones, while some of the other Chinese languages have as many as nine. For example *ma*, has a number of meanings in Mandarin depending on which tone is used:

high tone	*mā*	'mother'
rising tone	*má*	'hemp' or 'numb'
falling-rising tone	*mǎ*	'horse'
falling tone	*mà*	'scold' or 'swear'

There is also a 'neutral' tone, which is usually not indicated by a tone mark.

Mastering tones is tricky for the untrained Western ear, but with discipline it can be done. Try practising the following tongue-twister: *Māma qí mǎ. Mǎ màn. Māma mà mǎ.* (Mother rides a horse. The horse is slow. Mother scolds the horse.)

Don't let yourself be discouraged by the language. Apart from the problem of tones, Mandarin is not especially difficult to master. Most people in Taiwan are very friendly and will praise your linguistic skills if you manage to say even a few words in one of the island's languages.

CHARACTERS

The greatest difficulty associated with the language is its written form: Chinese characters. To borrow from a Chinese proverb, it can take a lifetime and a little bit more to learn how to read and write Chinese. The reason for this is that, unlike most languages, written Chinese does not employ an alphabet. This has led many to the false conclusion that Chinese characters represent a system of 'idea-pictures' or ideograms; in reality, the vast majority of characters consist of a phonetic element and another element called the 'radical', which provides a semantic clue to the meaning.

Some dictionaries list more than 55,000 characters, but many of these entries are no longer used or they are variants. The 2400 most frequently used characters account for 99% of most texts. A further complication in learning to read Chinese is that some 20% of characters have more than one pronunciation.

The sounds represented by Chinese characters are each one syllable long, but few Mandarin words are monosyllabic. As a result, many characters cannot stand alone as words, much as the the prefix 'im-' in 'impossible' is a unit of meaning, but not a complete word in itself.

Taiwan doesn't use the system of 'simplified' characters that was progressively introduced in China after the communist takeover. Instead, Taiwan has retained the use of traditional characters, which are also found in Hong Kong and in many Chinese communities abroad.

ROMANISATION

Romanisation is the rendering of non-Roman alphabet languages, such as Arabic, Mandarin, Thai or Russian, into a form that can be read or spoken by anyone familiar with the Roman alphabet (ie a, b, c etc) and the sounds it represents. Contrary to popular belief, it is entirely possible to Romanise Mandarin, but travellers to Taiwan are unlikely to encounter much Romanisation other than for names of people, places and streets. Unfortunately, Taiwan's approach to Romanisation has been slapdash, resulting in the island's road signs and maps displaying a veritable Babel of Romanisation systems, and even outright misspellings. There are many tales of signs exhibiting a variety of spellings for the same street – even at the same intersection!

Further complicating the matter is the fact that, until recently, Taiwan tended to use the Wade-Giles Romanisation system, which most native English speakers find counterintuitive due to the use of apostrophes to represent phonetically related sounds (such as 'b' and 'p', written in Wade-Giles as **p** and **p′** respectively). This explains why English has the spelling *Taoism* for what would be represented in most other systems as *Daoism*. Although there are sound linguistic reasons for this approach, the problems for the uninitiated are obvious. To make matters worse, the apostrophes are often routinely omitted, making it impossible even for those few who are familiar with the Wade-Giles system to be able to read it reliably. Without the apostrophes, for example, what is written *Kuting* could be pronounced 'Kuting', 'Guting', 'Kuding' or 'Guding'. Although Taiwan officially switched to the less ambiguous MPS2 Romanisation system in 1986, implementation was spotty and halfhearted, resulting in perhaps even more ambiguity and confusion than before.

The good news is that after years of complaints from foreigners Taiwan has finally begun to take steps to correct its use of Romanisation. The bad news is that the new signs tend to be in one of two different Romanisation systems: Hanyu Pinyin, which is used in China (and has become the international standard for Mandarin), and Tongyong Pinyin, a home-grown alternative born in the late 1990s of the desire to help differentiate Taiwan from China. Although advocates of Tongyong Pinyin often claim that the systems are 85% the same, in reality only about half of place names are spelled the same way in the two systems.

The major differences between the two systems are as follows:

HANYU PINYIN	TONGYONG PINYIN
zh-	jh-
q-	c-
x-	s-
-ü*	-yu
-ui	-uei
-iu	-iou
wen	wun
weng	wong
feng	fong
jiong/qiong/siong	jyong/cyong/syong
zi/ci/si	zih/cih/sih
zhi/chi/shi/ri	jhih/chih/shih/rih

*ü is written u (ie without the umlaut) when no ambiguity would result. Thus, *ju, qu, xu,* and *yu* should be pronounced as if they were written *jü, qü, xü,* and *yü.*

Although the central government has declared Tongyong Pinyin to be Taiwan's official Romanisation system for both Hakka and Mandarin (but not for Taiwanese), it left local governments free to make their own choices. Taipei has selected to use Hanyu Pinyin and has applied the system consistently. In times of budget constraints, however, most local governments have priorities other than putting up new signage for the benefit of foreigners, so progress toward standardisation in any form of Pinyin is slow in most of the country.

Taipei has also introduced a system under which major roads have been assigned numbers. Although this 'nicknumbering' system might at first glance seem like a boon to visitors to the city, don't bother asking for directions to '4th Boulevard', because no-one in Taipei knows what streets the numbers are supposed to match. This system is best ignored.

To sum up the situation, signage in Taiwan can be found in MPS2, Wade-Giles (which most people also use inaccurately for spelling their names), Hanyu Pinyin (mainly in Taipei), Tongyong Pinyin (mainly on highway signs and at train stations), plus a range of other possibilites employed with varying degrees of inaccuracy.

Given such a range, what is the poor traveller to do? When something written in Romanisation doesn't seem to make sense, a few guidelines can help you make an educated guess as to what is actually being referred to. Anything with **x**, **q** or **zh** will be in Hanyu Pinyin. Anything with **jh**, **iou** or **uei** will be in Tongyong Pinyin. Anything with **r** used as a vowel (eg *shr*) will be in MPS2.

If you're going to learn only one Romanisation system, your best bet is to learn Hanyu Pinyin and study a few of the most common differences (such as those listed below) to help you navigate through the other systems you'll likely encounter.

The following Hanyu Pinyin conversion could fairly safely be assumed where different systems are used:

WRITTEN	HANYU PINYIN
c	q
ch	zh/q/j/ch
jh	zh
k	g
p	b
s	x
t	d
ts/tz	z/c
h (at the end of a syllable)	– (no letter)

For example, Chihpen and Chihben are sometimes seen for Zhiben, and Kueishan for Gueishan/Guishan.

More Info on the Internet

For a list of Taiwan's city names, street names, and names of railroad stations in Hanyu Pinyin and traditional spellings, see www.romanization.com.

For loads more information on Chinese characters, Pinyin and Romanisation, including a full comparison of the main Chinese Romanisation systems, check out www.pinyin.info.

If you'd like more information on the ins and outs of Chinese characters there are many suitable books on the subject listed at www.pinyin.info/readings/. 'The Ideographic Myth' at www.pinyin.info/readings/texts/ideographic_myth.html is an extract from *The Chinese Language: Fact and Fantasy* by John DeFrancis (University of Hawai`i Press, 1984). DeFrancis gives an interesting and detailed history of the widely-held belief that Chinese characters are ideographic (ie pictorial) in nature.

LANGUAGE

PRONUNCIATION

The following is a description of the sounds produced in spoken Mandarin Chinese. The letter **v** is not used in Chinese. The trickiest sounds in Pinyin are **c**, **q** and **x**. Most letters are pronounced as in English, except for the following:

Vowels

a	as in 'father'
ai	as the word 'eye'
ao	as the 'ow' in 'cow'
e	as in 'her'
ei	as in 'weigh'
i	as the 'ee' in 'meet'; also as the 'oo' in 'book'*
ian	as the word 'yen'
ie	as the word 'yeah'
o	as in 'or'
ou	as the 'oa' in 'boat'
u	as in 'flute'
ui	as the word 'way'
uo	as 'w' followed by the 'o' in 'or'
yu	as German 'ü' – round your lips and try saying 'ee'
ü	as German 'ü'

* The letter 'i' is pronounced as 'oo' only when it occurs after **c**, **ch**, **r**, **s**, **sh**, **z** or **zh**.

Consonants

c	as the 'ts' in 'bits'
ch	as in 'church', but with the tongue curled back
h	guttural, a bit like the 'ch' in Scottish 'loch'
q	as the 'ch' in 'cheese'
r	as the 's' in 'pleasure'
sh	as in 'she', but with the tongue curled back
x	as the 'sh' in 'ship'
z	as the 'ds' in 'suds'
zh	as the 'j' in 'judge' but with the tongue curled back

Consonants other than **n**, **ng**, and **r** can never appear at the end of a syllable.

In Pinyin, apostrophes are occasionally used when a syllable in the middle of a word begins with a vowel, eg *ping'an* ('ping-an') compared with *pin'gan* ('pin-gan').

PHRASEBOOKS & DICTIONARIES

Conflicting Romanisation systems aside, reading place names or street signs isn't too difficult, since the Chinese name is usually accompanied by some form of Pinyin; if not, you'll soon learn lots of characters through repeated exposure.

Lonely Planet's *Mandarin Phrasebook* includes script throughout and loads of useful phrases – it's also a very useful learning tool. A small dictionary with English, Pinyin and Chinese characters is also useful for learning a few words.

ACCOMMODATION

I'm looking for a ...
Wǒ yào zhǎo ...   我要找 ...
  camping ground
  lùyíngqū   露營區
  guesthouse
  bīnguǎn   賓館
  hotel
  lǚguǎn   旅館
  tourist hotel
  fàndiàn   飯店
  hostel
  zhāodàisuǒ/lǚshè   招待所/旅社
  youth hostel
  lǚshè   旅社

Where is a cheap hotel?
Nǎlǐ yǒu piányi de lǚguǎn?
哪裡有便宜的旅館?
What is the address?
Dìzhǐ zài nǎlǐ?
地址在哪裡?
Could you write the address, please?
Néngbùnéng qǐng nǐ bǎ dìzhǐ xiě xiàlái?
能不能請你把地址寫下來?
Do you have a room available?
Nǐmen yǒu fángjiān ma?
你們有房間嗎?

I'd like (a) ...
Wǒ xiǎng yào ...   我想要 ...
  bed
  yīge chuángwèi   一個床位
  single room
  yījiān dānrénfáng   一間單人房
  double room
  yījiān shuāngrénfáng   一間雙人房
  bed for two
  shuāngrén chuáng   雙人床
  room with two beds
  liǎng gè chuángwèi de   兩個床位的
    shuāngrénfáng   雙人房
  economy room (no bath)
  yǎfáng (méiyǒu   雅房(沒有
    yùshì)   浴室)

LANGUAGE

room with a bathroom
  tàofáng (yǒu yùshìde fángjiān)
  套房(有浴室的 房間)
standard room
  biāozhǔn fángjiān
  標準房間
deluxe suite
  háohuá tàofáng
  豪華套房
to share a dorm
  zhù sùshè
  住宿舍

How much is it ...?
... duōshǎo qián?　　... 多少錢?
  per night
  yīge wǎnshàng　　一個晚上
  per person
  měigerén　　每個人

May I see the room?
  Wǒ néng kànkan fángjiān ma?
  我能看看房間嗎?
Where is the bathroom?
  Yùshì zài nǎlǐ?
  浴室在哪裡?
Where is the toilet?
  Cèsuǒ zài nǎlǐ?
  廁所在哪裡?
I don't like this room.
  Wǒ bù xǐhuān zhèjiān fángjiān.
  我不喜歡這間房間.
Are there any messages for me?
  Yǒu méiyǒu rén liú huà gěi wǒ?
  有沒有人留話給我?
May I have a hotel namecard?
  Yǒu méiyǒu lǚguǎn de míngpiàn?
  有沒有旅館的名片?
Could I have these clothes washed, please?
  Qǐng bāng wǒ bǎ zhèxiē yīfú xǐ gānjìng.
  請幫我把這些衣服此乾淨.
I'm/We're leaving today.
  Wǒ/Wǒmen jīntiān líkāi.
  我/我們今天離開.

CONVERSATION & ESSENTIALS

Hello.
  Nǐ hǎo .　　你好
  Nín hǎo. (more polite)　　您好
Goodbye.
  Zàijiàn.　　再見
Please.
  Qǐng.　　請
Thank you.
  Xièxie.　　謝謝
You're welcome. (don't mention it)
  Bùkèqi.　　不客氣
Excuse me, ...
  Qǐng wèn, ...　　請問, ...

EMERGENCIES

Help!
  Jiùmìng a!　　救命啊!
emergency
  jǐnjí qíngkuàng　　緊急情況
There's been an accident!
  Fāshēng yìwài le!　　發生意外了!
Could you help me, please?
  Nǐ néng bùnéng bāng wǒ ge máng?
  你能不能幫 我個忙?
I'm lost.
  Wǒ mílùle.　　我迷路了
Go away!
  Zǒu kāi!　　走開!
Leave me alone!
  Bié fán wǒ!　　別煩我!

Call ...!
  Qǐng jiào ...!　　請叫 ...!
  a doctor
  yīshēng　　醫生
  the police
  jǐngchá　　警察

When asking a question it is polite to start with the phrase *qǐng wèn* 請問 – literally, 'may I ask?' – this expression is only used at the beginning of a sentence, never at the end.

I'm sorry. (forgive me)
  Duìbùqǐ.　　對不起
May I ask your name?
  Qǐngwèn nín guìxìng?　　請問您貴姓?
My (sur)name is ...
  Wǒ xìng ...　　我姓 ...
Where are you from?
  Nǐ shì cóng nǎlǐ lái de?　　你是從哪裡來的?
I'm from ...
  Wǒ shì cóng ... lái de.　　我是從 ... 来的
I like ...
  Wǒ xǐhuān ...　　我喜歡 ...
I don't like ...
  Wǒ bù xǐhuān ...　　我不喜歡 ...
Wait a moment.
  Děng yīxià.　　等一下

Yes & No

There are no specific words in Mandarin that mean 'yes' and 'no' that are used in isolation the way they are in English. When asked a question the verb is repeated to indicate the affirmative. A response in the negative is formed by using the word *bù*, 不 (meaning 'no') before the verb. When *bù* (falling tone) occurs before another word with a falling tone, it is pronounced with a rising tone.

Are you going to Taichung?
Nǐ qù Táizhōng ma? 你去台中嗎?
Yes.
Qù. (literally 'go') 去
No.
Bù qù. (literally 'no go') 不去
No. (don't have)
Méi yǒu. 没有
No. (not so)
Bùshì. 不是

DIRECTIONS
Where is (the) ...?
... zài nǎlǐ? ... 在哪裡?
Go straight ahead.
Yīzhí zǒu. 一直走
Turn left.
Zuǒ zhuǎn. 左轉
Turn right.
Yòu zhuǎn. 右轉
at the next corner
zài xià yīge zhuǎnjiǎo 在下一個轉角
at the traffic lights
zài hónglǜdēng 在紅綠燈
Could you show me (on the map)?
Nǐ néng bùnéng (zài dìtú shàng) zhǐ gěi wǒ kàn? 你能不能(在地圖上)指給我看?

behind	*hòumiàn*	後面
in front of	*qiánmiàn*	前面
near	*jìn*	近
far	*yuǎn*	遠
opposite	*duìmiàn*	對面
beach	*hǎitān*	海灘
bridge	*qiáoliáng*	橋樑
island	*dǎoyǔ*	島嶼
main square	*guǎngchǎng*	廣場
map	*dìtú*	地圖
market	*shìchǎng*	市場
old city	*jiù shìqū*	舊市區
palace	*gōngdiàn*	宮殿
sea	*hǎiyáng*	海洋

HEALTH
I'm sick.
Wǒ shēngbìngle. 我生病了.

I need a doctor.
Wǒ děi kàn yīshēng. 我得看醫生.
Is there a doctor here who speaks English?
Zhèlǐ yǒu huì jiǎng yīngwén de yīshēng ma? 這裡有會講英文的醫生嗎?
It hurts here.
Zhèlǐ tòng. 這裡痛.

I'm ...
Wǒ yǒu ... 我有 ...
  asthmatic
  qìchuǎnbìng 氣喘病
  diabetic
  tángniàobìng 糖尿病
  epileptic
  diānxiánbìng 癲癇病

I'm allergic to ...
Wǒ duì ... guòmǐn. 我對 ... 過敏.
  antibiotics
  kàngshēngsù 抗生素
  aspirin
  āsīpǐlín 阿司匹林
  penicillin
  qīngméisù 青黴素
  bee stings
  mìfēng dīng yǎo 蜜蜂叮咬
  nuts
  jiānguǒ 堅果

anti-diarrhoea medicine
  zhǐxièyào 止瀉藥
antiseptic cream
  xiāodú yàogāo 消毒藥膏
condoms
  bǎoxiǎn tào 保險套

contraceptive
  bìyùnyào 避孕藥
diarrhoea
  lā dùzi 拉肚子
headache
  tóutòng 頭痛
medicine
  yào 藥
sanitary napkins (Kotex)
  wèishēngmián 衛生棉
sunscreen (UV) lotion
  fángshàiyóu 防曬油
tampons
  wèishēngmián tiáo 衛生棉條

LANGUAGE DIFFICULTIES
Do you speak English?
  Nǐ huì jiǎng yīngwén ma? 你會講英文嗎?
Does anyone here speak English?
  Zhèlǐ yǒu rén huì shuō 這裡有人會說
  yīngyǔ ma? 英語嗎?
How do you say ... in Mandarin?
  ... zhōngwén zěnme shuō? ... 中文怎麼說?
What does ... mean?
  ... shì shénme yìsi? ... 是什麼意思?
I understand.
  Wǒ tīngdedǒng. 我聽得懂
I don't understand.
  Wǒ tīngbùdǒng. 我聽不懂
Please write it down.
  Qǐng xiěxiàlái. 請寫下來

NUMBERS
0	*líng*	零
1	*yī*	一
2	*èr, liǎng*	二, 兩
3	*sān*	三
4	*sì*	四
5	*wǔ*	五
6	*liù*	六
7	*qī*	七
8	*bā*	八
9	*jiǔ*	九
10	*shí*	十
11	*shíyī*	十一
12	*shí'èr*	十二
20	*èrshí*	二十
21	*èrshíyī*	二十一
22	*èrshí'èr*	二十二
30	*sānshí*	三十
40	*sìshí*	四十
50	*wǔshí*	五十
60	*liùshí*	六十
70	*qīshí*	七十
80	*bāshí*	八十
90	*jiǔshí*	九十
100	*yìbǎi*	一百
1000	*yìqiān*	一千
2000	*liǎngqiān*	兩千

PAPERWORK
name
  xìngmíng 姓名
nationality
  guójí 國籍
date of birth
  chūshēng rìqí 出生日期
place of birth
  chūshēng dì 出生地
sex (gender)
  xìngbié 性別
passport
  hùzhào 護照
passport number
  hùzhào hàomǎ 護照號碼
visa
  qiānzhèng 簽證
visa extension
  yáncháng qiānzhèng 延長簽證
Foreign Affairs Police
  Wàishì Jīngchá 外事警察
credit card ...
  xìnyòngkǎ 信用卡
  number
  hàomǎ 號碼
  expiry date
  yǒuxiào rìqí 有效日期

QUESTION WORDS
Who?	*Shéi?*	誰?
What?	*Shénme?*	什麼?
What is it?	*Shì shénme?*	是什麼?
When?	*Shénme shíhòu?*	什麼時候?
Where?	*Zài nǎlǐ?*	在哪裡?
Which?	*Nǎge?*	哪個?
How?	*Zěnme?*	怎麼?

SHOPPING & SERVICES
I'd like to buy ...
  Wǒ xiǎng mǎi ... 我想買 ...
How much is it?
  Duōshǎo qián? 多少錢?
I don't like it.
  Wǒ bù xǐhuān. 我不喜歡
Can I see it?
  Néng kànkan ma? 能看看嗎?
I'm just looking.
  Wǒ zhǐshì kànkan. 我只是看看
It's cheap.
  Zhè bùguì. 這不貴

Is there anything cheaper?
  Yǒu piányi yìdiǎn de ma? 有便宜一點的嗎?
That's too expensive.
  Tài guìle. 太貴了.
I'll take it.
  Wǒ mǎi zhège. 我買這個.
Can I pay by travellers cheque?
  Kěyǐ fù lǚxíng zhīpiào ma? 可以付旅行支票嗎?

more
  duō 多
less
  shǎo 少
smaller
  gèng xiǎo 更小
bigger
  gèng dà 更大
too much/many
  tài duō 太多

Do you accept ...?
  Shōu bùshōu ...? 收不收 ...?
  credit cards
    xìnyòngkǎ 信用卡
  travellers cheques
    lǚxíng zhīpiào 旅行支票

Excuse me, where's the nearest ...?
Qǐng wèn, zuìjìnde ... zài nǎlǐ?
請問, 最近的 ... 在哪裡?
I'm looking for a/the ...
Wǒ zài zhǎo ...
我在找 ...
  ATM
    zìdòng guìyuánjī/ 自動櫃員機/
    tíkuǎnjī 提款機
  bank
    yínháng 銀行
  chemist/pharmacy
    yàojú 藥局
  city centre
    shìzhōngxīn 市中心
  ... embassy
    ... dàshǐguǎn ... 大使館
  foreign affairs police
    wàishì jǐngchá 外事警察
  currency exchange
    wàihuì duìhuànchù 外滙兌換處
  hospital
    yīyuàn 醫院
  hotel
    bīnguǎn/ 賓館/
    fàndiàn/ 飯店/
    lǚguǎn 旅館

  market
    shìchǎng 市場
  museum
    bówùguǎn 博物館
  police
    jǐngchá 警察
  post office
    yóujú 郵局
  public toilet
    gōnggòng cèsuǒ 公共廁所
  telephone
    diànhuà 電話
  telephone office
    diànxìnjú 電信局
  the tourist office
    guānguāngjú 觀光局

change money
  huàn qián 換錢
telephone card
  diànhuà kǎ 電話卡
international call
  guójì diànhuà 國際電話
collect call
  duìfāng fùfèi diànhuà 對方付費電話
direct-dial call
  zhíbō diànhuà 直撥電話
fax
  chuánzhēn 傳真
computer
  diànnǎo 電腦
email (often called 'email')
  diànzǐyóujiàn 電子郵件
internet
  wǎnglù/ 網路/
  wǎngjì wǎnglù (more 網際網路
    formal name)
online
  shàngwǎng 上網

Where can I get online?
  Wǒ zài nǎlǐ kěyǐ shàngwǎng?
  我在哪裡可以上網?
Can I check my email account?
  Wǒ jiǎnchá yíxià zìjǐ de email xìnxiāng, hǎo ma?
  我檢查一下自己的 email 信箱, 好嗎?

TIME & DATES
What's the time?
  Jǐ diǎn? 幾點?
... hour ... minute
  ... diǎn ... fēn ... 點 ... 分
3.05
  sān diǎn líng wǔ fēn 三點零五分

When?
  Shénme shíhòu?   什麼時候?
now
  xiànzài   現在
today
  jīntiān   今天
tomorrow
  míngtiān   明天
day after tomorrow
  hòutiān   後天
yesterday
  zuótiān   昨天
in the morning
  zǎoshàng   早上
in the afternoon
  xiàwǔ   下午
in the evening
  wǎnshàng   晚上
weekend
  zhōumò   周末

Monday	*Xīngqíyī*	星期一
Tuesday	*Xīngqí'èr*	星期二
Wednesday	*Xīngqísān*	星期三
Thursday	*Xīngqísì*	星期四
Friday	*Xīngqíwǔ*	星期五
Saturday	*Xīngqíliù*	星期六
Sunday	*Xīngqítiān*	星期天

January	*Yīyuè*	一月
February	*Èryuè*	二月
March	*Sānyuè*	三月
April	*Sìyuè*	四月
May	*Wǔyuè*	五月
June	*Liùyuè*	六月
July	*Qīyuè*	七月
August	*Bāyuè*	八月
September	*Jiǔyuè*	九月
October	*Shíyuè*	十月
November	*Shíyīyuè*	十一月
December	*Shí'èryuè*	十二月

TRANSPORT
Public Transport
airport
  jīchǎng   機場
long-distance bus station
  kèyùn zhàn   客運站
subway (underground)
  jíeyùn   捷運
subway station
  jíeyùn zhàn   捷運站

train station
  huǒchē zhàn   火車站

What time does ... leave/arrive?
  ... jǐdiǎn kāi/dào?   ... 幾點開/到?
  the boat
  chuán   船
  intercity bus; coach
  kèyùn   客運
  local/city bus
  gōngchē   公車
  minibus
  xiǎoxíng gōngchē   小型公車
  the plane
  fēijī   飛機
  train
  huǒchē   火車

I'd like a ...
  Wǒ yào yìzhāng ...   我要一張 ...
  one-way ticket
  dānchéng piào   單程票
  return ticket
  láihuí piào   來回票
  platform ticket
  yuètái piào   月台票
  1st-class ticket
  tóuděngcāng   頭等艙
  2nd-class ticket
  èrděngcāng   二等艙

I want to go to ...
  Wǒ yào qù ...   我要去 ...
The train has been delayed/cancelled.
  Huǒchē (wǎndiǎn le/   火車(晚點了/
  qǔxiāo le).   取消了).

When's the ... bus?
  ... bānchē shénme shíhòu lái?   ... 班車什麼時候來?
  first
  tóu   頭
  last
  mò   末
  next
  xià   下

boarding pass
  dēngjīzhèng   登機證
left-luggage room
  jìfàng chù   寄放處
platform number
  yuètái hàomǎ   月台號碼
ticket office
  shòupiào chù   售票處
timetable
  shíkèbiǎo   時刻表

ROAD SIGNS

讓	*Ràng*	Give way
繞行	*Ràoxíng*	Detour
禁止進入	*Jìnzhǐ Jìnrù*	No Entry
禁止超車	*Jìnzhǐ Chāochē*	No Overtaking
禁止停車	*Jìnzhǐ Tíngchē*	No Parking
入口	*Rùkǒu*	Entrance
保持暢通	*Bǎochí Chàngtōng*	Keep Clear
收費	*Shōufèi*	Toll
危險	*Wéixiǎn*	Danger
減速慢行	*Jiǎnsù Mànxíng*	Slow Down
單行道	*Dānxíngdào*	One Way
出口	*Chūkǒu*	Exit

Private Transport

I'd like to hire a ...
Wǒ yào zū yīliàng ... 我要租一輛 ...
  car
  qìchē 汽車
  motorbike
  mótuōchē 摩托車
  bicycle
  jiǎotàchē 腳踏車

How much is it per day?
Yītiān duōshǎo qián? 一天多少錢?
How much is it per hour?
Yīge xiǎoshí duōshǎo qián? 一個小時多少錢?
How much is the deposit?
Yājīn duōshǎo qián? 押金多少錢?

road	*lù*	路
section	*duàn*	段
street	*jiē*	街
No 21	*21 hào*	21號
diesel	*cháiyóu*	柴油
petrol	*qìyóu*	汽油

Where's the next service station?
Xià yíge jiāyóuzhàn zài nǎlǐ? 下一個加油站在哪裡?
Please fill it up.
Qǐng jiāmǎn. 請加滿
I'd like ... litres.
Wǒ yào ... gōngshēng. 我要 ... 公升
Does this road lead to ...?
Zhè tiáo lù dào ... ma? 這條路到 ... 嗎?
How long can I park here?
Zhèlǐ kěyǐ tíng duōjiǔ? 這裡可以停多久?
Can I park here?
Zhèlǐ kěyǐ tíngchē ma? 這裡可以停車嗎?

Where do I pay?
Zài nǎlǐ fùkuǎn? 在哪裡付款?
I/We need a mechanic.
(Wǒ/Wǒmen) xūyào qìchē wéixiūyuán. (我/我們)需要汽車維修員
The car has broken down (at ...)
Chēzi (zài ...) pāomáo le. 車子 (在…) 拋錨了
The car/motorbike won't start.
Qìchē/mótuōchē fādòng bùqǐlái. 汽車/摩托車發動不起來
I have a flat tyre.
Lúntāi pòle. 輪胎破了
I've run out of petrol.
Méiyǒu qìyóu le. 沒有汽油了
I had an accident.
Wǒ chū chēhuò le. 我出車禍了

TRAVEL WITH CHILDREN

Is there a/an ...?
Yǒu ... ma? 有 ... 嗎?
I need a/an ...
Wǒ xūyào ... 我需要 ...
  baby food
  yīng'ér shípǐn 嬰兒食品
  baby formula (milk)
  yīng'ér nǎifěn 嬰兒奶粉
  baby's bottle
  nǎipíng 奶瓶
  children's menu
  értóng càidān 兒童菜單
  (disposable) nappies/diapers
  niàobù 尿布
  (English-speaker) babysitter
  (huì jiǎng yīngwén de) yīng'ér bǎomǔ (會講英文的)嬰兒保姆
  highchair
  yīng'ér cānyǐ 嬰兒餐椅
  potty
  yīng'ér mǎtǒng 嬰兒馬桶
  stroller
  yīng'ér chē 嬰兒車

Also available from Lonely Planet:
Mandarin Phrasebook

LANGUAGE

Glossary

See also Language (p361) for useful phrases, and Food & Drink (p58) for an explanation of Taiwanese food terms.

aborigines *(yuánzhùmín)* – the original residents of Taiwan, of which there are currently 13 recognised tribes; considered possibly the ancestors of all Austronesian people
ARC – Alien Resident Certificate; foreign visitors must apply for one if planning to stay for long-term work or study
Ami – Taiwan's largest aboriginal tribe; lives on the coastal plains of eastern Taiwan
Atayal – Taiwan's second-largest aboriginal tribe; lives in mountainous regions of the north

bàngqiú – baseball
Baochung – type of oolong tea grown around Pinglin
bensheng ren – Taiwanese people whose ancestors came to Taiwan prior to 1949
black gold *(hēi jīn)* – in Taiwan this refers to political corruption and not oil
Bunun – Taiwan's third-largest aboriginal tribe; lives in Central Mountains

catty – unit of measure (600g)
chá – tea, especially Chinese tea
chi (qì) – vital energy
Chu-kuang *(Jǔguāng)* – 2nd-class regular train
congee – rice porridge
cūn – village

dàgē'dà (literally big-brother-big) – mobile phone
DPP – Democratic Progressive Party; Taiwan's first opposition party

Forest Recreation Area – similar to a state or provincial park in the west
Fujianese – people originally from Fujian province in China who migrated to Taiwan; the Taiwanese dialect is derived from that of southern Fujian
Fu-hsing *(fùxīng)* – 2nd-class regular train

gǎng – harbour/port
gāosù gōnglù – national highway
gōng – Taoist temple
guānxi – the art of giving and receiving favours; mutually supportive and cooperative relationships

Hakka – nomadic subset of the Han Chinese, the Hakka were among the first Chinese to settle in Taiwan; many prominent Taiwanese are also Hakka people

Hanyu Pinyin – system of Romanisation used in mainland China; though there is some crossover, most signs in Taiwan outside Taipei use the Tongyong Pinyin or Wade-Giles systems
HSR – High Speed Rail, Taiwan's newly built 'bullet train'

Ilha Formosa – the name Portuguese sailors gave Taiwan, meaning 'beautiful island'

jiǎotàchē zhuānyòngdào – bike path
jié – festival
jiē – street
jīn – unit of measure; see *catty*
jīngjù – see *opera (Taiwanese)*

Kaoliang – liquor made from sorghum; made in Matsu and Kinmen
KMT – Kuomintang, Nationalist Party of the Republic of China
KMRT – Kaohsiung's MRT system
koi – carp

láojiǔ – medicinal rice wine made in Matsu
laver – edible seaweed
liǎng – unit of measure (37.5g)
Lu Tung Pin – one of the eight immortals of classical Chinese mythology; couples avoid his temples as he likes to break up happy lovers

Matsu (Māzǔ) – Goddess of the Sea, the most popular deity in Taiwan; one of the Taiwan Strait Islands
miào – general word for temple
mínsù – B&B, homestay
mountain permit – special permit you pick up from local police stations to allow you to enter restricted mountainous areas
MRT – Mass Rapid Transit; Taipei's underground railway system

National Trail System – a system of hiking trails running over the entire island

One China – the idea that mainland China and Taiwan are both part of one country: People's Republic of China
oolong (also *wulong*) – semifermented tea, most popular kind in Taiwan
opera (Taiwanese) – also known as Beijing or Chinese opera, a sophisticated art form that has been an important part of Chinese culture for more than 900 years

Paiwan – small aboriginal tribe
píng – unit of measure for property: land, apartments etc (4 sq metres)
PFP (People First Party) – offshoot of KMT started by James Soong
PRC – People's Republic of China
pùbù – waterfall
Puyuma – small aboriginal tribe

qiáo – bridge
qū – district/area

ROC – Republic of China; covered all of China before the PRC was established
suòxī – river tracing; popular sport that involves walking up rivers and streams with the aid of nonslip shoes
Rukai – small aboriginal tribe; lives in southern part of Central Mountains

Saisiyat – very small aboriginal tribe, lives in mountains of Miaoli County
sēnlín – forest
shān – mountain
shěngdào – provincial highway
xiàndào – county road
sì – Buddhist temple
Sinicism – Chinese method or customs
shoji – rice paper

tael – unit of measure; see *liǎng*
taichi – graceful but powerful slow-motion shadow-boxing commonly practised as the sun rises
tái kè – describes someone or something as very Taiwanese in style; formerly a derogatory term for low class, now embraced by many young people looking to assert a local Taiwanese identity
Taipeiers – people from Taipei
Three Nos – refers to no support for Taiwan independence; no support for 'two Chinas' and no support for Taiwan's entry into any international organisation for sovereign states
Three Small Links – the opening of cross-Strait trade between China and Taiwan's offshore islands
Tieguanyin (Iron Buddha Tea) – type of oolong tea grown in Maokong, south of the Taipei Zoo
Tongyong Pinyin – system of romanisation used in parts of Taiwan
Tsou – small aboriginal tribe
tuántǐfáng – youth hostel dormitory
Tze-Chiang (*Zìqiáng*) – the fastest and most comfortable regular train

VAT – Value-Added Tax
waisheng ren – Taiwanese who immigrated from mainland China following the KMT defeat in the Chinese civil war
Wade-Giles – a Romanisation system for Chinese words; widely used until the introduction of Hanyu Pinyin
Wang Yeh – a Tang dynasty scholar, said to watch over the waters of southern China; worshipped all over the south
wēnquán – hot spring
White Terror – a large-scale campaign started by the KMT to purge the island of political activists during the 1950s; one of the grimmest times in Taiwan's martial-law period
xiàng – lane

Yami – A small aboriginal tribe inhabiting Lanyu island
yèshì – night market
Youth Guesthouse Network – program set up by the National Youth Commission to establish cheap hostel accommodation around the island.

zhàn – station
Zhuyin – Also known as 'Bopomofo'; system of symbol-writing used to teach children and foreign students how to pronounce Chinese words

The Authors

ROBERT KELLY
Coordinating Author, Northern, East Coast & Western Taiwan

Robert Kelly arrived in Taiwan 11 years ago, after five long years of not having the same fixed address for more than six months. He quickly found a land he could call home and one that could appreciate his ability to spin a good yarn. Though never one to go native, Robert has picked up a few new traits including a deep love for tea, a respect for poisonous snakes, an appreciation for self-control, and a hunger for all things soy. This is Robert's second go at the *Taiwan* guide and his final remarks remain the same: he has no intention of leaving this country now that he's seen even more of what it has to offer.

JOSHUA SAMUEL BROWN
Taipei & Taiwan Islands

American-born expatriate Joshua Samuel Brown has lived in Taiwan, Hong Kong and China since 1994. A prolific traveller and writer, his features have appeared in an eclectic variety of publications around the globe, including the *South China Morning Post*, *Clamor* magazine and *Cat Fancy*. The late subgenius philosopher Lago Von Slack infamously summed up Brown's work, calling him 'the Mahatma Gandhi of restaurant criticism' and 'the Rudyard Kipling of professional boxing'. To this day, no one knows quite why Lago said these things. Joshua's debut book, *Vignettes of Taiwan,* offers tales of betel-nut beauties and how to avoid jail time by impersonating a Mormon. *Taiwan* is Joshua's first book for Lonely Planet; his other work can be found at www.josambro.com.

Behind the Scenes

THIS BOOK

This 7th edition of *Taiwan* was researched and written by Robert Kelly and Joshua Samuel Brown. The first five editions were written by Robert Storey. The 6th edition was written by Andrew Bender, Julie Grundvig and Robert Kelly. This guidebook was commissioned in Lonely Planet's Melbourne office, and produced by the following:

Commissioning Editor Jane Thompson, Errol Hunt, Tashi Wheeler

Coordinating Editor Shawn Low

Coordinating Cartographer Helen Rowley

Coordinating Layout Designer Jim Hsu

Managing Editor Liz Heynes

Managing Cartographer David Connolly

Managing Layout Designers Celia Wood

Assisting Editors Charlotte Orr, Michelle Bennett

Assisting Cartographers Kusnandar

Cover Designer Pepi Bluck

Project Manager Eoin Dunlevy

Language Content Coordinator Quentin Frayne

Thanks to Jessa Boanas-Dewes, David Carroll, Louise Clarke, Barbara Delissen, Kate James, Evan Jones, Margot Kilgour, Rebecca Lalor, Betsy & Henry Lin, Adam McCrow, Susan Paterson, Averil Robertson, Mark Swofford, Gina Tsarouhas, Jeanette Wall

THANKS

ROBERT KELLY

The Tourism Bureau was invaluable in my researching for this edition, especially Joseph Cheng who tirelessly helped arrange meetings with knowledgeable people around the island. I am very grateful to Audrey for showing me some incredible wild hot springs in Wulu and Niwa in Taitung, and for her deep insights into aboriginal culture.

LONELY PLANET: TRAVEL WIDELY, TREAD LIGHTLY, GIVE SUSTAINABLY

The Lonely Planet Story

The story begins with a classic travel adventure: Tony and Maureen Wheeler's 1972 journey across Europe and Asia to Australia. There was no useful information about the overland trail then, so Tony and Maureen published the first Lonely Planet guidebook to meet a growing need.

From a kitchen table, Lonely Planet has grown to become the largest independent travel publisher in the world, with offices in Melbourne (Australia), Oakland (USA) and London (UK). Today Lonely Planet guidebooks cover the globe. There is an ever-growing list of books and information in a variety of media. Some things haven't changed. The main aim is still to make it possible for adventurous individuals to get out there – to explore and better understand the world.

The Lonely Planet Foundation

The Lonely Planet Foundation proudly supports nimble nonprofit institutions working for change in the world. Each year the foundation donates 5% of Lonely Planet company profits to projects selected by staff and authors. Our partners range from Kabissa, which provides small nonprofits across Africa with access to technology, to the Foundation for Developing Cambodian Orphans, which supports girls at risk of falling victim to sex traffickers.

Our nonprofit partners are linked by a grass-roots approach to the areas of health, education or sustainable tourism. Many projects we support – such as one with BaAka (Pygmy) children in the forested areas of Central African Republic – choose to focus on women and children as one of the most effective ways to support the whole community.

Sometimes foundation assistance is as simple as helping to preserve a local ruin like the Minaret of Jam in Afghanistan; this incredible monument now draws intrepid tourists to the area and its restoration has greatly improved options for local people.

Just as travel is often about learning to see with new eyes, so many of the groups we work with aim to change the way people see themselves and the future for their children and communities.

BEHIND THE SCENES

Once again, special thanks to my wife, Hui-ming, especially for her patience and help with scripting. And final thanks to my hiking partners for helping explore some of the fantastic places that made it into this book – and for not minding my sharing these places with the world.

JOSHUA SAMUEL BROWN

I would like to thank Phillip and Tammy at Pristine Communications (Taipei) for looking over some of my more dubious assertions, the Mooney clan for providing copious moral support, Zippo of Hsin-chu for always being interesting, and, most of all, to Laurie, for sticking around through the writing of this guide. This book (my chunk of it, anyway) is dedicated to the memory of my oldest friend, Clifford Heller. Cliff passed on with great and terrible velocity on 30 December 2006. Though he came close, he never quite made it to Taiwan; his presence in my world is sorely missed.

OUR READERS

Many thanks to the travellers who used the last edition and wrote to us with helpful hints, useful advice and interesting anecdotes:

A Alex Aaron, Alice, Jeffrey Anderson, Mark Anderson, Thomas Andersson, Nike Annys, Michaela Atterer **B** Sara Bannerman, Kevin Bertman, Todd A Born, Jim Boyden, David (Dick) Boyes, Matthew Boyter, Jude Bradley, Bryan Brandsma, Carol Brash, Jacob Brown, Jeff Brown, Chris Bryant, Will Burris **C** Paul Cawsey, Sophie Chang, Jason Chang, Amanda Chen, David Chen, Deborah Chen Pichler, Jessica Chen, Vincent Chen, Yoon-Jung Choi, Chungwah Chow, Helle Christensen, Barry Climate, Thatcher Collins, Jean-Marc Compain, Jeff Conquest, William Cox, Geoffrey Cranch, Terry Crossley **D** Larry Daly, Arnaud De Coster, Frans De Lange, Carey Ditmars **E** Kim Eberle-Wang, Koh Ein Lit, Keith Ekstam, Andrew Essen **F** Angela Faries, Paul Fielding, Alan C Fitton, Andy Foltz, Isaac Forbes, Holger Fricke, Phyllis Fung **G** Lasse Gerrits, Walter Gillies, Irene Goedhart, Ben Goren, Yves Goulnik, Francine Grandsard, Danny, Gad & Merav Gudovich, David Guest **H** Bashar Hamarneh, John Hanna, Judy Harrison, Simon Hay, Abraham Held, Rocio Hernandez-Viciana, Chua Hian Koon, Jochen Hoheisel, Christopher Holsman, Tony Horrigan, Celia Hsu, Katrin Huber, Wei Jean Hui **J** Laurent Jalabert, Jessie, Scott Johnson, Sian Jones-Enomoto **K** Oded Kafka, Arlene & Alan Karpel, Kun Kemp, James Kent, Hildur Knútsdóttir, Olaf Kotzke, Robert Kurtz **L** Ashley Lacourse, Nancy Lai, Steven Lai, Suzanne Laird, J Lamare, Moa Largerman, Jose Laroy, Mikelson Leong, Elton Levingston, Bethe Lewis, Brian & Lorna Lewis, Ken Leysen, Wilson Liao, William Lieder, Lily Lin, Belinda Lintern, Maria Lit, Jimmy Liu, Michele Loewen, Nick Lucchetti **M** Donald Mac Donald, Marianne Macdonald, Daniel Machanik, Jon Major, Chee Keong Mak, Daniel Marshall, Paul Maslowski, Thor May, Paul-Jack Mayska, Susan Mclachlan, Shane Mcnamara, Robert Mccoy, Darren Meachem, Ken Merk, Francois Mes, Bernhard Messerli, Joris Michielsen, James Miller, Doug Milliken, Teresa Moore, Christopher Morris, Raaamen Mukherji **N** Ole Naehle, Chris Nelson, Anders Nilsson, Erin Noose **O** Neil Oliver, Brandon Ou, Nancy Oxford **P** Ashwin Panicker, Ryan Parker, Wayne Peterson, Cory Pettit, Hsuan-Yun Pi, Nelson Pires, Katherine Pitts, Anne Podoll, Lauren Powell **Q** Erik Quam **R** Stefan Ratschan, Thomas Reckers, David Reid, Christof Rimensberger, Millie Rivera, Christine Robinson, Nicky Robinson, Yann Roffiaen, Cassandra Ryce **S** Gloria S, Alan Sargent, Gerrit Schilder Jr, Johannes Schilli, Ed Schlenk, Gil Schneider, Renee Shaeffer, David Shirk, Tanit Sindin, Mike Sluchinski, George Stair, Steve, Eduard & Wendy Stiphout, Alan Stone, Mary-Ann Stone, Guy Summers, Yee Szemen **T** Erin Tate, Martin Tate, Christopher Tsai, Ian Turner **U** Elaine Uang **V** Amy Vallis, Richard Van Der Meij, Erik Van Der Molen, Shirley Van Essen, Hakime Vanelli, Ray Varnbuhler, Milou Veling, Andrei Vermont, Jerry Vochteloo, Peter Voelger **W** Derek Walker, Hsinyi Wang, Julie Wang, Frances Waszkiel, Alastair Watts, James Weiler, Pohsuan Weng, Dave Wilson, Angie Wong, Kim Woo, Joy Wood **Y** Chi Y, May Yu **Z** S Zangpo, Oliver Zoellner, Guangcai Zou

ACKNOWLEDGMENTS

Many thanks to the following for the use of their content:

Taipei metro transport map © 2006 Taipei Rapid Transit Corporation

Globe on title page © Mountain High Maps 1993 Digital Wisdom, Inc.

Index

INDEX

INDEX

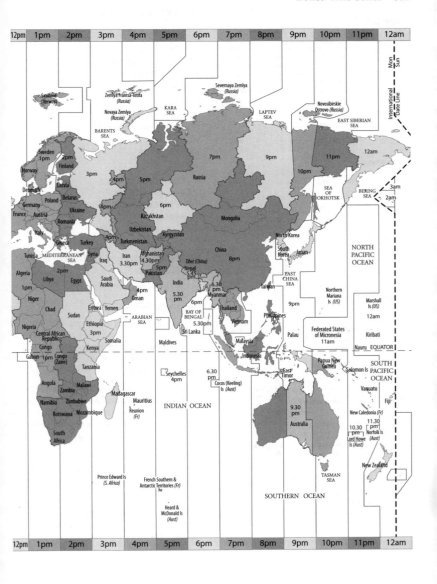

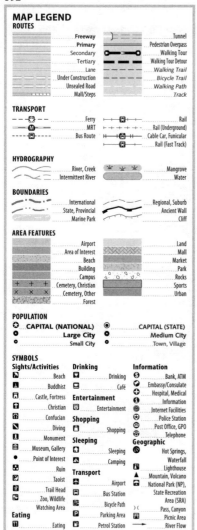

MAP LEGEND

ROUTES

- Freeway
- Primary
- Secondary
- Tertiary
- Lane
- Under Construction
- Unsealed Road
- Mall/Steps
- Tunnel
- Pedestrian Overpass
- Walking Tour
- Walking Tour Detour
- Walking Trail
- Bicycle Trail
- Walking Path
- Track

TRANSPORT

- Ferry
- MRT
- Bus Route
- Rail
- Rail (Underground)
- Cable Car, Funicular
- Rail (Fast Track)

HYDROGRAPHY

- River, Creek
- Intermittent River
- Mangrove
- Water

BOUNDARIES

- International
- State, Provincial
- Marine Park
- Regional, Suburb
- Ancient Wall
- Cliff

AREA FEATURES

- Airport
- Area of Interest
- Beach
- Building
- Campus
- Cemetery, Christian
- Cemetery, Other
- Forest
- Land
- Mall
- Market
- Park
- Rocks
- Sports
- Urban

POPULATION

- ◎ **CAPITAL (NATIONAL)**
- ● **Large City**
- ● Small City
- ◉ CAPITAL (STATE)
- ● Medium City
- ○ Town, Village

SYMBOLS

Sights/Activities
- Beach
- Buddhist
- Castle, Fortress
- Christian
- Confucian
- Diving
- Monument
- Museum, Gallery
- Point of Interest
- Ruin
- Taoist
- Trail Head
- Zoo, Wildlife Watching Area

Eating
- Eating

Drinking
- Drinking
- Café

Entertainment
- Entertainment

Shopping
- Shopping

Sleeping
- Sleeping
- Camping

Transport
- Airport
- Bus Station
- Bicycle Path
- Parking Area
- Petrol Station

Information
- Bank, ATM
- Embassy/Consulate
- Hospital, Medical
- Information
- Internet Facilities
- Police Station
- Post Office, GPO
- Telephone

Geographic
- Hot Springs, Waterfall
- Lighthouse
- Mountain, Volcano
- National Park (NP), State Recreation Area (SRA)
- Pass, Canyon
- Picnic Area
- River Flow

LONELY PLANET OFFICES

Australia
Head Office
Locked Bag 1, Footscray, Victoria 3011
☎ 03 8379 8000, fax 03 8379 8111
talk2us@lonelyplanet.com.au

USA
150 Linden St, Oakland, CA 94607
☎ 510 893 8555, toll free 800 275 8555
fax 510 893 8572
info@lonelyplanet.com

UK
72–82 Rosebery Ave,
Clerkenwell, London EC1R 4RW
☎ 020 7841 9000, fax 020 7841 9001
go@lonelyplanet.co.uk

Published by Lonely Planet Publications Pty Ltd
ABN 36 005 607 983

© Lonely Planet Publications Pty Ltd 2007

© photographers as indicated 2007

Cover photograph: Members of Taiwan Meimen Oigong and Culture Centre organisation perform taichi during a ritual ceremony outside the Chiang Kai-shek Memorial Hall in Taipei, May 12 2006, Wu Yi-Hua/Eyepress News Photo. Many of the images in this guide are available for licensing from Lonely Planet Images: www.lonelyplanetimages.com.

Printed by SNP Security Printing Pte Ltd, Singapore